COMMENTARY

ON

THE GOSPEL OF ST JOHN.

BY

E. W. HENGSTENBERG, D.D.,
PROFESSOR OF THEOLOGY, BERLIN.

TRANSLATED FROM THE GERMAN.

VOLUME II

PUBLISHERS
Eugene, Oregon

Wipf and Stock Publishers
199 W 8th Ave, Suite 3
Eugene, OR 97401

Commentary on the Gospel of St. John, Volume 2
By Hengstenberg, E. W.
Softcover ISBN-13: 978-1-6667-3250-4
Hardcover ISBN-13: 978-1-6667-2629-9
eBook ISBN-13: 978-1-6667-2630-5
Publication date 7/8/2021
Previously published by T&T Clark, 1865

This edition is a scanned facsimile of the original edition published in 1865.

EXPOSITION

OF

THE GOSPEL OF ST JOHN.

CHAPTER XI. 1–46.

THE RAISING OF LAZARUS.

WE begin here with the investigation of the question whether the sinner of Luke vii., Mary Magdalene, and Mary the sister of Lazarus, were different persons, or only different designations of the same person. The result of this inquiry is of great importance in the explanation of the present section.

The more ancient material for its solution Deyling gives in his Observ. Sac. iii. 291 seq. Clemens Alexand. assumes only *one* anointing, which he ascribes to the woman who was a sinner. Tertullian says that the sinner, by the washing of Christ's feet, presignified and presymbolized His burial, and therefore identifies her with the sister of Lazarus. Origen (Tract. 35 in Matt.) remarks: "*Many* think that the four Evangelists have written concerning one and the same woman." He himself declares against this opinion, though it was the current one of his time.[1] The reason which he lays most stress upon,—"It is not to be thought that Mary who loved Jesus, the sister of Martha, who had chosen the better part, was a 'sinner of the town,' "—exerts with most people a strong influence,

---

[1] Origen seems sometimes inconsistent. In Tract. 12 in Matt. App. 3, he proceeds on the supposition of the identity of the sinner and the sister of Lazarus and Mary Magdalene. But this is not a real contradiction. In the former place he follows tradition; in the other, he introduces his own hypothesis, which he mentions as such.

although its force is destroyed by what the Saviour, who came into the world to save sinners, the friend of publicans and sinners, in Luke vii., says to the Pharisee Simon. (Lücke, for example, says: "The word ἁμαρτωλός, in Luke vii. 37, is so fatal to the identification, that a single glance at this hypothesis is quite sufficient.") Irenæus has been without reason quoted in favour of the distinction between the sinner and Mary. But Chrysostom, in the sixty-second Homily on St John, treads in the footsteps of Origen. "Mary," he says, "the sister of Lazarus, who anointed Christ, is not the harlot, but a different person, honourable and excellent."

While to the Greek Church, with her predominant spirit variously touched by the heathen Greek morality, it must have been exceedingly hard to reconcile herself to the theory which identifies the sinner and Mary the sister of Lazarus, that theory found in the Latin Church, especially in consequence of the authority of Gregory the Great, absolute and universal acceptance. In the Breviary it is taken for granted that what is said of the sinful woman, of Mary Magdalene, and of Mary the sister of Lazarus, refers to one and the same person. The antiphone to the Magnificat in the Feast of St Mary Magdalene (22d July) runs thus: "Jesus Christ came into the world to save sinners; and He who did not scorn to be born of the Virgin Mary, did not count it unbecoming to be touched by Mary the sinner. This was that Mary whose many sins were forgiven because she loved much. This was that Mary who was thought worthy first of all to see Him who was raised from the dead."[1] In the Catholic Church of France there arose, in the seventeenth century, a very strenuous opposition to this theory. The defenders of the identity appeared, in the domain of learning, to be altogether vanquished. This went so far, that in a whole series of dioceses, with Paris at the head, the new editions of the Breviary were issued without those portions of the office of St Mary Magdalene which referred to Luke vii. and the sister of Lazarus,[2]—a remarkable instance of the freedom which has always more or less opposed in that Church the intolerance of

[1] In a current Roman Catholic hymn we read: Maria soror Lazari, Quæ tot commisit crimina, Ab ipsâ fauce tartari, Redit ad vitæ limina.
[2] There are two editions lying before the author, the Breviary of Nancy and that of Metz, which show the difference.

dead uniformity. But soon after this change a reaction took place, and the old Catholic view regained the predominance.

In the theology of the churches of the Reformation, the current hypothesis was that the three persons were distinct. This was supported, among others, by Lyser, Calovius, and Bengel. It needs no proof that, with men of such views as theirs, the Pharisaic bias against the "sinner" exerted no influence. It was not until the Rationalist period that such a bias began to manifest itself again, and then a sentimental element entered into the question. A strong feeling of repugnance displayed itself against admitting the censorious Simon "into the loving company and household fellowship of the brother and sisters in Bethany." If the sinner, Mary Magdalene, and the sister of Lazarus were identified, their family circle must be regarded with an essentially different consideration from that usually accorded. Martha must be connected with her husband, the repulsive and harsh Simon. Mary, whom we have been accustomed to regard as a silent soul involved in meditation, who has opened her pure heart to the Redeemer, "as the tender flowers silently unfold themselves to the sun," becomes " a wild and tameless woman;" who first found in Christ stillness for her passions, and convulsively clings to Him still, lest the calmness of the waters of her soul should be exchanged again for tempest. Probably, too, Lazarus has undergone a similar development. He eats, after having led the life of the prodigal son, in the house of his brother-in-law, the bread of mercy; and she loves him, not on account of any natural worthiness to be loved, not as the type of those who continue in the grace of baptism, but like Him who has come to seek and to save that which was lost, and rejoices when He has found it. To some it is hard to accept all these changes. Others will love Bethany all the more, if an honest investigation should establish that the old idyllic view has rested upon illusion. It would then yield them pure consolation in the consideration of their own circumstances, and in the remembrance of melancholy passages of their own religious development.

There have not been wanting those who have sought to mediate between these opposite views. At their head is Grotius, who on Matt. xxvi. 6 maintains the identity of the sinner in Luke vii. with the Mary of Lazarus, but doubts whether this latter Mary were identical with Mary Magdalene. The reasons which he alleges for the now generally admitted identity of the anointing in Matthew, Mark, and John, and the now generally renounced identity of the anointing in Luke vii. with theirs, we shall proceed to consider; for the presentation of this argument forms an excellent preparation. " In Matthew and Mark," he says, " *everything* coincides. In Matthew, Mark, and Luke, the accounts agree that the occurrence took place at a feast in the house of Simon; and that the woman came with an alabaster box of ointment, ἀλάβαστρον μύρου, from which she anointed Jesus. Matthew, Mark, and John agree that this took place in Bethany, at a feast; that the ointment brought by the woman was very precious; that she was therefore blamed among the disciples (John mentions Judas) as guilty of waste, under the pretence that the expenditure might better have been devoted to the poor; that Christ defended the woman, with the intimation that the honour had reference to His burial. These details are too specific and peculiar to have concurred at different times. Again, Luke and John agree that the woman washed Christ's feet, and wiped them with the hair of her head, which was certainly so singular a proceeding, as not to allow the supposition of being repeated. Let it be added, that John gives this token as characteristic of Mary the sister of Lazarus, that she was the person who washed the feet of Jesus, and wiped them with her hair. But a thing which happened more than once, could hardly be mentioned as a sufficient distinguishing mark of any one."

We shall now proceed, first, to examine the reasons alleged against the identity of these seemingly different persons, and then proceed to an exposition of the reasons in favour of that identity.

1. It is asserted that chronological data will not allow the anointing in Luke to be one with the anointing in Bethany; and therefore that the sinner cannot be identified with the sister of Lazarus. " The anointing recorded in Luke," says Bengel on Luke vii., "took place in a Galilean town before the Transfiguration, indeed before the time of the second Passover; while the other anointing took place at Bethany, six days before the third Passover." But this argument rests upon the unsound hypothesis, that chronological principles must alone rule the

order of events in the Gospel of Luke,—a view by which Bengel was so far led astray, as to assume that there was a double pair of sisters Mary and Martha, one Galilean, Luke x., and another of Bethany, and which in other respects has introduced such inextricable confusion. Luke announces, in ch. i. 3, that he purposed giving the events in their order. But the analogy of the book of Judges teaches us that we are not to extend this purpose to every detail. The author of that book says, in the first words of it, that he intended to write what took place after the death of Joshua. But he then forthwith, throughout the first chapter, recapitulates events that occurred during Joshua's life, which were of importance for the right understanding of events which took place after his death; and in ch. ii. 6 seq. he returns back to the times of Joshua. The words, "And it came to pass after Joshua was dead," at the beginning, were designed, therefore, only to lay down the *rule*, which would admit of exceptions where circumstances rendered them necessary. So also is it with Luke. The beginning and the end of his Gospel relate events in their chronological succession. But in the middle, after he has brought down the history to the verge of the Passion, between the active work and the sufferings of the Redeemer, we have in ch. ix. 57–xviii. 34, an entire circle of events which he did not purpose to adjust chronologically; thereby intimating, that in this section everything bears an indefinite character, so far as time and place are concerned,—a testimony against those who would enforce chronological rules upon matter that obstinately resists them. In this part of Luke's Gospel, which is not fettered by chronology, and which is justified by the consideration, that in Holy Scripture everything gives way to edification, stands the narrative of the visit of Jesus to Mary and Martha, ch. x. 38 seq. In reference to the chronological position of this visit we are left perfectly free: the writer gives us not the least intimation. But the same Spirit from whom proceeded the interpolation of this whole chronologically unconnected mass, manifests its influence in various ways, even in those parts which are chronologically connected. Luke even in them also combines the succession of time with the connection in the nature of the events: he introduces parentheses, and places things related by their character in juxtaposition. Such a parenthesis occurs in the narrative of the feast in the house of Simon the Pharisee, concerning the sinner and her anointing, ch. vii. 36–50. This is not an arbitrary supposition: it rests upon plain and obvious grounds. The narrative is given as an appendix to the Lord's declaration in ch. vii. 34: " The Son of man is come eating and drinking; and ye say, Behold a gluttonous man, and a winebibber, a friend of publicans and sinners !" The Pharisaic offence at " the friend of publicans and sinners," could not be better exemplified than by this narrative. The catchword ἁμαρτωλός serves to connect the event related in its chronological sequence and the interpolation with each other. Thus the account of Luke's anointing is perfectly free as to its chronological place: what that place is, must be found in the other Evangelists. Luke says nothing about the time of its occurrence.

2. " Martha and her sister," it is said, " were of Bethany, but Magdalen of Galilee." But there is no contradiction here. The name Magdalena certainly points most probably to Magdala as the home of Mary, and thus of Martha also,—a place mentioned in Matt. xv. 39 as on the west coast of the sea of Gennesareth, a few miles from Tiberias, and now *el Medschdel*. The free communication between Jerusalem, in a certain sense the metropolis of the whole people, and the country, easily explains how Martha came to Bethany. Simon may have made her acquaintance at one of her visits to the feasts. With the change of her dwelling, the change of her designation would concur. The original name we know not. Martha, " the lady," was certainly not her original name, but the honourable designation which was given her when she became the mistress of the rich Simon's household affairs, just as in earlier days she who was called as a virgin Iscah (Gen. xi. 29), obtained as Abraham's wife the name of Sarai, " my dominion," honourable lady. In Jerusalem the name Martha would not have been very distinguishing, only having value within the house; but it was quite sufficient for the little village of Bethany, where there was only one lord, the rich Simon, whose property was there, and also one " lady."[1] Mary had remained in Galilee, and

---

[1] Instead of בעלת הבית in 1 Kings xvii. 17, the Targum has מרת ביתא. The maid in 2 Kings v. 3 speaks למרתה, to her mistress. In Isa. lx. 2, the maid and her mistress, מרתה, are placed together. In Bereshith Rabba, sec. 47, we read: " The Rabbis say מרתא for בעלה, mistress of the house."

there led a life of sin. After the Lord had cast seven evil spirits out of her, she had followed Him in His travels through Galilee, Luke viii. 1–3. She could not separate from Him with whom she had received the death of her sinful passions. He had become the magnet of her life. Darkness came upon her inner being when she no longer saw this light. About half a year before His death Jesus had left Galilee. During the entire period between the last Feast of Tabernacles and the last Passover, He remained in Jerusalem and its neighbourhood (Bethabara and Ephraim). Mary had accompanied Him in the journey from Galilee to Jerusalem, Matt. xxvii. 55, 56; Mark xv. 40, 41; Luke xxiii. 49, 55; John xix. 25. What should she do in Galilee, when the "great light" which had risen upon the darkness of that country had retired from it? Nothing remained for her then but the remembrance of her sins. When Mary went to Judea, she was directed to take up her abode with her sister. There she could "sit still in the house," and show that the words of Prov. vii. 11 no longer applied to her ("she is loud and stubborn; her feet abide not in her house"); she could at the same time continue her communion with the Healer of her soul. The visit to the sisters which Luke x. 38–42 records, took place during the time of our Saviour's abode in Jerusalem after the Feast of Tabernacles. That Jesus often went to Bethany, we learn from the history of His last days, when He was wont to pass the night in that village, after spending the day in Jerusalem. In Bethany Lazarus also had found a new home. That he abode in the house of his brother-in-law, and such a brother-in-law, leads us to the conclusion that he had adopted a similar course to that of his sister Mary; and this is confirmed by the special love that Jesus bore to him, Matt. xviii. 10–14; Luke xv. 4–7, xix. 10. That his position in the house of his brother-in-law was a humble one, we may gather from the conduct of the latter to his sister-in-law; and we have a direct assurance of it in the parable concerning Lazarus. This parable, which Jesus probably delivered on the same occasion, forms the counterpart to the transaction between Jesus and Simon touching Mary Magdalen.

3. "If Luke," it is urged, "meant the same woman, why does he designate her by different names, and speak no other-

wise in chs. vii. viii. x. than if he intended to introduce to us three different women? In ch. x. 38 he speaks of Mary the sister of Lazarus as of one unknown, while in ch. viii. he had already referred to the Magdalen. Mary the sister of Martha is never termed Magdalene, and Mary Magdalene is never termed the sister of Martha or Lazarus." This argument is at first glance very plausible; but it loses its force when we remark that the Evangelists, in their communications concerning the relations of Mary and Martha, were under a certain degree of restraint. As to the reasons of this reserve, we are left to conjecture. One reason was probably a regard for Gentile readers. In the writings of the Old Testament we meet with only exceptional instances of such regard—for instance, in the preacher Solomon. These writings were, as a whole, ignored by the Gentile world. But it was otherwise with the writings of the New Testament. They were written in the language then universal; and the tendency of the Christian Church, from the beginning, was to make incursions upon heathenism, while the Church of the Old Testament was content to maintain its own existence. The result corresponded with the design. It was natural that the spirit of defence in heathenism would fasten its keen observation on the written archives of the new religion, and use them in its own service. This being the case, it seemed perilous to lay open very explicitly the life of Mary; it might be surrendering to the rude mockery of the Gentiles one of the leading persons of Christianity, and with her the Christian cause itself. It seemed more appropriate to give mere hints, so that only the deeper investigators might understand the whole connection of things, which would remain hidden from superficial readers. A second design was, as it seems to us, one of pious respect to Martha. It was not desirable to expose to all the world the strange household relations in which she stood as the wife of Simon the Pharisee. But whatever view we may take of the reasons of it, the fact of an intentional reserve lies clearly before us; and with it the argument we now consider falls to the ground. *Luke* introduces to us in ch. vii. 36, "a woman which was a sinner." That he knows her name, but will not mention it, is shown by what immediately follows, where he retrospectively, and with a secret hint, alludes to her name. When in ch.

viii. 1 seq. he returns again to the chronological order, he makes mention of "certain women which had been healed of evil spirits and infirmities," placing at their head Mary Magdalene, "out of whom went seven devils." There we have the "sinner." But even in this gentle and prudently hinted solution of the mystery which the previous section presents, we have the same reserve again. The expression, which had already occurred in Mark xvi. 9, retains a certain ambiguity, so that it might be explained of an "infirmity," a merely bodily infliction. The sin is at the same time disguised under the veil of this expression. *Matthew* and *Mark* record the anointing in Bethany as performed by "a woman." That they know the name, and that it was concealed only for the time, is plain from the fact that they record the declaration of Christ, "Verily, verily, I say unto you, Wherever this Gospel shall be preached in all the world, there shall this 'that this woman hath done be told for a memorial of her." Name and memorial are inseparably connected together. In *John's* account of the last feast in Bethany, the giver of the feast is designedly unmentioned. "They," it is said, "made Him a feast." Lazarus was not the host; for he is expressly mentioned as one of the *guests*. Who the host was, is indirectly contained in the remark that "Martha served;" that is, according to New Testament phraseology, played the hostess. That Martha was married, is plain from her name: she appears as the head of the house in Luke x. 38, "A woman named Martha received Him into *her* house;" she requires of Mary only that she should lend her co-operation, and help her in her many cares as the mistress of the house. Bengel properly compares 1 Cor. vii. 32 seq. If Martha was the hostess, her husband must have been the host. His name had been mentioned already in Matt. xxvi. 6, "When Jesus was in Bethany, in the house of Simon the leper," and in Mark xiv. 3. But there Martha is not mentioned, and the name of Mary is also wanting. John, on the other hand, omits to give the name of the host, although well known to him. We see that all the Evangelists have it in view, that the unpleasant family relations of this house should not, at the first glance, be laid bare. Simon is in Luke plainly mentioned, but not the husband of Martha. Luke isolates him, in order to show his title to make his comment. Never are Simon and Martha brought together in the narratives. We are obliged to supply the inference that he was the husband of Martha. The same design appears in John also, in the circumstance that in ch. xix. 25 he suddenly introduces the name of Mary Magdalene, without giving the reader any further intimation about her, without giving any answer to the obvious question as to her relation to Mary the sister of Lazarus. For the great mass of readers this relation was, for the time, to remain uncertain. For this there was probably another reason, in addition to those already suggested. Many readers would find more edification in these things when distributed among several persons, than when united in one. And the Evangelists would not prevent this. But, at the same time, care was taken that the true relation of things might be known by those to whom their occurrence in one person would not be an offence, but yield edification, who were thoroughly free from the Pharisaical spirit of Simon,—a thing more difficult than to many it might appear. That the Apostles themselves were not altogether free from this spirit, is plain from the fact that Judas was able to infect them with his murmuring displeasure. Had not Mary been a "sinner," this would not have been possible.

4. "It is said concerning the sinner of Luke, that she was *a woman in the city.* The Mary of Lazarus, on the contrary, dwelt in Bethany, which is by Luke himself, in ch. x., described as a village." But there is no real contradiction in this. The connection in which Luke communicates the narrative of the sinner in ch. vii., as a mere appendage to the assertion that Christ was the friend of publicans and sinners, independently of all chronological sequence, of itself intimates that external relations would be given only in the vaguest generality. Exactness would in such a case be not an advantage, but a defect. Where the account was so general, Bethany might appropriately be spoken of as the suburb of "a city." The article does not denote a definite city, but stands as often generically—the city in opposition to the country : so *the* mountain in Matt. v. 1, is really *a* mountain, and thus translated by Luther; and *the* ship of Matt. ix. 1, *a* ship. Bethany was a *suburbium* of Jerusalem: according to John xi. 18, it lay "nigh to Jerusalem," only 15 stadia removed; and the citizens had there their resort, according to vers. 19, 45, 46, and the

narrative of the feast, Luke xi. 37 seq. The property of Simon was related to the city, as a detached country-house to a village. Jesus was wont to retire there to spend the night during His last week. As here the city, in a wider sense, includes its surroundings, so Jericho is used for the district of Jericho in Matt. xx. 29. Jesus had spent the night in the neighbourhood of the city. When he left that lodging, a blind man met Him near the city who sat and begged, according to Luke xviii. 35, who does not here contradict Matthew, but only, as a later writer, gives the more exact details.

5. "The sinner" comes, as Augustin says, first to Jesus, and obtains through her humiliation and tears the forgiveness of her sins. This seems to show that she must be distinguished from the sister of Lazarus, with whom Jesus at the anointing in Bethany was already well acquainted, and who was the only sister-in-law of Simon the leper, at whose house the feast was made. But Schleiermacher, in his work upon Luke, has shown in what difficulties we are entangled, if, deceived by appearances,—which here result from the fact, that Luke takes a particular incident in the life of the sinner, and interweaves it into a complete exhibition of Christ's life,—we assume that the sinner had been hitherto a perfect stranger to Jesus and the circle into which she entered. "Is it indeed probable," he asks, "that a respectable Pharisee at a great feast would have permitted entrance into the guest-chamber to a person whose reputation was so foul, and so justly foul, in the whole neighbourhood? The person who should venture on and accomplish such an act —without being rejected with abhorrence and removed, or appearing in a very adventurous and ridiculous light—must, on the one hand, have had a right to be there, and to enter among the guests, and, on the other, have stood in some well understood relation to Christ Himself." The appearance as if the sinner now for the first time obtained forgiveness of sins, has arisen from the fact that Jesus defends her against the attack of her Pharisaic brother-in-law; as also that she had been constrained by the uncourteous conduct of this brother-in-law towards Jesus to give a new expression to the fulness of her heart's love and gratitude towards Him, and thus to retrieve the Christian honour of the house. To Simon the Pharisee, Mary is never anything but a sinner. A supernatural gift he

has never himself experienced in his own heart, and so can never acknowledge it in another. In opposition to his spiritual rudeness, Jesus confirms to the humiliated Mary, before all the guests, the forgiveness of her sins. A similar position to what he assumed towards his sister-in-law Mary, Simon assumed towards his brother-in-law Lazarus. The parable concerning Lazarus, which Jesus delivered probably at the same meal, is the counterpart of the colloquy between Simon and Jesus concerning Mary Magdalene. That this parable had a historical basis, was shown by the Fathers.[1] If we deny the connection between John's Lazarus and the Lazarus of the parable, we pave the way for modern destructive criticism, which uses the parable in order to bring into suspicion the historical truth of the narrative of John.[2] It is a striking circumstance in itself, that any name is mentioned in the parable. This occurs in no other parable of the New Testament. But if Jesus had purposed to use a name, He certainly would not have used this one in particular, which must have made all think of the Lazarus so nearly related to Himself, if He had not had this same Lazarus in His eye. With the historical Lazarus, who dwells in the house of his brother-in-law, a rich man, and eats at his table, the Lazarus of the parable has this in common, that he satisfies himself with the crumbs that fell from the rich man's table: the historical relation is presented to us here only with a poetical clothing. The Lazarus of the parable *dies*, and goes into Abraham's bosom: and the starting-point for the poetry lies in the history itself. And even for the *resurrection* of the historical Lazarus we have a point of connection in the parable. It is said in Luke xvi. 31, "If they hear not Moses and the prophets, neither will they be convinced if one should rise from the dead." This passage has close affinity with John xi. 46, where we read, after the record that many believed in consequence of the resurrection of Lazarus, "But some went to the Pharisees, and told them what Jesus had done." We may well assume that Simon was among the

---

[1] Tertullian, *de Animâ*, says: Imaginem existimas exitum illum pauperis lætantis et divitis mærentis? Et quid illic Lazari nomen, si non in veritate res est? Feuardentius on Irenæus, B. iv. c. 4, has collected similar testimonies from the Greek and Latin Fathers.

[2] Baur, über die Evangelien, s. 249.

number of these. Even the name "leper," which he bears in Matthew and Luke, awakens no favourable prejudice towards him. A man would not continue to be designated by such an opprobrious name, after being healed of the disease, unless his spiritual nature suggested a certain analogy with that disease. And what is recorded of him in Luke vii. excellently suits this name. If after the resurrection of Lazarus he retained the same disposition towards Christ which that narrative displays, where he denied to the guest obtruded upon him the most common courtesies, we may well rely upon it that he was the centre of what is recorded in John, ver. 46. Thus, probably, from the same house in which Mary sat at Jesus' feet, and Martha served Him with joyful heart, where Lazarus dwelt whom Jesus loved, proceeded the first impulse to the Saviour's death. It is obvious to assume that Simon nourished a mortal hatred towards Him who had disturbed the peace of his house, Matt. x. 34. Finally, even the five brothers in the parable belong, as Bengel perceived, not simply and solely to the region of fiction. The originals might well have sat at this same table. We have, in Luke xi. 37 seq., yet another scene which seems to belong to this same feast. A Pharisee there also invites Jesus to his table : not a Pharisee like Nicodemus, but, as the conversation at the table shows, one of the ordinary stamp. There we have certain quite peculiar relations in the house of this Pharisee, such as could scarcely have been found in any other than the house of Simon. This circumstance leads us only to identify the house, in which probably the scene also of Luke xiv. 1–24 is to be placed, where Jesus is invited by one " of the chief Pharisees" to eat on the Sabbath. But while the latter scene probably belongs to the time of the abode of Jesus in Jerusalem, before the journey into the country beyond Jordan, John x. 40,—the same time in which the visit of Jesus to Mary and Martha, Luke x., falls,—in Luke xi. 37 seq. there are definite reasons which lead us to the last meal in Bethany,— namely, the fact that, according to ver. 49, this meal must have occurred in the last days of our Lord; and again, the coincidence of the discourses which Jesus uttered against the scribes and Pharisees with Matt. xxiii.[1] The description of the vivid

[1] Probably there is some internal connection between the facts, that Jesus to the Pharisee's offence does not wash His hands, Luke xi. 38, and that

conflict of Jesus with His fellow-guests, the Pharisees and scribes, in vers. 53, 54, assures us of the originals of the rich man's five brothers. This further sets aside the remark of Bengel, "Simon the Pharisee doubts whether Jesus were a prophet; Simon the leper could not doubt, in the presence of Lazarus raised up." That he could doubt, is clear from John xi. 46, according to which eye-witnesses of that resurrection told the Pharisees with an evil motive what Jesus had done; and that he did actually doubt, from the combination of the parable of Lazarus with this passage. That there must be a connection between Luke xvi. 31, "If they hear not Moses and the prophets, neither will they be persuaded though one rose from the dead," and John xi. 46, has forced itself upon the convictions of many expositors. Stier, for example, remarks on the latter passage, "Now Luke xvi. 31 has its impressive fulfilment;" which proceeds, however, upon the unfounded supposition that the parable of Lazarus belonged to an earlier period. The possibility of the doubt in itself could not, however, be denied. A Pharisee like Simon is a poor psychologist when the light side of human nature comes into question. He judges all things according to his own perverted heart, and after the fashion of his party, so rich in wiles and self-deception. A preconcerted plan between Jesus and the three Christian members of his household was to the cunning Jew the solution of the whole problem; and, in fact, he could not go further who was morally so low as not to recoil from the supposition of such a concerted scheme.

6. "The Pharisee Simon says, in Luke vii. 39: This man, if he were a prophet, would have known who and what manner of woman this is that toucheth him; for she is a sinner. According to this, the sinner was till now unknown to Jesus, while the Mary of Lazarus had stood in the nearest relation to Jesus long before the meal at Bethany." But we have already shown in what perplexities we involve ourselves, when we assume that this woman then for the first time entered into the presence of Jesus and the circle which joined Him around the table. The

the Pharisee, Luke vii. 44, gives Him no water for His feet. A guest who neglected the most sacred customs, seemed to the Pharisee deserving of no civility. He rejoiced that what sprang from his own inclination was thus in some sense justified.

objection, however, is robbed of its point by observing that the word *prophet* here only includes the idea of holy man, and sent of God; and that the *knowing* here, as often, is not a merely superficial and purely theoretical knowledge, but real and practical—such a knowing as that of Isa. lxiii. 16, where Israel says to God: " Doubtless Thou art our Father, though Abraham be ignorant of us, and Israel acknowledge us not: Thou, O Lord, art our Father, our Redeemer; Thy name is everlasting;" as also that of Hos. xiii. 5. Simon does not stumble at Christ's theoretical ignorance, but at the fact that He *ignores* and pretermits the earlier sinful course of this woman. It is not said in vain, " When the *Pharisee,* which had bidden Him, saw it." It was as a Pharisee that Simon took offence at the conduct of Jesus. The whole narrative is recorded as an adjunct to the remark that the Pharisees took offence at " the friend of publicans and sinners." If the knowing here is understood of being acquainted with the mere fact, Simon does not interpose as a Pharisee, and the connection with ver. 34 is lost. According to our view, we have here a distinct parallel to Matt. ix. 11 : " And when the Pharisees saw it, they said unto His disciples, Why eateth your Master with publicans and sinners?"

7. " At the anointing of Luke vii. no one murmured on account of the waste of the ointment; only the Pharisee thought within himself that Jesus, if a prophet, would not have let this woman touch Him; but in John xii. Judas murmurs on account of the waste of the precious substance, and Christ defends this act. In Luke, Christ instructs Simon in the nature of true love as the undeceiving sign and assurance of justifying faith, and announces to her who had anointed Him the forgiveness of her sins. In John there is nothing of all this." But there is no contradiction here: nothing more than agreement and supplementing. The narrative of Luke was required by its object to bear a partial character. He gives it only as an illustration of the Pharisaic complaint against Christ as the " friend of publicans and sinners." Weisse (die evang. Gesch. ii. s. 143) has rightly stated this one-sided characteristic of the narrative: " The peculiar essence of the narrative is brought out by the parable of the two debtors, with the appended application. Jesus would plainly show how a converted sinner—that is, one who knows and repents of her sins—is of

more value than such righteous persons as have never attained to a true consciousness of their sinful condition." A second scene which was enacted at the anointing—that which contains the displeasure and murmurings of the disciples, as already recorded by Matthew and Mark—it did not comport with Luke's object to introduce. This scene stands in an internal connection with the former, as we have already intimated. After Simon's assault upon the woman had been decisively repelled by our Lord, there arose a murmuring against her even in the circle of the disciples. These were disposed, after she had been so highly exalted by Christ, to prepare for her a slight humiliation; for they themselves were as yet not quite exalted above the prejudice excited by the fact that she had been such a sinner. John almost expressly points to the representation in Luke, when he describes the anointing in words taken from that Gospel; and he then supplements Matthew and Mark by the information that the centre of the opposition to Mary in the apostolical circle was Judas the traitor. This gives a very significant contribution to the understanding of the transaction. It suits well the character of Judas that he should come to the help of Simon, and lead up another seemingly justifiable assault against Mary. Simon and the son of Simon understand each other. The others, or at least several among them, are carried away by the specious argument; they exhibit the relics of a Pharisaical spirit still within them, and which could not be destroyed and entirely disappear until the outpouring of the Holy Spirit. The collision between the believing and the unbelieving portion of the guests, inevitable at such a time of intense excitement, gave occasion to Jesus, during the progress of the meal, to deliver the parable of Lazarus,—in consequence, probably, of offensive allusions which Simon made to the disparagement of his brother-in-law, as he had formerly done in the case of his sister-in-law. And with all this there is abundant room also at this feast for what is recorded in Luke xi. 37 seq. The intimation there, that the conflict began with the commencement of the feast, ch. xi. 38, completely coincides with Luke vii. 45, 46. We might expect a plenitude of events at a feast which occurs in the eventful period of our Lord's last days.

8. Finally, "The sinner in Luke," it is affirmed, "cannot be

identical with Mary Magdalene. For what is said of the latter —that Jesus cast out of her seven spirits or 'demons'—does not infer a life of sin, but rather a derangement for which she was not responsible. Where demons are introduced, possession, as commonly understood, is meant." But the demons do not stand in any particular relation to possession: they everywhere signify the "angels of Satan," Matt. xxv. 41, Rev. xii. 7, whose ministry he uses for all his evil works. This appears most plainly in 1 Tim. iv. 1, where the teachings of error are termed "the doctrines of demons," thus ascribing to them an influence in the purely spiritual domain; and from 1 Cor. x. 20, it is evident also, where the Gentiles are represented as sacrificing to demons, and not to God, and those who partake of Gentile sacrificial feasts as entering into the fellowship of demons. Here also the demons appear as presiding over a moral region, and from whom a kind of moral contagion proceeds. When James, ch. ii. 19, says, "The demons believe and tremble," he evidently has in view the whole of the "spiritual powers of wickedness," Eph. vi. 12. And when our Lord, in Matt. ix. 34, describes Satan as the "prince of the demons," He doubtless meant all the powers of evil spirits which exist apart from Satan, and not one individual class of them. We are led to the same result by the fact that the expressions, "evil spirits," Luke vii. 21, and "unclean spirits," Matt. x. 1, Luke iv. 33, Mark iii. 11, are used interchangeably with demons. These expressions are too general to allow of their being restricted to any special classes of evil spirits. Moreover, to these "unclean spirits," identical with the demons, there is expressly attributed by our Lord, in Matt. xii. 43 seq., an influence in spiritual things: "When the unclean spirit is gone out of a man, etc.; then goeth he and taketh to himself seven other spirits more wicked than himself." Thus the Lord speaks when depicting the growing depravation which would follow upon the beginnings of repentance among the Jews, who, in consequence of the manifestation of Christ, would degenerate into a "synagogue of Satan." This passage is all the more important, since here, and in the whole New Testament *only* here, we find the *seven* demons or unclean spirits of Mary Magdalene recurring.

But the fact remains, that throughout the Gospels the demons are commonly introduced with reference to so-called possession; while, on the other hand, the morally evil influences which come from hell are referred directly to Satan, who, for example, put it into the heart of Judas to betray the Redeemer, John xiii. 2, and enters into Judas, Luke xxii. 3. But this is explained by the consideration, that moral surrender to the dark powers, as being the more awful, leads the thought more obviously and directly to that "old serpent," whose working was manifested in the moral region at the first commencements of human history. No unchangeable rule can be deduced from this. Even as possession in Acts x. 38 is referred directly to the devil, so in certain circumstances moral degradation may be represented as resulting from the influence of demons. The reason why this was the case with Mary Magdalene, we have already indicated. Thus there was a veil thrown over her former melancholy condition.

These, then, are the reasons which may be urged against the personal identity of the Sinner, Mary Magdalene, and Mary the sister of Lazarus. It remains that we exhibit the positive arguments which support the hypothesis of that identity.

If Mary Magdalene and the sister of Lazarus are made two persons, the latter was not present at the crucifixion, had no connection with the embalming (Mark xvi. 1; Luke xxiii. 55 seq.), and was not amongst the witnesses of the resurrection. The place which we should assign to the woman so inwardly bound to the Lord, to Mary the sister of Lazarus living so near as Bethany, is everywhere appropriated to Mary Magdalene. At the cross there is only one Mary present, the wife of Cleopas, besides Mary Magdalene and the mother of Jesus, John xix. 25. At the entombment of Jesus we miss the sister of Lazarus all the more, as she had, John xii. 7, already pre-symbolized the burial of the Lord. Was she likely to have left the actual embalming to the hands of others?

As Peter regularly stands at the head in the lists of the Apostles, so does Mary Magdalene when women are mentioned. This place of honour is given her in all the four Evangelists. Thus it is in the enumeration of the women who followed Jesus in Galilee, Luke viii. 2; in the narratives of the crucifixion, Matt. xxvii. 56, Mark xv. 40, 47; of the entombment, Matt.

xxvii. 61, Mark xvi. 1; of the resurrection, Matt. xxviii. 1, Mark xvi. 9, Luke xxiv. 10. The only exception is John xix. 25. There, Mary the sister of the Lord's mother is mentioned before Mary Magdalene. But this was done evidently to avoid sundering her from the previously mentioned mother of Jesus, who naturally took precedence of Mary Magdalene, and formed the centre of the occurrence there mentioned. How absolutely Mary Magdalene took the first place in John's Gospel, is plain from ch. xx. 1, 18, where she alone is mentioned, and those who accompanied her are left unmentioned. Now, if we distinguish Mary Magdalene from the Mary of Lazarus, and from the sinner of Luke, we lose all reason for such a distinction—the uniformity of which, however, shows that it, like the distinction of Peter, must rest upon some definite fact, and some express word of our Lord connected with that fact. For the isolated Mary Magdalene there remains no reason but this one, that Jesus cast seven devils out of her; but this is not sufficient. We need some fact which exhibits Mary as more than merely suffering and receiving. The anointing and the glorious commendation which Jesus gave her on occasion of it—this is the true solution of the mystery of the distinction of Mary Magdalene.

The anointing in Bethany is recorded by Matthew, Mark, and John. We might naturally expect that Luke also would include it. For it was in reference to it that Jesus said, " Verily, verily, I say unto you, Wheresoever this Gospel shall be preached in all the world, this also that this woman hath done shall be told for a memorial of her." But Luke contains this memorial, only if we recognise the identity of the sinner in ch. vii. with Mary the sister of Lazarus.

John, in ch. xi. 2, gives it as a characteristic mark of Mary of Lazarus, that she anointed the Lord, and wiped His feet with the hairs of her head. But this token would lose its distinctiveness, if we suppose that another woman, the sinner in Luke vii., had performed the same act; and this passage excludes the notion of a double anointing on the part of Mary herself, for here only *one* anointing is spoken of. Had there been two, then, in the time that John wrote, the anointing recorded by him in ch. xii., and already before him by Matthew and Mark, would not less than the earlier have passed out of remembrance.

John must then necessarily have separated off the one from the other. Moreover, we are otherwise involved in the greatest difficulties by the assumption that the one Mary anointed twice. What, once performed, was an expression of deep and true feeling, must partake, on repetition, of another and forced character. The whole transaction of the anointing is perfectly intelligible only if we combine all the elements which on the one hand occur in Luke, and on the other in John, as forming its conditions; and thus assign to it one motive, and rescue it, once only performed, from all imputation of extravagance on the part of Mary. The things to be assumed are, that Mary had been a sinner, and had found mercy through Jesus; that our Lord had given to her, feeling so deeply as she did her own unworthiness, the very highest proof of His love in the resurrection of her brother; that Jesus was dishonoured by the master of the same house that had received such a deliverance; and that thus a mighty impulse had been given to show " that gratitude had not died out upon earth," and that Simon had not infected the whole house with his leprosy. This house was disinfected by the savour of Mary's ointment from the pestilential vapours with which Judas had previously filled it. If it had before represented the germ of the synagogue of Satan, now it became a type of the future Church of Christ. Mary was urged the rather to present the very utmost in honour of Jesus, and to go to the very verge of the extravagant, inasmuch as she knew that the sufferings and death of Jesus impended, that she was paying Him the *last* honour—a circumstance to which our Lord expressly gives prominence for her justification: comp. ch. xii. 7.

The hypothesis of two distinct anointings is encountered by the insuperable difficulty of both having occurred in the house of a *Simon;* but his designation, on the one hand, as a Pharisee, and on the other as a leper, presents no contradiction, but rather the reverse. By what figure could Pharisaism be better designated or described than by that of leprosy, by which man in a living body becomes an offensive and abhorred thing? Both anointings, further, took place at a *feast*, and both have in common the highly characteristic circumstance of the wiping of Jesus' feet with the hair of the anointer's head. But the Evangelists have so carefully ordered their expressions, that he cannot err who very carefully follows their hints. There are phenomena here which are very characteristic in regard to the relation of the Evangelists generally. The later writers adopted the most characteristic expressions of the earlier, thereby as good as expressly citing them, while declaring their purpose to be only supplementary; just as, in the narrative of Moses, his manner when returning to the same object is not expressly to adopt the same words again—which would not suit the popular character of Holy Writ—but to connect the latter with the former by verbal repetition, mingled with inserted supplementary matter. Luke borrows the very peculiar ἀλάβαστρον μύρου, " an alabaster box of ointment," from Matt. xxvi. 7, Mark xiv. 3, and intimates thereby that his anointing is the same with that of Bethany. John indicates the identity of the anointing related by him with that of Matthew and Mark, by adopting from the latter the commercial expression πιστική, unadulterated (Mark xiv. 3, νάρδου πιστικῆς πολυτελοῦς; John xii. 3, νάρδου πιστικῆς πολυτίμου). On the other hand, by the literal adherence to Luke vii. 38, in ch. xi. 2, he intimates that the anointing by Mary, recorded by him, is identical with the anointing by the sinner in Luke vii. (John xi. 2, ἦν δὲ Μαρία ἡ ἀλείψασα τὸν Κύριον μύρῳ, καὶ ἐκμάξασα τοὺς πόδας αὐτοῦ ταῖς θριξὶ αὐτῆς; Luke, τοὺς πόδας αὐτοῦ—ταῖς θριξὶ—αὐτῆς ἐξέμασσε—καὶ ἤλειφε τῷ μύρῳ). How closely John adheres to Luke, is emphatically shown by the fact that his " who wiped His feet with her hair" is explicable only by comparison with Luke. John thoughtfully refers the wiping, not to the ointment, but to the feet. The precious ointment, which was rubbed in, could scarcely be regarded with any propriety as the object of the wiping. This points to water or the like: comp. ch. xiii. 5. But nothing of this kind has been mentioned in John; nor can the mystery be solved but by a comparison with Luke. According to ver. 38, Mary washed the feet of Jesus with her *tears*, and dried them with the hairs of her head: comp. ver. 44. John could not have written thus, had he not designed that the supplement should be taken from Luke; unless the notion of the Fathers be the correct one, that the Evangelists form a four-sided whole.

The account in Luke on the one side, and of John on the other, mutually supplement and are necessary to each other.

The questions which force themselves upon us in Luke,—How came Jesus in the house of the Pharisee, who displayed so unfriendly, yea, so decidedly inimical a feeling towards Him? What could have induced such a man, who stood in absolutely no internal relation to Him, who denied Him the commonest courtesies which a host shows his guests, to invite Jesus; and what could have induced Jesus to accept the invitation? How came the sinner in this company?—are questions which receive their answers in the narrative of John. But in his narrative also there are many things which compel us to go back to Luke. If we regard the family circle in Bethany as limited to Lazarus and his two sisters, we can hardly understand the mixed company which was assembled there for condolence, and cannot see why Jesus did not at once go to the house, but remained outside at a distance; why Martha goes out to Him there; why she *secretly* calls her sister; and why that sister goes out without letting her company know the reason of her departure. Only when we regard the evil-minded Pharisee Simon as standing in the background, whose friends have met the personal acquaintances of Mary and Martha for the purpose of condoling, can we understand what is written in ch. xi. 46: "But some went to the Pharisees, and told them what Jesus had done." The intimation, "but Mary sat in the house," with its reference to Prov. vii. 12, is seen in its true light only when we recognise in the Mary of John the sinner of Luke. To this we are led also, that Mary has so large a quantity of precious ointment at her disposal. This ointment was not provided by Mary originally for the anointing of Jesus. It was already before in her possession; for otherwise the complaint would not have been that she had not sold the ointment, but that she had bought it instead of giving the money to the poor. Christ says in her justification, that she had *kept* the ointment against the day of His burial, John xii. 7, in opposition to the declaration of Judas, that she ought to have sold it. This possession of ointment infers a previous life of vanity. And the otherwise unaccountable wiping with her hair is only then rightly intelligible, when we consider that Mary had formerly made the hair of her head minister to sin, so that the present use of it was an act of penance: comp. 1 Pet. iii. 3. Both the ointment and the hair are similarly united in Judith x. 3. There we read that Judith, when she prepared herself to go to Holofernes, in order to attract him by her arts, "anointed herself with precious ointment, and braided the hair of her head." There is an analogy also with the women who, in the wilderness, dedicated their precious mirrors, previously the instruments of their vanity, to the service of the sanctuary, Ex. xxxviii. 8. So also the tears of her eyes and the kissing of Jesus' feet would refer to an earlier misuse both of her eyes and of her lips. The early Fathers noticed all these things. Gregory the Great says, in his 33d Homily on the Gospels (the passage is found in the Romish Breviary): "It is manifest that the woman, who had formerly abandoned herself to evil courses, applied the ointment to the perfuming of her flesh. What she had shamefully provided, she now worthily dedicated to God. With her eyes she had sought earthly vanity, but now she wept with them in penitence. With her mouth she had spoken proudly [but see rather Prov. v. 3, vii. 13], but now she kissed with it the Lord's feet." That the Mary of Lazarus, like the sinner, had led a passionate career, is intimated by John xi. 32: "When she saw Him, she fell down at His feet, and said, Lord, if Thou hadst been here, my brother had not died." Martha had used the same words; but the passionate falling at the feet of Jesus is peculiar to Mary. Here it is to be observed, that the preference for a place at the feet of Jesus is a tender bond, which connects the sinner of Luke with the Mary of Lazarus: comp. Luke vii. 38, x. 39; John xi. 32, xii. 2. That was the place most desirable to the state of her feeling, most appropriate to the profoundness of her inward sorrow. Also the coincidence between "which *toucheth* Him," in Luke vii. 39, with the words spoken to Mary Magdalene, "Touch Me not," John xx. 17, is not without significance. But it can here be only hinted at.

How strictly the accounts of the anointing interpenetrate and complete each other, may be further seen clearly in one small speciality. According to Matt. xxvi. 7, Mark xiv. 3, the woman pours the ointment on the head of Jesus. According to John xii. 3, Mary anoints the feet of Jesus. There can be no contradiction here, inasmuch as Matt., ver. 11, Mark, ver. 8, show that the anointing only began with the head, and had a more general character; and the quantity of the ointment requires us to assume that it was more general. The reconciliation we have in Luke. The feet there are the main concern. But there is an indirect allusion to the head in "My head with oil thou didst not anoint," in the words of Jesus to Simon. It belonged to the polemical character, so to speak, of the anointing, that she began with the part of the body which Simon had omitted to anoint. Then she turned to the part which the heart's feeling of the "Sinner" must have thought of most.

Do we lose anything if we recognise in the Mary of Lazarus the "woman that was a sinner?" Gregory gives us the answer to that question: "If I think of the penitence of Mary, I can better weep myself than say anything. For who has so hard a heart, that the tears of this sinner cannot soften it to repentance?"

The raising of Lazarus is recorded only in the Gospel of John. The silence of the other Evangelists need not perplex us, even if there were no specific reasons for it. Niebuhr (Geschichte Assurs und Babel, s. 6) says: "The Oriental historian is extremely precise in the chronological frame, but in the proper historical narrative very imperfect; so that omission of the most important incidents is no impeachment of his truth." The historical books of the Old Testament share in this peculiarity of Oriental historical writing; so that we need not wonder at finding it reproduced in the New Testament, where it was all the more natural, from the fact that the Divine plan provided for the supplementing of the earlier Evangelists by the later — just as in the canon of the Old Testament the Chronicles were introduced as supplementary. In the books of Kings, for instance, the combination of the tribes of the wilderness against Israel, under Jehoshaphat, is passed over in silence; a circumstance the deep importance of which we learn, not only from the historical account in 2 Chron. xx., but also from the psalms referring to it, xlvii., xlviii., lxxxiii., which confirm every feature in the account of the Chronicles. Viewed in the light of our own historical writing, the silence of the books of Kings is all the more unintelligible, inasmuch as nothing less than the very existence of God's people was at stake, and the wonderful deliverance which was vouchsafed to Israel was rich in edification for all generations of the people. So also in

2 Kings xxi. there is no trace of the carrying away of Manasseh to Babylon, nor of his conversion and restoration. The omission of the former point is all the more striking, since his carrying away captive was the punishment of Manasseh's guilt, on which the writer has dwelt at length.

John expressly says, in ch. xx. 30, xxi. 25, that it was not his design to exhaust the infinite treasures of the acts of Christ's life in his narrative, but only to make prominent some of them. This declaration holds good of all the Evangelists. This is supported by the fact, that the first three, apart from the history of the Passion, remain mostly in the Galilean domain ; and that Matthew expressly announces his intention to do so. If the Evangelists aimed only at an eclectic treatment, we might expect that the assertion, "the dead are raised up," in Matt. xi. 5, would be illustrated by the communication of at least one example in each Gospel. Luke has only two instances of the raising of the dead ; the others are content with recording only one of these.

The resurrection of Lazarus was assuredly an event of high importance. Yet we must be careful not to exaggerate that importance. We must not overlook the fact, that all miracles are essentially alike, and that it is altogether wrong to measure their greatness, as it were, by the ell. The Lord Himself, at the healing of the man born blind, ch. ix. 6, declared that it was a creative work, and thus that in reality it was on a level with the raising of Lazarus. If we observe that this very miracle formed, according to John, the occasion of the final catastrophe in the life of Jesus, it is not to be overlooked that also, according to John, the matter stood so, that even without this miracle that final catastrophe must have come. Ch. xi. 8 is sufficient to prove this. The raising of Lazarus was not the essential cause of the catastrophe, but only the accidental cause.

Let us turn now to a consideration of the special reasons which have been adduced for the silence of the first three Evangelists. We must first repel the notion that their silence sprang from ignorance of the event. The Lord went to the scene of Lazarus' resurrection in the company of His disciples, and Matthew was one of these. The three Evangelists record that feast of Simon which, according to John, stood in close connection with the raising of Lazarus. The anointing of Jesus at that meal was based upon that fact as having already occurred. But all doubt is removed by the parable of Lazarus in Luke, especially by the close of it, the connection of which with John xi. 46 has forced itself always upon expositors. How little right we have to infer ignorance from silence in their narratives, is plain enough from Matt. xxvi. 61, xxvii. 40, Mark xiv. 57-59, compared with John ii. 19. The first two Evangelists do not record the event contained in John, but they afterwards refer to it.

They have more show of reason on their side who explain the silence of the first three Evangelists by reference to Lazarus as being still alive. If these Gospels were written in the last days of the Jewish state, in which, as the Epistle to the Hebrews shows, excitement against the Christians had reached a very high pitch, the resurrection of the narrative might have led to a renewal of the danger which, according to John xii. 10, threatened the risen life of Lazarus. That personal regards were not without influence upon the inspiration of the Gospels, we have already seen in the example of Mary and Martha: another example Heumann refers to: " The first three Evangelists do not publish that Peter was the disciple who cut off the servant's ear. All three relate the fact; all three knew that Peter did it; but none of the three mentions him." We must not, however, forget that this only amounts to possibility, and that the hypothesis is not adequately supported by a historical basis.

Nor can we account for the omission by explaining that the first three Evangelists restricted themselves to the Galilean region until the Passion week. Matthew leaves that region in ch. xix. 1. Luke might, in that portion of his Gospel which is not fettered by chronological law, have as well related this fact as the parable concerning Lazarus. This reason is not, indeed, without some force. The communications relating to the time from the departure from Galilee to the festal entrance in Jerusalem, are in the first Gospels in the highest degree imperfect, as is evident from the fact that in Matthew they occupy only two chapters.

But the chief reason must doubtless be looked for in another direction. The great men of the Old Testament were instructed to change their voice. Among David's psalms, for example, there are those which, like the sixteenth, lead us into the mysterious depth of the life in God, and the characteristic name of which is מכתם, *secret;* and there are also those in which he condescends to the simple, plain alphabetical psalms, in which we find only a collection of proverbs. This twofold manner we find also in connection with our Lord and His Evangelists. The mysterious side of His nature was presented more especially in the metropolis, where He had to do with " those who see." For a colloquy like that with Nicodemus there could have been found in Galilee no immediate occasion. This double-sidedness of our Lord's manifestation rendered it necessary that the Gospel should not be written by any one single writer. The vocation of each Evangelist had reference to that only which was to him accessible. For the deep and mysterious that disciple had a special mission whom Jesus loved, and who lay on His bosom, as Christ in the bosom of the Father. It was not merely in the Divine plan for these writings that John was reckoned on and provided. In the apostolical circle also they looked upon him from the beginning as designed for this; and we cannot suppose that John's Gospel took the Church by surprise. The narrative of the raising of Lazarus belonged to the class of things reserved for John. That the mysterious character which it bears has its ground in the event itself, and not in the mere record, is plain from the comparison of the perfectly plain narrative of the healing of the man born blind in ch. ix., as also from the narrative of ch. iv. 43-54, which is nearly related in its character to the first three Evangelists. We can hardly imagine the history of Lazarus' resurrection told in the manner of the first three Evangelists. It belonged essentially to the " spiritual Gospel."

Let us now investigate the meaning of the event before us. It had this in common with all the miracles and signs of Christ —to serve for the glorification of the Son of God, ver. 4. But its individual and specific purport was, to typify and represent *the future resurrection of the dead.* Christ issues no mere bulls, or letters of simple authority. All that He will perform in that other world, He had already, during His earthly life, pretypified and symbolized in act; having by that type and symbol given an assurance of that which hath not yet appeared. We have here, as it were, the embodiment of the utterance which our

Lord gave in ch. v. 25, 28, 29 : " The hour cometh, when the dead shall hear the voice of the Son of God; and those that hear shall live. The hour cometh, in the which all that are in the graves shall hear His voice, and shall come forth; those which have done good, to the resurrection of life." The καὶ νῦν ἔστι of ch. v. 25 expressly points (see the commentary on the passage) to this typical significance of our Lord's resurrection acts : and thus the early Church interpreted them.[1] Vers. 23-27 of the present chapter, which can be understood only in this point of view, have special relation to the present event. The raising of Lazarus constitutes the climax of the pledges, given in act, of the future resurrection. Jesus re-awakened the daughter of Jairus, just dead, upon the very couch where her spirit departed; and the young man of Nain, on his way to the grave ; but He here signalizes His absolute dominion over death, by calling back to life one who had been four days dead, and in whom corruption had already begun to take place. The chronological position of this event corresponds with this internal relation which it bears to the other resurrections. It was not accidental that it befell at the end of the life of Jesus. This was its appropriate place ; and thus Christ, immediately before He gave Himself up to death, declared Himself to be the supreme ruler of death; thus He assured us of the voluntary character of His sacrifice, and gave warranty to the hope of His own resurrection.[2]

Besides being a pledge of the dominion of Christ over death in the more limited sense, this event also gives us assurance of the power of Christ to dispense salvation to all the

---

[1] Augustin: Oportebat ut modo aliqua faceret, quibus datis velut suæ virtutis indiciis, credamus in eum, et ad illam resurrectionem præparemur, quæ erat ad vitam, non ad judicium. Domini facta non sunt tantummodo facta, sed signa. Calvin : Fuit hic quasi extremus actus et clausula, jam enim mortis tempus appropinquabat : vivam imaginem ante oculos posuit futuræ nostræ resurrectionis.

[2] Lyser : It cannot be doubted that Christ reserved this celebrated miracle for the time when His own death was imminent, that He might heal the offence of His own cross and death, and render His resurrection after three days more credible. Inasmuch as Christ did not raise only the recently dead, but one who had been in the grave over three days, it was made more credible that He Himself after three days would arise, and did arise.

wretched, whose misery is living death: comp. on ch. v. 21. The Apostles were destined to experience such death in a living body after the death of Christ. But by His own resurrection the Saviour redeemed the pledge which, in regard to the salvation of His disciples from such a death, He had given them in the resurrection of Lazarus.—Bodily death is the figure and reflection of spiritual death. Instead of "In the day thou eatest thereof, thou shalt die," we may read, "In the day thou (spiritually) diest, thou shalt also (bodily) die." According to ch. v. 21, 24, Christ demonstrates His lifegiving power even in the present state by awakening sinners from the death of sin. Sinners are termed *dead* in Matt. viii. 22. "This my son was dead, and is alive again," is the language of his father concerning the prodigal son, Luke xv. The Apostle Paul describes believers as those who have become alive from the dead, Rom. vi. 13. He speaks in Eph. ii. 1 of those dead in trespasses and sins; and appeals to the sinner in ch. v. 14, "Arise from the dead." From this death too, the most frightful of all deaths, and the primitive form of death, we have the pledge of a joyful and blessed resurrection in the resurrection of Lazarus. It teaches us further that help is near, and help which is sufficient, even when death has gone very far, even when the ἤδη ὄζει has begun to take place.[1]

We have here the last of three manifestations of Christ's glory in Judea, which form a counterpart to three manifestations of His glory in Galilee: comp. on ch. ix. 1–x. 21. The second of them, recorded in ch. ix., the restoration of the man born blind, is referred to here in ch. xi. 37. As the manifestation of Christ's glory in ch. vi. is divided into two parts—the feeding, and the stilling of the tempest—we may reckon altogether seven manifestations in St John: three pertaining to Judea, and four to Galilee. This distribution is recommended by the fact that the number seven plays an important part elsewhere in John—both in the Gospel and in the Apocalypse.

In vers. 1–16 we have what preceded the journey to Bethany, as connected with it. The words of Lampe aptly express the

---

[1] Augustin: Quam difficile surgit, quem moles consuetudinis premit; sed tamen surgit: occulta gratia intus vivificatur, surgit post vocem magnam.

leading idea of this section: Primum indicia omniscientiæ Domini in ejus susceptione commemoratur. The Lord knew beforehand with supernatural assurance that the sickness would not issue in permanent death, but would tend to the glorification of the Son of God; that this journey would be without any peril to Himself; that Lazarus, whose sickness alone the message announced, was already dead; and that He Himself would raise him from death.

Ver. 1. "Now a certain man was sick, named Lazarus, of Bethany, the town of Mary and her sister Martha."—The "But," in opposition to what had been recorded in ch. x. 40-42 concerning the abode of Jesus on the other side Jordan, intimates that here begins the narration of the circumstances which occasioned His suspension of His work there. "Now a certain man was sick, named Lazarus:" this kind of introduction shows that we shall now have to do with a personage who had never yet (either in first three Gospels or in John) been mentioned. And this introduction was all the more appropriate, as the name Lazarus had already occurred in the Gospel of Luke; the Lazarus of whose parable stands in a certain relation with John's, so that it seemed proper to prepare the way for their identification. Bethany needed not to be distinguished from any other town of the same name. There was no such other town in existence; it is only a false reading which has introduced it into ch. i. 28; and if there had been another Bethany, some note of distinction would have been necessary. The expression, "the town of Mary and her sister Martha," was not introduced for that purpose; for Bethany had never been mentioned before as the dwelling of Martha and Mary, either in John or in the first three Gospels. These also speak of Bethany without any distinguishing note, and take it for granted that there was only one such place. The prepositions ἀπό and ἐκ do not demonstrate that Lazarus was born at Bethany; sufficient that at the time of the event he was dwelling there. The prepositions are used from the standing-point of the city, in which the whole people annually assembled for the high feasts, and which was the centre of the nation in a far higher sense than any other capital. ’Aπό, in respect to locality, does not ordinarily indicate derivation; but simply the place from which one comes to another place: comp. Matt.

CHAP. XI. 1.

xxvii. 57, ἄνθρωπος πλούσιος ἀπὸ 'Ἀριμαθαίας. If Mary came from Magdala, then the brother and sister came also from the same place. We find Lazarus in the house of his brother-in-law. He cannot therefore have been a resident in Bethany, as would have been to be expected, if he had originally sprung from Bethany.

Κώμη, village or hamlet, is, as it were, to be enclosed in quotation marks. That Mary and Martha dwelt in one κώμη had already been mentioned in Luke x. 38. John here supplementarily names the place, which Luke had designedly omitted to do. The veil which had been thrown over the earlier relations of the sisters is here at least partially withdrawn. John speaks of Mary and Martha as of persons known through the earlier narrative of Luke x. 38–42: the "certain man, named Lazarus," is introduced, by being connected with their names, into a circle already known to the readers. That Mary is mentioned before Martha, who is introduced as Mary's sister, is explained by the same passage in Luke, which represents Mary as spiritually the more important person. Ver. 2 gives a further reason. There we have the explanation, that the "sinner," who according to Luke vii. anointed the Lord; the "woman," who according to Matt. xxvi. 7, Mark xiv. 3, performed that act, in reference to which the approving word of Christ was spoken, "Verily, verily, I say unto you, Wherever this Gospel shall be preached in the whole world, there shall also this that this woman hath done be told for a memorial of her,"—was no other than Mary, to whom consequently the place of pre-eminence before her sister belonged by the best right. The selection of the expressions points so specifically to Luke vii. as to be equivalent to a simple quotation. The order here, in which Mary takes precedence,—John being guided pre-eminently by the spiritual relation,—is, however, not the only one. In ver. 19, Martha and Mary are mentioned in an order which has reference to their civil and social relation. In this last Martha was first, as Luke x. 38 shows, where Martha is represented as receiving Christ into her house, and Mary assumes a subordinate place. What Jesus says to Martha in Luke x. 41, μεριμνᾷς καὶ τυρβάζῃ περὶ πολλά, suits very well the character of a thrifty housewife ruling over a large establishment, and who has to consult the wishes of a man like Simon. What Paul, in 1 Cor. vii. 34, says of the difference between the virgin and the married, serves to illustrate the relation between the two sisters; and shows that the difference between them did not arise so much from any original difference in nature, as rather from their diverse position in life and training.

Ver. 2. "It was that Mary which anointed the Lord with ointment, and wiped His feet with her hair, whose brother Lazarus was sick."—Hitherto it had been said only that Mary and Martha belonged with Lazarus to the same place. Thus it was necessary to define still more closely the relation in which he stood to them. That he is described as the brother of Mary, and only indirectly as the brother of Martha (the latter having been mentioned as the sister of Mary), is not to be explained only by the circumstance that Mary was the one last spoken of. Lazarus stood nearer to Mary as an unmarried sister, than to the married sister. Hence also in ver. 45 (if the current reading is the correct one) it is said of the Jews, that they came to Mary to testify their sympathy. She is therefore regarded as the chief mourner.—The Mary whose brother Lazarus was sick, is thus described as the same with the person who anointed our Lord. This way of mentioning it presupposes that there never occurred more than one such anointing: the token would otherwise have had nothing characteristic in it. The Aor. Partic. indicates the "closed past" (Buttmann). John afterwards touches upon the anointing in ch. xii.; not giving a full detail, but merely adding one particular that had been passed over by the rest. To this account we cannot refer the ἀλείψασα; for the object evidently was to describe Mary to the readers by a sign already well known to them. Nor can the ἀλείψασα be explained as referring to tradition. John in no one instance can be proved to have referred to traditional reports. All that he presupposes is found in the first Gospels. Nor does the ἀλείψασα countenance those who assume a double anointing by Mary: the participle cannot be made to mean, "who once more anointed the Lord." The anointing of the Passion week was, at the time John wrote, long past; and the fact that he afterwards touches upon it is left out of sight. But a double anointing by Mary is decisively set aside by the circumstance that the ἀλείψασα would not have been sufficient for the purpose of separating between the earlier and the later, since the former also would belong to the region of the past. It might be thought that, according to the view now given, ἦν would not be the reading, but ἔστι; but this objection is obviated by the remark, that the leading idea is contained in the words, "It was Mary, whose brother Lazarus was sick;" and that the words ἡ ἀλείψασα—αὐτῆς do not contain more than a subordinate clause, "that Mary who was well known by the anointing which she afterwards performed."

Ver. 3. "Therefore his sisters sent unto Him, saying, Lord, behold, he whom Thou lovest is sick."—The degree of the sickness is not indicated. That was rendered needless, inasmuch as their mission to Christ of itself proved that all human aid was valueless, and that it was a sickness "unto death," ver. 4. The message to the "Lord" declared that they were not uttering a request; but that they were content to state the case, and leave it to the Lord to do as seemed good to Him. But that a certain request lay concealed under these words, is evident from "whom Thou lovest;" hinting the thought that Jesus, who had already come to the help of so many persons not directly connected with Himself, had now in the case of a dear friend a manifest call to interpose with His aid. Heumann supposes that "the good sisters knew not as yet that the Lord was omniscient, and needed no intimation of theirs." But the message should not be regarded in the light of information, so much as in the light of a request. Quesnel observes, "A sinner, who feels his unworthiness and his misery, should often come to Jesus with the same words, following the example of these two sisters: Lord, he whom Thou lovest is sick."

Ver. 4. "When Jesus heard that, He said, This sickness is not unto death, but for the glory of God, that the Son of God might be glorified thereby."—Jesus shows that He is better acquainted with the circumstances of the sickness than the sisters were who sent Him the message. He not only knows that it exists, but can explain also its origin and its end. "Jesus said' —to whom is not mentioned. It seems obvious, in the nature of things, that He spoke primarily to the messengers, who were not to be sent home without answer; and this is confirmed by ver 40, where Jesus, speaking to Martha, appeals to this word as having been spoken to her, as well as by the earlier ver. 22, for

Martha could have founded the hope which she there utters only on that declaration of Christ. The whole transaction between Christ and Martha in vers. 24–27, takes it for granted that Christ had already given His utterance as to what would first of all befall her brother. But ver. 12 shows that the Apostles were also present; for it speaks of their knowing the fact of Lazarus' sickness. The εἶπεν is designedly used in this indefinite manner, in order to intimate that the word of Christ was not intended for this or that person. The object of the declaration required the greatest publicity. The assurance of Jesus' foreknowledge of the issue of the sickness—which assurance was thus certified by as many witnesses as possible—was part and parcel of the miracle. Only thus could the thought of happy accident be obviated.

The words do not expressly say that Jesus would raise up Lazarus. They rather seem to imply that He would heal the man who was sick unto death. Not until Lazarus' death had become a reality is it clearly expressed that Christ will raise up the dead man; then it is made plain that "not unto death" refers to a permanent condition of death,—a transitory death not being termed such,—just as in Matt. ix. 24, "The maiden is not dead, but sleepeth (not dead, as others die)." (Heumann: The Lord speaks of a death by which Lazarus should be lost to his sisters.) Mary and Martha had already this illustration from the fact, when the message arrived; for Lazarus was already dead. Of the four days that Lazarus is said to have been in the grave when Jesus raised him, two must be reckoned for Jesus' continuing in the place where he was, ver. 6, one was occupied in carrying the message, another by the journey of our Lord; so that Lazarus must have died shortly after the departure of the messenger, and have been, as was the custom amongst the Jews, almost immediately buried. When the messenger returned, he had been already two days in the grave.

The road from the Jordan to Jerusalem took about seven hours: five for the plain from Jericho, two from Jericho to the Jordan.[1] It leads over Bethany, and thus required for Christ as well as the messengers not much over six hours. Bethabara

---

[1] Compare von Raumer, S. 60. Maundrell went with the pilgrim-train to the Jordan. With reference to the valley of the Jordan, he says that he reached it five hours after leaving Jerusalem, and that he spent two

lay in all probability in the same position as the pilgrims' baths placed there as a memorial.—Jesus knew that Lazarus was already dead. He must have intentionally so ordered this message, that the sisters could not at once understand its meaning. It seemed at first thought that Jesus had erred,—that, in fact, He supposed Lazarus would not die at all. This semblance of error was designed to evoke the energy of their faith. As soon as the sisters were firmly established in the living faith that Jesus was the Christ, the Son of God, ver. 27, the true interpretation of His words dawned upon their minds.—What Jesus says holds good of every mortal sickness of believers, and was intended so to do: for everything here has, in connection with the obvious sense, a symbolical and typical character. The sickness of believers does not lead to permanent death: it tends rather to the glorification of the Son of God in their resurrection. But so long as the time has not yet come when Jesus should finally demonstrate Himself to be the Son of God, and give the last pledge of His hidden power to raise the dead, it was necessary that some palpable glorification of the Son of God should be given as an earnest; and that the present occasion was selected by our Lord for the purpose of giving such assurance, is evident from a comparison with ch. ix. 3.—" This sickness is not unto death" may be illustrated by Isa. xxxviii. 1, where it is said of Hezekiah, that he was "sick unto death." And the passages are all the rather analogous inasmuch as in that case also the sickness, which was in itself mortal, became a sickness " not unto death" through the intervention of a messenger sent from God. If we observe that the meaning is here also, "This mortal sickness is not unto death," the passages become very closely related.—It is first said that the sickness should be for the glory of God; and then this is more expressly defined, that the Son of God should be thereby glorified. The Jews placed the glory of God and the glory of Christ in absolute opposition, just as unbelief and half-belief do even to the present day. Christ teaches us that the honour of God coincides with the honour of His Son; that it is effectually secured only by the glorification of the Son. Bengel: Gloria Dei et

hours over the way from Jericho to the Jordan. So also Robinson spent a little more than two hours, deducting stoppages, on the latter part of the journey.

gloria Filii Dei una gloria. It is for us to purge out all the Rationalist leaven in respect to this which still remains among us.

Ver. 5. "Now Jesus loved Martha, and her sister, and Lazarus."—We have here, on the one hand, the motive assigned for the saying of Jesus in ver. 4, which presented the prospect of Lazarus' deliverance from death; and, on the other, the motive for His subsequent act, in journeying towards Jerusalem for the purpose of accomplishing that saying. That the latter is not to be excluded, is evident from the " Our friend Lazarus," etc., which our Lord says to His disciples, ver. 11. That gives His friendship to Lazarus as the motive of the journey. $Ἀγαπᾶν$ is used, and not $φιλεῖν$, as in ver. 3, because women are the first mentioned. $Ἀγάπη$ is the love which does not so much rest upon individual inclination as upon the purely ethical basis, and which accordingly does not find its expression in tenderness. That the relation even of the Son of man to women was under certain restrictions which were not observed towards men, and that these restrictions were in force until the ascension, is shown by a right interpretation of the $μή\ μου\ ἅπτου$ which Jesus speaks to one of the women here alluded to, that is Mary, who would, in the passion of her fervour, prematurely overstep these limits.—As it respects the order of the three persons, Lazarus takes the last place, because death for him who dies in faith is not an evil, or, if an evil, one which is followed by an abundant compensation. It was not Lazarus who sent to Christ,—he doubtless rejoiced in the prospect of being received into Abraham's bosom, Luke xvi. 22,—but his sisters. Martha could not be sundered from Lazarus, as she was most severely affected by his death: comp. on ver. 2. Thus Martha must come first.

Ver. 6. " When He had heard therefore that he was sick, He abode two days still in the same place where He was."— The love of Jesus was approved, not in His tarrying two days, but, in spite of that tarrying, by the fact that He afterwards, without any regard to the machinations of the Jews, journeyed into Judea.—The $μέν$ is not followed by the $δέ$ which usually corresponds with it, in order to make the direct introduction of the contrast more striking.—Wherefore did Jesus abide two days where He was ? The answer is given by ver. 15. Christ there expresses His joy that He was not in Bethany before

Lazarus' death; because the raising him from the dead would tend more certainly to strengthen His disciples' faith than the healing which would have resulted from His being present. Thus it was for the same reason, to give opportunity for a stronger development of His miraculous power, that Christ here delayed. If He had set out at once, He would have reached when Lazarus had been dead two days.[1] The reason why He would go later to Bethany is given by the words of Martha in ver. 39. The dead man was to be raised up at the time when corruption begins generally to do its vigorous work. This gave occasion to that climax in the resurrection-acts of Christ which the Gospels set before us.

But was not this delay a hard one to the poor sisters? Those who maintain this will find difficulties enough in almost everything else. In all ages the Lord has been pleased to subject His people to more severe probation than this. He spares not the flesh, that the spirit may thrive. And this we see plainly cared for here. Jesus had previously given the sisters the staff of His promise. And it was a high grace that He, before the fulfilment of the promise, accustomed them for a while to fight against fear in dependence upon His word. Nor is it to be overlooked that they themselves, as well as the universal Church, derived benefit from the enhancement which the miracle gained from delay. Moreover, we must throughout the entire narrative direct our regard rather to the whole work of Christ, than to His personal relation to Mary and Martha, which only subordinately comes into view. How many faithful sisters have to give up their brother for ever, so far as this life is concerned, and not merely to wait for his restoration a few short days! We have here an exhibition beforehand of what was to happen to all. This gives the true key to the whole narrative.

Ver. 7. " Then after that saith He to His disciples, Let us go into Judea again."—Ἔπειτα and μετὰ τοῦτο are often connected in the classical authors. The tautology does not indicate remissness of style, but directs attention to the strange

---

[1] Without paying attention to the relation of time, many have assumed that Jesus designed to let Lazarus die before going to him, in order that He might raise him up. We have already shown, however, that Lazarus was already dead when the message reached our Lord.

circumstance that Jesus *afterwards* did that which, if He intended doing it at all, it seemed that He should have done *at once*, and suggests reflection upon that circumstance. This impressed the Apostles themselves. At the first, as Jesus did not set out at once, they had inferred that He had done what He purposed to do from a distance. From this agreeable delusion they were unexpectedly aroused by the summons to this perilous journey. Jesus does not say, to Bethany, but to Judea, in order to suggest what made the journey perilous, and to excite the opposition of the disciples. He had left Judea in order to place Himself beyond the reach of the persecution with which His enemies threatened His life. That He, in going to Judea, was going to Bethany, was self-understood, according to vers. 3 and 4, and needed not therefore to be expressly mentioned.

Ver. 8. " His disciples say unto Him, Master, the Jews of late sought to stone Thee; and goest Thou thither again ? "— Νῦν, so recently. In order to make their dehortation more forcible, they bring what had lately happened into the immediate present.

Vers. 9, 10. " Jesus answered, Are there not twelve hours in the day ? If any man walk in the day, he stumbleth not, because he seeth the light of this world. But if a man walk in the night, he stumbleth, because there is no light in him."— Jesus repels the objection of the Apostles, by showing from His own indwelling higher knowledge that the journey would be without danger. Heumann is essentially right when he says, " The time in which He should (could), according to His Father's will, teach and preach, and work miracles *unhindered*, He terms His day of twelve hours; and at the same time gives it to be understood that this day would be followed by a night, the time, namely, when He should fall into His enemies' hands, be condemned to death, and die a death both shameful and painful." Jesus does not give, as it were, a comparison and its application, but the figure and the application run into each other. It follows that we must not seek to distinguish between what belongs merely to the figure and what to the application; but that each individual trait belongs to the matter in hand, and all has a double meaning. The lower sense is very clear. The " light of the world" is the sun, according to Gen. i. 15, 16. Men *stumble* generally in the night alone. When this occurs exceptionally in the day (Isa. lix. 10, "We stumble at midday;" Hos. iv. 5, "And thou stumblest in the day"), extraordinary circumstances must be assumed which have caused the day to be turned into night, Job xvii. 12. These exceptions are not here taken into account, and the rule only is regarded. Βλέπει and ἔστιν ἐν αὐτῷ correspond to each other. The light of the sun is in a man, because the eye receives it into itself, and thus enables him to avoid the obstacles in his path. Now let us look at the figurative meaning. How far the day and the night come into consideration is shown in the clauses, "because he seeth the light of this world," and "because the light is not in him." Accordingly it is intimated that the day is light, the night is darkness. But light is in Scripture the ordinary image of salvation, night of an unsaved state. Now the Lord says the time of salvation is not quite run out, and therefore now there is nothing to fear. But a time will come when it shall have run out, and then danger will ensue. Day and night are contrasted also as the time of help and of helplessness in ch. ix. 4. So also the night is introduced in ch. xiii. 30: "And it was night" when Judas went out. There can be no question that the words have something mysterious in them; that the external night is to John here the symbol of spiritual night, when the light of the sun ceased to shine, when therefore the power of darkness began, and the hour came for successful assault upon the people of God. As descriptive of an unsaved state, night is used also in Rev. xxi. 25, xxii. 5, where it is said of the kingdom of glory, "And there shall be no night there." The grievous interchange of day and night, to which the militant Church is here subjected, will there cease for ever. A like distinction of a twofold time for Christ and His disciples, a time of safety and a time of suffering, occurs also in Luke xxii. 35, 36.

Jesus does not speak of the day generally, but of the twelve hours of the day. The fact that He thus represents safety as the characteristic of the entire day down to its perfect close—so that he who only walks generally in the day has no more cause of fear in the twelfth hour than in the eleven preceding—leads to the conclusion that the day, or the time of salvation, still continued, and would continue, during the whole journey, although very near its close nevertheless. (Bengel: Jam longe processerat cursus Jesu; jam multa erat hora, sed tamen adhuc erat dies.) Elsewhere in John we have stress laid upon the hour: comp. ch. vii. 30, viii. 28. So also in Luke xxii. 53, with which passage this stands in a close internal connection. Lyser: Necdum adesse horam passionis, de qua ad pontifices et seniores dicit: hæc est vestra hora.—Προσκόπτειν, בשל, in the Old Testament, is generally used without any moral meaning, but only of proceeding onwards. But the former is here necessarily required by the connection of the figurative with the proper meaning.—The antitype of the "light of this world," the sun, is the saving grace of God. This appears under a similar image in Job xxix. 3, where Job says of the time of his prosperity, "When His candle shined upon my head, and when by His light I walked through darkness." In Isa. lx. 19 we read: "The sun shall no longer shine upon thee, but the Lord shall be thine everlasting light." And in Rev. xxii. 5: "They need not the light of the sun, for the Lord God giveth them light." There the sun is the figure of the saving grace of God, which is now in the most real sense imparted to the Church. Even in Jesus there was at the time of His suffering "no light." Because the sun of salvation was gone down in His heaven, He knew not how to counsel or to save Himself. And, looked at in a higher sense, we have here a general proposition which is spoken primarily with reference to Christ and His disciples (Bengel: τις, indefinite pertinet hoc ad discipulos, qui etiam sibi timebant; with reference to the extension of it to the disciples, we may compare Luke xxii. 35, 36), but which has also a universal applicability. The separation between the time of unhindered active vocation and passion, as seen in Christ, recurs also among His disciples. There is a time which comes also to them, when they see not the light of the world, and no light is in them; when they must say, "Now there remains for me no more than to lie down in my suffering." "And since, then," says Lyser, "every man's day at last goes down, we must not, when we see that the time is come, withstand, but say, Thy will be done, O Lord; Thou hast given life, and Thou hast power to take it; Thou wilt for it give life everlasting. The hairs of our head are all numbered of Thee.—Meanwhile, let it be our comfort, that it lies not in the power of the devil, or of the ungodly world, to make our sun go down, but only in the hand of God. He has given to the day twelve hours, and of not one of these can our foes rob us against His will."

Ver. 11. "These things said He: and after that He saith unto them, Our friend Lazarus sleepeth; but I go, that I may awake him out of sleep."—The circumstantiality at the beginning was intended to guide the reader before he proceeds further to reflect upon the meaning of this mysterious word of Christ. It serves the same end which probably was served by a pause in the Lord's oral colloquy with His Apostles, and in the Psalms by *Selah*. After their Master had obviated the disciples' objections to the journey, He gives the reasons which induced Him to take it. He says, "*Our* friend," in order all the more to excite the Apostles' sympathy. This *our friend* shows that the relation between Christ and Lazarus must not be regarded in the same light as human friendships generally, such as that between David and Jonathan, but that it belonged entirely to the Christian sphere. Individual friendship would not have been common to Christ and His Apostles. Bengel is not correct here: "Christ says this at a time when Lazarus was just dead." Lazarus had died three days before. But Jesus says this now for the first time, because it is His will to go now and reawaken him. He is, however, perfectly right when he proceeds: "No man had given Him information of the death, and yet Jesus knew it." The description of the death of believers as *sleep* has been derived into Christian phraseology probably from the present passage, and Matt. ix. 24. The answer to the question, "Why did not Jesus speak at once of death and the resurrection, and thus prevent the misunderstanding of the Apostles?" is simply, that Christ intended by this word to introduce a milder view of death, as a mere falling asleep. (Augustin: "The Lord awakened him from the sleep of the sepulchre with the same ease with which thou arousest a sleeper from his bed.") The scriptures of the Old Testament not seldom exhibit death under the image of sleep: *e.g.* in Jer. li. 17, "They shall sleep a perpetual sleep;" Job xiv. 12, "So man lieth down, and riseth not: till the heavens be no more, they shall not awake, nor be raised out of their sleep." But Dan. xii. 2 is the only preparation among all these passages for the New Testament phraseology. The others do not include the idea of awaking out of the sleep; but only the sealing up of life and strength. But this one is adapted to fill us with contempt of death, the terror of which beset the saints of the Old Testament.

Vers. 12, 13. "Then said His disciples, Lord, if he sleep, he shall do well. Howbeit Jesus spake of his death: but they thought that He had spoken of taking of rest in sleep."—The disciples would not indeed have misunderstood Christ's meaning, if the saying of ver. 4 had not made it obvious that the sickness of Lazarus would not issue in death, but that it would be removed by the healing power of Jesus. Accordingly, they could hardly understand how the actual *death* of Lazarus should be meant by κεκοίμηται. They supposed that the Lord brought about a salutary crisis from a distance, as He had done on several other occasions: comp. ch. iv. 49 seq. That Christ's miraculous power had to do with the supposed sickness, was a supposition all the more natural, as Jesus could in the ordinary way have had no knowledge of the fact. Supernatural knowledge and supernatural action go hand in hand. Under these circumstances, the journey seemed to them without object; and they had not been so completely pacified respecting its danger by Christ's assurance, as not to desire still to be relieved from it. (Calvin: They gladly lay hold of this occasion for flying the danger.) What the words of Christ, "But I go to wake him out of sleep," meant to express, was indeed still very obscure to them; but as they conceived themselves to be quite certain as to the Lord's intention in using the word κεκοίμηται, they did not give themselves much trouble to investigate further the sense of the other words. Suffice that they had found reason sufficient for dissuading Him from the journey, which they persisted in thinking a fatal one. Anton: "Among these disciples was John, the narrator of this circumstance, and a sharer in this opinion. But now he is ashamed of it."

Vers. 14, 15. "Then said Jesus unto them plainly, Lazarus is dead. And I am glad for your sakes that I was not there, to the intent ye may believe; nevertheless, let us go unto him."—Jesus rejoices that He had not been there; because His disciples would derive more confirmation to their faith from the resurrection of one who had been long dead, than they would have derived from the healing of a man sick unto death. "That ye may believe" is the explanation of "for your sakes." Faith *is* as it were when it *grows*, and not before. At every new stage of faith, that which preceded is regarded as belonging, so to speak, to the region of unbelief.

Ver. 16. "Then said Thomas, which is called Didymus, unto his fellow-disciples, Let us also go, that we may die with Him."—How necessary it was that the Apostles should be thus strengthened in faith, this word of Thomas shows. He believes in Christ, otherwise he would not have desired to go with Him unto death. (That μετ' αὐτοῦ refers to Christ, and not to Lazarus, is proved by the connection with ver. 8. Only *with* a living person can one die. If any doubt remained, Matt. xxvi. 35 would remove it.) But that Thomas, notwithstanding the assurance of Jesus in vers. 9, 10, is so convinced that He is going to meet His death, shows that there was still in him an evil alloy of unbelief, a contest between doubt and confidence. The word of Christ has less force and effect upon him than the evident fact of the fierce hatred of the Pharisees, who wanted nothing more than an opportunity to get Him in their power. —There is no reason whatever for the supposition that Thomas bore the corresponding Greek name Δίδυμος in addition to this Hebrew name. The words, "called Didymus, or twin," rather give the explanation of his original name. It is the same in ch. iv. 25, where ὁ λεγόμενος Χριστός is equivalent to "which is in Greek Christ;" as also in ch. i. 39, the ὃ λέγεται ἑρμηνευόμενον. John usually gives such explanations of names only where the name is important to the matter in hand : compare on ch. ix. 7. And the reason of this is obvious: explanations of ordinary names would be, as a rule, extremely insipid. In the present case we are led to expect something important, from the fact that no less than *three* times we find it said of Thomas, "who is called Didymus," ch. xx. 24, xxi. 2; these two instances occurring so near to each other as to show that something significant in the meaning suggested the repetition, more especially as John is a writer who measures every word. Accordingly, there can be no doubt that the name Thomas, which never occurs in the Old Testament as a proper name, was imposed upon the Apostle by our Lord as descriptive of his character, and that the words "called twin" were designed to point to this significance in his name. Many such characteristic names are found in the Old Testament, especially in the prophets (comp. on ch. i. 43); and we also find them among the Apostles (comp. on ch. vi. 71). The Apostle who is always in the lists paired with Thomas, Matthew, bears a name which belonged to him as a disciple, and referred to his relation with the Lord. His original name was Levi.[1] But what is the meaning of the name Thomas? It signifies one at sight of whom we are reminded of twins.—תאם occurs only as a plural in the Old Testament; an $ἀνὴρ\ δίψυχος$, a double-minded man, Jas. i. 8, comp. $δίψυχοι$ in ch. iv. 8. Inward discordance is, alas, common to all who still live in the flesh; but the vehement disposition of Thomas brought his double-mindedness into special exhibition, so as to make him an apt exemplification of an undecided character. The proper key to the name is found in Gen. xxv. 23, 24: "And the Lord said unto her, Two nations are in thy womb, and two manners of people shall be separated from thy bowels; and the one people shall be stronger than the other people; and the elder shall serve the younger. And when her days to be delivered were fulfilled, behold, there were twins in her womb:" Sept. $τῇδε\ ἦν\ δίδυμα\ ἐν\ τῇ\ κοιλίᾳ$. Thomas had his Esau also, the first-born, and his Jacob—the old and the new man. But this reference to the passage in Genesis is not only humiliating; there is in it consolation also for Thomas, and for all of whom he is the type: the elder must at last serve the younger, and this was gloriously exemplified in the later self-sacrificing character of the missionary Thomas. The interpretation we have given is confirmed by the fact that it gives a sufficient reason for the appendage, $ὁ\ λεγόμενος\ Δίδυμος$, which does not indeed always accompany the name of Thomas. In the two earlier passages the affix is added to the name under circumstances which especially display the undecided character of Thomas: the word of doubt in ch. xx. 25 belonged to the one twin, to the other the energetic confession of faith in ver. 28. In ch. xxi. 2, Thomas is paired with Simon Peter,—the man of

---

[1] It is characteristic in evidence of the authorship of Matthew, that only in him we have the order $Θωμᾶς\ καὶ\ Ματθαῖος$, ch. x. 3; Mark, in ch. iii. 18, and Luke, in ch. vi. 15, have the names in the inverted order. Matthew himself, in his humility, would not assign to himself the first place, although it obviously belonged to him. And it is in harmony with this that he alone gives the appendage to his name, "the publican." His humility preferred to point back to his earlier despised condition.

rock and the man of double-mind—unity and doubleness. This juxtaposition points out to us what we are by nature, and what we ought more and more to become by grace.

We have now, in vers. 17-44, the narrative of the raising of Lazarus.

Vers. 17, 18, 19. "Then, when Jesus came, He found that he had lain in the grave four days already. (Now Bethany was nigh unto Jerusalem, about fifteen furlongs off.) And many of the Jews came to Martha and Mary, to comfort them concerning their brother."—As to ἔχειν, ver. 17, see the notes on ch. v. 5. The ἀπό, ver. 18, is used of distance from a place. This peculiar phraseology is found in the New Testament—besides the Gospel, where it occurs in ver. 8 of the disputed chapter xxi.—only in the Apocalypse, ch. xiv. 20. The use of the πρό, in ch. xii. 1, is analogous, as well as its employment by the Sept. in Amos i. 1, iv. 7. The statement of the distance of Bethany from Jerusalem serves to explain the following statement, viz. that many sympathizers came thence to the house of mourning. It it said that Bethany *was* nigh to Jerusalem. John's design required him only to observe that such was at that time the relation between the two places: whether that relation still continued, was in itself an indifferent matter. It can hardly be inferred from the ἦν that John meant to speak of Jerusalem and Bethany as already destroyed: in that case it must also be inferred from ch. xviii. 1, that John spoke of the *garden* as having disappeared: comp. also ch. xix. 41. Quite parallel is "Nineveh was a great city," Jonah iii. 3, which does not mean to say that it was no longer—the continuance of Nineveh in the time of the author is an assumption which lies at the basis of the book—but only that Jonah found it ch.— It is clear that the Jews, in ver. 19, are not the "Jewish party in opposition to Jesus." The position of affairs in the house requires us to suppose that the company was a mixed one, and so we find by the result it was: comp. on ch. i. 19. The words are literally, "to those *about* Martha and Mary." The phrase was originally employed in classical Greek only of eminent persons, who were surrounded by attendants; its use as a mere circumlocution was a later debasement. The New Testament never sanctions this degenerate use. In Acts xiii. 13, those around Paul are the Apostle and his companions; a mere pleonasm is not to be thought of in John. The expression points to the fact that the house was an important one, and that we must regard Mary the mistress, in whose honour her sister partakes, as surrounded by a number of female servants; and the connection with the name Martha is in favour of the same view. Esther iv. 16 throws some light upon it, where Esther says, "I also and my maidens will fast." The mistress and the maidens make up one whole. In harmony with the αἱ περὶ Μάρθαν we have the statement of ver. 20, that Martha, the real centre of a circle, knows at once of the arrival of Jesus, while Mary, who only virtually partakes of her dignity, has heard nothing about it.

Ver. 20. "Then Martha, as soon as she heard that Jesus was coming, went and met Him: but Mary sat still in the house."—Connecting with this the parallel, Luke x. 39, we must explain "sat as usual in the house." (Berl. Bible: "Here John refers us to Luke x. 39, he having written after Luke.") It forms a contrast to Prov. vii. 12, where it is said of the adulteress: "Now is she without, now in the streets, and lieth in wait at every corner." This had been true of Mary in former days, but now, after her conversion, she is all the more anxious to live in still seclusion. That word of the Old Testament had now become a sharp goad (Eccles. xii. 11). It is probable that Martha had *secretly* been informed of the arrival of Jesus, ver. 28, so that neither Mary nor those around her knew of it. This secrecy sprang from the internal relations of the house at the time.

Vers. 21, 22. "Then said Martha unto Jesus, Lord, if Thou hadst been here, my brother had not died. But I know, that even now, whatsoever Thou wilt ask of God, God will give it Thee."—If Thou hadst been here—at the time of the sickness. It is a clear misapprehension to suppose that Martha, in ver. 21, utters a reproach against Jesus. The word of Christ, in ver. 4, forms the foundation for vers. 21 and 22. That word guaranteed, if Jesus were present, the healing of the sick man, as Jesus Himself admits in ver. 15; but if Lazarus died before His coming, it guaranteed the resurrection of the dead man. Martha does no more, therefore, than give expression to her faith in the word of Christ. That He would be able to make good even this word, which would indeed involve very great things (ὅσα), she could all the less doubt, inasmuch as His miraculous power had already approved itself in raising the dead, and given practical demonstration that even death, the most awful of all our enemies, had no power against Him: and the νεκροὶ ἐγείρονται, Matt. xi. 5, had already had its glorious illustration. And Calvin's remark as to the utterance of Martha's hope being the result of wandering, rests upon a total misunderstanding of the matter. This charge would be well-founded only if Jesus had not given the word of ver. 4 as a staff for her hope. Then, indeed, she must have been contented with the consolation common to all believers; and then it would have been wild presumption to expect anything extraordinary for herself. And such presumption would not have been rewarded by the granting of an irrational request.

Jesus makes trial, before He proceeds to verify His word, in ver. 4, whether the subjective conditions necessary in the two sisters (represented by Martha) for the realization of that word are present in them; or rather, as the presence of those conditions was taken for granted by His words, He gives her opportunity of expressing herself satisfactorily on the matter. Her faith that the power of Jesus could call back the dead to earthly life, she had already freely spoken out in ver. 22. But that was not enough. It must be clearly established that she also stood firm in the fundamental truth as it respects the resurrection. This was all the more important, as the whole transaction was to have a symbolical meaning; as Jesus purposed to exhibit in it a prelude of the general resurrection at the end of the world,—a practical demonstration of the power by which He will then call back all believers from death to life. This colloquy between Martha and Christ has, as it were, a liturgical significance. Nothing occurs in it which does not hold good of all who bury their beloved dead. There is no allusion in it to the recalling of Lazarus back to this poor earthly life. Assurance of that had been given in ver. 4. Jesus tests first Martha's faith in the resurrection itself, vers. 23, 24; and then He requires her to confess, in the presence of the Church represented by the Apostles, her faith in Himself, as the author of the resurrection.

Vers. 23, 24. "Jesus saith unto her, Thy brother shall rise

again. Martha saith unto Him, I know that he shall rise again in the resurrection at the last day."—The "Believest thou this?" of ver. 26, is in effect to be understood also in ver. 23. This is evidenced by the answer of Martha, who recognises in the address of Christ a demand for her faith in the great article of the resurrection of the dead. Jesus propounds the objective Divine truth; and it is for Martha, as the representative or mouth of all believers, to avow her faith in it. Primarily, she represents her sister with herself. That the examination into her subjective standing-point of faith is not here the great matter, but only the bringing into exhibition a faith which was present and known to Jesus, is plain, from the circumstance that our Lord does not pursue the same examination with Mary. The whole transaction was intended to be significant for all ages of the Church of God upon earth.—The ἀναστήσεται, "he shall rise again," cannot, in the Lord's mouth, refer to a return into the sphere of the present miserable earthly life. This is shown by the answer of Martha, as well as by the current Christian and Jewish phraseology. In this it signifies the transition into a new glorious condition, which lies beyond the present existence of men. Ver. 25 altogether excludes the reference to a mere restoration to life: the ζωή, the ζήσεται, accord not with the present state of existence.—The New Testament teaches a twofold stage of being in that other world: the one which begins for believers with their departure from this life; the other which begins with the last day. To the former refers what the Lord said to the thief on the cross; as also John xiv. 2, 3, xiii. 36, xvii. 24; Rev. xiv. 13, "Blessed are the dead who die in the Lord *from henceforth;*" vii. 9-17, xiv. 1-5, xv. 1-4. To the latter refer, for example, Matt. xix. 28; John v. 25, 28, 29, vi. 39, 40; Rev. xix. 9, xxi. 22. In the Revelation the two stages are often combined in the unity of life or salvation, *e.g.* ch. ii. 7, 10, 17, iii. 5. That the *former* may be included under the term "resurrection," is evidenced by Rev. xx. 5, where it is expressly described as the first resurrection. There can be the less objection to this, inasmuch as the figurative use of the resurrection holds extensively, and in various ways, throughout the Scripture; every transition from misery to blessedness, from a lower to a higher condition, being described by the terms: comp. my commentary on Rev. xx. 5. Martha, in her answer, here looks alone on the *second* stage of blessedness, the resurrection at the last day; and it cannot be doubted, taking the current phraseology, and especially ch. v. 25, 28, 29, into view, that Jesus pre-eminently referred to the same. But that in connection with this, He has also the former in view,—that the resurrection here means the whole of that future life—that we consequently have here the basis of the "first resurrection" in the Apocalypse,—is plain from ver. 25, where Jesus unites resurrection and life inseparably together, so that the sphere of the resurrection must be just as extensive as that of life. If there is, according to the most unambiguous and oft-repeated declarations of our Lord and His Apostles, a life, a blessedness, before the commonly so-called resurrection, so must there be also a resurrection before the resurrection commonly so-called, or before the last day. With such an all-comprehending meaning the resurrection occurs in Matt. xxii. 30. For the idea of resurrection is there also, according to ver. 32, as extensive as that of life. But it is the first stage which is in that chapter predominantly in question. For when we read there (and also Mark xii. 25), "In the resurrection they are as the angels in heaven," we must not refer the ἐν οὐρανῷ to the angels; in that case the οἱ must have come first, as many MSS. in Mark have interpolated the οἱ before ἐν οὐρανοῖς. We must rather construe ἀλλ' ἐν οὐρανῷ εἰσι ὡς ἄγγελοι: but in heaven are as the angels. The explanation of Fritzsche and others, "But they are as the angels of God in heaven (are)," is not so obvious; and the reason which is made to sustain it, "that in the New Testament the Messianic kingdom for the dead recalled to life is not heaven, but on this earth itself," rests, according to the intimation already given, upon a partial apprehension of the truth. It is the first stage of the resurrection which is especially regarded, because, among the blessed spirits *in heaven*, the inappropriateness of marriage is especially prominent. Phil. iii. 20 is parallel: ἡμῶν γὰρ τὸ πολίτευμα ἐν οὐρανοῖς ὑπάρχει. The blessed spirits, in their resurrection, attain to the place where already, during their earthly life, their proper *home* was.

Vers. 25, 26. "Jesus said unto her, I am the resurrection, and the life; he that believeth in Me, though he were dead, yet shall he live: and whosoever liveth, and believeth in Me, shall never die. Believest thou this?"—From the resurrection the Lord turns to its Author and Agent. "I am the resurrection and the life." Christ is the antitype of the tree of life in Paradise: he that eateth of Him shall live for ever. He is the resurrection and the life, not only as the giver, but as the procurer of both. The root is His atoning death, by which He hath assuaged the wrath of God and vanquished death, 2 Tim. i. 10; Heb. ii. 14. It reads, "I *am* the resurrection and the life." Jesus *is* this already virtually, according to His indwelling power; just as, according to ch. i. 4, the life was in Him before He appeared in the flesh. But not until the resurrection will the power already existing in Him approve itself in act. Bengel is not correct here: Ego præsens, non adstrictus ad longinquum. Noli putare, Martha, te differri in longinquum. Mors cedit vitæ ut caligo luci, protinus. The recall of Lazarus to this wretched life stood in no direct and immediate connection with the words, "I am the resurrection and the life;" it had to do with them only so far as the power immanent in Christ, which will one day effect the resurrection and life, had its prelude in Lazarus' restoration. In the Old Testament we find that all salvation, whether in the world to come or in the present world, is connected with the name of the Messiah. Of the Messianic age we read in Isa. xxv. 8, "He will swallow up death in victory, and the Lord God will wipe away tears from off all faces,"—the tears which flow with peculiar bitterness on account of death. In ch. xxvi. 19 it is said, "Thy dead men shall live, together with my dead body shall they arise. Awake and sing, ye that dwell in dust: for thy dew is as the dew of herbs (light or salvation), and the earth shall cast out the dead." According to Dan. xii. 2, in the Messiah's days "many of them that sleep in the dust of the earth shall awake, some to everlasting life, and some to shame and everlasting contempt." That the "life" of believers begins immediately after death, is proved by the parable of Lazarus. The poor man is, according to Luke xvi. 22, carried, when he dies, by the angels into Abraham's bosom, where he is comforted, ver. 25. The distinctive character which hell with its torments bears in that description—the wide gulf which is firmly established between the one and the other, go to prove that life also in that world must bear a not less distinctive character. If *life*, according to this parable, which stands in a near and peculiar connection with the event before us, commences with the departure from the present state, the resurrection also, which goes hand in hand with it, must have a similar beginning. Resurrection and life are, in Hos. vi. 2, connected together; and both as describing the transition from a miserable to a happy existence. Πᾶς ὁ ζῶν, whosoever liveth, forms the antithesis to κἂν ἀποθάνῃ, though he die, and must therefore refer only to the natural life. The οὐ μὴ ἀποθάνῃ, shall not die, corresponds to the ζήσεται, shall live; and thus the dying here cannot be used in the ordinary sense, as in the κἂν ἀποθάνῃ, but with an emphasis: death, which is no more than the transition to true life, is not death at all. The two members of the clauses are an advance respectively on each other's meaning. In the former, life after death is assured to believers; in the latter, it is declared that they shall not die at all. The death of which Jesus speaks in the former clause, accommodating Himself to our common phrase, is, when more clearly viewed, no real death. There is not here any distinction of two classes. It is true that the former clause holds good only of those who, with Lazarus, are already dead; but for living believers like Martha, both clauses are valid. Jesus, however, has the living primarily in view. The ζήσεται of itself shows this. His design is to arm His living believers against all the terrors of death.

Ver. 27. "She saith unto Him, Yea, Lord: I believe that Thou art the Christ, the Son of God, which should come into the world."—Martha does not avow her faith distinctively in Jesus, as the resurrection and the life, but as the super-worldly (comp., in reference to "coming into the world," on ch. i. 9) Redeemer and Son of God. If He be this—if the triple honour which Martha ascribes to Him be truly His, then it is sufficiently plain of itself that He must be the resurrection and the life. Quesnel: "Nothing in respect to Christ seems incredible or transcending hope, when we have a living faith in His divinity; but the whole building falls to the ground when this foundation is disturbed." Martha says, "I have believed." The perfect (comp. ch. vi. 69) is significant, as showing that she does not now attain for the first time to that faith, but is only avowing the faith which she already possessed; that, consequently, it is not His design to produce faith in her soul, but only to give her opportunity to confess the faith she had.

Ver. 28. " And when she had so said, she went her way, and called Mary her sister secretly, saying, The Master is come, and calleth for thee."—Why did not Martha earlier give Mary information? It was natural that at first she was wholly possessed by the thought of going out to meet Jesus, and of strengthening her faith in the promise sent to her (ver. 4), by beholding Him, and hearing His words. As soon as her heart had received this invigoration, she hastened at once to her sister. " Secretly," leads to the inference that, among those who according to ver. 19 were present, many were included who stood in a hostile or alienated relation to Christ. In Martha's purpose these were to be kept aloof. God's purpose, however, was different from hers. All who were in Bethany should be present at the miracle. " The Master is come." Quesnel: " Jesus had no other name in this family than Lord and Master; for it was a family of faith and of obedience." That Jesus *called for* Mary, was the necessary consequence of His presence, and of the end of His coming, according to ver. 4. Those out of love to whom the miracle took place, must needs be present to behold it.

Ver. 29. " As soon as she heard that, she arose quickly, and came unto Him."—Mary, says Quesnel, leaves without delay comforters who were a burden to her grief, in order to find out the true Comforter. It is only at His feet that we can find a consolation that penetrates the heart.—Ver. 30. " Now Jesus was not yet come into the town, but was in that place where Martha met Him." Why did not Jesus come to the place? It appears that He remained outside, in the neighbourhood of the sepulchre. For it is evident from what follows, that the sepulchre was very near the village. The Jews followed Mary on her way to Jesus, supposing that she was going to the place of sepulture: therefore that must have been near to the place where Jesus was. Our Lord's conduct on the occasion was shaped by the unequal character of the visitors at the house. The mixed multitude were to be present at the raising of Lazarus (ut tam grande miraculum quatriduani mortui resurgentis testes plurimos inveniret,—Augustin), but yet Jesus would not go to the scene accompanied by such a crowd. They were to be present, but it must be without any seeming or direct arrangement on His part. He would come into contact with them at, but not before, the performance of the sacred act.—

Ver. 31. "The Jews then which were with her in the house, and comforted her, when they saw Mary, that she rose up hastily and went out, followed her, saying, She goeth unto the grave to weep there."

Ver. 32. "Then when Mary was come where Jesus was, and saw Him, she fell down at His feet, saying unto Him, Lord, if Thou hadst been here, my brother had not died." —There is not the most distant hint of any reproach here. Reproaches are not lightly uttered against the Lord by one who sits at His feet. The words of Mary are the very same which Martha had spoken in the former part of her first address, ver. 21. Doubtless the sisters had often interchanged this kind of observation with each other. To the second part of Martha's address corresponds Mary's prostration: comp. the προσκυνοῦσα, καὶ αἰτοῦσά τι παρ' αὐτοῦ, Matt. xx. 20. This form of supplicating the salvation which ver. 4 had placed before her vision, was appropriate to the forgiven sinner, whose consciousness was anew and most vividly affected by a sense of unworthiness in the presence of that new manifestation of grace which was especially intended for her: comp. the "Lord, I am not worthy" of the centurion, in Matt. viii. 8. The whole deportment of Mary evidences her firm confidence in the miraculous power of Jesus, which, according to ver. 4, He must put forth upon her dead brother, though it had not pleased Him to put it forth upon her brother while sick and alive.

Vers. 33, 34. "When Jesus therefore saw her weeping, and the Jews also weeping which came with her, He groaned in the spirit, and was troubled, and said, Where have ye laid him? They say unto Him, Lord, come and see."—It has long been fully established that the ἐμβριμᾶσθαι can denote no other passion than that of holy anger. That the phrase accepts no other meaning, is confessed even by those who, not knowing how otherwise to evade it, enforce another signification upon the word here. Lücke, for example, says: "The lexical definition of a scholiast upon Aristophanes, Equit. 851, βριμᾶσθαι, τὸ ὀργίζεσθαι καὶ ἀπειλεῖν, is accepted by all lexicographers. If we hold to the strict meaning, then Jesus was angry, and saw Mary and the Jews weeping with displeasure." The ancient Greek expositors, who had still before their eyes the living phraseology, gave the verb the signification of anger. "Only this interpretation, that of loud and violent indignation, is the literal one that ἐμβριμᾶσθαι accepts," Gumlich asserts and amply proves in his exhaustive tractate on the resurrection of Lazarus (S. and K. 1862). But the indignation of our Lord could not have been directed at the weeping of Mary and the Jews; this is plain from the fact that Jesus Himself afterwards wept. The same reason decides against the assumption that Jesus was wroth with and strove against His own emotion, excited by the weeping of those around him; an assumption which is also refuted by the consideration that there is nothing recorded of any such preceding involuntary emotion on the part of our Lord. Moreover, it would then have been more in keeping that He should have composed rather than excited Himself. No further illustration is necessary to show how little any thus or thus originated anger is worthy of Jesus the Saviour, who sympathizes with us in our infirmities. His vehement wrath being occasioned by the weeping, it must have been excited only by that which caused this weeping. And that was no other than the great enemy of the human race, Death. To this our thoughts are at once directed by the words which follow the mention of our Lord's deep feeling. He asks, "Where have ye laid him?"—a question which is the introduction to His actual advance towards Death, and His wresting from him the prey which he had carried off. The anger was manifestly the internal feeling which precedes the act of revivification, and in which that act had its psychological root.[1] It is not the passion which brings about the resolution of Jesus; that, according to ver. 4, had been long fixed. The weeping around Him was only a subordinate factor. It would be altogether out of harmony with the Divine dignity of Jesus, to regard Him as raised solely by the weeping to so high a state of emotion, and to the sublime act that followed upon it. The weeping could not be wanting; but it was only one of the subordinate circumstances: the Lord's determination was already formed.—The Redeemer's wrath will appear all the more appropriate when we consider that the event had a symbolical meaning; that Lazarus was the representative of all believers fallen asleep; and that we have here the pledge

---

[1] Lyser: Indigne fert, quod atra mors hunc bonum suum amicum rapuit et hoc fremitu se ipsum excitat ad aggrediendum grande hoc opus, quo Lazarum ex faucibus mortis eripere vult.

and assurance of the abolition of the last enemy, ἔσχατος ἐχθρὸς καταργεῖται ὁ θάνατος, 1 Cor. xv. 26. It may be objected that the anger seems to be directed against a personal enemy; but such an objection comes very flatly. We are accustomed, in the Old Testament, to see impersonal and transitory powers assuming life, personality, and form, in order that their defeat and destruction may be all the more effectually exhibited: comp. *e.g.* Hos. xiii. 14. Jesus, according to Matt. viii. 26, not only threatens the wind and the sea,—to abate the force of this analogy, it may be pleaded that the act was symbolical, living powers lying concealed behind the wind and the sea: comp. on ch. vi. 14–21,—but He rebukes the fever also in Luke iv. 39. If we take into view the whole Scripture doctrine, it will be plain that behind death also there is concealed a personal enemy. Death, according to Gen. ii. 17, iii. 19, came upon the human race through the deceit of Satan: comp. the book of Wisdom, ch. ii. 24. Our Lord calls Satan a murderer from the beginning, ch. viii. 44; and in Heb. ii. 14 Satan is described as the ruler of death himself destroyed by Christ. Thus, when our Lord advances against death, He at the same time advances against Satan. Death and the devil are in the Scripture view inseparably connected.

Jesus was angry *in spirit.* A comparison with Mark viii. 12, Luke x. 21, John xiii. 21, Acts xvii. 16, παρωξύνετο τὸ πνεῦμα αὐτοῦ ἐν αὐτῷ, will show that τῷ πνεύματι defines the passion to have been an internal one, and consequently full of force, in contrast with emotions which are merely put on for appearance, or go no lower than the surface. The רוּחַ is, in the Old Testament, the seat of all strong passions: Gen. xli. 8; Prov. xxv. 28; Ps. xxxiv. 19. The remark that "the spirit, as contradistinguished from the soul, the seat of natural human sensibility, is here named as the sacred domain in which that violent emotion was exhibited," will not stand the test of the passages we have quoted. It is a mistake also to conclude from the τῷ πνεύματι that the anger of Jesus was restricted to the inner spirit. It is rather self-understood that His passion, which had its proper seat in the spirit, must have had an external expression,—as generally the measure of the internal strength of an emotion is the measure of its outward utterance,—otherwise it could not have been matter of historical record. Vatable rightly observes : Vultum mutavit Jesum et vocem et gestum præ dolore. "And was troubled." Τάρασσειν occurs in the New Testament, so far as it refers to men, always and only of mental emotions; and it must here, in opposition to those who think of a "bodily shivering," all the rather be referred to the spiritual sphere, inasmuch as the ἑαυτόν is defined by the preceding τῷ πνεύματι. Ἐτάραξεν ἑαυτόν is the same as ἐταράχθη τῷ πνεύματι, ch. xiii. 21, with this difference, that in the other instance the emotion was more passive, while here it is active and intentionally called up. Jesus excites Himself to an energetic conflict with the wicked enemy of the human race. Any reference to the Divine nature of Christ, and His elevation above all mere passivity of physical emotions, as resting upon that Divine nature (Augustin : Turbaris tu nolens, turbatus est Christus quia voluit. In illius potestate erat sit vel sic affici. And even Lücke: " A purely involuntary emotion would be too passive for the Johannine Christ "), is not to be sought in the ἐτάραξεν ἑαυτόν. The same would be said of a human hero, who roused himself to a sharp contest. Isa. xlii. 13 gives us some illustration : "The Lord shall go forth as a mighty man, He shall *stir up jealousy* like a man of war; He shall cry, yea roar; He shall prevail against His enemies." If we explain the active sense of the emotion by reference to the Divine nature of Christ, there is no reason why the same active verb was not used in ch. xii. 27, xiii. 21.

The question which immediately follows the Lord's excitement, Where have ye laid him? serves only to introduce and prepare for the act which flowed from it, and has, as it were, a liturgical significance. We can no more conclude from His asking the question, that Jesus knew not the place of sepulture, than we can conclude from *Where art thou?* in Gen. iii. 9, that God knew not the retreat of Adam. How little our Lord's questioning generally was based upon His ignorance (as if He asked because He knew not) we have seen in ch. vi. 6, and still more clearly in the style in which the disciples going to Emmaus were questioned, Luke xxiv. 17-19. If Jesus, at a distance, and without any human information, knew that Lazarus was dead,—if He was so sure beforehand that the sickness would issue to the glory of God, and that the journey would be without peril to Himself,—if we move in the sphere of miracle from the beginning to end of this whole transaction,—it seems a strange transition to another sphere when Christ is made to ask information about the burial-place because He knew it not. (Augustin: Scisti quia mortuus sit et non ubi sit sepultus?) We have already seen that our Lord had remained in the neighbourhood of the sepulchre, and this of itself proves that He was acquainted with it. The question was not intended to furnish Him with information upon a matter in which He was ignorant; it served only to define the boundary between the domain of the Son of God and that of men, who have to transfer as it were their dead to Him, being unable to accomplish aught themselves. Men can only lay their dead in the grave. One alone can raise from the dead.

The Κύριε, Lord, reflects the impression of the dignity of His person which the deportment of Jesus had created in the mourners' minds. The "come and see" is seemingly a reminiscence of Ps. lxvi. 5, xlvi. 8, springing from the impulse to use Scripture language in solemn moments; and the very words were all the more carefully preserved by the narrator, because those passages in the Psalms—" Come and see the works of God: He is terrible in His doings toward the children of men;" and, " Come, behold the works of the Lord, who doeth wonders in the earth"—were to receive a new confirmation. The ἔρχου καὶ ἴδε can scarcely be used indifferently here, seeing that John everywhere else uses it with a significant reference.

Ver. 35. "Jesus wept."—Gumlich rightly observes that both His wrath and tears were occasioned by one thing, death. That Jesus wept at the death of Lazarus is proved by ver. 36, on which Heumann, holding the opinion that the tears had another cause, is obliged to say, "The Jews were mistaken, when they supposed that He wept over the death of Lazarus." Surely there is no need to seek diligently for any other reason than the same which called forth the tears of all who were present. Had there been any such reason, the weeping of our Lord would have been carefully distinguished from that of all others. Death and tears are connected in the Old Testament, e.g. in Isa. xxv. 8,—"He will swallow up death in victory; and the Lord God will wipe away tears from off all faces; and the rebuke of His people shall He take away from off all the earth: for the Lord hath spoken it,"—a passage with which ours stands in close external connection; for here Jesus pours out the tears in order to make that saying true, in order that He might be able to wipe away all other tears. It is thrice recorded that Jesus wept: in this passage,—over Jerusalem,—and in Gethsemane, Heb. v. 7. Δακρύειν, only here in the New Testament, is milder than κλαίειν: it signifies only that tears filled the Lord's eyes. That literal weeping was not in itself improper for Jesus, is evidenced by Luke xix. 41, Heb. v. 7; but it is out of keeping with the present case, because our Saviour's tone is pre-eminently active, and the excitement of sympathy with the suffering race of mankind serves only as a foundation for His rigorous resolve to come to the rescue of that race. In Gethsemane it was otherwise. There the tone of our Saviour was predominantly passive. So also was it when He wept over Jerusalem, when He was enforced to give it up to ruin. But in the present instance, the tears which are devoted to the misery of mankind as exemplified in Lazarus, are preceded by the wrath of His spirit against the wretched enemy of mankind. —With the weepers Jesus had not wept. When He saw them weeping—the only thing by which they could exhibit their love to the deceased—He, the only one who could do more than that, was angered in spirit, preparing Himself for practical help. This shows us, by the way, that in circumstances when human help may be of service, He who can be helpful should not spend much time in inactive tearful sympathy. But when He comes to the very place and abode of death, He gives Himself up to softer sensibility, that He may by His pattern sanctify sympathy. (Augustin: Flevit Christus, fleat sc homo. Quare enim flevit Christus, nisi quia flere hominem docuit.) But in the Lord this sympathy does not so much accompany the vigorous assault on death, as form part of its foundation. Lampe's remark, repeated by Baur and others, is based upon a thorough misunderstanding: "There was no reason for weeping over Lazarus, who, as Jesus certainly knew, would now be awakened to God's and His own glorification." Lampe concludes, that the Lord must have wept over the Jews; Baur decides for the spuriousness of the narrative. They overlooked the fact that the weeping of Jesus was the necessary postulate of His action, even as all the miracles of Christ proceeded out of a similar profound emotion of soul.[1] A cold or stony-hearted raiser of the dead would belong to the region of fiction. The living Saviour could only as a helper approach the place of corruption; and only with tears in His own eyes wipe away the tears of ours.

Vers. 36, 37. "Then said the Jews, Behold how he loved him! And some of them said, Could not this man, which opened the eyes of the blind, have caused that even this man should not have died?"—That the exclamation and question of the Jews proceeded from sincere hearts, and that they had some foundation of truth—the thought, to wit, that Jesus at the death of Lazarus could not consistently maintain a purely passive attitude—is evident from the influence which both have, according to ver. 38, upon our Lord. His indignation at the enemy is excited by it afresh. That shows that the Jews had given prominence only to one element in the matter, which has still its force when those die who love Jesus. Both His love and His power warrant the supposition that He cannot be in such a case simply passive, but that He must recall them to life. Certainly there is concealed behind the "Behold how he loved him!" the question, "How has he then thus let him die?" And behind the question of ver. 37, another, to wit, "If he could have done so, why did he not?" But that they do not put these secret questions in the spirit of reproach, is shown by the fact that the reverence which, at this crisis, impressed the most violent minds, hinders them from speaking out what they think. It is not in itself sinful to question in uncertainty and awe the ways of God and His message, provided only the hand be laid on the mouth, and the questioner does not murmur, or make himself a judge. This latter is that sinning with the tongue against which, in all the unsearchable providences of God, we have to be on our guard. We cannot doubt, however, that there was something else latent in their thoughts. "Will he not even now give some further demonstration of his love and power?" The thought was only a germ, and did not take expres-

---

[1] Melanchthon: Nullum miraculum sine magno aliquo motu Christi factum est, sicut ipse dicit, Luc. viii. Apparet autem imprimis magnos æstus animi, magnos agones fuisse in hac resuscitatione, fremit, dolet, indignatur, lacrymat. Hic motus nobis ignoti sunt, sed significant luctam acerrimam, cum decrevisset resuscitare Lazarum.

sion; but that it was there, is proved by the influence which the Jews' words excited upon our Lord.—The question of ver. 37 could be answered by every one only with *Yes*. They believe in the opening of the eyes of the blind man; and that was so absolutely a creative work, that He who could perform it could also heal a man sick unto death. Why do they not rather mention the resurrection of Jairus' daughter, and the young man of Nain? Because they simply confine themselves to an event that had occurred only a short time before, and in their own midst; and the rather as, in the present case, it was *primarily* the healing of a sick man that was concerned, and not the raising of a dead one.

Ver. 38. "Jesus therefore again groaning in Himself, cometh to the grave. It was a cave, and a stone lay upon it." —The new access of our Lord's indignation is chiefly excited by the words of the Jews. They tend to renew and quicken His zeal against the fearful foe of the human race. "Because Christ," says Calvin, "does not come to the grave like an idle spectator, but as a strong hero, who prepares himself for war, it is not to be marvelled at that He is again angry; for He sees only that awful tyranny of death which He is come to vanquish and destroy." And Gumlich well observes, "The finished act of the miracle was the goal, at which alone the Lord's displeasure would find its perfect solace, and His zeal its perfect satisfaction."

Ver. 39. "Jesus said, Take ye away the stone. Martha, the sister of him that was dead, saith unto Him, Lord, by this time he stinketh: for he hath been dead four days."—It is a very unfortunate supposition which some have hazarded, that Martha did not believe the Lord purposed to restore her brother's life when He came to the sepulchre, but only desired to see the remains of His friend once more,—a design from which therefore she dissuaded Him. The right view is, that Martha, by reference to the corruption begun, would place before Jesus the greatness of the work which He designed to accomplish. We see by what follows what end she wished to attain. She would thereby give occasion to Jesus for a new confirmation of His promise, and thus strengthen her own faith: "Lord, he already stinketh: I believe, help Thou mine unbelief." Death and corruption seem to the natural reason to lie beyond the domain in which even miraculous power may display itself; and believers have evermore to struggle against the same natural reason. It is more especially vigorous in Martha here, inasmuch as the crisis of decision was immediately impending.[1] "The sister of him that was dead:" the most vehement conflict would naturally begin in her mind, at this moment of supreme decision, because she was most nearly affected. She, whose heart and soul were directed entirely to the dead man, would be specially affected by the signs of corruption. That "he stinketh" was only her inference—cannot be proved by "he hath been dead four days." For this latter gives the reason of the witnessed fact: he stinketh, as it could not be otherwise with one who has been four days dead. The ἤδη ὄζει must necessarily have been an actual truth. For—that is the reason why the Evangelist records the expression. It was intended to show emphatically the greatness of the miracle. But even if it be made a mere inference, the ἤδη ὄζει asserts still its actual truth. "The reason," remarks Gumlich, "for Martha's confident assertion is, in fact, so plain, that nothing but the vain imagination of a miracle before the miracle prevents its being seen."—From the words "by this time he stinketh," as connected with ver. 44, it has been justly concluded that the body was not embalmed. And this bears testimony to the faith which Mary and Martha reposed in the word of their Master, ver. 4. They did not bury their brother after the manner of the Jews, ch. xix. 40, because they hoped that he would not permanently inhabit the grave.

Ver. 40. "Jesus saith unto her, Said I not unto thee, that, if thou wouldest believe, thou shouldest see the glory of God?" —Jesus affords the desired help to the rising unbelief of believing Martha. In the presence of corruption He renews His promise. "If thou wouldest believe" refers only to vers. 23-27. There Jesus had based the demand for faith, not on the confirmation which the present case would afford to His miraculous power, but on His own person, and on His own absolute power over death. The words, "thou shouldest see the glory of God," refer solely to ver. 4. Only there do we find mentioned that glory of God which was to be manifested in Lazarus. The *seeing* God's glory points us back to Isa.

[1] Lyser: Quando ad rem ipsam ventum est, tum demum infirmitates sentimus—rem nimis diu dilatum esse ac proinde omnem conatum irritum fore.

xl. 5 : " And the glory of God shall be revealed, and all flesh shall see it together."

Ver. 41. "Then they took away the stone from the place where the dead was laid. And Jesus lifted up His eyes, and said, Father, I thank Thee that Thou hast heard Me."—The old covenant furnishes repeated instances of prayer offered in the form of anticipated thanksgiving. "The Church is distinguished from the world by this, that she does not pray in the way of experiment; she rests in her petitions on God's word and promise; so that she can ask in faith without wavering, James i. 6." This is the explanation of the fact that in the Mosaic economy there were no specific prayer-offerings; these were latently involved in the thank-offerings, which we not seldom find presented amidst circumstances of sorrow, when they could refer only to a deliverance expected, and not a deliverance attained. (See further in my Treatise on Sacrifice.) The anticipatory confidence which, even in the Old Testament, gave birth to this form of petition from the lips of believers, was infinitely more appropriate to Christ on account of His unity with the Father. Looking away from the mere form of the petition, Jesus here announces that He will perform, in the strength of God, the work which present circumstances brought before Him. It is not the hearing of any former prayer that is referred to. No such prayer is alluded to; the actual granting of the prayer does not in any sense follow until ver. 44, which altogether excludes the notion that Lazarus had here already begun to rise from the dead and live again. Accordingly, the words can be explained only on the ground of that anticipating confidence which was already inwardly assured of the actuality of the future salvation from death. We have something similar in Ps. liv. 6, where David in the midst of his distress expresses a full confidence of deliverance: "I will freely sacrifice unto Thee; I will praise Thy name, O Lord, for it is good;" and also Ps. lvi. 13.

Ver. 42. "And I knew that Thou hearest Me always: but because of the people which stand by I said it, that they may believe that Thou hast sent Me."—Our Lord refers to 1 Kings xviii. 37, where Elijah says, "Hear me, O Lord, hear me; that this people may know that Thou art the Lord God." The express petition, uttered in the form of confident assurance, was not designed to obtain the granting of the request; it might indeed have been omitted, since the relation of Jesus to God was so intimate and perfect that no express utterance of a request was ever needed: every the slightest wish of His soul, every glance of His eye, was regarded; and to Him the words of Isa. lxv. 24 applied in their fullest sense, "Before they call, I will answer." It is not signified here that His prayer generally is, in relation to God, superfluous,—this would contradict Mark vi. 46, which shows that Jesus went up to the mountain to pray, Luke ix. 28, etc.,—but prayer as formally expressed in words. So far as concerned His relation to God, "He lifted up His eyes" was enough, and more than enough. Something analogous to these high prerogatives of Christ we find in the experience of advanced saints, Rom. viii. 26. There is even among mere men a stage of sinking into God, in which the words of prayer rather recede and are lost. The ἀκούειν of itself shows that, not prayer generally, but a certain kind of prayer, is declared to be unnecessary. That Jesus on this occasion did, however, express His prayer in words, was solely on account of those who were around; in order that the connection between the sequel and the person of Christ might be abundantly clear, and thus faith in His Divine mission might be wrought in their minds.—That which our Lord here says in the form of address to God, He might, as in ch. xii. 30, have said in the form of an address to the multitude. But that, on the present occasion, would have been less solemn, and less befitting the sublimity of the crisis. The effect of the Lord's act upon the standers-by, was produced by the circumstance that they were raised with Jesus into the posture of prayer; they were elevated to that prayerful sentiment which was the habitual frame of Christ, the ceaseless breathing of His soul, and which made the present form of words the most appropriate to Himself.—Πάντοτε, *ever*,—whether I expressly put the petition or not.

Ver. 43. "And when He thus had spoken, He cried with a loud voice, Lazarus, come forth."—In regard to the cry of Jesus here, that holds good which He had said in regard to the praying, ver. 42. The loud voice, the outward demonstration of confidence and decision (comp. on ch. i. 15), was intended only to symbolize to those around the connection between the will of Jesus and the resurrection act. The parallels in the other Evangelists, Mark v. 41, Luke vii. 14, viii. 54, in which Jesus utters His cry on occasions of raising the dead, show that the call was addressed to the dead man, and that the revivification was simultaneous with that call. Comp. also ch. v. 25, according to which the *dead* shall hear the voice of God. Further, as Lücke observes, "If we compare ver. 43 with ver. 11, the δεῦρο ἔξω is the moment of revival itself." Lampe's objection, that Jesus addressed Lazarus not as a dead man, but as a living, is dismissed by a reference to Ezek. xxxvii. 4: "Ye dry bones, hear the word of the Lord." There also the dead were addressed. That which Jesus here does, is the type and prelude of that which He will do at the last day. This is shown by the connection of our passage with ch. v. 28, 29.

Ver. 44. "And he that was dead came forth, bound hand and foot with grave-clothes; and his face was bound about with a napkin. Jesus saith unto them, Loose him, and let him go."—The grave-clothes that bind the dead express the consolatory assurance that the departed has now rest from his hard toil upon the earth, which lies under the Lord's curse. They say symbolically what Isaiah said in words: "They enter into *peace*, they rest upon their beds." The hands and feet were bound by them, for a sign that, with death, the painful toil of hand and foot is over; as Paul Gerhard sings, "The head, and *hands*, and *feet* rejoice, that rest has come at last." The grave-clothes proper were there besides. The wrappings, which are here expressly limited to the hands and the feet, were added over and above the shroud; and as they served no practical purpose, but had only a symbolical use, their binding was of a looser nature, and the raised man could, although not without some trouble, move forward a few steps. By the supposition that each foot was specially bound about, the significance of the whole is lost. Why then would the word "loose" have been used? The napkin corresponds to these grave-clothes. It had its origin in Gen. iii. 19: "In the sweat of thy face shalt thou eat bread, till thou return unto the ground." It intimated that the dead had departed from labour and sorrow, Gen. iii. 17, Ps. xc. 10, Rev. xiv. 13, and out of "great tribulation," Rev. vii. 14; that they "rest from their labours." According to chap. xx. 7, the napkin was "on the head." Accordingly ὄψις, the face, is here used as *pars pro toto*. It covered the forehead, on which the sweat stands. That the eyes were covered, is plain from the words, "Loose him, and let him go," which refer to the napkin also, and show that the napkin was a hindrance to going. Nor is it a mere accident that the countenance is here designated by a word which is derived from seeing.—In the "let him go" it is not signified that Lazarus went alone to the house, which would have been unnatural. They were to let him go, inasmuch as they were to remove those bandages which they had laid upon the supposed dead man. The "*let* him" refers to the restraints which they had caused, and which were the only ones left, after Jesus Himself had removed the main hindrance. As in ver. 34 the burial is ascribed to the whole company present, so here with the unloosing.—"Death, sin, devil, life, and grace are all in His hand. He can save all who come to Him—that is the great practical result which the whole narrative teaches."

In vers. 45, 46, we have the effect of the miracle upon the people around.—Ver. 45. "Then many of the Jews which came to Mary, and had seen the things which Jesus did, believed on Him."—It does not mean many of the Jews who had come to Mary, τῶν ἐλθόντων, but many Jews (among those present generally) who had come to Mary. It is taken for granted that they had not all come to Mary. What is alone intimated here, receives its illustration from the relations of the household as we have explained them. Mary had come solely on Simon's account. Mary is mentioned, and not Martha, because the latter, the mistress of the house, could not be separated from Simon. The *believing* acquaintance had come to Mary in the first place, and only subordinately to Martha, who in this point of view depended on Mary. And we must suppose that they brought with them the beginnings of faith. When they saw what Jesus had here done, their germ of faith was more fully developed; comp., for a similar process and use of faith, the remarks on John vii. 5. But we may also assume that οἱ ἐλθόντες here stands irregularly for τῶν ἐλθόντων—as an abbreviated relative clause. Mary would in that case be mentioned as the chief mourner. (In favour of this a whole series of analogies may be adduced from the Apocalypse: comp. Winer and Buttmann.) We have a similar construction in ch.

i. 14. But such irregularities seldom occur in the simple historical style; and the fact that only Mary is mentioned here, differently from ver. 19, leads to the grammatically obvious interpretation. That αὐτῶν, in ver. 46, refers to those who came to Mary, is a construction which will not harmonize. But we must suspend our judgment.

Ver. 46. "But some of them went their ways to the Pharisees, and told them what things Jesus had done."—'Εξ αὐτῶν —if we adopt the former of the explanations offered upon ver. 45, τῶν 'Ιουδαίων,—some of those who, in contradistinction to those who came to Mary, had come to Martha, in her character of mistress of the house and wife of Simon, probably in concert and co-operation with that Pharisee (Luke vii., "chief of the Pharisees"), Luke xiv. 1. Grotius remarks: Impios hos fuisse necesse est, quod genus hominum ne conspecta quidem mortuorum resurrectione resipiscere solet, Luke xvi. 31. "He contrasts them, as untouched and uninfluenced, with the many believers; and gives it plainly to be understood that their zealous information occasioned the assembling of the synagogue, and the bloody counsel of Caiaphas." Bengel: Citius cedit mors virtuti Christi quam infidelitas. Death yields to Christ's virtue sooner than unbelief. The difference in disposition among the Jews had not appeared during the course of the event itself. The majesty of Christ had, for the time, overcome their unbelief. But it afterwards betrayed itself among those whose minds were unfriendly; and ch. xii. 10 probably gives us the true solution of the manner in which the matter was solved. Then the rulers of the Jews resolve to kill Lazarus as well as Jesus. This presupposes that they had found some fault in him. Doubtless they imagined some preconcerted plan between Jesus and the family in Bethany. Lazarus had acted the part of death.

In ver. 47–53 we have the plans which were devised by the Council in consequence of this event, and their result

Vers. 47, 48. "Then gathered the chief priests and the Pharisees a council, and said, What do we? for this man doeth many miracles. If we let him thus alone, all men will believe on him; and the Romans shall come and take away both our place and nation."—Anton: "When God displays His greatest works before the world, the world is provoked to the highest pitch of bitterness and wrath." For ἀρχιερεῖς and Φαρισ. see on ch. vii. 32. The precedence of the high priests shows that by the Pharisees are meant the Pharisaic party among the assessors of the council. Συνέδριον here signifies a session. The word was chosen in allusion to the *nomen proprium* of the supreme spiritual authority. This proper name does not occur in John, as it does in the first Evangelists and the Acts; just as he omits to mention the scribes and the νομικοί. Having the most accurate acquaintance with Jewish institutions, he always avoids expressly alluding to them. Thus he names not the Sanhedrim, but describes its sitting by a word which alludes to the proper name. "What shall we do?" is the ordinary question of those who are pondering: Judg. xxi. 16; 1 Sam. v. 8; Jonah i. 11; Acts iv. 16. Here it is strictly, What *do* we? Since the circumstances are urgent, and demanding instant action, and since there can be no doubt that something must at once be done, the present and the present of the indicative is strictly appropriate.—The proper motive of the opposition to Jesus was, among the Pharisaic members of the high council, a different one from that exhibited in ver. 48. It was, in one word, that which Matt. xxvii. 18 gives, where it is said of Pilate, "He knew that through *envy* they had delivered Him." Compare what was said on ch. x. 8 concerning the true character of the conflict between Christ and the Pharisees. But this self-seeking ground of their hatred to Jesus they cannot lay bare. They make pretence of another reason, and represent it as if they were alone actuated by love to the people. The specifically Pharisaic reasons were the less brought forward because the council had in it many Sadducee members, and the influential high priest himself belonged to that party. Had the Pharisees urged any of their own characteristic arguments, some such conflict might have arisen between the two parties as Acts xxiii. 10 records. They therefore abandoned the domain of theology, and contented themselves with such political arguments as were common to the Sadducees with themselves. Their anxiety was not altogether baseless. Although the kingdom of Christ was not of this world, yet at that time of general excitement insurrectionary movements might easily have connected themselves with His appearance (comp. John

vi. 15); the Romans might give a political interpretation to events which had in them no political meaning, entirely ignorant as they were of the spiritual character of the new kingdom. Characteristic in this view is Pilate's "Thou art a king then?" The intelligence of the Jewish Messianic expectations had at that time penetrated far and deep in the heathen world. Percrebuerat toto Oriente vetus et constans opinio, esse in fatis ut eo tempore Judæa profecti rerum potirentur, says Suetonius (Vespasian, iv.); and Tacitus (Hist. v. 13) speaks in the same style (comp. Christol. iii. 2). And as these expectations bore a political character, it was obvious that the same political character would be referred to the historical appearance of the Messiah. Nor was it a contradiction that those who longed for the Messiah as a deliverer from the hateful Roman dominion, were disposed to league against Christ on account of the danger threatened from the Romans. For Christ would never from the beginning yield Himself up as the instrument of their insurrectionary schemes; and they, on their part, were not inclined to lose what they had in favour of a passive Messiah, who would not favour them in their dearest desires. Of any spiritual victory over the heathen world which Christ was preparing for, they had no presentiment. But what they did in order to prevent the ruin of the Temple and the destruction of their national existence, precisely brought about that ruin and destruction. (Augustin: Temporalia perdere timuerunt et vitam æternam non cogitaverunt; ac sic utrumque amiserunt.) "Behold, your house is left unto you desolate," says the Christ whom they rejected in Matt. xxiii. 38, and history has approved His word. Lyser: "As the Evangelist tells us that Caiaphas unwittingly prophesied concerning the fruits of Christ's death, so we may say of these counsellors that they unwittingly prophesied concerning the future destinies of the Jewish people." In the prophecies of the Old Testament, the rejection of the good Shepherd is followed by the wasting of the land, and the destruction of the people, Zech. xi.; and, according to Dan. ix. 24–27, the consequence of the murder of the Anointed was that the greater part of the people became a prey to the army of a strange prince, which, an instrument in the hand of an avenging God, should utterly destroy the fallen city and the desecrated Temple.

"The Romans will come:" comp. Jer. xxxvi. 29, "The king of Babylon shall certainly *come* and destroy this land;" Dan. ix. 26, "And the people of the prince that shall come shall destroy the city and the sanctuary"—he that shall come being a non-theocratic ruler coming from without. To these passages the Pharisees here refer. We have shown in the Christology that the passage in Daniel was generally understood of an impending destruction of Jerusalem. Αἴρειν, to take away, remove, destroy (comp. xix. 15, 31), so that the place, as such, and the people should no longer exist. The ὑμῶν preceding the *place* is to be well noted; those who omitted it were ill-advised. That the word place here of itself signifies the Temple, cannot be established from 2 Macc. v. 19,—ἀλλ' οὐ διὰ τὸν τόπον τὸ ἔθνος ἀλλὰ διὰ τὸ ἔθνος τὸν τόπον ὁ κύριος ἐξελέξατο),—for it is only the connection with ver. 15 that makes the place the Temple in that passage. But "*our* place" can only be the Temple. It is the habitual style of the New Testament not to mention the city so much as the Temple, the seat and dwelling-place of the entire people. In the books of Moses we read of the "tabernacle of the congregation," the place where the Lord had communion with His people, and dwelt with them. Ps. lxxxiv. 4 refers to the Temple, "The sparrow hath found an house, and the swallow a nest for herself;" and so also ver. 5, where the Israelites are spoken of who dwell in the house of the Lord; Ps. xxvii. 4, xxiii. 6, lxi. 5, lxiii. 3. The Temple is called in Isa. lxiv. 10 our holy and beautiful house. "Your house" the Lord in Matt. xxiii. 38 calls the Temple, referring to these Old Testament passages. If Jerusalem is included in our present passage, it can only be on account of the Temple.—*Place* and *people* correspond to each other. The Temple was the spiritual centre and the soul of the people. Were the Temple gone, there would be no people. Israel is an ἔθνος, as a people among the peoples; ὁ λαός, as the elect people. Τὸ ἔθνος could hardly be used concerning Israel without some addition like ἡμῶν here. If ἡμῶν had been wanting, it must have been τὸν λαόν. The Pharisees feared that the Romans might say, with the sons of the wilderness, in Ps. lxxxiii. 5, δεῦτε καὶ ἐξολοθρεύσωμεν αὐτοὺς ἐξ ἔθνους. Anton: "They thought only of the ruin *ad extra;* about the ruin *ad intra* they made no question."

Vers. 49, 50. " And one of them, named Caiaphas, being the high priest that same year, said unto them, Ye know nothing at all, nor consider that it is expedient for us, that one man should die for the people, and that the whole nation perish not." —The name of Caiaphas is the same as Cephas, the difference being merely that between the Syriac and the Chaldee pronunciation. The same change of forms is found in the name of the town Kaifa (v. Raumer, s. 156), called by William of Tyre *Porphyria*, which was probably a translation of Kaifa. Caiaphas was only a surname: his proper name was Joseph. Josephus says, in Antiq. xviii. 2, 2, καὶ Ἰώσηπος ὁ καὶ Καϊάφας διάδοχος ἦν αὐτῷ; and in xviii. 4, 2, καὶ τὸν ἀρχιερέα Ἰώσηπον τὸν καὶ Καϊάφαν ἐπικαλούμενον ἀπαλλάξας τῆς ἱερωσύνης. No doubt Joseph took the name Caiaphas when he entered on his office: it was, properly speaking, his official name. It designated the high-priesthood as the rock on which the edifice of the theocracy rested. Caiaphas bore that name at the very time when Jesus gave it to the first of the Apostles, the rock on which He built His Church. It may therefore be assumed that the Lord had a polemical object in giving Simon his new name, setting against the imaginary rock the true one. Consequently the name Cephas was a declaration of war against the religion of the times, and an announcement of a new building to be set up: comp. ch. x. 8.

The remark that Caiaphas was high priest that year occurs three times, vers. 51, 18, 13. Josephus gives evidence of the frequency with which the high-priesthood changed hands during his time, Antiq. xviii. 2, 2; and it is a remarkable fact, that several high priests, and specially the immediate predecessors of Caiaphas, had enjoyed the dignity only *one* year. " And not long after, having displaced this man, he appointed Eleazar, the son of Annas, the high priest; and the year having passed, he gave the high-priesthood to Simon, he having held the dignity not more than one year, Joseph," etc. The more the high-priesthood became the centre of the national existence, the more it became the interest of the Romans to provide that single persons should not establish their roots too firmly. The words, " being high priest that year," stand in special and plain relation to these facts. Although Caiaphas administered the high-priesthood during several years (in connection with which it is to be remembered that Vitringa, Obs. vi. 13, 2, has suggested doubts as to the continuance in office ascribed to him by Josephus), yet every year the people expected a change; and if he remained in office after the current year, it was only for the next year that he was supposed to hold it. Very characteristic is the delicate reference to these peculiar relations of time, which are not recorded so much as taken for granted. Eusebius, H. E. 1, 10, recognised these relations, but he apprehended them too vaguely. Caiaphas, according to Acts v. 17, belonged to the party of the Sadducees; and that very circumstance, doubtless, enabled him to retain his office longer than others. The rough manner peculiar to this party may be discerned here. " Ye know nothing at all, nor consider," seems to be a rather needless impertinence. He might have begun his answer to the question, " What do we ?" without any such rough introduction, by the simple words, " It is expedient for us." We have here only a single example of that which Josephus says generally in the Jewish War, ii. 8. 14 : Καὶ Φαρισαῖοι μὲν φιλάλληλοί τε καὶ τὴν εἰς τὸ κοινὸν ὁμόνοιαν ἀσκοῦντες, Σαδδυκαίων δὲ καὶ πρὸς ἀλλήλους τὸ ἦθος ἀγριώτερον. It is usually explained, " Ye consider not that it is expedient for us." But it is better to give ὅτι the meaning *for* or *because*: first, the objection that they had spoken inconsiderately what they had said, " What do we?" then the establishment of this objection, by showing them that the course to be taken, about which they were in doubt, was plainly marked out. In the two other passages, where ὅτι follows διαλογίζεσθαι, Matt. xvi. 8 and Mark viii. 16, 17 (in John, διαλογίζεσθαι occurs only here), the ὅτι does not bear the signification *that*, but means *because*, and is independent of the verb. Even in Luke v. 21, the διαλογ. stands without direct connection with the verb. The notion that διαλογίζεσθε is not appropriate, as connected with ὅτι, gave occasion to the reading λογίζεσθε. First comes ὁ λαός, the people in their specific character and dignity ; then ὅλον τὸ ἔθνος, the people in mass, in opposition to the one man. Ἔθνος is like גוי, the most comprehensive designation. It means, properly, host or crowd, and is used by Homer even of swarms of flies. Ὁ λαός, העם, is the preferential name of Israel, because the people of God were the only people in the fullest sense, as united by an internal bond : the heathen were לא עם, οὐ λαός, according to Deut. xxxii. 21,

1 Pet. ii. 10, because they were without the true and real bond of unity, fellowship with God.

Vers. 51, 52. "And this spake he not of himself: but being high priest that year, he prophesied that Jesus should die for that nation; and not for that nation only, but that also He should gather together in one the children of God that were scattered abroad."—What Caiaphas said flowed, as is evident, from an evil fountain, and had a wicked intention; but John regards the Divine influence that was upon him as so overruling his words, that the spiritual ruler of the covenant people should express his bad purpose in such words as might most aptly utter a profound truth.[1] He who, with John, believes in a living God, whose secret operation pervades the hearts of the ungodly, scarcely needs the express assurance that the Evangelist gives. Without the Divine influence, another instead of Caiaphas might have delivered the sentiment, or Caiaphas might have been able to express his opinion in words which could not have admitted a sacred interpretation. In the προφητεύειν there is regarded only the Divine suggestion or inspiration, which had for its foundation the fact that Caiaphas was the high priest at the time. It was appropriate and so ordered that he, in that office, should bear testimony to the true propitiation which the true High Priest would effect by His representative death. It was a parallel to this when Pilate, the holder of the civil authority, was constrained to bear witness, in the superscription on the cross, that Jesus was *King* of the Jews, and to reply to those who urged the change of this inscription, that "what he had written he had written."[2] Pilate was under the same Divine guidance as that which here makes Caiaphas prophesy. And it was also a parallel, when the people cried out, "His blood be on us and on our children," Matt. xxvii. 25; when the high priests and scribes mocked Christ on the cross, with words

---

[1] Calvin: Thus Caiaphas was at this moment *bilinguis.* He poured out his impious and cruel purpose of rejecting Christ which he had conceived in his mind; but God gave his tongue another turn, so that he should at the same time utter a prophecy in ambiguous words. It was God's will that a celestial oracle should issue from the pontifical seat.

[2] Bengel: Caiaphas and Pilate condemned Jesus: each, however, gave his own specific testimony in his own sense. Caiaphas, in this passage, concerning the sacrificial death of Christ; Pilate, in the title on the cross, concerning His kingdom.

which they, as it were involuntarily, borrowed from Ps. xxii., and by which they spoke their own condemnation, Matt. xxvii. 43; when the soldiers, to fulfil Ps. xxii., must cast lots upon the vesture of Christ, ch. xix. 23. In regard to all these things, the "not of himself" holds good, as well as the positive answering to this negative, that the persons concerned prophesied, without on that account being prophets. For more appertains to the being a prophet, than such momentary and partial influences.

It is noteworthy that John does not, like Caiaphas, say ὑπὲρ τοῦ λαοῦ, but ὑπὲρ τοῦ ἔθνους. He could not have made Caiaphas say anything but ὁ λαός when speaking of the Jews: comp. ver. 50, xviii. 14. He himself speaks from the standing-point of his own time and the Church of Christ. Then the distinction between ὁ λαός and τὰ ἔθνη had vanished: comp. Isa. xlii. 6; Gesenius, Thes. i. v. גוי. Another people of God had taken the place of the Jews, 1 Pet. ii. 10; Rev. xviii. 4, xxi. 3. The Jews were only an ἔθνος, like the rest. That the Jews were in question here, is evidenced by the article pointing to the word of Caiaphas. But this delicate distinction itself shows how faithfully John reproduced the expression of the high priest. In ver. 52 John supplements the saying of Caiaphas, which, in its divinely-designed meaning, contained the truth indeed, but not the whole truth. In relation to the "children of God," that is most fully applicable which was remarked upon the sheep not of this fold, ch. x. 16. The children of God *scattered abroad* are not single believers, or individuals predisposed to believe, who were scattered amongst the unbelieving Gentiles, but the Dispersion generally. This has been, since Gen. xi., the essential character of the whole world of heathenism, as the kernel and centre of which the children of God here appear: the abandoned refuse of them, not predestined to become children of God, are not taken into account. The correctness of this view is manifest from the original passages in Gen. x. 5, 32, compared with vii. 35. Local dispersion is here regarded only as the reflection of the internal dispersion. From the tower of Babel the bond of fellowship was broken which previously united the human race, and all had been dissolved and confused. With the external dispersion, the most decisive separation of temper and spirit between the several national personalities runs parallel. The commencement of the regathering was made in the Old Testament by the call of the Israelitish people. That created a centre of aggregation. Christ gathers into this fold the scattered sheep of the Gentile world (comp. on ch. x. 16), and that by His atoning death, the result of which was, that " a great multitude, which no man could number, of all nations, and kindreds, and people, and tongues," enter into the fold. A fundamental passage in the Old Testament is Isa. xlix. 6, where the Lord says to His servant, " It is a light thing that Thou shouldest be My servant, to raise up the tribes of Jacob, and to restore the preserved of Israel; I will also give Thee for a light to the Gentiles, that Thou mayest be My salvation unto the end of the earth." But Isa. lvi. 8 still more closely touches our present passage. There we read, after the reception of the " sons of the stranger" into the kingdom of God had been spoken of, as it would take place in the Messiah's days: " The Lord God, which gathereth the outcasts of Israel, saith, Yet will I gather others to Him, besides those that are gathered to Him" (LXX.: συνάγων and συνάξω).

Ver. 53. "Then, from that day forth, they took counsel together for to put Him to death."—Among the Pharisees as a party the death of Christ had been long decided on, ch. v. 16, 18, vii. 1, 19, 25, viii. 37; but the council itself only now adopted that resolution, and from this time onward plotted for its accomplishment. Thus they realized, remarks Lampe, the type of Joseph's brethren, who took counsel concerning his death, Gen. xxxvii. 18.

Vers. 54–57. Jesus, who would die at the Passover as the paschal lamb, repairs, on account of the persecution which threatened Him, to Ephraim.

Ver. 54. "Jesus therefore walked no more openly among the Jews; but went thence unto a country near to the wilderness, into a city called Ephraim, and there continued with his disciples."—Ephraim is thus specifically mentioned as the name of the tribe; and all expository combinations which do not bear this in mind must be rejected. Thus we must give up the combination with Ophra, a town of the Benjamites, עָפְרָה, Josh. xviii. 23; or with Ephron, עֶפְרוֹן, 2 Chron. xiii. 19, where the Masorites led the way in this confusion. For the *Keri*, Ephrain, appears there to rest upon the collocation with Ephraim; and the suggestions of the Masorites have no more weight than those of a modern critic. We are assisted in defining the locality of Ephraim, not only by the name itself, which suggests a place hard upon or beyond the borders of the tribe of Ephraim, but by a passage of Josephus also (De Bell. Jud. iv. 9, 9), the existence of which enables us to confute the evil-disposed industry of our moderns, who strive to prove that the Evangelist has made the name of the tribe into the name of a town. Josephus says there that Vespasian had conducted from Cæsarea an expedition of horsemen to subdue the hitherto unsubdued parts of Judea; that he went into the hill country and occupied two districts, the Gophnitic and the Acrabatene, afterwards seizing the little towns Bethel and Ephraim, μεθ' ἃς Βηθηλᾶ τε καὶ Ἐφραὶμ πολίχνια; and that, finally, after he had left garrisons in these places, he journeyed to Jerusalem. Accordingly Ephraim must have lain in the mountain country, near Bethel; which agrees very well with the fact, that Bethel in the tribe of Benjamin was situated near the border of the tribe of Ephraim. As there is no record in the Old Testament of any town named Ephraim, we are obliged to assume that the place is there represented by some other name; and we are disposed to find it in the "Baal-hazor, which is by Ephraim"—עם, *near*, as in Gen. xxxv. 4; Josh. vii. 2—where Absalom, according to 2 Sam. xiii. 23, held his sheep-shearing. The place, like Ephraim, lay hard by the border of the tribe of Ephraim; and it is quite consistent with John's intimation, of Ephraim being close upon the desert, that Absalom kept his flocks there (מדבר is properly pasture). The name Baal-hazor might have been all the more easily rejected, because it was not strictly speaking a proper name of a town, but merely the designation of a place by the name of certain property in it (Gesenius: villam habens), which the narrative in Samuel makes prominent. That the name Baal-hazor no longer existed in the time of Jesus is plain, from the fact that Josephus mentions instead Baal-zephon, the name currently known to him of the Egyptian town, and transposes this Baal-zephon into the Ephraimite territory. This could hardly have occurred to him if the place had still borne its old name.

Ephraim was situated in the district "near to the wilderness." That was the reason why our Lord chose this locality. The wilderness forms an antithesis to publicity, the παρρησία. It isolated the place, and excluded it from human intercourse: it afforded also a refuge from approaching persecution, and gave opportunity for seeking yet deeper seclusion. We have, in Matt. xxiv. 26, an echo of this sojourn of our Lord (comp. on the διέτριβε, iii. 32) near and in the wilderness. At an earlier period also Jesus had occasionally repaired to the wilderness, Luke v. 16. His retreat at the present time was the beginning of the end, a prelude to the fulfilment of Deut. xxxii. 20: " And He said, I will hide My face from them, I will see what their end shall be;" and of Hos. v. 6 : " They shall go with their flocks and herds to seek the Lord, but they shall not find Him; He hath withdrawn Himself from them." The article in ἡ ἔρημος stands generically (comp. Acts xxi. 38); it does not denote a particular wilderness, but the wilderness in opposition to other localities. The wilderness is meant which, according to Josh. xvi. 1, "goeth up from Jericho throughout Mount Bethel," the hill-range in the neighbourhood of Bethel. "This desert," observes Keil, "is no other than that which, in ch. xviii. 12, is called the wilderness of Bethaven, since Bethaven lay east of Bethel." In Josh. viii. 15, 24, reference is made to the same desert. Epiphanius mentions a man who accompanied him in the wilderness of Bethel of Ephraim, when he went up from Jericho to the hill country (συνοδεύσαντός μοι ἐν τῇ ἐρήμῳ τῆς Βαιθὴλ καὶ Ἐφραΐμ). This was indeed the same way which Jesus took when He returned from Ephraim to Jerusalem. John goes on in what follows to describe the impression which was produced by the circumstance that our Lord retreated from publicity into seclusion.

Ver. 55. "And the Jews' Passover was nigh at hand; and many went out of the country up to Jerusalem before the Passover, to purify themselves."—We learn from Acts xxi. 24, 26, that this cleansing consisted primarily in external ceremonies; but more reflecting souls regarded these as only the symbol of the sanctification of hearts, Jas. iv. 8; 1 Pet. i. 22 ; 1 John iii. 3. The law contains no specific injunction with regard to this purification before the Passover. But the propriety of such a preparation, for the highest and holiest of the feasts, was obvious in the nature of things; and it was, moreover, sanctioned by a series of historical types, which taught the doctrine, that every approach to God, and every reception of His grace, must be preceded by a worthy preparation. In Gen. xxxv. 2, Jacob says to his people, when he would go with them to Bethel to celebrate Divine service, "Be clean, and change your garments." In Ex. xix. 10, 11, we read: "And the Lord said unto Moses, Go unto the people and sanctify them (Sept. καὶ ἅγνισον αὐτούς) to-day and to-morrow, and let them wash their clothes, and be ready against the third day; for the third day the Lord will come down in the sight of all the people upon Mount Sinai." In Josh. iii. 5, Joshua says to the people, "Sanctify yourselves (Sept. ἁγνίσασθε), for to-morrow the Lord will do wonders among you." That the doctrine lying at the basis of all these passages was applied also to the Passover, we learn from 2 Chron. xxx. 16–20. There we read of an exception in favour of those whose circumstances would not allow them to be cleansed and prepared for coming to the Passover. "If the Jews," says Lyser, "during several days prepared themselves for eating the shadowy and transitory Passover, with what earnest prayer and careful examination should Christians approach the mysterious table on which the true Passover of the New Testament is exhibited!" comp. 2 Cor. vii. 1.

Ver. 56. "Then sought they for Jesus, and spake among themselves, as they stood in the temple, What think ye, that he will not come to the feast?"—These questions start from the fact of the seclusion of Christ. According to their tenor, "the mixed multitude, who in religious matters are full of variations and uncertainty," doubt whether Jesus will or will not come to the feast: that He will not come, seems the more probable supposition. "Wait only a while, ye good people," says Lyser, "and ye will see with what publicity and stately dignity He will enter your city." In John's record of the impression which the seclusion of Jesus made upon the people, there is evident a certain gentle irony. It was somewhat as if they had been dubious whether the sun, for the moment hidden behind the clouds, would ever come forth again. We have two questions before us: What think ye about his concealment? Do ye think that he will not come to the feast? (comp. Winer.) If we assume only *one* question, and explain it, " What can be the cause that he does not come to the feast ?" we disturb the connection with ver. 54, and overlook the chronological relations. It was still a long time to the feast, and Jesus might yet come. Nothing is in harmony with this but the question whether the Lord would come at all.

Ver. 57. " Now both the chief priests and the Pharisees had given a commandment, that, if any man knew where He were, he should show it, that they might take Him."—The " also " is not to be overlooked. In the preceding we saw the impression which the concealment of Jesus made on the multitude. Here we have the measures which the spiritual authorities were thereby induced to adopt. Not merely the people, but their religious rulers also, deduced from the transitory seclusion of Jesus the inference that He desired to withdraw altogether from publicity; and they therefore proceeded against Him in the full confidence that their measures, even if they failed of any tangible result, would at least stamp Jesus as an impostor shunning the light. How must they have been confounded when our Lord suddenly appeared among them free and unrestrained !

Ch. xii. is occupied with the occurrences of the last six days before the final Passover of Jesus. First, we have in vers. 1-8 His anointing in Bethany. John's narrative does not profess to record the incident as a whole, with all its attendant circumstances; but only to give a series of supplements to his predecessors. He briefly sums up the fundamentals of the event, and as much as possible in their words. His additions are: the specification of the time of the supper; its connection with the resurrection of Lazarus; the name of the woman who anointed Christ; the name of the particular disciple who stimulated the opposition to Mary's act in the circle of the Apostles, connected with a remark upon the motive of that disciple.

Ver. 1. " Then Jesus, six days before the Passover, came to Bethany, where Lazarus was which had been dead, whom He raised from the dead."—The narrative connects itself with the end of the previous chapter by οὖν. Jesus confounded the thoughts and machinations mentioned in ch. xi. 55-57, and which had their origin in His seclusion, by His actions: at the right time He came forward with the utmost publicity, and thus overturned all their notions.—With reference to πρὸ ἐξ ἡμερῶν τοῦ πάσχα—about six days before the Passover—comp. on ch. xi. 18.—Which way did our Lord take from Ephraim to Bethany? John does not say: we must therefore assume that the former Evangelists had given an account of this; and our expectation is found to be warranted. They all agree that our Lord in His last journey to Jerusalem passed through Jericho: comp. Matthew, in which the account of this last journey begins ch. xx. 17, and goes on to ver. 29; Mark x. 46 (the beginning of the narrative in ver. 32); Luke xix. 1 (the beginning in ch. xviii. 31). John's predecessors also give us the reason why Jesus took the circuitous route through Jericho: the time of seclusion, John xi. 54, had run out; and Jesus would now enter Jerusalem in full publicity. To the stately entrance which He contemplated, a large retinue was necessary. To gather these together, our Lord took the road leading through Jericho, which was in the high pilgrim-road through Perea. As soon as Jesus joined this track, great multitudes of people began to surround Him, Matt. xx. 29: comp. Mark x. 46; Luke xviii. 36, xix. 3. These crowds, who doubtless came to Jerusalem the same day on which Jesus entered Bethany, spread there the report of His coming, set the whole city in commotion, and were the occasion that many came to Jerusalem even on the Sabbath; and that still more fetched the Lord on the ensuing day. The circuitousness, therefore, of the road gives no difficulty. Probably Jesus during the last time did not remain in Ephraim, but sought out the perfect solitude of the wilderness which lay between Ephraim and Jericho: comp. on ch. xi. 54.

How are the six days to be reckoned? The word Passover is, in the law, used only of the paschal lamb, and in Matthew and Mark only of the paschal meal. If here also in John it describes the whole festival, we must assume that the festival took its beginning from the meal, the name of which passed over to the whole week. Ch. xiii. 1 makes this certain. There the "feast of the Passover" commences with the paschal meal; and the definition of the time there is all the more decisive, as the account is connected with our present one, and refers to the same feast. The paschal meal belonged to the evening of the fourteenth of Nisan, which, according to Jewish reckoning, begins at the same time the fifteenth Nisan. The paschal meal fell then on the Thursday evening. If we reckon six days backwards, Jesus came to Bethany on the evening of the Friday, the eighth of Nisan,—which, according to Jewish computation of time (Lev. xxiii. 32), also began the ninth of Nisan,—before the rest of the Sabbath had begun. The first day went from the Friday evening to the Saturday evening; the second from Saturday evening to Sunday evening, and so forth. The "Supper" of our Lord must belong to the day of His arrival; for otherwise the words "on the next day," ver. 12, would be meaningless,—a thing which, in John's chronological style, is inconceivable, and more especially here, where the Evangelist defines precisely those points in the Passion week which were left undecided in the first Gospels. The "Supper" of Bethany was, doubtless, the principal meal of the Sabbath-day. The entrance into Jerusalem followed on the Sunday: the second or next day extended, according to Jewish reckoning of time, from Saturday evening to Sunday evening. Jesus tarried in Bethany at least thirty-six hours. It has been erroneously urged, that the chronology in the text interferes with the sanctity of the Sabbath. The Sabbath is still among the Jews preferred for the enjoyment of feasts. But the food was prepared previously; and even the tables must have been arranged in order before the Sabbath began. Nor does the fact that guests came from Jerusalem militate against the feast having been on the Sabbath. The ecclesiastical district of Jerusalem extended beyond the walls. "Lightfoot, in the Hor. Heb. p. 73, cites a mass of passages from Jewish writers, which establish that Bethphage was altogether regarded as if it had been situated within the walls of Jerusalem. The wall was thus considered as pushed outwards; and Bethany was no more than a Sabbath-day's journey for the citizens of Jerusalem, although it was no less than fifteen stadia" (Wieseler, s. 435). The narrative of Luke xxiv. 50-53, compared with Acts i. 12, makes it clear that Bethany was not more than a Sabbath-day's journey from Jerusalem. Accordingly, the Sabbath would not throw any impediment in the way of the Jews' coming to Bethany in order to see Jesus, as recorded in ch. xii. 9-11.

The other Evangelists make no express mention of the sojourn of Jesus in Bethany before the entrance into Jerusalem. But they do not imply that He passed by that place without spending the night; which is rendered improbable by the fact, that in their own accounts Jesus went out to Bethany every evening of the last week of His life upon earth: Matt. xxi. 17; Mark xi. 11, 12; and especially Luke xxi. 37. Jesus had spent the previous night with Zaccheus in Jericho: thus He had already made a long day's journey when He reached Bethany. It is not probable that He first passed by Bethany and went to Jerusalem, and then returned back to the former place. There is a distinct intimation of the sojourn in Bethany before the entrance into Jerusalem in Mark xi. 1: "And when they came nigh to Jerusalem, εἰς Βηθφαγὴ καὶ Βηθανίαν πρὸς τὸ ὄρος τῶν Ἐλαιῶν, unto Bethphage and Bethany, at the Mount of Olives;" and Luke xix. 29. Bethphage and Bethany form in these passages a geographical unity. Bethphage, alone mentioned in Matt. xxi. 1, is placed first in order, to intimate that Jesus had already left Bethany behind Him. Mark's introduction of the latter word intimates that the Evangelists knew more than they narrate—that Jesus made Bethany His point of departure that day. The hint in Mark and Luke is fully developed in John.—But for what reason did the earlier Evangelists omit expressly to record the sojourn of Jesus in Bethany before the entrance into Jerusalem? The answer is simply, that their accounts had no point of connection with that sojourn, and did not require it for the sake of supplement. Luke had already, in ch. vii., independently of chronology, narrated the anointing, as an illustrative appendage to our Lord's designation of Himself as the friend of publicans and sinners. Matthew places the account of it in ch. xxvi. 6, etc., immediately before that of the treachery of Judas. He gives it without any reference to time. The τότε, corresponding to τότε in ver. 3, comes in ver. 14. So also with Mark in ch. xiv. 3-9. Their narratives of the anointing are in both these Evangelists parenthetical insertions, without reference to time. They separate the account of the consultations of the high priests from that which records Judas' offer of himself as their instrument. Both Evangelists subordinated chronological sequence, interrupting it in order to insert for a purpose an event which they had both reserved. But the reason why they mention the fact just where they do, is not what many, following Augustin, assume, viz. that Judas, in consequence of the anointing, and the waste which Jesus permitted, was filled with hatred and anger, and conceived the project of the betrayal. That Judas derived his instigation to treachery from that event is a mere fiction, for which there is no definite ground in the narrative. And it is decisive against this hypothesis, that Matthew and Mark do not mention Judas —whom John alone names; but they must have mentioned him had there been such a connection between the two events. The first two Evangelists place the story of the anointing immediately before the account of Judas' treachery, in order to make more prominent the darkness of the traitor, in contrast with the light of Mary. The avarice of Judas, who sold Christ for thirty pieces of silver, is the perfect opposite of the $ἀπώλεια$ of Mary upon Christ's person. She gives what she has in perfect sacrifice, probably the last relics of her substance (comp. the ὃ εἶχεν αὕτη, ἐποίησε, Mark xiv. 8); Judas, on the other hand, turns Christ Himself to gold. John only assigns here to the residence in Bethany, which the other Evangelists leave chronologically indefinite, its appropriate and true place in our history.— Bethany is described as the place where Lazarus was: he, since his resurrection, was the principal person in Bethany. The circumstance that he was there probably occasioned Jesus' going—the remembrance of the miracle would thereby be freshened; it occasioned the feast which celebrated that event; and attracted the concourse of multitudes who came to seek Jesus, ver. 9. The fact that Jesus had called Lazarus from his grave, brought to Him the crowds which fetched Him from Jerusalem, vers. 17, 18. The description of Lazarus, on this mention of him, has a solemn amplitude, which was intended to arrest the reader's attention to this person, and his high importance. Many copyists did not understand this. Hence some of them omitted ὁ τεθνηκώς as superfluous; others, for the same reason, ὁ Ἰησοῦς.

Ver. 2. "There they made Him a supper; and Martha served: but Lazarus was one of them that sat at the table with Him."—The phrase "making a feast" is commonly used of a greater and more special repast: comp. Mark vi. 21; Luke xiv. 12, xvi. 17. And the feast before us was of that kind. It served to celebrate the resurrection of Lazarus. The coming of Jesus was doubtless expected. All things had been prepared for the feast, and the guests had been summoned. That Martha played the hostess in her own house, is shown by Luke x. 38, 40 : comp. Matt. viii. 15 ; Mark i. 31. It would not have been becoming for an eminent woman to have discharged such a service in another house than her own. Martha, the housewife, who had under her a company of servants, waited even in her own house only because the circumstances were extraordinary. Where "the Master" is present, who in ver. 26 says, "If any man serve Me, him will My Father honour," it is perfectly becoming that the mistress should serve. That Lazarus was among the guests, had a theological significance : it was a demonstration of the truth and greatness of the miracle. Perfect reinstatement in the former life—and not merely the change from death into the state of a sick man— was required by the symbolical significance of the event.

Ver. 3. "Then took Mary a pound of ointment of spikenard, very costly, and anointed the feet of Jesus, and wiped His feet with her hair: and the house was filled with the odour of the ointment."—The whole conduct of Mary is, as Chrysostom remarked, that of a "broken-hearted soul." Wichelhaus (Comm. on the Passion-history) observes, "She must have been similarly affected as the sinner of Luke vii." That she anoints the feet of Jesus, that she unlooses her hair, to do which was held among the Jews a great disgrace, that she wipes with it the feet of Jesus —all exhibit her as the sinner and the penitent. Wichelhaus, who acknowledges all this, seeks in vain to prove that ch. xi. records a great transgression on the part of Mary. The nard, to which Pliny assigns the first place amongst unguents (H. N. xii. 26 : de folio nardi plura dici par est, ut *principali* in unguentis), is mentioned only by Mark of the earlier Evangelists. Matthew speaks only in general of a costly ointment. The pound here corresponds to the "alabaster box" of Matthew and Mark. According to the metrological investigations of Boeckh, λίτρα was not merely a weight of twelve ounces, but also a measure for liquids. A vessel which contained twelve ounces of water was the *libra mensuralis*, the metrical pound for liquid; and the ointment boxes were probably so made as to contain just one such metrical pound. Πιστικός is not, with many, to be understood in the sense of *liquid;* for an adjective derived from πίνω never occurs, and, moreover, potable in the sense of liquid would be a strange application of the word. It must rather be interpreted, with the old Greek expositors, that which might be trusted, real, genuine. The word πιστικός is not to be found in classical authors; for in the passage commonly adduced from Aristotle's Rhetoric, πειστική is the reading now generally acknowledged. Yet we find in an Attic inscription (Boeckh, Corp. Inscript. i. 382), a Πιστοκράτης Πιστικοῦ, both proper names of father and son, probably meaning the same. In later Greek, πιστικός was the supercargo, to whom the ship and its freight were entrusted; and then the man who stood representative of the company, and was bound to make provision for it. It was probably an expression of common life, and specifically a commercial *terminus technicus*. This interpretation is made the more probable by the fact that nard was so frequently adulterated. Pliny, xii. 26, says: Adulteratur et Pseudonardo herba . . . *Sincerum* quidem levitate deprehenditur. Again, xiii. 1 : Conveniet meminisse herbarum quæ nardum Indicum *imitentur*, species novem a nobis dictas esse : tanta materia *adulterandi* est. Tibullus speaks of the nardus pura; and in Galen we find the expression ἀκέραιον applied to it. Pliny, xii. 26, assigns to genuine nard the value of a hundred denarii to the pound. But that could not have been its highest price; for Pliny gives to nard the supreme place among unguents, but at the same time mentions another species which he declares to be worth from 25 to 300 denarii : comp. ver. 5.

Vers. 4, 5. The εἰς ἐκ τῶν μ. αὐτοῦ refers to the οἱ μαθηταὶ αὐτοῦ, not as a correction, but as supplementary. That Judas was only the originator of the complaint, is plain from the reproof administered to more than one in ver. 8. What Judas alleges is so specious and plausible, that the record of the other Evangelists may easily be believed as quite natural. " For luxurious and prodigal feasts," says Wichelhaus, " such an anointing might have been appropriate; but what end could such luxury upon Jesus serve ? What reasonable man would not have agreed with Judas in this censure ?"—Merely for distinction from the other Judas, the Σίμωνος alone would have been sufficient. The surname *Iscariot*, the man of lies, is added, because it was now that Judas declared himself to be essentially what that name signified; he disguised his covetousness and lust of thieving under the semblance of pious care for the poor: comp. ver. 6. "Who should betray Him" has also its special significance here. While he in his avarice was exhibiting his anger against this expression of love to Jesus, he was proving himself a worthy candidate for betraying Jesus through avarice. Three hundred pence or denarii, nearly ten pounds, was to these disciples a large sum. It is characteristic of Judas, the type of later money-making Jews, that he so accurately knows the price of a thing with which he had nothing to do. Even if we had not the narrative of John, this valuation of the ointment, which Mark also gives, would of itself have pointed to Judas.

Ver. 6. "This he said, not that he cared for the poor; but because he was a thief, and had the bag, and bare what was put therein."—$Βαστάζειν$ always in the New Testament means to carry; so even in ch. xx. 15, where the bearing is only by the context determined to be a carrying away. $Βαστάζειν$ itself never stands for appropriating, or spending on itself; nor is the $ἐβάστασε$ pleonastic, if we take the verb in its usual meaning of carrying. The new element lies in the $τὰ\ βαλλόμενα$, which specifies the contents of the common bag, and shows that it was filled by affectionate gifts. This new appendage to the sentence required a new verb. That Judas had the bag is remarked also in ch. xiii. 29; whence we see that this bag served both for the supply of the necessities of the company, and for charities to the poor. The contributions to this common stock came, according to Luke viii. 3, principally from women. As Judas had the bag and carried these contributions, he had good opportunity for appropriation. Obviously, he must have often given occasion for such a suspicion; but his fellow-disciples, observing the law of love, had kept down this fearful suspicion, receiving his justification, however little plausibility it might have. After his betrayal, all these grounds of suspicion returned to them in full force.

It can scarcely fail to be acknowledged, that the provision of this bag stands in some relation to 2 Chron. xxiv. 8, the only passage in which the Septuagint employs $γλωσσόκομον$. There we find that, by command of king Joash, they made a chest, and deposited it in the forecourt of the Temple; that all the princes and all the people brought joyfully their Temple tribute, ἐνέβαλον εἰς τὸ γλωσσόκομον: comp. βάλλειν, used of throwing gifts into God's treasury, Matt. xxvii. 6; Mark xii. 41; Luke xxi. 1. Jesus explains, in Matt. xvii. 26, that He, as the Son of God, was rightfully free from the obligation of Temple tribute. By adopting as a pattern the institution in 2 Chron. xxiv., He arrogated to Himself what in that passage was devoted to Jehovah. The negative in Matt. xvii., and the positive, rest upon the same ground. It was in the most proper sense a Divine chest, and theft from it was robbery of God. Christ appointed this provision as a type and example for His Church. Origen calls the ecclesiastical poor-steward τὸν τῆς ἐκκλησίας ἔχοντα γλωσσόκομον.—We do not read that Jesus gave the bag into the charge of Judas: probably he pressed himself into this service, and Jesus suffered it to be so. But how could He have done this, when, as the Son of God, He knew what was in man, ch. ii. 25, and had, in particular, penetrated the heart of Judas from the beginning? (Comp. on ch. vi. 71.) Lampe answers this question with perfect propriety: "It is part of the adorable ways of Divine Providence in regard to sin, that sinners are placed in circumstances in which their wickedness must break out." Jesus let Judas have the bag, not although he was, but because he was, a covetous man. The promise contained in the petition of the Lord's Prayer, "Lead us not into temptation," like the promises contained in all of them, applies only to the sincere and rightly disposed. That Judas was not one of these, was manifested by the fact that he forced himself into the keeping of the bag. Had he been honestly disposed, he would, considering his bias to covetousness, have been anxious to keep himself as far from money as possible. But as he served avarice, it was part of his doom that the bag was committed to his hands. Criminal records present in relation to this the most manifold analogies. Most transgressors become such by opportunity presented to them. That which slumbers within them is often aroused by remarkable concatenations of events pointing plainly to the finger of God's providence. To keep them back from such temptation would not make them better; it would only hinder their sin from reaching maturity, and showing its full fruits, which is the condition of thorough reformation if this be still possible, and the foundation of judgment if not. To doubt that Jesus marked the defalcations of Judas, is to doubt of His Divinity. The abomination of covetousness He had probably often dilated on to His disciples, with express reference to Judas. Having done that, He did all. Since Judas had no hearing ear, the Lord would not violently break in upon the development of his sin. He must fulfil his destiny.

Ver. 7. " Then said Jesus, Let her alone: against the day of My burying hath she kept this."—The gentleness of Jesus in His reproof shows that, as the other Evangelists expressly record, the murmuring was shared in by such as had no evil thought, and required to be gently dealt with. *Burial* is not the interment itself, but the preparations for it. The day or the time of burial was already come, inasmuch as the death of Jesus was immediately impending. We are not justified in having recourse to the notion of a providential arrangement of circumstances, or to explain the keeping and the using of the ointment "as an unconscious prophetic act," and to go on with Stier: " Mary designed only to pay the Lord a tribute of honour appropriate to the feast, and does not, for her own part, think of any burial or embalming." We may rather regard it as on all accounts probable that the thought of the impending death of Jesus filled Mary's soul, and was the reason why she reserved for future use the ointment, which otherwise she would have sold for the good of the poor. What Jesus had already plainly declared in Galilee, Matt. xvi. 21; what He had so expressly told His disciples at the outset of the present final journey, Matt. xx. 17, Mark x. 32–34, Luke xviii. 31–34; what was not unknown even to His enemies, Matt. xxvii. 63—could not have been concealed from Mary, occupying the position which she did. She who hung on the Lord's lips, Luke x. 39, had hidden this deep in her heart. The extravagance of her honour to Jesus sprang in part from the consciousness that it was the last honour she would do Him, the last expression of her thankfulness for all that He had done for her, the unworthy. This consciousness must be appealed to as the only moral justification of her act. The mere providential significance of the act would not be sufficient for that purpose. The reading ἵνα εἰς τὴν ἡμέραν τοῦ ἐνταφιασμοῦ μοῦ τηρήσῃ αὐτό is, notwithstanding its high authentication, a mere correction introduced by those who supposed the ἐνταφιασμός could only be effected on the person of one already dead. It is opposed by the preceding narrative in John and the other Evangelists, according to which the whole of the ointment was then and there expended (it was the waste of it all that was the main element); by Matt. xxvi. 12, Mark xiv. 8, according to which Mary anointed Christ *beforehand;* by Mark xiv. 6, where the ἄφετε αὐτήν forms a clause of itself; as well as by the current use of ἄφες, ἄφετε, in the Gospels, which usually indicates a brief despatch. Ewald explains, "Let her keep it for the day of My burial." But αὐτό too evidently refers to the μύρον, as Mark xiv. 8 also vouches. Τηρεῖν is used precisely as in ch. ii. 10.

Ver. 8. "For the poor always ye have with you; but Me ye have not always."—Jesus alludes to Deut. xv. 11, "For the poor shall never cease out of the land: therefore I command thee, saying, Thou shalt open thine hand wide unto thy brother, to thy poor, and to thy needy in thy land," with which ver. 4 there does not stand in contradiction, "there shall be no poor among you;" for there it is asserted that, on the whole, wealth and well-being should be the rule, which would naturally admit exceptions. That the "Me ye have not always" does not contradict the "I am with you always," needs no demonstration.— The words of Jesus show that we must be on our guard against admitting the common utilitarian principle too largely in the Church. What, looked at in the light of this principle, appears to be waste, may have its full justification as the expression of thankful love and glowing devotion. A deeper consideration will make it plain that this seeming waste often accomplishes more than those applications of money which plainly proclaim their practical uses. The cathedrals are not less necessary than the parish churches to the maintenance of Christian worship.

In vers. 9–11 we have the excitement which the coming of Jesus produced in the city.

Ver. 9. "Much people of the Jews therefore knew that He was there: and they came not for Jesus' sake only, but that they might see Lazarus also, whom He had raised from the dead."—It is plain enough that the word Jews here is not used with a hostile meaning, but that only their nationality is thereby denoted: comp. on ch. i. 19. Persons are here spoken of who are under an attraction to Christ. These were found especially amongst the strangers who came up to the feast (comp.

ver. 12); for the people of the place would have had earlier opportunities of seeing Lazarus. If Jesus tarried thirty-six hours in Bethany, there was ample time for their coming. The report of His arrival in Bethany was doubtless soon spread in Jerusalem by those who had accompanied Him.

Vers. 10, 11. " But the chief priests consulted that they might put Lazarus also to death; because that by reason of him many of the Jews went away, and believed on Jesus."— "Lazarus also," no less than Christ, ch. xi. 53. Such a thought, albeit transitory, came to the high priests when they observed the great excitement of the people: ἐσείσθη ἡ πόλις,—which Matthew, in ch. xxi. 10, remarks concerning the entrance of Christ,—was already true here. The fact that they wanted to kill Lazarus, shows that they regarded the miracle of his resurrection as a concerted scheme, just as the Pharisees endeavoured to set aside the greater fact of the resurrection of Christ by an imputation of deceit. All that Christ gained was so much lost to the high priests. In ὑπῆγον, which simply corresponds to the ἦλθον of ver. 9, Lampe sees too much meaning, when he makes it signify the people's forsaking the priestly chair to express their contempt of the priests.

THE ENTRANCE INTO JERUSALEM.

VERS. 12-19.

The Apostle first gives the chronological specification which was wanting in the earlier Evangelists. Then he briefly sums up, down to ver. 15, what they had already written on the subject. To this *resumé* he appends his own contribution. First comes the remark, that the connection between this event and Zech. ix., already observed upon by Matthew, was not perceived fully until Christ was glorified; then the relation it bore to the resurrection of Lazarus; and finally, how the Pharisees were affected by the whole proceeding. The arrangement of the whole section can be understood only when we perceive that the Apostle first recapitulates, and then supplements.

Vers. 12, 13. " On the next day much people that were come to the feast, when they heard that Jesus was coming to Jerusalem, took branches of palm-trees, and went forth to meet Him, and cried, Hosanna: Blessed is the King of Israel that cometh in the name of the Lord."—On the next day: after the arrival of Jesus in Bethany, and after the supper held on the same day. The entry followed doubtless on the Sunday forenoon. It cannot be detached from the tenth Nisan, inasmuch as it was on this day that the typical paschal lamb was set apart, Ex. xii. 3. As Jesus declares Himself to be the antitype of the Passover, it was doubtless with reference to this that He chose the day of entrance. Nor is it without significance that it was on the same day the people under Joshua went up from the Jordan, to begin their warfare with the powers of Canaan, Josh. iv. 19. That war was the type of "the judgment of this world," which was by Jesus, the true Joshua, to be accomplished. The "great multitude" consisted, doubtless, for the most part, of Galileans. In the capital, where the Pharisaic spirit was concentrated, and which the prophet had always indicated as the centre of destruction, Micah i. 5, the number of susceptible spirits was much smaller than in the provinces. *Baïa* are of themselves palm-branches; but τῶν φοινίκων is added, because that botanical technical term might not be understood in lands where the palm did not grow. "The branches of the palms" are simply palm-branches; and the repeated article has here, as in so many other cases, been made much more of than necessary. They are palms in opposition to other trees, and their branches to other parts of the tree.—The meaning of palm-branches we learn from Lev. xxiii. 40. There the children of Israel were commanded, in the Feast of Tabernacles, to take green branches of *palms*, and the boughs of thick trees; and they were to rejoice before the Lord seven days. The present festal rite was therefore an expression of joy, the object of which was the coming of the so long expected King. In the prophetic passage, which forms the centre of the whole event, the "Rejoice, O daughter of Zión!" corresponds to the bearing of palm-branches. This rejoicing found in the palm-branches its external expression: so the bearing of green branches and palms is in 2 Macc. x. 7 the symbol of joy. Parallel with this passage is Rev. vii. 9. "If the palms are to be understood as palms of joy, the symbolical acknowledgment of the salvation which the name of Jesus pledges, then these two passages harmoniously coincide. As the people once expressed by this symbol their rejoicing in salvation, when Jesus the Saviour entered into the earthly Jerusalem, so now the elect express their joy when they are with Christ in the heavenly Zion."—The acclamation of the multitude is taken from Ps. cxviii. 25, 26, " Save, Lord, we beseech Thee; blessed is He that cometh in the name of the Lord,"—words the application of which to the present occasion was all the more obvious, because, as Jewish writings testify, they were on other occasions used as a cry of joy in the public worship of the people. The psalm is a song of the Church's gratitude, exalted by the goodness of God from the deepest depression to the highest glory. What befell Israel, when saved from the captivity, was only the type of the people's deliverance in Christ.

That in the Hosanna, "Save now," the people pray on behalf of their *King*, and only indirectly for their own salvation (in harmony with the prophecy, where the King ישעו, is defended of God), is manifest from Matthew, who makes the people cry "Hosanna to the Son of David," as well as from the correspondence of the following "Blessed be." The word Hosanna must, in the time when John wrote, have become naturalized among the Christian congregations, even the Gentile ones; therefore he does not add the translation, as his wont is on occasion of introducing other Hebrew words. In the original Hebrew passage, the accents require us to construe " May He that cometh be blessed in the name of the Lord" (comp. my Comm. and Hupfeld): the name of the Lord, His historically manifested glory, is the *source* of blessing, ch. v. 43. "I am come in My Father's name," furnishes no sufficient reason for construing otherwise. Luke xix. 38 makes it manifest that $\dot{\epsilon}\nu$ $\dot{o}\nu\acute{o}\mu\alpha\tau\iota$ is to be connected with $\epsilon\dot{v}\lambda o\gamma\eta\mu\acute{\epsilon}\nu o\varsigma$. There the order is, $E\dot{v}\lambda o\gamma\eta\mu\acute{\epsilon}\nu o\varsigma$ $\acute{o}$ $\dot{\epsilon}\rho\chi\acute{o}\mu\epsilon\nu o\varsigma$ $\beta\alpha\sigma\iota\lambda\epsilon\grave{v}\varsigma$ $\dot{\epsilon}\nu$ $\dot{o}\nu\acute{o}\mu\alpha\tau\iota$ $Kv\rho\acute{\iota}ov$, not $\acute{o}$ $\beta\alpha\sigma\iota\lambda\epsilon\grave{v}\varsigma$ $\acute{o}$ $\dot{\epsilon}\rho\chi\acute{o}\mu\epsilon\nu o\varsigma$. $B\alpha\sigma\iota\lambda\epsilon\grave{v}\varsigma$ $\tau o\hat{v}$ $'I\sigma\rho\alpha\acute{\eta}\lambda$ serves more closely to define Him that was coming, and thereby at the same time to give the reason of the benediction imprecated on Him. Since the benediction manifestly should, as in Matthew, consist of three clauses, we must add, in thought, " Blessed be," or " Hosanna," to the King. The passages of the Old Testament in which the Messiah is described as King of Israel, have been adduced already on ch. i. 50. Christ is here primarily marked out only as King of Israel. If he be King, it is self-understood that He is also *the* King absolute, the King without fellow. For He could be acknowledged as King by the multitude only on the ground of His Messianic dignity. But the people expected in the Messiah the King whom no other king should equal.

Vers. 14, 15. " And Jesus, when He had found a young ass, sat thereon; as it is written, Fear not, daughter of Sion: behold, thy King cometh, sitting on an ass's colt."—Why did Jesus, just at that time, enter so majestically into Jerusalem, with His passion before Him, and, as it were, beginning that passion by entering? The following section gives the answer. It will show that Christ demonstrated Himself by His sufferings to be King; that His death was the means of the realization of His dignity and attainment of His dominion; that by His death the prince of this world was to be cast out; and that Christ should, when He was lifted up from the earth, draw all men unto Him: comp. vers. 23, 24, 31, 32. This strict connection between the sufferings and the dominion was set forth in the prophet Zechariah. There the King cometh *meek* or *afflicted*, and riding upon an ass; and in this character of sufferer He speaks peace to the Gentiles, and obtains dominion over the whole earth.

The entry of Christ into Jerusalem had also, apart from the prophecy of the Old Testament, to which Matthew and John place it in relation, its own independent significance, otherwise we should hardly be able to understand the fact that Mark and Luke do not expressly intimate its connection with the prophecy. That our Lord enters Jerusalem in this festal manner, was intended to exhibit Him as now about to assert that royal dignity which until now He had in a measure concealed. But that He enters upon an ass was intended to symbolize the manner in which He would assert His royalty: to wit, in the way of humility that He ever pursued, as an example for His Church, which should never forget that her Head rode forward upon an ass when He assumed His kingdom upon earth. The ass signifies the *Cross* aspect and condition of the Church. The old Gentile Romans, who, according to Tertullian, called the Christians *asinarii*, in allusion to this event, understood it better than superficial expositors, who want to make the ass a symbol of peace. Into that same city which David and Solomon had so often entered amidst a retinue of proud horsemen, and upon magnificently caparisoned mules and chargers, the Lord now entered upon a borrowed ass, a pitiful "ass's colt," never before used for riding on. The trappings were represented by the poor garments of His disciples; His retinue consisted of those whom the world accounted mere rabble, upon whom the wise Pharisees and rich men of Jerusalem looked down with contempt. To him who had no eye for the glory that was concealed beneath, the whole matter must have seemed a pitiful comedy. That the ass was not in the East essentially more honoured than amongst ourselves, is proved by the Son of Sirach, ch. xxx. 24 (xxxiii. 25), as also by the original passage in Zechariah, where the riding upon the ass is conjoined with the predicate עני, which can mean only *afflicted*. That a king should ride upon an ass at all, was, in the East, a thing unexampled; but here the King, as such, in His royal progress, rides upon it, and indeed upon a mere ass's colt. The remembrance of this should be our encouragement when the Lord's sad humiliation upon earth is reproduced in the providential course of His Church, and our warning against seeking too high things as His people. It should also be a caution to those who are always so ready to magnify every little stumbling-block in the Scripture into an argument against its divinity. Even in Scripture the Lord wears the garb of a servant; and in reference to it also holds good the word, "He comes riding on an ass's colt," as also, "Blessed is he that shall not be offended in Me."

The remarkable εὑρών, having *found*, altogether inappropriate had Jesus brought the ass with Him from Bethany, has an entire history behind it, which John, who omits all merely subordinate circumstances, and presupposes details as known, almost in express terms tells us to seek in the earlier Evangelists. The watchword, with the whole history resting upon it, is found in those earlier writers: comp. Luke xix. 30, εὑρήσετε πῶλον δεδεμένον; ver. 32, ἀπελθόντες δὲ οἱ ἀπεσταλμενοι εὗρον καθὼς εἶπεν αὐτοῖς; Matt. xxi. 2; Mark xi. 2, 4. Mark and Luke mention only the young ass. The mention of the she-ass occurs only in Matthew, whose eye is ever keenly directed to the minutest details which exhibit fulfilment of Old Testament scripture. The original in Zech. ix. 9 runs fully thus: "Rejoice greatly, O daughter of Zion; shout, O daughter of Jerusalem: *behold, thy King cometh unto thee*: He is just, and having salvation (saving Himself); lowly, and *riding* on an ass, and *upon a colt* the foal of an ass." The variations here have been usually, but very superficially, explained on the ground that John cites from memory. But then they would not have been omissions; the quotation would not then have so literally coincided with the original as it does, apart from the first words, where the change, as will presently be seen, is an intentional one. The reason of the variation was rather the Evangelist's design to direct attention to the main point which John had in view in narrating the accordance between the prophecy and its fulfilment, the riding upon a young ass. The *lowly* it was the less necessary to reproduce, because in the original it was covered by the "riding upon an ass."—Instead of the "Rejoice greatly, daughter of Zion," in the original, John has "Fear not, daughter of Zion." But, so far as the meaning goes, the "Fear not" does not vary much from the original. The matter of the *joy* is here especially the redemption from the power of an oppressor, the Gentile power. This is shown by the connection with ver. 8, "And no oppressor shall pass through them any more, for now have I seen with mine eyes." Accordingly, the "Fear not" is latent in the "Rejoice." Lampe: Non nudum gaudium præcipitur, sed tale quod præcedentem timorem exactorum excipiebat. The "Rejoice" is only the negative translated into the positive. But John did not introduce the change in his own fashion simply; he rather derived the "Fear not" from Isa. xl. 9 : " O Zion, that bringest good tidings, get thee up into the high mountain ; O Jerusalem, that bringest good tidings, lift up thy voice with strength: lift it up, be not afraid ; say unto the cities of Judah, Behold your God ;" and at the same time, from Zeph. iii. 16, a passage dependent on this of Isaiah: "In that day it shall be said to Jerusalem, Fear thou not ; and to Zion, Let not thine hands be slack ;" with ver. 15 preceding it, "The Lord hath taken away thy judgments, He hath cast out thine enemy: the King of Israel, even the Lord, is in the midst of thee: thou shalt not see evil any more." The change of the "Rejoice greatly" can all the less be fortuitous, inasmuch as Matthew also has introduced a remarkable variation upon these same words. He has instead, from Isa. lxii. 11, εἴπατε τῇ θυγατρὶ Σιών, pointing in a most suggestive manner to the connection of these passages, and weaving the isolated utterance of Zechariah into the great tissue of passages dwelling on the same theme. We can, indeed, hardly doubt that John decidedly chose the universal formula of citation, καθώς ἐστι γεγραμμένον, in order to intimate that in his view the single passage of the original took its place in the midst of a much wider and larger connection.

The "Fear not" denotes, according to the original passages, the absolute security of salvation. The miserable and lowly condition in which Zion lies as it were buried, and the apparent omnipotence of her foes, must not mislead her, and abate her confidence. The daughter of Zion must not fear, in spite of the lowliness of her King, and in spite of His sufferings. That which might seem to warrant fear, will in fact serve to remove it for ever. The King will vanquish the world, not merely despite His deep humiliation, but by the very means of that humiliation. Even to the present day He is then greatest when He seems to be least; and still with His disciples death is the way to life. Just when they are sinking deepest into the depths, the "Fear not" is most applicable to their case. John, quoting the Old Testament passage, must, in harmony with the phraseology of the Apocalypse, behold another daughter of Zion, still continuing to exist in the Christian Church, concealed behind that daughter of Zion whose destruction was impending when Jesus entered (indeed, the weeping over Jerusalem recorded by Luke, ch. xix. 41, was among the circumstances of the same entry), and was accomplished when John wrote. The μὴ φοβοῦ, as spoken to the common Zion, would have been meaningless. The true daughter of Zion meant by the Evangelist was for the moment represented by the multitude who cried Hosanna. It consisted really of those from among the Jews who believed in Jesus. And these were increased by believers from among the Gentiles. Both the exclusion from Zion and the adoption into Zion proceeded according to a spiritual principle. That in the time of the Evangelist the separation from the external Zion was perfectly accomplished, is shown by the manner in which John speaks concerning the Jews : comp. on ch. i. 19.[1]

[1] The true and spiritual notion of the daughter of Zion, which was variously prepared for even in the Old Testament, is given by Augustin : " In that reprobate and blind people nevertheless was the daughter of

Ver. 16. "These things understood not His disciples at the first: but when Jesus was glorified, then remembered they that these things were written of Him, and that they had done these things unto Him."—There is a similar remark in ch. ii. 22. The opened understanding, and the glorification of Christ, stood in the relation of cause and effect. That event gave the Apostles an entirely new standard. They saw that beneath the deepest humiliation the highest glory might be hidden; that greatness could not be measured by the ell, but must be estimated according to a spiritual standard. Moreover, the outpouring of the Holy Ghost was connected with the glorification of Christ, ch. vii. 39, xiv. 26; and that great gift raised the Apostles to a higher stage of knowledge and perception. Till that time their eyes were holden by their carnal Messianic expectations. The present event had too poor an aspect to allow them to discern in it the royal entrance of the King, who should speak peace to the Gentiles, and whose kingdom stretched from sea to sea, from the Euphrates to the ends of the earth, Zech. ix. 10. But when they learned to discern spiritual things spiritually, and to understand the hidden process of the Redeemer's power, and the great difference between the kingdom of Christ, with its concealed glory, and the kingdoms of this world, their eyes were opened, and they obtained an insight into the connection between prophecy and fulfilment. The ἐποίησαν includes especially the action of the people just recorded, and which also belonged to the fulfilment of the prophecy,—especially the Hosanna in correspondence with the designation of the Messiah as יְשׁוּעַ, *saved of God*, in the prophecy. What Christ, and at His command the Apostles, did, cannot be brought under this point of view; because that was done with the design to bring the prophecy to its fulfilment. But we may include the free action of the Apostles, which rested not upon the command of Christ, and did not recognise the refer-

Zion, to whom it was said, Fear not, behold thy King cometh, sitting upon the foal of an ass. This daughter of Zion to whom these words were divinely uttered, was found amongst those sheep who heard the voice of the Shepherd; she was in that multitude who praised the coming Lord with so much devotion, and escorted Him with so great a band. And it was said to her, Acknowledge Him who is the object of thy praise, and be not afraid when thou seest Him suffer, because that blood is being poured out by which thy crime will be blotted out, and thy life restored to thee."

ence to any prediction; as also the circumstance, that they found the ass, and that the owner of the ass suffered them to take it away. The relation which John sustained to the earlier Evangelists will not allow us to limit the ἐποίησαν merely to what he recorded: we may, and we must, borrow the supplement of his account from his predecessors.

Ver. 17. "The people therefore that was with Him when He called Lazarus out of his grave, and raised him from the dead, bare record."—The next verse shows that their testimony did not rest upon their own personal eye-witness, but upon what they had heard from others. The same is made plain by ver. 12, according to which "the multitude" consisted of those who had come from abroad to the feast. But these could not have been eye-witnesses of the resurrection of Lazarus: they were at the time of that event far away from Jerusalem. Luther, translating "but the people who were with Him when He called Lazarus out of the grave, and raised him from the dead, published the fact," follows the incorrect reading ὅτε (Vulg. *quando*), which sprang from the false notion that μαρτυρεῖν must needs infer the testimony of an eye-witness. Luke xix. 37 gives us the general foundation for all that is peculiar here.

Ver. 18. "For this cause the people also met Him, for that they heard that He had done this miracle."—The people here are identical with the people of vers. 17, 12. The supposition of another and different crowd is altogether baseless. In ver. 17 we have what the people did after they had joined Christ; in ver. 18, what they did when they came out to meet Him. Ver. 17 brings in a supplement to ver. 13; ver. 18, a supplement to ver. 12. The καί does not "distinguish between the crowd already accompanying Him and that which came to meet Him," but points to the fact, that the resurrection of Lazarus was not only the matter of their praise who met Jesus, but the very reason that they came at all.

Ver. 19. "The Pharisees therefore said among themselves, Perceive ye how ye prevail nothing? behold, the world is gone after him."—*Among themselves* is the same as *to each other*: the mere thoughts of the heart cannot be matter of historical record. That John was so well acquainted with the projects of the Pharisees (comp. ver. 10), suggests a middle person, who had some common relation to the disciples and to the Pharisees.

And we naturally think of Martha as such—the wife of Simon —who must have heard in the family circle of her husband much that would otherwise have been concealed. Θεωρεῖτε is not to be taken as a question: comp. Acts xxi. 20. The Apostle rejoices over the embarrassment of the Pharisees: this is the only point of view in which we can regard the verse. Paraphrases like that of Grotius—"We must adopt stronger measures to carry out the decree of the council"—spring from a total misapprehension of John's design. Everywhere we see that he takes pleasure in recording the opposition brought to bear against Jesus, and the shame to which his Master's enemies were always put. In the contest between evil and good, the saying, "Ye see that ye prevail nothing," must always hold from age to age. Ver. 24 shows that the deepest prostration of the good cause can never make this doubtful.—We have an Old Testament parallel in 1 Sam. xxiv. 21, where Saul is obliged to say to David, "And now, behold, I know well that thou shalt surely be king, and that the kingdom of Israel shall be established in thine hand:" comp. ch. xxiii. 17, where Jonathan says, "And thou shalt be king over Israel, and I shall be next unto thee; and that also Saul my father knoweth." The relation of Saul to David was a kind of type of the relation of the Pharisees to Christ. The representatives of a bad cause have the secret consciousness that they fight against God. Therefore they must needs lose heart on every fresh reverse. That here also "This spake he not of himself" holds good—that the Apostle regards these words, which were extorted from the enemies of Christ, as a kind of prophecy, is plain, from the connection in which the succeeding narrative so manifestly stands with these words: Yea, verily, ye do nothing at all; all the world goeth after Him—not only the Jews, but even the very Greeks! These last were already sending their deputation; and as the result of their request, Jesus, in ver. 32, utters the word, "And I, if I be lifted up from the earth, will draw all men unto Me." Bengel here observes: A hyperbole springing from indignation. If the whole world, say they, were ours, it would desert us to go after Him. There lies in their words something prophetical.

JESUS AND THE GREEKS.

VERS. 20–36.

It was a remarkable coincidence, that on the very day when Jesus took leave of the Jews, and withdrew into seclusion, certain Greeks expressed the desire to see Him; and that Jesus was led by this desire to announce the near approaching extension of His kingdom among the Gentiles. Like the wise men from the east at Christ's birth, these Greeks are to be regarded as types and representatives of the heathen world, destined to be received into the kingdom of Christ. But Bengel is not altogether right in describing the proceeding as "prelude of the transition of the kingdom of God from the Jews to the Gentiles." Such a transition never in fact took place. This is proved by a glance at the multitude shouting Hosanna from among the Jews in the preceding section. Believers from among the Gentiles did not take the place of the Jews generally, but of the unbelieving mass of the Jewish people. The stem of God's kingdom consisted of believers from the Jews, and into this stock the Gentiles were to be grafted: and it is this which the coming of the Greeks pretypified.[1] That the scene occurred in the Temple, is evident from the circumstance that this was the ordinary scene of Christ's work in the last days: comp. Luke xxi. 37, but specially from ver. 36, compared with Mark xiii. 1.

Ver. 20. "And there were certain Greeks among them that came up to worship at the feast."—It has been already shown, on ch. vii. 35, that "Ελληνες never means Hellenistic Jews, but always Gentile Greeks. We must not think here even of circumcised Gentiles: these by their circumcision became Jews. Only in relation to born Gentiles, who had never been received by circumcision into the community of Israel, can the scruple

[1] Augustin gives us here the right view: Behold, the Jews desire to kill Him, the Gentiles to see Him; but they also were Jews who cried, Blessed is He that cometh in the name of the Lord. Behold those of the circumcision, and those of the uncircumcision, like two bodies from different parts, coming together and uniting with the kiss of peace in the one faith of Christ.

of Philip and Andrew be understood; and only to them was appropriate the answer of Christ, who declined the desired audience, with an allusion to the fact that the wall of separation would soon by His death be done away. The true religion exercised, even in its imperfect Old Testament form, a mighty influence upon those deeper intellects in the Gentile world who had the opportunity of becoming more closely acquainted with it. Solomon says in the prayer at the dedication of the Temple, 1 Kings viii. 41 : " Moreover, concerning a stranger, that is not of Thy people Israel, but cometh out of a far country for Thy name's sake ; (for they shall hear of Thy great name, and of Thy strong hand, and of Thy stretched-out arm ;) when he shall come and pray toward this house : hear Thou in heaven Thy dwelling-place, and do according to all that the stranger prayeth unto Thee for; that all people of the earth may know Thy name." In the days of Christ, the number of those Gentiles who were inclined to the Israelitish religion was rendered greater than ever before by the deeper degeneracy of the Gentile religions at that period. They appear in Acts xiii. 43, 50, xvi. 14, xvii. 4, 17, under the name of σεβόμενοι. They formed an admirable bridge for the passage of the Gospel from the Jews to the Gentiles. It could not be otherwise than that these " God-fearers" would receive the tidings of the great works of God with peculiar delight and desire. Mark vii. 26, ἦν δὲ ἡ γυνὴ Ἑλληνὶς, Συροφοινίκισσα τῷ γένει, shows that by the term Greek, Gentiles generally of Greek tongue and culture were meant. Accordingly we need not assume Greeks from Greece to be signified here. That they applied to Philip of Galilee—by Isaiah called Galilee *of the Gentiles*—makes it presumable that they themselves also dwelt there, in one of its Greek towns. The present participle, ἀναβαινόντων, is used, as in ch. ix. 8, in the Hebrew sense, without any definition of time. The notion of habitually going need not be introduced: that would have been much more specifically noted. It means certain from among the number of those who then had come up to the feast. The words " to *worship*" indicate that they were not the visitors generally—so that ch. xi. 55 might be brought into comparison—but the *Gentile* visitors, whose participation in the feast was limited to the προσκυνεῖν, attributed to them by Solomon, and who had not received the sacramental rite. It is said of the chamberlain of Candace, in Acts viii. 27, ἐληλύθει προσκυνήσων εἰς Ἱερουσαλήμ.

Ver. 21. " The same came therefore to Philip, which was of Bethsaida of Galilee, and desired him, saying, Sir, we would see Jesus."—Why did they apply to Philip in particular? His name gives the answer; he was the only one among the Apostles who bore a Greek name. Greek name and Greek culture went hand in hand. The respectful request κύριε shows that they were deeply concerned for the attainment of their desire. Κύριε is certainly the word which Mary uses to the gardener; but only at a crisis when she thought that she was dependent on him in a matter of supreme importance to her. The Greeks did not venture to go straight to Jesus Himself; they thought they must take hold of the skirt of him that was a Jew, Zech. viii. 23, like the Gentile centurion who sent the elders to Jesus, Luke vii. 3. Their special desire had reference to a private and confidential colloquy. As Jesus taught openly, they might easily enough see Him in passing. But that kind of seeing was not of much value in itself.

Ver. 22. " Philip cometh and telleth Andrew: and again Andrew and Philip tell Jesus."—Philip and Andrew are united also in ch. i. 45. That Philip did not venture himself to go directly to Jesus, that he first lays the matter before Andrew, and takes counsel with him,—whence many expositors have deduced the doctrine that it is expedient in difficult cases to resort to the counsel of at least one trusted friend,—shows that there was a For and Against in reference to the wish of the Greeks. As it respects the For, the participation of the Gentiles in the kingdom of Christ was unanimously attested by the whole of prophecy. Compare, for example, Isa. lv. 4, 5: " Behold, I have given Him for a witness to the people, a leader and commander to the people. Behold, Thou shalt call a nation that Thou knowest not, and nations that knew not Thee shall run unto Thee;" with ch. lvi. 3, 7. According to the first personal Messianic announcement, Gen. xlix. 10, the people should gather to Shiloh. Christ had predicted, in the most express manner, the extension of His kingdom to the Gentiles, Matt. viii. 11; He had held intercourse with the Gentile centurion, with the woman of Canaan, and with the Samaritan woman. But, on the other side, Christ had communicated to His

Apostles the command not to go in the way of the Gentiles, and to enter no city of the Samaritans, Matt. x. 5; He had said to the woman of Canaan, " I am not sent but unto the lost sheep of the house of Israel;" He had just before the present occasion, John x. 16, represented the calling of the Gentiles as dependent on His own atoning death, and thereby indirectly declared, that until His death the wall of partition which separated Him and His people from the Gentiles should continue. Thus it is explained why Philip first talked over the matter with Andrew, and that the two proffer no specific request to Jesus, but simply report to him the wish of the Greeks. The answer of Christ was a negative. The exclusion of the Gentiles was, until His atoning death, which broke down the middle wall, the rule. This rule admitted, indeed, certain exceptions, in order to pretypify the calling of the Gentiles. But this design had been already subserved; and it was specially befitting that the separation should be maintained inviolate now at the end, in order that the distinction between the two ages should be distinctly marked.

It does not follow from Philip's consulting Andrew about the request, that the latter was the more spiritually advanced. Yet there are not wanting passages in which Andrew is the more prominent: Mark iii. 18, xiii. 3; Acts i. 13. There his name follows those of the three most confidential disciples of Jesus.

Ver. 23. "And Jesus answered them, saying, The hour is come, that the Son of man should be glorified."—"To them" —Andrew and Philip. There is no trace of any reception of the Greeks; on the contrary, the specific reference to the disciples, in ver. 26, shows that Jesus had to do with them alone. Moreover, the final result of Christ's answer tends to this one thing, that the time for the admission of the Gentiles was not yet come. The criticism which asserts that "it is quite uncertain here whether the desire of the Greeks was granted, and to whom the address was uttered," falls before a deeper consideration of the text.—"The hour is come:" the Gentiles therefore must only wait a little longer with patience, since, with the glorification of the Son of man, their union with Christ was immediately connected; and this is the issue of the whole discourse in ver. 32. As to the reason why our Lord here and elsewhere speaks not of the time generally, but of the

hour, Beza makes a very subtle remark,—which will, by the way, serve to show with what propriety the Erlangen critic asserts the time to be come for dismissing the old veterans in exegesis to the rest they have merited : "The word hour seems more expressly to denote that providence of God which is not only universal, but most specific in all things, and especially in the mystery of our salvation : that providence in which God has ordered from eternity, not only the years, months, days, but even the most minute portions of time ; and certainly this doctrine, as it is most sure, and harmonious with the nature, power, and will of God, so it most wonderfully confirms us in our faith and patience, in opposition to distrust and impatience."
—" That the Son of man may be glorified" has its commentary in ch. xvii. 5, "And now glorify Thou Me, O Father, with the glory which I had with Thee before the world was." It pertains to the glorification of Christ, according to what follows, that He has much fruit, ver. 24, that He draws all to Himself, ver. 32 ; but that is not the proper essence of that glorification, which is rather the ceasing of the servant form, and His reception into the glory of the Father. Bengel gives us here the correct view : Apud Patrem, c. xvii. 5, et in conspectu omnis creaturæ. Christi glorificatio et gentium conversio in unum tempus incidit.[1]

Ver. 24. "Verily, verily, I say unto you, Except a corn of wheat fall into the ground and die, it abideth alone : but if it die, it bringeth forth much fruit."—In what has preceded there was the fact that the glorification of Christ was immediately at hand ; here we have the *hour* of its accomplishment : the essential way and means to it, its inevitable foundation, was death. But because this was contrary to all natural reason, and because the disciples' minds would recoil from it, and all the more as Christ's suffering was the prophecy of their own, calling upon them also *per aspera ad astra,* therefore Christ here set out with a strong preliminary encouragement. In His words there is a remarkable blending of figure and fact. The spiritual seedcorn is Christ. That His death was absolutely

---

[1] Augustin : "He saw the Gentiles who should believe in all nations after His passion and resurrection. On occasion, therefore, of those Greeks who desired to see Him, He forcannounces the future plenitude of the Gentiles; and foretells that the hour of His glorification was already come."

necessary in order to His bringing forth much fruit, and drawing all to Him, ver. 32, has its foundation in the expiatory, vicarious significance of His death: comp. ch. x. 11, 15. In the fact of the atonement accomplished by Christ, the whole process of His dominion has its root. Isa. liii. clearly taught that doctrine, especially in ver. 10: "When His soul hath made an offering for sin, He shall see His seed." The thought is this, that in the sacrificial death of the Servant of God there was a quickening power; on that death He would found His living Church. "It bringeth forth much fruit" points back to Isa. xi. 1, where the branch out of the root of the stem of Jesse, the Messiah appearing primarily in humiliation, should spring forth and bear fruit; as also to Ezek. xvii. 23: "In the mountain of the height of Israel will I plant it (the tender twig, ver. 22); and it shall bring forth boughs, and bear fruit."

Vers. 25, 26. "He that loveth his life shall lose it; and he that hateth his life in this world shall keep it unto life eternal. If any man serve Me, let him follow Me; and where I am, there shall also My servant be: if any man serve Me, him will My Father honour."—Following Christ's pattern, all His servants also must willingly sacrifice all things to their calling; and thus shall they all share His glory. The two verses form a parenthesis. All the Gospels show it to be Christ's manner to avail Himself of any opportunity to represent Himself as the pattern of His disciples. The death of Christ is distinguished, on the one side, from the voluntary offering up of life on the part of His servants. It is only Christ's death that has consequences for all the world, brings forth much fruit, and effects that all are drawn to Him; the results of the death of His servants are only personal, in that they themselves attain eternal life, go where Christ is, and are honoured by His Father. But in the most general and comprehensive fact—the necessity of spiritual self-sacrifice, and death being not loss but gain—the Lord and His servants are alike. And it is only this general aspect of the matter that is here regarded. Expressions bordering on those of ver. 25 had been earlier uttered by our Lord, according to the other Evangelists; evidence how important it was, that this great thought should be deeply and indelibly engraven on the minds of the disciples: comp. Matt.

x. 25, 26, 39; Luke xiv. 26.—"He that loveth his life," his soul: that is equivalent to "He that loveth his own individual existence," himself. The soul is not here used, as in Matt. x. 28, Luke xii. 22, in antithesis to the body; but it represents the whole person. In Matt. xvi. 24 we read, ἀπαρνησάσθω ἑαυτόν, and then follows, "for he that will save his soul," etc. Thus the soul is there also paralleled with the self. That in Luke·xiv. 26 a man's own soul is the man himself, is plain from the juxtaposition of these persons throughout, the father, the mother, etc. In the Old Testament the soul is frequently used for the whole personality: e.g. in Gen. xiv. 21, "Give me the persons (the souls), and take the goods to thyself;" Ex. i. 5: comp. Acts ii. 41. The ground of this phraseology is to be found generally in the fact that the soul, as the breath of God, Gen. ii. 7, the "honour," Gen. xlix. 6, is the better part of man, and hence well fitted to represent the man. But *here* there is probably a specific reason for designating the whole person as the soul, in the fact that the subject here is the preservation or the loss of the *life;* now the soul and the life are closely allied in Scriptural phraseology.—The position contemplated is that in which the soul or the individual existence, and the calling or duty assigned of God, are opposed to each other. Now the first and chief commandment, to love God with all the soul, excludes all love to the individual I; the individual I, so far as it places itself in opposition to the vocation, must be hated.[1] This hatred, directed not against the soul in itself, but against its undue claims, is at the same time the truest love to our own soul and life. It assures the soul of a secure place there where her proper home is alone to be sought. Μισεῖν means simply *hate;* to *love less* it never means, either here or elsewhere in the Scripture. The father and mother, and so on, must, according to Luke xiv., when they come into conflict with our relation to Christ, not merely be less loved, but be hated and energetically cast away. "In this world," which is so poor in true professions, which can give and take

[1] Augustin: When, therefore, it comes to this, that either we must oppose the precept of God or cease to live, and a man is forced to choose one of the two courses, under the pressure of persecution,—then he must prefer to die with God's favour than to live with His displeasure; he must hate his soul in this life, that he may preserve it unto life eternal.

away so little, and to give up for which the future world with that eternal life which alone is worthy of the name of life, is the greatest of all follies.

In ver. 36 we have first, in the words, "If any man serve Me, let him follow Me," the duty which is to be discharged by His servants; then the reward. In a certain sense, there is a *serving* of Christ predicable of the laity. But that official service is here meant, appears first from the circumstance that the address is directed to the special and peculiar servants of God in His kingdom; but still more clearly, in the second place, from the succeeding words, "There shall also My *servant* be." Διάκονος always denotes an official position: comp. Matt. xxii. 13; 2 Cor. iii. 6, vi. 4. Grotius rightly remarks: "He here silently terms Himself a King who has many servants, for the administration of the things of His kingdom." "Let him follow Me:" in the way of self-denial and consecration of life.[1] Matt. x. 38 gives us a commentary on ἐμοὶ ἀκολουθείτω: "Whoso taketh not up his cross and followeth Me, is not worthy of Me;" xvi. 24, "If any man will follow Me, let him deny himself, and take up his cross and follow Me," where ὀπίσω μου ἐλθεῖν corresponds to the διακονεῖν here. Beneath this challenge, "Let him follow Me," there lies a concealed promise. It is taken for granted that the way of the servants, no less than the way of their Master, is a way of the cross, to the voluntary assumption of which cross the ἀκολουθείτω is a challenge. In this aspect of it, Mark x. 38, 39, is parallel, where Jesus foreannounces to the sons of Zebedee that they will drink the cup which He drank, and be baptized with the baptism with which He was baptized.—"And where I am, there shall also My servant be:" the commentary on this is ch. xiv. 2, 3, xvii. 24. Christ takes His servants up into those heavenly dwellings whither He had gone before to prepare their place. As soon as they make their exit from this miserable life, they come to Him in Paradise, Luke xxiii. 43, into the condition of heavenly blessedness, 2 Cor. xii. 4: comp. ver. 2. Of any intermediate condition, or Hades-life, the Lord knows nothing: comp. 2 Cor. v. 8; Phil. i. 23.

[1] Augustin: What is the following Him but the imitating Him? For Christ hath suffered for us, says the Apostle Peter, leaving us an example that we might follow His steps.

Ver. 27. This saying of our Lord is connected with ver. 24. In very deed, the dying of the seedcorn is not so light a matter. The soul of our Lord in the prospect of it was deeply troubled. But it must be so; it could not be otherwise. It was inseparably bound up with the great work that Christ was bound to accomplish. This trouble and this death, therefore, were the way to glorification. The words ἡ ψυχή μου τετάρακται are taken from Ps. xlii. 6, ἱνατί περίλυπος εἶ ἡ ψυχή μου καὶ ἱνατί συνταράσσεις με, Why art thou disquieted? ver. 7; ὁ Θεός μου πρὸς ἐμαυτὸν ἡ ψυχή μου ἐταράχθη : comp. ver. 12; Ps. xliii. 5. To the same psalm, the expression of David's deepest lamentation in his misery, the Lord also refers in Matt. xxvi. 38, Mark xiv. 34. We obtain anything like insight into the nature and ground of this trouble of the Redeemer, only when we have obtained a right perception of the significance of His death. If the death of Christ was merely an "event" or "calamity" which befell Him in the way of His vocation, He would have gone to encounter it with cheerful confidence. Otherwise He would have stood on a lower level than His own martyrs,—Ignatius, for example, who wrote in the prospect of death, "It is glorious to give up the world to go to God, that I may have the sight of His face; let me be the food of beasts, so I may find my God. I am God's corn; I shall be crushed by the teeth of wild beasts, that I may become the pure bread of Christ." But that Christ's death was something altogether different from a death of self-sacrifice in the ordinary sense, is shown by ver. 24, according to which the full power for the extension of His kingdom has its root in the death of Christ; and vers. 31, 32, according to which the Redeemer conquered, by His death, the prince of this world, and draws all men to Himself, abolishes the wall of partition which had hitherto excluded the Gentiles from the kingdom of God. The root and centre of the work of Christ is everywhere the vicarious expiation accomplished by His death; and with this was inseparably connected His bearing for us the wrath of God. John describes Him in ch. i. 29 as the Lamb of God who taketh away the sin of the world. In ch. iii. 14 Christ sets Himself forth as the antitype of the serpent in the wilderness, inasmuch as He assumed unto Himself the most deadly of all deadly energies, sin, and vicariously made atonement for it. In ch. x. 11 seq.

our Lord refers to Isa. liii. 10, where the Servant of God is said by His death to make satisfaction. According to Matt. xx. 28, Jesus gives His soul a ransom for many; He presents for the sins of the human race, which could not without satisfaction be forgiven, a satisfaction which the sinners themselves could never have given, and thus effects and provides for the justification of sinners before God. God made Christ *sin* for us, 2 Cor. v. 21; He sent Him as a sin-offering, Rom. viii. 3; He is the propitiation for our sins, Rom. iii. 25.

We have in this passage the prelude to the conflict of Jesus in Gethsemane. The trouble here, and the trouble there, form a unity: one key unlocks both. But we have elsewhere remarked, with reference to that fact: " The problem to be solved is this, not how this bitter anguish generally, and specifically this anguish as coming just before His death, should lay hold of the Redeemer, but how this anguish should declare itself to be the supreme degree of the fear of death: the Lord prays for the removal of this fear of death; the fear of death extorts from Him the bloody sweat. Nothing of this kind is found recurring in the death of any Christian martyr or confessor. And yet this very circumstance makes the infinite difference between the Redeemer and His servants. The sting of death is sin. The more free man is from sin, the sweeter to him is death, as the way to the Father.—The only solution of this is the vicarious significance of the sufferings and death of Jesus. If our chastisement was upon Him in order that we might have peace, then in Him must be concentrated all the horror of death. He bore the sin of the world, and the wages of that sin was death. And death, therefore, must to Him assume its most frightful form. The physical suffering was nothing in relation to this immeasurable suffering of soul which impended over the Redeemer, and the full greatness and depth of which He clearly perceived. Therefore, in Heb. v. 7, a fear is described as that which pressed with such awful weight upon our Lord. When God freed Him from that, He saved Him from death. Thus, when the suffering of Christ is apprehended as vicarious, and accordingly as voluntary, all the accompanying circumstances are easily enough understood. Then we can understand the sudden transition in tone and feeling from that of the high-priestly prayer to that of the conflict in Gethsemane. With equal freedom the

Redeemer responded here to the one and there to the other side of His destiny. Then also we see how it was that the Redeemer, far from being surprised by the agony or overpowered by its prospect, provided everything with reference to it, and took the most advanced disciples with Him, that they might be witnesses of His infirmity, and also of that which He effected for us." Thus Augustin remarks with perfect correctness: "Christ's perturbation tranquillizes us, and His infirmity makes us firm;" and Beza: "The cause of this, the most awful and horrible distress in the mind of Christ, was the sense of the Divine wrath, than which nothing more terrible can be conceived." If the perturbation had had no actual significance, if it had been merely a variation of weakness, Jesus would not have given it such express and careful utterance.

Τί εἴπω is the expression of consideration, and intimates that the matter had two aspects; that what was recommended as desirable on the one hand, was on the other very doubtful: comp. Matt. xxi. 25, 26; 1 Cor. xi. 22. The "What shall I say?" standing first, *softens* the following "Father, save Me from this hour," shows that it was only under one aspect that the deliverance was desired, and that not without hesitation, thus paving the way for the following retractation. There is no reason for understanding the "Father, save Me from this hour" interrogatively. Stier very justly opposes this by saying, "To our feeling there is something discordant, at this time of profound spiritual emotion, in a prayer which just questions, Shall I ask this request?" There is nothing inappropriate in the fact, that in the midst of this circumscribing agony, the anguish of His soul expressed itself in an actual supplication. This is the most obvious interpretation; and were it otherwise doubtful, it would be confirmed by Matt. xxvi. 39, where Jesus prays that the cup might pass away from Him. And Heb. v. 7 is decisive against the *interrogatory* theory: there we read of strong crying and tears being offered to Him who was able to save Him from death. "But *to this end* came I unto this hour:" διὰ τοῦτο, that My soul might be troubled. The anguish which evoked this supplication of Jesus, "Save Me from this hour," was the very reason why this hour, the time of anguish, came upon Him. It was the basis of the work of redemption. Christ must endure horror, that we might be delivered from horror.

That which constituted the design for which the hour was appointed, could not be the occasion for the prayer that it should come to an end. The διὰ τοῦτο is important, because it exhibits the inmost connection between the agony of Christ and His atoning work. Those who explain the trembling after the manner of Lücke,—" as a sacred law of nature: death has a horror for man, especially death as coming upon young and fresh life,"—have to make their very beginning with the διὰ τοῦτο.— The petition, "Father, glorify Thy name," is fully apprehended when we regard it as the counterpart of the request, " Save Me from this hour," as well as in connection with " Therefore came I unto this hour." Glorify Thy name by causing that My soul-anguish and My death be not in vain, but that it serve to My own glorification, the salvation of the world, and the extension of Thy kingdom. Let Me suffer what I must suffer —let Me tremble and agonize, so that only this fruit may finally come from My sufferings. Since this request was a definite and absolute one, it has for its foundation the assurance that the Lord *would* in this manner glorify His name. The deepest depth of this suffering is for Christ the way to glorification.

Ver. 28. " Father, glorify Thy name. Then came there a voice from heaven, saying, I have both glorified it, and will glorify it again."—God glorified His name by the works which Christ accomplished by His power, the resurrection of Lazarus being the last; and He would further glorify His name by prospering the suffering and death of Christ to the end of His glorification, and the spread of the kingdom of God over the whole earth. According to ver. 29, the people heard thunder; and the question rises, whether the voice from heaven here was identical with the thunder, or whether there was some articulate voice distinct from the thunder. We decide in favour of the former view. There is no reason for assuming any voice shaped into words. Among the concomitants of the sound, immediately after " Glorify Thy name," the thunder did expressly say what John gives as its meaning, in connection with which it is not accidental, that after οὐρανοῦ the λέγουσα is wanting. 1 Sam. xii. presents the nearest analogy. There we have not a voice of the Lord separated from the thunder, but the thunder itself, following at an unusual time; and in immediate connection with the words of Samuel is the voice of the Lord. In ver. 18 of that chapter we read, " So Samuel called unto the Lord, and the Lord gave thunder (voices) and rain that day; and all the people greatly feared the Lord and Samuel." To describe thunder as the voice of the Lord, was only following the example of the Old Testament. Seven times it is so termed in one Psalm, Ps. xxix. In Job xxxvii. 4 we read, " He thundereth with the voice;" and in Ps. xviii. 13, " The Lord also thundered in the heavens, and the Highest gave His voice :" comp. also 1 Sam. xii. 17; Ex. ix. 23. If John had intended that we should distinguish clearly between the thunder and the voice, he would have recorded both in separate terms. But there is no trace of any such distinction. On the contrary, John points expressly to the fact, that the thunder and the voice were one and identical. He records that the multitude heard the voice, and said that it thundered. Thus the people recognised the voice itself as thunder. There is not the slightest hint that the people heard less than what took place; that on account of the dulness of their ears they received the impression only of a rumbling noise, but did not apprehend the articulate voice. The multitude heard no articulate voice at all. Accordingly our Lord speaks, with allusion to what they had heard, of a voice, and exhorts them to lay that voice to heart. Thus the thunder spoke, even to those who heard nothing besides the thunder. John himself intimates that only thunder was there, when he uses the ἐδόξασα and δοξάσω, words used with allusion to thunder, and thunder as repeated, קולות. The name, son of thunder, given by Jesus to John, Mark iii. 17, assumes and was based upon a sense of the symbolical language of nature. It is natural that the son of thunder should assign its true significance to the thunder, and that he should regard it less prosaically than, for instance, Stier, who remarks, " *Mere* thunder as the voice of the Father over His Son, were something altogether unworthy: with him who does not feel that, we have no disposition to argue." Certainly we do find in Scripture heavenly voices without thunder: comp. 1 Sam. iii.; Matt. iii. 17, xvii. 5; Acts ix. 4, xxii. 7. But we cannot find there any satisfactory instance of a connection between thunder and the articulated voice of God. In Ex. xix. 19, we read that Moses spoke, and God answered with His voice; but according to ver. 16, that voice was thunder; for the voices and the lightnings are there placed in juxtaposition. The idea of an articulate voice of God combined with the thunder at the giving of the law (præmissa tonitrua, quæ attentionem quasi excitabant et deinceps articulatæ voces), rests simply upon the expositor's caprice. The articulate voice there belongs to Moses alone, who comes forward as the interpreter of God, and is legitimated as such by the thunder. What Moses, according to Ex. xix. 25, uttered, could only have been the same ten commandments which, in ch. xx. 1, are referred back to God, who sanctioned Moses, as His speaker and representative, by the " voices" of thunder. In Ex. xx. 19, the people ask that Moses might speak to them *alone*, and not, as aforetime, with the accompaniment of the terrifying thunder-speech of God. True that in Deut. v. 4 we read, " The Lord talked to you face to face in the mount, out of the midst of the fire." But how that is to be understood, that the Lord spoke only by the " voices" of thunder, while the words spoken were those of Moses, is plainly declared in ver. 5 : " I stood between the Lord and you at that time, to show you the word of the Lord, saying." That Moses with reference to the ten commandments acted the part of an interpreter, is shown by the " saying," which is immediately followed by these ten commandments. In Rev. x. 4, the voices of thunder are introduced with specific meanings. But *here* also we may say there is a specific meaning : it is marked by the circumstances under which the thunder is introduced. If in that passage of the Apocalypse the thunder itself seems to speak, that belongs only to the vision. In all other Apocalyptic passages the thunder itself is the voice of God : ch. iv. 5, viii. 5, xi. 19, xvi. 18. Throughout the whole of Scripture there does not occur a single instance in which articulate speech is introduced, concealed beneath the thunder.—Thunder is in its nature, and the impression it produces upon every human heart, not merely in general a revelation of the glory of God, but a revelation of a threatening and terrifying character. Dread is the sentiment which always responds to it. This was the character it bore at the giving of the law. It proclaimed to the people that their God was a jealous God, who would inexorably visit their sins upon them. It presented to them the alternative between obedience and judgment; and it pointed to the great truth that whosoever should break the law must die. So also in Ps. xviii. and xxix. According to Ps. xxix. 7, the voice of the Lord divides with flames of fire; the thunder appears to be the symbolical threatening to the world, and therefore at the same time a symbolical promise to the Church of God oppressed by the world. In the Apocalypse, which it is obviously natural to compare with the Gospel of John, the thunder always has a polemical character; it has always a reference to terrible judgments, whether these are only threatened as to come, or actually accomplished: comp. ch. iv. 5, viii. 5, x. 3, xi. 19, xvi. 18. That here also the "voice" has not only an imposing, but also a threatening character; that it aims at the glorification of God's name by the subversion of the enemies of God and His Christ, is shown by ver. 31, where the thunder is introduced as a premonition of judgment upon this world and its prince.

Vers. 29 and 30 form an interlude. But Jesus immediately restores the connection. While in vers. 31 and 32 He more fully develops the meaning of the thunder, He comes to the thought which forms the direct answer to Philip and Andrew, the indirect answer to the Greeks: that the time was at hand when there should be closer relations with the Gentiles. That time, however, not being actually come, the wishes of the Greeks could not be granted. Had not the intervening words of the people been spoken, Jesus would at once have begun with ver. 31. Thus the close of the answer to the Gentiles is formally and primarily a part of the answer to the people.

Ver. 29. "The people therefore that stood by, and heard it, said that it thundered: others said, An angel spake to him."— The people regarded at first only the material phenomenon. But what this did not deny—under the circumstances of the occasion, the force of which, as at the raising of Lazarus, must have excited and carried away the minds of all, what it could not have denied—the deep *significance* of the material phenomenon, some individuals expressly declared in words, thus interpreting the general feeling of all. (Doubtless the saying "it thunders" was spoken not without agitation; and nothing would be more perverse than to interpret them as speaking of common thunder. In the "angel" the Divine energy and presence is embodied to them: comp. on ch. v. 4. They think that God gave

Christ His testimony by the thunder, and thus assured Him of the answer to His prayer.[1]

Ver. 30. "Jesus answered and said, This voice came not because of Me, but for your sakes."—The answer of our Lord has regard to the αὐτῷ, spake *to Him*. He points them to the fact that He, in the internal relation in which He stood to the Father, needed no such external token; and that they should think rather of themselves. Thunder is a solemn sign of the time: woe to him who does not understand and lay to heart this sign. Its voice announces a judgment: he who does not receive its warning will, in that judgment, fall. That which is in ver. 31 only hinted, finds its more full explanation, so far as it referred to the Jews, in vers. 35, 36, 44–50.

Ver. 31. "Now is the judgment of this world: now shall the prince of this world be cast out."—We have in ver. 31 the exposition of the voice's meaning. It announces that there is to be a judgment held upon this world. This judgment proceeds primarily on the prince of this world; but that it does not end there—that it at the same time proceeds upon those who are one with him in spirit and act—those who are of their father the devil, viii. 44—is plain from the fact that, before the prince of the world, the world itself is mentioned as the object of judgment (Stier is manifestly wrong: "The ungodly world is itself *in a certain sense judged* in its prince, when it is *saved*"); more especially from ver. 30, which warns the Jews against falling in the judgment; and vers. 35–44 seq. Ver. 32 shows that the judgment has its root in the death of Christ. There Christ represents Himself as, in consequence of His death, drawing all men to Him; but this positive energy must have the negative one of judgment as its inseparable concomitant. Christ cannot draw to Himself without at once condemning the prince to whom they had previously belonged, and who will not let them go unless he is judged and stripped of his power, and at the same time themselves whom He receives, so far as

---

[1] In what embarrassments expositors are involved who assume a distinction between the thunder and the voice of God, may be seen in Lampe's remark on this verse: "It cannot without difficulty be decided whether the people really heard thunder distinct from articulate voice, and without any such voice, or whether they called the sound of the voice, as it came to their ears, by the name of thunder."

their indwelling sin is concerned, the extirpation of which in judgment is the condition of their being drawn to Christ, to whom they could never come in the spotted garment of the flesh. Judgment and salvation go hand in hand.

The death of Christ has a condemning significance in two ways. First, as to those who receive it in faith: a condemning sword pierces their soul; the pain of penitence is the prerequisite of faith; the condemnation of their sin, which was accomplished upon the cross, approves its saving power in them only when they have gone through this severe discipline. And then the death of Christ has its judicial significance for those who reject it in unbelief. The destruction of Jerusalem had its root in the death of Christ: the blood of the Redeemer was upon them and their children. He who counts the blood of the covenant an unholy thing, Heb. x. 29, is doomed to eternal condemnation.—Ps. xcvii. exhibited the manifestation of Christ under the judicial point of view. " The appearance of Christ had a judicial significance also for those among the Gentiles who obeyed the Gospel: the nothingness of their past existence was thereby made manifest; and profound shame took the place of the pride with which they had despised Zion. Among those who would not acknowledge this 'The Lord reigneth,' that side of the judgment which is here prominent came into force." —" The prince of this world:" thus Satan is named only in the last discourses of Jesus in John; first here, and then in xiv. 30, xvi. 11. This dignity is attributed to him only where its subversion is immediately in prospect. As regards the fact, Matt. iv. 8, 9 corresponds, where the devil shows Christ all the kingdoms of the world and their glory, and says to Him, " All these things I will give thee, if thou wilt fall down and worship me." What he promises to give, he must himself possess. Then, again, the description of the devil in 2 Cor. iv. 4, as " the god of this world," is in strict keeping; but especially Eph. ii. 2, where Satan is described as the prince who has power over the air. The air, corresponding to the $\tau o\hat{v}$ $\kappa \acute{o}\sigma \mu o v$ $\tau o \acute{v}\tau o v$ of the preceding verse, the atmosphere of the earth, denotes the influences of Satan everywhere surrounding man, who breathes an air, as it were, infected by Satan.

The imagination and desire of the human heart is evil from youth up: there lies the foundation of Satan's power. That power does not rest upon any right of Satan which even God is bound to respect: the notion of such a right is opposed to all Scripture. But the being subjected to his power is only the deserved punishment and necessary consequence of sin; so that with the cause the effect also must cease. Man is too weak and insignificant to assume anything like an independent middle position between God and Satan. He must walk either with God or Satan. Since the fall, he has been reduced to bondage under the devil. But through the manifestation of Christ, and especially through His atoning death, the power of sin has been broken. Since that event it has been a great anachronism when a people or an individual remains subject to the broken power of Satan. From the time that sin was atoned for on the tree, punishment has ceased for all who enter into the new order of things; new powers of life have been provided and given to them. And thus Satan has now nothing in them.—" Shall be cast out:" not from dominion, but from the *world;* for that is the word which immediately precedes, and we are led to that also by the corresponding ἐκ τῆς γῆς, from the earth, in ver. 32. The removal of Christ from the earth, which thus seems to exclude Him from dominion over it, will have for its consequence the removal of Satan from the earth. The ἐκβληθήσεται ἔξω, the exclusion of Satan from the world, is virtually contained in and implied by the death of Christ on the cross. The realization of it goes on from stage to stage, until, in the casting of Satan into the lake of fire, Rev. xx. 10 marks its consummation. A very important crisis in that realization is the binding of Satan in Rev. xx. 2, the destruction of the Gentile power which was the firmest bulwark of Satan on the earth. But that realization actually began with the death of Christ. From that time it was demonstrated that powers were energetic against Satan which the human race had never before known.—Here Satan is cast out of the world; in Rev. xii. 7–9 he is cast out of heaven, as the result of the victory which Christ had won over him through blood and death. The difference is only a formal one. For that Satan cannot maintain himself in heaven, means in the Apocalypse simply that his power is broken through the blood of Christ, ver. 11. Everything mighty is translated into heaven.

" And I, if I be lifted up from the earth."—According to

the current interpretation, there lies in these words a double meaning: they are made to refer at once to the crucifixion and to the exaltation; and the crucifixion itself is regarded as the beginning of the glorification. Bengel: " In the cross itself there was already something tending to glory." But we must reject this double meaning, and adhere to the simple reference to the death of Christ. This is demanded by the explanation of the Apostle in ver. 33; it is suggested also by the interpretation of the Jews in ver. 34: they find in the ὑψωθῶ ἐκ τῆς γῆς the contrary of their expectation concerning the Christ, that He would μένειν εἰς τὸν αἰῶνα, abide for ever; and Christ confirms that interpretation, by warning them to avail themselves of the light which would only a short time remain among them. The relation to ver. 31 also demands such an exposition: by the same event which seemed to assure to the prince of this world his authority over it, he would in reality be cast out; and by the same event which seemed to displace Christ altogether from the earth, He would be exalted into supreme dominion over it, and enabled to draw all men unto Himself. To combine and include reference to the glorification, is to oppose the symbolism of the cross. The high place is to him who is hanged not a demonstration of honour; it points to the fact that he is no longer worthy to be found on earth, that earth rejects him, and that he is devoted to the vengeance of God: comp. Deut. xxi. 23, " He that is hanged is accursed of God;" and in our Lord's discourses the ὑψοῦν always refers to the crucifixion, never to the ascension; comp. on ch. iii. 14, viii. 28. There is no trace throughout the New Testament of any hint that makes the cross a symbol or type of Christ's exaltation. The Old Testament passage, Isa. liii. 8, refers to a violent death, " He was cut off out of the land of the living:" comp. Acts viii. 33. In ver. 24, dying simply, and as such, corresponds with the being lifted up from the earth.

" I will draw all men unto Me:" the Gentiles also, whom hitherto the prince of this world had held so entirely in his own power: comp. ch. x. 16. With the πάντας ἑλκύσω πρὸς ἐμαυτόν (Lampe: He thus teaches, that those whom Jesus draws are at the same time drawn away from the head and body of which they had been previously part and members), the answer to Philip and Andrew, and indirectly to the Greeks, is completed: Ye shall come to Jesus, but the time is not yet quite come. The corn of wheat must first fall into the earth. The power of the prince of this world, who has hitherto been, so to speak, your legitimate sovereign, must first be broken by My death. Then will the Gentiles experience My attracting power.—The drawing power exists for *all:* unbelief is the only thing which can exclude from this glorious benefit, ch. iii. 15, 16, and here, ver. 36. Anton: "Not, indeed, as if man could not oppose, for the will of man is free; but yet it is so mighty, that where a man will withstand it, he must do violence to himself in order to get the victory." He also remarks, in reference to the drawing of Christ: "That which, in ver. 24, is the grain of seed bringing forth fruit—but on the condition of its first dying—becomes here the drawing. For that drawing did not take place until after the death; but after Christ's death it proceeded with power: men's minds and hearts were mightily moved. When the world thought that they had now extinguished His name, the attraction of that name first began: and we must not regard this as if that attraction was merely to be the result; but that it was the influence of His death, as of a *causæ meritoriæ*, to which the Lord refers and declares: I will thus draw men to Me; I will now stretch out My hands unto them." The drawing of Christ does not consist merely in the power of attraction which His death itself exercises: as Anton remarks, " Then will My death powerfully draw men's minds, and lay on their hearts the tenderest obligation." The main point is rather the drawing of the Holy Spirit, who was to be obtained by the atoning death of our Lord, and who reveals to the heart the meaning of that death: comp. ch. vii. 39. Ch. vi. 44 alludes to an internal attractive power; and in ch. xvi. 8 Christ says that He would exercise, through the Holy Ghost, the power here described.

Ver. 33. "And I, if I be lifted up from the earth, will draw all men unto Me."—$\Sigma\eta\mu\alpha\acute{\iota}\nu\epsilon\iota\nu$ is simply to point out, and does not signify merely "hint." So in Acts xi. 28, xxv. 27; Rev. i. 1, and always in the Sept. and the Apocrypha.

Ver. 34. "The people answered Him, We have heard out of the law that Christ abideth for ever: and how sayest thou, The Son of man must be lifted up? who is this Son of man?"— The Lord says, in Matt. viii. 11, 12: "And I say unto you, That many shall come from the east and west, and shall sit down with Abraham, and Isaac, and Jacob, in the kingdom of heaven: but the children of the kingdom shall be cast out into outer darkness; there shall be weeping and gnashing of teeth." This word of Christ was, in the closing scene of His public life among the Jews, realized in a visible manner. Greeks come and desire to see Jesus. Jesus declares to them, as the representatives of the Gentile world, that the time would soon come in which He would draw the Gentiles to Himself. The Jews who were present derive from the reply which He made to the Gentiles a reason for their opposition. Jesus warningly points them to the fact, that there was a little space yet left to them; that soon the light would be removed, and that then darkness would come upon them in its might.—The opposition of the Jews sprang from a malignant will. That the abiding for ever formed no real contrast to the being lifted up from the earth, the words of Christ themselves might have shown them, in which the being lifted up from the earth appears as the mere point of transition, as the foundation of His glorification, of the casting out of the prince of this world, and of the extension of His dominion over all the earth. The same they might have learned from the Old Testament. In Isa. liii. the vicarious propitiation and death of the Messiah appears as the necessary basis of His abiding for ever: " When Thou shalt make His soul an offering for sin, He shall see His seed, He shall prolong His days." And in Daniel himself, to whom they appealed, the violent death of the Messiah is foreannounced, ch. ix. 26. Through suffering to glory is the law which approved itself in the lives of all the great men of the Old Testament, the types of Christ, and pre-eminently of David. That it was with them a mere subterfuge, or a prejudice resting upon a sinful disposition, and not from any scruple which honest minds felt at the thing itself, is plain from the fact, that Christ, in His answer to their objection, does not in any way enter into it, but only exhorts them to know the time of their visitation. (Anton : " After the manner of the so-called learned, they wrested a single little word against the evidence of the whole matter." Quesnel : " The law announces the humiliation and death of the Messiah, as well as His glory, and the duration of His kingdom; but self-love holds fast that which flatters its vanity and effeminacy, passing by what does not accord with its notions and fleshly inclinations.")

They said, We have heard out of the *law*. The passage they had in view is in Daniel. That they quoted this by the name of the *law*, demonstrates that this book, as a portion of the canon, had for them a binding force, and that they durst not oppose this surer authority in deference to the doubtful authority of Christ, who opposed it by His words: comp. on νόμος, ch. x. 34. The full meaning of their reference to the law, here emphasized, we see in ch. ix. 29: "We know that God spake to Moses (Daniel); but as to this man, we know not whence he is." Our passage shows that, among the Jews of the time of Christ, the book of Daniel had the fullest canonical authority, which indeed Josephus confirms in many places. "We have *heard*:" what the Scripture said was then known rather by hearing than by reading.—The idea of Christ's abiding for ever occurs in many passages of the Old Testament. In Isa. ix. 5 He is termed the "everlasting Father" (Luther: "who for ever nourishes His kingdom and Church"); in ver. 7 it is said, with reference to the Messiah, "Of the increase of His government and peace there shall be no end—from henceforth for ever." According to Ps. cx., the Messiah is a high priest for ever. According to Dan. ii. 24, the God of heaven would establish a kingdom which should never be abolished. And in Dan. vii. 13, 14, it is said of Him who cometh in the clouds like the Son of man, "His dominion is an everlasting dominion, which shall not pass away." Compare, in relation to the eternity of His government, Ps. lxxii. 5, 7, 17, lxxxix. 37, 38. That the Jews singled out from these passages that of Daniel, is evident from the fact that there only the Messiah is described as the Son of man. They said, instead of Christ's "I must be lifted up," the Son of man must be lifted up, in order to make more emphatic the contrast between what Christ had uttered concerning Himself, and that which is said concerning the Son of man in Daniel. And they held themselves all the more justified in making the substitution here, because Christ had so often, and so lately as the introduction to the last discourse, in ver. 23, described Himself as the Son of man, with allusion to that passage of Daniel. But the appeal to this alone cannot explain the substitution. This is evident, especially from "Who is *this* Son of man?" which points to the difference between the suffering Son of man whom Christ would enforce upon them, and that eternally glorious Son of man referred to in Daniel, whom alone they would receive, and know nothing of any other.—Δεῖ ὑψωθῆναι, *must* be lifted up. Jesus, in fact, had said so much, when He declared the lifting up from the earth to be the necessary condition of His dominion over it.

Ver. 35. "Then Jesus said unto them, Yet a little while is the light with you: walk while ye have the light, lest darkness come upon you: for he that walketh in darkness knoweth not whither he goeth."—Anton: " Christ says that there was no time now for sophistry and circumlocution with such phrases. It was a solemn matter. O how differently should they demean themselves in the residue of their little time, and not while it away with affected contradiction! O how should they seek at once for refuge to the light, to shield themselves against the coming darkness!" On light and darkness, equivalent to salvation and ruin, see ch. viii. 12. The light proceeds from Christ; but the contrasted darkness shows that the light in itself does not denote the person of the Redeemer. The light did not cease to be among them precisely at the crisis of Christ's death. (Bengel: lux ipsa manet, sed non semper est in vobis.) This is evident from the great movement at the day of Pentecost. The limit of grace, which, according to the Lord's saying, yet remained to them, did not consist merely in the two days which intervened between these words and the Saviour's death. First must the atoning death of Jesus and His resurrection unfold their power, and that which is spoken of in ver. 32 become true of the Jews also. Nevertheless, the period of light to the Jews was drawing swiftly to its close; and their giving up the Lord to death was the beginning of that end. In that act they invoked His blood on themselves and on their children. The time during which the light was with the Jews *here* corresponds to the time of their visitation in Luke xix. 44.—The *walking* stands opposed to an idle and indifferent rest. It denotes activity; and in what way activity should approve itself under existing circumstances, is shown by the "*believe* in the light" of ver. 36.—Instead of ἕως, *whilst* (compare the ἕως ἡμέρα ἐστί, ix. 4), many important witnesses have here and in ver. 36 ὡς. But there is no other example of such a use of ὡς, or anything like it.—St Luke, xix. 43, exhibits more fully the meaning of the darkness here: "For the day shall come upon thee, that thine enemies shall cast a trench about thee, and compass thee round, and keep thee in on every side." Yet that is only the external side of the darkness. With the external exposure to ruin, the internal want of salvation goes hand in hand. The fundamental place in the Old Testament is Jer. xiii. 16. The prophet says there, in view of the Chaldean catastrophe: "Give glory to the Lord your God, before He cause darkness, and before your feet stumble upon the dark mountains, and, while ye look for light, He turn it into the shadow of death, and make it gross darkness"—" and (that ye may know what this darkness means) he that walketh in darkness knoweth not whither he goeth," into what an abyss of misery he may fall: comp. ch. xi. 10; Prov. iv. 19, "The way of the wicked is as darkness: they know not at what they stumble."

Ver. 36. "While ye have light, believe in the light, that ye may be the children of light. These things spake Jesus, and departed, and did hide Himself from them."—So long as ye have salvation, believe in the salvation, and in its representatives and instruments. Sons, in the sense of adherents, is a phrase common to Christ throughout the Evangelists: Matt. viii. 12, xii. 27, xiii. 38; Mark ii. 19. In Luke xvi. 8 we read of the children of light, υἱοὶ φωτός, by the side of the children of this world.—In ch. viii. 59 it is said, "Then Jesus hid Himself, and went out of the Temple." But the case there is essentially different from the present. There Jesus concealed Himself because the Jews wanted to stone Him. He retired from the presence of a transitory danger, and thus His retreat was only a transitory one. But here there was no danger impending; and the concealing Himself was a definitive one. He retired into secret, that the catastrophe might not take place before the time. He was to suffer and die, and He would suffer and die, as the paschal lamb. It is to be assumed that Jesus from this time onwards retreated altogether from public life. This helps to define the chronological relations of vers. 20–36. We have already seen that the entry into Jerusalem belonged to the Sunday. On the following day, that is, Monday, Jesus cursed the fig-tree on the way from Bethany to the city, Mark xi. 12. When, in the early morning of the next day, Tuesday, He went again to the city, the disciples saw that the fig-tree had withered away, Mark xi. 20. On this day Jesus entered the Temple for the last time; and that which is here recorded must have happened on the same day: for the detail, see Wieseler. St John gives here no chronological specification, because the time might be gathered with sufficient certainty from his predecessors. There were now only two days to the Passover. These He spent in the circle of His disciples. The Old Testament original of "He went away and hid Himself" is Deut. xxxii. 20: "And He said, I will hide My face from them, I will see what their end shall be: for they are a froward generation, children in whom there is no faith."

VERS. 37–50.

We have here the concluding word of the first of the four groups which make up the main portion of the Gospel. It falls into two parts. In the first the Evangelist himself speaks. He makes observations upon a problem which sprang out of the facts recorded in the first portion: How could the unbelief of the Jews be accounted for? Must it not operate against the Divine mission of Jesus? In order to obviate this arising scruple, the Apostle first declares that this unbelief, far from witnessing against Christ, had been foreannounced in the prophecy of the Old Testament, and was to be viewed in the light of a Divine punishment upon the perverseness of the people, vers. 37–41. He then shows that this unbelief was only partial: many believed on Jesus, not only from among the people, but from among the rulers, although they did not make open avowal, because of their servile dependence upon men. In the second part of this concluding word, the Apostle introduces Jesus Himself as speaking. He has at the end, in ver. 36, the concluding word which Jesus addressed to Judas before His departure, but broken off in the middle. Here he communicates the second part of it. Jesus represents Himself as the true representative of the Father, and the only Saviour; proclaiming the judgment which must be hereafter the inseparable attendant of unbelief. This is the appropriate winding up, as of the whole relation in which Jesus had stood to the Jews, so also of the evangelical record of that relation. The division of what was originally united, the Evangelist must the rather have determined on, because the fundamental thought of the whole of the last discourse had been fully contained in vers. 35, 36.

Vers. 37, 38. " But though He had done so many miracles before them, yet they believed not on Him: that the saying of Esaias the prophet might be fulfilled, which he spake, Lord, who hath believed our report? and to whom hath the arm of the Lord been revealed?"—The first words of ver. 37 allude to Ps. lxxviii. 11, 12: "And forgat His works and His wonders that He had showed them. Marvellous things did He in the sight of their fathers in the land of Egypt, and in the field of Zoan." This allusion is significant: it has an apologetic importance. It had been the hereditary character of the people to be unbelieving, in spite of all signs and wonders. Reference had been made to this same passage in ch. x. 32. There the leading word which identifies the allusion is ἔδειξα; here it is ἔμπροσθεν αὐτῶν. It was only the old thing made new when the Jews were unbelieving. As their unbelief had no force as an argument against the divinity of Jehovah, no more had it any force against the Divine mission of Christ, in whom the Jehovah of the Old Testament was incarnate. As τοσαῦτα can only mean *so many*, and not *so great* (comp. vi. 9, xiv. 9, xxi. 11),—while our Gospel records only seven miracles, four Galilean and three Jewish,—we cannot fail to discern here a tacit acknowledgment of the existence of other Gospels.[1] The Evangelist points to the multiplicity of the miracles in ch. xx. 30, 31, xxi. 25 also. The climax of them all was the raising of Lazarus. That "they believed not," is not exhibited under the aspect of guilt, but of doom or Divine reprobation, and is shown by "that it might be fulfilled," according to which their unbelief must serve for the fulfilment of the prophetic word, and therefore stand under the Divine direction. We must not fritter away the ἵνα as Ebrard does : " The words do not refer to any design on the part of God ; but what the Jews brought on themselves as the result of their unbelief, is stated in such a way as if they had designed to fulfil God's word." We ought rather to say, that because the Jews could not have had any design to establish the truth of God's prediction by their unbelief, therefore the οὐκ ἐπίστευον

---

[1] Lampe: John relates only a few: he does not go beyond that Septenary. But closing the canon of the Gospels with his, he points to those things which not only himself, but others also before him, related.

must be referred to a Divine decree. Ver. 39 also establishes the same, where " they believed not" is reproduced as " they *could* not believe."—The fact that their unbelief is exhibited in the light of a Divine penalty, does not exclude their guilt, but rather presupposes that guilt. God has so constituted human nature, that man, if he does not withstand beginnings, has himself no longer under his own control: comp. on ch. viii. 43. But that which is a decree resting upon guilt, the consequence of the righteous judgment of God, could not, and ought not to be wrested to the disparagement of Christ. Rather it should have given the Jews occasion to smite upon their breasts, and cry, God be merciful to me, a sinner; harden not further my heart, that I cease to fear Thee; give me grace unto repentance.—The clause added, τοῦ προφήτου, points to the reason why the word of Isaiah must necessarily come to fulfilment. Ὁν εἶπε is solemn enlargement. Κύριε, which also the Septuagint adds, serves to mark it off from ch. lii. 13–15. There the Lord speaks. With ch. liii. 1 the prophet begins. The Evangelist did not mechanically adopt the κύριε from the Sept.; he never follows that version in arbitrary additions and omissions. The prophet begins the further exposition of that which had been said in brief by the servant of the Lord in ch. lii. 13–15; setting out with the complaint that so many did not believe his report concerning the servant of God, so many did not behold the glory of God manifest in Him. The words, according to their connection, specially refer to the Jews: the unbelief of the Jews, which went so far that the believers were only a vanishing minority, is mourned over in them. Joy over the many Gentiles who, according to ch. lii. 13–15, receive and apprehend with delight the tidings concerning the servant of God, goes side by side with grief over the many of Israel who believe not the tidings. And in that passage of Isaiah himself, unbelief is exhibited under the aspect of doom. They believe not, because the arm of the Lord, the unfolding of His Divine power in Christ, is not *revealed* to them, because God withdraws from them the knowledge of His power made manifest in Christ. Prophecy has not for its object generally the free actions of men, but the Divine decrees; and that there is such a decree in the quoted word of Isaiah, is shown by the expression in 1 Pet. ii. 8 : the disobedient are *appointed* not to believe. We have shown in the *Christology*, that שְׁמֻעָה in the original, ἀκοή here, is equivalent to that which we hear—that which has been made known unto us, the prophets, represented by Isaiah. Ch. xxi. 10 gives a comment on the words, "That which I have heard of the Lord of hosts, the God of Israel, have I declared unto you." And this view is supported by the correspondence of the two members. As the knowledge comes to the prophet, so it comes to the hearer also, only through supernatural revelation. Anton: "Lord, who believeth our report? We do not speak our own to the people, saith the prophet, but as we have ourselves heard, and as we have through hearing found its truth in ourselves. We do not set dreams before them, or inventions of our own. No, it is ἀκοὴ ἡμῶν."—Seemingly independent, the Jews were in fact only a plaything in the hands of God. Under this point of view, their unbelief was not an argument against Jesus, but a confirmation of His Divine mission, to the concomitant circumstances of which it belonged, according to the prophecy of the Old Testament.

Vers. 39, 40. "Therefore they could not believe, because that Esaias said again, He hath blinded their eyes, and hardened their heart; that they should not see with their eyes, nor understand with their heart, and be converted, and I should heal them."—*Therefore*, on account of the Divine decree announced by Isaiah in ch. liii. The ὅτι then introduces a second reason, or an elucidation of the former one, from the mouth of the same Isaiah: comp. ch. v. 16, 18; Matt. xxiv. 44. The forced supposition, that διὰ τοῦτο refers not to what precedes, but to what follows (when, according to the correct remark of De Wette, we might have expected a δὲ or καί of transition), sprang from a false apprehension of vers. 37, 38, which regards that passage as intimating only the *fact* of the Jews' unbelief. Rightly says Anton: "For again has Isaiah ex eodem fundamento spoken."—The cited passage of Isaiah, ch. vi. 10, runs according to the original: "Make the heart of this people fat, and make their ears heavy, and shut their eyes; lest they see with their eyes, and hear with their ears, and understand with their heart, and convert, and be healed." The quotation is not very strictly literal, but accords in reality nearly enough with the original. The address is there directed to the prophets; but he seems there to be only an instrument of the Divine decree, and that which is imposed upon him or the collective servants of God whom he represents, must be referred back to God. It lay in the scope of the Evangelist to make prominent this Divine causality; for it was his purpose to exhibit the unbelief of the Jews under the aspect of a Divine decree and judicial infliction. Properly speaking, the first person ought to have been used instead of the imperative, " I have blinded." But then it would have been too obviously natural to take the prophet as the subject, the rather that in the original of Isaiah he is the person to whom the words are addressed. Therefore John used first the third person; but that he selected it only for the reason assigned is shown by the fact that he uses the first person in the conclusion, ἰάσωμαι, or, according to another reading, ἰάσομαι. This is not an instance of "negligence;" but it shows, on the contrary, how precisely, down to the least minutiæ, everything is ordered in John's Gospel. Guilt was upon the Jews. But that they might not imagine that they defeated Christ's plans by their unbelief, and overturned the evidence of His mission, prominence is given to the Divine causation, in connection with their perverse determination. What they would not, they should not, might not, and could not. Situated as they were, everything that furthered the faith of the well-disposed only strengthened them in their unbelief. That is the Divine penalty, the doom which ruled over them, and hurried them to their destruction.

Ver. 41. " These things said Esaias, when he saw His glory, and spake of Him."—Αὐτοῦ refers back to ver. 37. The distinction from the Lord, ver. 38, who is still the subject in ver. 40, is all the less necessary because John, as he himself says in this verse, beheld Christ in the Jehovah of the Old Testament. —Isaiah saw " the Lord" sitting on His throne. He says in ver. 5, " Mine eyes have seen the King, the Lord of hosts." But, according to the tenor of the Old Testament, all visible manifestation, all revelation of the Lord, is made through His Angel, the brightness of His glory; and this was seen manifest in Christ in the flesh.—" And spake of Him:" thus that also refers to Christ, which in ver. 40 was quoted from Isaiah as the Lord's own act. It was He, therefore, who blinded the eyes of the Jews, etc. The Jews, while they vainly imagined that by their unbelief they discredited His cause, and stamped Him as a " deceiver," were falling under His condemnation. The refutation of the Jews' delusion, that Christ must be a false Messiah because they held Him to be such, becomes here a cutting irony.—We must be on our guard against supposing that the words here have no express reference to the case in hand, and bear only a cursory relation to the state of the Jews. The fundamental idea of the whole passage is the penalty of obduration, which the Lord threatened upon His apostate people; and the Lord, who held that doom over them, was no other than Christ Himself. That which He Himself brought to pass, could not be brought into evidence against His claims.

Vers. 42, 43. "Nevertheless among the chief rulers also many believed on Him; but because of the Pharisees they did not confess Him, lest they should be put out of the synagogue: for they loved the praise of men more than the praise of God." —The unbelief of the Jews, it has been hitherto unfolded, could not be urged as an argument against Christ's Messiahship. But certainly it pertained to the confirmation of the Divine mission of Christ, that faith in some should be found mingled with unbelief in others. For the people of the covenant could never sink so low as to rise up as one man against the most glorious manifestation of their God. With this consideration in his mind, the Evangelist has all along diligently set over against the outbreaks of unbelief in the majority, the expressions of faith in the few. And here he points to the fact, that this necessary condition of the Divine mission of Christ was present. Not only among the people (Augustin: Eorum autem qui crediderunt alii usque adeo confitebantur ut palmarum ramis acceptis venienti occurrerent, etc.), *also* among the rulers,—who had specially hard difficulties to overcome, in whom the perverse national tendency was concentrated, and who from their position were most likely to be affected by prejudices,—many believed on Christ; and although through the fear of men they were restrained from making open confession, yet their faith bore witness to the impressive majesty of the appearance of Christ, and the mighty drawing of the Father to the Son: comp. ch. vi. 44. By ἐπίστευσαν, *they believed*, John's phraseology allows us to understand only a true faith. That was the only faith which would enter suitably into the design of the Evangelist here. That their faith, indeed, had not attained its full energy, was shown by their shrinking from confession. But this was the condition of Nicodemus and Joseph of Arimathea for a long time, whose faith, however, afterwards broke through all impediments: comp. on ch. iii. 2.—When Augustin observes, Principes hos habuisse ingressum fidei, quo si profecissent, amorem quoque humanæ gloriæ superassent,—what he says is true, though one-sided. Even weak faith must make confession. The strong emphasis laid in Matt. x. 32, 33 upon the necessity of confession, shows that we are wrong in supposing that confession comes with the gradual strengthening of faith. The faith that makes no avowal, cannot attain its full power. And he who forgets the obligation to confess, is in danger of extinguishing his faith, in order to fly from the admonitions of his conscience. —" Lest they should be put out of the synagogue :" comp. on ch. ix. 22. The praise of men is, according to ch. v. 44 (comp. 1 Thess. ii. 6), the honour which springs from and is bestowed by man: the praise of God is the honour which comes from God. How must the image of God have become dim in such a man! God is, in His Old Testament name Jehovah, Existence, the personal necessary Being, out of whom all is nothingness and death, the only One about whom man need care, and for whose favour man should struggle. Men, whose name is weakness, cannot assure us of anything, cannot really hurt or really profit any.

Vers. 44, 45. "Jesus cried, and said, He that believeth on Me, believeth not on Me, but on Him that sent Me. And he that seeth Me, seeth Him that sent Me."—There can be no doubt that John here communicates a discourse actually delivered by Jesus. There is absolutely no proof that He puts words into our Lord's mouth (see on ch. iii. 16); this was forbidden by the deep reverence which he entertained for his Lord. Here it is also opposed emphatically by the ἔκραξε, which refers to the Lord's manner of uttering His discourse, just as in ch. vii. 28, 37. When this hypothesis is supported by argument drawn from the unoriginal and almost recapitulatory character of the discourse, we have only to remark, that while, on the one hand, this discourse is not *formally* a composition from the earlier recorded words of Christ in John, from which it has not verbally borrowed a single expression (ver. 48 even touches upon Luke x. 16; and there is no Johannæan parallel for the καὶ μὴ φυλάξῃ in ver. 47), on the other hand, to have given anything materially new would have been scarcely appropriate in a final discourse of our Lord. Vers. 35, 36 bear evidently the same character of material dependence on earlier words combined with formal independence.

It has been further argued, that there is wanting here the organic connection which is observable elsewhere in the Lord's discourses as given by John; but to us it seems that it must be the fault of the expositor if the clear process of thought is not here traced. The analysis is as follows: I am the truly Sent, ver. 44; and the visible image of the Father, ver. 45; and because I am this, I am the Saviour of the world, ver. 46; and on this account unbelief—although the proper design of My mission is not judgment, ver. 47—must, in the nature of things, bring on judgment: the rejected word of God, which offers the most glorious of all benefits, eternal life, must recoil in judgment upon the heads of those who scorn it in My lips. "For I have not spoken of Myself; even as the Father said unto Me, so I speak." In these words, in which the end of Christ's discourse returns to the beginning (οὖν), the Jews received a measure by which they might mete their future— their future in this world, and their future in the world to come. A profound woe lies concealed behind them.—The book of Judges, ch. ii. 1-5, presents us something strictly analogous. There a word of the angel of the Lord to the collected Israelites, without any specification of the historical relations, and of the organ through which the angel spake, is inwoven into the introduction, in which the author of the book, with his own hand, exhibits the points of view under which the time of the Judges is to be regarded.

When did Jesus speak these words? As John gives no note of the time, we must naturally think of the nearest point of connection; and with this agrees the entire character of the discourse, which J. Gerhard thus describes: "Christ would, in this grave and serious attestation, publicly take farewell of the ungrateful and unbelieving Jews, and throw the whole blame of their judgment upon themselves alone." Thus we have here the continuation of the former part of ver. 36; and the words, "These things spake Jesus, and departed, and did hide Himself from them," would have stood after "Whatsoever I speak therefore," etc., in ver. 50, if the Evangelist had not thought it appropriate to close his Epilogue by a portion of the concluding words of Christ. This view is supported also by the consideration, that vers. 35, 36 are too brief for the solemn crisis of His departure from the people; and then, that the figure of light and darkness which was employed in vers. 35, 36, returns again at once in ver. 46, after Jesus, in vers. 44, 45, had laid the foundation, by a reference to His own dignity and His unity with the Father, for the testimony that in Him light was given to the people, and that with His departure darkness would come upon them.

"He that believeth on Me, believeth not on Me, but on Him that sent Me." The Jews sought to isolate Christ, and to erect a wall of partition between Him and the Father: We believe not thee; we believe only in God; and because we believe in Him, we will know nothing of thee. Entering into this their delusion, Jesus says,—he believeth not on "Me." Ewald, who makes our Lord intimate "that, when He demanded faith in Himself, He did not thereby demand faith in Himself as a mortal man, but pure faith in God and His word"—changes the meaning into its direct opposite. Jesus denies here, as in Mark ix. 37, all distinction between Himself and God.—The clause in ver. 45 is peculiar to this concluding word; and it is explained by what was observed upon ch. i. 18. To believers and unbelievers the Father was in Christ exhibited; and this was the cause of the downfall of the Jews, that they had seen the Father in Christ, and had blasphemously fought against Him: comp. on $\theta\epsilon\omega\rho\epsilon\hat{\iota}\nu$, ch. vi. 40. Bengel is wrong here: Ea visione, quam fides comitatur.

Ver. 46. "I am come a light into the world, that whosoever believeth on Me should not abide in darkness."—Light and darkness signify here, as in vers. 35, 36, salvation and ruin. Jesus came into the world as the personal salvation, that whosoever believeth on Him should not *abide* in that darkness, which involves all who have either not known Christ, or are without Him: comp. on ch. i. 4, viii. 12.

Ver. 47. "And if any man hear My words, and believe not, I judge him not: for I came not to judge the world, but to save the world."—$\Phi\upsilon\lambda\acute{\alpha}\xi\eta$ (keep not) is much better authenticated than $\pi\iota\sigma\tau\epsilon\acute{\upsilon}\sigma\eta$ (believe not). The expression is borrowed from the language of the law: comp. *e.g.* Ex. xii. 17, xv. 26.

By the use of this language Christ places Himself on a level with the Supreme Lawgiver. The keeping His words forms an antithesis to the utter rejection of them. In the ἀκούσῃ we must not include a believing adherence. The Lord has to do in these words only with the decidedly unbelieving. To the μὴ φυλάσσειν here, corresponds the μὴ λαμβάνειν in ver. 48. "I judge him not:" in harmony with ch. iii. 17, this simply asserts that the proper vocation and position of Christ is not that of a judge, but that of a Saviour; that the judgment only unfolds itself subordinately and of itself, growing out of the rejection of the Saviour. Judgment has not its root in Christ, or in any joy He feels in pronouncing sentence; it has its root rather in the unbeliever, and in the wicked relation which he assumes towards the truth from God. He is αὐτοκατάκριτος, Tit. iii. 11. But on that very account the judgment is only the more unavoidable; and it is simple folly to suppose it can ever be escaped.

Ver. 48. "He that rejecteth Me, and receiveth not My words, hath one that judgeth him: the word that I have spoken, the same shall judge him in the last day."—The catastrophe of Jerusalem was to the Jews a prelude or type of this last day. Then did the apparently impotent word of Christ come up against them like an armed man. Here, as in ch. viii. 50, there is allusion to Deut. xviii. 19.

Ver. 49. "For I have not spoken of Myself; but the Father which sent Me, He gave Me a commandment, what I should say, and what I should speak."—It is frivolous to make a distinction between the εἰπεῖν and the λαλεῖν. The union of the two words only indicates emphatically that all things whatever Christ spake He spake under the commission of the Father.

Ver. 50. "And I know that His commandment is life everlasting: whatsoever I speak therefore, even as the Father said unto Me, so I speak."—This commandment, the fruit of the doctrine sent from Him, when it is believingly received and embraced in the heart. The practical result is, that Christ has nothing to leave to the people, which, on account of its unbelief, He must abandon, but death and destruction. In rejecting Him they had renounced the Father; and the insulted word of the Father must work its influence upon them, until it should leave them neither root nor branch. For them it was the worm which never dieth.

CHAPTERS XIII.–XVII.

The first four of the seven divisions of the body of this Gospel relate how Jesus wrought the works of Him that sent Him while it was day: the last three describe His departure. The first of these three, ch. xiii.–xvii., records how Jesus loved His own to the end; relates how, in the prospect of His passion, He prepared His disciples for His coming departure, thus furnishing for His Church of all times a rich treasure of consolation. The Old Testament types of this portion are: Deuteronomy, in which the departing Moses set before his people the memory of the way; the sayings of Joshua before his death, ch. xxiii., xxiv.; and the "last words of David," in 2 Sam. xxiii., model of the departure of St Paul from the elders of the Ephesian Church, in Acts xx.

In the early part, the narrative of what passed at the Last Supper, John bears only a supplementary relation to the earlier Evangelists. From ch. xiv. onwards he communicates what his predecessors had altogether passed over; they having modestly recognised the limits of their gift and vocation, and not having ventured on the province of that disciple who formerly lay on our Saviour's breast, and was initiated beyond the rest into His mysteries.

Ch. xiii. falls into three parts: the feet-washing, vers. 1–20; the conversation touching the traitor, vers. 21–30; the discourse to the disciples after the traitor's departure, vers. 31–38.

THE FEET-WASHING.

CH. XIII. 1–20.

Ver. 1. " Now, before the feast of the Passover, when Jesus knew that His hour was come that He should depart out of this world unto the Father, having loved His own which were in the world, He loved them unto the end."—The δέ points to the circumstance that we have before us, not a new book, but only a new section of it. That the connection is formed by an adversative particle, places the severity of Jesus against the Jews in contrast with His love towards His own. This first verse gives the sketch; vers. 2 seq. give the completion. The εἰδώς, *knowing*, here, is resumed in ver. 3. As we cannot in that verse interpret " *because*," but only " *although* He knew," so we are constrained to interpret here. This will appear the obvious interpretation, when we consider that the motive of the transaction is indicated by the words, " as He loved His own," etc. If we understand, " *because* He knew," there arise two motives for this action, placed unconnectedly together, which is scarcely tolerable. If we understand, " *although* He knew," we have first a reference to the hindrance which existed to the last display of love, and then, in " because He loved," a reference to the living principle through which that hindrance was overcome. Ἀγαπήσας alone contains the motive: the εἰδώς, placed before it, points to what opposed the motive, and must be vanquished by the energy of that love. The proof of love which Jesus now at the last gave to His disciples, beams out in all the richer light, because Jesus was clearly conscious that His transition into a state of glory was near at hand. That, notwithstanding this knowledge, He so profoundly abased Himself towards His disciples, and washed their feet, must fill us with thankful and adoring love. It was as if God had from heaven itself come down to wash the feet of sinful mortals! And this He did to men who immediately before had been contending for a pitiful scrap of worldly honour! " Can any one," says Heumann, " who reads this history, retain a spark of pride in his heart? Or if he, notwithstanding what he reads, remains proud, is he not unworthy of the name of a Christian?"—We must not understand " having *hitherto* loved His own;" for the *hitherto*, which would form the antithesis to εἰς τέλος, is not in the text; the " in the world" looks back to the " out of the world," and refers to the perilous position in which the disciples would be found after the impending departure of their Lord (comp. ch. xvii. 11: " I am no longer in the world; but these are in the world, and I come to Thee." Grotius: Quos relicturus erat in hoc rerum salo. J. Gerhard: " Because they still remained in the world, in the valley of tribulation, where they must expect nothing but trouble "),—leads expressly to the love which manifested itself in this last proof, and by which Jesus strengthened their hearts beforehand to meet the coming sorrow. We must therefore assume that ἀγαπήσας indicates His love in general, while ἠγάπησεν points to the particular act of love which now sprang from that source. —'Ἀγαπᾶν can of itself signify only the affection of love. But as this can be known only by the action that expresses it, such an action is indirectly indicated in the ἠγάπησεν. That this ἠγάπησεν must be primarily referred to the act of washing their feet, is evident from the words " before the feast of the Passover." The other tokens of love which are recorded in this section are part of the feast itself. Yet we may appropriately regard the remaining evidences of love as supplementary to the feet-washing. " To the end" seems to show that the Evangelist so regarded them. There is no difficulty in this, when we consider what followed as only the unfolding of what had been already displayed in the washing, and furnishing a commentary upon it. If we separate them, the εἰς τέλος loses its significance. The remaining acts of love, which were assuredly confirmations of the tender affection of the Lord towards His disciples, would then fall beyond and after the τέλος. We cannot argue that the supreme proof of His love, His death, lay nevertheless beyond the " end" here mentioned; for the words here refer to the love displayed to His own, and not to that which was manifested by the Saviour of the world.

It remains that we examine the chronological note at the beginning of the verse, " before the feast of the Passover." Remembering John's manner in giving marks of time (comp. ch. xii. 1), we cannot doubt that his words here refer to the event which he was about to record, primarily to ἠγάπησεν, or to the " riseth" in the narrative; or that the feet-washing occurred in the time before the paschal feast.

" Before the feast" either means nothing (and that can the less be assumed, inasmuch as John is the only one of the Evangelists who follows definite chronological leadings, all his other notes of time being thoroughly precise, such as that of the six days before the Passover in ch. xii. 1; on the following day, ver. 12), or it points to the fact, that the transaction to which this note of time refers, the feet-washing, belongs to the time *immediately* before the beginning of the paschal feast; that between the feast and the washing nothing else intervened; that, with the completion of the washing, the Passover immediately began for those here concerned. If we give up the closest proximity of the feast, we are left to most arbitrary hypotheses as to the time. We have no more reason to refer it to the day before than to any other day. But considering the high importance which the Evangelist himself attaches to the events here recorded, the feet-washing and what was connected with it down to ch. xvii., it is inconceivable that he would leave them chronologically indefinite, with absolutely no note of time; and more especially as they have been treated with very exact chronological precision by the other Evangelists, themselves much more careless on this point. It is plain that the last meal of Jesus, to which all in John's thirteenth chapter relates, was, according to those earlier Evangelists, the paschal meal; and that Jesus partook of it at the same time with the Jews, entirely according to the law and the universal custom of the feast. (Wichelhaus has thoroughly settled this point in his *Leidensgesch.*) If the Evangelist had had the design, attributed to him by many, of subverting this chronological decision of his predecessors, he could not have acted more perversely. He would have opposed to their chronological precision an absolutely vague indefiniteness.

That "before the Passover" means "*immediately* before" (just as, in Luke xi. 38, πρὸ τοῦ ἀρίστου refers to what immediately preceded the mid-day meal), has been well shown by Lange, who argues that such specific acts as the rising from the table, ver. 4, are not reckoned by days, but by hours and moments. Accordingly the sense here must be, that immediately before the beginning of the feast He rose up.

Having settled that this action took place immediately before the paschal feast, the further question arises as to when the feast itself began. It is to be taken for granted that the most important time of the feast, that of the fourteenth Nisan, cannot be excluded from the paschal period. Those who have attempted to do so have been labouring under a misapprehension. That which gave its name to the whole feast must necessarily have been included within its limits. But the question is, whether the feast had its beginning literally with the commencement of this meal, or whether, as Wieseler and

Wichelhaus maintain, the slaying of the lamb must also be included.

We decide in favour of the former view, and assume that the beginning of the feast coincided with the beginning of this meal. The very idea of the feast is in harmony with such a view. ʽΕορτή always corresponds in the New Testament to the Hebrew חג, and is never used save of joyful festivities, in which the people rejoiced before the Lord. The root חגג signified originally to dance, then to celebrate a festivity: "derived from the sacred choruses and dances with which the feasts were wont to be observed" (Gesenius). The joy which was accordingly associated with the idea of the feast, was based upon the presupposal of an accomplished atonement, obtained in the Passover through the slaying of the lamb. The great day of atonement, notwithstanding its profound importance (Lev. xvi. 31), was never termed a feast any more than our Good Friday falls under the Scriptural notion of a feast. The paschal feast was further, according to Isa. xxx. 29 (comp. Ex. xii. 42), a night-feast, and did not begin until darkness had set in; but the slaying of the lamb took place while it was yet day. The same passage of Isaiah shows that feast and song were always inseparably connected. According to Ps. lxxxi. 2–4, the feast pertained to the domain of the moon, and was begun with shouting and song: comp. 2 Chron. xxx. 21, 22. Finally, the feast is always called in the books of Moses the feast of unleavened bread. But the eating of the unleavened bread began, according to Ex. xii. 18, not till "the evening," the evening which opened the fifteenth Nisan, Lev. xxiii. 6. On the fourteenth Nisan, between the two evenings—that is, in the afternoon—there was indeed a Passover to the Lord; but that was the paschal *sacrifice*, not the paschal *feast*, with which we are here concerned. The two are carefully distinguished in Num. xxviii. 16, 17, "In the fourteenth day of the first month is the Passover of the Lord. And in the fifteenth day of this month is the feast:" comp. also 2 Chron. xxxv. 17.

It may therefore be regarded as fixed, that the paschal feast had its commencement with the paschal meal. But what defined the actual commencement of the meal? Having so entirely spiritual a character, we may assume that its commencement was not a material but a spiritual one; and we can the less doubt this, inasmuch as its conclusion is expressly described to have been a spiritual one : ὑμνήσαντες, Matt. xxvi. 30. The meal had its specific liturgy, which Jesus did not dispense with, so far as it adhered to holy Scripture, as the ὑμνήσαντες itself shows. The meal had indeed its unvarying introductory words. All that took place before the moment when these were spoken, was regarded as "before" the feast of the Passover, although immediately preceding and introducing it.

The further question arises, Did the Lord's act of washing take place before the beginning of the paschal meal, as thus indicated?

It may be argued from vers. 2 and 4, that the supper, and consequently the feast, had begun before the feet-washing. But the fact of the time having come, does not prove the beginning of the meal or of the feast; that depended on the liturgy, and the actual eating which then immediately followed. The καὶ δείπνου γινομένου (Tisch.: not γενομένου) points to the circumstance that in a certain sense, not coming into consideration here, the supper was already come. (Meyer: "While they were in the act of keeping the supper.") The supper was not yet; it was about to begin. The translation of the Vulgate, cœnâ peractâ, and Luther's "after the supper," would not be justified even by the reading γενομένου.

But we can positively demonstrate that the feet-washing preceded the actual beginning of the supper and of the feast.

That the washing of the feet was customary at all greater feasts, was a result of the Oriental equipment of the feet, the Oriental climate, and the Oriental habit of reclining at the table, which brought the feet into contact with the neighbour. To give the guest no water for his feet was, according to Luke vii. 44, regarded as something altogether unusual, and as a great indignity. The word of our Lord, in ver. 10, shows that the washing of the feet was a necessity at the feast. Least of all could it have been omitted at the paschal feast; that would have been in the fullest sense a profanation.

The very nature of the case demonstrates that the feet-washing preceded the actual meal; this is attested by the whole of Scripture, wherever the matter is mentioned, from Gen. xviii. 4, xix. 2, downwards. Classical antiquity affirms the same thing. Not only was the washing of the feet "usually" performed before the meal; it was so always, and without exception.

We gather from vers. 4, 5, that the apparatus for the feet-washing was quite prepared, but had not as yet been used. This leads us to the conclusion that our Lord's act had a specific reason; and that, in fact, He did what others had omitted. And those who had neglected the act must be sought within the circle of the disciples. The master of the house had only yielded his chamber to the Lord. He did not, as in Luke vii., act the part of the host. In this last feast our Lord Himself occupies the place of entertainer: comp. Matt. xxvi. 17. The master of the house was always bound to his family at the paschal season. Those expositors who hold the independent nature and significance of our Lord's act, are much embarrassed by the presence of the materials for washing; Lampe, for example, following the example of Euthymius, represents Jesus as having asked for these things at the hands of the host, etc. That would have had to be recorded, if the act had been one of independent origination; but as we see the reverse, we may fairly infer that the feet-washing was, so to speak, accidental in its origin.

In respect to the Lord's act, it must be taken for granted that no other washing had preceded. Now, if it is a settled point that such a ceremony was absolutely necessary before the beginning of the feast, then must the present one have occurred before "the supper" began, and consequently before the Passover. It would have been most inappropriate for Jesus to wash over again the feet that had been washed. "*He did not*," says Schweitzer, "*superfluously rewash their feet*: there would have been nothing but an artificial example in such an act, as it would not have been an act of necessity."

The fact that our Lord rose up from the table, ver. 4, shows that He assumed the place of others whose business it was to wash the feet, but who had pretermitted it. If He had had the independent design to wash the feet of His disciples, He would not have seated Himself at the table. And the act itself leads to the same conclusion. His washing their feet would have had, viewed apart from some specific occasion for it, a far-fetched and romantic character; and the objection which Weisse, for instance, urges against it as a "tasteless humiliation" (he remarks that he could find no edification in it, as it would have to every unbiassed feeling a touch of theatrical design in it), would, on such a supposition, be not altogether unfounded. Ewald remarks, on that theory : " A strange thought was seen suddenly to take possession of Christ's soul;" and Lücke observes : "Here all was unusual; the Master of the house performs the act Himself, and by performing it interrupts the supper." We cannot but see the confusion of all these observations; and that, by renouncing any specific reason for the Lord's act, they lose the only key to its interpretation. By recognising the, as it were, accidental occasion of the feet-washing, we get rid of the notion that Jesus apparently prescribed a rite to be observed in all times; and we are then justified in distinguishing between the eternally valid principle of the feet-washing, and the form of its expression as influenced by passing circumstances. If we ignore the fortuitous origin of the act, we can hardly refute the argument of Weisse, that as the symbolical rite never became a sacred usage of the early Church, the historical truth of the narrative may be impeached.

Finally, the assumption of a special reason for the act is strengthened by the urgent manner in which our Lord requires of His disciples that they wash one another's feet. It is obvious to infer that He exhorted them to perform in future, after His example, the service that they had just neglected. So also the emphatic exhortations to brotherly love, vers. 34, 35, shine out in brighter light when we consider that the Apostles had recently incurred the blame of neglect in that particular.

So far we draw our materials from John himself. But our view is enlarged if we compare the nearest predecessor of John among the Evangelists, Luke, with whom he everywhere has more contact than with any other. He relates, in ch. xxii. 7-23, the events of " the day of unleavened bread, when the Passover must be killed," in chronological order, and in harmony with his two predecessors. Then, in the manner with which in him we are familiar, he adds a supplement not chronologically connected with what precedes, vers. 24-38. There he narrates a contest that took place among the disciples as to who of them should be greatest, and the words which our Lord addressed to them in consequence. But we cannot imagine this contention to have occurred after the beginning of the supper : such a supposition would be utterly inconsistent with the solemn tone in which Jesus commenced the feast. But neither can we imagine it before the commencement of the feast, at a time so full of solemnity, unless we suppose that some circumstances surprised them into it, that something in the state of matters gave direct occasion for the contest. That occasion we must not seek in the selection of places at the table (Lichtenstein); it must rather be sought in the fact that a service was expected by some which was not rendered. This will appear evident from the exhortation of ver. 26, which refers to this contention: " He that is greatest among you, let him be as the younger; and he that is chief, as he that doth serve." We infer from this that the greater among the Apostles, those who were by the Lord distinguished above the rest, and were the appointed " pillars," with Peter at their head, had expected from the lesser Apostles a *service* which these had not rendered. The words of Jesus, ver. 27, show that that service was no other than the washing of the feet: " For whether is greater, he that sitteth at meat, or he that serveth? is not he that sitteth at meat? but I am among you as he that serveth." These words of Luke stand in undeniable connection with ver. 4, where Jesus assumes the garment of a servant, in order to wash the disciples' feet. If the serving of Jesus, which in Luke is exhibited as the corrective of the disciples' reluctance to serve,—a reluctance which gave occasion for the contest,—was actually this washing of the feet, the disciples' refusal to serve must have been no other than their having declined to wash each other's feet.

The matter then stands thus. Jesus had seated Himself at the table, and probably Peter enjoyed the honour of washing His feet. After this was done, he, with the other disciples *interioris admissionis,* also sate at the table, expecting that the "younger" would spontaneously assume the function of feet-washers for all the rest. But pride evoked pride. The younger Apostles, following a quick impulse, seated themselves also at the table. Thus a situation of deep embarrassment was the result: murmuring and contest. Who would be the first to rise up again? Jesus put an end to the embarrassment, by arising from the supper and washing the feet of His disciples. How much sorrow was caused by this fatal contention in the circle of the disciples, is shown by the fact that Matthew and

Mark pass over it altogether, while Luke and John touch it only by way of hint.

If our Lord's washing occurred immediately before the beginning of the last paschal meal, John is in perfect harmony with the other Evangelists. Such a harmony every one must certainly expect who only remembers and carefully considers the general relation in which John stands to his predecessors. He also will be incapable of doubting that in John the last supper and the Lord's death must fall within the paschal feast. This is the goal to which all that precedes tends. Jesus always withdrew from His enemies until the Passover was come; He goes up to the capital when the feast draws nigh, entering it on the day when the lambs were set apart. Ch. xix. 36 points the same way, where Christ appears as the antitype of the paschal lamb.

Vers. 2, 3, 4. "And supper being ended, (the devil having now put into the heart of Judas Iscariot, Simon's son, to betray Him,) Jesus knowing that the Father had given all things into His hands, and that He was come from God, and went to God; He riseth from supper, and laid aside His garments; and took a towel, and girded Himself."—Καὶ δείπνου γινομένου in ver. 2 means literally, "And the meal being about to begin." Καί announces the further development of what was given in epitome in ver. 1. The meal needed no more exact definition, as, according to the connection with ver. 1, it could only be understood as that which the other three Evangelists had made familiar, and which opened the paschal feast. Tobit ii. 1 is similar: "In the feast of Pentecost there was a good dinner prepared me, in the which I sat down to eat." There a good meal is spoken of quite indefinitely; but the connection shows that the chief meal of the feast is meant. The passage is also further analogous, inasmuch as the ἐγενήθη ἄριστον there also indicates the meal by its material preparation. It follows in ver. 4: "Then, before I had tasted of any meat, I started up." In harmony with this parallel passage, Heumann paraphrases our text: "When the last supper was provided for, and stood ready on the table." In ch. xxi. 20, the article secures to the feast its definite character, just as here the relation to ver. 1 does: τὸ δεῖπνον, the generally known and celebrated meal.

The scope of the remark that Satan had already put it into the heart of Judas to betray Jesus, must first be interpreted by the epitome of ver. 1, and then by the words of ver. 3. Vers. 2 and 3 serve for the development of the words of the epitome, εἰδὼς—πατέρα. Accordingly, the already determined treachery of Judas is here referred to only as involving the near approach of the death of Jesus, and, as connected with it, His approaching departure to the glory of the Father. That Jesus, in the prospect of that glory, abased Himself so deeply, and assumed, as never before, the form of a servant, showed the energy of His love to His own. Vers. 31, 32 also support this view. There the betrayal of Judas appears as no other than the prelude of the glorification of Christ. If, in interpreting the words, " the devil having now put it into the heart of Judas Iscariot," we omit to connect them with the first and third verses, we are left to mere conjectures, and the result must be a wide variety of opinions. But, dealing with them as above, vers. 1–3 present much simplicity and transparency of thought. The Apostle gives the utmost prominence to the circumstance that the demonstration of Christ's love derived its deepest significance from its having been exhibited at the end, at the period when His glory was about to attain its consummation, in which it might have been supposed that thoughts of greatness would leave no room for any other. A secret *Kyrie eleeson* is always, however, the undertone. While the Apostle so strongly illustrates the humble love of Christ, he at the same time mourns over the proud φιλονεικία of himself and his brother-disciples, whose darkness was only shone upon by the clear brightness of Christ's example. That is the proper key to the striking accumulation of the expressions.—That Satan at that time had already put it into the heart of Judas to betray his Master, was an internal fact of which the Searcher of hearts alone could be cognizant. But, inasmuch as it here enters as an historical element, it is to be taken for granted that the internal fact had already assumed an external form, and become known to man. Now, the other Evangelists expressly record this to have been the case; they prove that Judas had already concluded his compact with the high priests, Matt. xxvi. 14–16; Mark xiv. 10, 11; Luke xxii. 3–6. John would have appealed to these passages, had the question been put to him, How knowest thou this? It is plain that he had in view the passage of Luke, his immediate predecessor, for there also the trafficking of Judas with the chief priests is referred to Satan. The narrative in Luke begins with the words, "Then entered Satan into Judas, surnamed Iscariot, being of the number of the twelve," words to which John, in ver. 27, also expressly alludes. He reserves, however, the very strong expression used there for the last stage. —According to Rev. xvii. 17, it might have been stated that God put it into his heart. Satan everywhere serves only as the instrument of the plans of God. What Judas did, like all the works of the ungodly, stood under the secret direction of the Supreme. The sin belonged to himself. Since he would not separate from it, and be converted, in spite of all the means freely vouchsafed to him, he was compelled to be the involuntary instrument of the plans of Satan first, and then of God, whose servant even Satan is; and when he had done this, he was to be thrown away, and go to his own place. As his personal definition, to distinguish the traitor from the other Judas among the Apostles, $\Sigma i\mu\omega\nu o\varsigma$ was enough. The '$I\sigma\kappa\alpha\rho\iota\acute{\omega}\tau o\upsilon$ was added only to stamp the traitor with infamy: comp. on ch. vi. 71, xii. 4.

On ver. 3 Heumann observes: "This must not be viewed as if John repeated in ver. 3 his first $\epsilon i\delta\acute{\omega}\varsigma$ in ver. 1, 'although He knew.'" His amazement at this act of Jesus constrained him to say again what he had said already, and thus to excite the attention of his readers: "I say it once more, that He, knowing that His Father had made Him Lord of all lords, and that He was about to enter heaven in full triumph, nevertheless humbled Himself so much as to wash the feet of His disciples." The $\delta\acute{\epsilon}\delta\omega\kappa\epsilon$, "gave," is used by anticipation; the brief space of time which elapsed between the present and the bestowment of His power is ignored: compare the "will straightway glorify Him," ver. 32. That the $\pi\acute{a}\nu\tau a$, "all things," is to be taken in its full comprehensiveness, is evident from Matt. xxviii. 18, "all power is given unto Me in heaven and upon earth:" comp. Heb. ii. 8.—The consciousness of Jesus, that He had come *forth from* God, must have been pre-eminently vivid at the time when His return to God, and to the glory which He had with Him before the world was, immediately approached.

He laid aside His garments, ver. 4,—so far, that is, as they were an hindrance to the act He was about to perform. This, of course, applied only to the outer garment. That Jesus girded Himself *with* the napkin, is evident from ver. 5. That was specifically the equipment or *habitus* of a servant. In Luke xvii. 8, we read of a servant to whom his lord says, " Gird thyself, and wait upon me." That our Lord so formally prepared Himself for the act, not only had reference to the end He proposed, but served also to realize vividly before our eyes the depth of His humiliation. The matter might have been accomplished without all this formal preparation. But then the humiliation of the disciples would have been less profound, and the admonition less penetrating. Only on the consideration we have mentioned can the careful detail of the Apostle's description be understood.

Vers. 5, 6. " After that He poureth water into a bason, and began to wash the disciples' feet, and to wipe them with the towel wherewith He was girded. Then cometh He to Simon Peter: and Peter said unto Him, Lord, dost Thou wash my feet ?"—" He began" points to the circumstance that the act had to be performed over a wide circle. The ἔρχεται οὖν, in its reference to ver. 5, suggests that Jesus began with Peter; which has been denied only in the interests of a narrow and petty opposition to the Roman Church. Ver. 5 says in general, that Jesus began to wash the disciples' feet. Ver. 6 adds with whom He began; and the οὖν is specifically connected with the ἤρξατο: thus He came, or thus beginning He came. It is probable, on other grounds, that our Lord began with Simon Peter. The order of precedence among the Apostles, in which Peter always had the first place (comp. Matt. xvi. 18), could hardly, on such an occasion as this, have been ignored by Christ. And that would have been all the less appropriate, inasmuch as Peter had doubtless assumed the first place in the contention. When Christ commenced the feet-washing with him, it was all the more keen a humiliation of his aspiring natural man. Even the protest of Peter leads to the conclusion that Jesus commenced with him. Every other disciple would doubtless have protested in the same way; and if, through modesty, one or other had kept silence, the impetuous Peter would doubtless have in some way interposed. As the Lord had placed him at the head of the Apostles, he had, in a certain sense, a right to be their representative. But in that case the explanation which ensued between Jesus and Peter would have taken place before; we can understand it, as it lies before us, only on the supposition that Peter began the series. "But," observes Heumann, "as the Lord commanded the first to let it be so, the others kept silence when their turn came; however astonished, they nevertheless submitted obediently to receive the service which the Lord performed."—Peter was not wrong in resenting the Lord's humiliation in washing his feet. So long as he did not recognise the symbolical significance of this action, it must have seemed to him altogether abnormal and unaccountable; and even if he had come to the full consciousness of his own guilt and obligation, it must have seemed to him a too severe punishment that the Lord should dedicate Himself to so degrading a service. But any such symbolical meaning he would not, and could not, assume on his own suggestion. The Lord Himself must declare it. When He had done so, Simon Peter's opposition was withdrawn. All is here correct enough; and the censure which the expositors are generally disposed to cast upon Peter has no foundation.

Ver. 7. "Jesus answered and said unto him, What I do thou knowest not now; but thou shalt know hereafter."—Jesus intimates that there was a mystery in the matter. "Hereafter;" some light came to Peter through the following explanation of our Lord. Yet that was not sufficient. He did not thoroughly understand it until his fall had taught him to know the depth of his sinfulness, and to see how needful it was that he should be washed of Christ; until, in fact, he obtained through the Holy Spirit, whose outpouring depended on the glorification of Christ, the deepest insight into his own misery and Christ's abundant benefit.

Ver. 8. "Peter saith unto Him, Thou shalt never wash my feet. Jesus answered him, If I wash thee not, thou hast no part with Me."—Peter continues to protest. The Lord's allusion to the fact of a mystery was not sufficient to overcome his opposition. In order to that, he must at least have some elementary knowledge of what the mystery was. And that knowledge the Lord now gives him by His answer. The bodily washing was a type of the spiritual washing away of the defilement of sin. This alone saved it from being unnatural and unworthy of Christ, and made it for the Apostles no longer a piercing rebuke, but actually an evidence of the supreme love of their Lord. Jesus, whose name signifies that He would save His people from their sins, is only then truly in His element. Both things must concur in our estimate of the reason for the act: reference to the Apostles' omission of the service to each other, and this spiritual meaning. The latter justifies the act in its real signification, the former justifies its form.

That the washing must be understood in its spiritual sense, which the Israelites were prepared for by the Levitical washings —these having regarded external impurity as the figure of sin, so that the purifications were symbolical acts that typified what must take place on sin—is plain from the circumstance that nothing more is said about washing the feet, but only of washing generally; as also from the result that is said to follow from the not being washed by Christ. To have no part in Him, means to have nothing to do with Him, to be excluded from all communion with Him: Josh. xxii. 24, 25; 2 Sam. xx. 1; 1 Kings xii. 16; 2 Cor. vi. 15. Entire exclusion from the fellowship of Christ can befall only those who refuse to seek for spiritual cleansing from Him. With this agrees the undeniable reference to Ps. li. 4, which the saying of our Lord contains. David there prays to God: " Wash me thoroughly from mine iniquity, and cleanse me from my sin." When Jesus arrogates to Himself what is there supplicated from God, He assumes to Himself a Divine dignity. That passage in the Psalm teaches us also that the washing here refers directly to the bestowment of forgiveness ($\nu i\pi\tau\epsilon\iota\nu$ is equivalent to $\dot{\alpha}\phi\iota\acute{\epsilon}\nu\alpha\iota$ $\dot{\alpha}\mu\alpha\rho\tau\acute{\iota}\alpha\varsigma$, Mark ii. 10, Matt. ix. 6, which the Pharisees rightly regarded as arrogating a Divine prerogative), and not primarily to sanctification. Ver. 9 gives us the comment on ver. 4 of the Psalm: the blotting out of iniquity corresponds to the washing. " In the preliminary petitions, vers. 3, 4, 5, the subject is the main and prominent blessing in the forgiveness of sins. And the unfolded supplications are occupied primarily only with this, vers. 9–11. Then in vers. 12–14 the Psalm turns to the second gift, which necessarily follows from the communication of the first, the impartation of the sanctifying grace of God." But though the washing has primarily nothing to do with sanctification, yet Jesus, when He arrogates to Himself the power to forgive sins, indirectly assumes also the power of creating a pure heart; for He by the former places Himself in the province of God, with whom the commencement in justification is, according to Ps. li., inseparably connected with the termination in holiness.—The word about washing must have found an immediate response in Peter, who, in Luke v. 8, cries, "I am a sinful man, O Lord." The law of Moses has such a severe word as this (Num. xix. 20): "But the man that shall be unclean, and shall not purify himself, that soul shall be cut off from among the congregation." As certainly as Christ is the thrice Holy One, so certainly the man born and bound in sin remains separated from Him by a wide gulf, unless He should fill up the great gulf by the forgiveness of sins. When here the being washed by Christ is made the fundamental condition of all fellowship with Him, we are thereby assured that the knowledge of sin, and the desire to be washed from it by Christ, are the first principles of all Christianity. "Whatever purity a man may flatter himself that he has," says Quesnel, "unless Jesus purifies us, we are unworthy of His fellowship, of the communion of His body, and of the glory of His new life." That the basis of the doctrine of the water of forgiveness is the blood of the atonement, we learn from ch. xix. 34, 35; 1 John v. 6. The forgiveness, therefore, which Jesus imparted during the continuance of His earthly life, must have had an anticipative character.

Ver. 9. "Simon Peter saith unto Him, Lord, not my feet only, but also my hands and my head."—We must supply: If the matter is so, then wash, etc. Peter had but recently, in the contention, found how mighty sin was still in him. It was natural that he should lose all consciousness of what he already possessed through the grace of his Master, and that he should come to Christ as one who generally had not yet been washed from his sins, 1 Cor. vi. 11. Therefore Jesus must remind him of the condition of grace in which he stood.

Vers. 10, 11. "Jesus saith to him, He that is washed needeth not, save to wash his feet, but is clean every whit: and ye are clean, but not all. For He knew who should betray Him; therefore said He, Ye are not all clean."—Jesus had already transferred the matter into the spiritual domain. "He that is washed" must mean only "He that is washed in a spiritual sense." First comes the universal proposition, and then the specific application of it to the disciples.—Purity appears here as the consequence of the washing; and as, according to ver. 8, the bestowment of forgiveness of sins was signified by that washing, so purity must consist in the possession of forgiveness. How had the Apostles become clean? According to ch. iii. 5, and the other passages of the New Testament which we have there alluded to, the basis of that blessing was baptism. But this, in their case, required supplementing, inasmuch as it was the baptism of John, which could only imperfectly attain its end by assuring the future forgiveness of sins (Mark i. 4). This supplement the Apostles attained through their relation to Christ: comp. ch. xv. 3. They were led thereby to repentance and faith; and their faith led to forgiveness of sins, Acts x. 43, and the purification of the heart that rests upon forgiveness, Acts xv. 9. In consequence of their faith, the Son of man, who had upon earth the right to forgive sins, absolved them from their sins: because they were believers in Him, they became righteous in Him. They could say with David, " Blessed is the man whose iniquity is forgiven, whose sin is covered."— To the washing of the feet, ever coming into contact with the dust and soil of earth, corresponds in the spiritual domain the forgiveness of sins to which the man in a state of grace is liable, from the fact that he, by nature a sinner, dwells among a people of unclean lips—such sins as result from the mere daily walk in a corrupted world. The Apostles were men of sincere heart; they hated sin as those who had obtained forgiveness; and when, in their own despite, and to their deep sorrow, they were surprised into it, they had an intercessor with the Father, Jesus Christ, 1 John ii. 1, who, if we confess our sins, as Peter confessed them here, is faithful and just to forgive us our sins, and cleanses us from our unrighteousness, 1 John i. 9. —" But not all " was intended to pierce the conscience of Judas, whom the Redeemer did not give up until the last good impulse had died within him. Jesus must exhaust all the means of love and discipline, however plain it was that through the guilt of his obduration all would be in vain. Therefore He washed his feet also, for a sign that He still stood ready to wash even him spiritually from his unrighteousness. But the word was not spoken for Judas alone. In common with the later sayings of our Lord concerning the traitor, it serves to obviate the natural suspicion that Jesus, without observing it, had nourished a viper in His bosom,—a fact that would have been an argument against His true divinity. The clearly discerned and plainly foreannounced treachery weighed nothing against, but rather in favour of, the claims of Jesus as the Son of God: comp. ver. 19. Jesus thereby declared that He possessed the Divine prerogative of searching the heart and the reins. The Evangelist himself makes this emphatic in ver. 11.

Vers. 12-17. Our Lord's feet-washing presents a twofold aspect. It was, on the one hand, an act of ministering love, which had for its object the performance of that literal bodily washing which the pride of the disciples had left unaccomplished. On the other hand, the feet-washing symbolized the forgiveness of sins assured through Christ. When our Lord went on to impress it upon the Apostles that they should copy the example given by Himself, that must of course be interpreted only of the former of these elements. The latter—the washing of forgiveness—was peculiar to Christ. It rested on His divinity. No one man can spiritually wash another. Admonitory appeals, and attentive watchfulness over others' sins, have nothing to do with this washing; moreover, the danger incident to this is so great, Matt. vii. 3, that we cannot suppose it to have been recommended and made a duty in so absolute a manner. It was all the more obvious that the former—the setting an example of brotherly service—was the true interpretation, inasmuch as our Lord's act was occasioned, in its formal aspect, by the Apostles' own deficiency, and was really intended to have the significance of a pattern. Beza remarks, that by God's grace it had been given to the Apostles to respond in their conduct to the Lord's present requirement: this is attested by the Acts of the Apostles, in which there is no trace of the contentions that were formerly so rife, and also by their epistles.

Ver. 12. "So, after He had washed their feet, and had taken His garments, and was set down again, He said unto them, Know ye what I have done to you?"—This question demanded that they should reflect on the whole transaction; and in order to lead them to this after consideration, Jesus sets before them in full what the matter had to do with them, and what His design had been.

Ver. 13. "Ye call Me Master and Lord: and ye say well; for so I am."—The nominative is not used instead of the vocative: but φωνεῖν signifies to name. When the Apostles spoke of Christ, they were wont to say: The Master said this, the Lord did this. The article must be emphasized. The Master and the Lord simply: here we are carried beyond the mere human nature.[1] Absolute dominion over others in spiritual things would be a sinful claim, unless made by one who partook of the Divine nature.

Vers. 14, 15. "If I then, your Lord and Master, have washed your feet, ye also ought to wash one another's feet. For I have given you an example, that ye should do as I have done to you."—The washing is here to be taken in its literal sense. A spiritual meaning has no foundation; and it is obviated by reference to the disciples' omission of the material washing, as well as by the Lord's own present act. That which they had now omitted they must do in the future, moved by the example of Christ. That there are circumstances under which it is a duty literally to wash others' feet, is plain from 1 Tim. v. 10. Among the disciples themselves there might arise occasions for it. But the commandment must be understood with a certain reserve. Beneath the specific injunction there lies the universal precept which it symbolically exhibited—the precept of self-sacrificing love, to which no service is too mean. The form of the expression given to this precept is taken from the act then performed. If this is acknowledged, it will appear plain that the literal fulfilment does not by any means satisfy the injunction; indeed, that the literal fulfilment might be under certain circumstances a violation of the precept. The literal feet-washing is by it enjoined upon them only as a ministry of love. But that it is now as it were only in the relation of the woman to the man. Gomarus has well observed, that in our part of the world it is not so much the feet as the shoes that require the cleaning. The washing of the feet would be among us a burden: it presupposes the Oriental manner of clothing the feet, and the propriety that resulted from it. Where the feet are among the covered parts of the body,

---

[1] Placæus in Lampe observes: Præter Deum patrem et dominum nostrum, Jesum Christum, nemo in N. T. ὁ Κύριος appellatur, excepto Cæsare, qui a Festo, homine Romano et a verâ pietate alieno, sic appellatur.

decency demands that they should not be uncovered before strangers. As a symbolical act, and as an exemplification of ministering love, the washing of the feet is not inadmissible. But it is not here commanded. There is something strange and forced in such an injunction. The ancient Church was rightly advised, and followed a sure instinct, in giving it up.

Ver. 16. "Verily, verily, I say unto you, The servant is not greater than his Lord; neither he that is sent greater than He that sent him."—The name Apostle (he that is sent) Jesus confers in Luke vi. 13 upon His twelve disciples. From the fact that the Lord uses that name, we gather that the phrase, general in its form, is used with a special reference to the disciples.

Ver. 17. "If ye know these things, happy are ye if ye do them."—The *doing* is emphasized by the Lord in a manner similar to this in Matt. vii. 21; Luke vi. 46, xii. 47.

In vers. 18, 19, the Lord obviates the danger of their referring what was said for the Apostles alone, to the traitor found amongst them.

Ver. 18. "I speak not of you all; I know whom I have chosen: but, that the Scripture may be fulfilled, He that eateth bread with Me hath lifted up his heel against Me."—I speak not of you all: this points to that which, in ver. 10, Jesus had said concerning the Apostles' state of grace, and to the exhortation of vers. 13-17 based upon it. Vainly has it been attempted to place in opposition things immediately connected together. Only those who in essentials are pure, can mutually wash each other's feet.—The choosing spoken of here cannot be any other than that spoken of in ch. vi. 70, "Have I not chosen you twelve?" and there is in fact no reason to understand the choosing otherwise than as the reception into the number of the Apostles. Grotius paraphrases: Non de omnibus bene spero. Novi intime eos, quos mihi in comites elegi. The *knowing* is opposed to the partial not knowing which might seem to be inferred from the treachery of Judas: comp. ch. vi. 64 and ver. 11 here.—"I know whom I have chosen" involves that Jesus had not received the traitor among His Apostles through ignorance. With this negative is connected the positive, "but (I have chosen him) that," etc.: comp. ch. ix. 3; "but (he was born blind) that." Jesus chose Judas that he might betray Him, and that thus the Scripture might be fulfilled, according to which such a man belonged to the necessary surrounding of the Redeemer. Had our Lord not chosen Judas, the nature of the world, as it has been exhibited in the scripture quoted, would have been imperfectly represented in the apostolical circle; and this again would have been an unfaithful type of the Church in its later development. Judas belongs to the apostolical circle no less than Peter and John. We should miss something essential if there had been no Judas among the Apostles. We might, following Matt. xxvi. 56, Mark xiv. 49, John xix. 36, supplement τοῦτο γέγονεν. That would only come to the same thing. The τοῦτο γέγονεν would refer to the fact of the choice of Judas by Christ.

The passage quoted is from Ps. xli. The subject of that Psalm is the suffering Righteous One, not specially David. That which is there said of him must pre-eminently be fulfilled in Christ, in whom the idea of the Righteous One became a reality. When, then, after the wickedness of the open enemies has been depicted, we read in ver. 10, "Yea, mine own familiar friend, in whom I trusted, which did eat of my bread, hath lifted up his heel against me"—like a beast which strikes out against its master and feeder—there is at the foundation the general truth, that in the world of sin the righteous man cannot but have false friends; and this truth must have its realization in Christ. The quotation is according to the original text. The Septuagint has: ὁ ἐσθίων ἄρτους μου ἐμεγάλυνεν ἐπ' ἐμὲ πτερνισμόν. That Christ did not regard the passage as *directly* Messianic, is plain from the fact that He omits "in whom I trusted," which would not have been appropriate to Him who knew what was in man. That the μετ' ἐμοῦ does not merely denote the fellowship of eating, but the eating with Christ as the host, is evident from the original, where the words run, "who eateth My bread." From the relation in which Judas stood to Christ, he was, like all the Apostles, nourished by Christ: comp. ch. xii. 6, and Matt. xxvi. 17, where the Apostles ask, "Where shall we provide *Thee* the Passover?" (Bengel: Jesus est ut pater familias inter discipulorum familiam); and finally from ver. 26.

Ver. 19. "Now I tell you before it come, that, when it is come to pass, ye may believe that I am He."—'Ἀπάρτι, from this time onwards (instead of the ἀπάρτι, Matt. xxvi. 64, Luke has, ch. xxii. 69, ἀπὸ τοῦ νῦν), points to the fact that Jesus would still recur often to the same subject. Some interpret "just now, now at once." But New Testament phraseology furnishes no certain example of this interpretation (comp. ch. i. 52); and we have no reason for departing from the ordinary meaning, as our Lord does often return to the subject of the betrayal.—The foreannouncement of it not only obviates an obvious argument *against* Jesus; in connection with that foreannouncement, the betrayal becomes a positive argument in His favour.—" That I am;" that is, the absolute, the central personality: comp. on ch. viii. 24. For to that alone does it belong to try the heart and the reins, and to know the hidden before it is evolved in act. At the basis lie those passages of Isaiah, in which Jehovah proves His true divinity by His prediction of the future, such as ch. xliii. 11-13.

Ver. 20. " Verily, verily, I say unto you, He that receiveth whomsoever I send, receiveth Me; and he that receiveth Me, receiveth Him that sent Me."—Jesus had given to His disciples the pattern of self-humiliation, and had pressingly urged them to follow that example. The expression here is directly connected with this. Vers. 18, 19 in reality bear a parenthetical character. Its position at the close of the whole transaction requires us to assume that the Lord here returns to the act from which all had started, which had been the central subject, and with which all thus closes; and that He, glancing at the treachery of Judas, would fortify the other disciples in their fidelity by a reference to the dignity of their vocation. There is no evidence whatever that the treachery of Judas would have been a temptation to the remainder of the Apostles. The son of perdition they looked upon only with amazement and grief. That the Apostles might not mistake the real dignity of their vocation, in consequence of His exhortations to humility, Christ here at the conclusion points expressly to that dignity with designed allusion to an earlier utterance, Matt. x. 40 (comp. Mark ix. 37; Luke x. 16), the continued validity of which seemed to be endangered by those words of exhortation. It is to this seeming danger that the " Verily, verily, I say unto you," with its express assurance, refers. Berl. Bible: " This is said for consolation to those who must have received a severe lesson before." But we must not limit ourselves to the notion that Christ here exhibits the other side, in order to obviate misunderstanding of the lesson of humility. The two views are not placed in juxtaposition; but the consciousness of the dignity of their vocation must rather bring with it a willingness to humble themselves. He who is penetrated with the conviction that he is in the enjoyment of a divine mission, will not be ready to contend about the trivial honours of this world; he will freely surrender them to him whose worldliness of spirit finds nothing better to desire. True spiritual pre-eminence puts an end to all common ambition, and has below its feet all such questions as, whether one should wash the feet of others, or be washed. To contend about such pitiable matters is below its dignity. The Lord's word here stands in close connection with Luke xxii. 28-30, and finds there its commentary. Jesus, after He had commended the humble service of love and self-renunciation to His disciples by word and example (the feet-washing), now refers them to the dignity of their vocation, and shows them that they are called to high honour. That remained, notwithstanding their obligation to self-abasement; indeed, it rendered them all the more disposed to such humility. For all honour which the world could offer, would be in comparison only contemptible.—Lampe observes on "whom I shall send:" "Christ, although preparing Himself to suffer, nevertheless foresees His dignity as King of the Church; and as such He will have His legates, whom He will *send*." The Apostles were only the first in the great company. We have here the basis of the designation of ministers in the Apocalypse, as the *angels* of the Church. The principle *from above* is here as expressly as possible declared in relation to office in the Church. Lampe, the *Reformed* theologian, remarks: " The servants of God in the congregation of the Old Testament, as well the extraordinary like the prophets, as the ordinary like the priests, were regarded as *sent* of God. The same expression was transferred to the ministers of the New Testament, as well the extraordinary, the most eminent of whom were therefore called Apostles, as the ordinary, Rom. x. 15, who therefore were called *angels*, Rev. ii. and iii. The ἐάν τινα πέμψω is intentionally general, in order to intimate that the sending of Christ would not be restricted to the Apostles."

VERS. 21-30.

The feet-washing is now followed by our Lord's discourse concerning His betrayer. The ταῦτα εἰπών at the beginning places this in immediate juxtaposition with the address which Jesus had delivered to His disciples after the washing was finished, and Jesus had resumed His seat at the table. Matthew and Mark coincide upon this. According to Matt. xxvi. 21, Mark xiv. 18, Jesus uttered the words, "Verily I say unto you, One of you will betray Me," immediately after He had placed Himself at the table with the twelve, and the supper had begun. Matthew and Mark point not indistinctly to the fact, that our Lord's words concerning the traitor were closely connected with the commencement of the feast; Mark especially, who to the εἷς ἐξ ὑμῶν appends ὁ ἐσθίων μετ' ἐμοῦ. Ver. 18 in John shows what that connection was. "He that eateth my bread," in the Psalm, was, as it were, realized in act at the beginning of the meal. Such a special occasion is demanded for the "troubled in spirit," ver. 21. Luke omits the colloquy touching the traitor, and, instead of it, inserts another omitted by his predecessors, and which belonged to the *end* of the feast. We have already observed that, after the ἀπάρτι in ver. 19, a *series* of our Lord's utterances concerning the traitor was to be expected. There was a particular reason for that one which Luke records. It was to occasion the departure of the traitor, who, although he must be present at the institution of the supper, would have been altogether out of place during the subsequent outpourings of our Lord. That the words concerning the traitor in Luke closely resemble the earlier ones, is quite natural, as it is a designed repetition for a particular purpose. In the Old Testament we often find in such cases the echo-like recurrence of the same words: as may be observed, for example, in Ps. xlii. and xliii. But Luke's words are too closely connected with what Jesus had uttered at the supper, to allow us to suppose that he arbitrarily inserted them. Not only the πλὴν ἰδού comes here into consideration,—which, in spite of all that Wichelhaus says, cannot be regarded as an appendage of Luke, without throwing some suspicion upon his genuineness,—but also the τοῦ παραδιδόντος με in its undeniable reference to the τὸ ὑπὲρ ὑμῶν διδόμενον. That what is recorded by Luke in ver. 23 does not harmonize with the period after the institution of the supper, is an assertion which could be made only by those who take an incorrect view of the previous transactions concerning the traitor.

Ver. 21. " When Jesus had thus said, He was troubled in spirit, and testified, and said, Verily, verily, I say unto you, That one of you shall betray Me."—The *testifying* (comp. on ch. i. 7, iii. 11) is the opposite of speaking from mere supposition: it here declares what Christ utters was founded upon fact, and rested upon direct intuition. This, in connection with such events as we have here, lies beyond the human domain: Christ's possessing it was based upon His participation in the divine omniscience. The testifying has its counterpart in the " Verily, verily," of our Lord's discourse; intimating that He did not speak in the language of supposition, but of certain knowledge. That Jesus spoke only of one among the twelve, had probably for its reason the prevention of the excitement which the mention of his name would have raised among the Apostles, and of the premature departure of the traitor, who must needs partake of the holy supper. At the same time, all the others were thereby stimulated to a salutary self-examination.

Ver. 22. " Then the disciples looked one on another, doubting of whom He spake."—They looked at each other, not so much to detect the traitor in any other face, as to see whether in others' countenances they saw any suspicion of themselves. How weak is the flesh, how deceitful the heart, and how deeply had fallen many even of the believers of the Old Testament! This gives the point of connection for Matt. xxvi. 22-24. The Lord's word then, ver. 23, " He that dippeth his hand with Me in the dish, the same shall betray Me," not only contains a more specific designation of the traitor, but, in its repeated reference to Ps. xli., gives prominence to the indignity, that one of His table-companions should betray his Lord. Mark makes this very emphatic in ch. xiv. 20: " *It is one of the twelve* that dippeth with Me in the dish." Here follows, from ver. 23 to ver. 29, a scene peculiar to John, the communication of which was the reason that he made mention of the incident concerning the traitor. Vers. 21 and 22 serve only as an introduction or point of connection with what the other Evangelists had already recorded, and which is here briefly resumed. That which John communicates in vers. 23–29 is, as it were, his own private property. He alone could have imparted from the first source, and therefore the Evangelists who preceded him left it unmentioned.

Ver. 23. "Now there was leaning on Jesus' bosom one of His disciples, whom Jesus loved."—That the words "whom Jesus loved" occupy the place of a proper name (Heumann: "a title, a designation, by which John desired to be known"), appears from its being repeated often (ch. xix. 26, xx. 2, xxi. 7, 20), as well as from its being used in circumstances in which the love of Jesus is not under consideration. They are a paraphrase (as Bengel tells us) of the name of John, which signifies "him whom Jehovah loves." In the love of Jesus, the Jehovah manifest in the flesh, the pious wish became fulfilled from which the denomination arose. Meyer objects that it ought in that case to have been, not "whom Jesus loved," but "whom the Lord loved." But John speaks of Jesus as the Lord only twice before His resurrection, ch. iv. 1, vi. 23. Jesus, on the other hand, is the standing name. That was the name which belonged to the Son of man, Jehovah manifest in the flesh. To have designated himself as pre-eminently the disciple whom Jesus loved, would have been presumption on John's part (Grotius very incorrectly: Hac *modesta* circumlocutione se designare solet Johannes)—he would have shown himself a "babbler who on all occasions boasted that none of the other disciples were so highly esteemed as himself"—if this pre-eminence had not, like the primacy of Peter, rested upon some declaration of Christ Himself, and thus been removed out of the region of self-complacent fancy. Lampe's remark, "That he was much beloved by Jesus, was the conclusion he drew from the strong love towards Jesus with which he felt his own heart filled," is more specious than true. In all probability Jesus gave this declaration in the form of an interpretation of the name John, which even by this interpretation became a "new name." This is confirmed by the fact that Jesus on other occasions stamped the spiritual character of His Apostles by the imposition of a second name: comp. on ch. vi. 71, xi. 16. Where the proper name itself only needed to be expounded, it was obvious to retain it, and to sanctify it by an interpretation given.—The place which John assumed at the table, on the bosom of Jesus (comp. on ch. i. 18), was symbolically significant: it stood in close reference to his name; and thus rested doubtless on an appointment of Jesus.—Lampe is wrong here: " The Papists will find it hard to justify the primacy of Peter; John takes here the first place, not only at the table, but also in the heart, of Christ." Peter and John have each after his kind the first place in the apostolical circle; and both, inwardly bound to each other, were altogether without envy at each other's preeminence. Peter, between whom and the Pope of Rome there is no solid bridge, so that there is not the least necessity for explaining away the pre-eminence which the Lord gave him, is placed at the head with reference to the energy of action. The profoundly internal John, with his depth of love, his inwardness and devotion, stands nearest to the heart of Jesus. We may say, that because the relation between John and Jesus took the form of a relation of love, and was so far partial in its character, he was *not* called to the primacy, however necessary love was to that primacy: comp. ch. xxi. 15.

Ver. 24. " Simon Peter therefore beckoned to him, that he should ask who it should be of whom He spake."—The present νεύει is characteristic. The scene, which he himself witnessed, and with which he had particularly to do, is immediately before the Apostle's eyes. That a mere beckoning was sufficient, implies a closer relation between John and Peter, such as is attested by many other passages: ch. xx. 2, xxi. 7; Luke v. 10, xxii. 8; Acts iii. 4, viii. 14. Lachmann's text reads: καὶ λέγει αὐτῷ εἰπὲ τίς ἐστιν περὶ οὗ λέγει. Here again we may learn a lesson of caution in relation to this text. The *beckoning* presupposes that Peter, in his position at the table, could not communicate with John by word. The λέγει comes into contradiction with this. The εἰπέ is unpleasantly ambiguous. The obvious view of it would be that John should speak of his own accord. Then arises the difficulty as to how John came to know, or how Peter could take it for granted that he knew. According to another view, the "say" is equivalent to "ask." But then we should expect αὐτῷ, and "say" in the meaning of "ask" is strange. The reading arose doubtless from the difficulty felt in appreciating the spiritual *rapport* between John and Peter, and in understanding how a request could be made by a mere nod.—Peter was not urged by curiosity. He, the man of action, who cut off the high priest's servant's ear, thought that there was something here also for him to do. That Jesus entered into his desire, served to answer the end indicated in ver. 19. According to this, Jesus could not end with "One of you shall betray Me;" He must before the betrayal mention the name of the traitor, although it was preliminarily left in the keeping of the disciple whom Jesus loved. He would, in committing it to John, commit it to the whole apostolical circle. to the collective Christian Church.

Ver. 25. "He then, lying on Jesus' breast, saith unto Him, Lord, who is it?"—$Ἐπιπεσών$ points to a certain violence in the act, a strong impulse of affection, which the disciple of love must have felt when the Lord said, "One of you will betray Me." The reading of Lachmann's text, $ἀναπεσών$, sprang from an inconsiderate comparison with ver. 12 or ch. xxi. 20, in which passages the word refers to the habitual place which John occupied at the supper, and not this particular act. The address $Κύριε$ shows, that with John the tenderness of affection did not impair the awe of reverence.

Ver. 26. "Jesus answered, He it is to whom I shall give a sop, when I have dipped it. And when He had dipped the sop, He gave it to Judas Iscariot, the son of Simon."—Why did Jesus take this method? Not merely that He might be understood by John. If He could say softly the words $ἐκεῖνος$—$ἐπιδώσω$, He might just as easily have softly pronounced the name. The purpose of our Lord was rather, by this intimation of the manner of the betrayal, to make more emphatic the horror and the abomination of that act. He thus realized in act the words of Ps. xli. 10, "He that eateth my bread," which He had quoted in ver. 18, and to which in ver. 21 He had referred. Outwardly viewed, that which Jesus did was an expression of paternal favour to Judas. The other disciples, observes Bengel, doubtless thought that Judas was fortunate beyond them. It need not be proved that this was not mere semblance; and nothing can be more foolish than to speak of it as a "cunning designation by an act which had the force of a token of friendship and goodwill." Although the act had a complaining and condemnatory significance, it was doubtless, at the same time, a declaration that Jesus had not yet quite given up Judas, that He was still ready to receive him again into the fellowship of His love. He must and He would touch his heart once more, if haply he might yet be susceptible of better emotions. Besides John, to whom Jesus had previously given the commentary on the symbolical act, Judas also knew the meaning of the sign. His conscience gave him the interpretation, especially as Jesus had already alluded to that passage in the Psalm. In order, however, to be absolutely certain, he asked Jesus, according to Matt. xxvi. 25, "Master, is it I?" and Jesus answered him, "Thou hast said." This colloquy between Jesus and Judas must have proceeded *softly*, and so that no one perceived it except John, who had been already made acquainted with the secret, and thus was especially observant. This is on other accounts probable. Jesus could not have unmasked the traitor before all the Apostles without exciting the utmost commotion in their minds, and especially occasioning some premature explosion on the part of Peter. It is made necessary also by vers. 28, 29. That Jesus could exchange these words with Judas in private, renders it necessary to suppose that the latter sate near Him at the table. Probably Peter was first in the series on that side, and Judas ended it on the other; so that in one respect he was the nearest to the Lord, in another the most distant. This is supported by the fact that in all the catalogues Peter takes the first place and Judas the last: comp. Matt. x. 2-4; Mark iii. 16-19; Luke vi. 14-16.—The ψωμίον of itself points to bread. In later Greek, ψωμί was bread; and Suidas remarks, ψωμὸς ὁ ἄρτος. That it was a morsel of bread, is plain also from the frequent reference to the passage in the Psalm, "He that eateth my *bread*." We have here such an allusion to the paschal rite as forbids us to separate this feast from that of the Passover. In the paschal meal there was a sop called *charoseth*, made up of figs, nuts, and other fruits compounded with wine or vinegar. In this sop the householder dipped pieces of unleavened bread, and was followed in the act by the rest of the company. The sop was not a continuation into the paschal feast of a custom belonging to an ordinary meal; it belonged entirely to the paschal feast. It had a symbolical meaning. It represented the fruits of the blessed land to which the partaking of redemption gave them a right; just as in the law the

VOL. II.

benefits of nature were always conjoined with the grace of redemption. Matt. xxvi. 23 refers to this dish. If we refer it to the common bread of the daily meal, there is no connection with that passage. There remains no material to be dipped into.

Ver. 27. "And after the sop Satan entered into him. Then said Jesus unto him, That thou doest, do quickly."—*Τότε* serves to give prominence to the frightful crisis. The allusion, in the "Satan entered into him," to Luke xxii. 3, is all the less doubtful, as this peculiar phraseology never again occurs in the same way, either in reference to Judas or for any other purpose. In Mark v. 12, Luke viii. 32, it is used of *bodily* possession. There is an apparent opposition here, but it is only a formal one: it only intimates, that now first the word used by Luke reached its *fullest* truth. We ought not to say that Luke wrote "less exactly." "There were two stages," says Lampe, "of which it in a special manner held good that the devil entered the heart of the traitor: the first in the preparation for the betrayal, and the second in the accomplishment of it." As the indwelling of Satan, so also the indwelling of God by His Spirit, has its several degrees; and as the phraseology is relative, it may be used of the several crises of possession. The only question is as to the point from which we take our departure. The basis of the expression used by Luke and John was the word which Jesus had used at an earlier period, ch. vi. 70: "Have I not chosen you twelve, and one of you is a devil?"—an incarnate Satan.

Why did the final decision follow so close upon this sop? The colloquy recorded by Matthew between Jesus and the traitor is presupposed by John. It belonged to the sop, as a commentary upon it. The foundation of the entrance of Satan into the traitor was formed by the absolute assurance that he was detected. In the interest of his design he had overcome the shining evidences which Jesus had earlier given of His Godhead, otherwise the betrayal would be inconceivable: he who would betray the Son of God, must first be convinced that He is not the Son of God. The divinity of our Lord now suddenly shone out in the demonstration that He gave of His possessing the Divine prerogative of searching the heart and the reins. Not uttering a supposition, but with absolute assurance,

Jesus says, " Verily, verily, I say unto you, One of you shall betray Me." The rays of Divinity now beam still more brightly upon Him. By sign and word the Lord says to him, Thou art he who eateth My bread, and betrayeth Me. Then should he have been pierced to the heart, as Achan was in Josh. vii.; and all the more, as Jesus was at the same time attracting him, and declaring to him by this very sign that he was not yet struck out from the number of the twelve, and that there still remained space for his return. But he *would* not; and the vehement effort which he made to close his heart against heavenly influences, must at the same time have opened the door to the influences of hell: yea, he must have derived the very strength for that resistance from his union with those powers of evil. As it is said of David that he strengthened himself in his God, so Judas strengthened himself in Satan. This crisis decided his fate for all eternity.—The word, " What thou doest, do more quickly," does not command Judas to do anything generally, but to do more quickly what he will do, and must. He shows thereby that He does not fear the act of Judas; that His impulse to suffer, and to finish the work which the Father had given Him to do, was stronger than the impulse which Satan had given to Judas; that His desire for the salvation of the world was more vehement than Judas' desire for the reward of his sin. Judas sees himself by this word of Jesus profoundly degraded. He has not power over his Master, as he had imagined he would have, and soothed his vain thought thereby, like many others who follow in the footsteps of Judas; but his Master uses for His own purpose the designs of the traitor.

Vers. 28, 29. " Now no man at the table knew for what intent He spake this unto him. For some of them thought, because Judas had the bag, that Jesus had said unto him, Buy those things that we have need of against the feast; or, that he should give something to the poor."—This remark has so far actual circumstantial interest, as it shows what a thorough hypocrite Judas was, and how little the evidence of his treachery could be gained in a natural way. Even now the eyes of his fellow-disciples are not opened, so firmly had he closed all the issues of his heart, and watched over his words and looks. " No man knew" besides the disciple whom Jesus loved. This limitation is given by ver. 23. If the letter is pressed, Judas himself must be made unaware of it.—The supposition here referred to will appear "senseless and wild," only if we inadequately depict to ourselves the situation, and sunder the meal here described from the paschal feast. "For the feast" is more fully explained by ch. xiii. 1, which shows that only that part of the feast was meant which followed the opening of the Passover. Jesus had, in the anticipation of His passion and death, taken no care for the remainder of the feast. His disciples had doubtless been surprised at that; and it was all the more natural that they should refer the Lord's present words to that fact, as the things needed would be required in the next morning. It has been asserted, that to buy in the night of the Passover would have been a violation of the enjoined rest of the feast. But at the feasts, when men were to *rejoice* before the Lord, they were less rigorous than at the Sabbath. The law itself, in Ex. xii. 16, permitted on the first day of the feast the provision of food which was forbidden on the Sabbath. The immense multitudes of people in Jerusalem at the feast, and the wide variety of needs arising from it, caused doubtless a certain relaxation of rule after the great feast, in order that the remainder of the festival might be worthily cared for. In view of such pressing and decisive necessity, we may be sure that some resource must have been discovered for relief. "Necessity breaks law:" the Talmud gives express evidence as to how provision was made for buying during the feast, *Tract. Sabbath*, c. xxiii. 1. A difficulty arises only if we separate the meal in John from the paschal feast. In that case there would have been no urgency in the buying. Needless trouble has been raised as to the offices for buying and selling being open. The paschal feast certainly did not last elsewhere longer than that of the Apostles; and the sellers, who are always ready enough for gain, especially the Jewish, would not delay to open their stores.

Others thought that Jesus commanded Judas to give something to the poor: that is, for the same object, the procuring of provision for the further need of the feast. There were doubtless many whose slender resources were exhausted by the expenditure of the journey and the first part of the feast. It was the office of gratitude for the grace of redemption sealed in the Passover, to take charge of such as these. According to the prescription of the law, the people were to rejoice before the Lord in the great feasts, and to receive *personœ miserabiles* into the fellowship of this joy, by hospitality and alms. Deut. xvi. 14 : " And thou shalt rejoice in thy feast, thou, and thy son, and thy daughter, and thy man-servant, and thy maid-servant, and the Levite, the stranger, the fatherless, and the widow, that are within thy gates :" comp. ver. 11, xii. 12. This injunction had, as we may take for granted, been observed by Jesus at the earlier feasts which He had attended ; and that circumstance would render the supposition more natural. Quesnel : " The Redeemer sanctified the feast by mercy ; and He teaches us that we should give more liberal alms on those days on which God more richly dispenses His gifts. That is only a righteous requital ; but all the advantage is on our side." But the supposition of the text was obvious only if the feast in John was the paschal feast : the distribution of alms at such an otherwise unseasonable time would be accounted for as a necessary appendage of the feast. Under ordinary circumstances, the time—it being night—was altogether inappropriate. But the paschal night was the most excited of the whole year—the only one which, in this regard, was equal to the day : comp. Isa. xxx. 29. The supposition about Judas' errand would have been, on any other night, " senseless and wild."

Ver. 30. " He then, having received the sop, went immediately out; and it was night."—Instead of $εὐθέως$ $ἐξῆλθεν$, Lachmann and Tischendorf have $ἐξῆλθεν$ $εὐθύς$, following preponderating witnesses. The $ὅτε$ $ἐξῆλθε$, which many add at the end of this verse, omitting it at the beginning of ver. 31, is essential to that verse, since it gives emphasis to the connection between the utterance of Jesus and the departure of Judas. In ver. 30, however, it is superfluous and disturbing. John connected the receiving of the sop with the departure of Judas, because there was a link of causation between them. The $εὐθύς$ is pressed too far, if we draw from it the conclusion that he went out at that precise moment. The $εὐθύς$ soon after, in ver. 32, teaches us that, as also that of ch. vi. 21. Such an instantaneous departure cannot be conceived; for by it Judas would have betrayed himself before all the other disciples. It would have been just the same as if one among ourselves should withdraw from the rank of communicants : indeed much more surprising, when we consider the legal strictness of the Old Testament. He could not have gone away before the most holy feast of the nation—the feast on which their participation in redemption depended—reached its conclusion in the song of praise. The external reasons which forbade this were reinforced by a special internal reason. Hypocrites, like Judas, are particularly scrupulous in the observance of religious usages. He would not assuredly act like an ordinary knave, who tramples on all restraints; that would have been out of harmony with his whole past life: he concealed his wickedness under the garment of devotion; and the thirty pieces of silver were a slight and accidental matter to him. He would have forsaken his part, and have acted in opposition to that delusion by which he soothed his conscience, had he wantonly broken through the sacredness of the festal circle. There are also other reasons which assure us that Judas was present at the institution of the sacrament. Luke xxii. 21, 22, are of decisive import in relation to this. There, after the institution of the Supper, Jesus says: But, πλήν, behold, the hand of him that betrayeth Me is with Me on the table. So also "they *all* drank of it," Mark xiv. 23, after the mention of the Twelve just preceding, vers. 17, 20. Further, the passage in the Psalm, on which our Lord lays such decisive stress, "He that eateth My bread hath lifted up his heel against Me," would not have had its complete fulfilment if Judas had not partaken of the holy meal. So also the symbolical character of this first supper must not be left unconsidered in respect of this: there must have been present some representative of those who should eat and drink unworthily, and to their own condemnation, 1 Cor. xi. 29. The matter, then, must be viewed thus: after the transaction touching the traitor, and the completion of the paschal feast, followed the institution of the sacrament, which required only a few moments: Matt. xxvi. 26-29; Mark xiv. 22-25; Luke xxii. 17-20. When we consider the record given of this by the first three Evangelists, and the strictly corresponding account of Paul in 1 Cor. xi., we shall not need any further reason why John passed it over in silence. It was for him to supplement his predecessors; and they had already perfectly communicated these proceedings. After the institution of the sacrament, Jesus brought back the discourse to the traitor, Luke xxii. 21, 22, in order to occasion his departure, whose presence during the confidential utterances that were to follow would have been disturbing. Judas' going out followed after the psalm of praise had been sung, and consequently the official feast had ended. The intercourse of our Lord with His disciples now assumed a freer character; and Judas, the business agent of the society, could retire without exciting much attention, more especially as our Lord's word, "What thou doest, do quickly," furnished him with a cloak for his disguise.—The view we have taken is further supported by the consideration, that after ver. 30 we cannot find any room for the institution of the sacrament. Vers. 31–35 are most closely connected with the departure of Judas. Peter's word, in ver. 36, "Lord, whither goest Thou?" refers to ver. 33, and allows no interval. With ch. xiv. 1 we enter upon the last discourses of our Lord to His disciples, and we cannot imagine any interval during the utterance of them. In ch. xiii. 36 we are, according to the other Evangelists, beyond the *song of praise;* but the holy supper must, from its express explanation as given by our Lord, and from the nature of the case, have preceded that psalm.

That Judas partook of the supper, may with perfect propriety be regarded as the ecclesiastical view. It is supported by the far greater number of the more important authorities among the Fathers, as well as in the middle ages. As to the opinion of the Lutheran Church, the remark of John Gerhard is very characteristic: *qui aliter sentiat nemo mihi notus.* Those who have differed have been led by two classes of motive: some based upon ecclesiastical discipline (held by many Reformed theologians), and some based upon sentimentality (held by most moderns, with Neander at their head). Wichelhaus has most fully exhausted the historical material. He argues against the participation of Judas, on the ground that the known character of such a transgression as Judas' would necessarily exclude from the communion of the body and blood of Jesus. This is certainly not without force; but it is outweighed by another consideration still more important, namely, that the first supper had a symbolical significance, and was a prospective exhibition of the sacrament of all future times. Nothing more was absolutely necessary than the protest against him, and that was given with abundant force. Nor is it to be overlooked that the feet of Judas were washed with the rest. Now, if we press the argument of ecclesiastical discipline, the washing of his feet would be equally a stumblingblock. Signifying as it did the forgiveness of sins imparted by Christ, it would not seem to have been appropriate to Judas. But if we regard him as the type of those who, notwithstanding the proffer of the washing away of their sins by Christ, perish in their guilt, we find no further difficulty. Wichelhaus argues further: "According to Matthew, ch. xxvi. 25, Jesus had designated Judas, before the collected disciples, as the traitor; consequently he could not have remained any longer; and it is impossible that a detected traitor should have partaken of the sacred supper with the other Apostles." But all that he says about the "collected disciples" is an interpolation of his own. Matthew says nothing about it. All he thinks of is, that Jesus uttered the words, "Thou hast said." That had to him an apologetic meaning. It was sufficient if only one among the Apostles besides Judas heard it. That Jesus spoke it before all, is in itself highly improbable; and John intimates the very contrary.

The remark, "It was night," has no chronological importance. The whole festival was a night festival: comp. Ex. xii. 8, 42, "This is that night of the Lord, to be observed of all the children of Israel in their generations." It belonged to the domain of the moon, and not to that of the sun: comp. "in the new moon, in the time appointed, on our solemn feast-day," Ps. lxxxi. 4. It began בערב, after the light of the day had entirely departed. That had to do with the nature of the festival. The Lord arose upon His people in the night of their misery, as the Sun of their salvation. The night signified their Egyptian oppression, as the type of all oppression which the people of God should ever have to endure from the world.—Now, if the night mentioned in this verse had no chronological meaning, it had a symbolical one. What night meant from the moment when Judas went out—it existed, indeed, before his departure, but its full significance came out only with that—may be seen in what has been observed upon ch. ix. 4, 5, xi. 9, 10. In harmony with the symbolism of the paschal feast, the night signified the dark passion-season for Christ and His disciples, which really began with the vers. 31-38, departure of Judas.

With the departure of Judas began the profound humiliation of Christ. It was beyond all things needful to strengthen the disciples against the temptation that would spring from His abasement. Jesus did this by intimating, in vers. 31, 32, that suffering and abasement would be for Him only a short point of transition to supreme glory.

Vers. 31, 32. "Therefore, when he was gone out, Jesus said, Now is the Son of man glorified, and God is glorified in Him. If God be glorified in Him, God shall also glorify Him in Himself, and shall straightway glorify Him."—That ἐδοξάσθη, in ver. 31, refers to an actual fact that had already taken place, and not to an anticipated event (according to many the passion of Christ, which, however, is never viewed under the aspect of glorification; according to others, His state of éxaltation), is shown by the εἰ ἐδοξάσθη in ver. 32. The relation of the two verses to each other becomes entirely incomprehensible, if we do not perceive that in ver. 31 an accomplished fact is spoken of, and in ver. 32 the consequence that should be developed from that fact. The Son of man had been glorified through all that He had done while it was day, ch. ix. 4. With the departure of Judas, and the night that then and thereby set in, when no man could work, ch. ix. 4, xi. 10, xiii. 30, His course was so far ended; and a new one began, which, however, was to be one in reality closely connected with the former. The glorification of the Father by the Son is now followed by the glorification of the Son by the Father.

To the glorification of the Son of man by His *acts* the ἐδόξασα of ch. xii. 28 also refers. To the δοξάσω there corresponds ver. 32 here. According to ch. xi. 4, the sickness of Lazarus had for its end, that the Son of God should be glorified. We have, in ch. xvii. 4, 5, simply a commentary on these two verses. Accordingly, the glorification of the Son of man was to consist only in the consummation of His work upon earth, in the acts by which He at the same time manifested His own glory and the glory of God: comp. on ch. ii. 11.—Wherever the Son of man is mentioned, the Son of God is in the background, according to the precedent of the original passage in Daniel: comp. on ch. i. 52. The glorification brings the hidden background into the light.—That ἐν αὐτῷ signifies not *by* Him, but *in* Him, is shown by the corresponding ἐν ἑαυτῷ, ver. 32. Since the Son of man is the Son of God manifest in human form, the manifestation of God in the flesh, therefore God is, at the same time, glorified in Him: comp. on ch. xi. 4.

What was remarked upon ch. vii. 4 holds good in reference to the εἰ in ver. 32. It is still more emphatic; and intimates that the one must, so to speak, draw the other after it by logical consequence. In 1 Sam. ii. 30, "Them that honour Me I will honour," we have the proposition on which the inferential "if" here rests. As the particular instance here rests upon the general principle there expressed, so again out of this particular may be constructed a general proposition, calculated to excite our zeal to make the glory of God the aim of all our endeavours upon earth. But there is for the disciples a still more direct and potent encouragement here. If Christ was to be received up into the glory of God, then would His disciples be safe; if the fulness of omnipotence was at His command, they need not tremble though the whole world were in arms against them. How the glory of Christ turned to the advantage of His followers, is developed in ch. xiv. 12 seq.—The glorification assured by God to Christ began with the resurrection, and was consummated in His session at the right hand of the Father, with all the supreme prerogatives and glories connected therewith.— Ἐν ἑαυτῷ, in Himself, is stronger than παρὰ σεαυτῷ, with Thyself, in ch. xvii. 5. The latter might have spoken of the Arian Christ. Ἐν ἑαυτῷ leads to the equality with God in power and glory; intimates that the Son was to be received up into the sphere of the Father. In the Apocalypse, the Lamb in the midst of the throne, ch. vii. 17, corresponds to the ἐν ἑαυτῷ. As, during the earthly life of Christ, the relation of the Father to Him was not one of nearness and help merely, as God was manifested in Him, ver. 31, as the Father was in Him and He in the Father, ch. xiv. 10, 11; so also in glory we must conceive of no mere *nearness*, but Christ is to be received up into the Divine glory itself. The communion of nature which was declared in the earlier time, must have the latter as its consequence.—" And shall forthwith glorify Him:" immediately after death, not in some remote distance, allowing an interval during which the disciples might be left to themselves.

Ver. 33. "Little children, yet a little while I am with you.

Ye shall seek Me: and as I said unto the Jews, Whither I go, ye cannot come; so now I say to you."—From the contemplation of His glory, Jesus again descends to His disciples. That which He here tells them, forms the foundation for the solemn exhortation of vers. 34, 35. He would, by allusion to the impending separation, render their minds tender and susceptible, that they might receive the exhortation, and shut it up in their heart. That which, when leaving them, He had so emphatically laid on their hearts as His last request, they would never dismiss from their thoughts. This exhortation brings the holy supper to its conclusion. It began with uncharitable contention; it ends in the exhortation to love.

It was appropriate that our Lord, when He would exhort His disciples to love, should use the most affectionate address, τεκνία, never elsewhere occurring in all the Evangelists (τέκνα only once, Mark x. 24: comp. Matt. ix. 2; Mark ii. 5: comp. παιδία, ch. xxi. 5), but which finds a kind of echo in the First Epistle of John. And it was all the more appropriate, as our Lord lays down as the foundation of His precept of love—as I have loved you.—" Ye shall seek Me:" especially in the times of trial and tribulation. This word, as parallel with what Jesus had spoken to the Jews (comp. vii. 33, 34, viii. 21), points to the fact that even for the disciples, and for the faithful members of the Church, the ceasing of the bodily presence of Christ would be grievous and hard to be borne. Christ would be unapproachable to the Jews; and so He would be, in a certain sense, to His disciples, until they were received one by one into the heavenly glory, and He should return in visible form: comp. Acts i. 11. Assuredly, Jesus did not leave His disciples orphans; He came to them by the Paraclete; He is still and ever with them, present in the midst wherever two or three are gathered together in His name. But all this is not full compensation for His personal presence; does not hinder Christ from appearing as one who has gone away, ἀποδημῶν, Matt. xxv. 14; does not prevent His disciples from desiring, during the interval until His return, to see one of the days of the Son of man, Luke xvii. 22; and does not cause that, during this whole season, the fundamental tone of Christendom should not be sorrow. But it was profitable for them that it was so. Wrestling faith was thereby excited (comp. ch. xx.

29), and thus the best preparation secured for seeing Him in person.

Jesus says, "Yet a *little* while am I with you." This is to be referred to the short space until His imprisonment. The intercourse of the risen Lord with His disciples was essentially different from all His former intercourse, and led the way to that entirely spiritual communion which began after the Lord's ascension.—This is the only passage in which Jesus spoke to His disciples concerning the Jews. Elsewhere He uses the designation only in the conversation with the Samaritan woman, with Caiaphas, with Pilate. We have here the germ of the Johannæan phraseology: comp. on ch. i. 19. Just here, after the institution of the sacrament of the new covenant, before the mention of the new commandment, and where there is a sharp distinction made between the disciples and the enemies of Jesus, the designation is quite in place. How carefully John distinguishes between his own words and the words of Jesus, may be gathered from the fact that the Jews are never mentioned save here, without the Evangelist himself coming forward in his own person to use the name.

Vers. 34, 35. "A new commandment I give unto you, That ye love one another; as I have loved you, that ye also love one another. By this shall all men know that ye are My disciples, if ye have love one to another."—It is an arbitrary and baseless notion, that the love of the disciples to each other is here supposed to be the compensation, as it were, for the bodily absence of Christ. We have already exhibited the right connection with ver. 33: that verse is the soil for the seed of the present ones. It would also be a mistake to make the new commandment here the New Testament first and great commandment, as Ebrard does: "That same single new commandment which the New Testament brings in as a necessary supplement of the ten precepts of the Old Testament." The first and great commandment is even in the New Testament the love of God. That brotherly love is made prominent here, had its reason in the contention which had preceded. Knapp rightly observes (*De novo præcepto Christi*) that there is here a silent condemnation of the disciples, who had been unfaithful in some degree to this obligation of love. What they had neglected, while Christ was with them, they were, after His departure, all the more diligently to observe. A comparison with the Lord's saying in ver. 15, which has a manifest reference to the φιλονεικία of the disciples, shows that here also there is such a reference as the undertone.

The Old Testament foreannounced Christ as a new Lawgiver, Isa. ii. 3, xlii. 4. The difference between Christ and Moses in this domain appears in this, that Christ here comes forward independently as a Lawgiver, while Moses ordinarily referred back his laws to Jehovah, and represented himself to be only a mediator. In a certain sense, all the laws of the New Testament are old laws. The law of the Old Testament has eternal value, and belongs to the Church of the New Testament no less than to that of the old: comp. Matt. v. 17-20. In a certain sense, all the commandments of the New Testament are new. Even the first and chief commandment of the Old Testament, the precept of the love of God, shines forth in new brightness now that Christ has brought the Father near to us, and in the manifestation of His love laid the foundation for ours. It was to the disciples as if they had never received this precept before. Also the precept of brotherly love, the love of our neighbour, was in the Old Testament so clearly and rigorously set forth, that, viewing it merely as a commandment, it could not be more expressly enjoined. To love our neighbour as ourselves, Lev. xix. 18, is just the same precept in the New Testament as in the Old: Mark xii. 31; Matt. xxii. 39. Yet this commandment also has, in a certain sense, become new. First, it has received a new foundation in the love of Christ. The Lord has saved the expositors from speculating as to what the newness of the law consisted in, by adding, "as I have loved you." Christ exhibits the commandment as a new one, after He has come to the perfection of the manifestation of His own love, and His departure from the disciples was impending: comp. ver. 33. Secondly, in internal connection with the newness of the foundation stands the new limitation of the sphere of this love. In the Old Testament the neighbour is, according to grammatical and historical exposition, the member of the covenant established on Sinai, the fellow-partaker of the Old Testament covenant benefits. In the New Testament he is the member of the covenant sealed by Christ,—the new *commandment* here consequently corresponds to the new *covenant* of which Christ had spoken in the institution of the Supper,—the fellow-partaker in His redemption, the brother in His love. This is a relation which before Christ had never been in the world, and of all the bonds of love it is the most binding and internal.—'Αλλήλους refers to the true disciples of Christ, ἐμοὶ μαθηταί, ver. 35. Primarily the Apostles were meant; but these were the representatives of all believers: comp. ch. xvii. 11. But that which primarily was spoken of the stricter bond of Christian brotherhood, involves also the indirect obligation to the most universal love of man; just as the love of Christ to His own disciples, which is here set before us for our imitation, rests upon the foundation of His universal love to the world. Even under the Old Testament they were to love the *stranger* as themselves: this proves that the Pharisaical gloss on the precept of the love of their neighbour, which certainly in the letter referred only to fellow-Israelites, was not according to the mind of the Lawgiver. If we are to love the Christian brother as Christ loves him, so we are to love all men because Christ loves them, and died for them. Nevertheless, the violation of brotherly love is a heavier guilt than the violation of the universal love of man. The measure of the guilt is the greatness of the love of Christ.—The commandment is at first nakedly laid down, and then, after the reason given for it, it is repeated with an inserted καί, which refers to the reason given: ἵνα, καθὼς ἠγάπησα ὑμᾶς, καὶ ὑμεῖς ἀγαπᾶτε ἀλλήλους. The displacement of the ἵνα does not militate against this view, which is simple, and recommended by the comparison of ver. 15. We find the same elsewhere, *e.g.* in ver. 29, and 2 John 6.—Acts iv. 32 may be compared with ver. 35; and what the heathen used to say of the Christians (Tertull. Apol.): " See how they love one another."

Ver. 36. " Simon Peter said unto Him, Lord, whither goest Thou? Jesus answered him, Whither I go, thou canst not follow Me now; but thou shalt follow Me afterwards."—What Jesus had said concerning love had gone straight to Peter's heart, and the more as he had taken a prominent part in the contention which had given rise to the exhortation. But there was something in the Lord's words which smote him still more keenly: Christ had spoken of His speedy departure. On this point he earnestly desired more light; and, as the Lord's answer shows, in order that he might actively interfere, and unite his destiny with Christ's. Whither goest Thou? If Thou goest unto death, I will go with Thee: compare the word of Thomas in ch. xi. 16; and Elisha's word to Elijah in 2 Kings ii. 4, 6: "As the Lord liveth, I will not leave thee." The "canst not" in our Lord's answer has a psychological reason. Before Peter could die for Christ, Christ must have died for him, and have obtained for him by His death the Holy Spirit, who is, with other attributes, a Spirit of might. August.: Quid festinas, Petre? nondum te suo spiritu solidavit Petra. There were also other reasons for that inability. In God's counsel, Peter, before he followed his Lord in death, must strengthen his brethren, and feed the lambs of Christ. But that the inability was connected with the state of Peter's mind, is evident, as from the answer of Peter, so also from a comparison of Matthew: there " thou canst not follow Me now" is followed by "All ye shall be *offended* in Me this night."

Ver. 37. "Peter said unto Him, Lord, why cannot I follow Thee now? I will lay down my life for Thy sake."—As Peter could not follow Christ, so likewise he was ignorant of himself, and estimated his own strength far too highly. True self-knowledge could come to him only in consequence of the outpouring of the Holy Ghost. The Spirit searcheth all things, the deep things of God, and the deep things of the human heart. Nevertheless, Peter was like the young eagle, which is beginning to stir its wings. Of such stuff were the martyrs formed, when the full possession of the Holy Ghost was added. The spirit was already willing, though the flesh was weak: the strength was small, the will was good. Aug.: Quid in animo ejus esset cupiditatis videbat, quid virium non videbat.

Ver. 38. "Jesus answered him, Wilt thou lay down thy life for My sake? Verily, verily, I say unto thee, The cock shall not crow, till thou hast denied Me thrice."—When Jesus disclosed to Peter his real weakness, He assured him at the same time of the means of his recovery, after his fall, which would lead him to a much profounder knowledge of himself. That fall was itself a demonstration of the Divine omniscience of his Master, and must therefore have assisted to strengthen his faith. When he heard the cock-crowing, he must have remembered the word of Christ.

Vers. 36–38 coincide accurately with what the other Evangelists record of the same event. We have here, in ver. 36, the starting-point of the whole incident, which in the others is wanting. The question of Peter here refers to the words of our Lord, not communicated by the other Evangelists, immediately after the departure of Judas. And our Lord's answer here, "Whither I go, thou canst not follow Me now, but thou shalt follow Me afterwards," connects itself with vers. 31, 32, in Matthew. That the *answer* there also issues from Peter, harmonizes well with the fact that, according to John, the Lord's words were primarily addressed to him. John communicates the former part of that answer, Matthew gives the remainder in ver. 33. John supplements the answer of Jesus by the words placed at the beginning, "Wilt thou lay down thy life for My sake?" What Peter replied, Matthew had already recorded: hence John omits it here.—As to the particulars of time, there is no essential difference between John and Matthew. The τότε of the latter, in its reference to the καὶ ὑμνήσαντες, ἐξῆλθον εἰς τὸ ὄρος τῶν ἐλαιῶν, leaves us ample space in the interval between the hymn with which the Passover began, and the arrival at the Mount of Olives. Those only are embarrassed by it who place the departure of Judas, with which vers. 31-38 in John are immediately connected, before the institution of the supper, and the hymn that marked its commencement.

Mark adheres closely to Matthew; he gives only what the Lord had said concerning the cock-crowing, but in a rather more detailed form.

The address of Jesus to Peter in Luke, ch. xxii. 31, 32, forms the continuation of Matt., vers. 31, 32. That Peter, besides the words quoted by Matthew and John, added further, "Lord, I am ready to go with Thee to prison and to death," is quite in harmony with the vehemence of his character. He cannot do full justice to the absoluteness of His devotion and willingness to sacrifice himself; and he is all the more impetuous because a still voice within his inmost soul whispers to him that he has not yet the needed strength. This voice he thus strove to silence. To the threefold assurance of his readiness for self-sacrifice (John: Lord, why cannot I follow Thee now? I will lay down my life for Thy sake. Matt.: Though all men shall be offended because of Thee, yet will I never be offended.

Luke: Lord, I am ready to go with Thee, both unto prison and to death), corresponds the threefold denial in the Lord's reply, and in the event. The same heaping of affirmation we find at the denial itself in Matt. xxvi. 74.

CHAP. XIV.

The Lord's words in ch. xiii. 36-38 had concerned Peter alone. Here He turns directly to the disciples in general. The abruptness of the transition originated, in a series of many manuscripts, the clause which overwhelming authority decides to be spurious, καὶ εἶπεν τοῖς μαθηταῖς αὐτοῦ (Luther: and He said to His disciples). The transition is all the more startling, as Peter did not in the foregoing assume the character of representative of the Apostles, but appeared in his own personal relations. Further, the beginning, "Let not your hearts be troubled: believe in God, believe also in Me," and the sequel, in which all the resources of consolation and strengthening are suggested, presuppose that immediately before great dangers had been referred to, by which the disciples were threatened. Looking at John alone, that was not the case. In ch. xiii. 36-38, the Lord had to do with Peter alone; and it is not of external danger that He spoke, so much as of moral aberration. In vers. 31-35 the Lord had certainly spoken of His departure; but He did not there allude to the disconsolate condition into which the disciples would, as a consequence, fall. He had exhibited that departure to them in vers. 31, 32, under a cheerful aspect; and in vers. 33, 34, connected with it the exhortation to love. How little chap. xiii. furnishes the foundation of ch. xiv., may be noted from the fact, that expositors can by no means come to agreement as to the connection between "Let not your heart be troubled," and what precedes. Lampe's embarrassment betrays him into the remarks: "His mercy is so great, that before His people call upon Him He answers them, Isa. lxv. 24, and proffers consolation to those who have not in their thoughts the hope of experiencing it." Accordingly, we are driven to suppose, that between ch. xiii. and ch. xiv. there is a link which the predecessors of John, whom he everywhere only supplements, will supply, and which will form the starting-point and the key to the encouragements that now follow. We are especially referred to Luke, as the immediate predecessor of John, to whom his supplementary details are generally most directly attached. In Luke we have the middle clause surprisingly supplied. The Lord there, in ch. xxii. 35–38, turns from Peter to the disciples generally. He reminds them that, through the grace of God so visibly overruling them, they had hitherto prospered; that no distress and no need had invaded them, ver. 35. He tells them that now another time was coming, when God's manifest grace would be withdrawn—a time of need and danger—enemies around them, and nowhere a friend—everywhere persecutions, hardships, and dangers, ver. 36. He points in ver. 37 to the reason of this change: the days were to come to their Master of which the prophet Isaiah had written, when He was to be "numbered with the transgressors;" and shows them that if their Head suffered, the members must suffer also; that their Head suffered only in consequence of that power which had been given to darkness, and that the members must encounter the same. It would have been unnatural that the servants should be prosperous while the Master suffered and died. The disciples had misunderstood the word, "Let him that hath no sword, sell his coat and buy one," which in a proverbial form only expressed the thought that a very perilous period was at hand, which could not be met but by the most energetic and effectual means of defence, and in which they would have to sacrifice all in order to withstand the pressure of their foes. They supposed, though dubiously, with the feeling that they might be altogether wrong, and with the wish that the Lord would open to them the right understanding, that a defence with external weapons was recommended to them: "Lord, here are two swords." The Lord says, "It is enough;" thereby intimating that His words were to be taken with some qualification, and that their defence must be sought in an altogether different region. For if two only were enough, swords of that kind generally must have been useless. Against the forces of the High Council nothing could be effected with two swords. And with this rejection of the wrong weapons of defence against the impending danger—of weapons that would have no value in a contest in which the real opponent is the "prince of this world," ver. 30, is immediately connected the exhibition of those true and spiritual weapons which our chapter presents. It is enough: the visible sword is not to be your defence, but simple faith. *Sursum corda.* Seek your help above, from your God and your Saviour.

This explanation of the starting-point of our Lord's words in this chapter is of no slight practical importance. The imperilled situation in which the disciples were placed during the sufferings of Christ, is typical for the Church of the last days. Then will power be again given to darkness; the world will again go such lengths as to crucify Christ afresh; His Church will be threatened with danger on all hands; and the grace of God, which had through such long periods been with her, will seem rather to retreat and be concealed. Now this chapter teaches us how we must conduct ourselves at such a time; with what weapons we are to defend ourselves against the threatening danger; and what those helps are on which we may surely rely.

The whole chapter bears a consolatory character, in harmony with Isa. l. 4, lxi. 1, Matt. xi. 5, according to which it is the proper vocation of Christ to strengthen the feeble, to bind up broken hearts, and to bring glad tidings to the poor. The exhortations scattered here and there to love and to keep His commandments, vers. 15, 21, 23, are only subordinate: they only point by the way to the moral conditions on which the realization of His consolations and promises is suspended; they give the preparatory prospect of the unfolding of this most important aspect, the thorough exhibition of which could not be wanting in the Lord's last sayings in another connection, and thus serve as a link between the consolatory and the hortatory portions of the farewell discourses. They have precisely the same position which ver. 18 assumes in Ps. ciii.,—a psalm which, in its fundamental tone, is thoroughly consolatory. That "Let not your heart be troubled" is here the ground-tone of the whole discourse, is shown by the recurrence of these introductory words towards the close, in ver. 27.

We have evidently here a complete whole connected and rounded. The three interruptions of the disciples—of Thomas in ver. 5, of Philip in ver. 8, of Judas in ver. 22—do not disturb the connection; the Lord's discourse does not derive from them a character of irregularity; but they only give Him occasion to develop more fully what was in His original plan. The first interjection, that of Thomas, was excited by our Lord Himself.

The clause placed at the outset, " Let not your heart be

troubled: believe in God, believe also in Me," is developed through the exposition of those individual grounds of encouragement for the troubled heart, and of those individual means of defence against distress and danger, which are provided of God in Christ. The first thing is, that to the disciples of Christ heaven is sure; that no power of this world can exclude them from eternal life: turning to this refuge, they can look calmly at the confusion of things upon earth; their tribulation, because temporal, is light: " Who can rob us of the heaven which the Son of God gives to our faith?" The departure of Jesus is all the less grievous to them, because it enabled Him to prepare them places in heaven, and because, when their hour is come, He will return to receive them into their eternal inheritance, vers. 2, 3. But they are not only referred to the world beyond: into the confusion of this world shine down the clear lights of the Divine grace from above; and even in the time of their perilous pilgrimage upon earth, they are enriched with the best possessions. The second in the series of encouragements is this: They have in Christ the certain way to heaven, the assured preparation for eternal life; and the being obliged to renounce the world, robs this present being of all its importance, and empties it of all real substance. In Christ the Father has been made known to them; in the world of shadows the truth has shined, and in the world of death life has been revealed; and, united to Him, they can never fail of their participation in His glory, vers. 4–11. The third consolation: They need not fear, that with the departure of Christ His *works* will cease. That departure will rather, as being His entrance to the glory of the Father, enable them in His power to do yet greater works: the apparent end of Christ's manifestations of His power will in reality be the beginning of them, vers. 12–14. The fourth: If they must, in the coming hard conflict with the world, be without the visible presence and assistance of their Lord, He will instead send them another Intercessor, the Spirit of truth, vers. 15–17. The fifth: They need not fear that Christ will disappear from them. He would leave His people only for a short time; He would then come back again; and that not, as before, in a visible form, but secretly, and in such a manner as to be manifest only to His own; yet with a much more deep and effectual influence, so that His coming back brings true life with it, vers. 18-24. The sixth: The disciples must not despond because their understanding was as yet so dull, and because they had failed to penetrate the depths of truth. This defect the Holy Spirit would supply, whom the Father would send in His name: the same Comforter who was before promised as a Helper in the conflict with the world, is now promised as a Teacher, vers. 25, 26. Finally, the seventh consolation: The peace of Christ, ver. 27, where, after exhausting all grounds of encouragement, the "Let not your heart be troubled" returns again. After all this, the announcement of the departure of Christ to the Father would be no more grievous, but joyful. Christ passes thereby from the form of a servant into the full fellowship of the Divine glory, ver. 28. The conclusion of all is the declaration, that the catastrophe presented in the prospect was now very near at hand, and the summons to the disciples to go forth with their Lord to meet it.

We must suppose, that after "Arise, let us go hence," they arose and departed: this is evidently included. In such cases of request and performance the Scripture is often concise and condensed: so, for example, in Gen. iv. 8, what Cain said to Abel is omitted, so that the supplement must be sought in the sequel: comp. Ex. xix. 25. In Isa. viii. 2 we have a strictly analogous case. In our present passage we may find a particular reason for so brief a hint, in the solemn and stately character of the discourse of these chapters having something of a poetical tinge. If the Evangelist had not intended us so to understand him, he must needs have made some cautionary remark. The summons of itself excludes the idea of other discourses having been afterwards uttered in the same locality. It is inconsistent with the dignity of Christ, and the solemnity of the occasion, to assume that He followed arbitrary impulses, such, for instance, as Gerhard and others suggest, who compare it with the broken words of separating friends. Jesus repeats the "Rise, let us go hence," afterwards in Gethsemane, Matt. xxvi. 46; and there the departure follows hard upon the summons. Concurrently with the request to arise, the discourse itself reaches its full close in ch. xiv., issuing in a formal word of farewell: comp. especially ver. 28.—We gather from this, that the discourse could not have been carried on upon the same scene; and that, if other words were to follow, these would have a new starting-point, and belong to a new locality, which suggested new impulses, and formed as it were a new *station*, different from that of the last supper. Here we have one terminus, the departure from the feast-chamber; the other is in ch. xviii. 1, the passage of the Cedron. What intervened must have been spoken in the way from the chamber to the brook; and with this agrees the circumstance, that the vineyards on the road would give appropriate occasion for the representation of Himself as the true Vine (comp. iv. 35), and that the words, "He lifted up His eyes to heaven," ch. xvii. 1, suggest that the prayer was offered under the open heaven. So much of the way as led through the agitated city, the streets of which were in the evening especially excited, was probably passed in silence; outside the city, before that anxious passage of the Cedron with which John in ch. xviii. 1 expressly links the discourses of ch. xv.-xvii., Jesus stood and gathered the disciples around Himself. Robinson (vol. ii. 33) remarks with reference to this locality, that before the valley reaches the city, and opposite its northern part, it broadens into a space of considerable extent, which is built upon, and contains olive and other fruit trees. He adds, that at this place it is crossed obliquely by a path which leads from the north-eastern corner of Jerusalem over the northern part of the Mount of Olives.

Ver. 1. "Let not your heart be troubled: believe ye in God, and believe in Me."—"These words," observes Gerhard, "contain the sum of what was to be said; they are the theme which Christ would place at the head and bring in again at the close, that the main scope of the whole discourse might be perfectly clear." The words are an allusion to Ps. xlii. 5: "Why art thou cast down, O my soul? and why art thou disquieted within me? hope thou in God." There can be the less doubt of this, inasmuch as the Lord frequently elsewhere refers to this passage: comp. on ch. xii. 27.—Jesus Himself says in ch. xii. 27, "Now is My soul troubled;" and in ch. xiii. 21, it is said of Him that "He was troubled in spirit:" consequently He cannot have required in His servants anything like a stoical apathy, which is ever the sign of a withered and hardened heart; but only that their sorrow should never have the dominion over them. It must be observed that He is here speaking not to such as were enjoying a perfect tranquillity,—so that the dehortation would refer to a dismay possible in the future,—but to souls that were profoundly moved and disquieted. To these His exhortation is, that they should not remain in their disquietude, but rise through it to that consolation from above, the necessary condition of which is a previous sorrow, such a sorrow as dead insensibility can never know. Christians have tender hearts, and therefore deep sorrows; but they have also the privilege of consolation from above. But the dehortation and the exhortation have here—as a comparison of the original Hebrew, and especially the sequel of the chapter, show—a predominantly consolatory and encouraging significance: Ye need not disquiet yourselves, ye have reason to believe.

The original refers only to God. That God, however, was not the abstract God which could not be the object of true faith and living confidence; but rather the God who had been revealed through the ages, and had dwelt in their midst, the God of Abraham, Isaac, Jacob, Moses. That God had now in Christ become perfectly revealed; and that gave the *Believe in God* an altogether new significance. (Bengel: Fides antiqua in Deum novo quasi colore tingitur in Jesum Christum credendo.) —Each of the two clauses suffices in itself: *Believe in God*, and *Believe in Me*. The juxtaposition is only apparent. The God whom they were to trust was the Father of Christ; and the Christ whom they were to trust was the true revelation of God: they who believed in Him, believed on Him that sent Him, ch. xii. 44. If Christ and the Father are one, ch. x. 30, it is indifferent whether we place our confidence in God or in Christ. The form of juxtaposition, as of counterparts, is adopted in order to obviate the misunderstanding which would sunder God from His manifestation in Christ, and assign to Christ only a subordinate place. But, strictly speaking, the two clauses include and are the equivalent of each other. The passage, Ex. xiv. 31, is in a certain sense analogous: "And the people believed the Lord, and His servant Moses." Faith was reposed in Jehovah, who was revealed through Moses, and in Jehovah, who wrought great deeds by Moses. Here also the juxtaposition is merely apparent. Jehovah sundered from Moses would not be Jehovah, but an empty idea of the imagination, which could not be the object of faith and confidence. Another Old

Testament parallel is 2 Chron. xx. 20, where Jehoshaphat says to the oppressed people, " Believe in the Lord your God, so shall ye be established ; believe His prophets, so shall ye prosper." There also Jehovah is not the abstract God, but, as the appendage shows, the God who dwelt among the people; and, in His organs the prophets, assumed, as it were, flesh and blood.— Those who would separate the clauses which are here inseparably connected together, who would hold to the " Believe in God," but give up the " Believe also in Me," are involved in a ruinous error. A God sundered from Christ dwells in inaccessible light—not to be apprehended, and utterly obscure. Faith, however, can apprehend only a God become incarnate; which explains the fact, that Deism everywhere in history appears as the mere forerunner of Atheism, and as nothing but a developing Atheism. But more : as the πιστεύετε denotes rather the privilege than the obligation of believing, it is of great significance that God sundered from Christ has nothing left for forgiveness or bestowment. All the Divine gifts which are individually enumerated in the sequel are bestowed through the medium of Christ; God has poured upon Him all the fulness of His gifts; and He has reserved nothing more that He could give to those who come to Him without the mediation of Christ. They are worthily dealt with in that they are sent away empty. It is the appropriate punishment of that pride which is offended by the lowliness of Christ. (Calvin: Pudet superbos homines humilitas Christi. Ideo ad incomprehensibile rei numen evolant.)—That the πιστεύετε is in both instances to be taken as imperative, is now all but universally acknowledged. (The Vulgate is incorrect : Creditis in Deum et in me credite ; so Luther and the English translation.) The relation of the positive to the negative, with the comparison of Ps. xlii. 6, Ex. xiv. 31, and 2 Chron. xx. 20, are sufficient to prove this to be the correct view. Πιστεύετε is after εἰς ἐμέ emphatically repeated, in order to point to the supreme dignity and importance of Christ, who is not introduced as a simple adjunct, but is on a level with the Father as a proper and real object of faith. Luther : " Ye have heard that ye should trust in God ; but I would show you how you may come to that faith, so that ye may not set up for yourselves another idol under His name, after your own devices. If ye would assuredly come to Him with true faith, ye must come to Him in Me, and through Me: if ye have Me aright, ye have Him aright."—This saying shows us, on the one hand, that characteristic of our nature which everywhere and always inclines to fear and despondency; and it also shows us, on the other hand, the dignity of Christ, who in the fulness of love takes upon Himself our infirmity, who, Himself then going to meet Satan and death, yet is so sublimely exalted above His own suffering, that He can come to His disciples' help with consolation, and arm them against danger and dread.

In vers. 2 and 3 we have the first ground of consolation, the allusion to life eternal. This is very fittingly made the first, inasmuch as eternal life is the supreme benefit, for which every other paves the way. That He would give His people eternal life, Jesus had from the very beginning declared emphatically: comp. ch. iii. 15, 16. Then again it must be observed, that however glorious the gifts and graces are which Christ gives to His disciples in the present life, their condition in this life is, after all, a transitory and changeable one. The Divine gifts and influences themselves may suffer many interruptions. The sun often hides himself behind the clouds. The Church of Christ must be disciplined by the cross. There is one star of hope, however, which shines, and shines steadily, in always equal clearness. To this the Lord had pointed His people before, in the prospect of coming troubles and persecutions, Luke vi. 23: " Rejoice and be exceeding glad, for great is your reward in heaven." St Paul recommends this as an excellent defence against fear, in 2 Cor. iv. 17, 18: " For our light affliction, which endureth but a moment, worketh for us," etc.; and so in the Epistle to the Hebrews, ch. xi. 26. When once this hope is firmly rooted in the mind, the soil is at the same time and thereby prepared for the scattering of the seed of other consolations. He to whom the end is sure, cannot before the end, and in the way to it, be forsaken and lost. The heirs of eternal life must be kept by God, during the time of their pilgrimage, like the apple of His eye.

Ver. 2. " In My Father's house are many mansions: if it were not so, I would have told you. I go to prepare a place for you."—The Father's house is His heavenly abode. Comp. Deut. xxvi. 15, " Look down from Thy holy habitation, from heaven, and bless Thy people Israel;" Isa. lxiii. 15, " Look down from heaven, and behold from the habitation of Thy holiness;" Ps. xxxiii. 13, 14, " The Lord looketh down from heaven: He beholdeth all the sons of men. From the place of His habitation He looketh upon all the inhabitants of the earth;" 2 Chron. xxx. 27, " Then prayer came up to His holy dwelling-place, even to heaven." Comp. further, Ps. xx. 7, lxviii. 6; Jer. xxv. 30. The earthly Temple, the tabernacle of congregation, the place where God is wont to hold communion with His people, where He dwells upon earth and receives His people as guests, has its antitype in heaven: comp. Ps. xi. 4; Heb. ix. 24; Rev. vii. 15, xi. 19, xiv. 15. There the supreme God, who in all times and in all places is the dwelling-place of His people,—whether upon earth or in heaven, Ps. xc. 1; Deut. xxxiii. 27,—has His sacred abode, in which He dwells not alone, but receives to Himself all His saints after the cares and the conflicts of life.

" Many mansions:" so there is room there for you all, when the prince of this world shall leave you no more place upon earth: comp. ἔτι τόπος ἐστί, " yet there is room," Luke xiv. 22. Luther: " If they will not suffer you to be citizens and neighbours, or even guests, but would have all the world for themselves, let them have the world, but know that ye shall nevertheless have mansions enough." Many the mansions must be, since the Father's house will contain not only the multitude which no man can number, Rev. vii. 9, of the saints made perfect, Heb. xii. 23, but also the ten thousands of angels, Deut. xxxiii. 2; Heb. xii. 22. Allusion to the many gradations of dignity in that future life (Augustin: Multæ mansiones diversas meritorum in una vita æterna significant dignitates) introduces a discordant and foreign element into the passage. Here we can think only of what is common to all: if the earth has no more place for you, there is room enough in heaven. The phraseology reminds us of Gen. xxiv. 23, 25. To the servant's question, " Is there room in thy father's house for us to lodge in?" Rebekah answers, " We have both straw and provender enough, and room to lodge in." The allusion can be the less doubted, inasmuch as what follows, " I go to prepare a place for you," stands in undeniable relation to that narrative: comp. ver. 31, where Laban says, " Come in, thou blessed of the Lord; wherefore standest thou without? *for I have prepared the house."* Sept. ἐγὼ δὲ ἡτοίμασα τὴν οἰκίαν. We see from such an allusion as this, what high value the Old Testament had in the Saviour's estimation. From a matter of common history there He derives here the words for the presentation of a supremely important truth. There is a real parallel, though not verbal, with these many mansions, in Matt. xxv. 34, where Jesus speaks of that kingdom which had been prepared for the blessed of the Father from the foundation of the world.

"If it were not so, I would have told you," is, in another form, the same as "Verily, verily, I say unto you," in ver. 12. The disciples might absolutely rely upon it; and in this confidence might count it for nothing that the earth seemed to have no more place for them,—comp. ch. xvi. 2; Rev. xiii. 17,—and that the cry, ἆρον, ἆρον, John xix. 15, was lifted up on all sides against them. For He who gave them this assurance was the only True Being—He of whom it is written, "There was no guile found in His mouth," Isa. liii. 9, comp. 1 Pet. iii. 22; and who assuredly would not deceive His disciples with fallacious hopes. Heaven is an unknown land. It will be hard for men to obtain it by letters of commendation. If these are to have any value, the person who issues them must be absolutely confident, and enjoy an unlimited amount of personal confidence. Anton: "Here He speaks to His intimates. So great was their faith, that they believed what Christ said must be true, however hard they might find the application of it."

There can be no doubt that after "I would have told you" there must be interposed a period. If the connection is made, "If it were not so, I would have told you that I go to prepare a place," the going away to prepare a place is declared to be needless. But, according to ver. 3, Christ does actually go to prepare it. The ὅτι πορεύομαι, which is found in some considerable manuscripts, sprang from a false punctuation, and with a more correct punctuation must vanish. If we place a period after εἶπον ἂν ὑμῖν, the ὅτι can be justified only by a forced interpretation. That Christ goes away to prepare a place, is no apparent reason why there exist many mansions.

That the fact of there being many mansions does not exclude the Lord's work in preparing them, may be illustrated by the narrative of the patriarchal times, already referred to. Rebekah had said, "There is room to lodge in;" and yet Laban afterwards, "I have prepared the house, and room for the camels." The room may be there; but before it can be occupied, obstacles must be removed, and arrangements made.

In what way did our Lord provide a place for His people? He tells us Himself, in ch. xvi. 10. By His departure to the Father He obtained that righteousness which is the essential condition of entrance into the Father's house. By the propitiatory virtue of His sacrifice of His life for the sheep, ch. x. 11, the partition between heaven and earth was done away. Eternal life was won, when Christ, the antitype of the brazen serpent in the wilderness, took sin upon Himself, and expiated it as a substitute, ch. iii. 15. But with the atoning sufferings there was connected, in order to the preparation of heavenly places, the resurrection and ascension of the Redeemer. He must first enter as our πρόδρομος, our Forerunner, into eternal glory, Heb. vi. 20. The Head must be in heaven before the members can enter there. To be in heaven is to be with Christ. We can conceive of the glory of believers only as the participation in His glory, as their assumption into glorious fellowship with Him.

Our entrance into the glory of heaven being thus made so entirely dependent upon Christ, His atoning sacrifice and entrance into glory, it follows, that in the times before the Christian economy this entrance was not fully opened, and that the pious of the Old Testament were only in a state of preparation. Christ first perfectly abolished death, and brought life and immortality to light, 2 Tim. i. 10. The paradise in which, according to Luke xxiii. 43, the penitent thief was to be with Christ, was opened first by Him.

He who receives and retains in his heart the full force of this text, must attain to an estimate of temporal things quite different from that which is held by the world. He has in himself an inalienable heritage which infinitely transcends all earthly good. St Basil, when the prefect of the Arian emperor threatened that he would persecute him by land and sea, and tauntingly asked him where he would abide then, said, with allusion to this passage, "Either under heaven or in heaven." Luther answered Cardinal Cajetan in a similar way: "If the earth has no place for me, yet heaven will."

Ver. 3. " And if I go and prepare a place for you, I will come again, and receive you unto Myself ; that where I am, there ye may be also."—Here we have the third thing: the abodes are there; Christ prepares them; and He receives His own to Himself. That which is here said of the coming of Christ, receives illustration from the example of Stephen. He, at the hour of his death, Acts vii. 55, beholds the glory of God, and Jesus standing at the right hand of God. In his last word, " Lord Jesus, receive my spirit," he addresses Him as present, and yields to Him his soul, that He may introduce it into heavenly glory. We have here the comforting assurance that the Lord is personally present at every deathbed of believers ; and in harmony with this assurance, we have countless records of dying experience, in which faith has been in such energetic exercise as to become sight. To set aside this consolatory truth by any qualifying interpretation, is wrong; nor is there any reason for doing so, since, according to vers. 18 seq., the entire life of believers is pervaded by manifestations of the Lord; and it is to be understood as self-evident, that He accompanies His own through the valley. The angel of the Lord, who appeared to Abraham in a bodily prelude of His incarnation, says, in Gen. xviii. 14, " At the time appointed I will return unto thee, and Sarah shall have a son ;" and that He fulfilled His word, is manifest from ch. xxi. 1, " And the Lord visited Sarah, as He had said." If, at the hour of birth, the Son of God is near, why should He not much rather be near in the hour of death ? The Lord teaches us, in Luke xvi. 22, that in the last hour the heavenly powers are especially active : the angels carry Lazarus into Abraham's bosom. The other interpretations have sprung from the fact, that men have taken "I come again" separately from " and receive you unto Myself " (with which, however, it is so inseparably connected, that there is not even a comma between them), and have then compared with it other passages in which the coming of the Lord is spoken of, interpreting this by those. It is obvious, from the nature of the case, that the coming of the Lord is a manifold and various coming ; for He is the Living One. Where a cold faith thinks only of an indefinite working from afar, there a living faith apprehends a real coming down from above. Here we have not simply a figure derived from sense, but the actual truth of the matter. The Lord, according to Rev. ii. 1, walks in the midst of the seven golden candlesticks: He is everywhere present in His Church upon earth, and everywhere in ceaseless activity. And it is a fundamental view of the Apocalypse, that wherever He works He comes. With the coming of ver. 18 seq. the coming of our present passage has nothing to do. There it is not the receiving the disciples home that is spoken of, but rather the tokens and manifestations by which Christ declares Himself to His people during their pilgrimage to be the Living One. The eschatological interpretation (Origen: "He means His second coming from heaven;" so Lampe: "He speaks of His final coming visibly in the clouds of heaven," Acts i. 11) overlooks the fact that the Lord's utterance was primarily addressed to the Apostles, and that we must include here only what was an advantage to them personally; and it forgets the connection with the word spoken to Peter, ὕστερον δὲ ἀκολουθήσεις μοι, ch. xiii. 36. There is no reason why we should rob ourselves of the gracious consolation which this declaration of our Lord reserves for the time of our departure; we should rather receive it into our heart, and overcome by it all the terrors of death, which then assumes a friendly aspect, when we know that the Lord accompanies it, to take us to Himself.—"And receive you unto Myself:" heaven is made heaven really and truly only by our entering there into the most direct personal fellowship with Christ, whom upon earth we loved. Luther: "So that ye have most assuredly, both at once, the mansions in heaven and Me with you for all eternity." Christ Himself, without any veil, and without any medium, without anything that in our present life interposes between Him and us—that is the profoundest desire of the soul in this valley of tears. And that desire will be satisfied when He shall come and receive us home to Himself.

"After Christ," observes Lampe, "had, in vers. 2 and 3, shown that eternal salvation was connected with this going away, He now enumerates the several benefits which the disciples would have to expect upon earth through Himself and for His sake." First, in vers. 4–11, to His people, through their knowledge of Him the way is open to heavenly blessedness, and to that glorious house of the Father. To be in possession of the right way to heaven, is a precious consolation in our present troubled life ; through that we are enabled, in this miserable world, to wait patiently for the blessed time when we shall reach the house of our Father and the presence of our Lord.

Ver. 4. " And whither I go ye know, and the way ye know."—Jesus here passes over to the exhibition of the second ground of encouragement. The emphasis must be laid on the *way*. This is evident from what follows, where the way is spoken of simply and alone, not the place to which Jesus was going. Hence it does not refer to the way Christ Himself was taking, but to that way which His disciples must enter in order to reach His presence. We are led to the same conclusion by the relation in which the *way* stands to the last words of ver. 3, " that where I am, there ye may be also ;" as also by the whole tenor of the thought in vers. 2 and 3, which is this, that heaven is not for Christ alone, but also for His disciples.—The abbreviated reading, ὅπου ὑπάγω οἴδατε, τὴν ὁδόν, which gives a very uncouth construction, is not essentially different from the common one, since even in it the emphasis lies upon the *way*. Perhaps it was a right apprehension of this that led to the abbreviation.

The way is not generally the way to God, but the way to the Father's house ; the way, therefore, to eternal life, the method and manner of attaining it. That Christ Himself, or faith in Him, was that way, the disciples had had abundant occasion to learn. The Lord had at an earlier time emphatically and repeatedly so declared : for example, He had, in ch. v. 24, said, " He that heareth My word, and believeth on Him that sent Me, hath everlasting life ;" in ch. vi. 40, 47, " He that believeth on Me hath everlasting life ;" in ch. xi. 25, " I am the resurrection and the life : he that believeth on Me shall never die." He had in the words immediately preceding declared it to be Himself who would prepare for His people mansions in eternal life, and then receive them there. In such a connection, no other way to heaven could occur to the disciples' thoughts than Himself.

The definite words in which a knowledge of the way to heaven was here attributed to the disciples, were intended to expose to them the uncertainty in which they still remained, to give occasion for further instruction upon it, and to ensure for that other instruction a ready access. The taking their knowledge for granted served here the same purpose as, in Rev. vii. 13, the question by which the knowledge of ignorance was communicated, and occasion taken to impart instruction in the most effectual way. "Ye *know*," however, maintains its truth; and there is no reason for assuming, with Lampe, that Jesus attributed to them a knowledge of that which they might and ought to have known. The disciples knew more than they supposed. (Augustin: Sciebant discipuli, sed se scire nesciebant.) As certainly as they believed in Jesus, so certainly had they recognised in Jesus the true way to heaven. But their sorrow had thrown for a moment a cloud over their knowledge, and this cloud the Lord now sought to disperse.

Ver. 5. "Thomas saith unto Him, Lord, we know not whither Thou goest; and how can we know the way?"—It is not without significance that the words "called Didymus" are not added, as in ch. xi. 16, xx. 24, xxi. 2. It shows us that Thomas does not here exhibit his own peculiar spiritual character, but only expresses what was common to all. Accordingly, he does not speak in his own name, but in the name of all; and Jesus, in ver. 7, presupposes that it was the general spirit that spoke in him. Circumstances were already beginning to be such, that the differences between the man of rock and the man of doubt were done away. "*All* ye shall be offended because of Me this night," said Jesus, Matt. xxvi. 31, and this offence even now began to be developed.—"We know not whither Thou goest" must be more carefully interpreted than it has been by most expositors. Christ must have spoken altogether in vain to His disciples, if they had not understood that He was going to heaven, to the glory of the Father. He had, indeed, in so many words, told them that He was going to the Father's house; and that that Father's house was heaven, every child in Israel knew full well. "He that dwelleth in heaven" was, on the basis of Ps. ii., one of the most common designations of God. But the understanding of the disciples was only external. They were altogether sunk in grief at the departure of their Master, and in anxious solicitude on account of the abandonment and danger that impended over them. Heaven had become to them an unknown land; they could not spiritually accompany their Master on the way that lay before Him. And on that very account they could, in a realizing manner, apprehend the way for themselves to heaven. If the way of Christ was obscure, their own would be obscure also. Only when with clear glance they could accompany their Lord into the regions of light beyond, were they in a position to discern in Him the plain way to heaven. When the heavenly glory of Christ was obscured to them, their eyes were necessarily holden that they could not discern the shining path, the way of holiness, Isa. xxxv. 8, which would guide them from this world to the next. This way is no other than Christ Himself; and he who has not penetrated to a clear perception of the heavenly glory of Christ, must also lose His track upon earth. Berl. Bible: "The clearness of knowledge may, in the dark hour, be much dimmed. Christ the sun, however, is there, although behind the clouds."

Ver. 6. "Jesus saith unto him, I am the way, and the truth, and the life: no man cometh unto the Father, but by Me."—When our Lord calls Himself the way, that means more than merely the guide. "The example," says Luther, "of Christ is very precious, but it is too high for us, and we cannot follow it. I must have a firm and sure bridge which will carry me over." The word "I am the way," points to the fact that he who would enter heaven must be baptized and lost in Christ, so that not he himself shall live, but Christ in him. Jesus does not only show the way: He is the way. Only in absolute union to His person, only in the most internal fellowship with Him, can heaven be attained. This shows us the deep misery of our fallen nature, which of itself is altogether excluded from heaven. "Many paths paved by Divinity lead to happiness" is the maxim of the world; Christ declares these many ways to be only by-paths and ways of error. He teaches only one way—Himself; and to know only one, is the note and badge of His disciples. The "particularism," the individuality, which is now, under the dominion of rationalism, so much scorned, is the signature of the Christian Church. "With this one stroke," says an old expositor, "Christ rejects all the worship of the heathen, of Mohammedans, and Jews outside the Church;" and, we would add, the delusion of all deists, freemasons, and rationalists. "Here is," says Luther, "another marvellous thing; and this is what St John is evermore urging, that all our doctrine and believing must tend to Christ." "A Carthusian monk makes a way in which he would reach to heaven: I will forsake the world as wicked and impure; I will go into a corner, fast every day, eat no flesh, and plague my body; such vigorous spiritual life God will regard, and by it save me." The rationalist thinks that, in a way of righteousness much less anxiously sought out, he will attain to heaven. But the true Church of Christ knows, with Him, no other way than He Himself.

The words, "and the truth, and the life," must essentially intimate the same thing. For the clause, "No man cometh unto the Father but by Me," refers back to "I am the way." Accordingly, the clause intervening must present the same relation under another expression: I am the way, because the truth and the life. This is important in the consideration of many expositions given of the words, especially of καὶ ἡ ἀλήθεια. That exposition is the only right one according to which the truth does not remain apart from the way and the life: the only idea of truth appropriate here is that in which Christ, as the truth, is at the same time the way and the life; just as all definitions of the way are inadmissible which remain apart from the idea of truth and of life.

Hence "I am the truth" cannot refer to the truth of words, but only to the truth of being, from which indeed truth of words necessarily flows. I am the truth is the same as, I am Jehovah; for Jehovah, Jahve, means the Being, the pure absolute existence, independent of which all is delusion, in whom all must participate who would be partakers of that Being which is the only source of all creaturely existence.

"I am the truth:" thereby the Lord primarily places Himself in opposition to all that is created, to the world and all that therein is. But the exclusiveness refers in a certain sense even to the Father and the Holy Spirit. To men, Christ is the truth; if, passing by Him, they would seek the truth in God or the Spirit, they find nothing but delusion and a lie. Only in Him is the Father and the Holy Ghost accessible to man as the truth.

If Christ is the way, He must also in this sense be the truth; and were He not the truth in this sense, He could not be the way. No man can win heaven who does not, in personal union with the personal truth, attain to redemption from the miserable delusion of the present world, from the shining impiety of its virtues, the wretched phrases of its truths, the hollowness of its inspirations, and the hypocrisy of all its views. If Christ is the truth, He must also be the way. He who is baptized into the truth, and penetrated by it, he who is taken up into the fellowship of the personal truth, has heaven opened to him,—that abode of truth which is the absolute opposite of the vanity and the lie which from the Fall has set up its seat in the earth.

The Old Testament passage in which the word truth occurs in this sense is Jer. x. 10: "But the Lord is the true God, He is the living God, and an everlasting King." Jehovah as truth (Michaelis: veritas in re) forms here the contrast to the false gods, whose nature is nothing else than deception and nothingness. That passage is seen the more certainly to be connected with this one, from the circumstance that there also the truth is conjoined with the *life*. There it is the effect of the truth of God that before His wrath the earth quakes, and the nations cannot abide His indignation. This shows that truth does not there mean truth of words, but truth of being. That which is there uttered of Jehovah, is here appropriated by Christ to Himself; as truth is to lie, in Rom. i. 25, the relation of God is to the idols. The truth of God means there, that He is as such the possessor of all true being, and that out of Him there is nothing but vanity; whence the necessary consequence is, that he who would be a partaker of the truth must partake of it only in fellowship with God.

In ch. i. 14, Christ is spoken of as "full of grace and *truth;*" by that very word He is exalted above humanity, and placed in the Divine sphere, whose high prerogative it is alone to possess the truth. In Rev. iii. 7 we read, "These things saith He that is holy, He that is true." There we cannot limit the meaning to the truth of words. That truth of being is signified, may be inferred from the fact that truth is there in juxtaposition with holiness, absolute supremacy above all that is created. In Rev. xix. 11, Christ as the True One is the antithesis of Ps. cxvi. 11, "All men are liars," who deceive those who trust in them, and cannot help those who hope in them. The truth of the nature of Christ, which is based upon His almightiness and true divinity, appears there as the guarantee of His Church's victory. In 1 John v. 20, the True One is simply and as such identified with the true God; Christ is there first termed "He that is true," and then designated the true *God* and eternal life.

As Christ is the truth, so also He is the *life:* comp. on ch. i. 4. He who is not in fellowship with Him, has only the semblance of living; in reality he is dead, a walking corpse. Truth and life go hand in hand. Where truth is—true being, without the alloy of delusion and untruth—there is also life, and thence vanish all the miserable restraints which compass about on all sides the existence which is fallen into delusion and the lie.

There is no reason why we should restrict the *coming to the Father* to another world. Its meaning rather is generally a relation to the Father. Where such a relation is entered into, the way also to the Father's *house* is opened: it were impossible that He, after the pilgrimage of life is over, should leave those without who once belonged to Him; just as, on the other hand, it were impossible that those should enter the Father's house who never stood in any such personal relation to Him during their life upon earth. The words mean this: No man cometh to the Father, and therefore to the Father's house. That this phrase must be regarded as expressing generally a relation to the Father, is shown moreover by ver. 7, where *knowing the Father* corresponds to *coming to the Father* here; and with the negative the positive runs parallel: every man who receiveth Me cometh to the Father, and so to the Father's house.

This saying of our Lord is full of consolation. No crosses, no tribulations, however severe, can rob Christians of the confidence that they have in Christ, the way, the truth, and the life; that they are in Him redeemed from the oppressive empire of vanity, under which the soul that thirsts after true possessions, τὸ ἀληθινόν, Luke xvi. 11, is condemned, and from the thraldom of death, which has ever from the Fall compassed man about in all its variety of forms; that they are in the way to that heaven which has come down to earth in the truth and the life, and to which truth and life aspire back as their home. Those things which cannot deprive us of the truth and the life and the heavenly way, are in reality not afflictions; they are, indeed, if they tend to bring us into nearer connection with the truth and the life, to be esteemed rather as "pure joy," James i. 2. This is the right spiritual estimate of all the trials of life and all suffering in the world, which indeed are hard to human nature, and against which human nature continually rebels.

Ver. 7. "If ye had known Me, ye should have known My Father also: and from henceforth ye know Him, and have seen Him."—Luther: "If ye had known Me. This knowledge of Christ is not that of which St Paul speaks, the knowing after the flesh; but it is the knowing how to regard Him, what we have in Him, and how we may enjoy Him. This is not attained by high-minded hypocrites, but by the lowly, contrite hearts and troubled consciences; and by them not without care and trouble, so that they must concern themselves mightily about it." "If ye had known Me" intimates that the disciples had not yet pressed into a perfect knowledge of Christ, and therefore of the Father; of the Father who perfectly reveals Himself in Christ, the express image of His person, in whom, as St Paul says, Col. ii. 9, the fulness of the Godhead dwelleth bodily. "From henceforth ye know Him:" this shows that, objectively considered, this knowledge of God was assured to them by the manifestation of Christ in the flesh, and their internal communion with Him; the necessary consequence being, that, in their willing docility, this knowledge was to all intents and purposes already fundamentally in them. "If ye had known Me" certainly required some following qualification, otherwise there would have arisen a contradiction with ver. 4 (the way ye know); and the disciples would have been placed on a level with the Jews, to whom Jesus in ch. viii. 19 said, "If ye had known Me, ye would have known My Father also." The objective character of the γινώσκετε—that it primarily refers to a knowledge *offered*—is shown by the fact that ἑωράκατε, ye have seen, is added, this being afforded directly by the manifestation of Christ. That which was intended first of all to soften the asperity of the blame, and to save the disciples from the painful feeling which the parallel with the unbelieving Jews would have excited, served at the same time as an admonition that they should ponder what was given them, and not, by a denial of the knowledge already imparted, sink down to the low and melancholy level of the Jews, who, dishonouring the Son, had lost the Father also. Ἀπάρτι, from this time forward, ch. xiii. 19. The *now* does not mean the then present moment, but the time since they had learnt to know Christ. The Lord divides the existence of the disciples into two halves, formerly and now. The line of demarcation in their life was their relation to Christ. Before they had seen and known Him, they knew not the Father; in Christ they had learnt to know the Father, and thus gained the certain way to the Father's house. In 1 Cor. xiii. 12 also, ἄρτι occurs in the sense, not of a moment, but of a period.

If the γινώσκετε is at once referred to a subjective knowledge, we must either, with Lampe, interpolate an exposition, "Ye begin now to know;" or, with Lücke, we must give it a future application, and extract from it the consolatory assurance, "that the hour is not now far distant, when the former ignorance of the disciples would be exchanged for clear knowledge." Against the latter view it may be observed, that the present, γινώσκετε, and still more the perfect, ἑωράκατε, evidence that a knowledge is meant which the disciples already enjoyed. (Both are united, as here, in the passage of Demosthenes cited by Winer: ἀνθρώπῳ ὃν ἡμεῖς οὔτε γινώσκομεν οὔθ' ἑωράκαμεν πώποτε.) But ver. 9 excludes all doubt. There Jesus mourns that Philip had denied the knowledge already imparted. That such a knowledge was intended, is shown also by the word spoken to him in ver. 8, which on any other supposition is unintelligible.

Ver. 8. "Philip saith unto Him, Lord, show us the Father, and it sufficeth us."—The Apostles had hitherto seen Christ only in the form of a servant, in the humiliation under which the glory of the Father was profoundly hidden. At the Transfiguration it was only transitorily shone through; and that sublime spectacle was witnessed not by all the disciples, but only by the most advanced. Under these circumstances, it was natural that the disciples, having in their view the prophecies of the Old Testament, which always presented a prospect of the glorious revelation of the glory of the Lord, Isa. xl. 5, and having further in their view the impending severe trials and dangers which would demand a mighty auxiliary for their faith, should be unable altogether to reconcile themselves to the fact that they were so absolutely referred to Christ in regard to their relation to the Father, and should feel a disposition to ask for a revelation of the Father besides that of Christ, in order to their invigoration in their perilous path, more especially as their spiritual eye was not yet strong enough to discern the glory which was hidden under so thick a veil of humiliation. Their rising desire was gratified when the concealed glory of Christ burst through in the resurrection, in the ascension, and in those great victories which the Church through Christ gained over the world, ver. 12. Then the Father was plainly and obviously shown to them; although not in the way here desired by Philip, beside Christ, but in Christ. That which was natural and excusable in the Apostles, if not altogether justifiable, ver. 9, because it sprang from the dimness of their vision, which could not discern the glory behind the form of a servant, would be now, after the means for sharpening the spiritual vision have been afforded through the outpouring of the Holy Spirit, and when we have before us the glorious evidences and tokens of the ascended Lord, and of His triumph through the Christian ages, a melancholy anachronism. Where a similar desire now arises, it springs from a less excusable source. Christ must dwell in the heart by faith, if His spiritual glory is to be beheld. That man in whose heart, through his own fault, He has not taken up His abode, has eyes which see not, and ears which hear not. It is his righteous punishment that he is excluded, as from the Son, so also from the Father.

The Apostles exhibit their faith in Christ in this, that they ask of Him to bring about the manifestation of the Father which they desire. And they are all the more justified in putting that request, because in the earlier days of their predecessors and types, such a manifestation of the glory of the Lord was vouchsafed to the elders of Israel for the strengthening of their faith: comp. Ex. xxiv. 9-11. They did not consider that the mediator of the old covenant was, unlike the Mediator of the new, a weak man, who needed to exhibit to the representatives of the people an authentication direct from God, and who needed himself to be invigorated by such a manifestation to his faith. To desire such a revelation under the New Testament, was a virtual denial of the divinity of Christ, which could not but meet with such an earnest rejection. This refusal, however, could not be absolutely severe, but rather full of tenderness, inasmuch as the revelation of the Father in Christ had not yet finished its course and reached its consummation. Καὶ ἀρκεῖ ἡμῖν points to the fact that they had not reached full satisfaction through any revelation of the Father in Christ which they had yet beheld: comp. 2 Cor. xii. 9.

Ver. 9. "Jesus saith unto him, Have I been so long time with you, and yet hast thou not known Me, Philip? he that hath seen Me hath seen the Father; and how sayest thou then, Show us the Father?"—Jesus could not possibly have cut off all immediate relation of believers to the Father, and required that the Father be sought only in Himself, if it were not that the being of the Father and the being of the Son perfectly coincided with each other, and the whole fulness of the Gospel dwelt in Himself bodily, and the Father had poured into Him all the riches of His essence. Otherwise, it would have been a betrayal both of the Father and of the believers. The Supreme God cannot give His glory to another; and the human heart thirsts for God, for the living God, nor can it be satisfied with any quasi-god, with any mere "divine being."—The appeal by name served to prick the disciple's conscience, and to remind him that he had become *alius a seipso*, an alien to himself.— Bengel rightly deduces from the Lord's utterance here the inviolable rule: In omni cogitatione de Deo debemus Christum proponere. The duty, however, is subordinate here. The main thing is the consolation, the great grace, that the God who in Himself is a hidden God, has become perfectly revealed to us in Christ. "Have I been so long time with you," has now for us become a much wider and more comprehensive truth.

Ver. 10. "Believest thou not that I am in the Father, and the Father in Me? the words that I speak unto you, I speak not of Myself: but the Father, that dwelleth in Me, He doeth the works."—The two clauses, "I am in the Father," and "the Father is in Me," denote only the same relation under two aspects. From this it follows that the two clauses which serve for the illustration of that relation,—and of which the former formally refers to the "I am in the Father," the latter to "the Father is in Me,"—do, in reality, refer to both. It might just as well have stood, "The words which I speak, speaketh the Father Himself; and the works which I do, I do in the Father."—The explanation is at the same time proof.

This is shown by a comparison with such parallels as ch. x. 37, 38. The demonstrative argument in the *words* of Christ is seen in ch. vii. 46, where the servants of the high priests say, "Never man spake like this man," and ch. vi. 68, 69, where Peter says to Christ, "Lord, Thou hast the words of eternal life," and bases upon the words of Christ his faith that Jesus was the Christ, the Son of God. Christ Himself, ch. vi. 63, demonstrates from His words that He shared the Divine nature: "The words which I speak unto you, they are spirit, and they are life." With regard to the works, comp. on ch. v. 36, x. 25, 26. These works are not exclusively the miracles proper: *every* act of Christ is, as an outbeaming of His nature, demonstrative of His unity with the Father; yet the works have their climax in the miracles, because these form the most palpable evidence of the saying, "I and the Father are one." The "dwelling" or abiding indicates habitual indwelling, in opposition to a merely transitory influence and operation, such as men enjoyed under the Old Testament.

Ver. 11. "Believe Me that I am in the Father, and the Father in Me: or else believe Me for the very works' sake."— Heumann: "O how would the disciples be humbled by this address, in which our Lord spoke in such a manner as if He doubted as to their faith in Himself!" With this we must compare ch. x. 38. His disciples ought first of all to believe Christ's *utterance* as to His relation to the Father, as it was delivered by the impression of His whole personality. But if they were in circumstances which would not allow of this, they should at least believe on account of the works. In connection with these might, as in ver. 10, the *words* have been named, the whole sum of His spirit-breathing, life-breathing discourses, in contradistinction to the mere utterance concerning His being one with the Father. But the Lord falls back upon the *works* alone, because these furnished the most palpable evidence. The works themselves: this points to the fact that these alone were sufficient for demonstration. Luther: "This is the style in which St John and St Paul, before others, teach in this matter, firmly uniting together Christ and the Father, in order that we may learn not to think anything about God apart from Christ, and to hide and wrap ourselves in His Christ.—Here is a beautiful word and sermon for the Apostle Philip, in which not only is *he* answered, but the fluctuating thoughts of all men; for the whole world and thyself are here told by the Lord: Wherefore wilt thou seek God otherwise than in Me, or desire to see and hear any other word and work than that which I speak and do?"

In vers. 12-14 we have the *third* ground of consolation. Christ had finally, with express emphasis, referred to His *works*. Out of the consolation there sprang up to the disciples a new element of sorrow. These works must, it seemed to them, cease with the departure of the Lord. Left to their own poverty and impotence, they must, in opposition to the unfriendly word, fare but miserably. That was about to be removed which had given some measure of firmness to all. It is against this grief that their Master here consoles them. The works would not cease with His departure; they should rather, in consequence of His departure, rise to a higher level of energy and significance. He who should be elevated to the glory of the Father, would, by His disciples, perform yet greater works. They should only ask; and out of His inexhaustible riches they should obtain all that their necessities might demand.

Ver. 12. "Verily, verily, I say unto you, He that believeth on Me, the works that I do shall he do also; and greater works than these shall he do: because I go unto My Father."—This vigorous assurance shows at the outset how far beyond the horizon of the disciples lay the promise that followed. The Lord had, in ch. v. 20, described the works which He performed during His earthly life as the mere prelude to greater works. The greatest deeds which, in the Old Testament, were ascribed to the Messiah, were at this time scarcely even inaugurated. He was to be the light of the Gentiles, Isa. xlii. 6; and to rule from sea to sea, and from the river to the ends of the earth, Ps. lxxii. 8; Zech. ix. 10; all kings were to worship Him, all the heathen serve Him, Ps. lxxii. 11. The root of Jesse, which stood as an ensign to the nations, the Gentiles were to seek unto, Isa. xi. 10. Of all this there was as yet but the faint anticipation. And the great Messianic work of grace and judgment upon the Jewish people, as foreannounced by the prophets, was as yet far from accomplished. Instead of the hundreds of believers from among the Jews who were assembled during the Lord's life, 1 Cor. xv. 6, many myriads were won by the preaching of the Apostles after the Lord's resurrection, Acts xxi. 20. And as it regards the judgment upon them, the withering of the fig-tree of the Jewish people took place only in *symbol* shortly before the departure of Christ; and the actual rooting up of those plants which the heavenly Father had not planted was left to the future, to be the work of the exalted Redeemer, and to those prayers of believers which should evoke His work; for, according to Matt. xxi. 21, the withering of the fig-tree appears as the work, in this sense, of the believers themselves.

The antithesis is, in fact, not between Christ and His disciples, but between the humble and the exalted Christ. His disciples accomplish their works only as the organs of the ascended Lord, and by His assistance. The whole power of performance is here expressly placed in the disciples' faith in Christ; in the words " because I go to the Father" it is based upon the glorification of Christ, and the omnipotence connected with it; in ver. 13, whose ποιήσω refers back to the ποιήσει of ver. 12, Christ alone is exhibited as acting, while the co-operation of the disciples is referred to their *prayer*. Without Me, said the Lord in ch. xv. 5, ye can do nothing.

The Apostles are not specifically spoken of, but generally all who believe in Christ. We are therefore justified to seek the fulfilment of these words in the whole course of the history of the Christian Church.

With " The works that I do shall he do" we must compare Mark xvi. 17, 18. There the works are individually enumerated. But we must regard that enumeration as only an individualizing. Behind these palpable signs stand others, which are more concealed and less obvious, but in reality much greater: the miraculous power which Christ will assure to His people for the conversion of individuals and nations, for the effect of regeneration in a world corrupted to the very centre, for their victory over the whole hostile force of the world, and over its prince who wields that force. That of this we are especially to think, is plain from " greater things shall he do." In reference to miracles, commonly so called, Christ was not *surpassed* by His disciples; on the contrary, they were considerably inferior to Him. But in what domain we are chiefly to seek the works here spoken of, ch. xii. 32 teaches us: " And I, if I be lifted up from the earth" (this corresponds to the " going to the Father" here), "will draw all men unto Me." Hence the great work which was to be accomplished after the exaltation of Christ, and in the power of that exaltation, was *the conversion of the world*, specially the heathen nations. Further, in ch. x. 16, where our Lord thus exhibits the result of His atoning death, and the great task to be fulfilled after it: "And other sheep I have, which are not of this fold: these also must I bring, and they shall hear My voice; and there shall be one fold, and one shepherd." So also we may compare Matt. xxviii. 18–20. There the Lord bases upon the "power" given unto Him in heaven and earth as the result of His atoning passion, the injunction, "Go ye forth and disciple all nations," and promises that He would be with them to the end of the world for the accomplishment of a work immeasurably surpassing all human power. We have also an illustration of the "greater works than these shall he do" in the Apocalypse, which depicts the marvellous victory of Christ and His members over the Gentile world and its prince; compare particularly, ch. xvii. 14: "These shall make war with the Lamb, and the Lamb shall overcome them: for He is Lord of lords, and King of kings; and they that are with Him are called, and chosen, and faithful." But the proper commentary on our text is furnished by a word spoken some days before to the disciples, Matt. xxi. 21, 22: "Verily I say unto you, If ye have faith, and doubt not, ye shall not only do this that is done to the *fig-tree*, but also, if ye shall say unto this *mountain*, Be thou removed, and be thou cast into the sea; it shall be done. And all things, whatsoever ye shall ask in prayer, believing, ye shall receive." This passage is closely connected with that we are considering. Ver. 22 absolutely coincides with ver. 13. They have in common also the introduction by "Verily," and the emphasis laid on *believing*. We see from this that the greater works were to consist in the victory over Jerusalem, and over the Gentile secular power then concentrated in Rome. It needs no proof that the fig-tree signified the Jewish people; and, of course, what they were to do must have referred to an antitypical action in something else, since the natural fig-tree was already destroyed. "This which is done to the fig-tree" must have referred to something yet to be done to its counterpart. So also, in connection with the fig-tree, the mountain must have had a symbolical meaning: nor can this be obviated by the suggestion that *this* mountain is spoken of; for a specific fig-tree was also spoken of. This fig-tree, this mountain, were sanctified into symbols of hostile powers. The mountain, in contradistinction to the fig-tree, can only be a symbol of Gentile temporal power. In the Old Testament, mountains are used as the ordinary symbols of kingdoms. In Zech. iv. 7, the great mountain is the Persian empire, which was in an attitude of opposition to the building of the Temple. In Jer. li. 25, the mountain which endangers the whole earth is the Chaldean empire. So the mountain here is the universal empire that then was, that of Rome. The sea is, according to the common symbolism of Scripture, the sea of nations: comp. on ch. vi. 14–21; Rev. viii. 8, 9, out of which the universal empire had arisen mightily in the time of its prosperity, but into which it now sinks back again through the faith of the disciples and the power of Christ. Rev. xviii. 21 is parallel, where we read, with reference to the Roman empire, and in allusion to Jer. li. 63, 64: "And a mighty angel took up a stone like a great millstone, and cast it into the sea, saying, Thus with violence shall that great city Babylon be thrown down, and shall be found no more at all." On the ground of the same passage in Jeremiah, our Lord, referring to the then ruling power, had already spoken, Matt. xviii. 6, of those who offended His little ones being cast into the sea with millstones.

The foundation of the doing works like Christ's, and still greater works, is to be found in the "going to the Father." What follows is only the further development of the idea, that Christ's work would not cease with His death; that the disciples need not fear that they would sink back into the darkness when the light of His works, which during His earthly life had irradiated them, was withdrawn; and that they would not be left to the consequences of their own impotence. The independence of the clause is confirmed by a comparison with ver. 28, where the "I go to the Father" stands in a similar independent position, and where the "My Father is greater than I" develops the consolatory meaning lying in those words. The independence of the clause in ver. 13, "And whatsoever ye shall ask," etc., is plain from Matt. xxi. 22, which accurately corresponds with this present saying. So also, from the repetition in ver. 14,

Jesus was going to the Father, into the glory which He had with Him before the world was, ch. xvii. 5; and He therefore could most mightily assist His disciples in the performance of greater works than He Himself, in the days of His servant form, could accomplish. To go to the Father was to enter into His glory, Luke xxiv. 26; and this glory could not but have a most pervasive influence upon His people below. When Jesus went to the Father, the grief of the disciples must be turned into joy, and their despondency into confidence. The departure of their Lord, which seemed to make them helpless, and abandon them an easy prey to the wolves, was the very condition and foundation of their power and of their victory. It made their Master's omnipotence available for them. "How should we not expect something more glorious from the exalted than from the humbled Christ?" Luther: "Christ going to the Father means, that He is exalted to the Lord above, and placed on a royal throne at the right hand of the Father, all power and authority being subjected to His sway in heaven and in earth. And ye shall therefore have the power to do such works, because ye are My members, and believe in Me, so that ye shall be in Me and I will be in you.—Now I am weak, because I yet walk here below in this flesh; and do slighter and less considerable works, only raising a few from the dead and healing a handful of Jews; and I must submit to be crucified and slain. But afterwards, when I have been crucified, have been buried, and have risen again, I shall make my great leap from death into life, from the cross and the sepulchre to eternal glory, and Divine majesty and power; and will then, as I have said, draw everything to Me, so that all creatures must be subjected to Me, and I can say to you, Apostles and Christians: Thou, Peter and Paul, go and overturn the Roman empire, if it will not receive My word and obey Me; for it must either receive the Gospel, or stumble over it to ruin."

This present saying of our Lord is not merely rich in consolation; it also gives occasion to rigid self-examination on the part of the Church and of individual Christians. Christ has here given solemn asseveration, that whosoever believeth on Him shall do works like those which He did while on earth, and even greater works. Therefore, when these works are found wanting there must be lack of faith: as Augustin says, Si ergo qui credit faciet, non credit utique qui non faciet. The complaint, which is now so common, over the corruption of the world, the feeble wail of despondency over the unbelief of the age, must be abashed before this utterance of our Lord. Christ sits for ever at the right hand of the Father, equipped with irresistible arms against all His enemies. But "faith faileth upon earth." There is, indeed, a difference of seasons in the kingdom of God; there are times in which power is given to the darkness; and, doubtless, such a time is that wherein we live. But our saying avails even for such times as these. The greater is the opposition, the more plainly is it the task of faith to do " greater works," and the richer is the aid which is given from on high for the accomplishment of this task.

Ver. 13. " And whatsoever ye shall ask in My name, that will I do, that the Father may be glorified in the Son."—" And," when I have gone to the Father; or, in virtue of My departure, through which I shall be received into the fellowship of the Divine omnipotence. The connection with ver. 12 shows that petitions are referred to here which have relation to the things of the kingdom of God: their effect is the performance of the works. Prayer directed to that object is for ever being answered; although the arrangement of the time and hour must be left to the wisdom of Him who sitteth at the right hand of the Father, and although the answer may be impeded by many weaknesses and defeats on our part.—To the *name* all expressions and revelations of the nature converge: comp. on ch. i. 12, ii. 23, v. 43, xii. 13. It corresponds to the *memorial*, or memory, to the historical personality. He who would pray to Christ in such a way as to be heard, must not set before his eyes a phantasy of his own imagination: he must represent to himself the corporeal form of the historical Christ, in the outlines which the Apostolical Confession of Faith presents to us; he must thoroughly renounce all idealistic refuges. Christ has, by His deeds upon earth, made unto Himself a glorious name (comp. Isa. lxiii. 14); first of all, by those which He performed in His state of humiliation, and since by the victorious course of eighteen hundred years in His Church; and whosoever would pray to Him with acceptable prayer, must in faith embrace the whole fulness of these manifestations of His name. Experience bears witness that prayer dies out in feebleness, precisely in proportion as the name of Christ is obscured to the mind by doubt.

He to whom the prayer is directed is designedly not named, because it would be matter of indifference, after Christ had gone to the Father, whether petitions were addressed to Him or to the Father. Both would come to the same thing; for, as Christ is in the midst of the throne, Rev. vii. 17, prayer truly offered to the Father is offered to Him, and prayer offered truly to Him is offered also to the Father. That supplication cannot be presented to the Father, as contradistinguished from Christ, is plain from the τοῦτο ποιήσω. If there were an alternative in the case, this expression would oblige us to assume that the prayer was to be addressed to the exalted Christ.—The ποιήσω here refers to the ποιήσει, in ver. 12. Luther: "What He had said about their doing greater works, He again appropriates to Himself." This was to the disciples, altogether penetrated by the consciousness of their impotence, not discouraging, but full of consolation. It might appear that the sphere of the Lord's action and the sphere of the disciples' action were different; but this distinction vanishes when we observe, that even in those cases in which the act seemed to belong to Christ alone (such as the destruction of Jerusalem), the disciples were actually co-operating by their prayer, and that, on the other hand, there could be no work done by the disciples alone without the effectual aid of Christ.—" That the Father may be glorified in the Son:" the aim of the acting of Christ is primarily His own glorification. But this reflects back on the Father. When it is seen that the Son can do great things, says Theophylact, He is glorified who hath begotten such a Son.

Ver. 14. "If ye shall ask anything in My name, I will do it."—We have here an express repetition, which, with its ἀμὴν, ἀμὴν, at the beginning, springs from the same source. It is intended to furnish supplication with a yet firmer ground of confidence. Luther: "Our Lord Christ foresaw that this article would go hard with human reason, and that it would be much assailed by the devil." Comp. Ps. lxii. 12: "God hath spoken once, yea, twice have I heard this, that power belongeth unto God." God said it not once only, but confirmed it by a second assurance, that all power was His. So also in 1 John ii. 14, repetition has the effect of stronger assurance. The ἐγώ, which

CHAP. XIV. 15.

Gerhard describes as a word of majesty, gives great prominence to the supreme authority of Christ in His exalted state: it is as it were, I to whom all power is given in heaven and upon earth. Luther: "What ye ask, I will do: this is as much as to say, I am God, who may do and give all things."

In vers. 15-17 follows the *fourth* ground of consolation. Christ had foreannounced to His disciples, that they would be brought before judgment-seats, and princes, and kings. The contemplation of this must have invested His departure with every element of sadness. Their confidence in their conflict with the world had hitherto rested upon the fact, that they had Him in their midst as their champion and advocate. They were themselves ἄνθρωποι ἀγράμματοι καὶ ἰδιῶται, Acts iv. 13. What should they be able to attempt and accomplish after the departure of the Lord, when the contest with the world grew more and more fierce? The sorrow and anxiety of this prospect our Lord obviates here by His consoling word: He would send His people another Advocate in their process against the world,—an Advocate who should, during all the ages of the militant Church, abide with them, assist their infirmity, and conduct their cause with full efficiency—the Spirit of truth. Lampe thinks that the promise of the mission of the Holy Ghost was appropriately connected with the preceding, because in it was given the power for the accomplishment of the greater works. But the fact is, that with regard to the greater works, the disciples were referred not to the Holy Spirit, but to the power of the glorified Christ. The Holy Spirit appears here only in His proper function, as Intercessor, Advocate, or Comforter.

Ver. 15. "If ye love Me, keep My commandments."—This is the condition to which the fulfilment of the promise now to be given is attached. What is here, where the main point was consolation, only hinted at, is further dilated upon in ch. xv. And the hint given here leaves it to be expected that such a moral hortatory portion of the last discourses of our Lord was to follow. For if fidelity in the love of Christ, and in the observance of His commandments, is of such pervasive importance, surely it was not enough to deal with it only in the way of a brief and passing intimation. Jesus here most vitally and thoroughly connects together love to Himself, and the fulfilment of His commandments. He acknowledges no love which does not find its expression in the observance of His laws. These cannot be separated from the person : they are so many conditions, under which alone communion with His person is possible. On the other hand, our Lord recognises no fulfilment of His commandments which is not an outgoing of personal love to Himself. He condemns every other kind of fulfilment which springs only from temporal interest, from fear of punishment, from deference to public opinion, as mere illusion. It is expressly declared that love is the condition of all obedience to His commandments, and must approve itself in that obedience.

"*My* commandments :" Moses was not wont to speak thus. It implies the oneness of nature between Christ and the Supreme Lawgiver. Hence, in unison with this, we mark the intentional use of the same expressions which are used in the Old Testament with reference to Jehovah : comp. especially Ex. xx. 6, " And showing mercy unto thousands of them that love Me, and keep My commandments ;" Deut. vii. 9, " The faithful God, which keepeth covenant and mercy with them that love Him, and keep His commandments, to a thousand generations ;" ver. 11, " Thou shalt therefore keep the commandments, and the statutes, and the judgments which I command thee this day to do them ;" Ps. ciii. 17, 18, " But the mercy of the Lord is from everlasting to everlasting upon them that fear Him, and His righteousness unto children's children, to such as keep His covenant, and to those that remember His commandments to do them ;" Ps. xxv. 10. The two expressions of the Mosaic law come nearest to our passage. There the keeping of the commandments of God appears both as the guarantee and as the outflow of love to Him, as its inseparable attendant.—The commandments of the Old Testament were also the commandments of Christ; and they are included by Him when He speaks of *His* commandments. For He had solemnly recognised them, and exhorted His Church inviolably to keep them : comp. Matt. v. 17–20. But He did not simply receive them externally into His Gospel; He has everywhere modified, supplemented, and established them : comp. on ch. xiii. 34.—All old things in Him became new. For example, the first and greatest commandment of the Old Testament, that of the love of God, takes here, as we see in ch. xv., the form of a commandment to love Christ, who first loved His disciples; whilst the commandment to love our neighbour takes the form of a commandment to love the brethren who are sharers of the redemption in Christ. All Old Testament ordinances and precepts are baptized in Christ, and new-born in Him.

Ver. 16. " And I will pray the Father, and He shall give you another Comforter, that He may abide with you for ever." —Jesus does not supplicate His Father as a servant, but as the Son, to whom He can deny nothing. If we remember the τοῦτο ποιήσω, and the " because I go to the Father," in which Christ arrogates to Himself an absolute participation in the Divine glory, we might expect it to follow, " And I will send you another Intercessor," as we find it actually in ch. xvi. 7 : ἐὰν δὲ πορευθῶ πέμψω αὐτὸν πρὸς ὑμᾶς. But the phrase our Lord used received its character from the design, everywhere apparent (comp. ver. 13), to refer everything in its last issues to the Father, who was not, as it were, constrained by the mediation of the Son, but was to be brought nearer by Him to the spirits of men—infinitely nearer than He stood to them under the old dispensation. Luther says: " Christ asks the Father, not in His Divine being and nature, in which He is equally with the Father almighty, but because He is true man, Mary's son." But the Angel of the Lord also, the Logos, supplicated the Lord on behalf of His Church upon earth, Zech. i. 12 ; and the Lord assured Him that He was heard. " Another Intercessor:" Luther: " For I cannot be ever with you below in this manner. If I am to enter into My glory, and spread My kingdom by your means, I must die, and go to heaven, and leave you behind Me."

It seems at the first glance startling, that the sending of the Holy Ghost is here made conditional on the love of Christ and the keeping His commandments, while in 1 Cor. xii. 3 it is said, that no man can call Christ Lord but by the Holy Ghost. We have not, however, here to do with the mission of the Holy Ghost in general, but with His mission in a distinct relation, as the Paraclete, and as the Helper in that great process which the Church is ever vindicating against the world.

In regard to the Paraclete, expositors are very diverse. According to one party (Origen, Chrysostom, Cyril of Jerusalem, Theophylact, Luther), the word, which is used of the Holy Ghost only in the last discourses of Christ given by St

John (comp. ver. 26, xv. 26, xvi. 7; of Christ, in 1 John ii. 1), means comforter, consoler. According to another, it is a judicial expression to designate advocates in judicial processes. The upholders of this interpretation appeal to classical Greek usage, which is best explained in the treatise of Knapp, De Spiritu Sancto et Christo Paracletis (Opusc. t. i.), where παράκλητος, from παρακαλέω, to summon to aid, is used of those who, whether as agents or as influential friends, undertook the cause of those who stood before the judgment-seat.

But the interpretation *Comforter* has no trivial arguments in its favour. We read in Acts ix. 31, concerning the first Christian congregations, καὶ τῇ παρακλήσει τοῦ ἁγίου πνεύματος ἐπληθύνοντο, " and by the comfort of the Holy Ghost were multiplied:" comp. ch. vi. 1, 7, vii. 17. There the Holy Ghost is a comforting, encouraging Spirit. It is obvious to assume that we have here an exposition or paraphrase of the name Paraclete; and that He was called Paraclete on account of His consolation.

Further, the verb παρακαλέω is never used in the New Testament for summoning to aid; and therefore παράκλητος could not be derived from it as an adjective of passive signification, *advocatus*. It is always used in the sense of speaking to, or encouraging and comforting—in so many instances, indeed, amounting to more than a hundred, that the exclusiveness of this meaning can scarcely be accidental. In Acts xxviii. 20—the only place adduced by Knapp in support of the meaning, *summon to aid*—the common interpretation is appropriate: comp. ch. xxiv. 4.

Finally, παρακαλεῖτε παρακαλεῖτε τὸν λαόν μου, λέγει ὁ Θεός, is the beginning of the second part of Isaiah, to the commencement of which, especially ch. xl. 3–5, the New Testament repeatedly refers, and everywhere with the view that its fulfilment belongs to the time of the new economy: comp. on ch. i. 23, ii. 11.—St Luke, in ch. ii. 25, alluding to this παρακαλεῖτε, describes Simeon as προσδεχόμενος παράκλησιν τοῦ Ἰσραήλ. It is hard altogether to sunder this παράκλητος from that παρακαλεῖτε. The Son of man had hitherto fulfilled and realized this παρακαλεῖτε: after His departure, the Holy Spirit would take His place.

These are very plausible arguments; but their weight is overbalanced by those which support the other interpretation.

And first, the form is of decisive importance. Derived from the 3 Perf. Pass. it bears a passive character; παράκλητος can no more mean Comforter than κλητός can mean Caller. That the older Greek expositors attributed an active signification to this form, is a fact not sufficient to outweigh this argument. Nor is it of much moment that Aquila and Symmachus, in Job xvi. 2, use παρακλήτους where the Hebrew speaks of *comforters*, translated by the Septuagint παρακλήτορες and Symmachus παρηγοροῦντες. For even the παράκλητος, passively accepted, expresses the idea of supporting.

The second argument is, that we ought not, without due consideration, to forsake the classical Greek usage, in which παράκλητος always occurs in the sense of advocate-at-law. This has all the more force, inasmuch as the word bearing this meaning, and with it a series of other judicial expressions, had passed over into the Rabbinical phraseology; with the same meaning it is frequent in the writings of Philo (comp. Carpzov. Exerc. in Ep. ad Heb., p. 155; Loesner, Observ. ex Phil., p. 496), as also we find it in the epistle of Barnabas, who, in § 20, describes the wicked as πλουσίων παράκλητοι, πενήτων ἄνομοι κριταί.

In the document of the Church of Vienne (Eusebius, Hist. Ecc. v. 2) παράκλητος is used to designate one who represents the person of another in a judicial process. The passage is all the more remarkable, because it furnishes the first instance of an allusion to St John's sayings concerning the Paraclete, and because it goes on the supposition that they mention the word Paraclete with the meaning then current among Greek writers. Vettius Epagathus requests, when certain Christians were brought before the tribunal, that he might be heard ἀπολογούμενος ὑπὲρ τῶν ἀδελφῶν. This was refused him, and he was himself executed. It then goes on: ἀνελήφθη καὶ αὐτὸς εἰς τὸν κλῆρον τῶν μαρτύρων, παράκλητος Χριστιανῶν χρηματίσας, ἔχων δὲ τὸν παράκλητον ἐν ἑαυτῷ, τὸ πλεῖον τοῦ Ζαχαρίου, ὃ διὰ τοῦ πληρώματος τῆς ἀγαπῆς ἐνεδείξατο, εὐδοκήσας ὑπὲρ τῆς τῶν ἀδελφῶν ἀπολογίας καὶ τὴν ἑαυτοῦ θεῖναι ψυχήν. He receives the name of the Christian's Paraclete, not because he addressed comfort to them, but because he came forward as their advocate and intercessor; and he proved by this courageous intercession that he had within himself the Paraclete promised by Jesus to His disciples, who therefore was not to be a comforter, but only an intercessor.

The Christian's conflict with the world presents itself in many ways under the aspect of a judicial process; and it was with reference to this aspect of it that Jesus had already previously promised His people the assistance of the Holy Ghost. In Matt. x. 17, 18, He had predicted to His disciples, that "they will deliver you up to the councils, and they will scourge you in their synagogues, and ye shall be brought before governors and kings for My sake. But when they deliver you up," our Lord continued, "take no thought how or what ye shall speak; for it shall be given you in that same hour what ye shall speak. For it is not ye that speak, but the Spirit of your Father which speaketh in you." Here we have the full Paraclete, as he appears in classical writers, the agent and pleader at the bar; only the name παράκλητος is wanting. The parallel saying in Mark xiii. 9-11 is all the more appropriate in this connection, inasmuch as it occurs in a discourse which our Lord had delivered shortly before, on the Tuesday before the feast, and thus only two days previously.

If we understand Paraclete in the sense of comforter, it is hard to account for the narrowly restricted use of the word. As in our passage the Paraclete is promised to the disciples in connection with their relation to the world (comp. ver. 17), so also, in ch. xvi. 7, the promise of the mission of the Paraclete is connected with predictions of the world's persecutions (comp. ver. 1). Generally there is no passage in which the idea of representative or advocate is not appropriate. In ch. xv. 26, the Holy Spirit is called the Comforter only in reference to ch. xiv. 16: the same Person, whom I have promised to send as your advocate in the severe conflict with the world, will render you great assistances also in other respects. In 1 John ii. 1, Christ Himself exercises the function of an advocate for His own people with the Father. Christians have a hard double cause to carry through with God and with the world; and in neither can they succeed without a powerful representative. That such a relation of advocate to clients is not limited to classical usage, is shown by Job xxix. 12-17. Job describes himself there as availing himself of his powerful position for the defence of the poor and the miserable in the judgment, as a true Paraclete.

Hence, as there are reasons so decisive for giving the term Paraclete the meaning of advocate and intercessor, we must not be inclined to allow much weight to those weaker reasons which favour the signification comforter. The argument which rests upon the meaning of the word παρακαλέω in the New Testament is set aside by the remark, that the noun, as such, irrespective of its derivation, was imported and accepted from the then current judicial phraseology. And this observation has all the more weight, inasmuch as John, the only Evangelist in whose writings the word Paraclete occurs, is precisely the one who never uses the παρακαλέω elsewhere so common in the New Testament,—a remarkable testimony, also, in favour of the unity and connectedness of his writings. The coincidence of the term with the παρακαλεῖτε of Isa. xl. 1, we cannot regard as other than fortuitous; and must also assume, that in Acts ix. 31 we have not an exposition of the name Paraclete, but only an allusion to it.

When our Lord says, "He will send you *another* Paraclete," it does not lead necessarily to the conclusion that He had hitherto actually and effectually approved Himself their advocate. The meaning may be this: Be not afraid of the persecutions, the judicial processes, which threaten you in the world, whether the Jewish or the Gentile world. If I cannot be your παράκλητος in them, I will provide for you another advocate in My stead. Yet there had been occasions when Jesus had, in a certain sense, literally shown Himself their judicial advocate: comp. for example, Matt. xii. 1-8. And then the whole contest with the world may be regarded as a judicial process with it, as we find in the Old Testament the epithets of legal contention are applied frequently to all contests, so that the idea of the Paraclete is enlarged to mean help in every kind of conflict with the world. A yet further extension, to mean help in every other kind of difficulty, cannot be established here. Paraclete and process are inseparably connected.

The first fulfilment of the promise lying before us we find in the fourth chapter of the Acts. The Apostles were asked, before the high council, by what authority and in what name they did those things. Peter answered the question, " filled with the Holy Ghost," ver. 8. The members of the high council wondered at what they heard, and were unable to reconcile it with the position and education of the Apostles, so mightily did their Advocate make His presence and aid known, ver. 13.—The εἰς τὸν αἰῶνα, equivalent to πάσας τὰς ἡμέρας, ἕως τῆς συντελείας τοῦ αἰῶνος, Matt. xxviii. 20, gives us the comforting assurance that the promise was given to the Apostles not as individuals, but as representatives of all believers; that, so long as the world lasts, the Paraclete will discharge His function in the Church; and that the Church, in her conflict with the world, need never despair, however superior may be the world's numbers, dignities, and endowments. "Wherefore," says Luther, "there is no wrath, or threatening, or dismay; nothing but confident laughter, and sweet consolation in heaven and upon earth."

Ver. 17. " Even the Spirit of truth; whom the world cannot receive, because it seeth Him not, neither knoweth Him: but ye know Him; for He dwelleth with you, and shall be in you."—The Spirit of truth is the Spirit to whom the truth belongs, who possesses it as His own, ch. xv. 26, and who imparts it to those to whom He is given, ch. xvi. 13; 1 John iv. 6. The Spirit approves Himself as the Paraclete, by imparting the truth to those whose cause He defends in their severe process with the world. Of all weapons, this is the noblest. This will bring the Church finally and triumphantly through all beleaguerments. Truth is mightier and nobler than all science, than all hair-splitting reasonings, than all specious eloquence, than all cunningly conceived speculations. On their possession of this truth rested the confident fidelity to their confession displayed by the confessors of the faith, independent of all external relations, and unshaken even in the presence of death. It was the basis of that joyful acceptance of martyrdom, by which the Church made such an impression on the world. He who has a firm hold on the truth, knows that his interests and his person are hidden above, and that all his discomfitures are but the passage to victory. Luther: " Hence let it be to thee no small consolation; for there is nothing upon earth that can so comfort in the time of need, as for the heart to be confident in its cause." But the truth not only evidences its influence upon the spirit of its confessors; it also impresses the world. From the Fall downwards the world has been overrun with lies; yet it can never evade the influence of the truth. The uncreated Divine image retains still some measure of its prerogatives. Truth makes its sure appeal to the conscience.

The world cannot, so long as it maintains itself to be the world, become partaker of the Spirit; for that Spirit it has no receptivity: its eyes, defiled by sin, cannot perceive Him; and therefore it is excluded from the independent possession of the high and noble blessedness of truth, access to which can be obtained only through the Spirit. For the truth belongs to God alone, and can become the heritage of the creature only through the Spirit, who is the bond between the Creator and the created. The truth impresses the world; but proper access to that truth is sealed against the world, because it cannot receive the Spirit. Believers, however, perceive and know the Holy Ghost by intimate communion, and not afar off. The example of the world shows that no discernment of the Spirit can be attained at a distance; and it is because the Spirit is immanent within them, that believers are established in the possession of the truth.

The world has also its own $\pi\nu\epsilon\hat{\nu}\mu a$, the spirit of lying who proceedeth from Satan, Matt. xiii. 38, 39; Acts xvi. 13. That spirit the world knoweth and seeth, although it is no less immaterial than the Spirit of truth. Hence we must not seek the reason for His not being seen, and not being known, in the fact of the immateriality of the Spirit of truth (Grotius: Mundus non curat nisi ea quæ oculis corporeis conspiciuntur; quale non est ille spiritus); but only in this, that the eyes of the world were beclouded and holden by sin. Berl. Bible: For no man can know God, unless he is converted from his sins.—In the double present, $\gamma\iota\nu\dot{\omega}\sigma\kappa\epsilon\tau\epsilon$, and $\mu\acute{\epsilon}\nu\epsilon\iota$, our Lord, abstracting from all relations of time, places the character of His disciples and the character of the world in contrast. But in order to obviate misapprehension, the timeless present is accompanied at the close by the future $\ddot{\epsilon}\sigma\tau a\iota$, to show that the whole matter belongs to the domain of futurity. Many copyists could not appreciate this delicate turn: hence they displaced $\ddot{\epsilon}\sigma\tau a\iota$ by $\dot{\epsilon}\sigma\tau\acute{\iota}\nu$.

In vers. 18-24 we have the *fifth* ground of consolation: Christ comes again.

Ver. 18. "I will not leave you comfortless (orphans); I will come unto you."—Our Lord does not place His own coming in opposition to the coming of the Holy Ghost. He does not say, I Myself will come; for even in the Divine Spirit it is He who comes to His disciples. He says positively, I come, that the disciples might not fall into the comfortless notion that they would not henceforth have to do with Him directly, and that the Holy Ghost would interpose as a separating medium between Him and them. He gives them the assurance, that even after His departure they would remain in the most immediate connection with Himself. The evidence that Christ, even after His return to the Father, held personal intercourse with His disciples, in harmony with this promise, and therefore that the being in the Spirit furnished only the basis of this intercourse, we find primarily in the appearances of the risen Lord, but also in the history of Stephen, who, according to Acts vii. 55, 56, saw the heaven opened, and Jesus standing at the right hand of God, and who, in ver. 59, said to the immediately present Redeemer, "Lord Jesus, receive my spirit;" and in ver. 6, "Lord, lay not this sin to their charge." Then the Apocalypse, the first chapter of which records a manifestation of Christ to the Apostle; a manifestation which, however, presupposes the ἐγενόμην ἐν πνεύματι, ver. 10. How little the Spirit is to be regarded as a restricting medium of partition, which precludes the Lord from any direct operation upon earth, is shown by the history of Saul's conversion, in which Christ comes to the persecutor without even any preliminary reference to the Holy Ghost at all.

What coming of Christ is here spoken of? Certainly not His return at the end of the world; for in that case He would have left His disciples long orphans, and the consolation would have been comfortless enough. According to ver. 19, the coming was *soon* to begin; and the characteristic distinction, "the world seeth Me not," would not be at all suitable to the eschatological return, inasmuch as at His final coming all the nations are to be gathered into His presence, Matt. xxv. 32. Nor can the manifestations of the risen Lord exclusively be meant; for the Redeemer does not speak of what should be the prerogative of a few elect, but of what should be the portion of all His believers in every age and continually: comp. especially the μονὴν παρ' αὐτῷ ποιήσομεν in ver. 23, which cannot be referred to the appearances after the resurrection; and generally vers. 21 and

23, which, taking their whole contents, cannot, without great violence, be limited to those appearances of the risen Lord, as is all the more evident if we compare the strikingly coincident parallel in Rev. iii. 20. There the Redeemer stands before the door of every one who belongs to the number of His people; and His coming notes a relation, the effect of which runs through the whole earthly existence of believers, "like heaven upon earth, and the brightness which irradiates the night." The promise, "I will not leave you comfortless," was but very imperfectly fulfilled in the manifestations of the Lord occurring in the interval between the resurrection and the ascension. It points to a *permanent* connection. On the other hand, we must not by any means exclude those intermediate manifestations of the risen Lord. When Jesus says here, in ver. 19, "Yet a little while, and the world seeth Me no more; but ye see Me," every one must refer the words primarily to the appearances after the resurrection, especially as these have that characteristic mark in common with all later spiritual manifestations, that the world does not participate in them, but that they belonged exclusively to believers: comp. Acts x. 40, 41, "Him God raised up the third day, and showed Him openly, not to all the people, but unto witnesses chosen before of God." This view is confirmed by the parallel passage, ch. xvi. 16, 22, which may well serve as a comment upon our ver. 19. But the appearances of our risen Lord must not be excluded; and all the less as the result of the coming of Christ here in ver. 19 is seen to be the *invigoration* of His disciples, a result which notoriously first followed at the resurrection of their Lord. When the risen Redeemer first appeared to His disciples, they rose immediately from the death of languor and despondency: comp. Ps. lxxii. 15. It is evident that a false apprehension of the resurrection has placed in opposition things which are in fact perfectly accordant. When Christ arose with a glorified body, His appearances were a type and prelude of that living intercourse which, according to Matt. xviii. 20 and xxviii. 20, is to subsist between Christ and His Church to the end of the world; and what in Acts i. 3 is recorded as historical fact, bears at the same time the character of a prophecy, which in its fulfilment runs through all the ages of time. Only thus is it to be explained, that St Paul, in 1 Cor. xv. 7, 8, places the manifestation of that which was given to himself after the ascension on the same level with the manifestations of the risen Lord before the ascension.

Here we have the real secret of the strength of believers in their conflict with the world, which in number and equipments far preponderates. It is their concealed intercourse with that Jesus to whom all power in heaven and earth is given, that enables them to look down upon the earth far below their feet. When the waves of the world's wrath run high, they say to Him, "Be not a terror unto me; Thou art my hope in the day of evil," Jer. xvii. 17.—God in the Old Testament bears the honourable appellation of the God of the orphans, Ps. lxviii. 6; He is described as one with whom the fatherless findeth mercy, Hos. xiv. 3; and also with special reference to His suffering Church upon earth. This His high title God will make good, so far as concerns the disciples, and especially the Apostles, through Christ, with whom all the treasures of His mercy and power are laid up, and who, in Old Testament prophecy, was once called the Everlasting Father, Isa. ix. 6. Their orphanhood, their abandonment, their misery, must not make them dispirited; it must rather fill them with deeper joy. For the greater their orphanhood, the more confidently might they rely upon the consolation of the Father of the fatherless.

The orphan condition of the Apostles lasted from the beginning of the passion to the resurrection. It was the type of conditions which are ever recurring in God's dealings with the whole Church and its individual members. When these circumstances occur, it is "our duty to weep with our mother as fatherless, and to lift up our hands to our Father" (Quesnel). Then will the word be fulfilled to us, as it was formerly to the Apostles: I have forsaken thee for a small moment, but with great compassion I will gather thee.

Ver. 19. "Yet a little while, and the world seeth Me no more; but ye see Me: because I live, ye shall live also."—That the world which was to be excluded from seeing Christ is *primarily* the unbelieving Jewish people, is shown by ch. vii. 33, where Jesus says to the Jews, "Yet a little while am I with you: ye shall seek Me, and shall not find Me." To see Christ no longer is the climax of all misery: for in Him is the fountain of all true joy; and when He departs, the Divine judgments throng in on all sides. The words, "Because I live," etc., are the foundation of the promise that the disciples should see Christ. In the life of Christ Himself lies the guarantee that His disciples should live. But the condition of that life was, that they should see Him. Seeing Christ and living are, with the Apostles, everywhere and inseparably one and the same: He is the centre of their being. When they see Him not, they are as dead in a living body. The life of Christ must develop itself in His disciples further and further until the joyful resurrection: comp. ch. xi. 25. But, according to the connection, that life alone is here pre-eminently meant which unfolded itself in the Apostles immediately with the resurrection. Life is, in the Old Testament, wherever there is contentment and joy: comp. Job xxi. 7; Prov. xvi. 15.

According to some critics, the present, $\zeta\hat{\omega}$, stands here instead of the future. But that would involve the necessity of the present being substituted afterwards for the future, $\zeta\acute{\eta}\sigma\varepsilon\sigma\theta\varepsilon$. Jesus had described Himself in ver. 6 as the life. There is, therefore, no ground whatever for an enfeebling interpretation. Jesus not merely will live, but He is, under all circumstances, the Living; and in the fact that He lives is the pledge given that He will live, and that His disciples shall live with Him. Berl. Bible: "Life is His essential nature; dying is a strange thing, but now necessary to Him." That which is a strange thing can only be transitory. In Luke xxiv. 5, 6, the angels say to the women, "Why seek ye the living among the dead? He is not here, He is risen." Christ did not become alive again—the $\mathring{\eta}\gamma\acute{\varepsilon}\rho\theta\eta$ does not accord with that—but He is the Living One under all circumstances; and in the fact that He is always the Living One lies the ground of His resurrection. In Acts ii. 24, Peter says concerning Christ, "Whom God raised up, having loosed the pains of death, because it was not possible that He should be holden of it." The impossibility rested upon this, that He was the essentially Living. The $\zeta\omega\grave{\eta}$ $\mathring{\alpha}\kappa\alpha\tau\acute{\alpha}\lambda\upsilon\tau\sigma\varsigma$ which, according to Heb. vii. 16, dwells inherently in Christ, elevates Him above the law of death. In Rev. i. 18, we read that Christ approved Himself the "Living One" by the overcoming of death.

The life of His disciples is the necessary consequence of the life of Christ. As the Living, He is also the life-distributing: He cannot rest until He has vanquished for His people death in all its forms, and abolished it utterly. In the Old Testament God is called the living God, for the consolation of His people who sink into death. David thirsts for the living God, Ps. xlii. 3, because, as such, He was the God of his life, ver. 9, distributing life to His own. But as the Living One is the source of life to His own, so He is the source of death to His enemies. Because He liveth, they must die. The first form of that death is their seeing Him no more.

Ver. 20. "At that day ye shall know that I am in My Father, and ye in Me, and I in you."—Primarily the day of the resurrection; yet this only as the beginning of a whole period of time, during which the annunciations of this resurrection continued. By the resurrection, and the manifestation to the disciples connected with it, was actual demonstration given that Christ is in the Father, and that He stands in the most intimate and essential fellowship with Him: comp. Rom. i. 4. The disciples learnt this by living actual experience, from the fact that the life of the Father manifests itself in Him. As by the resurrection it was demonstrated that Christ is in the Father, comp. ver. 10, so also it was proved that the relation of the disciples to Him was not an imaginary one, but a real one; that He was truly the life of their souls: comp. Gal. ii. 20. That could He be, only if He is actually the only Son of God. But, as it regards the latter point, their knowledge depended not upon a mere inference. Concurrent with this conclusion, was the flowing of Christ's life into them at His resurrection. Only by this communion of His life could a true assurance arise that they were in Him and He in them. Luther: "I had not such power in me before, for I was, like others, under the devil's power, and under the fear of death. But now I have another spirit, which Christ gives me through the Holy Ghost; by which I trace that He is with me, and that I may scorn all the threats of the world, death, and the devil, and joyfully glory in my Lord, who lives and reigns for me in heaven."

Ver. 21. "He that hath My commandments, and keepeth them, he it is that loveth Me; and he that loveth Me shall be loved of My Father, and I will love him, and will manifest Myself to him."—Lampe remarks: "The expression is changed. Earlier He had addressed the disciples; now He proceeds to speak in the third person, because the promise of His coming which precedes, specifically concerned His disciples, but this concerns all His people." Instead of *specifically*, we would say *especially*. That Lampe distinguishes too nicely, is shown by the ἐμφανίζειν in ver. 22.

As the impartation of the Holy Spirit, ver. 15, so also the manifestation of Christ, is conditional on love to Christ approving itself in the keeping of His commandments. The high reward promised must fill with glowing emulation towards this obedience. What under one aspect is recompense, is under another the consequence of Christ's manifestation. But before that manifestation there must be the full bias and earnest effort of the soul to keep His commandments. Christ cannot manifest Himself to an indolent and careless soul.—The καὶ τηρῶν αὐτάς more closely explains the *having*: it points to the fact that our Lord did not mean the unreal and merely outward remembrance of the law. To refer the ἔχων to this latter, and assume that the καὶ τηρῶν αὐτάς is an appendage, equivalent to "He that not merely has My commandments, but also keepeth them" (Augustin: Qui habet in memoriâ et servat in vitâ), would scarcely be in harmony with the emphasis of the Johannæan phrase. Grotius rightly compares (on ἔχειν) ch. v. 28, where it is used concerning the vital and real possession of the word of God. Christ Himself shows how the merely external having is, when closely considered, no having at all, Matt. xiii. 12: "But he that hath not, from him shall be taken away that which he hath." The ἐκεῖνος—He and no other—intimates that the human heart is eminently prone to yield itself to the delusions of a mere semblance of love to Christ, of a mere love of feeling and fancy.—The love of the Father comes into consideration only as the foundation of the love of Christ; and this only as the foundation of its form of expression, its *manifestation*, which involves in itself the fulness of all blessedness, and is the foretaste of eternal happiness, enabling the soul to say, in the time of affliction, "Yea, though I walk through the valley of the shadow of death, I will fear no evil; for Thou art with me."

Ver. 22. "Judas saith unto Him, (not Iscariot,) Lord, how is it that Thou wilt manifest Thyself unto us, and not unto the world?"—"The disciples," says Lampe, "did well in confessing their ignorance, and in asking questions for their further instruction. Their questions bring us excellent fruit, because they gave the Lord occasion to add further explanations and encouragements." "Not Iscariot:" that was obvious of itself. But care for the honour of the true Judas, to whom it was a severe grief to have a name like the traitor's, required that provision should be made against the possibility of ever so fleeting a confounding of the two persons, by keeping them absolutely distinct. Matthew, in ch. x., takes pains to avoid naming the true disciple by his name of Judas: he introduces him by a double surname, Lebbeus and Thaddeus, and makes the former take the place of his proper name. Mark also calls him Thaddeus in ch. iii. 18. Luke, in the Acts, describes him as Judas the brother of James, at a time when Judas Iscariot was already dead, and confusion was not possible any longer. The paraphrastic name in Matthew and Mark, and the addition Ἰακώβου in Luke, sprang from the same reason as the "not Iscariot" here.

"How is it," *what has happened?* (Lachmann omits the καὶ; but it has been struck out here on the same grounds which secured its omission in ch. ix. 36): there must, in his opinion, something extraordinary have taken place, indeed some *fatal* incident must have interposed, that Jesus should limit His revelation to His disciples, and withdraw it from the world. Christ's universal dominion, as predicted by the prophets, and so many earlier announcements of our Lord Himself—for example, that He would draw all men unto Him, and that many should come from the east and west, and sit down with Abraham, Isaac, and Jacob in the kingdom of God—appeared to him to be altogether out of keeping with such a word as this. There would have been much to reply, indeed, to such a difficulty. For example: that Jesus did not renounce His absolute victory over the world by not revealing Himself to it; that the exclusion referred only to the world which should refuse to abandon its wickedness; and that Christ would adopt the most effectual means of redeeming it from that sinful nature. But Jesus limits Himself in His answer to one thing. After express repetition of the encouraging promise to His disciples, He indicates that the world excludes itself from participation in this glorious promise, inasmuch as it does not fulfil the absolute and unchangeable condition on which it is suspended. Thus nothing had taken place;

no hindrance had occurred to baffle the Lord, constrain Him to change His plans, and give up His vast enterprise; the world simply made itself unworthy of so high an honour. We may compare Eccles. vii. 10 for the τί γέγονεν : " Say not thou, *What is the cause* that the former days were better than these?"—what has brought in this fatal change?—Stier is not quite correct in making it the only word uttered by this Judas. It must be placed in connection with ch. vii. 4. There the " brethren" of Jesus say to Him: "If Thou doest these things, show Thyself unto the world." The view is very common, that in the mission of Jesus a revelation to *the world* was necessarily given; that it is not enough if a little company in quietness enjoy His manifestations. The nearest connections of Jesus after the flesh were least satisfied with the notion of a seeming dominion in a corner. But by the appeal, "Lord," Judas shows that he laid his scruples humbly at his Master's feet.

Ver. 23. "Jesus answered and said unto him, If a man love Me, he will keep My words: and My Father will love him, and we will come unto him, and make our abode with him."— The promise which had been given in ver. 21 to the disciples, receives here an addition. Not He alone comes, but the Father with Him, and with Him the inexhaustible fulness of all consolation, the most abundant compensation for the impending departure of Jesus, the Son of man.—The love of Christ and the performance of His commandments is, as for the individual, so also for the churches, the measure of the participation in this glorious manifestation. To deal lightly with the least among the precepts of Christ, is wilfully to fight against our own blessedness. "The soul," says Quesnel, "which aspires to be the Temple of the Sacred Trinity, must have, as it were, an eternal longing to do His will." What holds good of the soul, holds good also of the Church. The μονὴν παρ' αὐτῷ ποιήσομεν points to "that I may dwell among them," Ex. xxv. 8, xxix. 45, 46 : compare Ezek. xxxvii. 27, "My tabernacle also shall be with them." The beginning of the true fulfilment of these Old Testament sayings was the revelation of Christ in the flesh (comp. on ch. i. 14); its eternal realization we shall find in the new Jerusalem : here have we the middle fulfilment. In the parallel place, Rev. iii. 20, the reference to the Canticles comes out more prominently than even here, where, however, the tender and internal tone points the same way.

Ver. 24. "He that loveth Me not keepeth not My sayings: and the word which ye hear is not Mine, but the Father's which sent Me."—He "keepeth not My words," and therefore the Father cannot love him; we cannot come to him, and make our abode with him. Thus nothing has "taken place," but the world excommunicates itself. The saying, "and the word which ye hear," etc., gives the reason wherefore the not keeping Christ's commandments entails such ruinous consequences. If Christ's word goes back to the Father's authority, then arise in full power all those sayings of the Old Testament in which the keeping of the commandments of God is exhibited as the condition of fellowship with Him, from Gen. xviii. 19 downwards. Compare particularly Lev. xxvi. 3, "If ye walk in My statutes, and keep My commandments, and do them;" vers. 11, 12, "And I will set My tabernacle among you, and My soul shall not abhor you. And I will walk among you, and will be your God, and ye shall be My people;" Deut. vii. 12 seq., xxviii. 1, 15. And the reference to these passages of the Old Testament shows further, that, over and above the application to individuals, the application to religious communities must not be forgotten. In the proportion in which they are filled with zeal for the obedience of the words of Christ does the Father love them, and make His abode among them. When this zeal dies out, the Father with Christ retires, and leaves nothing but darkness behind. This the Jews were to find out in sad experience, to which the word of Christ primarily refers: comp. ch. xv. 20.

In vers. 25, 26, we have the *sixth* consolation. With the thought of their Master's departure, the thought of their own *immaturity* must have painfully risen in their consciousness. "Ye are yet without understanding," the Lord had not long before said to them, Matt. xv. 16. Even as disciples and learners they felt themselves insecure, and thought they could not go on without the guidance and further instruction of their Teacher. And now, after the departure of Christ, they were alone to represent His cause. How should they step forward as teachers who had scarcely as yet clearly and sharply seized the very first elements of Christian doctrine, who were always stumbling at unsolved mysteries, and encountering difficulties everywhere? comp. ch. xvi. 25. They might well indeed cry out, with Jeremiah, " Ah, Lord, I know not how to speak: I am young." The Lord now intimates to them that His departure would not be, as they vainly supposed, the end of His instruction among them; but that, in the mission of the Holy Spirit, He had provided them with an abundant compensation for His own departure.

Vers. 25, 26. " These things have I spoken unto you, being yet present with you. But the Comforter, which is the Holy Ghost, whom the Father will send in My name, He shall teach you all things, and bring all things to your remembrance, whatsoever I have said unto you."—The words, " These things have I said unto you," indicate that the discourse of Christ to them was drawing near its end. They do not primarily refer to the whole of His discourses during His public ministry, but to the discourse which He was then uttering. Yet this particular portion was a representative of the whole. In this last discourse of Christ there was, as in all the former, much that remained obscure to the disciples; they did not yet feel themselves satisfied; everywhere there were chasms in their knowledge, and riddles unsolved. It was in view of the scruples and difficulties which this fact caused, that Christ uttered the present consolations.

This promise is essentially different from that of vers. 15–17. There the Holy Ghost was promised to them as an advocate in their conflict with the world; here, as the teacher who should save them from their ignorance.—Here also the Holy Spirit is a Paraclete, an intercessor or advocate. But this designation was only to indicate the identity of the Helper in both cases: " the same whom I earlier promised to you as an advocate in your process with the world." We are not at liberty to assume that the original idea of an advocate at the bar is enlarged into that of one who, under difficult circumstances, speaks in behalf of another. For it is not a Helper in their teaching office that is primarily promised to the Apostles—one who should speak for them to others—but one who should help them out of their ignorance. There is, however, no reason whatever for the assumption, that the specific idea of an advocate is here weakened down to the very general one of an assistant or helper. The term Paraclete never occurs in so general a sense. In ch. xvi. 7, where He is named again, He is, as in ch. xiv. 16, the advocate in the process against the world; and in ch. xvi. 13, where our promise recurs, and is further unfolded, it is not the Paraclete who is mentioned, but the Spirit of truth. This shows plainly that the Paraclete here only lays down the stepping-stone for ver. 16, indicating that the Holy Spirit was a person already known to them by what had been spoken before. If this is forgotten, all that is characteristic is removed from the idea of the Paraclete.

"The Holy Ghost:" comp. on ch. vii. 39. "In My name" indicates that the mission of the Holy Spirit has for its foundation the historical personality of Christ (comp. on ver. 14),—all that comes to mind when we hear the name Christ, all that He did and suffered upon earth, of which the atonement accomplished by the Redeemer's suffering and death is the great result: comp. on ch. vii. 39. Before Christ had, by His passion and sacrifice, made Himself a glorious name, the Holy Spirit could not be sent forth.—We have here Father, Son, and Holy Spirit together, as in Matt. xxviii. 19, where the *name*, the measure of personality, is attributed to the Holy Spirit no less than to the Father and the Son. The sending from the Father is here spoken of the Holy Ghost, even as in ver. 24 of the Son.—That the *teaching* is not explained simply by the *bringing to remembrance* that follows, as many of the older expositors thought, in their polemical zeal against the Romish Church; that the teaching is either the generic notion, which includes the specific reminding, or refers to the impartation of new elements of instruction, with which the bringing instruction already received from Christ to mind was to go on concurrently, —is plain from the parallel passage, ch. xvi. 12, 13, according to which the teaching function of the Holy Ghost was far to transcend that of a mere remembrancer, and to refer to very much that Jesus Himself could not tell His disciples, because they were not able to bear it. The limitation of the teaching to the mere bringing to remembrance, is in opposition to the fact as we find it throughout the books of the New Testament. The doctrinal substance of the Apostolical Epistles, and of the Apocalypse, cannot by any means be referred back to the discourses which Christ delivered during His life upon earth; although the germs and principles of all, down to the minutest details, were contained in them. But it is self-evident that the teaching office of the Spirit could not come into contradiction with the reminding office; as also, that the promise is here given primarily to the Apostles, through whose instrumentality the Holy Spirit imparted His instructions to the churches of all ages. Assuredly the Divine Spirit continues still His teaching function in the Church; but it is limited now to the penetrating ever deeper into the meaning of that which Christ and His Apostles taught. That the promise here primarily referred to those who received it, and was mainly limited to them, is obvious from the second member of it. The *reminding* function of the Holy Spirit could be exercised only upon those who had been the companions of Jesus during His life upon earth. But the teaching and the reminding offices go hand in hand. That the "will teach you all things" was, as to essentials, closed with the completion of the canon, is made obvious by the "show you things to come," in ch. xvi. 13, which manifestly found its fulfilment in the book of Revelation. For us, the consolation here given assumes a different form from what it had to the Apostles. As the result of its fulfilment to those to whom it was primarily given, we have received the Holy Scriptures of the New Testament, and in them the remedy of all our ignorance; especially as, depending upon the promises given first to the Apostles, we may be confident that we are not left to ourselves in its interpretation, but that the Holy Spirit will continue His teaching function by the exposition of the truth of Scripture. Here is the never-ceasing prerogative and pre-eminence of the Church before the world; with all the boasted advancement of its science, the world is left to the natural ignorance of man, and deals in the dark with the highest problems of life.—The bringing to remembrance was obviously not to be of a merely mechanical or internal kind; but such as at the same time opened up a deeper understanding. Bengel rightly observes, that in these last discourses of our Lord, so faithfully reproduced by St John, we have a document of the fulfilment of this promise itself.

In ver. 27 is the *seventh* and last consolation—the promise of peace. Enemies all around them, sheep in the midst of wolves—such was the position of the disciples on the departure of Christ. Nevertheless, Christ guarantees to them, and through them to the Church of all ages, His peace. This is, at the first glance, and to the judgment of carnal reason, an absurd promise; and yet it has its reality, and experience confirms its truth.

Ver. 27. " Peace I leave with you, My peace I give unto you: not as the world giveth, give I unto you. Let not your heart be troubled, neither let it be afraid."—Peace is the condition of one who is not hurt by enemies. We must not set in the place of peace a mere state of prosperity. The original Hebrew שלום, from שלם, to be whole, denotes the condition of one who is unhurt by inimical influences, by those hostile powers which, from the Fall downwards, have hemmed in human life on all sides,—human nature, " beset with original sin, infirmity, distress, and death." But εἰρήνη never has, even ostensibly, any other meaning than that of peace, which is the meaning entirely in harmony with the derivation of the word. The antithesis of εἰρήνη, according to ch. xvi. 33, is θλίψις, tribulation or oppression.—'Αφίημι is here, as in Matt. xxii. 25, used of that which one leaves behind on departing. Christ seemed as if He was about to leave His disciples nothing but an inheritance of warfare and oppression : comp. ch. xv. 18-21; but, when we look closely into the matter, He really leaves them peace. The words, " My peace I give unto you," intimate that this peace would rest upon His positive influence, and spring directly from Himself. First comes the paradox, that after His departure they would have peace; then more definitely the source whence that peace would come, which, indeed, was slightly indicated in the ἀφίημι. The explanation, that " Jesus did not take away the peace of His disciples with Him, but rather gave them of His own peace," devises a peace which the disciples had independent of their Lord, and overlooks the fact that it is not said, " *your* peace," which such an antithesis would have required.—The severest trials awaited the Apostles; nevertheless, they found themselves more and more in a condition of peace. For, 1. They were, through Christ, established in the possession of eternal life, and no enemy could rob them of that blessed state and experience. 2. Hostile oppression was a disturbance of their peace only to human apprehension, and so far as fleshly sensibility went; in reality, it furthered their religious welfare, helped to prepare them for eternal life, and was therefore a concealed benefit of grace. And during their tribulation the Lord was peculiarly near to them; then more than usually He fulfilled His own word, "We will come to him, and make our abode with him." Had they much tribulation in their hearts, the consolations of Christ all the more quickened their souls. 3. Oppression, persecutions, and contempt, bore, even upon earth, only a transitory character. Final victory over them all was guaranteed, ch. xvi. 33; and, in the confident expectation of that victory, their momentary degradation could not overmuch affect their hearts. The death of Christ seemed essentially to peril the peace of the disciples: comp. Luke xxiv. 17. But after His resurrection, the Lord welcomed them with the greeting, Peace be unto you! ch. xx. 19, xxi. 26, and thus intimated that the promise given to them before His departure had begun its accomplishment. This is a type of the ever recurring dealings of our Lord with us. The most perfect realization of the words, "My peace I give unto you," belongs to the perfect kingdom of God.—That the promise of peace stands here just at the end, probably has allusion to the circumstance, that men were wont to utter the wish of peace at the time of separation: comp. 1 Sam. i. 17, xx. 42; 2 Sam. xv. 9. In the place of the impotent wish, the saving efficacy of Christ's promise comes in. The objection, that Christ is not immediately departing from His disciples, but they go along with Him, has no force. We sometimes take farewell more than once. Here this takes place at the close of the last and highest festival, at the end of their last mournful interview, before the stress of conflict with the prince of this world begins.

"Not as the world giveth, give I unto you." According to the current exposition our Lord here says, that He does not give peace, or gifts generally, as the world gives them, delusively; that is, merely seeming peace and hollow blessings. But such a thought would thus be very imperfectly expressed. We must not arbitrarily introduce the idea that the world's peace is an illusion or an empty phrase, and that its good things are only the semblance of good things. Nor do we clearly see that there is any antithesis of Christ's peace as the true. But the main point is, that with its principle of selfishness, the world does not like to give at all, not even its seeming peace and its seeming good things. Especially in relation to the disciples, who come prominently into view here, the world must be regarded as manifestly and only hostile. The key to the right interpretation is found in ch. xvi. 33, " In the world ye shall have tribulation :" this is all the more obvious, inasmuch as we have there the last farewell of Christ to His disciples, just as here we have the preliminary farewell. Tribulation, $\theta\lambda\hat{\iota}\psi\iota\varsigma$; that is the world's gift in regard to all the disciples of Christ. For them it has nothing better. It seems, indeed, sometimes as if Christ also had nothing better for them; as if He left them, without help, a prey to the oppressions of the world. There lies the essential sharpness of the sting; that was the strong temptation to which the Baptist had sometime been exposed. But in reality it is far otherwise. As the world gives them tribulation, so He gives them peace: only this is required, that His disciples should know how to appropriate that peace, that they should take a spiritual estimate of things, and await the right time. The $\hat{\upsilon}\mu\hat{\iota}\nu$ belongs also to the $\kappa\alpha\theta\grave{\omega}\varsigma\ \acute{o}\ \kappa\acute{o}\sigma\mu o\varsigma\ \delta\acute{\iota}\delta\omega\sigma\iota$. Instead of *as*, we might read equally well *what*. The difference in the gift connects with it also a variation in the manner of giving, an unfriendly or a friendly. The tribulation which the world inflicts upon the disciples of Christ, is with a touch of irony described as a *gift*, in reference to those good gifts which they ought to have been ready to give. Such a use of the word giving is often found in the Old Testament: for example, in Deut. xxxii. 6, " Do ye thus requite (give) the Lord, O foolish people and unwise?" 1 Sam. xxiv. 18, where Saul says to David, " Thou hast rewarded me good, whereas I have rewarded thee evil:" I, who should have given thee that which was good, have instead thereof brought thee a *wicked* gift: comp. my commentary on Ps. vii. 5.—The recurrence of $\mu\grave{\eta}\ \tau\alpha\rho\alpha\sigma\sigma\acute{\epsilon}\sigma\theta\omega$ indicates the conclusion of the grounds of consolation.

After the Lord has so powerfully and in such various ways comforted His disciples, He can now go further, and declare that they ought to *rejoice* over that which had been the source of their deeper sorrow.

Ver. 28. " Ye have heard how I said unto you, I go away, and come again unto you. If ye loved Me, ye would rejoice, because I said, I go unto the Father: for My Father is greater than I."—Christ exhibits His return to the Father as a matter of joy to the disciples, first of all on the ground of their love to Him; but what would redound to His honour would serve at the same time their best interests. He enters into a condition of eternal glory, which will allow Him to fulfil the high promises that He had made to them in the previous words. That He made prominent the former point, had respect to the sentiment of the disciples, that it was the obligation of their love to mourn over His departure. But if reference to the good of the disciples had not been in the background, Christ would not have added " and come again unto you" to the " I go away." That would have had no meaning, if the personal interests of Christ alone had been involved. If, on the other hand, there is a latent reference to the salvation of the disciples, these have their due significance. Through His departure to the Father, who is greater than He, He can fulfil His promise of return. This return, in which He would impart to His disciples much more than He had imparted during His earlier earthly life, was to be a result of His assumption into the glory of the Father. That the personal interests of the disciples were in the background, and that they were coincident with those of Christ Himself, is shown by the relation in which " ye would rejoice" stands to " Let not your heart be troubled, neither let it be afraid," in ver. 27. There the subject was solicitude about their own danger, and therefore the corresponding joy must have reference to their own salvation. Quesnel is perfectly right in saying, " The interests of Jesus Christ ought to be dearer to us than our own. But we cannot seek His things without at the same time finding our own."

Christ does not demand of His disciples that they should rejoice. He knew that their love was not yet purified enough for that. But when He says to them that they ought, if they loved Him, to rejoice, the result was doubtless attained that their sorrow was mitigated. So from us He does not demand at once that we should rejoice when our beloved are taken away. He leaves nature its rights; He has sympathy with our weakness, which is bound up with the best elements of our nature. It is the healthy development of love, that it is first blended with earthly admixtures, and only by degrees sublimates itself into the pure heavenly flame.—In a certain sense, every one who dies in the Lord may say to his friends what Christ says here to His disciples. Every believer goes at his departure to His Redeemer, and thus into the glory of the Father.[1]—That

[1] Cyprian: Dixit Dominus: si me dilexissetis gauderetis quoniam vado ad Patrem, docens et ostendens, cum cari quos diligimus de sæculo exeunt, gaudendum potius esse quam dolendum.

the Father was greater than Jesus, makes His departure to the Father matter to be rejoiced in, only if Christ in His departure was received into the fellowship of the glory of the Father (comp. ch. xvii. 5). If I shall be with My Father, I shall be greater than I am now. It is clear from this, that Christ is not here set over against the Father in His original essence, nor in His human nature generally; for this shared the exaltation to the Father's right hand, whereas a condition is here meant which was laid aside by going to the Father. But He is placed in opposition to the Father according to His entire personality, as the Christ come into the flesh, and in the form of a servant, as He was then incorporate and lived among men. The Arians had no right to use this passage in the interest of their doctrine; on the contrary, the assumption of Christ into the supreme glory of the Father, as it is here taught, serves most effectually to refute their error. Equality in glory presupposes, and is based upon, equality in essence. According to Lücke, the word, "For My Father is greater than I," must express, "not the transitory human consciousness of the Redeemer in His earthly humiliation," but "the essential, indissoluble consciousness of His subordination to the Father." But indeed the going to the Father made no difference in that essential consciousness. But only such a being greater can be attributed to the Father as came to an end when Christ went home to Him. Other explanations, such as "God can better protect you than My earthly presence with you," or "the Father is a mightier defence than I am," are negatived by the consideration that Christ's going to the Father is primarily exhibited as a matter of joy and advantage to Christ Himself. "If ye loved Me" plainly shows that the disciples were to rejoice on Christ's own account at His departure to the Father.[1]

---

[1] We select a few striking sayings from the older expositors. Augustin: Hæc est forma servi, in qua Dei filius minor est, non Patre solo, sed etiam Spiritu Sancto: neque id tantum sed etiam se ipso: quid idem ipse in forma Dei major est se ipso. Unum sunt (ch. x. 30) secundum id quod Deus erat verbum: major est Pater, secundum id quod verbum caro factum est. Infidelis, ingrate, ideone minuis tu eum, qui fecit te, quia dicit ille quid factus sit propter te? Æqualis enim Patri filius, per quem factus est homo, ut minor esset Patre factus est homo: quod nisi fieret, quid esset homo? Luther: "Going to the Father, means receiving the kingdom of the Father, where He is like the Father, known and honoured in the same

Ver. 29. "And now I have told you before it come to pass, that, when it is come to pass, ye might believe."—Comp. ch. xiii. 19. "I have told it you" refers to the departure of Christ, and His return to His disciples, as this had its glorious beginning in the resurrection. Of like significance with the ὑπάγω καὶ ἔρχομαι πρὸς ὑμᾶς, is the πορεύομαι πρὸς τὸν πατέρα. For the going of Christ to the Father must have its announcement or declare itself in His resurrection and glorification. The prediction, therefore, refers to the suffering of Christ, and His entrance into His glory, Luke xxiv. 26.

After the Lord had strengthened His disciples, Himself doing that which He appointed Peter to do, "Strengthen thy brethren," Luke xxii. 32, He can challenge them to go forth with Him to the decisive conflict.

Vers. 30, 31. "Hereafter I will not talk much with you; for the prince of this world cometh, and hath nothing in Me. But that the world may know that I love the Father; and as the Father gave Me commandment, even so I do. Arise, let us go hence."—In relation to the prince of this world, comp. on ch. xii. 31. "As often as we hear this name," says Calvin, "we should be ashamed of our wicked condition. For, let men vaunt themselves as they may, they are the devil's slaves, and no better, until they are born again through the Spirit of Christ." Those who boast of their free spirit, and of being freethinkers, are entangled in their own great folly. It is well for them to say,

majesty. Therefore I go hence, He says, that I may become greater than I am now; that is, I go to the Father. For the kingdom which I am to receive at the right hand of the Father is over all; and it is better that I should go from this humiliation and weakness into the power and dominion which the Father hath, in which He governs with almighty majesty.— Thus He goes out of a narrow space into the broad heaven, out of this prison into a great and glorious kingdom, where He is much greater than before. Before He was a poor, sad, suffering Christ; but now with the Father, He is a great, glorious, living, Almighty Lord over all creatures.— In His nature He abides equal to the Father, eternal God, and yet condescended, upon earth to the most abased and feeblest ministration of a servant for us, and for us sank into death. But by dying He overcame death, and takes us with Himself above, where His kingdom is the Father's, and the Father's kingdom is His." Anton: "According to ver. 12, the disciples were to be greater than Christ in His present condition." Bengel: Ante ipsam profectionem minor fuerat etiam angelis, Heb. ii. 9, post profectionem major se ipso, ver. 12, patri par, xvii. 5.

"We will not have this man to rule over us;" but that does not make them free, and they are enslaved still in the most abject bondage. "When the people of the world," says Quesnel, "follow their passions, they think they are doing their own will; but in reality they are only, on the one hand, obeying the will of the prince of this world, whose desires and plans they execute, and, on the other, they serve, through the overruling power of God, His plans, and do His will, which is, and must evermore be, supreme over that of His creatures." Satan never approved himself more fully the prince of this world, than when he incited the Jews and the Gentiles to contend against the Son of God.

Judas was in the confederacy of the multitude: comp. ch. xviii. 3. But Jesus introduces us into the concealed background of the manifestations of his life, the mere external part of which is all that the world in its melancholy superficiality beholds. Before His profound glance Judas vanishes, the Roman soldiers vanish, the servants of the high priests and Pharisees vanish, and one only remains, whom they, with their superiors, serve as poor unconscious instruments,—the prince of this world, who sets in motion their schemes and their arms. This view of the matter gives us to perceive, on the one hand, the full solemnity of the conflict, and urges us to take the whole armour of God, since in such an assault we can do nothing by our own power (comp. Eph. vi. 11, 12); on the other hand, it is full of encouragement, since, when Satan is on the scene, we may be very sure that God will be on the scene likewise.—In Luke xxii. 53, again, our Lord refers to Satan what the Jewish rulers undertook against Him with seeming success. All rested upon this, that power was given to the darkness. So also, in ch. viii. 44, He had indicated Satan as the proper originator of the assaults of the Jews. In ch. vi. 70, too, the traitor was connected with Satan. But we must not limit our thoughts to Satan's manifestations in the persons of his instruments. We are led to perceive that Jesus had to do immediately with the enemy himself, by the parallel of the temptation at the outset of our Lord's ministry, and by Rev. xii. 7-9, where Christ is in direct conflict with Satan and his angels. At the agony in Gethsemane, which preceded the appearance of Satan in his instruments, we must regard Satan himself as actively engaged. There, as formerly in the beginning, he assaulted Christ as a tempter.—In the present passage the prince of this world and the Redeemer are in contest; in the parallel passage of the Apocalypse, ch. xii. 7–9, Michael and the dragon contend : these are only different names of the same persons. "Michael and Satan are the proper factors of history. All others, however they may push themselves forward, and however much also they may draw upon themselves the eyes of a shortsighted world, are but subordinate agents and instruments." (Comment. on Apocalypse, Clark's Trans.) This note on the Apocalyptic passage holds good here also. The obscuration of the true nature of this conflict involves the greatest peril. The spiritual eye of the believer must be open to discern the real opponent.

"He hath (indeed) nothing in Me" (οὐκ is not superfluous; the double negation strengthens the emphasis—absolutely nothing): this is to be interpreted by reference to the ἄρχων, the meaning being regulated by the fact that Satan is called the *regent* of this world. The *having* is accordingly that of a ruler and possessor ; and the ἐν ἐμοί marks the territory of the possession. The reference to the *prince of this world* makes the mere ἔχειν equivalent to the ἔχειν ἐξουσίαν, the having authority, in ch. xix. 11. Christ was absolutely beyond the domain of his authority, because He was not of this world, which since the Fall has been subject to the dominion of Satan, and consequently by a righteous judgment exposed to his assaults : comp. on ch. xii. 31. To be in constrained subjection to Satan is the wretched lot only of the children of Adam ; Christ is in His divine nature sublimely elevated above it. But in His obedience to God, and in His acceptance of the work of redemption committed to Him—which demanded that He should submit to Satan's assault for one moment, that He might vanquish him for ever—our Lord would not evade or withdraw from the contest. "He hath nothing in Me :" these words are in fact equivalent to "I am not of this world," to which the domain of Satan was limited, but "from above," ch. viii. 23; the cause and the effect are here both intimated.— "Hath nothing in Me :" One only upon earth could ever utter these words. All who come into being according to the ordinary course of nature, are, in consequence of sin, Satan's subjects. But this One, who voluntarily placed Himself before the enemy, and confronted all his power, broke down his dominion for all those who should become one with Himself through faith. "Hath *nothing*," absolutely nothing, points primarily and obviously to the Lord's perfect freedom from sin. But His divinity is thereby assumed. A sinless man is an unreality; as certainly so as Adam, according to Gen. v. 3, begat a son in his own image and likeness.—Lücke is wrong here: "The reason why Satan had no power over Christ lay in this, that Christ had overcome the world, and already glorified it." The true reason was no other than this, that Christ was not of the world, and that there was in Him nothing of that element which gives Satan his power over the world. This being sin, the reason why Satan had nothing in Him was simply this, that He was "holy, and undefiled, and separate from sinners," Heb. vii. 26, and therefore absolutely apart from the human race, and "higher than the heavens."—Our Lord uttered the words, "he hath nothing in Me," as a protest against those erroneous conclusions which have been drawn, or might be drawn, from the fact that He seemingly became subject to the power of Satan. Luther: "My suffering this, is not because I am not strong enough for Satan, whom I have so often cast out." Lampe: "Not through any flaw in Him, but through the exuberance of His love; not through the power of the devil, but the will of His Father."

"But that the world may know;" the world which lieth in the wicked one, but which includes in itself the yet future children of God, ch. xi. 52, who through faith in Christ are to be drawn out of the world and introduced into the Church of God, ch. iii. 16. It is only under this aspect that the world comes here into consideration. The world embraces all the children of Adam; all are by nature children of wrath, Eph. ii. 3. Nevertheless there is here a great distinction. There is a world which is capable of being drawn, ch. vi. 44, xii. 32, does not serve its prince with perfect joy, but sighs to be free from his dominion. This is the aspect of the world that comes into view here. The world only on its susceptible side, and not the hardened, it is the design of the Lord to enlighten and bring to true knowledge.

The true reason why our Lord confronted Satan and submitted to his assaults, was His love to His Father, and the great commission entrusted to Him. The Father gave Him this work to do out of love to the world (comp. on ch. iii. 16); and the Father's motive was no secret unshared by the Son. But while He also loved the world, it was primarily out of love to the Father that He accomplished the work of redemption. That He entered into the contest with Satan under these particular circumstances, in this so to speak dramatic form,—so that the Church has bequeathed to her a passion-*history* with all its affecting and heart-piercing crises, and can, on the basis of that history, celebrate a passion-week,—took place in order "that the world might know," etc., that there might be given to it the true and urgent impulse to behold and meditate upon the scene.

The words, "Rise, let us go hence"—which must be preceded, not by a full stop, but by a comma—contain, in the form of a command to the disciples, the intimation of what was to be done in order that the world might know, etc.; they are equivalent to, "Therefore I will set forth with you, that I may encounter the assault of the prince of this world." Ἐγείρεσθε, ἄγωμεν· ἰδοὺ ἤγγικεν ὁ παραδιδούς με : thus Jesus speaks, according to Matt. xxvi. 46, in Gethsemane immediately before the arrival of Judas. He designedly repeats the "Rise, let us go," when the conflict directly impends. On the ἐγείρεσθε Augustin remarks: Discumbens discumbentibus loquebatur. The word in Matt. xxvi. also signifies rising up in opposition to sleeping and continuing to rest.

Chap. xv. 1–xvi. 11.

The fifteenth and sixteenth chapters contain the discourses which our Lord uttered shortly before His passage over the brook Kedron; the seventeenth chapter contains His prayer to the Father. In His discourse to the disciples, the Lord first unfolds, in the section before us, the threefold relation in which they stand, first to Him, then to one another, and lastly to the world.

The Lord first gives to His disciples a commentary upon the first table of the Decalogue, " Thou shalt love the Lord thy

God." That, under the New Testament, takes the form of abiding in Christ. Since the existences or natures of the Father and the Son perfectly coincide and cover each other, Jesus could not, in a separate section, adjust His disciples' relation to the Father specifically. As they stood with respect to Himself, so they stood with respect to the Father; should they abide in Him, they would abide in the Father. Then, in ch. xv. 12-17, He turns to the second table. The commandment, "Thou shalt love thy neighbour as thyself," takes, in the kingdom of Christ, the form of Christian brotherly love. After the Lord had determined His people's relations to Himself as their Head, and to each other as brethren (Augustin: "For on these two commandments of love hang all the law and the prophets"), He sheds light upon their relation to the world, and what they would have to expect from it, and what resources they would be able to use in defence against its enmity.

The sections are clearly and sharply demarcated. The first is separated from the second by the concluding formula in ver. 11; the second from the third by the concluding formula in ch. xv. 17. The third is distinguished from that which follows by the circumstance that the watchword *world*—which, in the beginning of the section, is used with intentional frequency, in order to point attention to the theme which now begins to be treated—twice recurs at the end. And that all things down to the most minute are here ordered and sure, appears from the fact that, in the first section, the watchword *abide* occurs precisely ten times, as J. Gerhard long ago observed ($\mu\epsilon\acute{\iota}\nu\eta$, in ver. 11, is a false reading); that in vers. 12-17, which are entirely devoted to love, there are seven characterizations of that grace, the seven further being divided as usual into four and three: ἀγαπᾶτε, ἠγάπησα, ἀγάπην, ἀγαπᾶτε—φίλων, φίλοι, φίλους; that in the third section κόσμος also recurs seven times, the seven being divided into five at the beginning and two at the end—a division of seven which elsewhere accompanies that into four and three. We cannot attribute this to chance, especially as this kind of reckoning occurs so frequently, not only in the Gospel and the Apocalypse of St John, but also in the Lord's discourses, as recorded by the first three Evangelists. We have only to refer to the petitions of the Lord's prayer, the benedictions, and the seven words on the cross.

Ver. 1. "I am the true vine, and My Father is the husbandman."—In vers. 1 and 2 the relation is sketched in its general outlines; from ver. 3 onwards with specific reference to the disciples. The not observing this order of thought misled De Wette, who remarks that the fruitfulness of the branches is an idea that comes in too soon at ver. 2, and which, in the appropriate order, should follow ver. 5. Calvin gives the actual force of the figure of the vine thus: "He teaches that the life-sap flows only from Himself, whence it follows that the nature of men is unfruitful, and void of all good." So also Gerhard: "He would, by this figure, denote the most intimate union between Himself and His disciples, and all believers in Him." When Christ describes Himself as the *true* vine, He intimates the existence of false vines. These may be either the natural vines, according to the remark of Meyer and others: "Christ declares Himself to be the reality of the idea which is only symbolically exhibited in the natural vine; the material growth of the earth is not the true vine, but only its type and figure;" *or* the false vine is a spiritual power which promises life but does not bestow it, as Beza says: "He speaks of the true vine as that which alone has in itself that quickening life, and is alone able to communicate it, in opposition to all other means for the securing of spiritual life, which are altogether false and delusive." This last view is the only right one. It is in itself improbable that Christ would designate Himself the true in opposition to a common vine. That earthly things are only types and symbols of the heavenly, is indeed a theosophic idea, but not a scriptural one. It would be more suitable to Dionysius Areopagita than to the Redeemer. In ch. i. 9 Christ is termed the true light, not in opposition to the natural light, but in opposition to spiritual lights, like John the Baptist, imperfect and transitory. Christ is the true bread in chap. vi. 35, not as opposed to ordinary bread, but as opposed to the manna. The good (that is, the true) shepherd the Lord is termed in ch. x. 11, as the antithesis, not of ordinary shepherds, but of the wicked rulers and guides of the people, the Pharisees. The visible world has, according to the scriptural view, its own proper significance in itself, and it must not be degraded into a mere shadow and type. We can all the less doubt that the comparison points to a *spiritual* vine, because in the Old Testament *Israel* often is introduced as such, and because his destination to be a true vine is contrasted with his lamentable degeneracy, which needed grafting again, and renewal. This was promised in *Christ*. Israel, the vine of God, is the fundamental idea of Ps. lxxx. Concerning degenerate Israel we read in Deut. xxxii. 32, " For their vine is of the vine of Sodom, and of the fields of Gomorrah : their grapes are grapes of gall, their clusters are bitter." Hosea says, in ch. x. 1, " Israel is an empty vine, he bringeth forth fruit unto himself ; according to the multitude of his fruit he hath increased the altars," etc. According to Isa. v. 2, 4, the Lord planted His vineyard with the choicest vine, and "looked that it should bring forth grapes, and it brought forth wild grapes." In Ezek. xix. 10-14, Israel is a vine fruitful and full of branches, which was destroyed by the wrath of God. But the real original, to which the Lord here refers, even as in Matt. xxi. He refers to the parable of the *vineyard* in Isa. v., is Jer. ii. 21, " Yet I had planted thee a noble vine, wholly a right seed : how then art thou turned into the degenerate plant of a strange vine unto Me ?" LXX. : ἐγὼ δὲ ἐφύτευσά σε ἄμπελον καρποφόρον πᾶσαν ἀληθινήν, πῶς ἐστράφης εἰς πικρίαν ἡ ἄμπελος ἡ ἀλλοτρία. There we have the same antithesis between the true and the false vine. Since Israel is changed from a true to a false vine, another true vine must be substituted : such an one as should not be strange to Israel, but in which Israel finds again his true nature, as the Messiah is in Isa. xlix. 3 mentioned as He in whom Israel would attain to his destination, and in whom the idea of Israel would be realized. The false vine is not Israel generally, but Israel after the flesh, 1 Cor. x. 18 ; Israel degenerate from its true nature, and not gathered again into Christ its head. The thought is, that salvation does not come from out of the people themselves, but from above, from fellowship with Christ, who has been placed in its midst : comp. Rom. ix. 31, x. 3. The true vine is Christ, or the Church in its absolute dependence on Christ ; the false vine is the Jews establishing their own righteousness, and all those who tread in their footsteps, all communities which separate from the Head, and sever salvation from its absolute dependence upon Him. We may find a commentary on this passage in the beautiful golden vine over the gate of the Herodian temple, " a marvel both of size and of art to all beholders," as Josephus says, Ant. xv. 11, 3 : comp. also Bell. Jud. v. 5, 4, where we read, " The gate had also golden vines upon it, from which depended clusters as long as a man;" and the thorough description of this vine in the Mischna Cod. Middoth, c. 3, 8.

Our Lord convicted of error the Pharisaic notion concerning the vine, which in His own time was the prevalent interpretation, and at the same time He pointed to the real truth which was contained in the figure. Christ is the true vine only, *in the first place*, as opposed to Israel after the flesh, the synagogue of Satan (Quesnel: " The Church does not bear bitter fruit like the synagogue"), which became such because it assumed to have life in itself, and would not derive it from connection with Christ as the Head of the Church. " I am the true vine," our Lord cries out, through all ages of the Church, in opposition to those who either altogether or partially establish their own righteousness, and would set up in the Church other sources of life than those which it derives from connection with Him as its only and living Head.

" And My Father is the husbandman:" the husbandman here is identical with the vinedresser, the ἀμπελουργός of Luke xiii. 7, 9 ; γεωργός is the general term. We may seek explanation in Gen. ix. 20, " And Noah began to be an husbandman (Sept. γεωργός), and he planted a vineyard." There the work of the husbandman is the general designation, including, as a specific branch, the planting of the vineyard. No mention is made of any owner of the vineyard or the land ; the husbandman only is mentioned, because here possessorship is not referred to, but labour. That this labour had, first of all, the planting of the vine for its object, is shown by the example of Noah. And it corresponds, in the Divine vineyard, that the Father had sent His Son into the world, and caused Him to take flesh of our flesh. It may be questioned, however, whether that function of the husbandman is here alluded to. In the succeeding verses we read only of two works performed by the husbandman, the cutting off of unfruitful branches, and the cleansing of the fruitful. And that the Divine act which corresponds to these is not attributed to the Father in opposition to the Son, is evident, as Chrysostom and Augustin noted, from ver. 3, where the purity of the disciples is derived from the word which Christ had spoken;[1] while, as it respects the cutting off evil branches, ch. v. 22 is decisive, according to which the Father had given all judgment to the Son. Jesus terms Himself the vine, not with respect to His whole being, but only one aspect of it. He is the vine, inasmuch as He is immanent in the Church. But, so far as He rules over the Church, He is, along with the Father, the husbandman.

Ver. 2. "Every branch in Me that beareth not fruit He taketh away; and every branch that beareth fruit He purgeth it, that it may bring forth more fruit."—It may seem strange that our Lord should speak of branches in Him that bear no fruit; it is manifest that those are meant who have never borne fruit at all. It might seem that these could not be regarded in any sense as branches, especially as the beginning of fruit-bearing is, according to ch. vi. 29, faith in Christ. Yet Quesnel's observation is perfectly true, that "the good and the evil branches belong alike to the stock." The matter is resolved by the actual offer of the grace of Christ, and the voluntary acceptance of that grace. So long as this is proffered, and until Christ punishes the rejection of His gifts by exclusion from His kingdom (comp. ver. 6), the unbelieving and the wicked are branches in Him the vine. Predestinarianism, indeed, is much embarrassed by "in Me," as may be seen in the commentaries of Calvin and Lampe. What is spoken of is the unfruitful branches actually being in Christ the vine, and not their thinking themselves, or others thinking them, to be so. The matter is an actual offer of the gifts of Christ, and the assurance of the possibility of a full participation in them: an offer and an assurance which result in nothing only through the fault of those who receive them.[2]

[1] Augustin: When He spoke of the Father as the husbandman who should take away the unfruitful branches, but purge the fruitful that they should bear more fruit, He spoke also of Himself as the cleanser of the branches, "Now ye are clean through the word which I have spoken to you." Behold He Himself is the purger of the branches,—the duty not of the vine, but of the husbandman.

[2] Calvin: Multos censeri in vite *opinione hominum*, qui re ipsa radicem in vite non habent. Ita Dominus vineam suam apud Prophetas nominat populum Israel, qui *externa professione* nomen ecclesiæ habebat. Lampe: In a certain sense even hypocrites may be said to be in Christ, partly because, in the external fellowship of the Church, they partake of the

"Every branch in Me that beareth not fruit:" the Jewish branch is *primarily* meant; as by the contrasted fruit-bearing branch we are to understand primarily the Apostles, and the Christian Church having its germ in them. That even the Jews were a branch in Christ the true vine, is as certain as that, according to ch. i. 11, when He came to the Jews, He came to His own property. Accordingly, they belonged to Him from God, and by absolute right. It was because the Jews, in spite of their not bearing fruit, their unbelief and their enmity, were still a branch in Christ, that a final attempt was to be made after the death of Christ, and through the sending of the Paraclete, to win them: ch. xv. 26, xvi. 7-9. Those with whom this final attempt was vain, and who persisted in their stiffnecked rebellion, were cut off. But the evidence that Jesus had primarily in view the Jews, when He spoke of the branches not bearing fruit, is found in the fact that the same thought recurs in ver. 6, where the reference to Ezek. xv. places the allusion to the Jews beyond doubt. Further, that the general proposition, "Every branch in Me that beareth fruit," etc., refers first of all to the Christian Church, as existing in the germ of the apostolic company, is shown by ver. 3. But it is manifest that the reference of the unfruitful branches to the unbelieving Jews goes on parallel with this. A comparison of Jer. viii. 13 leads to the same result: "I will surely consume them, saith the Lord: there shall be no grapes in the vine, nor figs on the fig-tree, and the leaf shall fade; and the things which I have given them shall pass away from them." There also we have the *taking away;* and the reason, the not bearing fruit, is common to both. In regard to this latter, we may still further compare Deut. xxxii. 32, where it is said of the people of Israel, "Their grapes are grapes of gall, their clusters are bitter;" Isa. v. 2, "And He looked that it should bring forth grapes, and it brought forth wild grapes;" Micah vii. 1. Speaking of the Jews, John the Baptist uttered the general declaration, "Every tree that bringeth not forth good fruit, is hewn down and cast into the fire." The same words, with reference to the same people, are

sacrament of union with Christ, and therefore *boast themselves* of being in Christ; partly because they are *esteemed by others* to be such as belong to the mystical body, or at least are *tolerated* in the external communion of the disciples.

spoken by our Lord in Matt. vii. 19. For the αἴρει, we may compare Luke xiii. 7, 9. There the fig-tree which was to be cut down is the Jewish people; and the αἴρει has also its parallel in κακοὺς κακῶς ἀπολέσει αὐτούς, in Matt. xxi. 41. The branch bearing no fruit in our passage, is in Matt. xxi. 19 the fig-tree bearing only leaves. In Rom. xi., the olive-tree is another parallel to the vine; the ἐξεκλάσθησαν κλάδοι corresponds to the αἴρει αὐτό, as we find it stated of the Jews in Rom. xi. 19. The reference to the Jews in our present passage will hardly be misapprehended, if we bear in mind that the last discourses of Christ in the first Evangelists, and especially in Matthew, are predominantly concerned with the judgment which was to befall the Jews on account of their unbelief.

The alliteration between αἴρειν, to take away, and καθαίρειν, to purge, goes for nothing, as it exists only in the Greek, and the verbs themselves have nothing in common. (Bengel: Graceful rhythm, although καθαίρω is not, like καταίρω, from αἴρω.) That even the fruit-bearing branches also need purging, points to the deep and thorough corruption of human nature. Calvin: "He mentioned the purging, because our flesh abounds in superfluous and noxious vices, and is only too fruitful of them." The means of the cleansing are manifold; and many other passages of Holy Scripture, as well as experience, make it plain that, among those means, tribulations are prominent. Many therefore suppose them to be mainly intended. But that *here* we must think of the purifying power of the *word*, is clear from ver. 3. Luther: "In what way that purifying comes, and what the purification truly is by which they are incorporated into Christ as living branches, He plainly shows, when He adds, Now ye are clean, etc." All other means are but subsidiary to the energy of this first and main instrument.

Ver. 3. "Now ye are clean through the word which I have spoken unto you."—The Lord had, in vers. 1 and 2, spoken generally. Henceforth He speaks with specific application to the disciples. He says here, first, that they, for the present, belong to the *second* of the two classes indicated in ver. 2. That was consolatory to their minds; but consolation was not our Lord's real end. The Lord's admission that they were clean, forms only a transition to the following exhortation to abiding in Him, which is the real pith of the whole section, as is plain enough from the word being repeated ten times. As soon as they forget the abiding, they fall back into the former class. Thus it was equivalent to saying, "Now ye are *indeed* already clean; *but*—" Lücke's " Be ye therefore without fear, ye will never be cut off," misses altogether the right point of view.— The purity here corresponds to the fruit-bearing in ver. 2. That it was only a commencing purification which they had received, is shown by the relation to ver. 2, where it is seen to be a process continually going on in the fruit-bearing branches; by the following words, in which the urgent exhortation to abide in Christ rests upon the consideration that there were still in them impure elements which struggled to get the mastery again; and by ver. 13, according to which Christ must, even for His disciples, lay down His life, and deliver them by His blood from their sin.[1]

The source or cause of the purity of the disciples is stated to be the *word* which Christ had spoken to them. That excludes every notion that they had acquired their cleansing by any efforts of their own, or any inherent righteousness possessed. The Father, in whom, according to ver. 2, the purifying energy has its final source, wrought it in them through the word of the Son. It is not any single word that is intended, as some think, who appeal to ch. xiii. 10 as that word; but the sum of all that which Christ had spoken, as Peter said to Him, "Thou hast the words of eternal life." In ver. 7 corresponds " and My words abide in you," where the $\dot{\rho}\acute{\eta}\mu\alpha\tau\alpha$ is but the expansion of the $\lambda\acute{o}\gamma o\varsigma$ in our present passage. Out of the word of Christ sprang that faith to which, in Acts xv. 9, the purification of the heart is ascribed. Thus the word is the final and proper cause of purity. To the word of Christ a high importance is here assigned; and we are therefore led to set our affection upon it, to meditate upon it day and night, and absolutely to submit our wills to its influence. We are warned against the deceitfulness of modern theology, which assumes to be censor and judge of the word which cleanses us, and wrests and perverts it every

---

[1] Augustin: Mundi atque mundandi. Neque enim nisi mundi essent, fructum ferre potuissent: et tamen omnem, qui fert fructum, purgat agricola, ut fructum plus afferat. Fert fructum, quia mundus est: atque ut plus afferat purgatur adhuc. Quis enim in hac vitâ sic mundus, ut non sit magis magisque mundandus?

way. It is the direct consequence of the importance here attached to the word, that Christ has taken care that it should be transmitted to His Church in an uncorrupted and pure form. As the complement of the word which Christ Himself spoke immediately to His disciples, we have, according to ch. xvi. 13, 14, that which He has communicated by His Spirit for the Church of all ages.

Ver. 4. "Abide in Me, and I in you. As the branch cannot bear fruit of itself, except it abide in the vine; no more can ye, except ye abide in Me."—To the fact uttered in the preceding verse, is now adjoined an exhortation. Then the Lord develops the motives which must afford the disciples an argument to abide in Him: that abiding alone makes them capable of bearing fruit, vers. 4, 5. Not abiding, is to fall under the Divine judgments, ver. 6. He who abideth may pray with assurance of being heard, ver. 7. He enters into an intimate fellowship with the Father and the Son, ver. 8. He receives the portion of that which, to the Apostles, was the best and highest good—the love of Christ, ver. 9. Then, after the nature of this abiding is still further explained and developed, ver. 10, there follows the concluding formula, ver. 11, "Abide in Me." It is shown by what follows that the disciples could not do this of themselves, and of their own power: "Without Me ye can do nothing." But they could, like Judas and the Jews, close their own hearts; they could wickedly hinder the efficacy of the means employed by Christ in order to their abiding; and they are here urgently exhorted not to do that. The main instrument by which Christ effects our abiding, is, according to ver. 3, His word. Their preservation could be secured only by the same means which wrought the beginning. In the fundamental passage relating to our abiding in Christ, John vi. 56, we read, "He that eateth My flesh, and drinketh My blood, abideth in Me, and I in him." There the means of abiding in Christ appears to be, that we incessantly receive the flesh and blood of Christ, and thereby more and more tame and discipline and render divine our own flesh and blood. This factor goes hand in hand with the Word of God. That Christ should be more and more evidently formed within us, is the tone and substance of the Word of God. Everything in it points to that—Christ attaining a full life in us.

The emphasis thrown upon "abide in Me" by our Lord, serves for the refutation of the doctrine of the indefectibility of grace. If this were a sound doctrine, our whole section would have been needless. The ten times repeated *abiding*, shows that there is not merely an abstract possibility of falling, but the most urgent danger of falling, against which we need to be every moment on our guard.

"And I in you." Some explain this as if the *exhortation* were here continued: Do your diligence, that I may be able to abide in you; by your own abiding, so demean yourselves, that I may still abide in you. But it is simpler to take it thus: So I also abide in you. Ch. vi. 56 confirms this view. Only the μείνετε ἐν ἐμοί has a hortatory meaning; as is plain from the fact, that the motive and inducement presently introduced refer to that alone.—As, in the reason urged for the abiding in Christ, all fruit-bearing is made dependent upon that abiding, this is a strong denunciation of fallen human nature, which out of its own resources can produce only sin or delusive virtue; and therefore it is a direct refutation of all Pelagianism.[1]

Ver. 5. "I am the vine, ye are the branches: he that abideth in Me, and I in him, the same bringeth forth much fruit; for without Me ye can do nothing."—The first words do not contain a mere repetition. The words which had been formerly spoken generally are now specifically applied to the relation to Christ and His disciples, in order to draw the conclusion, that they can bear fruit only in fellowship with Him. "Ye are the branches" does not imply that the disciples were the *only* branches. It is rather equivalent to saying: My relation to you is that of the vine to the branches. This does not exclude the fact, that with them there were, and after them should be, other branches. That there were other branches, and that the Jews in particular were such, is shown by vers. 2 and 6. The absolute relation of vine to the branches, which Jesus assumes in declaring His relation to His disciples,—His thus making Himself to be unconditionally the source of all spiritual powers

---

[1] Augustin: Magna gratiæ commendatio. Nonne huic resistunt veritati homines mente corrupti, reprobi circa fidem, qui loquuntur iniquitatem dicentes: a Deo habemus, quod homines sumus, a nobis ipsis, quod justi sumus?—Qui a semetipso se fructum existimat ferre, in vite non est; qui in vite non est in Christo non est, qui in Christo non est, Christianus non est.

of life,—presupposes and rests upon the basis of His divinity. Augustin: Quamvis autem Christus vitis non esset nisi homo esset: tamen istam gratiam palmitibus non præberet nisi etiam Deus esset. "Without Me ye can do nothing" leads to the deep corruption of our nature, and presupposes the πονηροὶ ὄντες in Matt. vii. 11, and "that which is born of the flesh is flesh" of ch. iii. 6. Thence will appear at the same time the necessity of the closest adherence to the vine, and of the firmest continuance in a state, to relapse from which is to fall back again into the old impotence. Augustin: Non ait, sine me *parum* potestis facere, sed nihil potestis facere. Luther: "Thus there is a heavy sentence pronounced upon all life and action, however great and glorious it may seem to be, which is out of Christ: man can do nothing, and be nothing, out of Him."

Ver. 6. "If a man abide not in Me, he is cast forth as a branch, and is withered; and men gather them, and cast them into the fire, and they are burned."—In the former words the abiding in Christ was commanded, on the ground that it alone would capacitate them to bring forth fruit. The not bearing fruit is a miserable lot. Here the exhortation assumes a still more solemn character: the *fire* is the issue of not abiding. "If any man abide not in Me"—whether it be that he never made a beginning of fruit-bearing, or that he afterwards fell away again, and thus relapsed into the state of the not-bearing branch, ver. 1. The limitation to the latter part of the alternative is negatived by the fact that there is reference to the words, "Every branch in Me that beareth not fruit," ver. 2, which evidently here have their full development; as also by the fact that Jesus, in the whole verse, has primarily in view the unbelieving Jews, who were as certainly branches in Christ, as they belonged to the people of God: the Jews had originally stood in a relation to Christ—He was their divinely-appointed Shepherd, and they His flock; but they did not abide in Him, they violently sundered themselves from Him. A comparison with Ezek. xv. makes this allusion to the Jews indubitable. There the Jews appear under the image of a degenerate and wild vine, which was fit for nothing in the world but to be burnt: "Shall wood be taken thereof to do any work? or will men take a pin of it to hang any vessel thereon? Behold, it is cast into the fire for fuel." We are led to the same result by the parallel with the last discourses of Christ in Matthew, which for the most part refer to the Divine judgment impending over the degenerate people. Especially we must bear in mind the symbolical treatment of the fig-tree that bore no fruit, but leaves only, Matt. xxi. 18 seq., Mark xi. 12–14; as also the parable of the vineyard, Matt. xxi. 33, Mark xii. 1 seq. As this last refers back to Jer. v., so our present parable rests upon Ezek. xv. It is obvious, however, that the reference to the Jews is only the primary one, and not the sole. The Lord speaks, indeed, to such as have already become Christians. But that there is a certain latitude of interpretation, which will refer the not abiding, or the falling away, to the Gentiles who were to be called into the kingdom of God, is taught by the parable of the guest who had not on a wedding garment: comp. also Rom. xi. 22, "But toward thee goodness, if thou continue ($\dot{\epsilon}\grave{\alpha}\nu\ \dot{\epsilon}\pi\iota\mu\epsilon\acute{\iota}\nu\eta s$) in His goodness; otherwise thou also shalt be cut off." This apostasy shall increase in a special manner towards the final period of the kingdom of God. That the $\tau\iota s$ designates rather an ideal person than an individual, a unity which embraces a real plurality of persons, is shown by the following $\alpha\dot{\upsilon}\tau\acute{\alpha}$ in the plural, which in the $\kappa\alpha\acute{\iota}\epsilon\tau\alpha\iota$ returns back into the ideal unity. It is not accidental that our Lord here uses the third person; not saying, "If ye abide not in Me," although immediately afterwards the direct address returns in ver. 7. This serves to intimate that the not abiding and the cutting off of Judas would not apply to any other of the Apostles; that to the remainder belonged rather the promises addressed to such as should abide in Christ.—The two aorists, $\dot{\epsilon}\beta\lambda\acute{\eta}\theta\eta$ and $\dot{\epsilon}\xi\eta\rho\acute{\alpha}\nu\theta\eta$, emphatically indicate that the guilt is at once followed by the decree of punishment, although the execution of that doom may be a little longer delayed. The נכרתה of the Mosaic law strictly corresponds. The soul that broke the Divine command is cut off at the moment of the breach itself.

The being cast out refers to exclusion from the kingdom of God: comp. Matt. viii. 12, "But the children of the kingdom $\dot{\epsilon}\kappa\beta\lambda\eta\theta\acute{\eta}\sigma\text{o}\nu\tau\alpha\iota$ ($\dot{\epsilon}\kappa\ \tau\hat{\eta}s\ \beta\alpha\sigma\iota\lambda\epsilon\acute{\iota}\alpha s$) into outer darkness." Matt. xxi. 43 gives us a commentary on the $\dot{\epsilon}\beta\lambda\acute{\eta}\theta\eta\ \ddot{\epsilon}\xi\omega$, so far as Jesus had the Jews in His eye when He spoke: "The kingdom of God shall be taken from them, and shall be given to a nation bringing forth the fruits thereof." The guilt corresponding to this retribution we have in Matt. xxi. 39 : " And they took him, and cast him out of the vineyard." They thrust the Lord of glory out of the vineyard, and as the penalty they are now themselves thrust out; or, at the moment when they did this, they did really cast themselves out: comp. also Luke xx. 16.— The ἐξηράνθη has here the same meaning as in the case of the fig-tree, which signifies the Jewish people, Matt. xxi. 19. It points to the solemn fact, that with severance from Christ all life and prosperity cease. The first evidence of this is in the spiritual and ecclesiastical life, which dies away. What a fearful change has passed upon Judaism, in regard to this, since the rejection of Christ! How saltless and vapid has everything become! But the withering has its reference also to outward prosperity. All bloom and every sign of well-being passed away with the rejection of the Messiah.

The plural συνάγουσι, βάλλουσι, is significant : it can refer only to the instruments of the Divine judgment, and shows that that judgment is to be executed by men. Lampe : Hoc judicium non immediate a Deo infligitur. Pater amputavit palmites : sed plures sunt qui eos colligunt. Comp. Isa. xiii. 3, " I have commanded My sanctified ones; I have also called My mighty ones for Mine anger;" and the Lord's own word, " Where the carcase is, there shall the eagles be gathered together," in which the eagles point to the Roman standards. If we carefully note the double plural, we shall not hastily with Stier interpret the *fire* as meaning the " great furnace at the end of the world." It signifies rather the Divine judgment, as in Deut. xxxii. 22 : " For a fire is kindled in Mine anger" (here fire is evidently expounded as wrath), " and shall burn unto the lowest hell; and shall consume the earth with her increase, and set on fire the foundations of the mountains." Just before, we read, " And I will move them to jealousy with those that are not a people; I will provoke them to anger with a foolish nation." The executioners of the Divine judgments are, throughout the chapter, the Gentiles. The Baptist had early threatened the Jews with the fire of Divine judgment in case they scorned to be baptized by Christ with the Holy Spirit, the sole preservative against the fire, Matt. iii. 10-12. So also the Redeemer Himself in Matt. vii. 19. In the Apocalypse the fire is *commonly* the fire of the Divine wrath : comp. my commentary on ch. iv. 5, viii. 5, xiv. 18. The material fire in Matt. xxii. 7, " And he sent forth his armies, and destroyed those murderers, καὶ τὴν πόλιν αὐτῶν ἐνέπρησε," is only the embodiment of this spiritual fire. That we must not here think primarily of the fire of hell, the final manifestation of the fire of the Divine wrath, is shown by the original passage in Ezekiel, ch. xv. There the fire is that of the Divine judgment by the hands of the Chaldeans; and the material of the fire is not individuals as such, but the catastrophe has a national import. The final form, however, of this fire is of course the fire of hell, Matt. v. 22, xxv. 41, xiii. 40, 42. The general doctrine is this, that their relation to Christ involves those in heavier guilt and punishment who cease from His fellowship, and who thereby sink back into a condition which is far worse than that of those with whom He never entered into any such relation.[1] The truth of this declaration of the Redeemer was demonstrated not only in the Jews, but also in many early flourishing Christian communities and peoples, which were consumed by the fire of the wrath of God because they failed to abide in the Vine.

Ver. 7. " If ye abide in Me, and My words abide in you, ye shall ask what ye will, and it shall be done unto you."—A new motive. To have the privilege to pray with acceptance is a high prerogative; and the condition of that privilege is abiding in Christ. To " if ye abide in Me" is appended, " and My words abide in you," in order to impress it upon the disciples that they must attach supreme importance to the words of the Lord, and give them all their due. It was through His words that they came to Christ, and their retaining His words that would decide their abiding in Him. He who deals frivolously or capriciously with Christ's words, who partially rejects them, or evades them by one-sided interpretation, deceives himself if he thinks that he abides in Christ. Lachmann's reading αἰτήσασθε, instead of αἰτήσεσθε, is condemned by the fact that the imperative never occurs in that form. The future is in ch. xvi. 26 the same as here; and the imperative was doubtless adopted through failure to understand the passage. If we

---

[1] Augustin: Ligna vitis tanto sunt contemtibiliora si in vite non manserint, quanto gloriosiora si manserint. Unum de duobus palmiti congruit, aut vitis aut ignis. Si in vite non est, in igne erit: ut ergo in igne non sit, in vite sit.

lose sight of the strict and inseparable connection of these words with those which follow, we may suppose that the future yields no appropriate meaning—as if every man might ask what he would; and consequently the imperative, giving an authority for such asking, would seem necessary. But if we pass on immediately to " and it shall be done," it becomes manifest that the words speak of petition that *may be granted*.—The limitation to " what ye will" is given by what precedes. Supplication for temporal good, for instance, cannot proceed from one in whom Christ's words abide, Luke xii. 15; his mind is set, and set wholly, on the true riches. Augustin: Aliud volumus quia sumus in Christo, et aliud volumus quia sumus adhuc in hoc seculo. Here, however, we must think especially of such asking as is concerned with the universal interests of the kingdom of God; for the Lord is not so much speaking to individuals as to the Church as such, represented by the Apostles. If the Church abides in Christ, she cannot fail of victory over the world, particularly the Jews, and then over the whole power of heathenism: comp. on ch. xiv. 12. All the Church's power, as outward, is dependent on her internal relation to Christ. If all is well there, her enemies need cause no alarm.

Ver. 8. " Herein is My Father glorified, that ye bear much fruit: so shall ye be My disciples."—We have here also a motive to abiding in Christ. For, according to what has preceded, the bringing forth fruit is dependent on that abiding. But this has here a double blessed result. First, the Father is glorified by it, on whose ground the fruit is borne (Bengel: Multitudo uvarum honorifica est vinitori); and this is of itself a blessed thing, fruitful in the reward that follows: comp. ch. xiii. 32. And then, secondly, they thereby advance more and more into the blessed condition of the disciples of Christ, whose most characteristic token is the bearing much fruit. In the sermon on the mount, we have the glorification of the Father set forth as a motive to zeal in good works, Matt. v. 16. In regard to $\dot{\epsilon}\delta o\xi\acute{a}\sigma\theta\eta$, the proleptic aorist, comp. Winer. Before $\gamma\epsilon\nu\acute{\eta}\sigma\epsilon\sigma\theta\epsilon$, we must supplement $\dot{\epsilon}\nu$ $\tau o\acute{\upsilon}\tau\omega$. Beza: Ita glorificabitur Pater meus, et ita demum eritis mei discipuli, si multum fructum attuleritis. Some expositors interpret, " Thereby My Father is glorified in your bringing forth much fruit, and becoming My disciples." But, in harmony with the figure, the exhortation refers only to the bearing of fruit. The result that they become disciples in relation to Christ, is simply parallel with the result that the Father is glorified: comp. ver. 1; ch. viii. 31 also is in favour of the co-ordination, ἐὰν ὑμεῖς μείνητε ἐν τῷ λόγῳ τῷ ἐμῷ, ἀληθῶς μαθηταί μου ἐστέ. As there, so here also, the Lord makes the becoming disciples a *promise*. 'Αληθῶς may have passed over from that passage to this. The ἐμοί is also an argument for the co-ordination of Christ with the Father. The becoming disciples also could scarcely with propriety be made the condition of the glorification of the Father. The reading γένησθε originated in an incorrect notion concerning the dependence of ἵνα, which only in a few exceptional cases is connected with the indicative future. The saying teaches us that the final end of our actions should be the good pleasure of God and His glory, and that we cannot more effectually attain that object than by zeal in good works; and the fact that these are dependent on our abiding in Christ, should urge us continually to adhere to Him. Further, we are taught that we may only then assure ourselves of our intimate relation to Christ, when there is in ourselves that inseparable result of abiding in Him, the bearing of fruit.

Ver. 9. " As the Father hath loved Me, so have I loved you: continue ye in My love."—The last motive: Abiding in Christ is the only means of retaining the highest good, Christ's love. " As the Father hath loved Me:" the love of Jesus receives its highest significance in this, that it is the reflection of the Father's love to Him. The love of Him whom the Father loveth as His Son, should be preserved as the apple of our eye. The word is, " hath loved Me," because only those demonstrations of the Father's love to the Son which had been openly witnessed come here into consideration. " My love" can be only the love of Christ to His people, not the love of His people to Him. They would abide in this love, if they did not, like the Jews, constrain Him through their apostasy to withdraw His love from them; or, in other words, if they kept His commandments, ver. 10. Strictly parallel with this is, in Rom. xi. 22, the " continuing in His goodness," not losing it through apostasy. Christ's love is suggested also by a comparison of the abiding in the vine, " in Me," ver. 4. Accordingly, here also the discourse must refer to abiding in an objective person.

Ver. 10. " If ye keep My commandments, ye shall abide in

My love; even as I have kept My Father's commandments, and abide in His love."—That the ἀγάπη μου is the love of Christ to His people, is evident from the corresponding ἀγάπη ἐμή in ver. 9. Consequently, the love of God also at the end must be the love of God to Christ, not the love of Christ to God. To this we are led also by ch. x. 17 : " For this cause My Father loveth Me, because I lay down My life." The laying down the life there corresponds to the keeping the commandments of God here. This was manifested especially in the fact, that Christ, in obedience to the will of the Father, presented the atoning sacrifice. " Even as I have kept," etc., hangs on ver. 9. As Christ's love to His people is the reflection of the Father's love to Him, it is natural that its maintenance should rest on the same condition. We have here generally a thought which is the counterpart of ver. 9. To the exhortation of that verse, urging the disciples to continue in the enjoyment of His love, is here appended an indication of the means in order to that continuance.

Ver. 11. "These things have I spoken unto you, that My joy might remain in you, and that your joy might be full."—Properly " might be in you," not " might remain ;" it is ᾖ, not μείνῃ. *My joy*, in contradistinction to *your joy*, can only be the joy of Christ in His disciples or over them ; especially as the interpretation, " My *joyfulness* may be in you," is opposed altogether by the phraseology. The joy of Christ is described as being in His people, inasmuch as it is a transcendent passion or affection, which penetrates its object, and sinks into it entirely. In the Hebrew, verbs expressing joy are frequently connected with ב. In the same way as joy is spoken of here, it is spoken of also in Luke xv. 5, 7, 10. Comp. Eph. iv. 30, according to which the Holy Ghost is *grieved* by the sins of the elect. But there are Old Testament passages which expressly illustrate it : such as Ps. xlv. 9, where it is said, in reference to the bride of the Divine King of the future age, " Out of the ivory palaces, whereby they have made thee glad ;" Isa. lxii. 5, " As the bridegroom rejoiceth over the bride, so shall thy God rejoice over thee ;" and Zeph. iii. 17, " The Lord thy God in the midst of thee is mighty ; He will save, He will rejoice over thee with joy, He will rest in His love, He will joy over thee with singing."

The joy of the disciples keeps pace with the joy of the Redeemer. That joy is *fulfilled* when it attains its climax: comp. on ch. iii. 29. It therefore means, "And the highest joy shall be yours." The climax of all joy is the consciousness of being and abiding in Christ: comp. Song of Solomon i. 4, "The king hath brought me to his chambers. We will be glad and rejoice in thee. We will remember thy love more than wine."—We have here the concluding formula of the first part of Christ's farewell discourses. That which He lays down as the design of His words (comp. ch. xvi. 1, 33), which exhort to abiding in Him, is at the same time a motive to that abiding. Who must not wish that Christ may be able to rejoice in him? And who would rob himself of his own joy, which rises or declines in proportion as Christ's command to abide in Him is responded to?

There follows now, in vers. 12-17, the New Testament supplement of the *second* table of the law.[1] As in the former section abiding was the watchword, so now it is *love*. Jesus bases the commandment of Christian brotherly love upon the type and example of *His own* love, ver. 12. The greatness of His love He exhibits by intimating that it urged Him to lay down His life for His friends, ver. 13. To such great love they were to respond—this is a *second* motive—by obedience to His commandments, especially that of brotherly love, ver. 14. His love, however, did not declare itself merely in His sacrificial death; it finds expression also in this, that He makes His friends sharers and fellow-partakers of His knowledge of the mysteries of God, ver. 15; and this was all the more a reason why they should return His love by faithful obedience, especially in reference to His commandment of brotherly love. And they should further be urged to love by the consideration, that Jesus, vers. 16, 17, who elected them, and therefore had the right to impose the conditions of their relation to Him, specified as those conditions that they should bring forth fruit, and specifically that they should love one another. Thus we have here three motives: the example of Christ; the obedience to which they are bound by His love; and the fulfilment of the condition under which their election was vouchsafed to them.

[1] J. Gerhard: Duo exhortationis capita; primo ut vere credentes uniret sibi, secundo ut eos uniret inter se invicem.

Ver. 12. "This is My commandment, That ye love one another, as I have loved you."—This is My commandment: that is, in regard to your relation to each other. By ἀλλήλους the domain is indicated in which this commandment is all in all. If we fail to bear in mind the limitation prescribed by the context, we must needs interpret it by saying that brotherly love is only a single expression of a generally renewed and right Christian spirit, that it shows in one point the goodness of all, and that therefore this commandment is in a certain sense the only one. Augustin: "Where there is love, there must be faith and hope; and where there is brotherly love, there must be also the love of God." But the Scripture is not wont to speak thus; it does not place thus in the background the first and great commandment. We read in Rom. xiii. that "love is the fulfilling of the law;" the connection teaches us—especially ver. 8, "Owe no man anything, but to love one another: he that loveth his neighbour hath fulfilled the law"—that the fulfilment of the law is meant so far as it refers to our relation to one another.

Ver. 13. "Greater love hath no man than this, that a man lay down his life for his friends."—The injunction of brotherly love had been grounded on the love of Christ to His disciples. The strength of His own love our Lord here further declares, and thus points to the strength of the obligation entailed, and the height of the demand which gratitude urged. "He teaches us," says Quesnel, "as our Master, our love to the brethren; to copy the love which He bears to us." If I have loved you to the extent of sacrificing My life for you, ye must also have a fervent and self-sacrificing love to each other. We have the unfolding of the same thought in 1 John iii. 16, Eph. v. 1, 2. Jesus here speaks of the laying down of His life, in allusion to Isa. liii. 10: comp. on ch. x. 11, where the sheep correspond to the *friends* of this passage. That the death of Christ comes into view as a *sacrificial death*, is evident from the reference to a passage in the Old Testament that treats of the sacrificial death of the servant of God. A death of mere devotion is quite unsuitable here. Christ did not save the life of His disciples by dying for them. Even His *friends* need an atoning sacrifice ("And hath given Himself for us an offering and sacrifice to God, προσφορὰν καὶ θυσίαν," as we read in Eph. v. 2). So active is sin and the corresponding wrath of God. The friends here are, however, to be distinguished from the *sinners* and *enemies* of Rom. v. 8, 10; and Lücke's remark, that "only because He in His love thinks of sinners as friends, does He die for them," fails to meet the case. What Paul there wrote, St John could not here have written. The Apostles to whom Christ is here speaking were not sinners and enemies in the sense in which St Paul there speaks of sinners and enemies. "Greater love:" love is here spoken of in relation to the disciples, who were already friends. Hence there is no propriety in the objection that has been urged, viz. that love to enemies and dying for them was greater. In relation to friends, the offering up of life is the greatest demonstration of love. Luther says: "He is so gentle and tender to them, that He speaks into their heart this last commandment that He leaves them; impressing upon them that they should consider and think how He loved them, and what He had done for them. This is My commandment: I lay it upon you, and demand it as the return of My great and unspeakable love, *if indeed ye would that men should know you for My disciples.*"

Ver. 14. "Ye are My friends, if ye do whatsoever I command you."—We have here a *second* motive. In the preceding verse, the injunction of brotherly love had been based upon the example of Christ. Here it is based upon the obedience which the disciples of Christ as His friends are bound to render. As friends He treats His disciples, when He gives up His life for them; as friends they should approve themselves, by fulfilling His commandment, and thus loving one another.

Ver. 15. "Henceforth I call you not servants; for the servant knoweth not what his lord doeth: but I have called you friends; for all things that I have heard of My Father I have made known unto you."—The practical reasoning runs as in ver. 14. Christ treats His disciples as friends, not only by dying for them, but also by the free communication of all that which He had heard of the Father. Such love they should requite by fulfilling His commandments, especially that of loving one another. $\Delta o\hat{v}\lambda o\varsigma$ is here the antithesis of $\phi\iota\lambda \acute{o}\varsigma$: a servant and nothing more, a mere slave. The absolute dependence of the disciples on Christ can never cease: even as friends, they still are servants: comp. ch. xiii. 13, 16, and here, ver. 20.

Εἴρηκα refers to what had just been spoken. The Lord had at an earlier period termed the disciples friends, Luke xii. 4; but now the relation of friendship had reached its point of consummation through the perfected revelation of the Divine counsels, mysteries, and doctrines. " All things : " this is spoken generally, and does not exclude the fact that there was very much to be imparted to the disciples at a later period; which they were not as yet able to hear (comp. ch. xiv. 26, xvi. 12–14), as also that there was much which our Lord withheld from the disciples, as generally transcending human capacity, and having no tendency to further them in the way of salvation. Suffice that Jesus withheld nothing from them through lack of love; and the limitation which Calvin expresses is plain from the nature of the case: " Nothing of those things which concerned our salvation, and which it imported that we should know." The expression implies obviously the absolute supremacy of the person of Christ, and the infinite interval between Him and His disciples. What endless love was it, that the eternal Son of the Father should communicate to poor mortals those mysteries which He possessed through fellowship with His Father; and how urgent the obligation to requite that love with obedience! The form of expression suggests the similarity of Jer. xxi. 10.

The Old Testament revelation was a prelude of the revelation perfected in the Son, Heb. i. 1; and the rather, as even in the prophets it was the Spirit of Christ who spake, 1 Pet. i. 11.

Vers. 16, 17. " Ye have not chosen Me, but I have chosen you, and ordained you, that ye should go and bring forth fruit, and that your fruit should remain ; that whatsoever ye shall ask of the Father in My name, He may give it you. These things I command you, that ye love one another."—A new reason, the *third.* The disciples did not choose Christ, but Christ chose the disciples. Therein lay the propriety of His laying down the conditions of discipleship. One fundamental condition is, that they bear fruit; and it was therefore necessary that they should love one another, for brotherly love is part of the fruit of discipleship.—The *choosing* here, as in ch. vi. 70, xiii. 18, is the assumption into the number of the Apostles. And the enumeration among the faithful was of course included. To ask whether the election referred to the Apostles or to the believers, is as perverse as to ask whether in 1 Sam. xvi. 13 the gift of the Spirit, common to all believers, is spoken of, or the royal charisma. When applied to all believers, the term refers only to the Christian privilege or state, as such. The *ordaining* marks the high and independent prerogative of assigning their lot. The word ὑπάγειν, " that ye should go," is not superfluous; but it points to the fact that Christianity is such a continuous movement of life. The bringing forth fruit embraces at once the good works which are common to all believers, and those which were peculiar to the apostolical office. That it here stands specially connected with Christian brotherly love, is manifest from its connection with what precedes; and in ver. 17 it is expressly asserted.

The words, " that your fruit should remain: that whatsoever ye shall ask the Father in My name, He may give it you," forsake the main thought, and indicate, by the way, what would abundantly encourage the disciples in the fulfilment of the duty of their vocation to bring forth fruit. The fruit would approve itself to be abiding—as fruit that does not perish, but has the best results (comp. 1 Cor. xv. 58, " knowing that your labour is not in vain in the Lord")—by this, that it would place the disciples in the blessed condition of offering acceptable prayer, and prayer that would always be answered : comp. on ch. xiv. 13 and xvi. 23. By their fruit they would show themselves to be the genuine disciples of Christ; and to such the Father can deny nothing which they ask in the name of His Son. That every offence against love affects injuriously the offering of acceptable prayer, had been many times impressed upon them by their Master: comp. Matt. vi. 14, 15, v. 23, and Peter's words in 1 Pet. iii. 7.—Ver. 17 serves at one and the same time as the complement of the thought in ver. 16, and as the final formula for the whole section, corresponding to the close of the first section in ver. 11.

The relation of the disciples to Christ, to each other, to the world, are the three fundamental points which needed establishment, definition, and adjustment. Our Lord comes to the last in ch. xv. 18-xvi. 11, not as it were fortuitously, as if the injunction of brotherly love naturally suggested the hatred of the world. That is only the formal link of connection between the two sections, which does not affect the independent import of this latter. Still less are we to suppose that the hatred of the world is introduced merely to strengthen the motive, or add one to the motives, to enforce the exhortation to brotherly love contained in the previous section. (Lampe: Tacite novo argumento præceptum amoris fraterni stabilitur. Illis enim potissimum incumbit, ut vi unita fortiores se reddant, quibus multi et timendi hostes imminent.) There is nothing to warrant such a view; and the introduction of it tends greatly to imperil the independence of a section so important as this. It was of the greatest moment that the disciples should rightly apprehend their relation to the world—that they should be rightly persuaded at the very outset that they would have nothing to expect from the world but hatred and persecution—and that they should know the reason of this. Otherwise the "strangeness" of it, 1 Pet. iv. 12, would have led them into great temptations. In ch. xvi. 1, the Lord declares that the aim of His communication was expressly to obviate temptations from that source. If the disciples knew from the beginning what they had to expect from the world—if they discerned it as a necessity, based upon the relation of the world to Christ and to the Father,—then persecution, whenever it set in, could have no strength to mislead them as to their Master's cause; it would rather strengthen their faith in Him who had so clearly and expressly set before them what they had to expect from the world. But the Lord does not limit Himself to a description of their danger, and a development of its necessity: He refers the Apostles also to the *help* which they might look for; and the Church has, from the day of Pentecost downwards, gloriously realized that promise.

The formal articulation of the section is seen in the circumstance, that according to the common division of seven into five and two, the watchword *world* occurs five times at the beginning, and twice at the close. It may be distributed thus: the hatred of the world and its cause generally, vers. 18–25; and the preliminary reference to the help to be afforded in encountering it, vers. 26, 27. Then in ch. xvi. 1–4 we have the climax of the hatred, its paroxysms (to use Bengel's expression); and thereupon, in vers. 5–11, the still more developed reference to the sending of the Paraclete.—In ch. xv. 18–25, the arrangement is as follows: the Lord first, in vers. 18–20, exhibits the hatred of the world towards His disciples as the necessary fruit of their hatred to Him; then, in vers. 21–24, He refers back their hatred to Himself to their hatred to the Father; and finally, in ver. 25, He points to the fact, that the Jews, the portion of the world then before His eyes, only fulfilled, through their hatred to Him, the predictions of the Old Testament Scripture.

Ver. 18. "If the world hate you, ye know that it hated Me before it hated you."—That γινώσκετε is imperative, the corresponding μνημονεύετε in ver. 20 shows. The Lord's meaning refers to a *living* knowledge, which alone is able to furnish effectual aid against the assaults of temptation. If the world first hated Christ, its hatred must have rested on some essential principle of necessity; and true Christians must be conscious of a strong willingness to submit to a hatred which is the inseparable concomitant of membership in Christ, and the absence of which infers the absence of that union. Augustin: "Thou refusest to be in the body, if thou declinest to bear with Christ the hatred of the world." Bernard: "Do not the members follow the body? If we receive good things from our Head, why should we not also endure evil? Do we wish to reject the troublesome, and communicate with Him only in the pleasant? It is not a great thing that the member should suffer with the Head, when with the Head it will be glorified." Luther: "Had they not first hated Christ, they would not now hate me. But because they hated Him who died for them, what wonder that they oppose me: what am I in comparison of the Lord?" He who duly considers that the world hated Christ before it hated himself, will not, when the world's hatred presses him hard, yield to the temptation to think that Christ might have spared him these heavy assaults, and to murmur because He has not. He will rather regard his trial as the seal of his union with his Lord. In *the world* the Lord saw primarily that phase of the world with which the disciples had pre-eminently to do— Judaism. This is proved by the present, μισεῖ, in reference to the disciples; by the perfect, μεμίσηκεν, in reference to Christ; by the sequel, wherein Jesus speaks of those who had heard His discourses, and had seen His works; by ver. 25, where the Lord refers to those who were subject to the law; and by the ἀποσυναγώγους, in ch. xvi. 2. He introduces here a new principle of division, to which a Jew would find it hard to reconcile himself. Hitherto Judaism and heathenism had confronted each other. Now, however, the contrast is simply between the world and the Church; and unbelieving Judaism, in spite of the law, and circumcision, and the Passover, must needs sink into a subdivision of the world. But obviously the Jews were only primarily meant. The idea of the world embraces in itself " all nations," all the children of Adam who have not, by union with Christ, been redeemed from their natural ruin and regenerated, and by abiding in Him maintained their new estate.

Ver. 19. "If ye were of the world, the world would love his own: but because ye are not of the world, but I have chosen you out of the world, therefore the world hateth you."—The hatred of the world does not aim at human weakness in the disciples. It is evoked rather by their good side, that which they have specifically Christian, the image of Christ stamped upon them. In this the world beholds something strange and repulsive; something unfamiliar and intolerable, because it, in act and reality, is a continual protest against the world. On " the world would love its own," Luther says: " But He speaks as to matters concerning the Gospel. Here they all agree together—Pilate, Herod, Caiaphas, Judas, and all devils—against Christ and His people, however otherwise at enmity among themselves. Towards each other, apart from Christ, they are such friends as dogs and cats; but in all that concerns Christ they are quite unanimous in their hatred." With all subordinate differences, there remains ever an absolute concord in the essential matter. The election manifests itself in this, that Christ impresses upon those who, like others, were children of wrath (Eph. ii. 3), His own stamp; renews in them His own image; imparts to them thoughts, inclinations, and tempers, altogether different from those of the world, springing from a source quite other than that opened by the fall. Thence arises a contrast which has no parallel, and which conceals beneath it no latent principle of unity.—If the hatred of the world springs from the source thus indicated, it ought not to be matter of dismay, but rather to be rejoiced in as a sign of election, the highest prerogative of man.

Ver. 20. "Remember the word that I said unto you, The servant is not greater than his lord. If they have persecuted Me, they will also persecute you; if they have kept My saying, they will keep yours also."—The saying, "The servant is not greater than his lord," had been spoken, ch. xiii. 16, in another connection: the disciples were not to fail in or shrink from those manifestations of love in which their Master had preceded them as their example. This was His primary meaning; but the translation of this watchword into another region would be all the more easily understood by the disciples, inasmuch as Jesus had once before, Matt. x. 24, used it in precisely the same way. The τηρεῖν τὸν λόγον must mean, following the parallels, retaining the word in mind, as opposed to a thoughtless forgetfulness, and a scornful rejection of it: comp. ch. viii. 51, 52, 55, xiv. 15, 21, 23, 24, xv. 10. The Lord places the condition and the result in juxtaposition, and leaves it to the Apostles to decide which of the two propositions assumed is the existent state of the case, and so to shape their prognostic of the future. If we include the past and the present, then the Lord's word continues thus: "As they have persecuted Me, they will also persecute you; as they have not kept My word, but rather on account of it have laid snares for My life, ch. viii. 37, so will they not keep your word, but rather on account of it place your lives in danger. Thus ye see clearly what ye have to expect from them; and when the peril shall come, ye must not think it a strange thing, and take it ill." It is plain from the "all these things" of ver. 21, which cannot of course refer simply to "they will persecute," that beneath the alternative at the close, there is an announcement of snares and various dangers impending. When the Lord speaks of the Apostles' word as not kept, it is clear that He speaks of them as Apostles, as appointed ministers of the word, and not merely as representatives of believers. J. Gerhard: "He subjoins the mention of their word, that He may fortify them against the offence of their Gospel being despised when they should preach it." Luther hits the practical point well: "It is not fit that the Head should wear a crown of thorns, and the members sit upon cushions.— Therefore let it not seem strange to you; for thus it is with Me." The Saviour had, in vers. 18-20, opened up to the disciples a consolatory aspect of the sufferings which they had to expect from the world: they suffer "for My sake," as Christians. We perceive the strength of this consolation by examining Acts v. 41: "But they went from the presence of the council rejoicing, ὅτι ὑπὲρ τοῦ ὀνόματος κατηξιώθησαν ἀτιμασθῆναι:" comp. also 1 Pet. iv. 16. But the consolation was not yet perfect. There remained yet another important stumblingblock. Did not the matter stand as all the authorities, and the immense preponderance of the people, thought,—on the one side Jesus and His disciples, on the other side God and the Jews? This stumblingblock our Lord takes, in vers. 21-25, out of the way. The persecution which the world, or the Jews, directed against the disciples for the name of Jesus, rested upon ignorance of that God in whom they boasted, ver. 21. For as Jesus had approved Himself the Sent of God by His words, full of spirit and life, their hatred of Him was a hatred of God, His Father, as well as of Christ Himself, vers. 22, 23. And all the more, as His works, such as no other had done, ver. 24, had gone hand in hand with His words. The matter, therefore, stood thus: on the one side the disciples, Christ, the Father; on the other the world, with its princes, the Jews, who, by their rejection of Christ, had been transformed from the Church of God into the synagogue of Satan. Who would not rejoice to suffer at the hands of the world, in the fellowship of Christ and of the Father?

Ver. 21. "But all these things will they do unto you for My name's sake, because they know not Him that sent Me."— The ἀλλά points to the introduction of a new thought. Now that new thought we do not find in the "for My name's sake," equivalent to "on account of My historical manifestation and personality" (compare διὰ τὸ ὄνομά μου, Matt. x. 22, xxiv. 9; ἕνεκεν ἐμοῦ, Matt. v. 11). For it had been already taught in vers. 18-20, that Christ was the cause of the hatred of the world against His disciples. The new element lies rather in this, that the matter of vers. 18-20, the persecution for Christ's sake, is referred to ignorance of the Father as its primary source, and thus the disciples are saved from the solicitude of thinking that the Father was against them. If the Jews had known the Father, they must have loved Christ, whom the Father had sent, and in whom He had revealed Himself.

Ver. 22. "If I had not come and spoken unto them, they had not had sin; but now they have no cloak for their sin."— That the Jews, by their hatred to Christ, had revealed their ignorance of the Father, Christ *proves* first by His *words*, which exalted Him far above the level of mortality, and demonstrated that the Father had sent Him, and that the Angel of the Lord, whom the Old Testament magnified, had appeared in Him in the flesh. By the side of this proof from the *words*, comes in the proof from the *works*, in ver. 24. The καὶ ἐλάλησα αὐτοῖς is badly translated by Luther, "und hätte es ihnen gesagt," and *told them*. "And had spoken to them" refers rather to the whole substance and body of the discourses of Christ during His ministry, which had loudly and always protested against their separating Him from His Father. He was by them declared to be the Sent of the Father; for the words which He had spoken were spirit and life, and consequently argument of His superhuman life: comp. on ch. vi. 63; "Thou hast the words of eternal life," ver. 68; the avowal which the servants of the high priests were constrained to make, that never man spoke like this man, ch. vii. 46; and the testimony to His discourse, in Matt. vii. 28, 29, "The people *were astonished* at His doctrine: for He taught them as one having authority, and not as the scribes." The *words* and the *works* constituted the double evidence which Jesus adduced, as here so also in ch. xiv. 10, for His being in the Father. In Luke x. 23, 24, He said to His disciples, "Blessed are the eyes which see the things which ye see: for I say unto you, that many prophets and kings desired to see the things which ye see, and have not seen them; and to hear the things which ye hear, and have not heard them." There our Lord appeals to the great double evidence of His words and His works to attest His heavenly origin.

The ἦλθον has no independent meaning, but is connected with ἐλάλησα, and should not be separated from it by a comma. According to the connection with what precedes, where the Lord had spoken of the unbelief and hatred displayed by the Jews towards Himself, the words, "If I had not come and spoken to them," must mean, "If they had not been *unbelieving*, in spite of My having spoken to them, and demonstrated and made plain My Divine mission by My discourses."—"They had not had sin;" that is, no sin of such all-penetrating importance: comp. on ch. ix. 41, "If ye were blind, ye would not have sin." The universal disease of the human race scarcely comes into consideration, in comparison with *this* sin of unbelief in Christ, as attested and legitimated by His words. That this is, strictly speaking, the *only* sin, is involved in the fact that its essence is a guilty contempt of the only remedy for sin. Augustin: "For this is the sin by which all sins are retained; whosoever has it not, to him all sins are remitted." A disease for which there is offered a sure remedy, can scarcely be regarded as a disease. In ch. xvi. 9, also, the not believing on Christ appears as the climax of all sin, and in a certain sense the only sin. So also, in Matt. xi. 20-24, where Jesus condemns the cities in which He had performed most of His wonderful works, and declares their guilt to have been incomparably greater than that of Tyre and Sidon, cities notorious for their heathenish abominations, greater indeed than even that of Sodom.—"But now they have no cloak for their sin." For sin before Christ there was a πρόφασις, an excuse, that of ignorance, Acts xvii. 30, 1 Pet. i. 14: men knew not, and could not know, better; on which account in the Old Testament there is foreannounced a future restoration to the greatest sinners, doomed by the judgments of God to temporal destruction. This kind of excuse has indeed only a relative significance; but an excuse of that relative kind was expressed by the term πρόφασις. The antithesis here gives the preceding "had not had sin" its limitation and precise meaning; such sin as much may be said to apologize for, cannot in the fullest and deepest sense be called sin. Without this limitation, these words, "they had not had sin," would have been a contradiction to the law and the prophets of the Old Testament, would have been inconsistent with the Divine judgments preceding Christ, and with the language of Rom. i. 18.[1]

Ver. 23. "He that hateth Me, hateth My Father also."— This is not merely asserted here by Christ. It is rather an inference from that which had been laid down on the former verse. Since Jesus had by His words approved Himself the *Son*, it followed that the hatred displayed against Him was displayed against the *Father* also. The Jews professed that they loved God, and that on the ground of that love they

---

[1] Calvin: "He does not absolve them entirely, but extenuates the gravity of their wickedness. Nor was it the design of Christ to promise indulgence to others; but to hold His enemies, who had contumaciously rejected the grace of God, convicted of their sin; whence it appeared plainly that they were altogether unworthy of grace and mercy."

hated Christ; the God, however, whom they loved was not a true God, but a phantom which they named God. This was as certain as it was that Christ's words had declared Him to be the Son. The fact that they rejected Christ, in spite of all His words so full of spirit and truth, detected their hypocrisy, and showed them to be manifest enemies of that Father whom they professed to love.

Ver. 24. "If I had not done among them the works which none other man did, they had not had sin: but now have they both seen and hated both Me and My Father."—We have here the *second* proof of the proposition, that the Jews by their hatred of Christ had displayed their ignorance of the Father, and their hatred of Him. It lay in this, that Christ by His *works* had most amply declared Himself to be the Sent of the Father. That the Jews hated Him, in spite of His works, was a sin in comparison of which all former sin sank into insignificance. "Which none other man did" may be compared with Matt. ix. 33, where the multitudes cried on account of the healing a dumb and deaf man under demoniac influence, "It was never so seen in Israel." The miracles of Jesus acquired, through their connection with the dignity of His person, an absolute supremacy over all that had been wrought under the Old Testament; apart from the fact that some individual miracles—such as the healing of the man born blind (ch. ix. 32), and the raising of Lazarus—had no parallel or approximation in the Old Testament.

Ver. 25. "But this cometh to pass, that the word might be fulfilled that is written in their law, They hated Me without a cause."—The Lord now obviates another objection, which might be drawn from the Jews' enmity against Him, by pointing out that they were, and would be, only instruments in the fulfilment of that which was written in the Old Testament Scriptures, and consequently that their hatred would serve only as an authentication of His claims. It was an Old Testament fundamental principle, that no righteous man, and least of all the Christ, would fail to encounter the hatred and persecution of the world. Accordingly, Christ would not be Christ without the hatred of the Jews. So also, in ch. xii. 38, 39, the opposition of the Jews to Christ was regarded in the light of a Divine appointment, through which the fulfilment of Old

Testament prophecy was brought about. Seen from this point of view, the hatred of the Jews should have no power to dishearten, but rather to fill with the highest joy. We see in it the presence of the Divine hand, impressing upon Christ the seal of authentication. The ἀλλά points to the circumstance that a new point of view in regard to the hatred of the Jews is opened up. Accordingly τοῦτο γέγονεν must be supplemented: comp. xix. 36, and probably also xiii. 38, Matt. xxvi. 56, Mark xiv. 49. The name of the *law* is here, as in x. 34, xii. 34, referred to the entire Old Testament, because the remaining books divide with the Mosaic the whole. "In *their* law;" so that thus the criteria of the Messiah, given in the law, were such as they were obliged to accept and be regulated by.

In reference to the ἐμίσησάν με δωρεάν, we may collate the following passages of the Old Testament. First, Ps. xxxv. 19. There the suffering just man says, "Let not them that are mine enemies wrongfully rejoice over me; neither let them wink with the eye that hate me without a cause:" Sept. οἱ μισοῦντές με δωρεάν. Then, again, the fourth verse of Ps. lxix., which is so often cited and applied to Christ. There the suffering Righteous One says, "They that hate Me without a cause (Sept. again, οἱ μισοῦντές με δωρεάν) are more than the hairs of Mine head; they that would destroy Me, being Mine enemies wrongfully, are mighty." It will be seen that these two passages have in common "hating me without a cause," and "enemies wrongfully." These verbal resemblances and parallels, which are peculiar to the Davidic psalms of the Righteous One, have the effect of indicating that they are links of a great chain, parts of a great descriptive painting. So, finally, Ps. cix. 3, "They compassed Me about also with words of hatred; and fought against Me without a cause:" Sept. ἐπολέμησάν με δωρεάν. In this psalm too the suffering Righteous One speaks. "That the singer had in view, at the same time, the family of David, and especially Him in whom it would reach its crown;—that the psalm, as it proceeded from David, so also went back to him (in his offspring), and kept him ever in view,—cannot be doubted when we compare the *last* verse of the psalm with the first of Ps. cx., and with the fifth verse of the same. Here it is the help of the Lord, which He sends to His anointed in His sufferings; there it is the glory which He sheds upon the saved one. Here we see how He stands at the right hand to save him from those who condemn his soul; there we hear Him saying the great word, Sit thou at My right hand." This connection of the 109th Psalm with the 110th throws a wonderful light upon the remaining psalms of David which refer to the suffering Righteous One. The quotation here is designedly combined from the three passages quoted. From the first two we have the *hating;* the third is indicated by the fact that the verb there is in the preterite. The co-reference to this passage is of importance, inasmuch as there the final reference to Christ, which is rather concealed in most of the passages which treat of the suffering righteous, appears most expressly and plainly.

Ver. 26. "But when the Comforter is come, whom I will send unto you from the Father, even the Spirit of truth, which proceedeth from the Father, He shall testify of Me."—Jesus had hitherto fortified the disciples against the hatred of the Jews, by reminding them that it fell upon them on account of His name; that the hatred which they felt for Him had His *Father* also for its object; and finally, that this hatred subserved the fulfilment of Old Testament prophecy. A new element now enters. It might have been supposed from the previous considerations, that Jesus had already now finished with the Jews. But this issue would have been at variance with the prophecies of the Old Testament, which were not satisfied by all that had been yet attained. According to those prophecies, the calling of a special election was as necessary as the rejection of the mass. Hence our Lord intimates that the work of salvation among the Jews was not sealed and closed; and that He would oppose to their hatred such a power in the Paraclete as should subdue many into submission. The Christ of truth, coming from the Father, would with victorious power break down the opposition of many. Thus the disciples were prevented from making the enmity of the Jews a source of despondency.

These words concerning the Paraclete do not point back to ch. xiv. 26—that saying is not taken up again until ch. xvi. 13—but to ch. xiv. 16, where the question is the same as it is here, the warfare against an unfriendly world. The Holy Ghost is the Paraclete only inasmuch as He in this conflict lends His aid. The idea of the Paraclete is elucidated in 2 Tim. iv. 16: "At my first answer no man stood with me, but all men forsook me: notwithstanding the Lord stood with me, and strengthened me." The human paracletes, or judicial advocates—which service in ancient times was discharged not merely by counsellors, but also by distinguished friends—had forsaken the Apostle; but, instead of them, the heavenly Paraclete had faithfully stood by his side—Christ, that is, by the Spirit whom He sent. The ὑμῖν must be carefully noted. It shows that the Holy Spirit is considered here as having His indwelling in the Apostles, and not as simply exerting His immediate influence upon the minds of those to whom they preached the word. So, in ch. xvi. 8, it is only a false interpretation which finds anything like a direct relation of the Paraclete to the world. This is evident from the preceding πρὸς ὑμᾶς in ver. 7. We may compare the "filled with the Holy Ghost" in Acts iv. 8; and Luke xxiv. 49, where the Lord, after His resurrection, says to His disciples, "And, behold, I send the promise of My Father upon you: but tarry ye in the city of Jerusalem, until ye be endued with power from on high;" and also Acts i. 8, "But ye shall receive power after that the Holy Ghost is come upon you;" and ch. iv. 31. There is a distinction in ver. 27 between the testimony which the Holy Spirit would bear in His function as Paraclete by the lips of the Apostles against the opposing world, and the Apostles' own testimony, which would refer to the historical facts as such, and which they would bear as intelligent and honourable men: compare the same distinction in Acts v. 32, where Peter says, "And we also are His witnesses of these things; and so is also the Holy Ghost, whom God hath given to them that obey Him." There, however, the two testimonies are inverted. *Those that obey* are the *Apostles.* As here, so also in our Lord's word, Matt. x. 20, "It is not ye that speak, but the Spirit of your Father that speaketh in you:" the organ altogether retires behind the efficient Spirit. Quesnel brings out the practical element in these words with much force: "What have we to fear? The Spirit who is in the Church and dwelleth in our hearts, is stronger than the spirit which dwells in the world and in the ungodly.—We labour in vain when we seek to overcome error by merely human means, without the assistance of the Spirit of truth."

That the Holy Ghost finally proceedeth from the *Father*, the original source of all power, was a truth of such importance, so encouraging and quickening to the disciples, before whom Christ stood in His humble servant-form (compare "The Father is greater than I" in xiv. 28), that the words "from the Father" are immediately expanded into "proceedeth from the Father," in order to give this point its full prominence. Both were very important,—the proceeding from the Son, on which the emphasis falls in "whom I will send from My Father," and the proceeding from the Father; but the latter was under their present circumstances so important, that it might not be lightly despatched with a mere "from the Father." Calvin: "Nor in the face of such great forces, such and so impetuous assaults, would the testimony of the Spirit suffice, unless we were persuaded that He came from God." The explanation of the fact that the Spirit is, on the one hand, sent by Christ, while on the other He proceeded from the Father, is to be sought in the fact that He was sent by Christ, from the glory of the Father. The ἐκπορεύεται, taken in connection with the preceding πέμψω, shows that we have not to do here with eternal relations in the Godhead, but with the mission of the Spirit to the Apostles. The present, ἐκπορεύεται, is the timeless tense that stands in a general sentence: when He goeth forth, it is from the Father that He goeth. The more specific idea is given by the preceding future. There can be no reference to the going forth of the Spirit from Gen. i. downwards, through the whole period of the Old Testament economy (comp. Isa. lxiii. 11). The Spirit in this speciality—as Paraclete, as Spirit of truth (comp. ch. xiv. 17)—was specially linked to the atoning death of Christ; He was not yet in the world, because that Christ was not yet glorified: comp. ch. vii. 39. The Spirit of truth, the Paraclete, was what Peter lacked, says Augustin, when he was terrified by a little maid, and uttered his triple denial: "He giving His testimony, and making His witnesses most resolute, took away all fear from the friends of Christ, and converted the hatred of His enemies into love."

Ver. 27. "And ye also shall bear witness, because ye have been with Me from the beginning."—This is a *second* power for subduing the hatred of the Jews: which, indeed, derives its true significance from its strict connection with the first preceding it. This double testimony—that of the Holy Ghost and the historical—now goes on in the Church concurrently. But the thorough study and use of the latter is not so simple as in the apostolic age; and it demands a profound research. The present, μαρτυρεῖτε, is fully explained by the future that immediately precedes. The Lord places Himself in the future: "Ye then bear witness." We have a commentary on "from the beginning" in Mark i. 1; Luke i. 2; Acts i. 21. The beginning was the first manifestation of Christ: comp. 1 John i. 1, "That which was from the beginning, which we have heard, which we have seen with our eyes, which we have looked upon, and our hands have handled, declare we unto you."

Ch. xvi. 1. "These things have I spoken unto you, that ye should not be offended."—We find here expressed the ultimate aim of all that had been said from ch. xv. 18 onwards, and the point of view is shown under which all must be viewed. The design was, namely, to obviate the offence which the hatred of the Jews could not fail to occasion, especially as authority and scientific knowledge were on their side. "These things" does not refer merely to the foreannouncement of their hatred; it includes also everything that had been said to place their hatred in the true light, as well as the help which had been promised in the sending of the Paraclete. "That ye should not be offended" leads us into a circle of ideas which the first Evangelists had already exhibited as realized. In them we have seen the hatred of the world becoming to the disciples a sore σκάνδαλον, the source of a perilous temptation to apostasy from Christ,—comp. Matt. xiii. 21, xxiv. 9, xxvi. 31–33,—a temptation which had already hard beset the Baptist, Matt. xi. 3.

Ver. 2. "They shall put you out of the synagogues: yea, the time cometh, that whosoever killeth you will think that he doeth God service."—The Lord indicates what direction the temptation to offence would take, and thus shows the necessity of those communications which had for their object to encounter and overcome that temptation. In reference to ἀποσυναγώγους, comp. on ch. ix. 22, xii. 42: in these words there is involved the degenerating of the synagogue into a synagogue of Satan, Rev. ii. 9, iii. 9. The synagogue which could not tolerate Christians within it, would show by that fact that it was no longer a "congregation of the Lord." Casting out Christians, they would cast out Christ, and with Christ the Father.[1] The disciples were not voluntarily to depart out of the synagogue, but to await what would happen to them on a full proclamation of the Gospel. This gives a very intelligible hint to the faithful in times of the Church's decline, viz. that they should keep far from their thoughts the idea of arbitrary secession. The *new formation* is right only when the *casting out* has gone before.

The λατρεία in itself signifies *cultus* in general; but the προσφέρειν shows that sacrificial worship is particularly meant: comp. Ex. viii. 16, 21, 22; 2 Sam. xv. 8, where the sacrifice is certainly a λατρεία; Rom. xii. 1, where θυσία and λατρεία are combined. We may find the basis of the opinion or thought, here ascribed to the Jews, in Ex. xxxii. 29. There Moses declares the self-renouncing assault of the Levites upon the rebels to be an acceptable sacrifice which they had brought to the Lord: "Ye have to-day filled your hands [strictly, " Fill your hands;" the acceptance of what was done uttered in the form of command] in this, that ye have turned every man upon his son and his brother, and have thus obtained for yourselves a blessing." The fearful quid-pro-quo, however, was this, that in the present case the *rebels* would think to make the *faithful* a sacrifice. They made their beginning with Christ Himself. That this was accomplished at the Passover, rested upon the view here indicated.

Ver. 3. "And these things will they do unto you, because they have not known the Father, nor Me."—The Lord here opens up another encouraging aspect of their case, in reference to the persecutions predicted in ver. 2. Calvin: "That the Apostles might scorn with lofty minds their blind fury."

Ver. 4. "But these things have I told you, that, when the time shall come, ye may remember that I told you of them. And these things I said not unto you at the beginning, because

[1] Augustin: "Since there was not any other people of God than that seed of Abraham, if they would acknowledge and receive Christ, they would abide as natural branches in the olive-tree: there were not to be churches of Christ and synagogues of the Jews distinct; but if they would be one, they might be one. But as they would not, what remained but that, remaining out of Christ, they should cast them out of the synagogues who would not leave Christ?"

I was with you."—The ἀλλά in the preceding verse stated why they would do these things; here it states why the Lord spoke of it. Ταῦτα refers, as in ver. 1, not simply to that which the disciples had to suffer from the world, but also to those consolatory suggestions which Christ had opened to them in regard to their sufferings. In what immediately preceded, the prophecy of their future suffering had been lightened by a prospect of joy. Our Lord had certainly before spoken to His disciples of their coming persecutions, Matt. v. 10, x. 17; but it had been to them as if He had not so spoken, the blessed present having prevented their thoughts from lingering upon His words. The announcement never exerted a penetrating influence upon them until now, when Jesus, Himself on His way to death and deeply moved, addressed it to His deeply moved disciples; and when, without admixture of other elements, He made it the matter of one great division of His last discourses, placing it, by a fundamental and, as it were, systematic treatment, in an altogether new light. That Jesus, indeed, had earlier, and in a variety of ways, spoken to them on the same subject, is not only evident from the testimony of the first Evangelists, but is also obvious of itself, since His three years' intercourse with the disciples must have furnished Him many opportunities for such discourse, and, according to the fundamental views of the Old Testament, especially the Psalms and the prophecies of Jeremiah, the way of the disciples through a world of sin could not be other than full of thorns.—Their Master had not from the beginning spoken it in so affecting a manner, *because He was yet with them*, and Himself defended them, ch. xvii. 12, executing the office of their advocate in their conflict with the world, ch. xiv. 16. But now, when His departure was at hand, He must tell them more definitely, in order that, when the persecution should arrive, His word might take the place of His personal presence.

Vers. 5, 6. " But now I go My way to Him that sent Me; and none of you asketh Me, Whither goest Thou? But because I have said these things unto you, sorrow hath filled your heart."—The Redeemer now begins to lead on their thoughts to the consolation which, as the expansion of ch. xv. 26, He would assure to them in the presence of an unfriendly world. The transition is made by δέ, because in the preceding verse the presence of Jesus with His disciples had been finally spoken of. But any external connection with what goes before is not to be sought.

Peter had in ch. xiii. 36 asked, "Whither goest Thou?" But the Lord here means another kind of asking, such as would take pleasure in the subject, and spring from a heart never weary of hearing about it. The disciples ought in consistency to have besought Christ again and again to tell them of heaven, and the glory which He expected to enter there. This questioning would have been all the more reasonable, as on their adequate views of this subject rested all their joy in the prospect of the world's hatred and persecution. Thither, where He was going, He would fetch His disciples, that they might be received into the fellowship of His glory, ch. xiv. 3, 4; thence He would send them power to perform the greatest works, ch. xiv. 12; from heaven He would send the Holy Spirit as their advocate in their process with the world, and as their abiding teacher; from thence He would manifest Himself to them, clothed in the glory of the Father. But these questions had no impulse in their minds. They were altogether carried away by their sorrow at His departure.

Ver. 7. "Nevertheless I tell you the truth; It is expedient for you that I go away: for if I go not away, the Comforter will not come unto you; but if I depart, I will send Him unto you."—"*I* tell you the truth" (Bengel: *mentiri nescius*): comp. ch. xiv. 2, "If it were not so, I would have told you." Jesus makes it express and emphatic that He tells them the truth in this matter; because, as the sadness of the Apostles shows in ver. 6, the matter seemed to be very different. Bengel is not right when he says that there is here a double function of the Paraclete, towards the world in this passage, and towards believers in ver. 12. As Paraclete, the Holy Ghost has but *one* office: to assure to the Apostles, and generally to all the faithful, help in their conflict with the world. The πρὸς ὑμᾶς must be carefully noted. It shows that the Holy Spirit is regarded here only as *indwelling* in the disciples, and not as a power which, in connection with them, works upon men's minds. The ὃν ἐγὼ πέμψω ὑμῖν, in ch. xv. 26, is strictly corresponsive.—Wherefore was the Paraclete to come only after His departure? The answer is, because Christ was to procure for them and minister to them the Holy Ghost only through His atoning death; and He could be imparted only to those who were reconciled to God through the blood of His Son: comp. what was said upon ch. vii. 39, xii. 32. According to Gal. iii. 14, the sending of the Holy Ghost required as its condition that Christ should become a *curse* for us. J. Gerhard: "The corn of wheat falling into the ground produced this among other fruits, the gift of the Holy Spirit, John xii. 24, in token whereof Christ after His resurrection breathed on the Apostles, and said, 'Receive ye the Holy Ghost,' ch. xx. 22." Why did Jesus do this only after His resurrection? Manifestly because the Holy Spirit was a blessing obtained by His passion. Anton: "Father, Son, and Holy Spirit are not divided; and no one Person can, without violation of the Divine holiness, work good in man without the Redeemer's atoning entrance into heaven." That was the true reason. On the other hand, that the presence of Christ in the flesh placed a wall of partition between the disciples and the Holy Spirit, is an altogether unfounded idea, though Augustin led the way in it: "What is therefore *If I go not away the Paraclete will not come* but this, that they could not receive the Spirit so long as they persisted in knowing Christ after the flesh?"

Ver. 8. "And when He is come, He will reprove the world of sin, and of righteousness, and of judgment."—We have here the leading features of the preaching which the Apostles, under the influence of the Spirit, were to engage in. The meaning of the present verse must first of all be sought in its own terms. The further expansion in vers. 9, 10 can be regarded only as the touchstone of the interpretation found independently of it; especially as the Lord's saying in those verses can be rightly understood only on the basis of a right understanding of our present passage. The *world*, after what has preceded, must be regarded primarily in its Jewish manifestation: that is, *the Jews*. So Heumann stated it rightly: "The Lord here sets before the Apostles only their first apostolical work, since they were to urge upon the Jewish people the sin of their past unbelief, and were to convert a great multitude of them." So also the later preaching among the *heathen* population of the world had essentially the same foundation of principles. Yet these sustained a certain modification, inasmuch as the Apostles had not to apply their preaching to those who were already unbelievers, but simply to those who did not believe. The Jews were to be reproved because of their already present unbelief; but it was to be set before the Gentiles how great would be their sin and guilt if they did not believe, and thus despised the only remedy for their sins. In reference to the *righteousness* and the *judgment*, the heathen were to receive *exhortations*, in order that they might place themselves right, appropriate the righteousness, and escape the judgment, instead of the *condemnation* or reproof that the Jews required, who had already placed themselves in an attitude of contempt.

The *sin* can be only, according to ch. xv. 22, 24, unbelief in the manifested and gloriously authenticated Redeemer. For that was there pointed out as the single great sin of the Jews. Augustin: "He put this sin before all the rest, as if it were alone: because, this sin abiding, all others are retained; and, this sin departing, all others are remitted." This sin would be mightily detected in them, and pressed upon their consciences, by the Holy Spirit's demonstration accompanying the Apostles. —The *righteousness* must necessarily belong to the same to whom the sin belonged, that is, *the world:* else we are left to random conjecture. The righteousness of *Christ* would never have been thought of here apart from ver. 9; nor can that verse justify such an interpretation of the present passage. Still more remote is the righteousness of *God*, to which not even ver. 9 gives the slightest semblance of plausibility. But the righteousness cannot be regarded as having grown in the soil of their hearts to whom it belongs: from their hearts only the *sin* proceeds. By the preceding mention of sin, every notion of "a righteousness of their own," ἰδία δικαιοσύνη, Rom. x. 3, is excluded. Their righteousness must rather come to them from without. And whence it comes we gather from the foregoing words, "He shall convince the world of sin." If the sin, according to ch. xv. 22, 24, consisted in this, that they believed not in Christ, then the righteousness could be theirs only through their believing in Christ. The prophecies of the Old Testament Scriptures had, in the most various forms, referred to a righteousness coming from above, which would be part of the prerogatives and blessings of the Messianic age; so that there is no ground for the objection that this interpretation of the passage is a premature intrusion into the specific phraseology of St Paul. "In His days," we read, Jer. xxiii. 6, "Judah shall be saved, and Israel shall dwell safely; and this is His name whereby He shall be called, *The Lord our Righteousness.*" The Messiah was to bear the name of "The Lord our Righteousness," because He would be the channel through which the righteousness of God would flow to His people, and become *our* righteousness. According to Dan. ix. 24, the Messiah was to bring in an "everlasting righteousness." Isaiah says, in ch. liii. 11, "By His knowledge shall My righteous servant justify many; for He shall bear their iniquities." And in ch. xlv. 24, 25, " Surely shall one say, In the Lord have I righteousness and strength ; in the Lord shall all the seed of Israel be justified, and shall glory :" comp. further, ch. xlv. 8; Ps. lxxxv. 11. To this righteousness, which indeed belongs to the people of God, but did not grow up in the soil of their own nature, the Lord's saying in Matt. v. 6 refers, "Blessed are they which do hunger and thirst after righteousness: for they shall be filled," which again points us back to Isa. lv. 1.—And as the sins and the righteousness belong to the world, so also does the *judgment.* It can be no other than the condemnation which falls upon the world, and primarily upon the Jews, when they persist in the sin of unbelief towards Christ, and will not become partakers of the righteousness which springs from faith in Him.—Around these three centres, in fact, revolves all the preaching of the Apostles to the Jews after the outpouring of the Holy Spirit. For the περὶ ἁμαρτίας we may compare, for example, Acts ii. 22, 23, as also ch. iii. 13-15. For the περὶ δικαιοσύνης, ch. ii. 38, "Repent, and be baptized every one of you in the name of Jesus Christ for the remission of sins," and ch. iv. 12, "Neither is there salvation in any other ;" v. 31, viii. 37, x. 43, xiii. 38, 39, "Through this man is preached unto you the forgiveness of sins; and by Him all that believe are justified from all things, from which ye could not be justified by the law of Moses." For περὶ κρίσεως we must compare ch. ii. 19–21; and "fear was upon every soul," in ver. 43, with ch. iii. 23.

In all other parts of the New Testament, ἐλέγχειν stands for a reproving charge, the conviction which impresses guilt upon the conscience, and is everywhere used only of moral crimination. So ch. iii. 20, viii. 46, Rev. iii. 19. In 2 Tim. iv. 2, ἔλεγξον and ἐπιτίμησον go together. In Tit. i. 13 we read, ἔλεγχε αὐτοὺς ἀποτόμως. In Jas. ii. 9, ἐλεγχόμενοι ὑπὸ τοῦ νόμου ὡς παραβάται. Hence the ἐλέγχειν has always to do with *transgressors*, and this is its meaning in our present passage. Its reference to righteousness and judgment has also a reproving tone. It is directed, as the preceding "of sin" shows, against those who were involved in unbelief, who through their guilt robbed themselves of righteousness, and, unless they repented, would fall into condemnation. That the ground-tone of apostolical preaching after Pentecost was conviction and re-proof, is evident from its result in Acts ii. 37, " pricked in their heart," and the affrighted " What shall we do ? " In Bengel's note, " He who is convicted of sin, afterwards passes over into the righteousness (of Christ), or shares (with Satan) condemnation," the bracketed words-are unwarranted interpolations from ver. 9.

Vers. 9, 10. " Of sin, because they believe not on Me: of righteousness, because I go to My Father, and ye see Me no more."—The righteousness forms the antithesis to the sin (δέ); the judgment, the antithesis to the righteousness (δέ). The ὅτι is—" with reference to the fact that," John ii. 18. In the first clause, it means " consisting in this, that;" in the second it is equivalent to " thereby attained, that;" and in the third, once more " consisting in this, that." Righteousness *consists* not in the going of Christ to the Father, and His not being seen by His disciples; but through this the righteousness was obtained for us. The form which the statement assumes is explained by reference to the state of the Apostles' minds. That which filled them with the deepest grief would bring to them the wholesome fruit of righteousness;. and was therefore, rightly viewed, not matter of sorrow, but of joy. It is not " because *they* see Me no more," but " because *ye* see Me no more." The appearances of the risen Lord are here taken no account of, because they were of a transitory character, and served only as means to an end, viz. the full conviction of the Apostles.—The judgment is, in ver. 8, that which impended over the unbelieving Jews, in case they should continue in their unbelief. And that here also we are to understand, beneath the judgment already accomplished on Satan, a latent reference to the judgment threatening the Jews, is plain from the "convince the world," which must be the supplement of each clause, and in harmony with which the mention of the judgment upon Satan must have a condemnatory meaning for the world and the Jews. In fact, the already executed judgment upon Satan, the prince of this world, contains in itself a denunciation of judgment upon the κόσμος of his subjects, provided they do not in good time release themselves from their bond of subjection to him, which they can do only through faith in Jesus Christ. Augustin: "Let those who follow him who is judged, take heed lest they be hereafter judged like their prince, and condemned." Quesnel: "Blind men, who still cling to the world and set your hopes upon it, what will become of you when your prince is already adjudged to eternal punishment?" The judgment upon Satan was accomplished through the death of Christ, comp. on ch. xii. 31; and with Satan the world itself is virtually condemned. In ch. xii. 31, the world, as the object of the judgment, is mentioned before the prince of the world. That world can, however, escape through penitence the execution of the suspended sentence; it may by faith pass over into the domain of another Prince, of Him who hath judged the prince of this world. It is a perilous thing to continue a subject of an already condemned prince, and to refuse submission to Him who hath condemned that prince. If the prince of this world is judged, the cry rings out, "Save yourselves from this untoward generation," Acts ii. 40—a generation which has Satan for its lord, ch. viii. 44.—The judgment upon Satan was not actually consummated but by the atoning death of Christ; but here it is regarded as already accomplished, κέκριται, because it was immediately at hand, and because it would be an actually effected judgment when the Holy Spirit should begin to exercise His reproving function.

Chap. XVI. 12–33.

After the Lord had regulated the Apostles' views of their fundamental relations, He now turns to His specific farewell discourse. This character we find in vers. 12–15. As Moses, when he departed, pointed to Joshua, Deut. xxxi. 23, so Jesus pointed to the Holy Ghost, who should lead His disciples into all the truth. With this is connected in ver. 16 an allusion to His immediate departure, and that seeing Him again which should follow upon it. So also the words of Christ in vers. 20-28, anticipating the question of the disciples as to the meaning of these words, lead back, according to the explanation given, into the track of the farewell discourse, inasmuch as they point to the impending departure of the Lord, and the advantage which should accrue from it to the disciples. So also the third paragraph, occasioned by the interruption of the disciples, bears a farewell character; it predicts to the disciples their approaching dispersion, but intimates that such calamities should never have the power to depress their spirit.

The fact that in vers. 12-15, just as in vers. 7-11, the Holy Spirit is the subject, has misled many expositors, leading them to think that a new section does not begin here. We have already pointed out, that, with ver. 11, there is a conclusion first of the section ch. xv. 18-xvi. 11, and then also of the whole discourse from ch. xv. 1 onwards. There is, indeed, a connection between the discourse beginning with ver. 12 and the general strain of the whole, inasmuch as here the internal work of the Spirit's edification follows the Spirit's operation as it respects the word. But that is only the connection of transition from one section to another; it serves only to connect what follows with the general body of the one discourse, and to show that it is not an absolutely new commencement that follows. That the work of the Holy Spirit, spoken of in vers. 12-15, is essentially distinguished from that of vers. 7-11,—and, therefore, that the link of connection is not very strict,—is plain from the fact that, in ch. xiv., these two operations of the Holy Ghost are exhibited as totally distinct. As vers. 7-11 of this chapter refer back to ch. xiv. 15-17, so vers. 12, 13 refer back to ch. xiv. 25, 26.

Ver. 12. "I have yet many things to say unto you, but ye cannot bear them now."—It is not "I might have," but "I have;" and it leads to the conclusion that Christ could not now say it to them on account of their weakness, but that He would say it at a later period. The Spirit of truth, who should impart it to them, would give what He received of Christ, ver. 14; and through that Spirit Christ therefore would speak to His disciples. The Revelation of John, which was included under this promise, and itself formed a considerable part of its matter, is in ch. i. 1 referred back to Christ as its author; and the Spirit in whom John found himself when he received the revelation (ch. i. 10) was only the medium of the reception of the contents which sprang from Christ, and finally from God. In ch. i. 10, xix. 10, xxii. 16, the substance of the Apocalypse is directly said to be derived from Christ.

Of what nature were the many things which Christ had yet to say to His Apostles? It appears from a comparison with ch. xv. 15, that in all great essentials the revelation already imparted through Christ had a certain completeness, and that the supplement promised through the Holy Ghost could refer only to specialities. What follows, shows that among the many things the future destinies of the Church occupied the first place. One instance we have in the revelation which St Peter recorded in Acts x., concerning the reception of the Gentiles into the kingdom of Christ. So also there were to be further revelations concerning the great facts of our Lord's passion, resurrection, exaltation, which should be based upon these facts, not yet accomplished, themselves.—Those to whom Christ had yet much to say, were manifestly the same to whom He had already spoken many things. And as these were the Apostles, we have no right to go beyond their circle for the fulfilment of the great promise of future communications; and Beza was quite justified in his zeal against those who " dare to continue into long ages after the Apostles' death, the revelations which our Lord promised to the Apostles whom He Himself chose."

Βαστάζειν does not mean " apprehend." The sense is, that the Apostles must not generally be overweighted. Their weakness required that the truth should be gradually imparted to them, as the Lord, in Luke xii. 42, required that the wise householder should divide the food in due season, ἐν καιρῷ. Much of that which they had already heard was not less beyond their apprehension than what had been hitherto withheld (comp. ver. 25). The victory of Christianity over the power of heathenism was not in itself harder to be understood than its victory over Judaism. But the Lord contents Himself with depicting the latter point in lively colours; He speaks of the victory over Gentile powers only in hints: the full expansion of the truth He reserves for the Apocalypse, after the catastrophe of Jerusalem had already taken place.—These disclosures, prematurely imparted, would have been to the Apostles only a useless *burden;* they would have been only distracted, by matters of no immediate practical significance, from the point to which now their attention should be supremely directed. Matt. xxiii. 4 furnishes a comment on the $\beta\alpha\sigma\tau\acute{\alpha}\zeta\epsilon\iota\nu$: Jesus says of the Pharisees, "They bind heavy burdens, and grievous to be borne, $\delta\upsilon\sigma\beta\acute{\alpha}\sigma\tau\alpha\kappa\tau\alpha$, and lay them on men's shoulders." Jesus would not lay doctrinal burdens upon the shoulders of the Apostles which they could not yet bear, and in this He gave His Church a pattern: we also, following His example, should avoid overloading. J. Gerhard is wrong in saying, that by naming the Spirit, Christ gives the reason why the Apostles could not bear what He had yet to say,—because they were yet *carnal.* The Spirit of Christ would tell them what Christ did not, simply because, after the Lord's departure, He would take His place.

Ver. 13. " Howbeit when He, the Spirit of truth, is come, He will guide you into all truth: for He shall not speak of Himself; but whatsoever He shall hear, that shall He speak: and He will show you things to come."—P. Anton: "As He will rebuke the world upon the three points of which we heard in ver. 8, so He will not forget His other office. He will lead you into all truth." That the "you" must refer only to the Apostles, has been shown in our remarks upon ver. 12. On this point Tholuck says: "The persons addressed are no other than the witnesses to the truth of ch. xv. 17,—those to whom vers. 17, 18 apply,—for whom He primarily prays in ch. xvii. 9, the rest being prayed for in ver. 20." We would add, that what is here meant is not the quickening of truths already present in the minds of the individuals (so that 1 John ii. 27 might be brought into comparison); but the first impartation of truths not yet made known. This is evident from the reference to ver. 12, according to which we can only include matters which Christ had not yet spoken of. It is plain also from the words which follow, "He will show you things to come," where we may, from the species, infer the *kind,* the revelation of hitherto unknown mysteries. The Apostles laid the most decisive claim to be the organs of such revelation. " Regarding this promise," says Grotius, " the Apostles say, It seemed good to the Holy

Ghost and to us." Acts x. records an important revelation made to Peter. John, in the Apocalypse, declares himself to be the organ of high revelations. With regard to the revelations and prophetic position of Paul, see 2 Cor. xii.; Eph. iii. 3; Gal. i. 1, ii. 2. It has been shown in my Commentary on the Apocalypse (Clark's Transl.), ch. i. 1, xviii. 20, that for the reception of new truths there is no other organ than the prophetic; and that this organ, under the New Testament, is intimately connected with the Apostolate, forming a portion of its prerogatives. We find no trace in the New Testament that any disclosures of secret truth, important for the whole Church, were made beyond the circle of the Apostles; or any revelations which affected the doctrine or the future destiny of the whole Church. What we read in the Acts of the manifestations made to other prophets, bears always a very subordinate character; we never read that they were the organs of any great and new revelations.

It has been maintained, entirely without reason, that the truths into which the Spirit of truth should lead them were not to be more closely defined. They were simply all those which first were clearly expressed in the Apostolical Epistles and Apocalypse, and concerning which the discourses of Christ had given in the Gospels no adequate disclosure. That the Apocalypse in particular occupies an important place among them, is plain from the triple ἀναγγελεῖ, in vers. 13, 14, 15, and from the corresponding high importance which, in the Apocalypse itself, is ascribed to its revelations and teachings. The promise given, as we have seen, to the Apostles alone, would have been wavering and useless, if it had not resulted in documents from which we might gather the nature of the disclosures communicated to them. Only by the presence of such archives could the appeal of enthusiasm and heresy to this promise be foreclosed and cut off. (Augustin: All the most senseless heretics, wishing to bear the name of Christians, have sought to give, by occasion of this passage, an evangelical colouring to lies against which man's common sense rebels.) The apostolical writings, the monuments of the fulfilment of this promise, form, notwithstanding their apparent independence, an organic whole, in the instruction of which the Spirit of truth has provided for all the needs of all ages of the Church. Stier's assertion, that this passage is not strictly a proof of the infallibility of the Apostles, inasmuch as the promise essentially belongs to us all (1 John ii. 27), is based upon an opinion which we have already rejected, viz. that the promise was given to all believers generally, while it was really given to the Apostles alone, who were consecrated as the organs of the establishment of the whole treasury of the truth needed by the Church. On the same false foundation rests the Romish view, which refers the saying to a revelation running through all ages of the Church.—The Spirit would lead into the whole or the full truth, inasmuch as He would supplementarily add what Jesus during His life had not communicated; and bring to their remembrance that which He had spoken to them. The difference between the two readings, $εἰς πᾶσαν τὴν ἀλήθειαν$ (for which Mark v. 33 speaks), and $εἰς τὴν ἀλήθειαν πᾶσαν$, into all truth, and all of it, touches not the sense.

That the Spirit would lead them into all truth, is *grounded* upon this, that He would not speak of Himself, but speak that which He had heard. The Spirit cannot absolutely speak of Himself, because He exists in the most intimate communion of nature with the Father and the Son; because it belongs to His essence to be the Spirit of the Father and of the Son. Augustin: " He will not speak of Himself, because He is not of Himself. But whatsoever things He shall hear, He will speak: whatsoever He shall hear of Him from whom He proceedeth." That which is self-understood is, however, here emphatically stated, because there is a false "spirit," which speaks of itself, and on that account can lead not into truth, but only into error. (Luther: " His preaching would not be like a dream of man, like that of those who bring matter of their own,—such things, to wit, as they have neither seen nor known. But He would preach such things as had a foundation under them; that is, what He received of the Father and Me.") That was the spirit who was active in the false prophets of the Old Testament: comp. Jer. xxiii. 16, " Thus saith the Lord of hosts, Hearken not unto the words of the prophets that prophesy unto you: they make you vain: they speak a vision of their own heart [Michaelis: 'Ex corde suo tanquam principio oriundam,' corresponding to the $ἀφ'$ $ἑαυτοῦ$ here: in ver. 26 they are called 'prophets of the deceit of their own heart'], and not out of the mouth of the

Lord:" comp. Isa. xiv. 14, 27, ix. 14. In 1 Kings xxii. 21 this spirit appears personified, in harmony with the character of the vision, and offers to deceive Ahab, by being a lying spirit in the mouth of all the prophets of the calves. In Zech. xiii. 2, the Lord promises, "And also I will cause the prophets and the unclean spirit to pass out of the land." That this spirit still existed in the times of the New Testament, and that there was needed a rampart against him in the Spirit who should not speak of Himself, and in the trustworthy monuments of His revelation, is plain from Matt. xxiv. 11, 24; Rev. xvi. 13, 14; 2 Thess. ii. 2.

As the "not of Himself," so also the "what He hath heard," points back to the Old Testament. "That which was heard" was the term by which the true prophets (see Isa. liii. 1; Obad. 1) designated their announcements, in order to express that they had nothing to communicate which they had not received, and thus to arrogate to themselves absolute authority. In Isa. xxviii. 9, the prophets take their taunting word out of the mouth of the mockers, who cried, "To whom shall he teach שְׁמוּעָה?" the comment on which is ch. xxi. 10: "That which I have heard of the Lord of hosts, the God of Israel, have I declared unto you." Of *whom* the Spirit heareth, is not here declared, because the main point primarily was to emphasize His hearing. According to ver. 14, He hears primarily from Christ; according to ver. 15, what He hears goes back to the Father. Against those who at once supplement "of the Father," Kling rightly observes: "If we suppose the Spirit hearing, as it were *by the side of* the Son, from the Father, the whole relation is disturbed, and the subordinate and false position of the Greek Church theory is assumed."

"And He will show you things to come." Τὰ ἐρχόμενα—here we have the most distinguished species of the class. "Things to come" is an expression which a series of prophetical passages in Isaiah use to designate the events of the future, which form the object of prophecy: ch. xli. 22, 23, xliv. 7, xlv. 11. Τὰ ἐρχόμενα, so far as they were peculiar to the revelation given to the Apostles, can be only the future destinies of the kingdom of God. We are led to this conclusion by the original in Isaiah, where, on the ground of the revelations made by the prophets concerning the future of the kingdom of God, the false gods are tauntingly challenged: "The things that are coming and shall come, let them show unto them." Nor is it very difficult to determine what theme those future revelations to the Apostles would mainly dwell upon. Concerning the destruction of Jerusalem, the Lord had Himself given clear prediction; so clear and perfect, that the boundary line was reached which separates between prophecy and history. Hence we expect disclosures concerning the history of the Church, in its relation to the Gentile secular power. This had been lightly indicated by our Lord as the second hostile agency; even as it is exhibited in the scenes of the crucifixion, which bear upon them a symbolical character. In Matt. xxi. 21, the Lord sets over against the fig-tree of the Jewish people the symbol of a *mountain* for the Gentile power, to remove which was the task assigned to the faith of the Church. In Matt. x. 18, "And ye shall be brought before governors and kings for My sake, for a testimony against them and the Gentiles," the Lord gives an intimation of the persecutions which threatened the Church from the heathen world, and of the judgment upon it which would ensue. In Luke xxi. 24, He speaks of the times of the Gentiles being accomplished, following upon the judgment upon Jerusalem. In Matt. xviii. 6, there is a reference to Jer. li. 63, 64, where Jeremiah gives to Seraiah, going to Babylon, the command to read his prophecy: "And it shall be, when thou hast made an end of reading this book, that thou shalt bind a stone to it, and cast it into the midst of Euphrates: and thou shalt say, Thus shall Babylon sink, and shall not rise from the evil that I will bring upon her; and they shall be weary." And this shows that, behind the reference to events immediately coming, there lay concealed a reference to the Gentile powers, which would one day in a more serious manner offend the little ones: comp. Rev. xviii. 21. These hints we expect to see expanded by the Holy Ghost, and with a precision, luminousness, and practical force, somewhat corresponding to the pattern given in our Lord's description of the catastrophe of Jerusalem. If this be so, Stier's observation is quite correct: "And now let him who hath ears to hear, hear what the Spirit saith to the churches, through the bosom-disciple in Patmos, who was *in the Spirit* on the Lord's day." The Church and the Gentile power are the theme of the Apocalypse. I observed in my commentary on that book as follows: "It is remarkable that this promise of our Lord should have been found in the Gospel of John. The intimations of what was to come, given elsewhere than in his writings, are only of an occasional scattered description. They are to be met with chiefly in Paul, who did not belong to the apostolic circle as it then existed. If we were to conceive of the Apocalypse dropping away, we should at once feel that the promise of Christ had found no adequate fulfilment. Even from the analogy of the fulfilment given to the parallel declaration, 'He will bring to your remembrance whatsoever I have said to you,' as it is to be found in the Gospels, especially in those of John and Matthew, we are naturally led to expect a book specially devoted to the announcement of what was to come; and this so much the more, as the prophecy of the Old Testament presented the type of something independent and complete. The Gospel itself thus looks beyond itself to another book, that should be peculiarly occupied with the revelation of things to come, as these belonged to the many things of which the Lord had said to His disciples that they could still not bear them." Our Rationalist criticism cannot confront the Lord's declaration in this passage; more especially after having, as it has, contended against the genuineness of the Second Epistle of Peter, the only book springing from an original Apostle, which, apart from the Apocalypse, contains a detailed foreannouncement of future things: comp. 2 Pet. ii. 1 seq., and the allusion to this passage in the Epistle of Jude, vers. 17, 18.

Ver. 14. "He shall glorify Me; for He shall receive of Mine, and shall show it unto you."—The Holy Spirit would *glorify* Christ, inasmuch as He would impart revelations which could not be explained from natural causes, leading the mind up beyond the human domain into the divine. This importance could not be attached to the doctrines generally, so much as to those special disclosures of the future. That these are more particularly to be considered here, is plain from the repetition, here and ver. 15, of the ἀναγγελεῖ, the triple recurrence of which serves to demonstrate what deep significance our Lord attached to these revelations of futurity. Grotius' observation is correct: "By this He will show forth My glory, inasmuch as through Me future things will be foreannounced to My people." In a long series of passages in the second portion of Isaiah, it is shown to have been the design of the many predictions of the future contained in the book, to demonstrate that Jehovah was God, or to *glorify* Him: see ch. xli. 25, 26, xliii. 9-11. As those prophecies were to serve for the glorification of Jehovah, so those of which our passage speaks were to serve for the glorification of Christ. They would show that to Him was applicable the word spoken, in Dan. ii. 22, concerning Jehovah: "He revealeth the deep and secret things; He knoweth what is in the darkness, and the light dwelleth with Him." The world would, in consequence of the confirmation which these prophecies should receive, say, as Nebuchadnezzar said, Dan. ii. 47, " Of a truth it is, that your God is a God of gods, and a Lord of kings, and a revealer of secrets, seeing thou couldest reveal this secret."

All that the Holy Spirit would communicate, should return back to Christ, and serve to His glorification. The Holy Spirit receives His disclosures from Christ (comp. Rev. i. 1, xxii. 16); and that they really belonged to Him, is plain from the fact that an actual knowledge of the future is found only within the domain of the Christian Church. When heathen Rome was still dreaming of immortality, the Christian Church, taught by the Apocalypse, was as surely persuaded of its impending fall, as if it had already sunk before its eyes.— The saying we now consider suggests to us that we should reverently dwell upon the Apocalypse, and, if we find in it obscurities, reflect upon the dimness of our own vision. If we do not take this book into the account, it is hard to indicate how the promise was fulfilled. We cannot then point to any apostolical revelations or disclosures of the future which contributed in any striking manner to the glorification of Christ. The prophecies of the destruction of Jerusalem were not such; for the Son of man had already, before the Spirit's revelations, preoccupied that theme. Nor the predictions of the end of the world; for the glorification ensuing was to be of a practical kind, and to serve to the extension of the Redeemer's kingdom upon earth. Thus, the communication of the Holy Spirit that should glorify Christ must move in the same circle as the predictions of the Apocalypse. In harmony with our passage is **the high significance which that book ascribes to its own prophetic revelations** (comp. ch. xix. 10, with my commentary):

there also the disclosures which the spirit of prophecy makes are referred back to Christ (compare my remarks on the same passage, ch. xxii. 16); further, the prophetic testimony of Jesus, according to that book, culminates in the Apostles. With ἐρχόμενα, compare ἃ μέλλει γίνεσθαι μετὰ ταῦτα, Rev. i. 19.

Ver. 15. "All things that the Father hath are Mine: therefore said I, that He shall take of Mine, and shall show it unto you."—Jesus now shows how great things the Apostles had to expect in the Holy Spirit's revelation of the future, by declaring that, in this matter as in all others, His domain was co-extensive with that of the Father; so that nothing was inaccessible to Him, nothing going beyond His own sphere. The "of Me" needed this explanation all the more, inasmuch as the Old Testament had always most decisively referred the disclosure of the future to God alone, exhibiting it as His supreme and sole prerogative. In harmony with the present passage, the Apocalypse in its very first words refers itself to God as its original: "The revelation of Jesus Christ, which God gave Him:" comp. also ch. xxii. 6. The triple ἀναγγελεῖ ὑμῖν, "will show you," must have had the effect of making the Apostles anticipate with the most anxious expectation the disclosures which were foreannounced with such deep emphasis. When they subsequently recalled this promise, and reflected who among them would be the instruments of these high revelations, the three, Peter, James, and John, would be the most prominent; for these three had been on every occasion distinguished by our Lord, and were among the Apostles "the greater." Of these three, again, that disciple who leaned on the Lord's bosom seemed the most adapted to the revelation of these deep mysteries, Amos iii. 7. His self-renouncing, contemplative, mystical peculiarity, placed him in the forefront.

Ver. 16. "A little while, and ye shall not see Me: and again a little while, and ye shall see Me; because I go to the Father."—The Lord utters here the proper farewell word. But He veils it in intentional mystery, in order that the difficulty which it presented to the understanding of the disciples might give opportunity for further explanation. The connection with what precedes is made plain by ver. 7. The sending of the Holy Ghost had His going to the Father, His death and His resurrection, for its condition.—The double μικρόν, a little while (comp. Isa. x. 25, Hagg. ii. 6), shows that we must interpret it of events which belonged to the immediate future. As the former, the not seeing, manifestly referred to the death of Christ, which was close at hand, so we must understand the second of an event which was the next in order of those then under consideration. For that reason alone we must prefer applying it to the resurrection (Bengel: In universum quatriduum) rather than to the outpouring of the Holy Ghost.[1] That the latter event does not satisfy the Lord's meaning seems plain, further, when we consider that at the Pentecost the disciples did not see the Lord, saving in a figurative and spiritual sense; whereas in the resurrection they saw Him literally, and that literal seeing preceded the other. The reference to the resurrection is, as Stier remarks, "incontrovertibly established by the simple antithesis between ὄψεσθε and οὐ θεωρεῖτε; if the one takes away the bodily visibility, the other must give it back again." Moreover, the ὄψομαι ὑμᾶς in ver. 22 corresponds to the ὄψεσθέ με in our present passage. If this latter might indeed in itself and in another connection be referred to the outpouring of the Holy Ghost, yet the former could not, since we hear nothing of a Christophany at the Pentecost. But it must not be overlooked that these terms, ὄψεσθε and ὄψονται, are used in Matt. xxviii. 7, 10, Mark xvi. 7, when recording the Apostles' seeing their risen Lord; comp. the ὤφθη in Luke xxiv. 34; Acts xiii. 31; 1 Cor. xv. 5, 6, 7, 8. But the verb ὄπτομαι is never once used with reference to the outpouring of the Holy Spirit. It is, generally, never used elsewhere save to express an actual personal beholding, πρόσωπον πρὸς πρόσωπον, face to face, 1 Cor. xiii. 12 : comp. Acts xx. 25; Rev. xxii. 4.

The clause "Because I go to the Father," gives the reason of both assertions, "A little while, and ye shall not see Me,"

[1] If we consider carefully the consolatory meaning of the second μικρόν, we cannot possibly go further for it than the resurrection. Lampe: "It was a supreme point of consolation, that the hour of temptation was to pass in so short a space of time. As nothing was more sad than the absence of their beloved Master amidst the deepest distresses, so nothing was more comforting than that the little cloud should be so soon dissipated by the new rising of the Sun of Righteousness."

and "again a little while, and ye shall see Me." Christ could not go to the Father otherwise than by that bodily death which made Him invisible to the disciples. But since going to the Father was the same thing as entering into His glory, therefore the resurrection was inseparably connected with the death. He who was thus going to the Father could not be holden by the bands of death. But the resurrection necessarily involved His appearance to His disciples; only through it would the death and resurrection produce their fruits.[1]

He went to the Father before the day of the ascension came: concerning the ascension, He says in ch. xx. 17, not ὑπάγω, but ἀναβαίνω πρὸς τὸν πατέρα. The resurrection, which was not merely a revivification, but a glorification also, showed that He had already gone to the Father.—The omission of the words ὅτι ὑπάγω πρὸς τὸν πατέρα, in several important MSS., may be explained partly by the difficulty of the sense, and partly by the fact that Jesus in ver. 19 omits these words. But their genuineness is vouched for by their recurrence in ver. 17. That the Apostles took the clause from ver. 10, and attached it arbitrarily to clauses with which it originally had no connection, and that they thus even wilfully aggravated the difficulty of the passage, is in the highest degree improbable. The words are here absolutely indispensable; for they alone give the Lord's saying its character of inexplicable mystery: the mere "A little while, and ye shall not see Me; and again a little while, and ye shall see Me," they would have been able to interpret, even as they had not failed to understand, according to ver. 22, the very similar declaration of Christ in ch. xiv. 19. It was the ὅτι ὑπάγω, "because I go to the Father,"—to the present day so full of embarrassment to expositors,—which made the saying hard to be understood by the Apostles. These words of themselves were not difficult. The thought had become familiar to them in the Lord's discourses: comp. ch. vii. 33, xiii. 33, xvi. 10. The difficulty arose from its being connected with what went before by ὅτι, "because." The former of the two clauses might be naturally so explained. "I go to the Father, and ye see Me no

---

[1] Lampe: "The departure to the Father demanded that He should presently make Himself visible again after the resurrection. For thus He would demonstrate that, by His former departure, He had appeased the Father."

more," had been said in ver. 10. But that the going to the Father should at the same time be the reason of their seeing Him again, was what the disciples could not understand; and the obscurity of this point was diffused over the whole. It was all the worse, as the matter concerned the most important catastrophes, which were immediately impending, and as they were robbed of that understanding of these important declarations which they thought they had. But their Master would exercise their spiritual discernment, and therefore designedly threw this stone of offence in their path. Luther remarks on the double " little while :" " Thus there is here on earth an everlasting change going on among Christians. Now dark and night, presently it will be day."

Vers. 17, 18. " Then said some of His disciples among themselves, What is this that He saith unto us, A little while, and ye shall not see Me : and again a little while, and ye shall see Me : and, Because I go to the Father ? They said therefore, What is this that He saith, A little while ? we cannot tell what He saith."—The proceeding is a natural one. First, they ask one the other what Jesus could mean; for they suppose that the cause of their not understanding might possibly be an individual defect in themselves. As they receive no satisfactory reply, they come to the conclusion, that in these words there was a mystery not to be solved by any of the company of the disciples. They do not venture to carry their difficulty at once to Christ; they are ashamed of their ignorance, and fear to augment their Master's sorrow, by exposing their slow progress in the school of His instruction.—The " little while" which they single out, and all that was immediately connected with it, was not preeminently the *obscure* part of His words, but the pre-eminently *interesting* to their minds. They would fain have an explanation concerning every part of an announcement which placed in the prospect a doubly momentous catastrophe. Their desire was all the more urgent, inasmuch as their half-won understanding had been abruptly taken away from them by the clause which the Lord had added.—How important the μικρόν was, and how it formed the centre of all the disciples' thoughts, may be gathered from the fact, that in vers. 16-19 it occurs no less than seven times, which was certainly no more accidental than the threefold repetition in vers. 13-15 of ἀναγγελεῖ.

Ver. 19. " Now Jesus knew that they were desirous to ask Him, and said unto them, Do ye inquire among yourselves of that I said, A little while, and ye shall not see Me: and again a little while, and ye shall see Me?"—That this knowledge on the part of Christ belonged to Him, as knowing what was in man, ch. ii. 25,—that is, that the Apostles had in no way given outward intimation of their determination to ask Him,—is plain from ver. 30, where the disciples concluded that Jesus knew all things, from the fact that His answer anticipated their question. The Lord designedly omits, in the repetition of His saying, the words, " because I go to the Father," which involved the greatest difficulty, and a difficulty which could hardly be removed at present; He limits Himself to the elucidation of the two former clauses, to understand which, as the "What is this that He saith?" shows, was the point of most immediate concern to the Apostles.

Ver. 20. "Verily, verily, I say unto you, That ye shall weep and lament, but the world shall rejoice; and ye shall be sorrowful, but your sorrow shall be turned into joy."—The strong affirmation at the beginning was intended, in the first place, to dissipate at once the illusion that events might take another and more favourable turn; but it must be regarded, at the same time, as equally belonging to the latter clause of the verse. Heumann: "Believe Me once more, when I affirm it most solemnly, that your sorrow will be followed by the greatest joy; and when that sadness shall come upon you, fail not to remember, in your distress and anxiety, what I now so solemnly affirm to you." "A little while, and ye see Me no more," is thus explained as meaning such a withdrawal as would cause deep sorrow to the disciples. Accordingly, it was plain to them that Jesus was speaking concerning His impending death; and the rather, as $\theta\rho\eta\nu\epsilon\hat{\imath}\nu$, $\theta\rho\hat{\eta}\nu os$, were used especially of lamentation for beloved persons departed: Mark ii. 18, xi. 17; Luke xxiii. 27.—The words, $\dot{a}\lambda\lambda'$ $\dot{\eta}$ $\lambda\dot{v}\pi\eta$, $\kappa.\tau.\lambda.$, echo Ps. xxx. 12: comp. also Esth. ix. 22.

Vers. 21, 22. "A woman when she is in travail hath sorrow, because her hour is come: but as soon as she is delivered of the child, she remembereth no more the anguish, for joy that a man is born into the world. And ye now therefore have sorrow; but I will see you again, and your heart shall rejoice, and your joy no man taketh from you."—According to the express exposition of our Lord Himself, nothing is to be imported into the figure of the bearing woman beyond the immediate transition, in which the deepest sorrow is followed by the highest joy; and the edifying meaning which the saying has, when thus simply viewed, is rather lessened than augmented by the other deeper significations which are sought in it. In the Old Testament, the image of the bearing woman is everywhere viewed under one aspect, that of sorrow; and the other, that of joy following, is not included: comp. Mic. iv. 9, 10; Isa. xxvi. 17; Jer. iv. 31; Hos. xiii. 13. Thus there is here an extension of the figure which is already familiar in the older Scriptures.—" And your heart shall rejoice" is taken from Isa. lxvi. 14.—The words, " and your joy no man taketh from you," point to the fact that their seeing Christ again would be, in contradistinction to or contrast with the transitory sorrow which the not seeing Him would cause, a source of imperishable and everduring joy and rejoicing. That their seeing Him again would be only transitory, the Lord had very explicitly intimated, when He referred the Apostles, in ver. 13, to the Holy Ghost; but this transitory seeing would be sufficient to lay the foundation of an abiding joy. From that time it would be true, " In whom, though ye see Him not, yet believing, ye rejoice with joy unspeakable, and full of glory," 1 Pet. i. 8. We see in Luke xxiv. 52, 53, that the ascension was not an interruption to the joy of the disciples: as surely as their Head was in heaven, so surely would it stand firm that He would be with them unto the end of the world: comp. Acts i. 11, iii. 21.

Ver. 23. " And in that day ye shall ask Me nothing. Verily, verily, I say unto you, Whatsoever ye shall ask the Father in My name, He will give it you."—Jesus had in the previous words answered the question of the disciples before it had been put. Here He takes into view the condition of the disciples, out of which the necessity for asking had arisen. The *day* is here the day when Jesus would see His disciples again, and they should see Him; but this day is, in the Old Testament manner, regarded as the beginning term of a new epoch, in which the Apostles should be elevated above the low position which they had hitherto occupied. From the moment of their first seeing

Him again, the Apostles were exalted into a new being. This developed itself, however, by degrees. That the outpouring of the Holy Spirit on the day of Pentecost did not constitute a new beginning, is plain from the fact, that on the evening of His resurrection the Lord said to His disciples, "Receive ye the Holy Ghost," ch. xx. 22.—" Ye shall ask Me nothing" stands in obvious connection with the purpose of the disciples, perceived by Jesus, to ask Him in ver. 19 : comp. ver. 30. That lower position of spiritual insufficiency and impotence from which their question sprang, would cease from that day : they would no longer need to seek instruction in that external way, wherein it could be only very imperfectly obtained; but approach to God, the source of all true internal perception, would be opened up to them, according to the predictions of the Old Testament, which foreannounced such an unmediated knowledge of religious truth : comp. Isa. liv. 13, " All thy children shall be taught of God;" and Jer. xxxi. 34, " And they shall teach no more every man his neighbour, and every man his brother, saying, Know the Lord ; for they shall all know Me, from the least of them unto the greatest of them, saith the Lord."

" Whatsoever ye shall ask" must be referred, as the " ye shall ask Me nothing" shows, specially to matters of uncertainty in their knowledge (Bengel : " Ye shall not need to ask Me ; for ye shall clearly know all things") : comp. Jas. i. 5, " If any man lack *wisdom*, let him ask of God, who giveth to all men liberally; and it shall be given him." Yet the promise goes beyond this specific reference : whatever ye may ask in those circumstances in which, during the time of your imperfection, ye were wont to ask Me ; and in all other cases : comp. Matt. xxi. 22.—" In My name :" this intimates that, in order to prayer being answered, the petitioner must have the whole historical personality of Christ before his eyes; that he must go to a God not concealed, but manifested in Christ; that in his prayer he must sink into and be absorbed by what Christ hath done and suffered for us, grounding upon that all his hope of acceptance : comp. on ch. xiv. 13, 14, xv. 16.—In Matt. xxi. 22 it is not " in My name," but " believing."

Ver. 24. " Hitherto have ye asked nothing in My name : ask, and ye shall receive, that your joy may be full."—The

Lord does not here throw any reproach upon His disciples. The reason that they had not hitherto asked anything in His name, was that that name had not yet been perfectly unfolded in all its meaning; that the main elements of its development, the atoning sufferings, the resurrection, and the glorification of Christ, were still in the future. Jesus must first perfectly exhibit Himself as a Saviour, before faith in His name could perfectly exert its power. Here, as frequently elsewhere (comp. for example, ch. i. 17, vii. 39), the opposition which is in fact only relative is uttered absolutely; to intimate, that in comparison of their future confidence in the name of Jesus, that which they had already exercised was scarcely worthy of regard. From the very beginning of the disciples' relation to Christ, there had been in their prayers an element of trust in the name of Jesus. The God of Abraham, Isaac, and Jacob—to whom alone the Jews turned—began to recede before the Father of Jesus Christ; and in consequence of that fact, the disciples' prayers had acquired a new element of inwardness and depth. But in comparison of their future prayer, in the name of Jesus, that was not to be regarded or remembered. The advancement was not merely matter of subjective joyfulness: that was only subordinate. The true root of the higher prayer was the elevation of the objective significance of the name of Jesus; that of itself would result in higher personal joy. From the time that Christ gave His life for His friends, ch. xv. 13, and for their salvation sat down at the right hand of God,—or, to use Luther's phrase, "atoned for sin, strangled death, ravaged hell, and opened heaven,"—His name would become to them, in quite a new sense, the pledge and guarantee of their prayer being heard. They would then have to do with a propitiated God, at whose hands all their prayers would be sure of immediate acceptance. The Father cannot withstand the name of Christ made perfect (comp. the τετίλεσται, John xix. 30), when it is urged before Him. Luther: "When that name is complete, and everywhere preached, there will be new prayer and new worship in all the world; ye will then pray in My name to good purpose, and the virtue of My name will be proved by your prayers being mightily heard and answered."—Their full joy was to be the antithesis of their former imperfect joy. It would grow out of their prayer being perfectly granted.

Ver. 25. " These things have I spoken unto you in proverbs: but the time cometh, when I shall no more speak unto you in proverbs, but I shall show you plainly of the Father."— That which is here spoken must be regarded as parallel with what was, in vers. 23, 24, held out to the expectation of the disciples: for, in vers. 26, 27, the Lord recurs to this latter. There was a strict connection between the disciples having an entirely different access to God generally and specifically in the domain of knowledge, and His words to them becoming clear and transparent: before, those words had been full of obscurities and unsolved mysteries; they had had to say, with Ezekiel's hearers, " Doth He not speak parables?" and everywhere they had been obliged to put questions, the answers to which were not always satisfactory. But they would be translated into an entirely new life; and both those results would follow from the Lord's being able to say to them, " Receive ye the Holy Ghost."—" These things " refer primarily to vers. 19 seq.; but really they refer to the whole course of our Lord's previous teaching. Everywhere they had encountered manifold obscurities. Not only in the Gospel of John, but often in the other Gospels, we find this illustrated: for example, Matt. xiii. 36, xv. 15 seq., xvi. 5 seq. For παροιμία, corresponding to the Hebrew משל, primarily a figurative saying, then generally any difficult and obscure saying, comp. the remarks on ch. x. 6. Παῤῥησία is boldness in speaking, then generally any open and unfettered speech: comp. ch. xi. 54, xviii. 20. Our Lord's words in ch. xi. 14 come nearest as illustration: " Then said Jesus unto them plainly, Lazarus is dead." Before He had said, " Our friend Lazarus sleepeth." It was not that Jesus would change His speech: the change would pass upon the disciples, who would see clearness where they had formerly seen only obscurity. They were to be raised to a higher position; and to them, therefore, the Teacher would be quite different. The *hour* of this passage is identical with the *day* in ver. 23, the time of the resurrection. That was the date of the elevated condition of the disciples. The Lord's prophetic promise referred especially to the words which He would speak as the risen Redeemer: comp. Luke xxiv. 44; Acts i. 3. But it includes also all the earlier words. These recurred after the resurrection anew to their minds: comp. ch. xiv. 26, according to which the Holy

Ghost would bring to remembrance all that the Lord had told them. Then it seemed as if Jesus was saying all anew; everything obtained a new meaning and force for them. We may add, that Jesus also spoke to them through the Holy Ghost: comp. vers. 12–14.—Jesus names the Father as the matter of the communication He would make. Everything in religion goes back to Him. His domain embraces at the same time that of the Son and the Holy Ghost: " Of Him, and through Him, and to Him, are all things," Rom. xi. 36.

Vers. 26, 27. " At that day ye shall ask in My name: and I say not unto you, that I will pray the Father for you: for the Father Himself loveth you, because ye have loved Me, and have believed that I came out from God."—The words are not, " I will not pray the Father for you," but, " I say not that I will pray the Father for you." This only means that the *emphasis* does not fall absolutely upon His intercession; that it was not needful that He should first render gentle the Father's countenance; that they would have not only the Son, but the Father also, unconditionally on their side. Grotius: Prætereo hoc quasi minus eo, quod jam inferam. They were to pray in the name of Christ, involved in Him, and wrapped up in His atonement: therefore they would have not merely a merciful Saviour, but a merciful Father also. It is perfectly clear that the Lord does not here deny, or exhibit as needless, that intercession for His own which is elsewhere so expressly insisted on: comp. ch. xvii. 9; 1 John ii. 1; Rom. viii. 34; Heb. vii. 25. That rather is indirectly confirmed by the " in My name." How could the Redeemer assume an attitude of indifference towards the details of the life and needs of those who, trusting to His accomplished work, come as suppliants before God? He does not take away from the disciples the prospect of His intercession, which was so consolatory to their minds; but it was His purpose to open, in connection with that, another and a *second* source of consolation and joy. Anton excellently remarks: " He would remove everything out of the way. For man is so constituted as willingly to turn everything into gall and bitterness; and this is true even of the intercession of Christ. That intercession is an excellent consolation! But then man comes to think that the good God must have a hard heart if He must needs be urged and impelled by an intercessor;

and thus the coarsest idea of intercession is interwoven into the material of Christ's intercession. That was one main reason of the subsequent multiplication of many intercessors besides Christ. For they said we must have as many intercessors as we can. One land has this, another that; one town this, another that: thus the blessed Lord is dealt with as if He were a Saturn. No, the fault was not with God, that ye so dealt with the matter. I tell you ye must not so think of My intercession as if the Father were not Himself well disposed, but must first be coerced into kindness. No, He Himself loveth you, and Himself ordained My intercession. He appointed the way of acceptable prayer, that ye might know whence to draw your confidence. But ye must not take away the blessedness of it again."

The love of the Father is here grounded upon the disciples' love to Jesus, and their faith in Him. But this love which has their faith for its condition, was preceded by another love which appointed the atonement, and opened up the way to faith: comp. ch. iii. 16; 1 John iv. 19. To those who stood only under the government of this love, our Lord would never have said, "I say not that I will pray the Father for you." In that case, the intercession of Christ occupies the foreground: that intercession, of which we read in Isaiah, " He will make intercession for the transgressors," Isa. liii. 12. Then the propitiation of the wrath of the Father, coexisting with His love, was necessary.

Ver. 28. "I came forth from the Father, and am come into the world: again, I leave the world, and go to the Father."— As in ver. 16, so here again at the end of this part of the discourse, our Lord speaks words which prepare the way for His *farewell*. The point of connection is provided by the last words of the preceding verse. Luther: "That He might show what that going to the Father meant, He says, 'I leave the world,' that thus the disciples might mark that He now spoke somewhat more clearly than before.—In the same way also, after the resurrection, He spoke of it (Luke xxiv. 44), and said, 'These are the things which I spoke unto you while I was yet with you.'" Jesus left the world at the moment of His death, and did not return to it in His resurrection. The existence of the risen Lord belonged to another world, and His appearances transitorily broke through the limits which generally distinguish the two spheres of existence.

Vers. 29, 30. " His disciples said unto Him, Lo, now speakest Thou plainly, and speakest no proverb. Now are we sure that Thou knowest all things, and needest not that any man should ask Thee: by this we believe that Thou camest forth from God."—The words of the Apostles in ver. 29 have special reference to the more than ordinarily clear and simple saying of Jesus in ver. 28. They are heartily rejoiced at their own understanding; they congratulate themselves that they can gladden their Master by the declaration that they understand Him. They recognise, in their thus understanding, a foretaste of the fulfilment of the promise given them in ver. 25, to which they verbally refer. Anton: " Now they breathe freely, and inhale the fresh air. The disciples did well in that they did not complain alone, but told freely out their lightened feelings. To be always complaining is no virtue. And as they had affected their Master with their sorrow, so they would now rejoice Him with their little glimmer of joy in faith.—And not with one little word alone do they attest their recovery; they three times as it were lift up their voices. And this is appropriate to thankfulness. These are the offerings of the lips that praise Thy name, O God."—In ver. 29 the Apostles had referred to the conclusion of Christ's words; in ver. 30 they go back to its beginning again, which was to them not less consolatory than the end. By anticipating their question by His instruction, ver. 19, Christ had manifested Himself the possessor of omniscience, the καρδιογνώστης, Acts i. 24, xv. 8, Jer. xi. 20. In this they behold, recurring to the close of the Lord's discourse, a great assistance to their faith in His saying that He came forth from God. These words of the disciples stand in no connection with ver. 23. There it was promised that they should not find it necessary to ask Christ; here the matter is, that Jesus did not need to be asked by the disciples. Ἐν τούτῳ, properly "in this, by this." The effect upon their minds is thus traced to its cause.

Vers. 31, 32. " Jesus answered them, Do ye now believe? Behold, the hour cometh, yea, is now come, that ye shall be scattered, every man to his own, and shall leave Me alone: and yet I am not alone, because the Father is with Me."—It makes no essential difference whether we take ἄρτι πιστεύετε as a question or as a declaration. For, even in the former case, Jesus concedes to His Apostles that they do now believe, and only warns them not to lay too much stress upon that uncontestable fact (comp. ver. 27, ch. xvii. 8). The question simply intimates that all was not yet *quite* right with their faith, that there was some reason why they should not so very confidently build upon it: Are ye so absolutely assured that ye now believe? The interrogatory construction is favoured by a comparison with ch. vi. 70, xiii. 38, where our Lord tests the confident faith of Peter by a similar question. If we drop the interrogation, and make it a simple affirmative, the antithesis seems too violent. Jesus could hardly declare the Apostles absolutely to have faith, and then forthwith, without anything intervening, attach to it a prediction of their utter weakness.

The announcement of their coming infirmity was not designed solely as a reproach. According to ch. xviii. 8, our Lord Himself paved the way for the flight of His disciples. It was, as it were, in the order of things that their company was scattered. Christ must die for them and rise again before they were to be equipped with invincible assurance and boldness. Cowardice in the cause of Christ could be objected to only after His death and resurrection. To require that the Apostles should have sacrificed themselves for Christ before He had sacrificed Himself for them, would be to demand from a child the work of a man. The word σκορπισθῆτε points back to Zech. xiii. 7, and suggests the Lord's recent quotation of that passage and application of it to the Apostles, Matt. xxvi. 31, 32. The passage contained in it an element of consolation, since there was connected with their dispersion, both in the original passage and the quotation, the renewal of the bond between the Shepherd and His scattered flock. Τὰ ἴδια, the individual refuges of the disciples, in contradistinction to the one rallying-point, Christ. For "leave Me alone," comp. Matt. xxvi. 56. Μόνος points to Ps. xxii. 21, where the Righteous One cries, "Deliver My soul from the sword, My darling (My only one) from the power of the dog."

Ver. 33. "These things I have spoken unto you, that in Me ye might have peace. In the world ye shall have tribulation: but be of good cheer; I have overcome the world."—We have here the close of the whole discourse continued in ch. xv. xvi. That discourse had for its end, after the hortatory portion, to lead the disciples to perfect peace in Christ. Abiding in Christ, brotherly love, stedfast fortitude amidst persecutions of the world, were all conditions on which was suspended the enjoyment of peace in Christ. This peace includes assurance against all hostile powers: comp. on ch. xiv. 27. The having is not to be referred so much to the state as to the consciousness of it. To the *having peace* corresponds the θαρσεῖν, *be of good cheer*. The words of Christ should lead them to the confidence that all the hosts of their enemies could not touch them. But the subjective consciousness of peace must rest upon the objective possession of that peace which Christ hath obtained. Νενίκηκα is anticipatory: the great work of redemption, now to be accomplished, and by which the victory was to be achieved, is regarded as done (comp. on ch. xii. 31, 32). By similar anticipation, we have ἐνίκησαν in Rev. xii. 11, and νενικήκατε in 1 John iv. 4.

CHAP. XVII.

"A good sermon must have a good prayer" (Luther). This prayer, which forms the climax of our Lord's last discourses to His disciples, has been termed the high-priestly prayer of Christ. And rightly so, in as far as we have here the most amply unfolded intercession of Jesus for His people. Intercession for the congregation was one of the most essential functions of the high priest, Lev. ix. 22, Num. vi. 22–27. But that Jesus, by this prayer, prepared Himself for the high-priestly act of atonement has no warrant in ver. 19; and the prayer itself stands in no demonstrable connection with the redeeming sacrifice of Christ.

According to the current exposition, Jesus first prays for Himself, vers. 1–5; then for His Apostles, vers. 6–19; and finally for those who should believe on Him through their word, the Church of all ages. But this distribution is not satisfactory; it takes too much account of the mere form of the prayer. In vers. 1–5 there is a petition for the glorification of His people concealed beneath the prayer for His own glorification;[1] and on

---

[1] Lampe observes, that only in appearance our Lord at the outset pleaded His own cause: "He seeks no other glorification than what consists in this, that He should make His people partakers of eternal life."

the principle of this distribution, vers. 24-26 present no slight difficulties. The Lord here returns back from believers generally to the Apostles; and the petition for the heavenly glorification of these Apostles, as it is contained in this conclusion, shows plainly that the previous petition was not general, but specifically referred to the Apostles, and those who should believe through their word. To the same conclusion we are led by the fact that in vers. 6-23 the word κόσμος occurs with unusual and plainly intentional frequency, while everything seems to point to the general position of Christians in the world.

A more correct distribution will be as follows. At the beginning, vers. 1-5, and at the end, vers. 24-26, the Lord prays that His people may have the great benefit and blessing of the kingdom of God, *eternal life*, the heavenly glorification, the foundation of which was His own glorification. In the middle, vers. 6-23, He prays to the Father on behalf of His people, that they might have help in the perilous position in which they would be found in the *world*, during the days of their pilgrimage on earth; His prayer being first for the Apostles, and then for all believers.

Ch. xiv. offers a perfect analogy. There the Lord first directs the Apostles' thoughts to the certainty that heaven was theirs; and then He speaks of the Divine assistance and grace which they should receive during the time of their pilgrimage. What the Lord there promises, He here prays for.

That the whole refers to the disciples, we gather from ver. 13, where the end of the prayer is represented to be their establishment in perfect joy.

It is of some importance for the understanding of this prayer, that we should not study it as an outpouring of the Son's heart to the Father; we must rather regard it as having much to do with the edification of the disciples: comp. ch. xi. 42. If Jesus had had only to do with the Father, it would have been enough that "He lifted up His eyes to heaven;" the needs of the disciples would not have been unfolded before us in such detail; the supplications on their behalf would not have been so minute, and so constantly referred to their grounds. Augustin says: "Not only the direct preaching of such a Teacher, but also His prayer to the Father for them, served for the edification of His disciples." Lampe: "The confirmation and salvation of these disciples was the primary scope of these prayers." Schmieder: " His words were not only an effusion of the heart to the Father, but also a pondered and careful exposition for the disciples."

Between this high-priestly prayer and the conflict in Gethsemane, as recorded by the first three Evangelists, there might seem at the first glance to be an irreconcilable opposition. It has been said, that whosoever was able to pray as Jesus prays in John, and was so confident of his victory over the world and his own glorification, could not possibly have immediately afterwards fallen into such trembling and despondency, into such bitterness of death. Either of the two might be imaginable, but not both together. But this contradiction vanishes at once, so soon as we apprehend the true significance of the conflict in Gethsemane. If our Lord struggled and suffered for us and in our stead, if the chastisement of our peace was laid upon Him, then in Him also it was necessary that all the horror of death should be concentrated. He bore the sin of the world, and the wages of that sin was death. Death must therefore appear to Him in its most fearful form; and the rather as our Representative alone could look profoundly into the depths of sin. The physical suffering was nothing in comparison to this immeasurable suffering of the soul. And if the struggle was vicarious, and thus voluntarily assumed, the suddenness of the transition should not seem strange to us. It is not our task to trace and explain the connection between His different emotions. With equal freedom, the Redeemer was equal now to the one, and then to the other, aspect of His destiny. Then we likewise understand how it was, that, with such clear consciousness, He went forth to encounter this conflict; how, far from being surprised by it, or being overcome by its agony, He prepared all things beforehand, left behind the rest of the Apostles, while He took with Him the three most advanced, as witnesses for the Church of all ages; how He went, as it were, *ex professo* to suffer and struggle, even as at the beginning of His manifestation He was not fortuitously encountered by Satan, but led by the Spirit into the wilderness *that* He might be tempted of Satan.

That St John has altogether omitted the conflict in Gethsemane, is at the first glance strange. He himself was, with

Peter and James, a *witness* of this struggle; and that it was of the greatest moment to the Church, is evident from the very fact that the three were taken by our Lord to behold it. But the anomaly vanishes as soon as we rightly discern the relation of St John to the three first Evangelists, and the supplementary character of his Gospel. The more momentous the event was, the more obvious it was that the first Evangelists should record it with the utmost circumstantiality, thus leaving for the fourth no *Paraleipomena*. The transition to St John's silence is seen in the comparative brevity with which Luke records the incident. He sums up briefly all that the two Evangelists had already communicated, inserting only three facts peculiar to his account: first, that the disciples slept *through sorrow;* then, that an angel from heaven appeared to the Redeemer, and strengthened Him; finally, that His sweat fell to the ground like drops of blood. While St Matthew draws from the unexhausted fulness, we see in St Luke the end of the historical material. St John could not, according to the design of his Gospel, repeat. Instead of that, he gives all the more perfectly the high-priestly prayer of our Lord, which his predecessors had not ventured to touch, it having been regarded from the beginning as reserved for St John.

Ver. 1. "These words spake Jesus, and lifted up His eyes to heaven, and said, Father, the hour is come; glorify Thy Son, that Thy Son also may glorify Thee."—The circumstantiality with which the prayer of our Lord is introduced bespeaks its high significance. That He lifted up His eyes to heaven is more than once recorded: ch. xi. 41; Mark vii. 34; Matt. xiv. 19. On all these occasions, Jesus was in the open air; and in that position the upward glance would be more conspicuous. There is not, indeed, in the words themselves actual demonstration that our Lord pronounced His last discourses under the open heaven. The eyes may obviously be lifted up to heaven within a chamber; and so we find, Acts vii. 55, that Stephen lifted up his eyes to heaven in the midst of the council. The expression, however, suggests it; and we have already, on other and strong grounds, proved that Jesus did speak in the open air.—The *hour* is in itself indefinite: the sequel alone will furnish its more precise specification. (Augustin: He shows that all time, and all that in time is permitted to be done or suffered, was appointed by Him who is above subjection to time.) Accordingly, it was not the hour of the passion, but of the glorification. In His spirit, the suffering was already past. The word is more fully uttered in ch. xii. 23 : "The hour is come, that the Son of man should be glorified."—"Glorify Thy Son:" glorify Me *because* I am Thy Son, from whose nature the perfection of glory is inseparable, and who only for a season could renounce that glory. The Divine glory attended the Son of God even in His state of humiliation (comp. ch. i. 14, ii. 11), and manifested itself most variously in His deeds: comp. ch. xi. 4, xiii. 31, xii. 28. But it was a deeply concealed glory; and the Son of God prays that now this concealment might cease, that His glory might beam forth again in its original brightness.

The Father was to glorify the Son, that the Son might glorify the Father : the glory of the Father, and the blessedness of believers given with it, was the final goal. The καί after ἵνα is spurious : it weakens the idea, so important in the present connection, that the glorification of the Son here comes into consideration only as means to an end. The glory of the Father could not of itself know any addition : His being glorified, therefore, can only refer to men's recognition of that glory. But men's knowledge and acknowledgment of His glory required Christ's glorification as its condition. It has its various gradations and degrees. But it is evident from what follows, that the Lord here contemplates the highest gradation of it—the perfected knowledge of the glory of God in eternal blessedness. But the idea, "that Thy Son also may glorify Thee," could not remain in this generality. It points forward by its very mysteriousness, left to conjecture, to a closer definition of its meaning. Luther: "It is also to be observed in this text, how Christ ascribes it to Himself that He alone was the man through whom the Father must be glorified. That goes clean beyond all creaturely degrees."

Ver. 2. "As Thou hast given Him power over all flesh, that He should give eternal life to as many as Thou hast given Him."—Jesus first justifies His request concerning His glorification. It was in perfect harmony with that glorification that God had given Him the power to impart eternal life to all His people. This power He could exercise only when He had

Himself entered into His glory; His saints could be nowhere but where He was; their glory should consist in beholding His glory, ver. 24, ch. xiv. 2, 3. Καθώς here is used just as כאשר in Ps. li., "When Nathan the prophet came unto him, after he had gone in to Bathsheba;" Mic. iii. 4. Primarily it is only correspondence that is meant, but the causal connection lies in the background. For ἐξουσία, compare the remarks on ch. x. 18. The giving Him power is to be regarded as simultaneous with the sending of ver. 3. It was the recompense which should crown the work, and the prospect of which would inspirit to its performance. As the Father gave the Son His power, so He must place Him in that condition in which He could exercise it. The power given is over all flesh, inasmuch as no man absolutely and of necessity is excluded from the range of it. The limitation of that power is in every case the result of the fault of individuals, who reject the salvation provided for all: comp. "Ye would not," Matt. xxiii. 37. Πᾶσα σάρξ embraces the whole of mankind, corresponding to the κόσμος, ch. iii. 16; the ἐν παντὶ ἔθνει, Acts x. 35. In Matt. xxiv. 22, Luke iii. 6, Acts ii. 17, 1 Cor. i. 29, πᾶσα σάρξ is used to express the idea of the entire human race. Men are so denominated, in contradistinction to purely spiritual natures: comp. the πνεῦμα σάρκα οὐκ ἔχει, Luke xxiv. 39.

Strictly, the words run, "That all which Thou hast given Him" (nominative absolute), "He may give them." The summing up of all believers into one ideal unity makes still more emphatic the impartation of salvation to all of them, without exception. "As many as Thou hast given Him" corresponds with "whosoever believeth in Him;" just as the κόσμος in ch. iii. corresponds with the πᾶσα σάρξ. All are given to Christ who do not wilfully seal their hearts against faith. The limitation cannot be in God, else would the bestowal of power over all flesh be illusory. But it is referred back to God, because He judicially excludes unbelievers from salvation, and judicially makes believers partakers of it.

The eternal life which is here spoken of can belong only to the sphere of the other world; for it is such an eternal life as was still future to the Apostles, whom the Lord had always pre-eminently in His eye. Further, it was only the eternal life of the other world which was absolutely dependent on the glorification of Christ. The conclusion in ver. 24, corresponding with the beginning, leads to the same result; as also does ch. xiv. 2, 3. But, apart from these clear and definite reasons, in the nature of things we must refer this eternal life to the other world. The expression itself suggests it; and there are only a few passages in the discourses of our Lord in St John which bring eternal life into this present state. Generally they are in harmony with the words of our Lord in the other Evangelists, where the ζωὴ αἰώνιος is everywhere limited to the other state: comp. Matt. xix. 29; Mark x. 30; Luke xviii. 30, where the ζωὴ αἰώνιος is appropriated to the αἰὼν ἐρχόμενος. Recent exposition, instead of recognising in the few passages of this Gospel exceptions to the rule, has fallen into gross exaggeration, and not shrunk from the assertion, that the Gospel of John contradicts, on the one hand, the other Evangelists, and on the other the revelation of the Apocalypse: compare my commentary (Clark's Transl.). In ch. vi. 40, xi. 25, the resurrection and life are inseparably united; and in ch. iv. 14, v. 39, vi. 54, xii. 25, eternal life is strictly referred to the other world. Luther: "This power over all that liveth, such authority to give eternal life, belongs to no creature: the creature may receive it, but God's power alone can give eternal life. For even the angels, though they live eternally, cannot impart eternal life."

Ver. 3. "And this is life eternal, that they might know Thee the only true God, and Jesus Christ, whom Thou hast sent."—Jesus not only has to give a reason for the "glorify Thy Son," but He must also show that His own glorification would be the condition of the Father's. The latter He does now. If the Father places Him, in harmony with the authority given to Him, in a condition to give eternal life to His people, the goal of the Father's glorification would be thereby attained. For the essence of eternal life is to know God as He is, and that is the only true glorifying of Christ: to give Him His honour, is simply to acknowledge the glory that He has.—The knowledge of God has, indeed, its beginnings in the present life; but in its full truth it belongs to the life to come: there we shall first see God as He is, 1 John iii. 2; there first know Him as we are known, 1 Cor. xiii. 12. If eternal life consists in the perfect knowledge of God, or the beholding of His glory, ver. 24, the foretaste of this knowledge must be the substance of spiritual life in this world, the only essential element in it, the highest goal to which we should in this world aspire. Those who neglect in this life to labour after this goal, rob themselves of eternal life. The *nature* of eternal life is at the same time the *way* to eternal life. "To know Thy power," it is said, in Ecclus. xv. 3, "is the root of immortality."—The added clause, "the only true God," is instead of a reason: because Thou art the only true God. To see Him as He is, must be the only absolute felicity. As the only true God, He is Jehovah, the pure, absolute Being, out of whom there is nothing but illusion and shadow; to know this essential God, and in that knowledge to be united to Him, is the only true life for His creatures.

The original passage for the designation of God as the *Only One* (comp. ch. v. 44; Rom. xvi. 27; 1 Tim. i. 17, vi. 15, 16; Jude 25), is Deut. vi. 4, "Hear, O Israel; the Lord your God is one God." One God is not merely an antithesis to common polytheism, but declares that out of Him no true being exists, that He is the one and all; it annihilates all imagination of independent strength, Hab. i. 11, and the deification of riches, Job xxxi. 24. As in the original passage, and in our Lord's saying based upon it, Mark xii. 29, 30, the unity of God is the ground of the command to love Him above all (comp. Matt. iv. 10, "Thou shalt worship the Lord thy God, and Him *only* shalt thou serve," where the μονῷ is inserted from ver. 4 of the original in Deuteronomy), so here it is the ground of the doctrine that to know Him is eternal life. If God is the Only Being, He alone must be loved, He alone must be served, in Him alone our honour is to be sought; He is alone the source of living water, Jer. ii. 13; of life, Ps. xxxvi. 10; He is the life, Deut. xxx. 20, and to know Him is eternal life. Besides Deut. vi. 4, we may compare Job xxiii. 13, "He is one, and who can turn Him?" There, from the unity of God, His irresistibility, the absoluteness of His omnipotence, is argued. As there is none beside Him, whoever has this Being against him must fall.

The ἀληθινός is parallel with the μόνος: the one serves for the elucidation of the other. Because He is the only, therefore He is the true, God; and because He is the true God, therefore

He is the only one. That being which is simply true, is alone the Divine; all other being is infected with illusion and untruth: compare my commentary on the Apocalypse, ch. iii. 7, " These things saith the Holy One and the True." As the truth of His being is here parallel with its oneness, so in that passage and Rev. vi. 10 the truth is parallel with the holiness, that is, with the absoluteness, of that being. The truth of being is in antithesis to the lie, the deceitfulness, the delusion, the vanity, and the hollowness which cling to all created things.—When God is declared to be the only and the true God, His unity is declared only in regard to everything out of Himself: it does not exclude the Son, who shares His honour, but the world, and the false gods which it invents. This is plain, from the fact that it is not the abstract Godhead which is declared to be the only true God, but the Father of Christ. Anton: "It is inclusive, and only in opposition to *Allotria*."—By the ἀληθινὸν Θεόν, the reason for which the "glorify Thy Son, that Thy Son also may glorify Thee," was urged, is made complete. The appendage, " and Jesus Christ, whom Thou hast sent," was necessary, in order that the Apostles—whom the Lord, according to ver. 13, had always in view—might not misunderstand the words concerning the only true God. He Himself must be named, as being, not only in time, but also in eternity, the only medium of the knowledge of the one true and only God.

That Jesus is not placed, as it were, in juxtaposition with God, after the Mohammedan manner—" There is no God but God, and Mohammed is His prophet"—but as participator in the essence and in the honour of the one only God, is plain from the fact that the full knowledge of Christ is reserved for eternal life, which presupposes His superabounding glory. It is evident also from this, that the knowledge of Christ is, not less than the knowledge of the Father, made one with eternal life itself. This presumes that He is, not less than the Father, holy and true: comp. Rev. vi. 10, where these predicates are given to the Father, with iii. 7, where they are given to Christ. In 1 John v. 20, Jesus Christ is taken up into the region of the Only True: the Father and the Son together form the opposite of idols. The predicate of Truth is first assigned to the Father; and then it is said of His Son, Jesus Christ, " This is the true God, and eternal life," in order to show that in Him the Father is perfectly revealed, and that in Him all the Father's fulness is. Luther says: "Since He bases eternal life upon the knowing Himself with the Father, and says, that without the knowledge of Him no man can attain unto eternal life, and thus that it is one and the same knowledge by which He and the Father are known, He must perforce be of the same essence and nature with the Father: that is, He must be the selfsame true God, yet a Person distinguished from the Father."

"Whom Thou hast sent" points to the Old Testament Angel of the Lord, like unto God: comp. on iii. 17. That we are not to think of a mere mission, like that of the prophets, but of that sending which was from heaven to earth, is plain from ver. 18.—Our Lord does not say, "Me, whom Thou hast sent," but, making Himself objective, "Jesus Christ." This was the name which He bore upon earth in His state of humiliation, "the man Christ Jesus," 1 Tim. ii. 5. Its use suggested evidently, that He whom the disciples saw before them in the form of a servant, would in eternal life assume an altogether different position. For the same reason, it was our Lord's good pleasure, in those passages which treat of His future glory, to designate Himself the Son of man: comp. ch. xii. 23. And how wont He was to speak of Himself in the third person, is seen, for example, in Matt. xi. 27. Luther: "This I have often said, and now say it again, that when I am dead it may be thought of, and men may learn to avoid all teachers, as sent and driven by the devil, who set up to talk and preach about God, simple and sundered from Christ. If thou wouldst go straight to God, and surely apprehend Him, so as to find in Him mercy and strength, never let thyself be persuaded to seek Him elsewhere than in the Lord Christ. In Christ begin thy art and study; in Him let it abide firm; and wherever else thy own reason and thinking, or any other man's, would lead thee, shut thine eyes and say, I must not, and I will not, know of any other God than in my Lord Christ."

Vers. 4, 5. "I have glorified Thee on the earth: I have finished the work which Thou gavest Me to do. And now, O Father, glorify Thou Me with thine own self with the glory which I had with Thee before the world was."—After Jesus had *grounded* His prayer for glorification, He repeats His request, now declaring that the condition on which that glorification was suspended was fulfilled, and that work finished, for the performance of which He relinquished the state of glory belonging to His nature, and assumed the form of a servant. Schmieder: " After our Lord had expressed the final design of the glorification, which He had asked on His own behalf,—to wit, the glorification of the Father in men, through the communication of eternal life to man,—He takes up once more the prayer for glorification, setting forth first the ground of His warrant to urge this prayer now, and declaring wherefore the hour of glorification had now actually come." For " I have glorified Thee," comp. ch. xiii. 31, 32; Matt. ix. 8; Luke vii. 16, xiii. 13. While Christ revealed His own glory, He at the same time bore witness to the glory of the Father; He raised His people with a mighty hand out of their indifference towards Him, made them lift up their hearts to Him, and consecrate themselves to His service; even as to the present day the way to the glorification of God is only through Christ. Luther: " The Lord Christ, when He was upon earth, so glorified the Father, that He made His praise, honour, and dignity great. And it is the whole life and being of a Christian man, as it was of Christ Himself, to exalt the honour and glory of God alone, to know and to magnify His grace and goodness."—To the ἐπὶ τῆς γῆς corresponds the παρὰ σεαυτῷ, that is, " in heaven."—When the Lord says, " I have finished the work," He anticipates what still remained of it, which was to be accomplished in the next approaching hours. It was not really fulfilled until the Lord could say, " It is finished."—Σύ, Thou, forms the antithesis to ἐγώ, I. Righteousness required that the Father should glorify the Son, who had glorified Him. On account of the antithesis to ἐγώ σε, we must point με σύ, πάτερ, not με, σὺ πάτερ, as in ver. 21; also, there must be a comma between σύ and πάτερ. The address, " O Father," recurs four times; besides " Holy Father" in ver. 11, and " Righteous Father" in ver. 25. From the glory, the restoration of which Jesus here prayed for, we must distinguish that glory which was inseparable from His nature, which indwelt in Him, even during His humiliation (comp. ch. ii. 11, xiii. 31), and which ever and anon beamed forth in His words and in His deeds. Even in the case of believers, there exists this difference between a glory inseparable from their nature (comp. vers. 10, 22), and that added glory, which will be theirs only in the future life. His transfiguration was a prelude and earnest of Christ's heavenly glory. With the παρὰ σεαυτῷ, compare the ἐν ἑαυτῷ, in ch. xiii. 32. This shows that Christ would be taken up into the fellowship of the Divine glory itself. The παρὰ σεαυτῷ is explained by the antithesis to ἐπὶ τῆς γῆς. It served to introduce the universal designation of the place of the glorification. "Before the world was" (compare "before the foundation of the world," ver. 24), involves Christ's participation in divinity; for, before the world was, was only God. To be before the world, is, in Ps. xc. 2, the Divine prerogative: "Before the mountains were brought forth, or ever Thou hadst formed the earth and the world, from everlasting to everlasting, Thou art God:" comp. on ch. i. 1. The angels belong to the κόσμος; their creation is included in Gen. i. 1, even if it does not fall under the work of the six days. With "which I had with Thee before the world was," we may comp. what Prov. viii. 22, etc., says concerning Wisdom having been with God in the beginning of His way, before His works, before the earth was, before the mountains were established, when He prepared the heavens. In harmony with our present passage, Jesus, in ch. viii. 25, also claimed for Himself a Divine glory before the world was. Luther: "Here is once more a stern and clear text for the divinity of Christ against the Arians, although they have thought to make a hole through it. He says plainly, that He had possessed His glory, and had been one with the glorious nature of the Father, before the world was made. What that was, believers will estimate. For before the world was, nothing could be but God alone; since between God and the world there is no middle thing, all must be either the Creator Himself or a creature."

After Jesus had prayed to the Father that He would, by the glorification of His Son, open the way to heavenly glory for His disciples, He turns to the petitions which refer to the procedure of the Apostles in the *world*. In vers. 6–11 He lays the foundation for these petitions, by mentioning the peculiarly near relation in which they stood to God, vers. 6–10, and that they needed His help in their perilous situation in the world, ver. 11. Then, in the latter part of ver. 11, He utters the petition.

Ver. 6. "I have manifested Thy name unto the men which

Thou gavest Me out of the world: Thine they were, and Thou gavest them Me; and they have kept Thy word."—" I have declared Thy name" immediately suggests Ps. xxii. 23, "I will declare Thy name unto my brethren." The name of God is usually His historically manifested glory. Here, where the name is present before the manifestation, the nature of God Himself is described as His name, inasmuch as it contains in itself the germ of the actual manifestation: comp. on ver. 11. " God is known in Judah, His name is great in Israel," we read in Ps. lxxvi. 2. God had ever, in the Old Testament, made Himself, through His acts, a glorious name, Isa. lxiii. 14. But these revelations of the name were, in comparison of that effected through Christ, of so little account, that the name of God had hitherto, as it were, not been made known. The *men* form the antithesis to the Father and the Son in the previous verse. "Whom Thou hast given Me" refers not to eternal predestination, but to election in time. They were given at the moment when they attained to faith.—The design of the words, "Thine they were," etc., was formally to pave the way for the petition in ver. 12, and in effect to turn the disciples' hearts to God.[1] God could not forsake them, even because of the love which He bears to all His creatures; how much more, then, would He defend them as believers, as those who had maintained their state of faith! "Thine they were, and Thou gavest them to Me." Both these were true, even of Judas: comp. ver. 12, where he also is numbered among those whom the Father had given to the Son. But because the *third* thing was in him wanting—the keeping God's word—the first and the second lost their force, yea, were changed in his case into a condemnation and a curse.

"Thine they were:" that is, as men, as belonging to the κόσμος, as Thy creatures. If we do not interpret this by referring to τοῖς ἀνθρώποις and to ἐκ τοῦ κόσμου, we are left to mere conjecture. We may compare Gen. i. and ii. 7, and "In

---

[1] Luther: "That He used so many words, was not in order that His petition might have more effect with the Father; for He knew it all before, and everything that Christ could ask or desire is and must be done. But He said so much, that our hearts, always so fearful and doubtful before God, might be encouraged; that they might joyfully and boldly look up to Him, run to Him with all confidence, and stand before His presence with delight."

Him we live, and move, and have our being," Acts xvii. 28, and "We are His offspring," ver. 29. The universal providence of God rests upon the creative relation; and that universal providence is the foundation of the special care which He has of believers. The Psalmists constantly refer to their relation to the Creator for the strengthening of their faith in the saving and helping mercy of God. In Ps. xxii. 10, 11, the singer dwells upon the fact, that God had been the sufferer's God, even from his earliest infancy, and exults that He will not leave him or forsake him. "Thou preservest man and beast," it is said in Ps. xxxvi. 6: how much more His saints! In Ps. civ. the greatness of God, in His care for all creatures living on earth, is exhibited, in order to invigorate the Church's confidence in the final victory of God's people over the world. In Ps. cxlv. 9 we read, "The Lord is good to all, and His tender mercies are over all His works:" over all, therefore how much more over His people! Our Lord Himself took pleasure in reminding His disciples of God's goodness in caring for all His creatures: comp. Matt. vi. 26, x. 29–31. In these passages we have His own comment upon "Thine they were." But it cannot mean that they were once the Father's, but not the Son's. That would be at variance with ver. 10, according to which the Father can have nothing that the Son has not; and with vers. 5 and 24, according to which the Son, before the foundation of the world, shared the glory of God; and with ch. i. 3, which shows that all things were made by the Word. Augustin rightly remarks: "Were they ever the Father's, and not the only-begotten Son's; and had the Father ever anything which the Son had not? Far be it. Assuredly God the Son had once that which He had not as man the Son." But it was not here the question to exalt the prerogative of the Son. Jesus would lay all His own in the arms of the Father.

"And Thou gavest them Me:" hence they have become Thine in an altogether different sense from that in which they were Thine as men. They were Thine as men: how much more are they Thine as Christians! In the *third* clause we find the word of the Father mentioned, and not the word of Christ; and this points to the fact, that the relation to Christ is here referred as involving in itself the deepened inwardness of the relation to the Father. Luther: "In their being My disciples, and hearing My word, they hear and keep not My word, but Thine." To the keeping of God's word, in this passage, corresponds, in ch. xv., the abiding in Christ. Where this third is wanting, the first two foundations for trust in the grace of God are robbed of all their strength.

Vers. 7, 8. " Now they have known that all things, whatsoever Thou hast given Me, are of Thee: for I have given unto them the words which Thou gavest Me; and they have received them, and have known surely that I came out from Thee, and they have believed that Thou didst send Me."—We have here the further development of " Thou gavest them Me," and " they have kept Thy word." They have become, in the fullest sense, God's own; and therefore He cannot withdraw from them His help.

Ver. 9. " I pray for them: I pray not for the world, but for them which Thou hast given Me; for they are Thine."— He does not say, " I pray not *now* for the world," nor " I pray not in the same sense;" but generally, " I pray not for the world." This shows that the world, as such, is simply shut out from the grace of God; that to pray for it would not be according to the will of God; that 1 John v. 16 holds good of the world, " There is a sin unto death: I do not say that he shall pray for it." The world may be viewed under two aspects. First, there is the susceptibility of grace, which, despite the depth of the sinful depravation of Adam's race, still remains in it. Of the world in this sense, Jesus says, " I came not into the world to condemn the world, but to save the world:" comp. ch. i. 29, iii. 17, iv. 42. Viewed under this aspect, the world is the object of Christ's intercession. The disciples themselves were won from the world. But the world may also be viewed as ruled by predominantly ungodly principles. Of the world in this sense, we read in ch. xiv. 17, that it could not receive the Spirit of truth. To pray for the world, thus viewed, would be as vain as to pray for the " prince of this world." It is an object not to be prayed for, but to be prayed against. To it apply all those objurgations in the so-called cursing psalms, which our Lord so emphatically and so repeatedly quoted and acknowledged as the word of God. Of that world Ps. lxxix. 10 says: " Let Him be known among the heathen in our sight, by the revenging of the blood of Thy servants which is shed." To it applies the word of Rev. vi. 10 : " And they cried with a loud voice, saying, How long, O Lord, holy and true, dost Thou not judge and avenge our blood on them that dwell on the earth?" Luther gives us what is in all essentials the right view : " But how can the two be reconciled, His not praying for the world here, and His commanding us, in Matt. v., to pray for our enemies ? The answer is ready : to pray for the world, and not to pray for the world, must both be right and good. As the world now stands, and as it rages against the Gospel, He will in no way have it prayed for, that God should wink at and suffer its evil nature and ways ; but we must pray against it, that God would hinder its projects, and bring them to nought. So Moses did, Num. xvi. 15, against Korah and his company : he was very wroth, and said unto the Lord, Respect not Thou their offering. Thus Christ shows us here the two companies : the first and small one, which keeps and must preach the word of God ; and the greater one, which aims to thwart that little flock in everything." Similarly Quesnel : " The world, that corporation of the wicked, which stands fast and ever will stand fast, though individuals of its members may be snatched from it, remains under the curse, and is treated as under the ban, as having no part in the sacrifice of Christ, and therefore none in His intercession. What an idea this must give us of the world !"

Ver. 10. " And all Mine are Thine, and Thine are Mine ; and I am glorified in them."—Only " all Mine are Thine" belongs to the present matter. " All Thine are Mine" is added only to place in full light the inwardness of the fellowship on which " all Mine are Thine" rests : it is equivalent to " even as all Thine is Mine." So also, in Matt. xi. 27, the clause, " No man knoweth the Son but the Father," does not immediately belong to the matter in hand, but serves only as a basis of support for " No man knoweth the Father but the Son." Luther remarks : " It were not so much to say, All Mine is Thine ; for every man may declare, that whatever he has is God's. But it is much greater when He inverts it, and says, All Thine is Mine ; for no creature of God can say that." We have an elucidation of " All Thine is Mine" in Rev. v. 12. There the ten thousands of angels cry, " Worthy is the Lamb that was slain, to receive power, and riches, and wisdom, and strength, and honour, and glory, and blessing." The seven ascriptions correspond with the sevenfold praise of God in ch. vii. 12.

Christ was glorified in His people, inasmuch as they perceived and acknowledged, beneath the veil of His servant-form, the true Son of God; and even on that account they became the object of more gracious care to the Father, who beholds His own honour in the honour of His Son: comp. ch. xi. 4. Luther: " By the world I am obscured, dishonoured, and condemned; but they, My disciples, because they hear the word that I am sent of Thee, and that I have all that is Thine, glorify Me. Thereby I am revealed and plainly set before them, so that they regard Me altogether differently from the world, even as Thy Son, the eternal and true God. No possessions and no honours in the world are to be compared with this, that He will be glorified in the infirmity of our poor flesh and blood, and that God the Father is so highly honoured and well pleased when we magnify and honour the Christ."

Ver. 11. " And now I am no more in the world, but these are in the world, and I come to Thee. Holy Father, keep through Thine own name those whom Thou hast given Me, that they may be one, as we are."—From the reference to the *worthiness* of the disciples the Lord turns, in the words " I am no more in the world, but come to Thee," to the *necessities* of their condition. That which is here simply hinted is in ver. 12 seq., after the petition uttered, more largely developed. Thence we see that the world is here regarded as a tempting power, and that the words " I am no more in the world" were intended to suggest that the defence which they had hitherto enjoyed would be withdrawn through the departure of Christ, near at hand, and therefore anticipated as already come.—It is not a contradiction that Jesus here says, " I am no more in the world;" while elsewhere He says, " Lo, I am with you always, even to the end of the world," and, " Wherever two or three are gathered together in My name, there am I in the midst of them." This latter presence with His disciples belongs to a higher order of things. He is now no longer with them in the world; He visits them from above. This belongs to the domain of the πάτερ ἅγιε.

The *holiness* of God is His absolute supremacy over all things created and temporal (comp. my comm. on Ps. xxii. 3;

Rev. iv. 8; Clark's Trans.). An erroneous notion has been entertained, that by the holiness of God is meant His condescension and mercy; and for this the designation in Isaiah, "The Holy One of Israel," has been appealed to. But the idea of love is there imported simply and alone by the relation of *status constructionis*. The Holy One of Israel is the Sovereign God, separate from all that is creature, and independent of all that is creaturely, the absolute and unending One, who belongs to Israel, and from whom an endless fulness of power, in opposition to the world, flows to Israel His people. The passage in Hos. xi. 9 is no stronger as an argument: "I will not execute the fierceness of Mine anger, I will not return to destroy Ephraim: for I am God, and not man; the Holy One in the midst of thee: and I will not enter into the city"—I will not be like men who go in and out of the city. The idea of mercy lies no more in that of the *Holy One*, as such, than in that of *God*; although freedom from human outbreaks of wrath is certainly *included* in the notion of separation from everything creaturely. But here the holiness of God, as the connection shows, comes into consideration only as excluding every idea of want of power. Calvin: "That out of His heavenly glory He may help our weaknesses. The whole prayer tends to this, to prevent the disciples' minds from sinking, as if their condition would be worse on account of the bodily absence of their Master." As the Holy One, God has absolutely in His hands the means of granting what was prayed for. The allusion to the Holy Father intimated to the disciples, that the departure of Jesus, their Protector in the past, need not fill their souls with anxiety. They were given over to a mightier One, who could do and who possessed all things. We may compare "My Father is greater than I," in ch. xiv. 28. What Jesus in His state of humiliation petitioned of the Father, the disciples might all the more confidently expect, inasmuch as He Himself entered into the fellowship of the Father's glory: comp. ch. i. 5.

The ᾧ δέδωκάς μοι, " through Thy own name, which Thou hast given Me," is now pretty generally acknowledged to be the right one: that of οὕς, which Luther [and the English translation] follows, sprang from a misapprehension of the meaning. The ᾧ, by attraction for ὅ, which many authorities substitute, points to Ex. xxiii. 21. There Jehovah says concerning His

Angel, "My name is in Him" (comp. Christ. vol. i.). The Angel, in whom was the name of God, was the Angel on whom it was incumbent to make a name for God—whose nature is repugnant to being nameless—by manifesting through His glorious acts the nature of God dwelling in Him. The name was, as it were, proleptically used for that aspect of the Divine nature in which the name of God culminates, which impels Him, as it were, out of Himself, and moves Him to manifestation and impartation of Himself: comp. on ver. 6. The addition only makes more expressly prominent that which already lay in ἐν τῷ ὀνόματί σου. The name of God is His character as forming history, His nature as issuing into manifestation; and the unfolding of this name is to be sought only in Christ (comp. ver. 6): only in Him has God a name. The disciples stood in no direct relation to the Father; they belonged to the Father only through the Son; they were kept in the name of the Father, only in so far as the name of the Father was at the same time the name of the Son. Around the name of God in Christ the disciples had gathered. This name alone builds up the Church. In this centre the Holy Father would keep His people. If they should fall out of that name, the Church would cease to exist. According to the connection with what precedes, the world was the power which would make every effort to rend the disciples from the name of the Father and of the Son, thus destroying their unity. Against their persecutions and seductions the Saviour appeals to the power of the Father: asking of Him what He Himself in the fellowship of the Father would do.

That the name of the Father is to be conceived as actually indwelling in Christ,—that we must not interpret it, " which Thou hast given Me *to declare*,"—is evident from the original text, Ex. xxiii. 21. There " My name is in Him" indicates equal Divine glory. For the words were used to enforce a warning against dishonour done to Him: " Beware of Him, and obey His voice, provoke Him not; for He will not pardon your transgressions: *for* My name is in Him." The *proclamation* of the name of the Lord was not incumbent on that Angel; it was His rather to make for God a glorious name by His acts.—" That they may be one, as we are." The unity of the disciples among themselves was only secondary; it was not to be independently laboured for, but it was to approve itself as real when God fulfilled the petition here uttered. That unity would be precious only if it was not enforced, but should grow out of their abiding in the name of God and Christ, just as spontaneously as the union between the Father and the Son. The type of all those attempts at unity which should be substitutes for this natural union, we have in the Babel of primitive times. That tended only to increase division. He who looks more deeply will not be deluded by it. Luther: " But it is no other than that which Paul in 1 Cor. xii. 12, and many other passages, says, to wit that we are one body in Christ; not merely of one opinion or one thought, but of one nature.—But this we can attain in no other way than by this, *that God keep us in His name :* that is, that we abide in the word which we have received concerning Christ. For the word holds us together, so that we all abide in one Head, and depend on Him alone.—The devil tries hard to break this bond, and by his cunning devices to rend us away from the word."

Vers. 12–15 serve for the further justification of the prayer uttered in ver. 11. The watchword " keep" recurs in ver. 15, and marks the conclusion.—Vers. 12, 13 dilate upon the element of *need*, which was briefly hinted at in ver. 11. Vers. 14, 15 return to the element of *dignity*, which was dwelt upon in vers. 7–10. The disciples are committed to the care of the Father, for Jesus leaves them, vers. 12, 13; they are the bearers of the word of God, and as such worthy of His protection, vers. 14, 15.

Ver. 12. " While I was with them in the world, I kept them in Thy name: those that Thou gavest Me I have kept, and none of them is lost, but the son of perdition; that the Scripture might be fulfilled."—To the being given by God corresponds the election by Christ in ch. vi. 70, xiii. 18. Faith is the subjective condition of both; and as Judas is numbered among those whom God had given to Christ, at the time of his call he must have possessed faith.—The Lord has Judas in His mind—without however mentioning him, because that would have been out of harmony with the solemn dignity of the prayer—in order to anticipate and obviate the conclusion which might be drawn to the prejudice of His shepherd fidelity, or, generally, of His shepherd ability, from the ruin of Judas. In his case it was necessary that the watchful care of Jesus should be wasted; for he was taken into the number of the Apostles to be dropped from it again. " It had not been the task of the Redeemer to save him, but to bear with him, and, despite his foreknown insalvability, to neglect nothing in his case which the relation between Master and disciple, appointed by the Father, demanded " (Schmieder).

Perdition is here used, as in Rev. xvii. 8, 11, 2 Thess. ii. 3, of ruin simply, of the perdition of hell, in contradistinction to ἡ ζωή, eternal life, in Matt. vii. 13. To the son of perdition here, corresponds the child of *hell* in Matt. xxiii. 15.—The son of perdition is he who belongs to perdition; and Luther's translation, *das verlorne Kind*—the lost son—does not exactly hit the point. We may compare the "children of the kingdom," Matt. xiii. 38; "children of the bride-chamber," Mark ii. 19; "sons of thunder," Mark iii. 17; "children of this generation," Luke xvi. 8, xx. 34; "children of light," John xii. 36. This mode of designation, which all the Evangelists show to have been current with Christ, frequently occurs in the Old Testament: compare, for example, the "children of death," those who were appointed to die and belong to death as personified, that is, the dying themselves, Ps. lxxix. 11 ; the "children of the needy," Ps. lxxii. 4. The designation of Judas as the son of perdition involves the reason why he must be lost; and thus his perdition could furnish no argument to the disparagement of Christ. He was one whose destiny was to be lost. The designation here corresponds to the words which derive his ruin from the necessity that Scripture should be fulfilled. Accordingly the subject, or child of ruin, means one who was devoted or given over to ruin.—Judas was lost, that the Scripture might be fulfilled. Christ knew, when He chose him, that notwithstanding his transitory gleam of faith, he would apostatize and betray Him. If, therefore, He received him notwithstanding into the number of the Apostles, it must have been that he might work out his own ruin, and thus that the Scripture might be fulfilled, which includes such a man among the necessary surroundings of the Redeemer. That he came to ruin was his own fault; but since, in spite of his foreseen fall, he was taken into the number of the Apostles, and would not have been thus ruined if he had not been taken into their number, it may be said that he was lost that the

Scripture might be fulfilled. As he *would* fall, he should and did fall. It was his doom that he was admitted into the near fellowship of Christ, and thus had this peculiar occasion of falling. His election, and the concurrent ruin, were to serve for the fulfilment of Scripture. In harmony with the present text, our Lord says, in ch. xiii. 18, that He had chosen Judas that the Scripture might be fulfilled.—The citation of Scripture would be matter of great uncertainty if any other scripture ould be meant than that expressly quoted in ch. xiii. 18; the only one which our Lord generally applied to the case of Judas. In that passage the perdition of Judas is not directly spoken of, but his traitorous act,—a traitorous act, however, which had perdition as its immediate consequence.

Ver. 13. "And now come I to Thee; and these things I speak in the world, that they might have My joy fulfilled in themselves."—After "But now come I to Thee," we must supply in thought, "and Thou must, Holy Father, keep them in Thy name;" and then follows the statement of the reason why Jesus commits them so emphatically to His Holy Father. *Ταῦτα*, these things, refer to the "Holy Father," etc. "In the world," yet being in the world, before My departure. Before He leaves the world, He says this for the consolation of the disciples whom He leaves behind Him. Luther: "Therefore He would by these words show them another secure place, where He would be much better able to keep them and save them; that is, with the Father, to whom He is now going, in order that He may receive all things into His own hands, and be able always to be with them, although outwardly and in the body He might be absent." "My joy:" that is, the joy which I prepare for them, by means of the prayer which I offer in their hearing and for them to the Holy Father; just as "My peace," in ch. xiv. 27, meant the peace which I give unto them. Joy is here, as in ch. xiv. 28 (ch. xv. 11 is not to be compared), the opposite of the sorrow which the disciples felt at the impending departure of Christ. The joy which Jesus provided for them, by committing them to the keeping of the Father, who was greater than He, would be *perfect.* That resulted from the fact that He to whom they were committed was the *Holy One.*

Vers. 14, 15. "I have given them Thy word; and the

world hath hated them, because they are not of the world, even as I am not of the world. I pray not that Thou shouldest take them out of the world, but that Thou shouldest keep them from the evil."—That Christ had given them the word of God, was the reason, on the one hand, of the world's hatred, as between Christ's people and the world a wall of separation had been set up by that word; and, on the other hand, of that committal of them to the protecting power of God which is pleaded for in ver. 15. The fact that the world hated them would serve to recommend them to God; it was the confirmation of their sincere relation to God. If they had not the word of God in themselves, the world would love them.—They might not be taken from the world; partly because they themselves must, while yet in the world, be prepared and matured for eternal life (ver. 17, and the γνωρίσω, ver. 26); and partly because they must first fulfil the mission entrusted to them for the world, ver. 18 (comp. Phil. i. 24, and "Ye are the salt of the earth"). Elijah cried in deep despondency (1 Kings xix. 4), "It is enough: O Lord, take my life." That Jesus did not pray the Father that He would take His disciples out of the world, was to warn them beforehand not to pray as Elijah did, when the hatred of the world should pierce them bitterly. Τηρεῖν with ἐκ is found only here and Rev. iii. 10: the construction is explained by noting that the idea of delivering from is included in the preserving. The ἐκ of itself shows that πονηροῦ is not the designation of a person, but of a domain of evil; that we must therefore not think of the great enemy, but only of evil generally: Luke vi. 45; Rom. xii. 9; 2 Thess. ii. 3, where τὸ πονηρόν corresponds to the wicked men of ver. 2; 1 John iii. 12, v. 19. It is decisive against taking πονηροῦ as masculine, that here, as well as in the Lord's Prayer, there is an undeniable allusion to Gen. xlviii. 16, where Jacob says, "The Angel who redeemed me from all evil," ὁ ἄγγελος ὁ ῥυόμενός με ἐκ πάντων τῶν κακῶν, a passage to which we may trace a reference in 2 Cor. i. 19; 2 Tim. iv. 17, 18; 2 Thess. iii. 2, 3. It is all the more difficult to establish that Satan was here meant, inasmuch as throughout the prayer the Lord has to do with the world, and never with Satan. As τοῦ πονηροῦ is capable of two meanings, it is obvious that we should adopt that one for which the context decides; and the context here introduces, not the one spirit of evil, but the evil spirit of the world. The evil comes into consideration here, more especially as assuming the character of an inward temptation; to this we are led by the correspondence between "from the evil" and "in Thy name." Schmieder: "The petition, Keep them from the evil, and the petition, Keep in Thine own name, stand in the strictest connection. Keeping them in the name of God, is keeping them in that which sanctifies; preserving them from the evil, is preserving them from that which would desecrate or rob them of sanctification." But the pressure of persecution on account of the word, Matt. xiii. 21, is not to be excluded. The world lieth in wickedness, 1 John v. 19: this evil besets the disciples of Christ in two ways, by two temptations which go hand in hand. That which they have to suffer from the evil in the world, may easily mislead them into making an end of their difficulties, by admitting the evil into themselves.

In vers. 16–19, Jesus prays the Father that He would *sanctify* the disciples, and gives the reason of this prayer.

Vers. 16, 17. "They are not of the world, even as I am not of the world. Sanctify them through Thy truth: Thy word is truth."—Ver. 16 repeats what had been already said in ver. 14. We may suppose, therefore, that these words are not inserted for their independent meaning, but serve as a foundation for the prayer ensuing in ver. 17. The disciples belong not to the world, because they are sundered from the world by the word of God given to them, ver. 14, by Christ. The Father, therefore, is prayed to make this separation from the world perfect and real by the continual operation of that word.—To *sanctify* is to separate from the world, and translate into the region of God—to consecrate. The σου after τῇ ἀληθείᾳ (Thy truth) is, according to preponderating testimonies, spurious. Bengel has made the remark that we often hear of the truth in John, but never of the truth *of God*. Ἐν τῇ ἀληθείᾳ is explained by the subsequent ἐν ἀληθείᾳ, from which it must by no means be severed: comp. ἀληθῶς, ver. 8. Now, since ἐν ἀληθείᾳ is always used adverbially (in 3 John 3, 4, " walking in truth" is " truly, truthfully walking"), the article "in *the* truth" must be taken generically; the truth forms the antithesis of semblance and defectiveness: comp. on ch. iii. 21. We find "*the* truth" for "truth" also in 1 John i. 6. The addition "*Thy*" in the present text (σου) sprang from a misconception of the adverbial character of "in truth." The Codex Vaticanus omitted the article from a right apprehension of this. And Luther also retained this right apprehension, although he followed the incorrect reading σου: "And that in Thy truth, so that it may be a sound and right sanctification,—as also St Paul speaks in Eph. iv. 24, *in justitia et sanctitate veritatis*, that is, in a right, pure, and true holiness." We might, indeed, be disposed to interpret "in truth" as hinting a contrast with Old Testament sanctifyings, which only accomplished an external holiness, "sanctifying to the purification of the flesh," Heb. ix. 13. But such a reference in this connection would be far-fetched. We are obliged to refer it to the imperfect sanctification of which the Apostles were already the subjects. "They are not of this world," in ver. 16, means, expressed positively, "They are now already holy;" and "in truth" intimates that this already existing holiness yet lacked its perfect reality: comp. ὁ ἅγιος, ἁγιασθήτω ἔτι, Rev. xxii. 11. —"Thy word is truth," and therefore the ground of true sanctification. The word, by means of which the first separation from the world was effected (comp. ch. xv. 3), is also the means by which this separation must be brought more and more to its true and perfect consummation.

Ver. 18. "As Thou hast sent Me into the world, even so have I also sent them into the world."—We have here a new motive to the fulfilment of this petition. The disciples were, in ver. 6, viewed as *Christians;* now they are viewed as *Apostles*. They were all the more in need of true sanctification, since they were destined for a *mission to the world*. If they themselves should be infected with the spirit of the world, they would not be able successfully to accomplish their mission. The καθὼς—κόσμον is not a superfluous parallel. He who sent His Son into the world must take care that, by the true sanctification of His messengers, the end of His Son's mission into the world should be attained. So also, in ver. 16, "Even as I am not of the world" is more than a mere parallel. Christ's effectual separation from the world was the *ground* of the sanctification of His disciples.—The Apostles had already received their mission: the Lord had Himself called them Apostles, Luke vi. 13, and given them the full authority pertaining to their office, Matt. x. 1.

Ver. 19. "And for their sakes I sanctify Myself, that they also might be sanctified through the truth."—The Father must assure to the disciples the means of true sanctification; because otherwise the Son would have vainly assumed His great undertaking. The thought of the preceding verse returns here in another form. To the sending Christ into the world, corresponds in this verse Christ's sanctification of Himself. The present is used, because the self-consecration which was to reach its climax in the Redeemer's atoning death still continues. (Calvin: This sanctification, although it pertained to the whole life of Christ, yet was most eminent in the sacrifice of His death.) The exclusive reference of the words to the impending sacrificial death (Bengel: Sanctifico me, mortem crucis tolerans), disturbs the connection with "As Thou hast sent Me into the world," which furnishes a comment on "I sanctify Myself," otherwise indefinite of itself; and it disturbs also the connection with ch. x. 36. As there, so here also, sanctification is separation to the service of God in His kingdom. The only difference is, that in ch. x. He who separates is God, while here it is Christ who separates Himself; and in that passage it may be observed that the sanctifying is simultaneous or coincides with the entrance into the world. "For them:" Christ sanctified Himself for the whole world, and His vocation He entered on as a Redeemer of all men; but the Apostles here come prominently into view, because the Lord is now praying for them, and their relations were central: comp. ver. 20. In ch. xv. 13 also, the atoning death of Christ is exhibited as undergone specifically for the Apostles.

After His prayer for the Apostles as to their position in the world, the Lord, in vers. 20–23, turns to the petition for *believers* in the same relation: comp. the ὁ κόσμος in vers. 21, 23. The transition to this part of the prayer we see in ver. 18, where the Lord had spoken of the sending of the Apostles into the world.

Ver. 20. "Neither pray I for these alone, but for them also which shall believe on Me through their word."—As to the present participle πιστευόντων, comp. the remarks on ch. ix. 8. All faith in the Church is dependent on the word of the Apostles, the oral or the written; the written, after the death of the Apostles, having of course greatly preponderated in influence over the oral. Following the analogy of the Old Testament, which is everywhere based upon written documentary archives, the Lord must doubtless have had the writings of the Apostles in view. The corruption of so-called oral tradition at that time infected all departments. Our Lord strenuously resisted it, everywhere turning men's thoughts from human ordinances to Holy Scripture: "it is written" was with Him the constant solution. This being the case, how can we suppose that He would have relied for the diffusion of truth in His Church upon a mere oral tradition? We have the earliest historical commentary upon the saying of this passage in Irenæus iii. 1 : "We have not received the knowledge of the plan of salvation from any others but those who delivered the Gospel; that Gospel which they had first preached, and afterwards, by God's will, handed down to us in writings, to be the pillar and ground of our faith."

Ver. 21. "That they all may be one; as Thou, Father, art in Me, and I in Thee, that they also may be one in us: that the world may believe that Thou hast sent Me."—The second ἕν is opposed by the most important testimonies; and it is condemned by a comparison with ver. 11. There also the being one is made a result of being in God and Christ: the unity has no independent significance; but comes into consideration only as far as it is the necessary result of being in God and Christ. The second ἕν was introduced into the text in consequence of a failure to recognise the truth, that being one and being in the Father and the Son are correlatives, and cover each other. The fact that their union absolutely rests upon their being in the Father and the Son, contains a striking warning against all enforced and self-made unions. Anton: "This wants more than a mere palliative, like the hundreds of union-writings which have been put forth by empirics in our days. All these are only Pelagian workmongering, that introduces worse confusion. The hurt must be healed by one only Physician, the true High Priest." Real union consists in this, that we become "partakers of a divine nature" through fellowship with the Son, and in Him with the Father, 2 Pet. i. 4. Where divisions appear, they must be rectified, not in themselves, but in their root—an interrupted relation to Christ. "All religion," says Quesnel, "all the counsels of God, point to unity. Jesus

Christ is Himself, through His incarnation, the centre and the bond of that union. The whole fulness of the Godhead dwells in Him essentially and perfectly through the word; and He dwells spiritually in true Christians through faith and love."

The second ἵνα, "that," resumes the first. The third is not co-ordinated to these, but serves to indicate the ultimate design which the being of believers in Christ subserves; it furnishes the Church with a power that overcomes the world, and thus serves to realize the end of Christ's mission into the world: comp. ch. iii. 16. If believers are in the Father and the Son, of one heart and one soul, if the life of Christ is continued in them, that must impress the world. The Church is mighty in its aggression upon the world, in proportion as "I dwell in the midst of her" holds good, in proportion as she approves herself to be the tabernacle of God among men: comp. on Rev. xxi. 3. The world judges the Teacher by His disciples, the Lord by His servants. When human impulses and passions rule in the Church, she cannot fail to go astray from Christ. But when His image is reflected from the Church, when she presents fruits which grow not in the rest of the world, the world may be induced to recognise in Him the Son of God, who has stamped His image on His people. In the faith that the Father hath sent Christ, the world renounces itself and its own character.

Ver. 22. "And the glory which Thou gavest Me I have given them; that they may be one, even as we are one."—The honour of the Son is to be one with the Father, who shares His nature with Him. From the Son this honour, consisting in unity, passes over to believers, who become one in this, that Christ lives in them, Gal. ii. 20, Phil. i. 21; that they eat His flesh and drink His blood, ch. vi. Their unity among themselves is their glory, only inasmuch as it rests upon their unity with Christ. Unity enforced by despotic power and the arts of policy confers no glory.—" Whom Thou hast given Me," before the world was, ver. 5. For the honour of unity with the Father is the foundation of that collective heavenly condition spoken of there. Schmieder speaks otherwise: "The glory which the Father had given Jesus consists in this, that the Father had already appeared in the Son, and so appeared that the Son spoke words which the Father had given Him, and performed works which the Father wrought through Him, and which no other man could perform." It will be best, following J. Gerhard, to unite the two: "That beatific communion between the Father and the Son, and also between the Divine and the human nature in Christ." The second phase of giving honour, here has the first as its basis. That the first cannot be excluded, is evident from ἐν τῷ ὀνόματί σου, ᾧ δέδωκάς μοι in ver. 11, with its allusion to Ex. xxiii. 21.

Ver. 23. "I in them, and Thou in Me, that they may be made perfect in one; and that the world may know that Thou hast sent Me, and hast loved them, as Thou hast loved Me."— The words, "that they may be perfected into one," resume the thought of ver. 22, in order to connect with it the statement of the end which this unity would subserve, the glorious result which would accrue from it: "And if they shall thus become one, the world will thereby know," etc. It is added, that this unity, in order to the attainment of that end, must be a perfect one—"perfected into one," that is, all merging into this unity. A blessed residuum of the unity which Christ prays for is even now present in the Church, notwithstanding all appearances. But Christ's people are as yet far removed from perfect oneness, and on that account the influence of their unity is only imperfect and partial. No other way, however, leads to the consummation of this oneness, but a sinking deeper into Christ; and the conflict which seeks to remove the obstacles to this deeper sinking into Him, is often more helpful to unity than the attempts to establish an enforced unity.

From the prayer for their preservation *in time,* our Lord turns, in the conclusion, which corresponds with the beginning, to a prayer for their *eternal salvation;* first the prayer itself, ver. 24, then the ground on which it is urged, vers. 25, 26. Luther: "This is the last but the most comforting thing in the prayer, for all who hang upon Christ, that thus we become confident as to what we have to hope for in the end, as to where we are to find our final rest, we who are in this world, poor and despised, and without any continuing city."

Ver. 24. " Father, I will that they also whom Thou hast given Me be with Me where I am; that they may behold My glory, which Thou hast given Me: for Thou lovedst Me before the foundation of the world."—Οὓς δέδωκάς με (Cod. Alex. and Vat. ὃ δέδωκας, summing up the many into an ideal unity:

comp. the παν in ver. 2), primarily the Apostles: comp. ver. 6, xiv. 2, 3. According to vers. 20–23, however, the prayer really extends to all believers generally, although to the Apostles there was assured a specially distinguished place in the Divine glory, Matt. xix. 28. The strength of this "I will" lies not in itself (comp. Mark vi. 25 and 35, the will spoken in prayer appears, by that fact, to be conscious of its limitation), but in this, that it is the Son of God who here speaks. That which He absolutely declares to be His will (differently in Matt. xxvi. 39), must also be the will of the Father. To behold the glory of Christ, and of the Father in Him, is, according to ver. 3, the essence of eternal life; beholding it, we become partakers of it. It is not here "the eschatological union of Christ with His people when He comes back in the clouds of heaven" that is meant; rather the blessedness into which the believer is introduced at the moment of death: compare on ch. xiv. 3, xi. 23. "Thou gavest," according to the current interpretation, is used by anticipation: the Lord regards Himself as already installed in the glory for which He had prayed in ver. 5. But the words, "because Thou lovedst Me before the foundation of the world," show that we must think of a giving *before the world was*, abstracted from the temporary interruption which it suffered through the incarnation. It is equivalent to "which Thou, in love, gavest Me before the foundation of the world." "Thou gavest" corresponds to "I had" in ver. 5. This ἔδωκας referred to a glory given before the world was, and confirms what we said upon the δέδωκας, in ver. 22, against those who would refer it merely to the Son of man.

Vers. 25, 26. "O righteous Father, the world hath not known Thee: but I have known Thee, and these have known that Thou hast sent Me. And I have declared unto them Thy name, and will declare it; that the love wherewith Thou hast loved Me may be in them, and I in them."—"Righteous Father" stands in this elevated discourse for "Father, Thou art righteous," Rev. xvi. 5; and what follows is, by a *constructio ad sensum*, continued in such a manner as if these words had preceded. The righteousness of God approves itself in this, that His procedure stands in harmony with His being and action: comp. 1 John i. 9; 2 Thess. i. 6, 7; Heb. vi. 10. The righteous one is not the "rightly disposed:" that is rather ישר, ὅσιος, comp.

on Rev. xv. 4. We have here the ground for the request in ver. 24. God must in His righteousness mark out His own before the world by the impartation of eternal glory. The reason given cannot go beyond the matter of the request. Thus we must not, after "the world hath not known Thee," supplement "therefore must Thou exclude them from eternal life;" but that which is said of the world here serves only to set the disciples in brighter relief by its shadow. That the world cannot attain to eternal life, is indeed involved *indirectly* in the passage. This follows from the reasons which our Saviour gives for His prayer concerning the eternal life of His people. "I have known Thee:" Jesus places the world first in opposition to Himself, because the knowledge which the disciples had received flowed from Him as the source.—In their knowing that God had sent Christ, they knew at the same time the Father, who in Christ revealed Himself, whose name dwelt in Him, ver. 11.—"And will manifest:" the work of Christ in His disciples will go on; they are to be raised to a higher stage; and, in consideration of that, the father will overlook their present imperfection. Schmieder: "In the disciples there was still a not-knowing, which must first be done away. But our Lord covers this by the promise that He will further reveal in them the Father's name. This pledge redeemed them from the deficiency still marked in them." The "I will manifest" was fulfilled in the resurrection of Christ, and the instructions following that event; in the presence of the risen Lord ever with His people; and in the outpouring of the Holy Ghost.—The clause with ἵνα gives the design of the manifestation: if this design were attained, God would not deny them eternal life. That would be to deny His own love, and to dishonour Christ, who dwelt in them. "That the love wherewith Thou lovest Me might be in them:" that Thou mayest love them with the love with which Thou hast loved Me. "In them:" according to the connection, common in Hebrew, between verbs or nouns of passion with the object of the passion, by means of ב: comp. on ch. xv. 11.

CHAPTERS XVIII. XIX.

THE SECOND GROUP OF THE SECOND DIVISION, THE SIXTH OF THE WHOLE: THE SUFFERINGS, DEATH, AND BURIAL OF OUR LORD.

First, we have, in ch. xviii. 1-11, His betrayal and capture. Here also St John gives only supplementary details. He passes over the kiss of Judas, the address of Christ to the band after His capture, and also the transaction with the young man, which is peculiar to St Mark. On the other hand, he explains how Judas came to seek Jesus in this place; describes more specifically the band of the captors, according to their several elements: he first communicates—and that is the proper centre of his description—the procedure of vers. 4-9; first mentions the name of the disciple who smote off the ear of the high priest's servant, and the name of that servant; and supplements the words addressed to the disciples according to St Matthew. All that St John has in common with the other Evangelists serves only for the introduction of what is peculiar to himself, and is therefore recorded as briefly as possible.

Ver. 1. "When Jesus had spoken these words, He went forth with His disciples over the brook Cedron, where was a garden, into the which He entered, and His disciples."—" He went out:" there was not any point of departure mentioned in the preceding chapter: we must derive it therefore from the πέραν. He went from this side Kidron to the other. As the passage of our Lord over the Kidron is immediately connected with His last discourses, ch. xv.-xvii. (ταῦτα εἰπών), these discourses must have been uttered in the neighbourhood of the border, on this side: compare the introductory remarks on ch. xiv. The brook Kidron is mentioned only here, in the New Testament: χείμαρρος, flowing in winter,—a description which perfectly suits the peculiarity of Kidron. "Nine months of the year the Kidron is without water" (v. Raumer). William of Tyre says, "The brook Kidron, swollen by rains, was wont to flow in the winter months." We have a comment on the name Kidron, *troubled*, in Job vi. 16, where Job compares his faithless friends to brooks: " What time they wax warm, they vanish; when it is hot, they are consumed out of their place." The reading τῶν Κέδρων for τοῦ Κέδρων sprang from the ignorance of copyists. St John, who everywhere goes back to the text of the Old Testament, cannot possibly have so written it, as the Hebrew name Kidron has nothing whatever to do with cedars. Lachmann retains τοῦ Κέδρων, in token that the external reasons for this reading are at least of equal force with those which sustain the other; and the internal reasons are altogether in its favour. Josephus knows nothing of the brook of the cedars: he always uses ὁ Κεδρών, or merely Κεδρών: compare the passage in Wetstein. While he declines the name χείμαρρος Κεδρῶνος, Antiq. viii. 1, 5, the more Hebraizing John avoids this by inserting the article: so, in 2 Sam. xv. 23, 1 Kings xv. 13, τῶν, instead of τοῦ, must be attributed to the transcribers, since no one who had the original before him could have so written. And the true reading there is not destitute of all external testimony: see Holmes. St John gives prominence to the passage of the Kidron probably with some reference to 2 Sam. xv. 23, where David, in his conflict with his rebellious subjects, went over the Kidron: ὁ Βασιλεὺς διέβη τὸν χειμάρρουν Κεδρών.—The *garden*, here alone mentioned, in which Jesus, according to the abundant testimony of the first Evangelists, overcame death for His people, is the counterpart of that garden in which the first Adam succumbed to death. Augustin: It was fitting that the blood of the Physician should there be poured out, where the disease of the sick man first commenced. The property to which the garden belonged is called, in Matt. xxvi. 36, Mark xiv. 32, Gethsemane. St John does not mention the name (any more than St Luke), because the first two Evangelists had made it known. These give the name; St Luke designates the place as on the Mount of Olives; St John places it beyond the Kidron.

Ver. 2. "And Judas also, which betrayed Him, knew the place; for Jesus ofttimes resorted thither with His disciples."—The owner of this place must have stood in a special relation to Jesus: this is evident, not only from His free resort to the garden, but also from the narrative of the young man in Mark xiv. 51, 52. The young man must have belonged to the family of the owner of the garden. This is plain from his clothing—in a cold night he had on only a linen garment—which did not permit him to be taken away from the place. Sympathy for Jesus, at the time of His imminent danger, must have led him suddenly from his bed into the open air. Curiosity could not have been the motive: in that case the Evangelist would not have mentioned the matter, which was worth recording only as showing that the Apostles had ground for flying. Πολλάκις, oft, cannot refer only to the few days immediately preceding the Passover. Jesus kept Himself, during the whole time between the Feast of Tabernacles and the last Passover, in Jerusalem and its neighbourhood. Yet it seems that in the last days before the Passover, Gethsemane was the special abiding-place; that He spent there the nights of Monday and Tuesday, Tuesday and Wednesday, Wednesday and Thursday; that He withdrew thither during the last two days before the festival for still seclusion; and thence sent the disciples into Jerusalem for the preparation of the Passover. If this were so, we have the reason why Judas was so sure of finding Him there. On the day of the entrance into Jerusalem, on Sunday, Jesus, according to Mark xi. 11, returned with the Twelve to Bethany. In reference to the next day, we read, in Mark xi. 19, "And when evening was come, He went out of the city." It is certainly not accidental that St Mark does not here, as in ver. 11, say, "to Bethany," but "outside the city." St Luke gives, in ch. xxi. 37, a general notion of the locality where Jesus spent the remaining nights after Sunday: "And at night He went out, and abode in the mount that is called the Mount of Olives." Certainly Bethany, according to St Luke, belonged also to the Mount of Olives, ch. xix. 29. That we must not stop there, however, but regard him as having Gethsemane also partly in view, is shown by a comparison with ch. xxii. 39, 40. What determined our Lord to change His abode, is not clear. Probably greater nearness, probably also the household relations in Bethany.—Judas knew the place; that is, in regard to the matter now concerned, as the abode of Jesus. Jesus went designedly to the place which Judas knew. The time for hiding Himself from His enemies was past: His hour was come. He must afford the traitor an opportunity, that He might show that His surrender to death was voluntary.

Ver. 3. "Judas then, having received a band of men and officers from the chief priests and Pharisees, cometh thither with lanterns, and torches, and weapons."—There can be no doubt that by the band Roman military were meant. Σπεῖρα is used everywhere in the New Testament only of Roman troops: comp. Matt. xxvii. 27; Acts x. 1, xxvii. 1. Chiliarch (comp. ver. 12) is everywhere the name of a Roman military authority; and when we find the σπεῖρα connected with the chiliarch, a cohort with its tribune is meant: comp. Acts xxi. 31; and Josephus, Antiq. xix. 2, 3, ἦσαν εἰς σπείρας τέσσαρας, οἷς τὸ ἀβασίλευτον τιμιώτερον τῆς τυραννίδος προὔκειτο, καὶ οἵδε μὲν ἀπῄεσαν μετὰ τῶν χιλιάρχων, Jud. Bell. xi. 11, 1. The band is here the cohort which was employed for such purposes as the present, and during the feast was stationed in the Temple. Josephus says, in Antiq. xx. 5, 3: " When the feast called Passover was come, on which it is our custom to provide unleavened bread, and a great multitude of people from all places having come together to the feast, Cumanus feared that some insurrections might occur, and therefore gave orders that a cohort of soldiers with their weapons should be established in the court of the Temple, in order to quell any such insurrections as might arise (καταστελοῦντας τὸν νεωτερισμὸν εἰ ἄρα τὶς γένοιτο). But the same thing was wont to be done by his predecessors in the government of Judea at the feasts." In his work on the Jewish war, he says of the Castle Antonia (v. 5, 8): " But where it was connected with the Temple, there were steps by which the watchers (there was always a legion of Romans there) went down armed, and planted themselves in the courts at the feasts, to observe the people, that no uproar might arise." In these two passages of Josephus we have a commentary on our present text, with its article. It is otherwise with the band, ἡ σπεῖρα, in Matt. xxvii. 27, Mark xv. 16: comp. John xix. 2. There it is the cohort which kept watch at the Prætorium, Pilate's residence, the earlier royal castle of Herod in the upper city. The chief station of the Roman troops, the παρεμβολή, in Acts xxi. 34, 37, was the Castle Antonia. From this a watch was provided, both for the Temple at the time of the feasts, and for the Prætorium when the procurator was in Jerusalem. These circumstances are clearly stated in Josephus (de Bell. Jud. v. 5, 8: compare the remark of Reland in Haverkamp's edition). There was always an entire legion in Antonia.

There is no reason for assuming that it was a mere detachment of the cohort which was sent. If the hierarchs would be safe, they must guard against the possibility of the matter becoming noised abroad, and a great insurrection among the people ensuing: comp. Matt. xxvi. 5. How numerous were the dependants of Jesus, especially among the Galileans then present at the feast, was shown by the entrance into Jerusalem. A mere detachment would not have required the presence of the chiliarch. He had reason enough for taking his whole force, in order to provide for all the contingencies which, amidst a people already excited, could scarcely be foreseen. It was important to suppress all thought of opposition at the outset by an imposing display of force: once suffered to begin, there was no end to its possible effects. Time had already been when the crowds of the people took Jesus by force and would make Him a king, John vi. 15.

The first three Evangelists do not give so much prominence to the part played by the Roman military. In effect it was not of extreme importance in itself. Even in St John we see that, down to the leading away of Jesus to Pilate, the Jews were the main and independent actors. But it may be shown that the earlier Evangelists do take for granted the intervention of the Roman soldiers. The double style of arms of itself hints at this: partly with swords and partly with staves,[1] Matt. xxvi. 47; Mark xiv. 43. It is improbable that the reason of this twofold equipment lay in the fact that swords fell short; in the highest degree improbable also, that the Romans would have tolerated, by the side of their militarily accoutred power, another force also in arms. To bear arms in travelling, as a defence against robbers, was permitted to individuals. But we find no trace of any Jewish force in the Temple provided with arms. More of this was not to be thought of; the first readers of St Matthew must have understood the intervention of the Roman military when the double armour was mentioned. Further, our Lord's word concerning the twelve legions, Matt. xxvi. 53, appears to suggest that Roman soldiers had to do with His capture: the twelve legions of angels form a contrast with the fragment of a

---

[1] The ξύλα were used by the Roman soldiers also, when the service was not properly military, but only that of police. In a tumult, Pilate, according to Josephus, Bell. Jud. xi. 9, 4, forbade his soldiers to use the sword, but ξύλοις παίειν, to strike with their staves.

Roman legion. Mark xiv. 51 points also to Roman military: there it is said of the young man who followed Christ, καὶ κρατοῦσιν αὐτὸν οἱ νεανίσκοι. This description will not suit the servants of the high priest: these were certainly for the most part old men. On the other hand, the Roman military were commonly regarded and spoken of as *juvenes, juniores, juventus:* see ἤδη ἐπιλελεγμένων τῶν 'Αχαικῶν νεανίσκων in Polybius, *adolescens* in Cic. pro Milone, and other passages in Schleussner. But we shall not trust ourselves to inquire, whether by the *sinners* in Matt. xxvi. 45 we are to understand, with Grotius, the Gentiles (comp. Gal. ii. 15; and ἄνομοι in Acts ii. 23, 1 Cor. ix. 21); or whether the κουστωδία in Matt. xxvii. 65 was the Roman Temple-watch, the use of which, in order to the watching of Jesus' sepulchre, Pilate permitted to the Jews, and which he spoke of as standing at their disposal: " Ye *have* a watch." But extremely important are the passages, Luke xxii. 4 and 52, where the commandants of the Temple are spoken of in the plural, the στρατηγοῖς τοῦ ἱεροῦ. The Jews had only one captain, στρατηγός, of the Temple, whose position was so eminent, that in Josephus he is mentioned immediately after the high priest, and a son of a high priest was invested with this dignity: comp. Antiq. xx. 6, 2; De Bell. Jud. ii. 17, 2. In the Acts, St Luke mentions only one chief captain, whose only following were the " officers," ch. iv. 1, v. 24, 26, ὁ στρατηγὸς τοῦ ἱεροῦ: this excludes the notion of several captains of the temple at other times than the Passover, and of these the Acts of the Apostles speaks. How then can the plurality of captains in Luke xxii. 4, 52, be otherwise explained, than that the one captain belonged to the Roman military stationed in the Temple at the time of the Passover? It will not suffice to say, that by the plural στρατηγοί is meant the Jewish commandant with his officers. Appeal may be made to Josephus, Antiq. xx. 9, 3, where, however, the secretary of the Jewish commandant is referred to: for στρατηγός always means one who in a subdivision of troops was clothed with the highest authority,—not the officer, but the chief captain; and this notion is further opposed by the concurrence between our present passage and Luke xxii. 4.

With regard to the high priests and Pharisees, comp. the remarks on vii. 32. Although it was full moon, the torches and lanterns were thought necessary in order thoroughly to investigate the dark spaces of the trees in the garden and the house. The most obvious matter here is the betrayal of our Lord with a kiss. St John hints at such an act, although he does not narrate it, but presupposes it to be already known. He describes Judas twice—the repetition would serve to point attention to the note of description—as he who betrayed Him, ὁ παραδιδοὺς αὐτόν, vers. 2, 5, the participle used in the Hebrew manner: comp. on ix. 8. Thus we expect, even according to St John, an act of betrayal. The indication which he gives has its comment in Matt. xxvi. 48–51; Mark xiv. 44, 45; Luke xxii. 47, 48. Further, the remark in ver. 5, " And Judas also, which betrayed Him, stood with them," is, if we do not supplement St John from the other Evangelist, a needless and irrelevant one. It repeats only, and in an inappropriate place, what had been said already in ver. 3. It leads to the thought, that Judas had separated himself from the band, though that is not here mentioned; and it stands in specific relation to the προήρχετο αὐτούς, " went before them," of St John's immediate predecessor, St Luke, ch. xxii. 47. The words expressly intimate the fact, that the scene was already over with the kiss of Judas. Judas had first come forward from among the number of his confederates; now Jesus comes forward after Judas had gone back again into their ranks. Only from misapprehension has it been thought that vers. 4 seq. conclude the idea of Judas' kiss having preceded. On the other hand, it is perfectly clear that we can imagine it to have taken place only before ver. 4.

Ver. 4. " Jesus therefore, knowing all things that should come upon Him, went forth, and said unto them, Whom seek ye ?"—Εἰδώς is used here as in ch. xiii. 1 : " as He knew," or " although He knew." That Jesus, notwithstanding this knowledge, presented Himself to His enemies, is made prominent to His honour. Humanly speaking, it was to Jesus perfectly impossible to evade His capture. This is quite obvious. But the Evangelist proceeds from the assumption that supernatural means were at His disposal; and it was to His glory that He did not use these supernatural resources : comp. Matt. xxvi. 53, where our Lord Himself says, " Thinkest thou that I cannot now pray to My Father, and He shall presently give Me more than twelve legions of angels ?

Ἐξελθών: this must refer only to our Lord's advancing beyond the circle of the disciples, or out of His concealment. For that Jesus did not withdraw from Gethsemane, is evident from ver. 3, according to which Judas with his band entered into the garden; as also from ver. 26, where one of the servants of the high priest says to Peter, "Did not I see thee in the garden with him?" Therefore the band must have penetrated, just as here the word ἐξελθών is used also in Matt. xiv. 14, Mark vi. 34 (comp. on vi. 3).—The question, "Whom seek ye?" is uttered on account of the answer; and to that answer was to be appended the command of Christ to let His disciples go,—a command enforced by the previous miracle of Christ's power. The express commission of the band went not beyond the taking Christ prisoner. This appeared to the high priests something so great, that they seem not to have spent a thought on the disciples. But it was obvious that the multitude, when their special duty was discharged, went beyond the letter of their function, and, in order to act in the spirit of the rulers and to deserve their thanks, laid their hands on the Apostles also. The "rulers of the Temple" who were with them were justified by their position in acting independently thus. Jesus would now suppress that desire, the presence of which the soldiers' treatment of the young man also reveals. The same narrative of the young man shows that it was only our Lord's interference that saved the Apostles from imprisonment. The Apostles they durst not touch; so they would at least lay hands on one belonging to the wider circle of the Lord's dependants.

Ver. 5. "They answered Him, Jesus of Nazareth. Jesus saith unto them, I am He. And Judas also, which betrayed Him, stood with them."—The band declare their commission in the same terms in which they had received it. Although the sign which Judas gave them, and perhaps in part their own earlier knowledge (comp. vii. 32, 45), assured them who it was that stood before them, yet the words "We seek *thee*," by which they would have been placed in direct personal relation to Jesus, would not pass their lips. Here was the beginning of the terror which presently afterwards threw them on the ground.

In the word ἐγώ εἰμι, the Lord uttered forth the dignity of His person. Accordingly He struck the multitude like a flash of lightning. Jesus thereby declared Himself to be He of whom the prophet said, "And He shall smite the earth with the rod of His mouth, and with the breath of His lips shall He slay the wicked;" and who says Himself, in Isa. xlix. 2, "And He hath made My mouth like a sharp sword." This was the earnest of that which is, in Rev. i. 16, written of the exalted Redeemer, "And out of His mouth went a sharp two-edged sword;" as also of what, in 2 Thess. ii. 8, is written to depict the destruction of antichrist by the Redeemer at His coming, "Whom the Lord Jesus will destroy by the breath of His mouth." If Jesus had not tempered the power of His word, its effect would now also have been annihilating, like the word spoken in the might of God by Elijah, 2 Kings i. 10, 12; by Elisha, 2 Kings ii. 24, v. 27; and by the Apostle in Acts v. 5 ("And Ananias, hearing these words, fell down, and gave up the ghost"),—although these were only feeble men. But the influence of our Lord's word was precisely what the end designed required it to be. Jesus must and would be taken, but His disciples must go free. For this it was enough that His captors knew with whom they had to do. This was needful also, in order that all inferences drawn from His capture to the disparagement of His divinity should be obviated, and that the voluntariness of His surrender to death should be fully established. That which Christ here did was sufficient to show what He could do, and what in due time He will do. Augustin: "He says *I am*, and casts down the ungodly. What will He do as Judge who did this when judged? What will He do as reigning who did this as about to die?"

We have already observed that the notice "Judas stood" serves only for the connection of St John's narrative with that of the first three Evangelists. We are lost in difficulty if we attempt to assign a meaning to these words without going beyond the sphere of St John's own narrative. If with Meyer the words are regarded as merely a "tragical point in the description of this assault, without any further significance," they could not—even apart from the fact that, according to ver. 3, they were perfectly useless—have stood here. Their position precisely where they are admits of only one explanation. They were intended to obviate the false notion that the word "I am He," addressed to the captors, was to say anything unknown to them; and to intimate the fact that the scene with the traitor had already preceded. On that account, also, the words "who betrayed Him" are here repeated.

Ver. 6. "As soon then as He had said unto them, I am He, they went backward, and fell to the ground."—The Evangelist speaks of the whole multitude; and Leo (Serm. i. de Passione) rightly observes: "Which word struck down that band, gathered up of all the most ferocious people, as if with a lightning stroke, so that all those fierce and terrible threatenings fell at once." If we contemplate the whole scene aright, we shall discern no difference between Jews and Romans, between those who had already a secret dread of Jesus, and those who knew nothing about Him, or looked down upon Him with the deepest scorn. The lightning flash struck all alike, the courageous and the presumptuous as well as the fearful. If St John saw the matter otherwise, it was not worth his trouble to communicate it. "They went backward," ἀπῆλθον εἰς τὰ ὀπίσω, is the נסוגו אחור which prophets and psalmists declare concerning the ungodly driven backwards by the omnipotence of God: Isa. xlii. 17; Jer. xlvi. 5; Ps. xxxv. 4, xl. 15, cxxix. 5. These words, "They went backwards," introduced as it were with the marks of quotation, are the theological description of the effect of Christ's word; "they fell to the earth" are the natural description. We have an analogy in the various descriptions of the potion which our Lord was presented with on the cross. St Matthew describes it theologically, on the ground of the passage in the psalm, as "vinegar mingled with gall," ch. xxvii. 34; St Mark physically, as "wine mingled with myrrh," ch. xv. 23. The falling to the ground was the form in which the retreating before Christ's word manifested itself.

Ver. 7. "Then asked He them again, Whom seek ye? And they said, Jesus of Nazareth."—After His object in confounding them was attained, our Lord, the Lion and the Lamb, speaks to them in a milder tone. He Himself gives them courage to accomplish the task they had undertaken; whilst, however, what they had just experienced would restrain them from transgressing the strict limit of their commission. "Jesus of Nazareth," they uttered in low tones. But when they found their task done, when they had bound Jesus, they give up all their fear, and are ashamed of their earlier cowardice. When the heart is far from God, the work of hardening goes on apace, so soon as the sensible impression is past, and God withdraws again into silence. This was most impressively manifested in the history of Pharaoh.

Vers. 8, 9. "Jesus answered, I have told you that I am He. If therefore ye seek Me, let these go their way: that the saying might be fulfilled which He spake, Of them which Thou gavest Me have I lost none."—Ἵνα πληρωθῇ: it took place, or Jesus so acted: comp. xv. 25, xix. 36; Mark xiv. 49. That which our Lord, in ch. xvii. 12, utters in the form of fact, referred to the whole of His life upon earth, and by anticipation included the whole space down to His death: it was in fact a prediction which, in this act of our Saviour's preservation, found its fulfilment.—Jesus, in ch. xvii. 12, spoke of His care for the salvation of His disciples' souls. The external protection which He here vouchsafes must therefore be regarded in connection with that: the disciples were not yet strong enough to endure the internal temptations which would have assailed them in imprisonment. They could not suffer for Christ before Christ had suffered for them. The greatness of their spiritual danger we see exemplified in the example of the most advanced of all, Simon Peter. The fall out of which he rose again might have been for the "little ones" an irreparable one. The external protection afforded by our Lord derived its main significance from the connection between their temporal danger and their spiritual. From purely external danger the Lord never protects His people. He predicted to Peter that He Himself would provide martyrdom for him.

Ver. 10. "Then Simon Peter, having a sword, drew it, and smote the high priest's servant, and cut off his right ear. The servant's name was Malchus."—The earlier Evangelists speak of one of the disciples: St John first mentions the name. But the other Evangelists lead us obviously to think of Peter, who, according to Luke xxii. 33, said, "Lord, I am ready to go with Thee to prison and to death:" comp. Matt. xxvi. 35; Mark xiv. 31. Their not naming Peter appears to be accounted for by the fact that they wrote in his lifetime, which, in the case of St Mark, an ancient tradition expressly states, representing his Gospel to have been composed with the co-operation of that Apostle. St John, writing long after Simon s death, was free from the restraint of that consideration.—That two of the disciples were furnished with swords—doubtless for protection against the robbers who made the roads very unsafe, Luke x. 30—is recorded by St Luke, xxii. 38. The weapon which Peter bore must have been for a purpose permitted by the Lord; otherwise He would have earlier obviated the misunderstanding of His words, " And he that hath no sword, let him sell his coat, and buy one," Luke xxii. 36 (compare the introductory observations to ch. xiv.), with a more full instruction. Peter was to fail, in order that the Lord might have occasion in rebuking him to instruct the Church of all ages; and He found an opportunity, through Peter's act, of putting forth His miraculous power, and thus of proving that He voluntarily surrendered Himself to the hands of men.—The multitude set themselves, after Christ's words, to seize Him, or had already laid hold on Him. This presupposal of Peter's deed must be inserted from the other Evangelists: Matt. xxvi. 50; Mark xiv. 46; Luke xxii. 49. Ver. 12 here records the act fully accomplished, after the obstacle of the interruption was set aside.

Peter's act requires the preceding scene for its explanation, especially when we remember that Roman military were present. That gave him to understand the power of his Lord. It was hard for him to understand how, possessed of such power, his Master would suffer Himself to be taken. He thought that if he boldly made a beginning of the assault, the Lord would be stirred up to make a glorious end of it.—The δοῦλος here does not belong to the ὑπηρέτας of ver. 3: comp. ver. 18, where a distinction is made between them. The ὑπηρέται are officials: accordingly, in ver. 12, they are called " officers of the Jews." They belonged to the people. Malchus was only a private servant of the high priest, and was not therefore officially present. Simon's stroke fell upon him probably because, though having no official warrant to be there, he was present, and made himself prominent as the officious tool of his master.—It has been assumed, probably without any reason, that Peter's design was to cut off the head of the obtrusive servant of the high priest. His external unsteadiness, rather, made him prudently limit himself to cutting off the ear. But it was the Lord who so guided his hand that he did not become an unintentional murderer, "and suffered him to do only so much harm to the servant as was necessary in order that He might have opportunity to do good to His enemies, to instruct His disciples, and to edify all the world."—That the ear was not quite cut off, seems evident from the fact that, according to Luke xxii. 51, Jesus healed him by simply touching it. St Luke alone expressly mentions this healing. But it is taken for granted in the circumstance common to all the Evangelists, that Peter was not seized, and not even his sword taken away: comp. ver. 11. Nor would Jesus have allowed it to go so far, if He had not had the healing in view.—The intimation that the ear was the *right* ear, is common to St John with his immediate predecessor, St Luke. St John first mentions his name. How he came to do that is explained by vers. 16 seq., where we find that he knew the high priest, and went in and out of his house. He recognised in Malchus an old acquaintance: according to ver. 26, he knew his family connections. The other Evangelists may have heard the name of the servant, but St John alone had any interest in communicating it.—Malchus means *king*. Josephus (Bell. Jud. i. 14, 1; Antiq. xiii. 5, 1) mentions an Arabian king Malchus. The celebrated heathen philosopher Porphyry was called Malchus; and his other name, Porphyrius, was only a translation of it. Suidas: "Porphyry, who wrote against the Christians, was called king." Jerome (in Wetstein) says: "There was there a certain old man named Malchus, a Syrian by nation and language, whom we might call in Latin king." Probably he was the head servant of the high priest, his chamberlain: probably called Malchus in sport, as the king of the servants—a name that then clung to him. That proper names in those days often had such a natural origin, is shown by the name Pannychis, pertaining to a concubine whom Herod gave to Archelaus (Joseph. Bell. Jud. i. 25, 6).

Ver. 11. "Then said Jesus unto Peter, Put up thy sword into the sheath: the cup which My Father hath given Me, shall I not drink it?"—St Matthew gives more copiously what our Lord said to Peter: ch. xxvi. 52, 53. John supplements it by communicating the allusion to one word which our Lord had spoken in the conflict of Gethsemane not recorded in his Gospel (comp. Matt. xxvi. 42). This word appropriately fits the close of the Lord's words in Matthew: "Thus it must be." The cup which God gives is in the Old Testament the destiny which He appoints. Upon the expression which Christ on this occasion uttered, rests the practice of the collective Church of Christ in the midst of the persecutions which the authorities may inflict.[1]

JESUS BEFORE ANNAS AND CAIAPHAS—PETER'S DENIAL.

VERS. 12-27.

With ver. 27 the narrative of our Lord's appearance before Caiaphas is closed, without our being told what occurred in it. This is all the more remarkable, as, according to St John himself, something very decisive must necessarily have taken place there. The examination before Annas was altogether of a preliminary character, and, as Jesus declined to answer the question of the high priest, led to no result. That Jesus must have been condemned to death before Caiaphas, to whom in ver. 24 He is led away, is plain from ver. 14, where, in allusion to the event now being prepared for, it is mentioned that Caiaphas had earlier counselled the Jews that it was good for one man to die on behalf of the people. It is plain also from the transactions before Pilate, which rest upon the supposition that the Jewish verdict of death had already taken place. The rulers of the people first desire that Pilate would, without further ado, confirm this condemnation, ver. 30, and are induced, by his persistent refusal, to raise a complaint; returning afterwards, when Pilate declared their charge to be unfounded, to their original demand, that Pilate must confirm the sentence they had decreed, ch. xix. 7. We are here as good as expressly pointed back to the earlier Evangelists. We are led to expect that we shall find in them a chasm concerning the transactions before *Annas*, which explains why St John so particularly describes what was comparatively of less importance; as also, that we shall find in them a selected and exhaustive account of the transactions before *Caiaphas* and the Sanhedrim, which relieves St John's silence of its strangeness. This expectation

[1] Cyprian ad Demetrianum: "None of us, when he is apprehended, resists; nor does he avenge himself upon your unjust violence (although our people are great and numerous)."

is found to be satisfied. The resultless appearance before Annas is entirely passed over in the first three Evangelists; on the other hand, they record the transaction before Caiaphas and the Sanhedrim with a minuteness which allows nothing to escape. But St Luke gives a point of connection for St John's narrative in Luke xxii. 61, where we find our Lord with Peter once more in the court, and the "without" and the "below" cease, which, according to Matt. xxvi. 69, Mark xiv. 66, had separated him from his Master. John xviii. 24 gives the solution of this difficulty. That St John, on the other hand, takes for granted what had been narrated by the first three is plain, apart from the other reasons we have assigned, from the fact that, while nothing had been said in vers. 12–27 of any co-operation of the Sanhedrim, but the high priest only was mentioned, in ver. 28 we are suddenly met by a plurality, ἄγουσι, αὐτοί; and in ch. xix. 6, 15, the "high priests" are spoken of, the term used currently by St John as a concise description of the High Council: comp. on ch. vii. 32. From the position which the High Council everywhere in St John assumes in relation to Christ's interests (comp. *e.g.* ch. xi. 47–53, 57), we are naturally led to suppose, that by them with Caiaphas the matter was decided.

The denial of Peter had been thoroughly described by the first three Evangelists. But St John must return to it, because that event could not, without the communication of the events before Annas, be adjusted in its historical connection. At the same time St John, touching as lightly as possible what they had narrated, adds only a few notices. In regard to the chronological position of Peter's denial, St Luke forms the transition to St John. While in St Matthew and St Luke the things concerning our Lord and Peter are simply narrated together, without regard to the sequence of time (the fact that Jesus is first spoken of refers not to time, but His dignity), we perceive from St Luke that the three denials of Peter had already taken place before the Sanhedrim assembled: comp. ch. xxii. 62, 66. "Concerning the penitence of Peter," says Bengel, "St John presupposes what the other Evangelists write." If his Gospel was meant to have an independent position and significance, it could not possibly have broken off here.

Vers. 12, 13. "Then the band, and the captain, and officers

of the Jews, took Jesus, and bound Him, and led Him away to Annas first (for he was father-in-law to Caiaphas, which was the high priest that same year)."—According to Matt. xxvii. 2, Mark xv. 1, Jesus appears not to have been bound until He was led away to Pilate. The apparent contradiction is removed by observing that the bonds were removed in order to His being examined. That it was the custom of the Jews to bind those who were brought as delinquents before the Sanhedrim, appears from Acts ix. 1, 2, 14, 21, xii. 6, which are quite in harmony with St John. Ver. 24 here makes it indeed probable that our Lord had already been loosed from His bonds when He stood before Annas in the preliminary examination, otherwise the δεδεμενον would be superfluous.—The reason why Jesus was first led to Annas—named by Josephus (Antiq. xviii. 2, 1) Ananus the son of Seth—is simply stated to be the circumstance that he was the father-in-law of Caiaphas. It was not, therefore, because of any official position on which he stood, but only as an expression of personal respect to him; and this leads us to infer that Caiaphas would not have so honoured him if his father-in-law had not been in office himself, and a man distinguished by competency in affairs.[1] We are led to the same result by the fact, that even in the chambers of Annas Jesus was questioned, ver. 19, by Caiaphas,—a proof this that *officially* only he had to hear Jesus. In Luke iii. 2, where we learn that the Baptist appeared ἐπ' ἀρχιερέως Ἄννα καὶ Καϊάφα, it is not meant that Annas held any official position; all that it signifies is the considerable independent influence which, as a person in high esteem, he exerted. The singular ἀρχιερέως, supported by the best MSS., is of moment, intimating that the official person who was high priest was largely

---

[1] Josephus (Antiq. xx. 9, 1) gives us a luminous view of the position occupied by Annas, which was the ground of his son-in-law's respect for him: "This aged Ananus was a most fortunate man: he had five sons, and all of these attained the high-priesthood. He had himself enjoyed the honour long. This happened to no other of our high priests." It is of no moment that the sons of Ananus did not reach the dignity until after this event. The honour in which Annas was held, and from which afterwards their elevation proceeded, was already considerable. Probably Caiaphas owed his elevation, too, to the respect in which his father-in-law was held. He here gave him back in some sense part of what he had received through his influence.

influenced by another person. The personage who exerted that influence stood first. With this passage of Luke our present passage strictly harmonizes: it may be regarded as the key for its explanation. In the enumeration of the leading members of the council, Acts iv. 6, Annas is named before Caiaphas: this further confirms the hint of our text, that Caiaphas, who officially preceded all others, was entirely under the influence of Annas. Only such a dominant influence could have occasioned his being mentioned first; any official position would certainly have placed him subordinate to Caiaphas. The fact of Christ being led away to Annas, shows not only the independent authority which he exercised, but also the intensity of his hatred to Christ. His son-in-law knew that he could not afford him a greater joy than by giving him some concern in this process. The hatred felt by Annas to Christ continued to burn in his son, the younger Ananus mentioned by Josephus. He perverted his high-priestly function so far as to trespass upon the Roman authority of life and death, and to bring about the destruction of James the Apostle, "the brother of Jesus, who is called Christ, and many with him;" for which abuse of authority he was displaced from his office: comp. Josephus, Antiq. xx. 9, 1.

Where was the dwelling of Annas? Doubtless chambers were assigned to him in the house of his son-in-law, in the high-priestly palace. To this we are led by a comparison with the first three Evangelists, who do not mention Annas, and place the three denials of Peter in the court of Caiaphas the high priest. Other reasons also decide for this. 1. It is of itself remarkable that St John represents Christ as led from person to person, not from place to place: they led Him to Annas, ver. 13; Annas sent Him to Caiaphas, ver. 14; they lead Jesus from Caiaphas, ver. 28. All this indicates that the locality was the same. When a change of place is referred to, it is expressly mentioned: "they led Jesus to the palace," ver. 28. 2. "That disciple," we read in ver. 15, "was known to the high priest:" the high priest, with the article, could only be Caiaphas. In Acts iv. 6 Annas is not described as high priest; but mention is made of Annas the high priest, in contradistinction to others of the name who had not been high priests. Caiaphas is, throughout St John, always the high priest, xi. 49, xviii. 24, 28;

and here he has just been alluded to as such, vers. 13, 14. But this disciple went with Jesus into the palace of the high priest. Thus Jesus, when He was led to Annas, was led into the palace of Caiaphas. 3. In the court of the building in which Annas dwelt stood the servants of the high priest (comp. vers. 18, 26), that is, of Caiaphas; to whom we are the rather pointed, because the relatives of him whose ear Peter cut off in all probability were in the service of the same master, and all the Evangelists say that Malchus was the servant of Caiaphas. If Annas had not dwelt in the high priest's palace, we should have found his own establishment gathered together. 4. The body of servants, according to ver. 18, stood round a fire of coals while Jesus was with Annas. Peter went to that perilous place only because he would be near his Master; he remained there, doubtless, not a moment longer than Jesus was in the place. In ver. 24 Jesus is led away to Caiaphas; yet Peter remains near the fire, and amidst the same company. This shows that the sending from Annas to Caiaphas was only a sending from one part of the house to another. The court was common to both houses. 5. After Peter's first denial, Jesus, according to St John, was led away to Caiaphas. According to Luke xxii. 61, Jesus turned, at the third denial, and looked at Peter. Thus at the third denial he was in the same place where he was before. Jesus, already with Caiaphas, is at the same time with Peter in the same place. This is to be explained only on the supposition that the court was common to the two dwellings of Annas and Caiaphas. The assertion of Baur (Kanon Evang.), " When Jesus was again led away from Annas and went over the court (of Annas), the two other acts of denial took place," is, looking at St John alone, untenable. At ver. 24 Jesus must not merely have been on the way to Caiaphas, but must have reached his presence; for to ver. 4 is joined " they led Jesus from Caiaphas" in ver. 28.—Moreover, we cannot tell why so much opposition has been encountered by the theory that Annas lived in the high priest's palace. According to the custom of the East, where the palaces of the great belong usually not only to the actual ruler, but to all his kin, it must always be probable in itself that in the high priest's palace the whole γένος ἀρχιερατικόν, Acts iv. 6, resided.—On the words, " who was the high priest that year," compare what was said upon ch. xi.

49. As high priest of that year, Caiaphas was at the same time *the* high priest.

Ver. 14. "Now Caiaphas was he which gave counsel to the Jews, that it was expedient that one man should die for the people."—Compare ch. xi. 50. To the unconscious prophecy which Caiaphas had uttered (compare ver. 51) St John now refers, because the *fulfilment* of that prophecy was now prepared for,—a fulfilment in which Caiaphas played no insignificant part. And this observation leads also to the same conclusion, that the high priest in what follows could be only Caiaphas.

Ver. 15. "And Simon Peter followed Jesus, and so did another disciple. That disciple was known unto the high priest, and went in with Jesus into the palace of the high priest."—The article before ἄλλος owed its origin to an unseasonable comparison of ver. 16, and probably also ch. xx. 2. The article must be given up. It would mark out this disciple as known to the readers. But how was he thus known? St John everywhere represents that only as known which had been found in the first three Evangelists. But these knew nothing of another disciple here.—It cannot be doubted that the other disciple was John: that alone gives the reason why his name was not mentioned. Peter and John elsewhere appear as united: compare on ch. xiii. 24. Judging from the entire character of John and his relation to Christ, we might have expected that he, beyond all the other disciples, would, with Peter, have refused to be separated from the Lord. Under the cross we find the disciple whom Jesus loved, xix. 26. After the resurrection he runs with Peter to the sepulchre, and faster, too, than Peter. As the "other disciple" he describes himself, just as here, in ch. xx. 2, 3, 4, 8. So far back as ch. i. 35, 41, he is the unknown disciple by the side of one whose name is mentioned; and the manner in which he there concealed and yet revealed himself, has much affinity with what we find here. That tendency to keep his own person as much as possible in the background which pervades the whole Gospel, culminates at its close in the οἴδαμεν, "we know," which has given the expositors so much trouble. We are led also to think of St John, by the circumstance that he alone, of all the Evangelists, shows any interest, in keeping with his being "known to the high priest," about the relations of the high priest's house: he intimates the relationship between Annas and Caiaphas, ver. 13; mentions the name of the high priest's servant whose ear Peter smote off; refers to another among the servants of the high priest who was related to Malchus, ver. 26; speaks of the portress, ἡ παιδίσκη ἡ θυρωρός, where the other Evangelists mention only a maid, μία παιδίσκη, παιδίσκη τίς; and in ver. 18 specifies the fire of coals around which the servants of the high priest were gathered in the cold night.—The language speaks of acquaintanceship, not of kindred. Acquaintances and kindred are distinguished in Luke ii. 44, and so also often in the Old Testament, Job xix. 13, xlii. 11.—St John stood in some relation to the high priest himself, not merely to his servants. This is here expressly said; in ver. 16 it is emphatically repeated, and all is in strict harmony. St John goes without any ado into the palace of the high priest. No introduction was needed for him; he had free access. To the servants he must have been a person of some eminence. They venture to say nothing against him, nor against Peter while he was there. The maid admitted Peter at his word; and that she did this somewhat unwittingly, is plain from her subsequent attack on Peter.— How the acquaintance originated can scarcely be conjectured; human relations are manifold. But the character of St John leads to the obvious supposition that it rested on religious grounds. Searching for goodly pearls, John had earlier sought from the high priest what, after he had gone through the intervening station of the Baptist, he found in Christ. With what eyes he had formerly regarded the position of the high priest, is indicated by the fact, that as a disciple of Christ he nevertheless assigned to the word of the high priest a prophetic significance, ch. xi. 51. John, by his internally devout nature, had so attracted the good-will of the high priest, that he did not wholly cast him off even after he had gone over to the true High Priest. Nor had John entirely abandoned him. Real love cannot be so easily rooted from the heart; and it is characteristic of St John to retain, τηρεῖν, a pious regard to earlier relations. In the love which hopeth all things, he might hope yet to win the high priest to Christ. Moreover, we find among the Apostles one, whose surname, ὁ Ζηλωτής, Luke vi. 15, Acts i. 13, shows that he had gone through a similar process of development. And the life of St Paul furnishes some analogies.

Ver. 16. "But Peter stood at the door without. Then went out that other disciple, which was known unto the high priest, and spake unto her that kept the door, and brought in Peter."—Expositors condemn Peter for having, in his weakness, ventured so much. Even Calvin says: "As Christ had declared by His own voice that He spared Peter and the others, it would have been far better to groan and pray in some obscure corner, than to go openly before the eyes of man when he was so little firm." That may be true; but love vanquishes reasoning, and after all Peter following Christ is dearer in his denial, than if, without denying, he had remained in some obscure corner. It must have been a mighty and irresistible impulse which urged Peter to follow Christ. He had more to fear than all the others; for it was he who had smote off the ear of the high priest's servant, ver. 26. That made his situation peculiarly dangerous; and explains how it was that he was embarrassed by addresses which under other circumstances would have been regarded as harmless mockery. At the time of the outrage, our Lord's healing act had restrained the servants from attacking Peter. But it was very natural that the act was revived in their remembrance. Since Peter had not a good conscience in relation to that act, and had been by the Lord Himself reproved, it must have been all the more natural that he should expect to suffer for it.—What John said to the portress is not told, because it may be inferred from what she thereupon did. Gen. iv. 8 is similar: "And Cain talked with Abel his brother: and it came to pass when they were in the field." What Cain said to Abel, "Let us go into the field," is to be supplied from what follows.

Vers. 17, 18. "Then saith the damsel that kept the door unto Peter, Art not thou also one of this man's disciples? He saith, I am not. And the servants and officers stood there, who had made a fire of coals (for it was cold); and they warmed themselves: and Peter stood with them, and warmed himself." — When was it that the maid spoke to Peter? Obviously not directly after she had admitted him,—for then her objections would rather have been urged against his entering at all,—but after John, whose person she respected, had gone away. John doubtless accompanied his Master to Annas, and records what he has concerning that interview from personal knowledge; he probably also went with Him to Caiaphas, so that the narrative of this examination which we have in the first three Evangelists was derived from his testimony. We must not connect ver. 17 with ver. 16, but with ver. 18, which is only then properly understood when it is regarded as supplying the circumstances under which the colloquy in ver. 17 took place. The fire of coals and its surroundings had a close connection with the first assault of the maid; and it was not accidental that all the assaults upon Peter took place near this fire. She was bent upon bringing the Apostle—whose entrance she could not prevent—into embarrassment before the whole company of the servants, and thus making herself also an important and interesting personage. She was in possession of a secret; she alone was aware that Peter had entered through the intercession of John, whom she knew as a follower of Jesus; whom but another disciple would he have introduced? And she might, with the official feeling of a portress, come forward (St Luke's καὶ ἀτενίσασα αὐτῷ, xxii. 56, is very remarkable) to demand, as it were, a warranty after he had entered instead of before. Thus St John is in full harmony with the other Evangelists, according to whom the first attack and the first denial of Peter took place while he warmed himself.—The matter was at the outset harmless enough. Yet it is not right to say that Peter was afraid, where there was no great reason to fear. It might, in further course, have taken a very critical shape for his safety.

"Thou *also*," says the maid, with allusion to John, and indicating the ground of her suspicion : " John, who brought thee in, is a disciple of this man ; thou also assuredly art the same."—The despondent spirit which led to his denial on this occasion was not inconsistent with the courage with which he cut off the high priest's servant's ear, ch. xviii. 10. That act did not spring from the tranquil courage of faith; it was the courage of a naturally strong feeling, which had lost itself in circumstances of momentary excitement. As everything natural has its risings and fallings, so also has the merely natural feeling. Hero and coward, in the ordinary human sense, are not pure opposites. Circumstances altered the case. Then Peter had been stimulated by a glance at his Lord, whose demonstration of miraculous power he had just witnessed in the prostration of the multitude. But now, when he saw that Lord so powerless, his courage fell. This was needful in order to his humiliation. Thus only could he become a true Peter, when his confidence in his own natural strength was utterly taken away.

The fire had been made by the servants of the high priest, in the expectation that they would have to wait out the night while the examination proceeded. Considerable time must elapse while the members of the High Council were being assembled. The co-operation of the Roman soldiers went no further than the bringing Jesus, and delivering Him up in the palace of the high priest. After that, the responsibility of watching Him rested with the Jews.—Tobler, writing from Jerusalem, says : " There are occasionally outbreaks of winter down to May. We sat in the evening trembling with the frost, wrapped up in mantles. The fact that Peter warmed himself in the palace of the high priest on the third of April, is quite in keeping with all modern observations of the weather, as well as with the customs of the inhabitants. On the third of April 1837, after sundown the temperature was +6° R."— The servants *stood:* this seems to be opposed to the record of the other Evangelists, according to whom the servants were sitting, Matt. xxvi. 58, Mark xiv. 54, Luke xxii. 55. But standing and sitting doubtless alternated; moreover, the first Evangelists also speak of the ἑστῶτες, Matt. xxvi. 73; παρεστῶτες, Mark xiv. 69, 70. Nor is there any contradiction between Peter's standing in this account, and his *sitting* outside in the court, Matt. xxvi. 69, when the maid came and looked at him. The standing here forms the transition to his going out into the porch in Matthew, ver. 71. The excitement caused by the question induced Peter to rise up.—It has been rightly observed that Peter, playing the bold man, and mixing among the soldiers as one of themselves, laid already the foundation for his subsequent denial.[1]

Ver. 19. "The high priest then asked Jesus of His disciples, and of His doctrine."—Not Annas, but Caiaphas, questioned Jesus. Annas presided, as it were, over the council at the

---

[1] Lampe: He thought he might be securely quiet in this crowd. But inasmuch as the word of Jesus could not be false, Satan followed him into this hiding-place. And he found him opportunely enough. This dissimulation was itself a tacit denial.

examination; but the strictly judicial function could not be committed to him by Caiaphas. The greater the injustice was, the more important it became not to violate judicial forms. Caiaphas doubtless was instructed and inspired by Annas, but formally Jesus had to do with him alone.—The question concerning the *disciples* coincided with that concerning the *doctrine;* the second served to explain and define the first. We gather from the answer of Christ, that the matter in question was not that He should indicate the persons of His disciples—as a culprit might be required to name his confederates—but rather that He should show the relation He bore to His disciples. But that was one with His doctrine, and upon His doctrine that relation rested. It was of importance to provide materials for the charge to be brought before the High Council—that Jesus made Himself the Son of God and arrogated Divine authority, and in this presumption elevated Himself above all legitimate authority, gathering around Himself a crowd of disciples, who, as such, were the enemies of that authority. It was of equal importance in order to their providing material for the second charge before the Roman Forum,— that Jesus made Himself a king, and thereby set Himself up against Cesar: comp. Luke xxiii. 2. If we regard the two questions as perfectly distinct, the answer of our Lord leads to embarrassment; for in that case it refers only to the second question.

Vers. 20, 21. " Jesus answered him, I spake openly to the world; I ever taught in the synagogue, and in the temple, whither the Jews always resort; and in secret have I said nothing. Why askest thou Me? ask them which heard Me, what I have said unto them: behold, they know what I said."— Jesus declines answering the high priest's question. The reason of that refusal must not be sought in His design to withdraw from the interrogation altogether. Before the assembled Sanhedrim He at once declared Himself to be the Son of God; before Pilate He avowed His royal dignity. His silence had rather an admonitory character; it gave the high priest to understand that he was not worthy of any reply, because he did not seek but flee from the truth. It sprang from the same reason that led to the silence at the outset before the council, Matt. xxvi. 63, Mark xiv. 61; the perfect silence before Herod;

the refusal to answer Pilate, after he had made it plain that he desired not to serve the truth, but his own personal interest, ch. xix. 9. The high priest set out with the determination to allow no entrance to the truth. He resolved, under all circumstances, to deliver Jesus to death, ver. 14. His questions had no other design than to provide materials for accusation and sure impeachment. When the authorities assume such a position, there is, looking at them alone, no room for the duty of confessing (1 Pet. iii. 15 takes for granted a certain measure of good-will); and it would have been unworthy of our Lord's dignity to commit Himself to a fruitless colloquy with the high priest. The duty of confession came later for our Lord; that is, when, before the Sanhedrim in open session, He was solemnly and publicly asked by the high priest whether He were the Son of God; as also by the human authority, " Art thou the King of the Jews?" Then our Lord stood before the great tribunal, and before the world. In Pilate there was a certain measure of good disposition; he had not, to such an extent as the high priest, closed the avenues of his heart against all good emotions. To have spoken to the heart of the high priest would have been perfectly vain. He had firmly resolved to give no access to the truth. The objective fact of our Lord's teaching, however, was plain enough: it needed no confession to make that sure. For the "good confession" which our Lord had to make before His death, a more fitting place and time would come afterwards.

The words in which Jesus accounted for His silence intimate that there was no secrecy in question, and that what was public might be known in another way.—This answer of our Lord threw the high priest out of his course. The end of his investigation was to obtain material for the charge to be brought against Him in the council. Upon this he had firmly reckoned: how firmly we may gather from the fact, that the insufficiently prepared testimonies of the witnesses at the great examination led to so impotent a result, Matt. xxvi. 59, 60; Mark xiv. 55-59. The difficulty which the first Evangelists present—the reconciling the character of Christ's enemies with their defect of foresight in this instance—finds in St John its explanation.—For παῤῥησία, see on ch. xi. 54, vii. 4, 26. Ἐν συναγωγῇ: the article is wanting, because no particular synagogue was to be indicated. In itself the article would not be inadmissible for the generic noun; but here it could not have been used, since in ἐν τῷ ἱερῷ it marks out the Temple specifically. Jesus had taught in the synagogues of Galilee, as is evident from a series of passages in the first Evangelists, and John vi. 59. The Galileans were then present at the feast, and it was easy therefore to ascertain certainly what Jesus had taught in their synagogues. In Jerusalem He had always repaired to the Temple. The reason of this was, that He always sought the utmost possible publicity, and everywhere, as much as in Him lay, spoke to the *world*. "Whither the Jews always resort:" that characterized the Temple, in contradistinction to the synagogues. In harmony with this passage, our Lord, in Matt. xxiii. 38, speaks of the Temple as the house of the Jews. Three times in the year, according to the ordinance of the law, all the males were to appear in the Temple, in the house of "convocation," in the place where God was wont to hold intercourse with His people, Deut. xvi. 16. The words, "In secret have I said nothing," point to Isa. xlv. 19. There Jehovah says, in allusion to the prophecy communicated by Him, "I have not spoken in secret, in a dark place of the earth;" to the parallel clause the Lord refers in Matt. x. 27. If He sometimes taught in a narrower circle, and there unfolded "the mysteries of the kingdom of God," Matt. xiii. 11, He did this only on account of the want of susceptibility in the multitude; He uttered nothing to His disciples which He did not in another form and at another time publicly teach, nothing that was by those disciples to be kept secret. This is evident from Matt. x. 27, in harmony with our present passage. Augustin: And even this, which seemed to be spoken by Him in secret, in a certain sense was not spoken in secret, inasmuch as it was not so spoken as to be concealed by those to whom it was spoken; but rather so that it might be everywhere proclaimed.

Ver. 22. "And when He had thus spoken, one of the officers which stood by struck Jesus with the palm of his hand, saying, Answerest thou the high priest so?"—In Matt. v. 39, the verb ῥαπίζειν occurs for striking on the cheek; the same is probably its meaning here also. The blow on the cheek, as inflicted for a supposed offence, may be compared with 1 Kings xxii. 24, where the false prophet Zedekiah smote the true prophet Micaiah. The servant probably had in view that passage of the law, Ex. xxii. 27, which St Paul quoted under similar circumstances, Acts xxiii. 5.

Ver. 23. "Jesus answered him, If I have spoken evil, bear witness of the evil; but if well, why smitest thou Me?"—According to Deut. xxv. 2, the judge alone might inflict blows on the wicked man worthy to be beaten. Our Lord doubtless spoke these words in a low and gentle tone. It was His love that did not reckon it below His dignity to convict this servant of his evil. Quesnel: "To speak on such occasions with truth, with gentleness, and with righteousness, is much harder than to present the other cheek." The word of Jesus to a servant, as well as that to the high priest, shows that St John's Christ also knew how to condescend from His high dignity.

Ver. 24. "Now Annas had sent Him bound unto Caiaphas the high priest."—Here again the high priest is Caiaphas, in contradistinction to Annas. The οὖν was dropped from the text by those who thought it inappropriate, because it excluded the possibility of taking ἀπέστειλεν in a pluperfect sense; by others, it was expunged in favour of δὲ or καί. Between Annas and Caiaphas, as already shown, there was locally only a courtyard; or rather Jesus was with Caiaphas as soon as he left the apartments of Annas. And while He was with Annas He was still in the palace of the high priest, Luke xxii. 54; indeed, in a certain sense, He was with Caiaphas himself, Matt. xxvi. 57, Mark xiv. 53; not merely because he was the occupant of the house, but also because the examination was had before him. But because Caiaphas had honoured Annas by placing the prisoner before him, and caused the examination to be conducted under his honorary presidency, Jesus might be said, as in ver. 13, to have been led to Annas, so also in this verse to have been sent from Annas to Caiaphas. St John adheres to the forms of expression which Annas and Caiaphas themselves used. The δεδεμένον here indicates that Jesus was not at once led from the apartments of Annas before the Sanhedrim, but that a certain period of waiting intervened. With the present statement, which informs us that Jesus was led from Annas to Caiaphas before the second and third denial of Peter, agrees that of St Luke, who relates that on the third denial our Lord turned and looked upon the Apostle. Accordingly He was, on the third denial, with Peter in the court. Between the second and the third denial there elapsed, according to St Luke, about an hour. During this time our Lord must have remained standing in the court. Such a longer continuance in the court is also demanded, by the fact that the High Council did not assemble until it was day, Luke xxii. 66.

Ver. 25. " And Simon Peter stood and warmed himself: they said therefore unto him, Art not thou also one of his disciples? He denied it, and said, I am not."—In ver. 17 τοῦ ἀνθρώπου τούτου, here αὐτοῦ, as in ver. 26. Jesus, at the second and third denial, was in the court. The αὐτοῦ points to the Lord as present. The entrance of Jesus into the court probably gave occasion for the renewal of the assault upon Peter. According to St Mark, the initiative was taken again by the same maid who stirred the matter at the first. On the former occasion she had addressed Peter; now, repelled by him, she addresses the bystanders. According to St Mark, " another maid" spoke to those around, " This man also was with Jesus of Nazareth." According to St Luke, " another " spoke to Peter on the matter, " Thou art also of them." St John embraces the various persons introduced by the others in one εἶπον, " they said." Apart from the statements of the Evangelists, it is obvious that, in the midst of the idle circle, whose thoughts naturally were fixed upon the business that laid upon them this disagreeable night's service, one word begat another, and the several scenes were hastily enacted, one being made prominent by one Evangelist, another by another.

Vers. 26, 27. " One of the servants of the high priest (being his kinsman whose ear Peter cut off) saith, Did not I see thee in the garden with him? Peter then denied again; and immediately the cock crew."—The third denial was a scene composed of sundry incidents. An indifferent word spoken by Peter probably gave occasion for the beginning of the encounter. This enabled them to detect the Galilean; and the first three Evangelists agree in giving prominence to this moment. A relative of Malchus then joined in the attack; he said he saw Peter in the garden with Jesus. This is St John's account. That many were mingled in the assault, is indicated by St Matthew and St Mark, when they speak of those who stood around.

CHRIST BEFORE PILATE.

CHAP. XVIII. 28–XIX. 16.

In communicating his facts concerning the interrogation in the dwelling of Annas, and the examination before Caiaphas and the High Council, St John refers back to his predecessors in the narrative, contenting himself with indicating the place where their record is to be inserted; but, in the present section, he has the material for essential supplements, so that he indeed first gives us a complete view of the whole transaction. Here also, however, he is in reality only supplementing, as is very plain from ch. xviii. 28, as also from ver. 33, where Pilate's question to Jesus, "Art thou the King of the Jews?" is based upon the charge brought by the Jews as related by St Luke; and from ver. 40, where "they cried *again*" refers to an earlier cry recorded only by St Mark; and from ch. xix. 2, where a comparison with St Luke alone tells us where the soldiers obtained the royal staff.

Ver. 28. "Then led they Jesus from Caiaphas unto the hall of judgment: and it was early; and they themselves went not into the judgment-hall, lest they should be defiled; but that they might eat the Passover."—The persons who "led,"—the rulers of the people who had condemned Jesus,—we must supplement out of the earlier Evangelists. Prætorium was originally the name of the locality in Rome where the prætors sat in judgment; then it came to signify generally the private and official residences of the high Roman officials. The Roman procurators of Palestine had their proper residence in Cesarea; but at the great feasts, and especially at the Passover, they betook themselves to Jerusalem to prevent uproars. They then occupied what was once the palace of Herod (Joseph. de Bell. Jud. ii. 19, 4; compare, on the locality of the royal castle, Lightfoot, in the *Centuria chorographica Matthæo præmissa*, c. 23). It is not "into the prætorium," but "to the prætorium." Αὐτοί, *they*, not in antithesis to Jesus, as if He had gone away, but to Pilate, who went out to them. That Jesus Himself did not enter the prætorium, but remained standing before it with the rulers, is implied in "they lead,"—not "they send," but "they lead." Lücke incorrectly: "The Jews sent Jesus with the soldiers into the prætorium, to show that they were come;" but the soldiers had long withdrawn, having only aided in the capture of our Lord. Not till ver. 33 does Pilate take Jesus into his palace.

Πρωΐ, the period of the morning from three till six, appears in Mark xiii. 35 as a part of the common sleeping-time. The Roman judicial sessions did not usually take place until nine o'clock. That Pilate was already prepared to receive the Jews, is to be explained by the supposition that he had been already notified. The Jews urged the matter with the greatest despatch, in order to leave no time for the development of the people's excitement, and that they might be able to enjoy uninterrupted the mid-day meal, and, finally, for the reason assigned in ch. xix. 31. Pilate received the summons probably the evening before, at the same time that he received intelligence of Christ's capture. The dream of his wife points to the same conclusion (Matt. xxvii. 19), occasioned as it was by what she had just heard before retiring to rest.—The care with which the Jews avoided external contamination forms a fearful contrast to the levity with which they burdened themselves with the heaviest of all sins. It may be asked what the phrase "eating the Passover" means. If it was eating the paschal lamb, John is irreconcilably at variance with the other Evangelists, his predecessors: according to them, the great feast of the Passover, which they represent as eaten by Christ at the same time with the Jews, was long over.

The phrase "eat the Passover" signifies eating the Passover in its widest extent of meaning. This, at the first feast, was the eating of a lamb, with bitter herbs and unleavened bread; for the remainder of the time it consisted of the unleavened bread and the peace-offerings, the so-called *chagigah*, the name of which shows that it was an essential part of the Passover-eating. The peace-offerings were presented according to legal ordinance. We read in Deut. xvi. 16 concerning the *three* high feasts, "Ye shall not appear before Me *empty*;" and in Ex. xxiii. 15 this is specifically said of the feast of unleavened bread. That the practice was in accordance we see in 1 Sam. i., according to which Elkanah yearly brought at the Passover his peace-offering, and the whole family partook of the sacrificial meal thus provided. In 2 Chron. xxxv. 7–9 we find that oxen, as well as lambs and kids, were necessary to the feast of the Passover.[1] According to the Mishna, those festal offerings were presented every day.[2] But the first day of the feast, 15th of Nisan, was specially chosen for the presentation of these offerings.[3] The chief feast of this day was, on the one hand, the chief feast of the whole festival. The character of the first meal was solemn and stately. With the feast of the 15th, on the other hand, *joy* was predominant, according to the characteristic Israelite view of all festivals: comp. Deut. xvi. 14. To have been prevented from sharing this feast must have been particularly disagreeable.

Which particular portion of the paschal eating was here meant, cannot be gathered from the phrase, but must be determined by the context. If the first day is spoken of, *that* defines the phrase, in itself indeterminate, and including all the eating of the feast, as meaning the paschal lamb with its accompaniments; if any following day is meant, then reference is made to the eating of the unleavened loaves and the flesh of the peace-offerings, without its meaning being anywise changed. That φαγεῖν τὸ πάσχα, eating the Passover, occurs throughout the first Evangelists only in reference to the first meal, is purely accidental; the explanation being that they never had occasion to mention the other meals of the feast. In our passage the first meal cannot be referred to. We find ourselves, after xiii. 1, in the domain of the ἑορτὴ τοῦ πάσχα, the Feast of the Passover generally, which began with the eating of the paschal lamb. The night was past which followed the evening on which the whole nation were under obligation to eat the feast. We are thus introduced by the Evangelist into the general feast of unleavened bread in the narrower sense. The most obvious meal which presents itself to our consideration here is, as we have clearly seen, that pre-eminent mid-day meal so

---

[1] Comp. Annot. uber. in Hagiog. Ad holocausta nimirum et sacrificia salutaria, isto Paschalis festo offerenda, ut simul haberent homines, unde copiosius convivarentur. Bertheau: "Many thankofferings were presented, the flesh of which was consumed by the offerers and those who were invited to partake."

[2] *Chagigah*, c. 1, m. 6. *Rabe*, ii. 287.

[3] Comp. Lightfoot, Opp. i. p. 741. The Lexicon *Aruch* says under חג: Edebant et bibebant et laetabantur et sacrificium chagigae offerebant, ad quod adducendum tenebantur die decimo quinto.

joyfully partaken of on the 15th. That the remark of Bleek—that the writer had, in what precedes, given no hint that the time of the legitimate slaying and eating of the paschal lambs was over—is altogether incorrect, is plain from the investigations entered into on ch. xiii. 1.

That the phrase, "that they might eat the Passover," may refer to the eating of the Passover generally, in all its comprehensiveness, demands no proof, being self-understood. It must be admitted that the word Passover signifies not merely the opening feast of the 14th, but the whole seven days' feast; there is no ground for the assertion that the eating of the Passover can refer only to the meal of the 14th: it cannot be denied that the following days also, and especially the 15th, had their eating essentially connected with the nature and purpose of the feast. Nevertheless, while the admissibility of this phraseology is self-evident, we ought to expect that it would be found elsewhere. And this expectation is abundantly confirmed.

In the law itself we are furnished with a fundamental passage, all the more important because it must have contributed to mould the current phraseology. We read in Deut. xvi. 2, 3, "Thou shalt therefore sacrifice unto the Lord thy God, of the flock and the herd, in the place which the Lord shall choose to place His name there. Thou shalt eat no leavened bread with it (therein, עליו): seven days shalt thou eat unleavened bread therewith, even the bread of affliction." Here we have, in reference to the sacrifice which ran through the seven days, not merely the phrase *sacrifice* the Passover, but also that of *eating* the Passover: for when it is said, "Thou shalt eat no leavened bread *therewith*," this means, "When thou eatest the Passover, thou shalt not eat with it leavened bread." Keil: "As עליו can only be referred back to פסח, it is hereby plainly declared that the sacrificing and eating of the Passover should last seven days." We must not explain ver. 2, with Lücke and Meyer, "Thou shalt sacrifice the lamb of the Passover to the Lord, and (besides that) of the flocks and the herds." For, apart from the fact that פסח must necessarily have had the article; that, as the Passover, in the narrower sense, certainly consisted of the flock, Passover and flock could not have been thus coupled together; and, finally, that if this view were permissible, at least there would have been a copula;

—apart from all this, the explanation we refer to is refuted by the suffix in ver. 3, which points back to פסח. This shows that sheep and goats could mean only the material of the Passover. If Passover, sheep, and goats were co-ordinate simply, there would have been a plural suffix. Therefore it remains certain, that in ver. 2 the Passover is spoken of in its most comprehensive sense, and in ver. 3 the eating of it, which was to last seven days.

Another important passage in the Old Testament is 2 Chron. xxx. 22 : "And they did eat throughout the feast (את המועד) seven days, offering peace-offerings, and making confession to the Lord God of their fathers." Here we have the identical language of our passage, only that instead of the Passover it is the feast they eat, according to ver. 21 the feast of unleavened bread : a difference which is of no moment, since it is admitted by all that the whole feast was also called the Passover. How much this passage troubled Bleek, we may gather from his attempt to alter the reading.

These proofs are so abundantly sufficient, that we are not disposed to cite the parallels out of the Talmud which the older expositors quote.[1] The very name *Chagigah* shows that the peace-offerings were counted among the Jews as part of the paschal eating.

Movers, in his treatise on the last Passover and the day of Christ's death, alleges, in opposition to this reference to the mid-day meal of the 15th Nisan, that, according to the Talmud (Tr. Sanhedrim, fol. 63), none of the parties to a sentence of death passed by the Sanhedrim might eat anything on the day ; so that the members of the council who had condemned Jesus to death could not, if this had been the 15th Nisan, have eaten even the sacrificial offerings of the *Chagigah*. But Friedlieb (*Archæol. der Leidensgeschichte*) asserts that there is no proof that this late tradition of the synagogue had continued to influence the practice of the Sanhedrim in Jerusalem. We are in the habit of doing too much honour to these outgrowths of Jewish fantasy, which were so abundant while the Temple still stood. It is with this imaginary custom, as with the supposed custom which forbade the keeping of cocks in Jerusalem.

[1] Comp. *e.g.* Otto, Lex. Rabbin. v. 511 ; Bynæus, de morte Christi ; Reland, Antiq. Sac. p. 271.

Granted that such a custom existed, Jewish sophistry would find it easy to remove, in this case, the burden from itself. There was no capital sentence on this occasion; that proceeded only from Pilate. "It is not lawful for us to put any man to death," was the confession of the Jews themselves in ver. 31.

On the other hand, there is a reason which forbids us, apart from the relations of time, which do not agree with the reference to the paschal lamb, to think of the feast which commenced the Passover. Lightfoot (on John xviii. 28) and Bynæus (*de morte Christi*) point to the fact, that the entering a Gentile house belonged to that order of defilement which lasted only until the end of the day, until sundown. Now the first paschal meal fell after sunset; it did not begin, as Lücke supposes, "between the two evenings of 14th Nisan;" that was the period for the slaying of the paschal lambs: it began rather not until evening, after darkness had fully set in (comp. on ch. xiii. 1); and therefore the entering of a Gentile house had no influence on this. It follows that we can only think of a feast which was held in the course of the same day; of the feast, namely, which was the joyful mid-day meal of 15th Nisan.

This argument is an absolute demonstration. *All* defilements that arose from contact with unclean persons lasted, according to the law, only through the day on which they arose, and ended with the sundown, when the defiled persons washed themselves: comp. Num. xix. 22: "And whatsoever the unclean person toucheth shall be unclean, and the soul that toucheth it shall be unclean till evening." That the defilement which resulted from entering a Gentile house belonged to this class, is obvious enough. Further, the law says nothing about defilement contracted through entering a Gentile house, or intercourse with Gentiles. This was a later Jewish ordinance, which, however, as always, endeavoured to prop itself on a definite law. What this law was, we learn from Maimonides (in Bynæus and Reland). The ground of general defilement was, that the specific cause could not be determined. "Our customs," says Maimonides, "have settled that all Gentiles, whether men or women, are like those who are always affected with the flux, whether the fact be known or not, when viewed in the light of purity or impurity." Thus the Gentiles were regarded as in the same class with those who were affected with flux, and laid under the same law. But the defilement that resulted from touching such a person lasted only till evening: comp. Lev. xv. 5 seq., 19 seq. So was it with all similar defilements. Finally, we have in the book of Judith a weighty testimony to the fact, that defilement through intercourse with Gentiles had no influence upon the time of the institution of the Supper. According to ch. xii. 7-9, Judith went in the evening from the Gentile camp, and purified herself from the defilement to which she had been exposed: then she took the evening meal. After adducing all these convincing reasons, we scarcely need suggest how improbable it is in itself that defilement through commerce with Gentiles should have lasted more than one day: the defilement of one day, as things were, was felt to be a very heavy burden; but seven days' defilement would have had the effect, that a great portion of the people would never have been undefiled.

Lücke and others have objected, that this defilement would have been a hindrance, if not to the eating, yet to the killing of the paschal lamb. But St John does not say, "that they might *slay* the Passover," but "that they might *eat* the Passover." The not slaying and the not eating were not necessarily connected, since the slaying might be done by a representative; and even if such a connection had existed, it was much more obvious to mention the slaying, which was a condition of the eating. We might, not content with parrying the thrust of our opponents, turn their weapons against themselves. On the morning of 14th Nisan, it would have been more natural that the Jews should avoid defilement because it would hinder the slaying the lamb, than because it hindered their eating it. Bleek (*Beit.* S. 113) says: "In any case, the entering a Gentile house effected a defilement, which for its removal would require particular ceremonies, with which, as may easily be supposed, the Jews would have been very loth to burden themselves on 14th Nisan." But the burden of "particular ceremonies" consisted in one simple washing, to which the Jews were long accustomed, and the apparatus for which was everywhere at hand: comp. ch. ii. 6.

Steffert (*über den Ursprung des Ev. Matthæus*, S. 137) adopts another expedient. He observes, that the paschal meal, although after sundown, and therefore at the end of the day, yet belonged, properly speaking, to the 14th Nisan. Thus he thinks, that in this exceptional case the defilement also must have gone on with it into the evening. But the conclusion is an unsound one. The Jews laid down the general rule, that in reference to holy feasts and evening prayer the evening was reckoned with the preceding day.[1] This exception was based upon the nature of the case. The points concerned are precisely those which make the Jewish reckoning of time seem unnatural. All the preparations and concomitants of the Last Supper belong to the passing day: thus the meal itself, although really belonging to the domain of a new day, must be reckoned in the current day. No law could transform the evening supper into a morning meal. So also with evening prayer, the guilt for which pardon was sought, the benefits for which thanksgivings were offered, belonged to the day that was gone. These were the things that, according to Jewish statements, occasioned the exception to the rule, that a new day began with sundown. That *defilement* under any circumstances stretched into the evening, cannot be established by the slightest historical proof;[2] nor can it be shown how this could ever have been made an exception to the rule.

Ver. 29. " Pilate then went out unto them, and said, What accusation bring ye against this man ?"—Pilate is supposed to be a personage well known, from the earlier Evangelists. The first among them describes him, when he is first introduced, in ch. xxvii. 2, as the Roman governor, like Josephus, Antiq. xviii. 3, 1, " Pilate, the governor of Judea," and adds his prænomen Pontius. He was the fifth in the list of the Roman procurators of Judea. Concerning the character of Pilate, Philo gives some remarkable information in the *Legatio ad Caium* (Opp. p. 1033). According to him, he was a proud and obstinate man : $\mathring{\eta}\nu\ \tau\grave{\eta}\nu$ $\phi\acute{\upsilon}\sigma\iota\nu\ \mathring{\alpha}\kappa\alpha\mu\pi\acute{\eta}\varsigma\ \kappa\alpha\grave{\iota}\ \mu\epsilon\tau\grave{\alpha}\ \tau o\hat{\upsilon}\ \alpha\mathring{\upsilon}\theta\acute{\alpha}\delta o\upsilon\varsigma\ \mathring{\alpha}\mu\epsilon\acute{\iota}\lambda\iota\kappa\tau o\varsigma$. The threat of the Jews to appeal to Cæsar in a certain matter provoked

[1] Comp. Roland, S. 263 ; and Wähner, Antiq. Heb. ii. p. 18.

[2] It may, however, be shown, that the defilement of the preceding day did not hinder partaking of the paschal feast: comp. *e.g.* the passage from *Pesachim* in Lightfoot (Mar. xiv. 22 : Lugens lavat se et comedit Pascha suum vespere) ; but especially *Pesachim*, c. 81, the substance of which is thus stated : " All unclean persons, those excepted who were defiled by the dead, might eat the Passover on the day on which they cleansed themselves by the bath."

him to the uttermost; for he feared that this opportunity would be taken to bring to light all the other offences of his government: the bribes he had taken, the misappropriations he had permitted, the deaths he had inflicted without law or justice, and the intolerable severity he had in many cases manifested. His unquiet conscience came into sharp conflict with his proud and wrathful nature, which made submission exceedingly hard. We have here the key to Pilate's conduct in the matter of Jesus. The two accounts are mutually supplementary. Pilate had a great desire to decide righteously concerning Jesus, since in this case his great passions, covetousness and ambition, were not played upon. The person of Christ made upon him a deep impression. His better nature came out, when he had standing before him personal innocence and righteousness. But his energy was subdued by the consciousness of his earlier crimes, which did not permit him entirely to break with the Jews. While in the end he was obliged to give way, the energy of his character went so far as the circumstances would allow, as we see in the obstinacy with which he persisted in his attempts to save Jesus, and at last in the superscription on the cross. Pilate goes out to the rulers of the Jews. He had not been long in his office before he had occasion to learn that nothing was to be done with the Jews, unless concessions were made to their religious views. He had been obliged to yield to their petition, τηρεῖν αὐτοῖς τὰ πατρία (comp. Josephus, de Bell. Jud. ii. 9, 2, where Titus says to the Jews, " We have kept your country's laws"), after he had received evidence of the ἄκρατον τῆς δεισιδαιμονίας αὐτῶν (Joseph. Bell. Jud. ii. 9, 2 ; Antiq. xviii. 3, 1).—The address which Pilate made to the Jews gave them to understand at once that they would not attain their greatly desired object, to make him confirm without further ado their sentence of death. An illustration of this we have in Acts xxv. 16, where Festus says to the Jews, who long for judgment upon Paul : " It is not the manner of the Romans to deliver any man to die, before that he which is accused have the accusers face to face, and have licence to answer for himself concerning the crime laid against him." Pilate was previously acquainted with the cause of Jesus. He knew, according to Matt. xxvii. 18, that the rulers of the Jews had delivered Him out of envy; that they who constituted themselves His judges were at the same time a party; and that the question was that of a judicial murder. The warnings of his wife, who doubtless dreamed about what had occupied her thoughts much before she slept, shows that, and in what sense, the cause of Jesus had been talked about in Pilate's circle.

Ver. 30. " They answered and said unto him, If he were not a malefactor, we would not have delivered him up unto thee."—The Jews demand of Pilate that he should make of his judicial dignity a merely formal use, relying on their integrity, and mindful of the fact, that a short time before the power of life and death was still in their hands. On κακοποιός Beza says: " Guilty, not of a vulgar crime; but what kind of crime, that is, blasphemy, for which they condemned Him, they do not say." Together with blasphemy, they have in their eye the assumption of royal dignity: comp. Luke xxiii. 2. On παρεδώκαμεν, comp. Matt. xxvii. 2.

Vers. 31, 32. " Then said Pilate unto them, Take ye him, and judge him according to your law. The Jews therefore said unto him, It is not lawful for us to put any man to death: that the saying of Jesus might be fulfilled, which He spake, signifying what death He should die."—Pilate refers them to the Roman law, the decision of which was, *Ne quis indictâ causâ condemnetur*: no man could be condemned but on the ground of a formal judicial process. If the Jews would not have that, they must judge Him according to their own law. The judging includes the execution. Since the matter was one of life and death, and criminal cases were withdrawn from Jewish authority, the answer of Pilate was in plain fact a rejection of the wishes of the Jewish rulers. That we must so regard it, is shown by a comparison with ch. xix. 6, where Pilate says to the Jews, " Take him, and crucify him." That this must be understood with the qualification, " if ye can and dare," is plain from the fact, that the punishment of the cross was not a Jewish but a Roman punishment. But Pilate used the ambiguous word κρίνειν, judge. It is probable he did this designedly. Probably his intention was to involve the Jews in a snare. If they took this seeming permission, he had them in his power. They lost then the advantage which they had over him. How dangerous, under certain circumstances, the independent execution of a capital sentence might be, is seen in the narrative given by

Josephus (Antiq. xx. 9, 1). The younger Ananus, the son of Annas, took advantage, as high priest, of a favourable opportunity, when the governor Festus was dead, and Albinus his successor was not yet come, to put to death James and some others. But he was charged with this before Albinus, who threatened him, in an angry letter, with punishment. The result of it was, that he was deposed by King Agrippa. That the Jews, notwithstanding the passionate fury with which they were wont to be led away,—as, for instance, in the case of Stephen's martyrdom, Acts vii. 57,—made no use of Pilate's seeming permission, but rather contented themselves with prosecuting the matter further before the Roman tribunal, is regarded by the Evangelist as the work of God's influence, who thus brought about the accomplishment of that which Jesus had earlier spoken touching the manner and circumstances of His own death. The punishment of the cross was inseparably connected with the Roman condemnation, as stoning was with that of the Jews. To the manner of His death, Jesus had referred in ch. iii. 14, "The Son of man must be *lifted up;*" ch. viii. 28, xii. 32. That the Evangelist had this last passage in view, "I, if I be lifted up from the earth, will draw all men unto Me," is plain when we reflect that he had there added the observation, "This He said, signifying what death He should die." The mere hints of the passages in St John need, however, the commentary which is found in the sayings of Christ, found only in the three Evangelists: Matt. x. 38, xvi. 24, xx. 19; Mark viii. 34, x. 21; Luke ix. 23, xiv. 27. On the ground of these more precise utterances, St John explains that the less distinct sayings recorded by himself refer to the crucifixion.

God so ordered all, that the word of Christ as to the manner of His death was fulfilled. But this word of Christ rested upon an actual necessity. The Gentiles must take part in the death of the Redeemer, in order that that death might be exhibited as the collective guilt of the human race, even as it was the pre-intimation of what one day the degenerate Church of the Gentiles would independently strive to do against Christ, and has already begun to do. The death of the cross has a profoundly edifying significance. It gave occasion to reveal overcoming power in its most effectual manifestation. Christ as the atoning sacrifice is therein most luminously set forth,

Gal. iii. 1. How the bearing of the cross was typical for the self-denial of believers, Jesus Himself had often taught.

Ver. 33. " Then Pilate entered into the judgment-hall again, and called Jesus, and said unto Him, Art thou the King of the Jews ?"—Pilate had set the alternative before the Jews, either to bring a formal accusation against Jesus, or to judge Him according to their own law. They declined the latter; and we may suppose they adopted the former. St John, who brings the matter down to the point when the accusation *must* come forward, but does not record it, points back as certainly as if he said so to his predecessors. We find what is here presupposed in Luke xxiii. 2, the words of which are strictly applicable here : " They began to accuse Him, saying, We found this fellow forbidding to give tribute to Cesar, saying that he himself is Christ a king." With these last words are connected the recurring question of Pilate to Jesus, " Art thou the King of the Jews ?" St Luke records only two words as to what followed the question : Jesus answered, " Thou sayest it." St John gives the transaction fully.

Pilate repairs with Jesus into the prætorium, to avoid being disturbed in the investigation by the uproar of the Jews, the θόρυβος peculiar to them, Matt. xxvii. 24 ; Acts xxi. 34 (" And when he could not know the certainty for the tumult, θόρυβον, he commanded him to be carried into the castle "). The ἐφώνησε suggests that Jesus had hitherto stood outside the prætorium, otherwise Pilate would have needed only to go in to Him. For an illustration of the " called," we may refer to the " commanded him to be carried into the castle" in the passage just quoted. That the calling might take place through the instrumentality of others, is evident from ch. xi. 28. It appears that St John, who did not depart from Jesus, followed Him into the palace : there was no prohibition which hindered the Jews from entering ; they had refused to enter only for a reason that had no force to him. The exact report which St John gives of the proceedings within the prætorium, leads to the conclusion that he was present at these proceedings. The publicity of all Roman legal procedures allowed no man to be excluded who was disposed to witness these proceedings.

As the Jews were under the necessity of bringing forward a formal charge, they could not limit themselves to the offence which had led to His condemnation in the council—that of assuming to be the Son of God; this had no force whatever in a Roman forum. It was necessary that they should have a *political* offence to urge; and the fact that Jesus had arrogated royal dignity, gave them some assistance in this matter. Lampe is wrong in asserting that Jesus only in consequence of the Jewish charge vindicated to Himself a kingdom. The entrance of Jesus into Jerusalem had for its end the enforcement of His kingly authority, and He exhibits Himself as a King in Matt. xx. 20, 23, xxv. 34, 40. The word of the malefactor, " Lord, remember me when Thou comest in Thy kingdom," shows that Jesus had earlier represented Himself as a King. The royal prerogative was inseparable from the Messianic. But the Jews degraded the kingly authority of Jesus into a lower sphere. They charged Him with political sedition, and thus, like Potiphar's wife, laid upon Him their own sins. But Pilate knew with whom he had to do, and gave our Lord opportunity to defend Himself against the charge.—The *Thou* beginning the sentence certainly intimates a contrast between the appearance of Jesus and the idea of kingly dignity; but Lampe observes, in opposition to those who think that Pilate spoke in a tone of *mockery*, that Pilate was from the beginning seized by a holy awe of Jesus, which effectually restrained every movement of scorn, and impelled him fundamentally to investigate the Saviour's cause, and bring His innocence to light.

Ver. 34. " Jesus answered him, Sayest thou this thing of thyself, or did others tell it thee of Me?"—Jesus was present throughout the whole of this transaction with the Jews. The Roman law required this, and it is not only affirmed by the first Evangelists, Matt. xxvii. 12, Mark xv. 4 seq., Luke xxiii. 14 (ἐνώπιον ὑμῶν ἀνακρίνας), but attested by ver. 33 here, according to which Jesus had been with the Jews all this time before the prætorium. Our Lord's question, therefore, was not intended to give him explanation of anything that he did not know, but rather to move and awaken Pilate's conscience. It was designed to excite within him distrust of the Jews' accusation. Had Jesus been the King of the Jews in the sense in which the accusation had so termed him, Pilate himself must have found it out: seditious movements and insurrections could not well be concealed. But, as he must admit that nothing of that sort had come to his knowledge, he, who knew the complainants well, would attach very little importance to their assertion, but investigate the matter independently of them, and especially give attentive heed to the explanation of Jesus Himself.[1]

Ver. 35. " Pilate answered, Am I a Jew? Thine own nation, and the chief priests, have delivered thee unto me: what hast thou done?"—Pilate confesses that he has no personal knowledge of Jesus, that the matter hitherto had moved altogether in a Jewish sphere; and that there was nothing against Jesus but the allegation of the Jews. Since he is far removed from attaching final and decisive importance to the Jewish charge, he asked the Lord Himself what He had done. Thus the answer of our Lord had gained its end.

Ver. 36. " Jesus answered, My kingdom is not of this world. If My kingdom were of this world, then would My servants fight, that I should not be delivered to the Jews: but now is My kingdom not from hence."—Jesus is not speaking of the *nature* of His kingdom, but simply and alone of its *origin*. Augustin: He does not say, But now is not My kingdom *here*, but *hence*. Lampe: To be erected indeed in the world, but not of the world. To " of this world" and " hence" is opposed " of heaven:" comp. ch. viii. 23 and Jas. iv. 1, where " hence" forms a contrast to " from above," ch. iii. 17 ; comp. " ε thly," ἐπίγειος, ch. iii. 15. Bengel: "Whence it is, that is from heaven, He does not plainly say; but He hints it when He says that He had come into the world." The best comment on the words c͞ Christ is furnished by the original passages of Daniel, on which it rests. The four universal kingdoms of Daniel are followed by a *fifth* of absolutely *heavenly* origin, the Messianic kingdom, which, on account of that origin, was all-comprehensive and eternal. It is all the more obvious that we must have recourse to that passage, inasmuch as Jesus ever has it in His eyes when speaking of the kingdom of God or the kingdom of

---

[1] Grotius hits the right point, missed by many others, such as Lücke and De Wette: " Thou hast been so long ruler, and so careful a defender of the Roman majesty, and hast thou ever heard anything that would impeach Me of a design to usurp authority against Rome? If thou hast never known anything of thyself, but others have suggested it, beware lest thou be deceived by an ambiguous word."

heaven. We read in Dan. ii. 34, 35: "Thou sawest till that a stone was cut out *without hands*, which smote the image upon his feet that were of iron and clay, and brake them to pieces. Then was the iron, the clay, the brass, the silver, and the gold, broken to pieces together; ... and the stone that smote the image became a great mountain, and filled the whole earth." Again, ver. 44: "And in the days of these kings shall the *God of heaven* set up a kingdom, which shall never be destroyed: and the kingdom shall not be left to other people, but it shall break in pieces and consume all these kingdoms, and it shall stand for ever." Finally, ch. vii. 13, 14: "I saw in the night-visions, and, behold, one like the Son of man came with the clouds of heaven, and came to the Ancient of days, and they brought Him near before Him. And there was given Him (by the Ancient of days) dominion, and glory, and a kingdom, that all people, nations, and languages, should serve Him: His dominion is an everlasting dominion, which shall not pass away, and His kingdom that which shall not be destroyed." To the last quoted prophecy our Lord refers also in Matt. xxviii. 18, "All power is given unto Me." There is perhaps no passage of the Old Testament to which the Lord so frequently alludes as this (comp. my *Christology*, vol. iii.).—The word of Jesus, "My kingdom is not of this world," has often been perverted in the interests of a theory which would sunder the state from the dominion of Christ. Rightly understood, the passage subserves the very opposite purpose. The kingdom that sprang directly from heaven must have absolute authority over all the earth, and it will not submit to be put into obscurity or into a corner. The necessary consequence of the saying, "not of this world, not from here," is what we find written in Rev. xi. 15: "The kingdoms of the world are become the kingdoms of our Lord, and of His Anointed; and He shall reign for ever." In the original of Daniel, all peoples are represented as serving this kingdom. It does not occupy, by the side of this world's kingdom, a sphere sundered from it, and not occupied by it; but it breaks that power down under itself. The fact that all the Evangelists so carefully relate the Lord's assumption of His Kingship before *human authority*, is explained only on the ground that He is, as the Apocalypse styles Him, the King of kings, and that kings and states do not exist with Him, and concurrently with His kingdom, but are absolutely under His authority.

Christ does not say to Pilate, "My kingdom has nothing to do with yours;" but He intimates that His kingdom, not being of earthly origin, could not be contended for or against with earthly resources. Pilate would perfectly understand what was enough. The accusation was of political insurrection, of a course of conduct like that of the Egyptian, Acts xxi. 38; Theudas, Acts v. 36; and Judas the Galilean, ver. 37. If Jesus kept aloof from all such courses, if He expected the foundation of His kingdom only "from heaven," "without hands," then He was either a harmless enthusiast, or that for which He gave Himself out, in which case all opposition to Him would be blasphemous and vain : the word of Gamaliel would hold good, "But if it be of God, ye cannot overturn it, lest haply ye be found fighting against God."—The reference to Pilate's question, "Art thou the King of the Jews?" exhibits the βασιλεία, the kingdom, not in a passive, but in an active sense : meaning "My kingly power, My dominion." So also "kingdom" is used in Rev. i. 6, xi. 15, xii. 10, xvii. 18.

"My servants," not the angels, Matt. xxvi. 53, for these belong to a heavenly region; but here servants, ἐκ τοῦ κόσμου, are spoken of: they are rather the disciples of Christ, who, not reckoning the abortive act of Peter, never did anything of this kind; or the servants whom Christ would have in the future for such a case. The latter is better, as in the Gospels the disciples are described as the ὑπηρέται of Christ. It does not say, "They would have fought," but "they would fight," Vulg. *decertarent;* for the surrender to the Jews was not yet complete : it was then only perfect when Pilate fulfilled the desires of the Jews, comp. xix. 16.

Ver. 37. " Pilate therefore said unto Him, Art thou a king then ? Jesus answered, Thou sayest that I am a king. To this end was I born, and for this cause came I into the world, that I should bear witness unto the truth. Every one that is of the truth heareth My voice."—Jesus had declined to be a king in the Jewish sense; it was not His *ambition* to be a king. Yet He had spoken of His kingdom. This was ground enough for Pilate's deeper investigation, although he was convinced that there was nothing politically dangerous in Christ, and that the matter was more that of the man than of the judge. Οὐκ οὖν, *so*, is conclusive with regard to the foregoing words : Accordingly, thou art then a king. The notion of an " ironical by-meaning" is altogether to be excluded. In all Pilate's intercourse with Jesus, there is not the slightest trace of mockery. The impression of Christ's person was so powerful, that such feelings could not but be suppressed.—Jesus answered, "Thou sayest it, that I am a king," according to My own declarations : so let it be ; I have nothing to oppose to this, but avow Myself freely and publicly a king. This was the "good confession" which Jesus witnessed before Pilate, 1 Tim. vi. 13. Luke xxii. 70 is similar : "Then said they all, Art thou then the Son of God? He said unto them, Ye say that I am." The point before ὅτι is to be rejected in both cases. For the avoidance of ambiguity a "this" would, according to that pointing, have been necessary after " ye say," since λέγω commonly has *what* is said connected with it by ὅτι. Certainly the formula σὺ λέγεις of itself affirms perfectly and unambiguously ; but, considering the high importance of the confession of Christ, it was proper that the object of the avowal should not be derived from what precedes, but that it should be expressly stated : Yea, I am a King.

According to the current exposition, Jesus, in the words, "Therefore was I born," etc., defines more closely the nature of His kingdom. Bengel : To a kingdom of this world is opposed the kingdom of truth. Lücke : " Assuredly I am a King, but My kingdom is the truth." But in fact there is not the slightest reference to the kingdom.[1] The words refer rather to the prophetic office of Christ. Our Lord, after having avowed His royal dignity, turns the discourse from a subject which Pilate could scarcely apprehend, to another aspect of His nature and vocation which would be easier of apprehension to Pilate. It is true that the right understanding of this would serve materially to make the kingship more intelligible, and to place it in a true light. He who describes the immediate end of His mission to be the annunciation of the truth, would not be a king in the ordinary sense, in that sense in which the Jews had falsely charged Him with assuming it ; nor could He con-

---

[1] Lampe : He does not state the scope and design of His kingdom, but only of His advent into the flesh.

descend to involve Himself with mere political insurrectionary movements. The transition from the kingly to the prophetic office of Christ was all the more obvious, inasmuch as Isaiah, ch. lv. 4, described the Messiah as at once the *Witness* and the Leader and Lawgiver of the nations: the μαρτυρήσω here evidently refers to the *witness* there. So, in Rev. i. 5, Jesus Christ "the faithful Witness" distinguished from Christ "the Prince of the kings of the earth." If we would set in a closer connection the two offices of testimony and ruling, we cannot do that without establishing the fact that the testimony paves the way for the dominion. But in the present colloquy, that would have required to be more clearly intimated. On μαρτυρήσω, comp. iii. 32, 33. The words, "for this end was I born," of themselves point beyond the common sphere of humanity. No one born in the ordinary way of mortals could ever say that he was born for any particular destiny or vocation. The other words, "for this end am I come into the world," do the same still more emphatically: they show that the being of Christ in time and upon earth was preceded by another being. Jesus came into the world in order to bear testimony to the *truth*, that truth about which Gentile thinkers had made so much stir, but which could be truly known only through the communication of Him who came down from a higher sphere, and testified what He had seen and heard: comp. ch. iii. 31, 32. In the words, "Every one that is of the truth," the Lord turns, like Paul before Felix and Festus, from the judge to the man. Bengel is wrong here: "Jesus here appeals from the blindness of Pilate to the intelligence of believers." Under the general statement we incline rather to see, "If thou art of the truth." The very fact that our Lord entered into such close conversation with Pilate, of itself shows that he must have stood in some relation to the truth. Jesus made no answer to Herod, Luke xxiii. 18; His answer to Caiaphas, at the first hearing in the chambers of Annas, was a refusal, vers. 20, 21; before the High Council He at first kept silence; and the answer which He at length gave, under the high priest's adjuration, was manifestly meant only for publicity. Pilate was the only one with whom He really held discourse; and the circumstance that He afterwards denied him an answer, ch. xix. 9, shows that previously, and while He did enter into discourse with him, there was something in him yet to be worked upon. He then freely presented the side of his nature which gave a point of connection for the truth. But at the moment when he gave the preference to his own lower interest, Jesus turned away from him. The portion which Pilate had in the truth was this especially, that he did not count himself good, and did not, like the Pharisees, justify himself. He was a man of the world, but he had no desire to be or to appear anything else. He was no hypocrite: like Nathanael, he was free from guile, ch. i. 48. Although he did not think much of the sin which he admitted, yet it sometimes enforced itself upon him: when he came in contact with personal truth, he was seized with its awe; and the desire stirred within him to unite himself with that truth, and so reach a higher element.

"Every one that is of the truth:" the truth appears as a domain from which those spring who, in any sense whatever, partake of truth. A similar kind of expression we have in "of nothing and vanity," Isa. xl. 17; "of nothing," Isa. xli. 24; "of vanity," Ps. lxii. 10; $\dot{\epsilon}\kappa\ \tau o\hat{v}\ \pi o\nu\eta\rho o\hat{v}$, of the region of evil, Matt. v. 37; $\dot{\epsilon}\xi\ \dot{\epsilon}\rho\iota\theta\epsilon\iota\alpha\varsigma$, Rom. ii. 8. In 1 John iii. 19, "being of the truth" refers to the full possession of truth, as that is the privilege of Christians. In our present passage, the limitation is given by the connection. It cannot mean, in this context, the full possession of truth — that could be attained only by the testimony of Christ—but only a susceptible disposition. The beginning of this was in Pilate. But in order to be of the truth, he must have released that disposition from all its entanglements, and mightily striven against the impulses which would check it. That he failed to do this was his condemnation.—Jesus speaks categorically: "Every one that is of the truth heareth My voice." Accordingly, the man who loudly boasts of his striving after truth, and yet heareth not Christ's voice, but glories in the free spirit of his illumination, is not of the truth, is no *philosopher*, but the opposite.

Ver. 38. "Pilate saith unto Him, What is truth? And when he had said this, he went out again unto the Jews, and saith unto them, I find in him no fault at all."—That the question "What is truth?" was not uttered by Pilate in the spirit of desire to know, but that it was intended to break off the colloquy, is plain from the fact that Pilate with those words *departed*. He observed, like Felix, Acts xxiv. 25, that his heart was going where he was loth to follow; and that he might easily be brought to a point where he must outrage all his dearest inclinations. The question thrown out, "What is truth?" was to serve, as it were, for a justification of his breaking off a conversation that took a disagreeable turn. Talking about truth ends in nothing; about it there must be many opinions, and so many heads so many minds. It was not the language of a theoretical sceptic—the historical character of Pilate contradicts that—but of a worldling who, entirely given up to the " real interests of life," or to his passions, had lost the sense for truth, and had taught himself to regard it as a mere chimera. Every heart swayed by passion, or filled with avarice and ambition, asks internally like Pilate, although all are not as sincere as he was, in openly uttering their despair as to truth. Concerning truth, that holds good which is said of wisdom in Wisd. of Sol. i. 4: " For into a malicious soul wisdom shall not enter, nor dwell in the body that is subject to sin."—The three words " What is truth?" were for Pilate full of destiny. By them he put away that truth from himself which so graciously and invitingly appealed to him. By them he laid the foundation for the suicide by which, according to the report of Eusebius, who appeals to Greek historians, he ended his days under the Emperor Caius.—Pilate declined the truth. But he could not defend himself against its representative; and he who was not very scrupulous at other times about an act of injustice, more or less, strove hard to save Him, but always with the reservation that his own existence was not imperilled. Here again we see, that " being of the truth " was not absolutely far from him, and that he stood higher than Herod or Caiaphas. Doubtless he uttered the question " What is truth?" with a certain sorrow, with the consciousness that he, such a man as he was, sold under sin, was obliged to put the question, but that he was to act so contrary to it.—The words " I find no fault in him" are a point of coincidence with Luke xxiii. 4. Between these words, and what in ver. 39 he said to the Jews, lies the sending to Herod, which St Luke alone records. St John could immediately add the "but ye have a custom," especially as Pilate, according to St Luke, had, after He was sent back, again declared Christ's innocence.

Ver. 39. "But ye have a custom, that I should release unto you one at the Passover: will ye therefore that I release unto you the King of the Jews?"—The first three Evangelists had already recorded, but most copiously St Matthew, the free choice offered between Jesus and Barabbas. St John briefly touches it, and only to preserve a point of coincidence with his predecessors. It is perfectly plain that the proposal of Pilate was not free from additional wrong. Only the guilty were interceded for. In this way he would at once save Jesus, and give the rulers an opportunity of retreating honourably out of the matter. His own guilty conscience permitted him not to oppose these rulers decisively. But they were only rendered more obstinate in their demand by a proposition, the motive of which they divined. "At the Passover:" Bengel rightly observes, "Therefore that day was the Passover; and on that day the congregated people asked Pilate." The opinion which makes Jesus to have stood before Pilate at the early morning of the day between the two evenings of which the Passover was to be slain, is altogether irreconcilable with this "at the Passover." The earliest beginning that we can assign to the Passover was the time of the slaying of the paschal lamb, Lev. xxiii. 5, which must now have been already past, since we here find ourselves already in the sphere of the Passover. But, according to the first three Evangelists, who substitute *feast* for Passover, Matt. xxvii. 15, Mark xv. 6, Luke xxiii. 17, we are already on the other side of the first paschal *meal*, for this began the *feast*: comp. on ch. xiii. 1. To the same result we are led by the meaning of the usage. There can be no manner of doubt that the prisoner in it represented Israel. He served first of all as a *remembrancer* of the deliverance of the children of Israel from Egypt: that was the aspect which alone, as it regards the Romans, was exhibited. But with this there was connected the external aim, to express the hope that the Lord, through His redeeming grace sealed by the Passover, would one day again deliver His people from the bondage of earthly power. But the deliverance of the children of Israel, which this usage commemorated, followed on the 15th. Israel went out after the Passover was not only slain, but eaten. That fact rested upon the necessity of the case: the objective exhibition and the subjective appropriation of redeeming grace formed the root of the exodus. It formed also

CHAP. XVIII. 40.

the basis of their hope in their future deliverance from this world's power. This deliverance rested upon the atoning blood: comp. Zech. ix. 11, " As for thee also, by the blood of thy covenant I have sent out thy prisoners out of the pit wherein is no water." Thus there can be no doubt that the usage belonged only to the 15th Nisan, and consequently that St John, in perfect harmony with the other Evangelists, refers the examination of Jesus before Pilate to the 15th Nisan. The only possible escape from this, that Pilate in this case anticipated what properly belonged to the feast, is rendered impossible by Mark xv. 8. This shows that the initiative in reference to the release of a prisoner was taken by the *people.* The request of the usual release of the prisoner was a parenthesis quite independent of the transaction, and of which Pilate skilfully availed himself. Pilate speaks of the King of the Jews. " His perverseness in intermingling exasperating mockery by this *King of the Jews,*" belongs only to the expositors. Pilate intimates to the Jews that they would act against their own interests, if they persisted to extremity against Jesus. In the eyes of the Romans He was the representative of the Messianic hope of the Jews, and this would be in Him mocked and hung upon the cross. If passion had not blinded the rulers, they would have adopted every expedient to obviate such a scandal. The scorn which the Roman soldiers afterwards would manifest against Jesus, would in His person fall upon the Jews. But in the background there lay a presentiment of Pilate, that Jesus was actually the King of the Jews, and that therefore they were outraging their most sacred treasure in delivering Him up to him for crucifixion.

Ver. 40. " Then cried they all again, saying, Not this man, but Barabbas. Now Barabbas was a robber." — The word " again " is of no small moment in regard to St John's relations with his predecessors. No earlier cry is mentioned by St John, nor does he give us the antecedents for any such cry. We cannot admit De Wette's observation: " It may be referred to vers. 30 seq., where indeed no crying is mentioned, but where it may be supposed." For there Pilate had to do only with the rulers: the people are not introduced until the transaction connected with the release of the prisoner. St John refers here specifically to St Mark: the " again " stands in a similar connection with the "again" of Mark xv. 13, "They cried again, Crucify him," and, like this, points back to Mark xv. 8, the only passage where mention had been made of any loud cry of the people, "And the multitude, crying aloud, began," etc. (Fritzsche: Πάλιν belongs to the clamour raised in ver. 8, not to the words pronounced with a loud voice.)—The πάντες of St John (comp. παμπληθεί in St Luke, ver. 18) serves as a confirmation of the statement of St Matthew, that Pilate placed Barabbas with Jesus before the people for their choice, with the supposition that the decision would be in favour of the light, when they saw opposed to Him the utter blackness of the other. They certainly would not have been so unanimous in favour of Barabbas; the voices would have been very discordant, if this alternative had not been simply set before them. Barabbas, according to the accounts of the Evangelists, had nothing in him that could recommend him particularly to the people. Such a wretched representative of their national hope they would not have chosen, if their choice had been entirely free.

Ch. xix. 1. "Then Pilate therefore took Jesus, and scourged Him."—Between this verse and the preceding lies Matt. xxvii. 24, 25, the mention of Pilate's washing his hands; as between ch. xviii. 39 and 40, the message of Pilate's wife, Matt. xxvii. 19. After the popular will had been uttered in so express a manner, Pilate yielded to it. He paved the way for the crucifixion when he gave up Jesus to be scourged. But he hoped to be able to restrain in the midst of its course the punishment itself. When he presented to the people the sad image of suffering innocence and righteousness, he thought they would be smitten by it. That was the reason why he permitted the soldiers to indulge all their mockery of Jesus, to which the scourging had given them a kind of right. The more deeply He was humbled, the more tragical the spectacle was which He exhibited, the better would Pilate's end be subserved. "It is a poor policy," says Quesnel, "when we undertake to win the world, and at the same time indulge them with part of what they desire; and when we think to satisfy our duty by denying them the other part. Fidelity cannot divide itself in relation to God."

Crucifixion was usually preceded, among the Romans, by *scourging*, which was so painful and horrible, that the delinquents not seldom gave up the ghost during the process. Heyne has devoted a special treatise to the question, *cur supplicio addita fuerit virgarum sævitia* (Opusc. iii.). The true reason was, the determination to heap upon the malefactor all kinds of torment. This we learn from Josephus, who mentions the combination of scourging and crucifixion in several passages. In the *Antiq.* v. 11, 1, he says the malefactors were scourged and tormented in every possible way before death. In another passage, De Bell. Jud. ii. 14, 9, scourging is mentioned as the prelude of crucifixion: "And taking others, they led them to Florus, whom having scourged with rods, he crucified." The scourging inflicted by Pilate was evidently of this kind. As the question in St John concerned only life and death, we may suppose, after the attempt in ch. xviii. 39 had ended, that the scourging was the introduction to the penalty of death. The same is evident from a comparison of Matthew and Mark, where the scourging is the preliminary of the crucifixion: Matt. xxvii. 26, "And when he had scourged Jesus, he delivered Him to be crucified;" Mark xv. 15, "And so Pilate, willing to content the people, delivered Jesus, when he had scourged Him, to be crucified." As also in our Lord's own fore-announcement of His passion, Matt. xx. 19, "And shall deliver Him to the Gentiles, to mock, and to scourge, and to crucify Him;" and Luke xviii. 33, "And they shall scourge Him, and put Him to death." There is no sufficient reason for distinguishing the scourging of Matthew and Mark from that of John. The difference in the expression, there φραγελλοῦν, the Latin *flagellare*, here μαστιγοῦν, the genuine Greek expression, is of little moment, since in our Lord's prediction, Matt. xx. 19, we have μαστιγοῦν. St Matthew chooses the official term, since the execution itself was now in question. The historical portion of the scourging is, in Matthew, and Mark, and John, the same; the only difference being, that the former pass over the fruitless attempts of Pilate to arrest the natural course of things, and disturb the connection between the scourging and crucifixion. The assertion, that in the first Evangelists the scourging follows the sentence, while in St John it precedes it, is altogether erroneous. The Evangelists mention no other sentence than that which *in fact* was uttered in the scourging. The formal sentence of death spoken, according to St John, by Pilate afterwards, they pass over as less important.

It is misleading to connect the scourging in St John with Luke xxiii. 16, where Pilate says to the Jews, "Having punished him, I will let him go." There the matter was only of a disciplinary infliction, which Pilate offered to the Jews. What that infliction was to be is not plainly said, because nothing depended upon it: he desired only to pave the way for the Jews to retire with honour from the matter. The loud demand of the people, which, according to St Mark, was independent of the other transaction, and took place while Pilate was making the overture to the rulers—their loud and increasing cry that he would release a prisoner as usual, had such an effect upon Pilate, as to make him withdraw the proposition he had made, and adopt other means which seemed to present themselves for the same end. When these means failed, he reverted, according to Luke xxiii. 22, to his earlier proposal, but could obtain no hearing for it. St Luke alone gives us the account of Pilate's fruitless proposal. He omits the scourging. But that he did not omit it through ignorance, we learn from ch. xviii. 33.—The more terrible the scourging was, the more miserable was its contrast with Pilate's "I find no fault in him." But such contradictions are unavoidable, when a man with a guilty conscience, assailable at all points, attempts to withstand the evil of others. We, however, must never forget that Jesus endured the scourging for us: "He voluntarily withdrew from heavenly joys, and clothed Himself with all sorrows and agonies, that He might take away the sorrows of man and fill him instead with joy."

Ver. 2. "And the soldiers platted a crown of thorns, and put it on His head, and they put on Him a purple robe."—The *thorns* declared that the dominion, of which the crown was a symbol, should cost Christ, who attained it, dear. This was the truth, and therefore the crown of thorns in Christendom has been always regarded with deep interest. As certainly as the crown was the crown of a king, so certainly was the purple robe a royal robe, and the idea of a soldier's mantle is quite out of keeping. St Luke does not mention the mantle; but in ch. xxiii. 11, he relates of Herod, "And Herod, with his men of war, set Him at nought, and mocked Him, and arrayed Him in a gorgeous robe ($\dot{\epsilon}\sigma\theta\hat{\eta}\tau\alpha$ $\lambda\alpha\mu\pi\rho\acute{\alpha}\nu$), and sent Him again to Pilate." There we have an answer to the question where the Jewish soldiers obtained the royal robe (Herod says, in Josephus,

Bell. Jud. i. 23, 5, to his sons, δίδωμι ὑμῖν ἐσθῆτα βασιλικήν). On the renewal of the judicial investigation before Pilate, it had been laid aside, as below the dignity of the occasion; but when Jesus was handed over to the soldiers, they put it on Him again. St Luke speaks of a gorgeous or resplendent robe; St Matthew of a "scarlet robe" (χλαμύδα κοκκίνην, ch. xxvii. 28); St Mark xv. 17 (πορφύραν) and St John speak of a *purple* robe. There is no contradiction in all this. Λαμπρός does not signify white, but splendid or magnificent: it was therefore the most general designation. It simply says that the robe was a gorgeous robe—as may be supposed, an old one laid aside. That there is no contradiction between purple and scarlet, we learn from two passages in the Apocalypse: ch. xvii. 4, "And the woman was arrayed in purple and scarlet colour;" and ch. xviii. 16, where one and the same garment is called both purple and scarlet. Purple is the more general, scarlet the more specific, designation. Braun (*De vestitu sacerdotum*, i. 1, c. 14) has shown that in all ancient times, purple, as the leading colour for magnificent garments, often included in it the scarlet colour. When the soldiers laid on Jesus, and as the suffering Jesus, a purple garment, they unconsciously bore witness to the truth. For Christ is the "Prince of the kings of the earth," Rev. i. 5; the "King of kings," xix. 16; and the foundation of that dominion was laid in His sufferings.

Ver. 3. "And said, Hail, King of the Jews! and they smote Him with their hands."—The words ἤρχοντο πρὸς αὐτόν, received by Lachmann into the text after the Codex Vatic., appeared to many transcribers superfluous. But it serves to tell us that they in the most formal manner came before Him, in order to pay Him the obeisance due to royalty. The motive which induced the soldiers to practise their mockery is revealed in the words of the salutation, King of the Jews. They did not mock the presumption of Jesus. It was the kingdom of the Jews itself that they laughed at. The soldiers regarded Jesus as the representative of the Messianic hope of the Jews. They would turn into ridicule those royal hopes which were known far in the heathen world, more especially as those hopes took an external direction, and aspired to the dominion of the whole earth. The soldiers represented the Gentile world turning to scorn the lofty pretensions of the Jews. But there was here a remarkable irony of fate. The mockery, "Hail, King of the Jews," was to change soon into awful earnest.

"And they smote Him:" according to Matt. xxvii. 29, 30, with the reed which they had placed in His right hand as a royal sceptre, but which He had declined to accept. Lampe: "It had not seemed good to the Saviour so far to respond to their wickedness as to receive this reed in His hand He could, without disparaging His decorum, *suffer indignities, but not perform them.* Wherefore, when He refused to retain the reed in His right hand, they inflicted blows upon Him with it." These indignities presuppose that the condemnation had in fact taken place; and if the scourging had the significance which we have assigned to it, that was certainly the case. Only one who was condemned could be handed over to the violence of the soldiery. When Pilate surrendered Jesus to the scourge, he in fact pronounced thereby His condemnation. In the ordinary procedure of justice, the verbal condemnation should have preceded the scourging. But this did not take place, because Pilate was not without hope that he could restrain the punishment in its course. He wished to avoid the indecency of recalling a formally uttered sentence of condemnation. But as that hope was frustrated, he was obliged afterwards to pronounce the formal sentence.

Ver. 4. "Pilate therefore went forth again, and saith unto them, Behold, I bring him forth to you, that ye may know that I find no fault in him."—Here first it is definitely established that Pilate caused Jesus to be led into the prætorium to be scourged, and that there, where the watch was stationed, the indignities of vers. 2, 3 were inflicted. That Pilate once more led Him out, was itself a proof that he held Him innocent, because he otherwise would have made no further attempt to move His accusers in His favour. In the case of one who was pronounced a delinquent by the authorities, the crucifixion followed immediately on the scourging. On "I find no fault in him," Grotius remarks: "That is, not even so much fault as would warrant his being beaten with rods. Thus he condemned his own iniquity."

Ver. 5. "Then came Jesus forth, wearing the crown of thorns, and the purple robe. And Pilate saith unto them, Behold the man!"—Pilate preceded, that attention might be first directed to him and to his words, and that the impression of his words might not be damaged by a glance at Him whom they persecuted with such obstinate prejudice. Then he caused Jesus to come before them. Φορέω, as distinguished from φέρω, indicates that the crown of thorns and the purple robe then belonged to the proper costume of Christ. The subject in λέγει needed not to be mentioned, because it was plain enough that not Jesus, but Pilate, was the speaker. "Behold the man:" look once more on this man, this man who is man no more, Isa. liii. 3, a worm and no man, Ps. xxii. 7, in His deepest misery lustrous with innocence and righteousness, silent and patient in His sufferings, like a lamb led to the slaughter, and like a sheep that is dumb before her shearers. Pilate thought, judging others by himself, that they would need only to look upon Him in His humiliation, so full of innocence, and their hatred would pass away. But Pilate forgot two things: first, the abyss of wickedness opened up in those who stand in a near relation to religion, without admitting its transforming influence into their hearts; and then the all-penetrating influence which bigoted ministers of religion exercise upon the laity, when the latter are not armed against them by true religion.

Ver. 6. "When the chief priests therefore and officers saw Him, they cried out, saying, Crucify him, crucify him. Pilate saith unto them, Take ye him, and crucify him: for I find no fault in him."—"Take ye him, and crucify him," is only a vivid form of refusing to be their tool: comp. ch. xviii. 31.

Ver. 7. "The Jews answered him, We have a law, and by our law he ought to die, because he made himself the Son of God."—The Jewish rulers were emboldened by the spirit of concession which they already found in Pilate, who surrendered a man whom he pronounced innocent to the scourging which was reserved only for the guilty, and who supplicated them in favour of Jesus, when he ought to have enforced his own authority, and manfully defended against them the cause of innocence and righteousness. Thus, when their political accusation had come to nought (Grotius: Not being able to establish the crime against the Roman authority, they urge their own law), they return back to the position which they had taken at the beginning, ch. xviii. 30, and demand that Pilate should condemn

Him on their decision, whether he himself found Him guilty or not. They do not concede so much to Pilate as to point out the passage in the law which they had in view. That passage was Lev. xxiv. 16, which decrees that the blasphemer of God shall be punished with death. It was the same judicial decree on the ground of which Jesus before the high priest was adjudged to die. He had there, on the adjuration of the high priest, that He should say whether He was the Son of God, answered in the affirmative. Thereupon the high priest declared, "He blasphemeth;" and the council decreed, "He is guilty of death," Matt. xxvi. 63 seq. With "He made himself the Son of God;" comp. ch. v. 18, "He called God his Father, making himself equal with God." The claim to be the Son of God fell under the category of blasphemy only if it were a presumptuous claim. This was the sense in which Pilate took the words of the high priest; and if it had been untrue, Jesus would not by His silence have confirmed it as the right sense. That the members of the Sanhedrim were in earnest as to this claim of Sonship—that they regarded it as including the assumption of divinity, is plain from ch. x. 33. There the Jews accused Jesus of *blasphemy;* of blasphemy consisting in this, that though he was man, he made himself God.

Ver. 8. "When Pilate therefore heard that saying, he was the more afraid."—His present fear was distinguished from the former only by the *more*. Even before then he must have feared that he should draw down on himself the vengeance of God. Pilate had been already alarmed, when he thought he had to do only with a man under the special protection of Heaven. The words of his wife, "Have thou nothing to do with this just man," sank deep in his heart. But now that, according to the declaration of the Jews, Jesus made Himself the Son of God, a new aspect of the case was opened, and he might dread being in the fullest sense a $\theta\epsilon o\mu\acute{a}\chi o\varsigma$, a fighter against God. What Jesus, according to their statements, had uttered concerning Himself, he could not lightly dismiss from his mind. "He remembered," says Heumann, "His wonderful works, and with deeper reflection than before; he bethought himself that Jesus was a holy man, to whom lying and deception were impossible." The impressions of Christ's person, the majesty which shone through all His deep humiliation, led Pilate involuntarily to think of something beyond the sphere of mere humanity. He did not think of a son of the gods, of one *dei cujusdam filius*. The unity of God, a truth ineradicably implanted in the human mind, never entirely disappeared in polytheism; and this unity became more and more prominent in the period of the decline of Gentile culture. Pilate, in regard to this, like his centurion, Matt. xxvii. 54, Mark xv. 39, stood very much under the influence of the people among whom he had dwelt so many years. His conscience had been before this much wounded. He now feared, that by new guilt he should involve himself in the immediate judgments of Heaven.

Ver. 9. "And went again into the judgment-hall, and saith unto Jesus, Whence art thou? But Jesus gave him no answer." —Pilate went into the prætorium, and led Jesus with him. The auditory outside seemed to him too profane for the introduction of this question. That "Whence art thou?" could have but one meaning, "Belongest thou to heaven or to earth? art thou God, or mere man?" is now generally acknowledged: comp. ch. vii. 28, xviii. 36, 37. What our Lord in the latter passage said concerning His kingdom, that it was not of this world, not from below, applied also to His person. He was not, like ordinary men, $\dot{\epsilon}\kappa$ $\tau\hat{\omega}\nu$ $\kappa\acute{a}\tau\omega$, but $\dot{\epsilon}\kappa$ $\tau\hat{\omega}\nu$ $\mathring{a}\nu\omega$, ch. viii. 23. To the $\pi\acute{o}\theta\epsilon\nu$ here corresponds the $\mathring{a}\nu\omega\theta\epsilon\nu$ in ver. 11. Pilate designedly put the question in this general form. A holy fear restrained him from putting it more directly. He felt that in the region he now entered he was at a loss, and must reveal his inaptitude. Wherefore did not Jesus answer Pilate? The reason must be the same which occasioned the silence before Annas, before the council, and before Herod; as also the silence on the accusations of the rulers before Pilate, of which Matthew (vers. 12, 13) and Mark (vers. 4, 5) make mention. The supposition, that "Jesus kept silence because a heathenish notion of Sonship to God was in question," is, apart from the fact that it rests on a groundless supposition, wrong, simply because it severs our Lord's silence here from its connection with His other silences. Like the rest before whom Jesus kept silence, Pilate no longer deserved an answer. He had earlier declined to be led by Jesus into the knowledge of the truth, because he would not sacrifice the passions with which his soul was filled: comp. ch. xviii. 38. His whole bearing had shown that his personal interest was first in everything, and that he listened to the cause of right only so far as this consisted with his own interest. Jesus looked through his soul, and knew that he was incapable of practically following even the truth that he knew. There was no obligation incumbent upon Him to avow His divinity before the world. He had already solemnly avowed Himself to be the Son of God before the council. The " good confession" which Christ was to witness, and had already witnessed before the Roman power, touched not His divinity, but His world-embracing kingdom as based upon that divinity. Thus Jesus could and must make good on this occasion the prophetic word concerning the lamb which opened not its mouth, Isa. liii. 7. And all the more as, to the deeper glance, there was even in His silence an answer to Pilate's question whether man or God. " He showed," says Heumann, " by this silence the dignity of His person, and that it rested with Himself whether He would answer or not, while He by no means admitted Pilate to be His judge." Further, if He laid no claim to divinity, it would have been His duty to have absolutely repelled the allegation of the Jews, *that He made Himself the Son of God.* That would have been to give God His honour. His silence said, " I am from above, but thou art not worthy that I should admit thee into the mystery of My nature. For thine heart is not right before God." The silence was more significant than words. The " from above" was uttered in it; and at the same time an emphatic intimation of Pilate's insincerity, who belonged to that large class of whom these words have been used: " A man of the world is often touched by Divine deeds and Divine teaching, as we see in King Agrippa and the governor Felix, Acts xxiv. 24 and xxvi. 28; but, as the Lord says in Matt. xiii. 22, worldly thoughts choke the word, that it brings forth no fruit." How entirely our Lord's silence was justified, is manifest from the deep effect it produced on Pilate, here as well as in Matthew, vers. 12, 13,—an effect which it must have produced, inasmuch as assumed dignity is ever rich in words, while only true greatness can bear to be held in suspicion or denied.

Ver. 10. " Then saith Pilate unto Him, Speakest thou not unto me? knowest thou not that I have power to crucify thee, and have power to release thee?"—Pilate certainly did not speak in the sensitive and excited tone of offended dignity.

(Lampe: "Threatening anger is plainly opposed to the preceding fear.") That would have been contrary to the whole position which he assumed towards Jesus; and, moreover, his impression of Christ's majesty was too deep to allow it. He simply desired, half imploringly, to have from Jesus an explanation of the marvellous fact, that He thought him worthy of no reply who held, nevertheless, His life in his hands. "Power to *crucify*" precedes the "power to *deliver*," because the beam in the balance decidedly vibrated that way. The scourging had already taken place, which was the prelude to crucifixion, and Pilate's attempt to soften the rulers had already failed. The order has been inverted in many MSS., simply from a notion that the right of the magistracy was strictly "*jus vitæ et necis.*" That the emphasis fell upon the "crucify," is shown by what follows: "Thou couldest have no power over Me."

Ver. 11. "Jesus answered, Thou couldest have no power at all against Me, except it were given thee from above: therefore he that delivered Me unto thee hath the greater sin."—To the question Jesus had given no answer. Against the express denial of His dignity He must utter a protest. The words "Thou couldest have . . . given thee" declared that Pilate, to whom Jesus was apparently in submission, was in truth only an instrument in a higher hand which ruled over the destiny of Jesus; and that to it, not to him, was Jesus subjected. "Shall the axe boast itself against him that heweth therewith? or shall the saw magnify itself against him that shapeth it?" Isa. x. 15. The imaginary lord was thus reduced to a servant, not only of the Father, but of the Son, between whom there was the fullest concert. To this connection between the Father and the Son points the relation in which the ἄνωθεν stands to the πόθεν of Pilate. Grotius: Inde scil. unde ortus sum, tacite enim hoc indicat. Stier: "In this heavenly ἄνωθεν there is at the same time a late answer to the previously unanswered question as to *His* origin." The matter is not here the authority of the magistracy. Stier regards these words as a support for the "unassailable theory of the Divine right of the powers that be;" but the question was rather, as the reference to Pilate's words shows, the material power which Pilate as the representative of earthly dominion had over Jesus, whom no one as it seemed could wrest from his hands.—The leading thought is followed by an undertone. "Therefore:" that is, because thou hast obtained power over Me only through a special Divine ordering. The fact that Pilate had only a *permitted* power over Jesus, as, on the one hand, it overturned the conclusion which Pilate drew from his power in favour of his superiority, so, on the other hand, it served for his apology. He had not, like the Jews, voluntarily entered into the matter; he was by Divine destiny connected with it, he himself knew not how, and would with all his heart have been free from it.

All the enemies of Jesus, Herod and the Jews, no less than Pilate and the Gentiles, did against Him " what the hand and counsel of God had determined before to be done," Acts iv. 27. Even the act of the traitor Judas rested on a decree ὡρισμένον, corresponding to the δεδομένον ἄνωθεν here. But when a man against his will is involved in a matter, the Divine causality is in the foreground; when he deliberately seeks it, the human is predominant. In regard to this, Ex. xxi. 12, 13 is very instructive: " He that smiteth a man, so that he die, shall surely be put to death. And if a man lie not in wait, but God deliver him into his hand; then I will appoint thee a place whither he shall flee." The murderer no less than the manslayer stands under the decree of God, but no one would think of comforting an impenitent murderer by referring him to this Divine destiny. It was not until his brothers had attained to a penitent sense of their fault, that Joseph represented to them for their consolation the Divine causality, Gen. l. 20. As soon as the Jews repented, they also had presented to them the Divine causality. Till then their minds must be directed to their own guilt alone. —Our Lord does not acquit Pilate of guilt. The contrast presented to him was only a relative one. The relative admeasurement of guilt, according to its various grades, the allusion to the guilt of Israel, as deeper than that of the heathen, recurs often in the discourses of our Lord in the earlier Evangelists, Matt. x. 15; Luke xii. 48. When Jesus established the measure of Pilate's guilt, He declared Himself to be His judge's Judge, and intimated to him the place which He Himself would occupy at the great day of universal judgment.

" He that delivered Me to thee" must be, according to the comparison with Pilate, which leads us to expect that here person is set against person, as also according to ch. xviii. 28,

Caiaphas, not however Caiaphas as an individual, but as the representative of the Jewish people, whom Pilate opposes to himself in Matt. xxvii. 24, and who cried out in ver. 25 ($\pi\hat{a}\varsigma$ ὁ λαός), " His blood be on us, and on our children." Caiaphas was accordingly an ideal person as it were, the representative of the Jewish national spirit as it then was, in harmony with the representative position which the high priest assumes in the Old Testament. According to Lev. iv. 3, the sins of the high priest were reckoned to the people : " If the priest that is anointed sin according to the sin of the people." In Zech. iii. 1, the high priest appears before the Lord burdened with the sins of the whole people. Aben Ezra, on Lev. iv. 3, says : Ecce pontifex maximus æquiparatur universo Israeli.

Ver. 12. " And from thenceforth Pilate sought to release Him : but the Jews cried out, saying, If thou let this man go, thou art not Cesar's friend : whosoever maketh himself a king speaketh against Cesar."—Ἐκ τούτου, as in vi. 66, from that time onwards. Before ἐζήτει there might, as in ver. 8, be placed a μᾶλλον. Its omission rested upon the idea, that in comparison of his present striving, the earlier came not into consideration. John could have known this only in case Pilate had shown the earnestness of his present endeavour in a very demonstrative manner, coming out from the prætorium to the Jews. How he showed it, we are not told.—The Jews perceived that a change had come over Pilate, and that with their present means they could not accomplish anything more. They now laid hold on their most perilous weapon. They set simply before Pilate the alternative of giving up Jesus, or of losing himself. They threatened him, not ambiguously, with an accusation before Cesar.—" Friend of Cesar " was then the highest title of honour with which the high Roman officials, after praiseworthy government, were rewarded : comp. Wetstein on this passage. To be *not* a friend of Cesar, not to sacrifice all other interests to his, was the gravest charge against a man like Pilate, and one which the suspicious Tiberius was always sufficiently inclined to listen to. (Tacitus, Ann. iii. 38 : Majestatis crimen omnium accusationum complementum erat. Suetonius, Vita Tib. c. 58 : Qui atrocissime exercebat leges majestatis.)—
" Speaketh against:" Jesus had declared Himself to be a King, and thereby, according to the assertion of the Jews,

raised Himself into competition with the power of Cesar. The matter primarily moved in the sphere of words, and the ἀντιλέγειν preserves therefore its ordinary meaning. The Jews spoke really according to the mind of the Roman imperial power. We have nothing to do here with the inability of Cesar to apprehend the true nature of the kingdom of Christ. To the pretensions which the imperial power maintained, the kingdom of Christ actually stood in direct contradiction. This is plain from the conflict of life and death which arose afterwards between the imperial dominion and the Church of Christ, as well as the description of that conflict in the thirteenth chapter of the Apocalypse.—Jesus was to be condemned, but only after His innocence had been made as clear as day, and acknowledged by the judge in the most decisive manner, and in repeated ways. To attain this double end, there could have been chosen no more fitting instrument than Pilate, free from the malignity of the Jews, yielding to the impressions of truth, and filled with a certain zeal to put it in the true light; but yet too weak to enforce it at the price of his own interests or place.

Ver. 13. "When Pilate therefore heard that saying, he brought Jesus forth, and sat down in the judgment-seat, in a place that is called the Pavement, but in the Hebrew, Gabbatha."—Τῶν λόγων τούτων is the most approved reading: every word was to Pilate an arrow. Τοῦτον τὸν λόγον seems to have come from ver. 8.—Pilate, according to ver. 9, had gone with Jesus into the prætorium, in order that he might there speak to Him quietly. Ver. 12 requires us to assume that he then came forth to the people, and made known to them his full design to set Jesus at liberty. After his conscience had received that deadly blow from the Jews, he went back into the prætorium, and hastened Jesus out. The condemnation must be spoken under the open heaven, in the presence of the accused.—That the judgment-seat of the Roman governors stood in the open air, according to the tenor of our narrative, is proved by Josephus, De Bell. Jud. ii. 9, 3: "Pilate having sat down on the judgment-seat in the great stadium, summoned before him the people," etc. There he is speaking of Cesarea. In section 4 he speaks of the same thing at Jerusalem, around which "the people gathered themselves together with uproar." But still more explicit is ii. 14, 8. This passage shows, that when the procurator came to Jerusalem, the judgment-seat was placed before his dwelling, the old royal castle of Herod, identical with the prætorium here. We are presented with the same scene as here. Τοῦ before βήματος is omitted by Lachmann. Everywhere else in the New Testament this word has the article; but in two of the passages quoted from Josephus it is without the article. A judgment-seat might be mentioned, because, when the procurator left Jerusalem, the βῆμα also was taken away: the βῆμα, therefore, had not so permanent a character as the court of justice. We see in Matt. xxvii. 19, that Pilate, during the previous transactions with the people, had intermittently occupied the judgment-seat.—When St John approaches that crisis of universal interest, the proper pronunciation of Christ's doom by Pilate, everything becomes momentous to him: he designates places by their two names, the Greek and the Hebrew, or Aramaic, and specifies the day and the hour.—The Greek and the Aramaic names indicate the same place under different relations, yet so that these two relations are fundamentally connected. The Greek name points to the Mosaic work, which in its beauty indicated the dignity of the judgment: comp. Rev. iv. 6. The Aramaic name indicated the elevation of the place, suggesting the fact that absolute submission was due to the word of the judge. Λιθόστρωτον (we find the word in Josephus, Bell. Jud. vi. 1, 8) strictly means *inlaid with stone* generally, but was specifically used for Mosaic tessellation. Gabbatha signifies *hill*. The town, which is called in Hebrew Gibeah, Josephus mentions frequently under the name Gabbatha. So Antiq. v. 1, 29: " There is a tomb and monument of him in the city of Gabbatha." In vi. 4, 2, he says of Samuel, " Coming thence afterwards to Gabbatha:" comp. viii. 12, 4, 5, xiii. 1, 4. Josephus, Bell. Jud. v. 2, 1, calls Gibeah in Benjamin Γαβαθσαούλην, adding the explanation, "this means *hill of Saul*." The only difference, that Josephus spells it always with one β, is of small moment; for, apart from the fact that the reading Γαβαθά is not altogether unsupported, the reduplication of the letter might have been introduced for a euphonic purpose, the original word being otherwise harsh. So there is in the Hebrew a purely euphonic *dagesh forte*. Hence for the same reason we have μαμμωνᾶς instead of μαμωνᾶς, in a number of manuscripts of Matt. vi. 24.

The opposite we find in the case of the name עַיָּה, which the Septuagint translate Γάζα. There were other localities around Jerusalem which bore the name of *hill*, as the hill of the lepers, Jer. xxxi. 39. Iken's objection, that the name was too general, equally applies to Λιθόστρωτον; and, moreover, the specific characterization of the place was given in the preceding ἐπὶ τοῦ βήματος. These names were appropriate only in the immediate neighbourhood of the judgment-seat. When they spoke elsewhere of these localities, the reference to the βῆμα, or the connection with it, required to be expressly mentioned. According to the analogy of Λιθόστρωτον, we might expect that the word Gabbatha would be a general designation. The hill probably was an artificial one.

Ver. 14. "And it was the preparation of the Passover, and about the sixth hour: and he saith unto the Jews, Behold your King!"—The exact specification of the place is followed by that of the time. First the day of the week: "it was the preparation of the Passover." These words have been differently understood. According to some, they say that it was the preparation of the Passover, the day of preparation, on which the paschal lamb was provided; according to others, that it was the preparation for the Sabbath in the Passover feast. The latter interpretation is the correct one. Παρασκευὴ τοῦ πάσχα cannot mean the preparation for the Passover. Τὸ πάσχα meant either the paschal lamb or the whole feast. On that supposition, it must have signified the feast day of the paschal feast. But the word never occurs with that signification.

Further, παρασκευή never is used for the day that preceded the feast; only for the day that preceded its one Sabbath. Bleek has not been able to adduce the slightest proof that this word, and the corresponding Aramaic ערובתא, was ever employed to designate the day before the feast. There lies the point of the discussion: failing to prove this, the cause is lost. In the New Testament, παρασκευή is always the proper name of a week-day, the Friday. If the word was also used for the preparation days of the feasts, how was it that the preparation day of the Sabbath was always called the preparation day, or preparation day absolutely, ἡ παρασκευή, or παρασκευή, without the word Sabbath being ever added?—an addition which was all the more necessary, because all the passages which speak of the day of preparation refer to the feast, and ambiguity was therefore unavoidable. The passages are Matt. xxvii. 62; Mark xv. 42; Luke xxiii. 54; John xix. 31. St Matthew says, "The next day that followed the day of the preparation." He means thereby the Sabbath,—a strange note of time, if it were not quite settled that "day of preparation," standing alone, was synonymous with Friday. St Mark explains the day of preparation as "the day before the Sabbath." He gives his Greek readers this explanation of a term which in Jewish phraseology was more limited than its sound. But elsewhere than in the New Testament we find the same phrase. Josephus, Antiq. xvi. 6, 2, mentions an edict of Augustus, which gave the Jews certain exemptions on the Sabbath, and "on the day of its preparation from the ninth hour." There the word is used for the Friday; although Josephus or the edict explains it for Gentile readers, as being the day before the Sabbath, because the simple παρασκευή would have been unintelligible to them. So also in the language of the fathers, παρασκευή is always Friday: comp. Clem. Alex. Stromata 7; Dion. Alex. in Routh, Rell. Sac. s. ii. p. 385, and other passages in Suicer. The word is also expressly quoted as the Jewish phrase. Synesius in Ep. iv. says, "It was the day which the Jews term *preparation*." Thus the use of the phrase is absolutely on our side. The opposite view has here no ground to stand upon. Bleek has skilfully concealed the point on which all depends; but even he is obliged to confess, "that the expression in this form is not found elsewhere." The argument is not in the least degree weakened by the allegation, that the first day of the paschal feast, as being equal to the Sabbath, demanded its preparation. That would have force if the word bore only an appellative character,—if it had not been, in Jewish phraseology, the proper name of the last day in the week but one. Our opponents appeal to the fact, that in the Jewish writings ערב is frequently used for the eve of the feasts, and especially of the Sabbath. But there is no proof that ערב, evening, corresponds to παρασκευή, preparation day. Inasmuch as *ereb* is used of the eves of the feasts, but preparation day always denotes the day before the Sabbath, the two words, which are not coincident in meaning, have nothing in common. The Jewish word for παρασκευή is ערובתא, which had never any other meaning than that of the day preceding the Sabbath, and was simply the name of the week-day: Buxtorf, Lex. c. 1160. This same word is used by the Syriac translator for the word παρασκευή. In Syriac it so decidedly and so exclusively denoted the Friday, that the Syrians termed Good Friday the day of preparation for the Passion: comp. Castelli, Lex. (ed. Michaelis), p. 673.

It has been maintained that St John, if he had regarded the first feast day as the day of death, would not so indefinitely have designated as the Friday in the Passover that day which might have been any other of the seven feast days, especially here, where he is so exact in his record, that he defines the very hour. But what precedes had determined the day, in harmony with the first three Evangelists, who in regard to this point leave no room for doubt: comp. on xviii. 28, 39. Here the emphasis falls upon the determination of the *day of the week*, which had not yet been given.

It has again been asserted, that to regard the preparation day of the Passover as the preparation day for the Sabbath in the Passover, must always have the air of a forced evasion of a difficulty. But this assertion rests upon the supposition, already overturned, that παρασκευή signified preparation day generally. As soon as we settle it that the word standing alone meant the day before the Sabbath, the Friday, the ambiguity is at once removed. The parallel passages adduced by Reland (Antiq. Sac.) have then their full force. The pseudo-Ignatius, in the Epistle to the Philippians, c. 13, speaks of the Sabbath of the Passover, that is, of the Sabbath which fell in Easter, which in the Christian Church took its beginning in the week preceding the Monday of the resurrection. Socrates, Hist. Ecc. v. 22, speaks of the Sabbath of the feast, τὸ σάββατον τῆς ἑορτῆς.

Once more, it has been maintained to be unimaginable that the first day of the feast should be designated a preparation day. Now if the first day of the feast had been simply and as such denominated a day of preparation, it would have been something strange; for its character as the first feast day infinitely outweighed its character as a day of preparation. But it must be remembered, that whatever was peculiar to the day as the first of the feast, was now already over. For the *rest* of the day its characteristic as the preparation preponderated; or, at least, this characteristic might fitly be taken into consideration, especially as the Evangelist's design was to indicate the *day of the week*, and as such the day was only the παρασκευή. Moreover, while the main end of the statement was a chronological one, we may suppose that it was intended further to pave the way for the record that the Jews, in order that the bodies might not remain on the cross during the Sabbath, came to Pilate and asked that their legs might be broken and they taken away.

Finally, appeal has been made to the Jewish regulation, according to which the first day of the feast might never fall on the second, fourth, and sixth day of the week: nor on the last, the Friday, because in that case the first feast day would have been a mere preparation for the Sabbath. Ideler gave currency to this argument (Handb. der Chronologie i. S. 521); but it has been long since established that that Jewish decision was not extant in Christ's time, or centuries later. After Baronius maintained this, Bochart thoroughly proved it (Hieroz. i. 562, ed. Rosen. 638), Bynæus taking the same view. In the Talmud mention is frequently made of a case in which a feast might fall on the day of preparation; and Abenezra says, "Both in the Mishna and in the Talmud we may see that the Passover might come sometimes on the second, fourth, and sixth day." It may be proved also from Epiphanius, that this regulation was a recent one.

The determination of the hour follows that of the day: "it was about the sixth hour," ὥρα δὲ ὡσεὶ ἕκτη, or, according to Lachmann, ὥρα δὲ ὡς ἕκτη. Mark xv. 15 says, " It was the *third* hour, and they crucified Him." St John does not contradict this; but he supplements it. His statement was not to be isolated; it was in his design to be combined with that of his predecessors. St John had the records of the three Evangelists, in all their details, before his eyes; he never corrects them, but everywhere supplements. The two statements, when combined, furnish the result that the sentence of Pilate and the leading away to crucifixion fell in the *middle*, between the third and the sixth hour, that is, about half an hour after ten. The ὡσεί or ὡς in St John intimates expressly that he did not mean precisely the sixth hour, but that the sixth hour is only referred to as the period in the day. The idea of a contradiction has sprung only from the fact that the two Evangelists were supposed to have substituted the *current* hour in the place of the hour as the *time of the day*. The supposition that among the Jews the day was divided into four periods, each of three hours, rests not only upon the declarations of Maimonides and of the Talmud; it cannot be said that the division of the day was of late origin. That it existed in Christ's time, is made extremely probable by the analogy of the division of the *night* into four periods, each of three hours : comp. Mark xiii. 35; Luke xii. 38. It is still more forcibly suggested by Matt. xx. 3, 4. The reason why there is here a transition from dawn to the third hour, from this to the sixth, and from the sixth to the ninth, can only have been that the day was actually divided into spaces of three hours. We are led to the same result by the fact that, in the whole history of the crucifixion in the Gospels, only the third, sixth, and ninth hours occur, and that generally in the New Testament these hours are much oftener mentioned than the intervening ones. The fourth and the fifth hours, for instance, never occur in the New Testament; and the tenth only once, John i. 40, where it was the highest personal interest of the Evangelist to define with exactitude. Further, this supposition alone explains the fact, that precisely in connection with those hours which mark the quadrants of the day, the ὡσεί or περί is so often used: comp. Matt. xxvii. 46; Luke xxiii. 44; John iv. 6; Acts x. 3, 9. The intermediate time between the third and the sixth hour seems also in the nature of the case the most suitable. If we adhere to the *third* hour, the space is too much narrowed for the transactions before Pilate, and we come in conflict with the statement not merely of Matt. xxvii. 45, but also of Mark himself, xv. 33, that with the *sixth* hour the darkness began. As the darkness coincided with the crucifixion, as it was the answer in act to the crucifixion, and the concomitant mockery of the Jews, we can hardly suppose that Jesus at the commencement of the darkness had been hanging three hours on the cross. On the other hand, if we advance to the *sixth* hour, space is too much narrowed for the crucifixion itself.

Pilate said to the Jews, " Behold your King." Here also we must renounce the notion of mockery, which would so badly have served Pilate's ends; this would ill accord with the disposition of the wretched man, who, drawn hither and thither, this way by his conscience, that way by his interest, certainly was but little inclined to "sport with the King of the Jews." Jesus was assuredly a representative of the Messianic hope of the Jewish nation. According to Pilate's secret presentiment, He was yet more; and he could not, even at the moment of uttering the sentence, hold out to the Jews a more powerful motive to bethink themselves and stay their fury, than this, "Behold your King."

Ver. 15. "But they cried out, Away with him, away with him, crucify him. Pilate saith unto them, Shall I crucify your King? The chief priests answered, We have no king but Cesar."—The double ἆρον here, like the αἶρε, Luke xxiii. 18, Acts xxi. 36, points to Deuteronomy. Gesenius: Formula solennis Deut. ubicunque jubetur supplicium, hæc est בערת הרע מקרבך. Comp. xiii. 6, where it is said of false prophets, and xvii. 7, Sept. καὶ ἐξαρεῖς τὸν πονηρὸν ἐξ ὑμῶν αὐτῶν, xix. 9. The ἆρον was the judicial expression of their demand, which as such bore in it its own motive; σταύρωσον signified the form in which, under present circumstances, the supposed requirement of law might be satisfied.—"We have no king but Cesar:" they renounce their hope, that they may be rid of its hateful representative: comp. Acts xvii. 7. But their word had a deeper significance than they themselves meant; and therefore it was recorded. When they despised Christ their true King, and delivered Him up to death, they ceased, in fact, to be God's people and kingdom, and sank entirely under the power of this world, which God used for the execution of His wrath upon them: comp. Luke xix. 27. Lampe: "They elected Cesar to be their king; by Cesar they were destroyed, and that in the time of the Passover."

Ver. 16. "Then delivered he Him therefore unto them to be crucified. And they took Jesus, and led Him away."—Παρέδωκεν obviously must not be understood of material delivery over; it is equivalent to χαρίζεσθαι εἰς ἀπώλειαν, Acts xxv. 16: comp. ver. 11. A comparison with that passage shows that in the expression there lies a complaint against Pilate. According to the Roman law he acted unjustly, but still more so according to the law of God, which commands the ruler, "Ye shall not respect persons in judgment," Deut. i. 17. Παρέδωκε here is distinct from παρέδωκε in Matt. xxvii. 26. Here it denotes the last and definitive delivery, as it followed upon the solemn judgment; there it was the actual delivery, as it was expressed by the scourging. St Matthew has omitted the attempt of Pilate to undo the sentence which had been actually uttered by the fact of the scourging; he has omitted also the formal pronunciation of the sentence.

Despite the seeming humiliation of Jesus under Pilate, the transactions before him yielded a result which furthered the Divine plan of salvation. Jesus was to die for the sins of the world; but His innocence and righteousness must be attested by the judge himself who condemned Him to death. Pilate's triple "I find no fault in this man;" the declaration that he would be innocent of the blood of this righteous man; the adoption of all means that might have been available to rescue Him, down to the very moment when he pronounced the sentence; the message of his wife;—all these things utterly destroy the very root of the disparaging conclusions that might be drawn from the condemnation of our Lord.

We shall now cast a closing glance over the series of events that took place before Pilate. They present no real difficulty, still less any contradictions. Matthew and Mark are most brief; Luke and John communicate each his peculiar details with considerable minuteness. But in the matter common to all the Evangelists, we have a sure guide by which we can adjust the position of what is peculiar to each, so that the order is never arbitrary or doubtful.

John xviii. 29–32 forms the beginning. Then follows Luke xxiii. 2. The Jews, repelled in their request that Pilate would, without further ado, confirm the judgment they had pronounced, bring their accusation against Jesus, that He stirred the people to sedition, and hindered them from giving tribute to Cesar, saying that He Himself was Christ a King. This accusation was the point of connection for the question, common to all the Evangelists, "Art thou the King of the Jews?" From St John we gather that Pilate put this question to Christ after he had taken Him into the prætorium. The Lord's answer is communicated by the first three Evangelists only in its central words, σὺ λέγεις. St John records previously the explanations which Jesus had given Pilate touching the nature of His kingdom before that decisive answer. Then did Pilate, convinced of His innocence, betake himself with

Jesus to the people outside, and speak for the first time the words afterwards twice repeated, "I find no fault in this man," John xviii. 38; Luke xxiii. 4. The rulers are not pacified by that declaration; they renew, with increased vehemence, their allegations: Luke, ver. 5. Pilate challenges Jesus to defend Himself, but He answers nothing, so that Pilate greatly marvelled, Matt. xiii. 14; Mark, ver. 5. In the accusation of the rulers, mention had been made of Galilee. Pilate takes up that word, hoping that here would be an opening for his own extrication from the embarrassment. He asks (Luke) whether Christ were a Galilean; and on finding that it was so, sends Him to Herod. After Christ's return from Herod, Pilate, according to St Luke, summons the rulers of the people together, and declares a second time, "I find no fault in him;" but offers, that the hateful offence of false accusation and unrighteous judgment might not seem to rest with them, to inflict corporal punishment on Christ, and release Him. So far we follow St Luke. Now all the Evangelists concur. That the people's voice might be raised in favour of the accused, Pilate makes use of the popular cry, heard, according to St Mark, just at this moment, and before the answer to the proposal of chastisement could be given, demanding the release of a prisoner; and he gives them the choice between Christ and Barabbas. The conciseness with which St John touches this momentous event suggests that it had been already exhaustively treated by his predecessors. Between the proposal of Pilate and the answer of the people must be placed the message from his wife, which is peculiar to St Matthew. After this attempt had failed, Pilate a third time, despairing of the matter now, says, "I find no fault in him," Luke, ver. 22, and repeats his earlier proposition to dismiss Jesus with chastisement. But His enemies redouble their clamour, Luke, ver. 23. Still Pilate did not give all up. He declared by a symbolical action, the washing of his hands, that he would release himself from all responsibility. The multitude, regarding nothing but the readiness to fall into their plans which Pilate's words betrayed, declare themselves prepared to take the whole responsibility upon themselves, Matt. xxiv. 25. Then follows the scourging, Matt. ver. 26; Mark xv. 15; John xix. 1. Then come the indignities perpetrated by the soldiers, Matt. vers. 27-31; Mark, vers. 16-20;

John xix. 2, 3. Then Pilate renews his attempts to influence the people in favour of Jesus,—attempts which St John records in vers. 4 seq.; and, finally, when these availed nothing, the formal and final sentence.

THE CRUCIFIXION.
CHAP. XIX. 17–30.

Vers. 17 and 18 sum up briefly what the earlier Evangelists had recorded, to serve as a point of connection for what is peculiar to St John. Then there is a copious narrative of four facts, which either the other Evangelists altogether omit, such as the committal of the Lord's mother to the care of John, or in which St John has made remarkable additions: the superscription on the cross, the division of the garments, and the vinegar offered to drink.

Vers. 17, 18. "And He, bearing His cross, went forth into a place called the place of a skull, which is called in the Hebrew, Golgotha; where they crucified Him, and two other with Him, on either side one, and Jesus in the midst."—We might think, according to ver. 16, that the Jews were the subject of παρέλαβον. But the verbs "delivered" and "led" will not suit the Jews, inasmuch as the Roman punishment could be executed only by Roman instruments; still less "they crucified" (comp. ver. 23), which, however, belongs to the same subject. The agents in these verbs therefore must be those on whom devolved the crucifixion, the Roman soldiers, the same who, according to vers. 1–3, had performed the scourging which was the introduction to the crucifixion. But St John would have expressed himself more precisely, if he had not reckoned on being supplemented out of his predecessors: compare especially Matt. xxvii. 31, where, according to ver. 27, the soldiers of the governor are the subject to "led Him out to be crucified;" Mark, ver. 20, comp. ver. 16.—Executions must take place, according to the Roman as well as the Jewish custom, without the gate: Num. xv. 35; 1 Kings xxi. 13; Acts vii. 38. It signified that "this soul was rooted out from his people:" the culprit executed was cast out of the community of his fellow-citizens. The Epistle to the Hebrews, ch. xiii. 12, 13, grounds upon the fact that Christ suffered without the gate, the exhortation, "Let us go forth therefore unto Him without the camp, bearing His reproach."—'Ἐντεῦθεν καὶ ἐντεῦθεν occurs in the New Testament only here and Rev. xxii. 2. By the middle place assigned to Him, Jesus was marked out as the chief personage. It appears that this place was given Him at the urgency of the Jews. But there was a providence of God concerned in it. A malefactor on the right hand, and a malefactor on the left hand; so was it right for Him who, according to Isa. liii. 12, was reckoned among the transgressors, and was the representative of many sinners.

In his record of the superscription on the cross, vers. 19-22, St John is particularly copious, because he discerned in what Pilate wrote, and in the obstinacy with which he held to it, a remarkable leading of Divine providence. His predecessors had, as St John's copiousness itself might lead us to expect, touched this subject very briefly: compare Matt. xxvii. 37; Mark xv. 26. St Luke alone had mentioned the three languages. St John alone alludes to the contention with the Jews about the change in it.

Ver. 19. "And Pilate wrote a title, and put it on the cross. And the writing was, JESUS OF NAZARETH, THE KING OF THE JEWS."—Τίτλος, titulus, was the judicial name of the superscription. That St John gives the technical term, is in harmony with the significance which he attached to the whole matter. Naturally, the superscription was written and placed on the cross only at Pilate's order. "The King of the Jews:" a voice in Pilate's heart spoke in favour of His being so in reality. He had already done enough at the bidding of the Jews. In the consciousness of his injustice to Christ, he would not further afflict Him by charging Him in His death with making a presumptuous claim. Yet the determinations of men, especially of such men as Pilate, in whom diversified motives and impulses cross each other, are not to be reckoned upon. That this resolution, however, was held firmly, in spite of the counter influence of the Jews, was regarded by St John as resulting from the influence of God, who holds the hearts of men in His hands. Lampe: We believe that Pilate piously wrote this title under a certain Divine impulse.

Ver. 20. "This title then read many of the Jews: for the place where Jesus was crucified was nigh to the city: and it was written in Hebrew, and Greek, and Latin."—The observation that many of the Jews witnessed this, was not intended as a confirmation of the fact; but to intimate that Jesus was proclaimed the King of the Jews before many witnesses.—The three languages were significant to St John, inasmuch as their concurrence testified that the King of the Jews, as such, was at the same time the King of the Gentiles (comp. on i. 50); that through Him the prophecy of Japhet dwelling in the tents of Shem, Gen. ix. 27, and of Shiloh whom the nations would obey, Gen. xlix. 10, were accomplished. Calvin: The Lord thus declared that the time was at hand when He would make everywhere known the name of His Son. As it regards the order of the languages, the Greek precedes the Latin in St Luke also; but there is this difference, that the Hebrew comes last in his account, while in John it takes precedence. The inverted order may be most simply accounted for as due to St John's preference for the Hebrew. Ἑβραϊστί occurs four times in the Gospel, twice in the Apocalypse, but nowhere else in the entire New Testament. Neither of the two Evangelists professes to follow the actual order of the languages. It is probable that the Latin was really the first, as the tongue of the rulers of the land (the reading of Cod. B., Ῥωμαϊστί, Ἑλληνιστί, sprang from the erroneous supposition that John must needs follow the actual order, as in the original title); then the Greek followed, as the actual language of the country; and finally the Hebrew. St Luke placed the Greek first, because he wrote primarily for Greeks (Theophilus); and St John gives it the precedence of the Latin, because it was the more generally diffused language.

Vers. 21, 22. "Then said the chief priests of the Jews to Pilate, Write not, The King of the Jews; but that he said, I am King of the Jews. Pilate answered, What I have written I have written."—The representations of the Jews were made to Pilate, who was not himself present at the crucifixion, before the Lord was led away, when the superscription was just prepared. The whole section, vers. 19-22, does not stand to vers. 17 and 18 in the relation of sequence, but of juxtaposition. The superscription had been written and attached to the cross before Jesus was led forth. Ἀρχιερεῖς is used by Josephus, just as it is by the Evangelists, to designate all priests of the higher rank: comp. e.g. Antiq. xx. 7, 8; Bell. Jud. iv. 3, 6.

But often as the ἀρχιερεῖς are mentioned, the addition, "of the Jews," is found only here. We must seek therefore some special occasion for it. Evidently the high priests of the Jews stood in a peculiar relation to the King of the Jews,—a relation which explains the motive of the high priests. Between them and Christ a strife of life and death for dominion had been going on: comp. on x. 8, Matt. xxi. 28, xxvii. 18, according to which the high priests delivered Jesus for envy. In this rivalry between the high priests of the Jews and the King of the Jews, we may discern the impulse of that bitterness which led them to rob Christ of the honour which had been given Him by the superscription of Pilate.

Pilate's answer, ὃ γέγραφα, γέγραφα, doubtless suggests that obstinacy of character which Philo attributed to him (τὴν φύσιν ἀκαμπής). Still, as the preceding transactions show how little he was able, under the pressure of a guilty conscience, to persist in the object he set out with, we may justly refer his unbending determination in this particular point to the secret overruling of God, which secured that on the cross, where Jesus obtained the right to His dominion, He should be proclaimed King. Lampe: "As this title was written in the three cardinal languages of the world, so in a short space His kingdom was announced to all nations in the same tongues." What is expunged is as good as not written. Hence "I have written" is equivalent to "It must be so."

Vers. 23, 24. "Then the soldiers, when they had crucified Jesus, took His garments, and made four parts, to every soldier a part; and also His coat: now the coat was without seam, woven from the top throughout. They said therefore among themselves, Let us not rend it, but cast lots for it, whose it shall be: that the scripture might be fulfilled, which saith, They parted My raiment among them, and for My vesture they did cast lots. These things therefore the soldiers did."—All the Evangelists mention the division of Christ's garments, because this, of itself a less important circumstance, contained a fulfilment of the prophecy in Ps. xxii. 19. The interest which they all felt in this proceeding sprang from their sure conviction of the inspiration of the Old Testament, which of itself would attach significance to otherwise indifferent coincidences. The relation of the incident to the passage in the psalm was so plain, that the first three Evangelists held it needless to quote it (for the quotation in Matthew is spurious). In his allusion to the coincidence between the prophecy and its fulfilment, John goes more into detail; he testifies that inspiration in the Old Testament extended to the minutest matters, and that the overruling of Divine Providence is in these minute details of special moment. Now, as the individual words of the psalm were requisite to this object, he cites the passage itself. That passage speaks, in its first clause, of the division of the garments; in its second, of the lot cast for the לבוש, the long vesture, after the removal of which the body was left naked; so that it involves a climax: Job xxiv. 7-10; Ps. xxxv. 13; Esther iv. 2. Both were strictly fulfilled. The soldiers divided among themselves the other habiliments of Jesus: the covering of His head, the girdle, Matt. x. 9, Acts i. 13; the shoes, i. 27; the coat, Matt. v. 40; and then cast lots for the outer vesture. That which is here detailed St Mark hints at in xv. 24, "And when they had crucified Him, they parted His garments, casting lots upon them, what every man should take." Accordingly the lot was, at least in part, of such a kind, that one obtained something, while others obtained nothing. Strictly speaking, it is not "what every man should take," but "who should obtain something." As the value of the four parts was unequal, the first distribution also was probably by lot.

That four soldiers were usually employed in these matters by the Romans, is plain from many sources: *e.g.* Acts xii. 4; Philo *in Flaccum*, p. 981. John alone describes the vesture which the Son of man wore. And in harmony with his description, the glorified Christ appeared to him in a similar vesture, ἐνδεδυμένος ποδήρη, Rev. i. 13.—"Throughout," so that the web went through the whole, and no seam was visible. Before ἵνα πληρωθῇ we must interpolate, "This came to pass," or, "They must do this." "This, therefore, the soldiers did," forms of course the transition to the following scene. The act of the soldiers, however, in itself indifferent, would not have been made prominent by such a transition-formula, had not their act stood under the disposal of a higher power, which gave it importance. Apparently all is come to an end with the Redeemer. "The distribution of the garment served," as Luther יין, "for a sign that everything was done with Christ, just as with one who was abandoned, lost, and to be forgotten for ever." The soldiers doubtless, during this act, continued their mockery of the King of the Jews; and the matter, doubtless, derived its attractiveness rather from this pastime than from any material gain. We have here the continuation of the mockery in ch. xix. 2, 3. But the deed itself was under the hand of Providence; and, concurrent with the profane irony, there was a sacred irony upon the irony.

In vers. 25-27, Jesus commits His mother to John. This record is peculiar to the fourth Evangelist: it would seem as if the others regarded it as his property. The question arises, where we are to place the incident; and the most obvious thought is, that it occurred towards the close, as only on the border between life and death would our Lord have committed His mother to any other keeping. Moreover, the μετὰ τοῦτο, in ver. 28, would mean nothing, if the following occurrence were not in *immediate* connection with that we now consider. But that following occurrence, according to the express remark of John, fell in the near neighbourhood of the Saviour's death. Accordingly, the word which Jesus here addressed to His mother and to John must take the fourth place among the Seven Words spoken from the cross: the first, "Father, forgive them;" the second, "This day shalt thou be with Me in Paradise;" the third, "My God, My God, why hast Thou forsaken Me?" The sacred design in the number Seven will be seen, when it is observed that it is obtained here only by combining the records of the four Evangelists; so that their origin was not due to any artistic arrangement on the part of the several writers. Of these seven utterances, four were spoken in the near approach of His death, and had an immediate reference to it.

Ver. 25. "Now there stood by the cross of Jesus His mother, and His mother's sister, Mary the wife of Cleophas, and Mary Magdalene."—According to Matt. xxvii. 55, 56, at a certain distance from the cross of Jesus there stood "many women," among whom Mary Magdalene, Mary the mother of James and Joses, and the mother of the sons of Zebedee, are mentioned. Mark, in ch. xv. 40, 41, names also three women: Mary Magdalene, Mary the mother of the younger James and Joses, and Salome; the same therefore, with this only difference, that the name of James has the appendage τοῦ μικροῦ, and instead of the mother of the sons of Zebedee her name is stated. The appendage, "the less," was rendered necessary by Salome being mentioned instead of the mother of Zebedee's sons. There were only two prominent men with the name of James. The elder of these was the son of Zebedee. Thus Matthew, who introduces the mother of the sons of Zebedee, needed not to define more particularly the lesser James. John omits his own mother, the mention of whom would have been somewhat of an interruption in this scene, and substitutes the mother of Jesus, who forms here the centre of all. The two others are identical with those mentioned by the other Evangelists: this we might be led to expect, by the fact that Matthew and Mark certainly named those only who had a certain claim to be distinguished from the rest. The further difference in the order resulted from the mother of Jesus being mentioned first. She could not be otherwise than at the head; and her sister would naturally follow. Thus Mary Magdalene, who in all the other enumerations of holy women takes precedence, must needs have on this occasion the last place.

To Mary the mother of Jesus was now fulfilled the word of Simeon, Luke ii. 35, "And a sword shall pierce thy own soul also:" the same sword which, according to the prophecy of Zech. xiii. 7, was to smite and pierce the Shepherd of the Lord. Grotius aptly regards her presence at the cross as a prophecy of the Christian boldness which was to be exhibited even by the weaker sex.—" And His mother's sister, Mary the wife of Cleophas:" since we have no instance of actual sisters bearing the same name, the sister must be sister-in-law. The term sister is frequently used for near relations: Tobit viii. 4, 7, vii. 4, compared with ver. 2; Job xlii. 11. The designation had its specific reason, probably in the circumstance that after the death of Cleophas the two families were blended into one. The sons of this Mary are recorded by Matthew and Mark as being James and John. Accordingly Mary could be only the wife of Cleophas, which is indeed the most obvious relationship implied in the term. Cleophas is mentioned here only in the New Testament; but he must be identical with the Alphæus mentioned by Matthew, Mark, and Luke: for James, who in Matt. xxvii. 56, Mark xv. 40, is called the son of Mary, the wife, according to John, of Cleophas, was, according to Matt. x. 3, the son of Alphæus; as also according to Mark iii. 18, Luke vi. 15, Acts i. 13. The difference is to be explained by the fact that the name was originally Aramaic, and took the form חַלְפִּי. Now the ח might be translated variously in the Greek: compare the analogies in the Septuagint, which Gesenius has collected under the letter ח in his Thesaurus. Whether the Cleophas of Luke xxiv. 18 is the same name, may be doubted: it may have been a contraction of Κλεόπατρος. If he had been the same man as is mentioned in Luke vi. 15, the Evangelist would not in the same Gospel have adopted another Greek name. But if the two names were originally the same, that would be a reason why he should choose another Greek form, in order that personal identity might not be supposed to be implied. Mark ii. 14 shows us that the name was a current one: there we have another Alphæus, the father of Matthew. —We are led to suppose that Cleophas or Alphæus was already dead, from the circumstance that Mary is everywhere else indicated by her maternal relation. Supposing him to have died early, we can understand how Mary with her sons came into a close relationship with Joseph the husband of Mary, who would represent a father to them.—The James and John of Mark xv. 40 can be no other than those whom he had mentioned in ch. vi. 3, and with them Judas and Simon, also therefore sons of Mary. If it was not Mary mother of our Lord, but another Mary, who, according to Mark xv. 40, was the mother of these sons, then we must not think, in Mark vi. 3, of literal brothers of Jesus, but only of nearest kindred: comp., concerning the brothers of Jesus, the remarks on ch. ii. 12, vii. 3.—Many suppose that four, and not three women, are mentioned here. The (unnamed) sister of the mother of Jesus is supposed to be Salome the mother of John, and Mary wife of Cleophas to be a different person. But that this is a mere learned device, is rendered exceedingly probable by the simple circumstance, that the Christian Church has from the beginning regarded them as three in number. Where, in the earlier Evangelists, a great number of women had been previously mentioned, and then individuals are specified, three, and never four, are alluded to in connection with the cross. Hence we may naturally expect that here also three, and not four, are alluded to.

Only on the supposition that Mary wife of Cleophas was the sister of our Lord's mother, can we account for the postponement of Mary Magdalene, who everywhere else takes the first place among the women, as uniformly as Simon Peter takes the first among the Apostles. The καί also could be omitted only if there was no ambiguity. It could not possibly have been wanting if a description had preceded which required that the name of the same person should follow to make it clear. If the sister of the mother of Jesus and the wife of Cleophas are two persons, then the former lacks a name, and the latter is introduced without a reason given for the introduction. Nor is there ever given the slightest intimation of a relationship betwixt John and our Lord. The manner in which our Lord committed to him His mother leads to the conclusion, that a relationship of affinity did *not* subsist between the two. Finally, among the three Marys, here designedly placed in juxtaposition, we are not justified in interposing another, especially such a characterless and indefinite personage as this " sister of the mother of Jesus," about whom neither the earlier Evangelists nor St John give us any the slightest information.

Ver. 26. "When Jesus therefore saw His mother, and the disciple standing by whom He loved, He saith unto His mother, Woman, behold thy son!"—The fact that the women in Matt. xxvii. 55 looked on generally from afar, does not exclude the supposition that it was permitted to the mother of Jesus to approach nearer to the cross, especially as the Lord's mother did not belong to the circle of the women mentioned there. The address "Woman," occurring also in ch. ii. 4, is explained by Matt. xii. 48, where Jesus says emphatically to those who announced the arrival of His mother, "Who is My mother?" and intimated that, in the things pertaining to His vocation, into which His mother would intrude, the relation between them altogether receded. Thus here also the term *woman* suggests that at this crisis His relation to His mother retreated altogether in comparison of the high commission given Him by His Father to redeem a sinful world. We must carry this, however, no further than as teaching us that no such relation must hinder us from the discharge of our duty. We must not forget that, in the latest moments of His earthly existence, He, as a pattern to us, cared for His mother. He had honoured His Father by childlike obedience, in deference to the fourth commandment; and He honours His mother by careful provision for her external need.—" Behold thy son" presupposes that Mary had no sons besides Jesus. To honour parents by faithful care of them, is not merely the duty, but the privilege also, of children; and if she had had other children, Jesus would have infringed upon that privilege by committing His mother to John. He would have left His disciples but a poor pattern of the sanctification of the relations appointed of Heaven, if He had thus absolutely placed Himself in independence of those relations. The duty of the sons would have remained, even if the supposed brothers of Jesus had at that time been in a state of unbelief. Moreover, this supposition is based on a false exposition of ch. vii. 3: certainly the " brethren of Jesus" are a few weeks afterwards, Acts i. 14, in the number of the believers; and He who knew what was in man, who saw the future developments of the character of Peter and Judas from the beginning, would have fallen under the reproach of shortsightedness, if He had taken their mother from them on the ground of their temporary unbelief, and committed her for ever to another. The actual mother of the "brethren" of Jesus, Mary the wife of Cleophas, had been mentioned just before.—On the words of Christ to His mother and John, the Berlenberg Bible justly says: " Thus it is not opposed to the mind of Christ, when we extend the commandment for parents and children further than its mere letter."—Our Lord's design was not to provide for John, but to provide for His mother. He begins with her, and gives her a son, because as a feeble woman she needed that protection; and when He said to John, "Behold thy mother," this meant only that he was to pay her, from that time forward, the respect due to a mother. The result shows this. Mary does not take John, but John takes Mary to his house. Quesnel's remark springs from an entire inversion of the order: " The holy Virgin receives all Christians as her children in the person of John. This property over us gives us the right and the confidence to place all our interests in her hands."

Ver. 27. " Then saith He to the disciple, Behold thy mother! And from that hour that disciple took her unto his own home."—" From that hour" must be taken literally; but " to his own house" intimates that Mary was from that time the honoured companion of his home. The too literal view assumes that John had a house in Jerusalem, while ch. xxi. 1 shows that His abiding home was Galilee; and further, that he at once led our Lord's mother to his own house, which is contrary to ver. 34, and in itself unnatural. Bengel's remark is wrong here: "The sword had now sufficiently penetrated the soul of Mary: now she is guarded against seeing and hearing the most bitter things, the darkness, the abandonment of God [but both had already taken place], the death." It is the duty and the right of the nearest friends to abide until the last breath. It would have been severity towards His mother, and towards the disciple whom He loved, had He sent them both away.

In vers. 28-30, we have the potion of vinegar which was given to our Lord. It was customary to provide for those who were to be crucified a malefactor's potion, which should mitigate their pains, and still their horrible thirst. The vessel containing such a drink was, according to ver. 29, already there before Jesus said, "I thirst." Matthew, in ch. xxvii. 34, describes the potion *theologically* as vinegar mingled with gall, because he sees in it a fulfilment of prophecy, Ps. lxix. 21, "They gave Me also gall for My meat; and in My thirst they gave Me vinegar to drink." This description of the potion is a delicate and veiled quotation. As to its physical nature, it says—as every one must see who admits the reference to Ps. lxix. 21 according to which the words "gall and vinegar" must have, as it were, quotation marks—only this, that the potion was at once sour and bitter. Mark, who everywhere devotes a special observation to externalities, describes the potion in its physical quality, "And they gave Him to drink wine mingled with myrrh." The myrrh was designed to make the drink bitter, and rob it of its flavour. Galen (in Wetstein) says of myrrh, ἔχει πικρίαν. Accordingly, we must regard the wine as bitter vinegar. This drink was offered to Jesus by the soldiers before the crucifixion, but He rejected it: "And having tasted, He would not drink," Matt. xxvii. 34. It is significant here that the Lord first tasted: this pertains to the reason for rejecting it. In the bitter and sour wine, the entire relation of the ungodly to Jesus was exhibited; to Jesus, who through them and for them suffered. When He repelled this drink, He uttered His condemnation of this position, and rejected it as unworthy of Him. But this rejection can be viewed only as preliminary; and it intimated that an *acceptance* of it was afterwards to follow. Jesus, according to the psalm, must *actually drink*, but the circumstances stated there were not yet in existence. It is said, " In My *thirst* they gave Me vinegar to drink." Thus the thirst must first be experienced. Luke mentions the vinegar in ch. xxiii. 36, 37. According to his statement, the soldiers mockingly offered Jesus during the crucifixion the vinegar as His royal table-wine; and made much of the misrelation in which the malefactor's potion stood to His assumed royal dignity. This scene is peculiar to Luke. Matthew mentions the vinegar a second time in ch. xxvii. 48, " And straightway one of them ran, and took a sponge, and filled it with vinegar, and put it on a reed, and gave Him to drink." Mark xv. 36 is parallel. According to both, this incident followed hard upon the word which Jesus uttered about the ninth hour, " My God, My God, why hast Thou forsaken Me ?" and His death immediately followed. This is the same occurrence which John here touches, as immediately preceding the death. He adds the important clause which first places the whole incident in its true light, that they gave Him this to drink in consequence of His cry, "I thirst."

Ver. 28. "After this, Jesus knowing that all things were now accomplished, that the Scripture might be fulfilled, saith, I thirst."—The knowledge of Christ that all things were now fulfilled, was the motive which impelled Him to introduce that one last circumstance still wanting to the perfect fulfilment of Scripture. The question whether " all things" refers generally to the work which Christ was to accomplish, or to the predictions of it contained in the Old Testament, tends to divide things internally united. The work to be done by Christ was, in its fundamental principles, perfectly foreannounced and described in the Old Testament. That reference to the prophecies is not to be excluded, is shown by the following words, "that the Scripture might be fulfilled." So also in Luke xxii. 37 : " For I say unto you, that this that is written must yet be accomplished ($\tau\epsilon\lambda\epsilon\sigma\theta\hat{\eta}\nu\alpha\iota$) in Me, And He was reckoned among the transgressors : for the things concerning Me have an end." So also Luke xviii. 31, Rev. xvii. 17, which set aside the remark of Bengel, "τελέω refers to things, τελειόω to holy Scripture." The real distinction between the two verbs is this, that τελειοῦν is the stronger, and marks perfect fulfilment. Τελειοῦν is related to τελεῖν, as לְכַלּוֹת, in order to fulfil, *entirely* to fulfil, Jeremiah's word in 2 Chron. xxxvi. 22, is related to לְמַלֹּאות, to fulfil the word of the Lord through Jeremiah, in ver. 21. That, on the other hand, reference to the work committed by God to the Son of man, to all that which He had undertaken to do and suffer, is not to be excluded, needs no other proof than that this was the obvious interpretation of the words. Moreover, we must observe the relation in which the τετέλεσται here and in ver. 30 stands to the last word of Ps. xxii., עָשָׂה, "He hath done it," corresponding with the relation of "My God, My God, why hast Thou forsaken Me" to the *beginning* of that psalm. The *work of God* must be regarded, therefore, as what was *finished:* comp. ch. xvii. 4, "I have finished the work which Thou gavest Me to do."

"All things" receives a limitation in what follows: one point was in reserve, one thing which was yet wanting to the full fulfilment of Scripture, and therefore to the accomplishment of the work of God; hence all things with the exception of one point. The idea is evidently this: Jesus knew that all was accomplished, that one thing only failed as yet. In order to bring in the fulfilment of this one thing, He uttered the word "I thirst;" and when this was also fulfilled, He said again, "It is finished."—According to John, Jesus uttered the word "I thirst" in order to introduce a fulfilment of Scripture, the word of Ps. lxix. 21. To such a theological reason we are independently led by the declaration of the Evangelist. There can be no doubt that the "I thirst" was literally true. The most burning thirst was wont to torment the crucified. But in the immediate approach of death, our Lord would not assuredly have first desired to drink; He could not possibly have dedicated yet one of His sacred seven words to the relief of a mere bodily craving. That Jesus uttered the word in order to the fulfilment of a passage in the psalm is a stumbling-block only to those who, on the one hand, have surrendered the principle of the high import of the Old Testament, which Christ regarded as Divine down to its ἰῶτα and κεραία, and who, on the other hand, fail to discern that that word of the psalm utters a general truth, so that the incident retains its importance even for those who altogether look away from the psalm itself. That passage most luminously exhibits the position which the world assumes to the Sufferer, to righteousness suffering through the guilt of the world. In ver. 20 we read, " Reproach hath broken My heart, and I am full of heaviness; and I looked for some to take pity, but there was none; and for comforters, but I found none." After the enemies had brought the Sufferer so low that He was broken down in body and soul, they ought to have been amazed at the work of their hands, and their hatred should have turned to inward pity. But they give the Sufferer, instead of the refreshing potion, gall and vinegar. The situation here presented is dependent on the passage in the psalm, and yet at the same time independent of it. Jesus says in His suffering, which He endured for the world, "I thirst." What do they give Him in His thirst? Vinegar. This potion, presented to malefactors, was a benefit; presented to righteousness suffering incarnate, it was a harsh and bitter insult. To close His career with such a symbolical action was all the more appropriate to our Lord, inasmuch as what then took place was not an isolated thing, but reflected the attitude which the world would assume to Him in succeeding ages. The more vividly we see, in our own time, the counterpart of this offer of vinegar, the less reason have we to deal critically with it here as a symbolical action, and the less propriety is there in evading it by all kinds of forced exegesis. The better way is to turn it all to our profit. Quesnel: " See there the mortifications and amenities which men have to offer Him who gives His life for them. A vessel of vinegar for the blood which He shed for them. After this, can we complain of the ingratitude of men, and of the small consolation which we sometimes receive from our own friends?"

Ver. 29. " Now there was set a vessel full of vinegar: and they filled a sponge with vinegar, and put it upon hyssop, and put it to His mouth."—Meyer's remark here is erroneous: "Ὄξος is sour soldiers' wine, *posca*. John says nothing of the stupefying draught which Jesus rejected." It is against the soldiers' wine which expositors have invented, that besides the vessel with vinegar, the sponge also and the reed were in readiness. This shows that the provision was made for malefactors. Of any " stupefying draught" the other three Evangelists are quite unconscious. The potion must have been another and a worse one than mere soldiers' wine, otherwise the design for which our Saviour said "I thirst" would not have been accomplished, and Ps. lxix. 21 would be quite unsuitable. The necessary consequence of Meyer's view, "In Ps. lxix. 21 the offering of vinegar is the act of scorn and wickedness, which does not suit here," is sufficient, at the same time, for its refutation.—Instead of the reed, κάλαμος, in Matthew, John mentions specifically the hyssop. This would have been a refinement, if he had not viewed the hyssop with a theological eye. It is striking also, that instead of κάλαμος ὑσσώπου, he says barely ὑσσώπος. This of itself gives us reason to suppose that here there is an allusion to a passage of the Old Testament in which hyssop is mentioned, but not the reed of hyssop. The hyssop is in the Mosaic law (comp. Heb. ix. 13), and in Ps. li. 9, which comes strictly into consideration here, "Purge me with hyssop, and I shall be clean," the symbol of expiation. (Comp. my Commentary on the Psalms, and Egypt and the Books of Moses.) To the Evangelist the hyssop with the sponge of vinegar, the hyssop of *mockery*, forms a memorable contrast to the hyssop of *atonement;* and he regards it as a Divine arrangement that the reed was no other than a branch of hyssop. Celsius gives us the most complete explanations of the natural history of hyssop (Hierobotan. i. 407). In the Talmudic tract Succa, hyssop is mentioned among the branches which were used at the Feast of Tabernacles. Abulfadli (in Celsius) says that it reached nearly the height of an ell. The cross being so low, this was sufficient.

Ver. 30. "When Jesus therefore had received the vinegar, He said, It is finished: and He bowed His head, and gave up the ghost."—That was accomplished which the prophecies of the Old Testament had foreshown as the work of Christ, to accomplish which was incumbent on Christ in His state of humiliation, incumbent on the *Son of man:* comp. Luke xviii. 31, "All things that are written by the prophets concerning the *Son of man* shall be *accomplished*" (τελεσθήσεται). The limitation to the state of humiliation is obvious, from the fact that our Lord uttered it on the *cross*, where that humiliation had its end. "It is finished," peculiar to John, forms the foundation for Luke's last word of our Lord, "Father, into Thine hands I commend

My spirit." Lampe: "For the Father could not keep back from His bosom one who had so perfectly done the will of His Father." To these last words, as recorded by Luke, corresponds the " gave up" here, παρέδωκε. " Gave up," without mention of Him to whom, is as it were an express *allusion* to that last word, in which the imperfect expression finds its interpretation. Bengel well says: "There are seven words in the four Evangelists, all of which not one has recorded. Whence it is plain that these books are, as it were, four voices, which produce symphony when heard together."

Chap. xix. 31–37.

The Apostle relates here what ensued after the death of Jesus, and before He was taken down from the cross. John is silent as to the miraculous natural phenomena which were connected with the death of Christ, because he had nothing of his own to add to them. He records only what the others had omitted, that the legs of Jesus were not broken, like those of the malefactors crucified with Him; that one of the soldiers pierced His side with a lance; and that forthwith blood and water came thereout: three facts to which he assigns a high importance.

Ver. 31. "The Jews therefore, because it was the preparation, that the bodies should not remain upon the cross on the Sabbath-day (for that Sabbath-day was an high day), besought Pilate that their legs might be broken, and that they might be taken away."—According to Deut. xxi. 23, the bodies of persons suspended were to be taken down and buried the same day, and, " as we may see in the application of this law, Josh. viii. 29, x. 26 seq., before sundown" (Keil). Abhorrence of the offence was to be shown in this, that the delinquents were utterly destroyed as soon as possible, that the land might be no longer made unclean by them. That this law was in force at this time we see in Josephus, although, in a polemical interest, he assigns it to a wrong cause—the care for burial. He says, De Bell. Jud. iv. 5, 2, of the Idumeans: "They went to such a pitch of impiety, that they cast them out unburied [those whom they had slain], although the Jews were so anxious about burial that they were in the habit of taking down those crucified by the visitation of law, and burying them before the sun went down." If the new light of a common day was not to look upon the corpse of a malefactor, it is obvious that they would be especially solicitous when that new day was a *holy* day. In this case, the following day was not merely an ordinary Sabbath; it was one which derived a special dignity from its being also one of the days of the feast. The utter want of conscience on the part of the rulers was paralleled only by their excessive scrupulosity in such externalities. This is the common characteristic of hypocrites.

Παρασκευή here also is the proper name of the sixth day of the week. If it were a term that might indifferently designate the preparation of feasts, or this feast, there must have been an addition τοῦ σαββάτου. The words "for that Sabbath-day was a high day" have been made to serve as the basis of an argument that this Sabbath was at the same time the first day of the feast; for only that day could be great, like the seventh and last, because these two were termed holy in the law, but not every day of the feast. It is not said, however, that the day was great as a *feast-day*; it rose above the level of ordinary Sabbaths, because to its sanctity as the Sabbath there was superadded its dignity as being also a feast-day, though not one of the holiest days of the feast. The passage proves rather the reverse of these conclusions. The day spoken of here could not be the first day of the feast: for in the case of this day, as the most important day of the whole year, its festal quality would preponderate over its Sabbath quality; while here, inversely, its quality as a Sabbath is pre-eminent, and its quality as a feast-day only something superadded. In one point alone, in reference to its *rest*, the Sabbath outweighed the first feast-day. But this point comes not here into consideration. Here the question is only the sanctity and festal character of the day. In the interest of a higher festal character, the question of rest on the first day of the Passover would not have been so rigorously regarded. The Passover was the root of all the feasts, and was therefore instituted before the Sabbath, yea before the covenant on Sinai: compare, for the dignity of the Passover, on ch. v. 1. This, therefore, stands irreversibly firm. If the following day was the first feast-day, it would have been so described, and not as the Sabbath.

The *crurifragium* was among the Romans of itself a distinct punishment. The reason of its connection with the crucifixion is to be sought in the idea of a compensation. Instead of the longer continuance of the agony, there was a compromise in its greater acuteness. The breaking of the legs generally issued in death (Amm. Marc. xiv. 9 speaks of those *qui fractis cruribus occiduntur*), and would therefore, in the case of such as were already exhausted by the torments of crucifixion, soon hasten death. From the circumstance that the converted malefactor had to undergo this punishment, Bengel draws the conclusion: " Even to the converted there often remain sorrows, and an external bodily misery equal to that of the ungodly."

Vers. 32, 33. " Then came the soldiers, and brake the legs of the first, and of the other which was crucified with him. But when they came to Jesus, and saw that He was dead already, they brake not His legs."—Jesus, according to ver. 30, had said in the presence of the soldiers, " It is finished," had then bowed His head, and given up the ghost. Looking therefore at John alone, we should not infer that the soldiers came to Jesus with the design of breaking His legs. We are led to the opposite by marking that they did not come to Jesus until they had broken the legs of the two malefactors. Jesus was the chief person. If they had originally the intention of breaking His legs, they would have made their beginning with Him; or if they took the persons in order, Jesus must have come between the two in the operation. Their leaving the natural order must have had a specific reason. Accordingly, the note of the soldiers seeing that Jesus was already dead, can only mean that this confirmed their previous observations. A comparison of the other Evangelists leads to the same result. According to these, the centurion, and " those who were with him," were deeply impressed by the death of Jesus, Matt. xxvii. 54, Mark xv. 39, Luke xxiii. 47.—The intention of the piercing could not have been to ascertain the reality of Christ's death; for the soldier was no professor of medical jurisprudence. It could only have been to hasten the death, in case it had not, as circumstances seemed to indicate, taken place; and, as His death was absolutely probable, in a manner less rough than that of breaking the legs. With this design, the thrust would naturally be directed to the *heart*; for there, it was well known, was the seat of mortal wounds. Galen (in Wetstein) says: "That the piercing of the heart necessarily brings death, is among things universally acknowledged." Sextus Empiricus: " Piercing the heart is a cause of immediate death." So also Quinctilian.— That blood and water came forth (Lampe : " We must hold to the letter: blood first flowed, then water, so limpid that it might be seen by John and others around to be different from blood"), seems by what follows to have been something extraordinary, indeed miraculous. We might therefore expect that analogous facts are not to be found; nor is it strange that the *responsa* of the medical faculty in reference to our passage are so unsatisfactory. What Tholuck adduces goes far enough to show the conditions in human bodies which, under peculiar circumstances, might bring about the result here recorded. If more could be done, it would be possibly a disadvantage to the design of the Evangelist.

Ver. 35. "And he that saw it bare record, and his record is true; and he knoweth that he saith true, that ye might believe."—That the assurance refers to all the three points in the preceding, and not to the third alone—that the bones of Jesus were not broken, that His side was pierced, and that blood and water came forth,—is shown by the connection with vers. 36, 37, which, by γάρ, refer also to the two former incidents. But the Evangelist had the *third* matter in view pre-eminently; for the assurance is directly connected with it. The two former facts were so simply material, and of themselves probable, that the assurance, as referring to them alone, would seem almost superfluous. In connection with the *third*, on the contrary, deception of an excited fancy might easily be asserted. There was something unusual, under these circumstances something miraculous: that in the Lord's case blood and water came forth, symbols of the atonement and justification which His death obtained for us, was to the Apostle sufficient reason for saying so emphatically that he, the reporter, was not a *credulus*, but a *fidelis*. The assurance designedly takes a triple form. On ὁ ἑωρακώς Bengel says: " Hence it appears that John clave inseparably to the body of Jesus after His death." In regard to the perfect μεμαρτύρηκε, comp. on ch. i. 34. Testimony is called *true*, in opposition to a statement which rests upon delusion or lie. "Ἵνα introduces the design of the assurance so expressly given in the preceding words. There must be supplemented from the context, "This I say," or, "These things are written:" comp. ch. xx. 31. In the same elliptical way, ἵνα is used in ch. i. 22, "Who art thou? (we ask thee,) in order that we may give an answer." Πιστεύειν is used for believing generally, not for believing in the truth of a fact stated: comp. ch. xx. 8 and ver. 31, where, instead of the simple believing as here, we read, "Believe that Jesus is the Christ." Πιστεύειν not seldom occurs in John with this comprehensive meaning: ch. i. 7, 51, xi. 15.

Ver. 36. "For these things were done, that the scripture should be fulfilled, A bone of Him shall not be broken."—Γάρ justifies the connection which the preceding words established between the truth of the recorded facts and *believing*. Ταῦτα refers to those preceding facts generally. One of these, however, is prominently stated: "They brake not His legs." This was brought about in the providence of God, who caused Jesus to die before the soldiers came to break the bones, that in this way an utterance of the Old Testament might be fulfilled. This correspondence between prophecy and fulfilment is itself a strong motive to faith. By *scripture* is here meant, as in ch. xiii. 18, Mark xii. 10, xv. 28, an individual passage of Scripture: it is equivalent to τὸ γεγραμμένον τοῦτο, Luke xx. 17, 37. Scripture is whatsoever is written and is found in the Book simply. "That the scripture might be fulfilled" is equivalent to "that what is written might come to pass." John was not looking at the passage, Ps. xxxiv. 21: for there the bones of a *living* righteous man are spoken of; there the singular ὀστοῦν is not used; and the αὐτοῦ is wanting. We expect in relation to this something beyond what is common to all saints. The allusion was rather to two passages which treat of the paschal lamb: Ex. xii. 46, "Neither shall ye break a bone thereof," Sept. καὶ ὀστοῦν οὐ συντρίψετε ἀπ' αὐτοῦ; and Num. ix. 12, "Nor break any bone of it." John easily substitutes συντριβήσεται for συντρίψετε, συντρίψουσι, that their application might be more obvious to the Antitype, in regard to which the Evangelist makes most prominent the Divine causality. The view that the paschal lamb was typical of Christ is not found only in 1 Cor. v. 7. In ch. i. 29 of John's Gospel, Christ is the Antitype of the paschal lamb: ch. vi. 4 also points to

Christ as the true Paschal Lamb. Jesus declared Himself to be the Paschal Lamb, in that He withdrew before His enemies until He could die at the Passover; as well as by instituting the Supper in the place of the Jewish feast.

For a clear apprehension of the connection between this Mosaic ordinance and the fact we now consider, it is necessary that we should look at the design and significance of that ordinance. There can be no doubt that it was intended to obviate the profanation of the paschal lamb. No violence was to be offered to it: nothing which might tend to obliterate the distinction between the all-holy sacrifice of the Lord and a common sacrificial animal. In Micah iii. 3, the greediness is described of those who, not content with eating the flesh, broke the bones asunder that they might find out everything eatable. Such greediness was to be excluded from the holy meal. Ex. xii. 46 leads us to a similar reason of the ordinance: "Neither shall ye break a bone thereof" is there preceded by, "In *one* house shall it be eaten; thou shalt not carry forth aught of the flesh abroad out of the house." Both fall under the same law: the lamb was to be treated with sacred respect, and not as a common sacrifice. So also in Num. ix. 12, "They shall leave none of it until the morning, nor break any bone of it." The parallel clause leads to the same reason of the ordinance. If any part of the holy lamb remained over, it was not to be used as common food, nor given to other persons; it must be burnt. If we thus discern the reason of the Mosaic ordinance, the passage we now consider has some light shed on it. It was the same divine decorum which forbade all indignity to be offered to the typical paschal lamb, and hindered all indignity from being offered to the Antitype. To the distinction between the typical lamb and common sacrifices in relation to the breaking of the bones, corresponds the distinction between Christ and the two malefactors.

Ver. 37. "And again another scripture saith, They shall look on Him whom they pierced."—The passage is Zech. xii. 10. For an exposition of its meaning and its connection with the fact before us, we refer to the Christology (vol. iii. Clark's Trans.). John here contemplates only the *piercing* (ἐξεκέντησαν, as here also in Rev. i. 7: see on that passage), not the penitent looking at the Pierced One, which referred to another time. The Evangelist had recorded three facts in the preceding verses, as suited to work faith. Only in regard to two does he, in vers. 36, 37, suggest how fitted they were to produce this effect, as realizing what, according to the Old Testament, was to befall the Christ. In regard to the third fact, the issuing of water and blood is without such an intimation. The reason of this absence cannot have been that the Apostle attached less importance to it. We saw in ver. 35, that it was upon this event that John laid the chief stress. The reason was rather, that the Evangelist regarded the import of this event as perfectly plain, so that he could leave the reader to discern it for himself; even as the Christian Church of all ages has detected it without difficulty. This reason for silence may be supported by many parallels: for example, the three Evangelists omit referring to Ps. xxii. in their record of the distribution of the garments; and John, in ver. 18, does not quote Isa. liii. 12. Blood and water flowing from the side of the Redeemer dead upon the cross: what that signifies, no Christian heart can ever doubt. The *blood* is the blood of atonement, which is exhibited in Isa. liii. as the centre of the work of redemption: comp. on ch. vi. 53. The *water* signifies, in the symbolism of the Old Testament, the forgiveness of sins, which is shown to have its ground in the blood of atonement, by its being placed after that blood. We have the interpretation in 1 John i. 7, " The blood of Jesus Christ cleanseth us from all sin," where the cleansing pertains to the water. So also in 1 John v. 6: " This is He who came by water and blood, even Jesus Christ; not by water only, but by water and blood :" water without blood would have been forgiveness without satisfaction, according to the doctrine of those who regard the death of Christ as a mere event or concomitant. Rev. i. 5 is also parallel, " Who loved us, and washed us from our sins in His blood;" and vii. 14, " Who washed their garments in the blood of the Lamb :" the washing signifies the attainment of the forgiveness of sins, through the appropriation of the blood of Christ. These parallels are of all the greater importance, as they are John's own : at the same time there is a reference to the two sacraments of the Christian Church. The water signifies baptism, which is connected with the forgiveness of sins, comp. on ch. iii. 5; the blood points to the holy communion, comp. on ch. vi. 53.

THE BURIAL OF JESUS.

CHAP. XIX. 38–42.

It is peculiar to John's account of this, that Joseph of Arimathea came forward publicly with his confession of Christ, which Mark in the τολμήσας, xv. 43, had only slightly intimated; and that Nicodemus co-operated with Joseph in the interment of Jesus. He further gives the particulars of the spices, the statement that the sepulchre was in the neighbourhood of the garden, and that this was the reason why they placed Him there. The rest is simply taken up from the earlier Evangelists, in order to add these additional traits. "Wonderful power of the death of Christ!" cries Quesnel, "which gives courage to avow Him in His deepest humiliation, to those who, when He was performing His wonderful works, came to Him only in secret."

Ver. 38. "And after this, Joseph of Arimathea (being a disciple of Jesus, but secretly for fear of the Jews) besought Pilate that he might take away the body of Jesus: and Pilate gave him leave. He came therefore, and took the body of Jesus."—Ἄρῃ, with its allusion to ἀρθῶσιν, ver. 31, can refer only to the taking the body from the cross, not to the removing of the body already taken down. The καθελών of Mark xv. 46, Luke xxiii. 53, points to the same conclusion. Pilate had given orders that the legs of the crucified should be broken, and they taken down and removed. The soldiers, acting on their own responsibility, had failed to break the legs of Jesus. The removal of the body, as having that condition connected with it, they durst not attempt themselves or permit to others, notwithstanding the piercing of His side, until Pilate gave permission. This permission Joseph sought, and Pilate conceded it, after having called the centurion, and made satisfactory inquiries as to the actual death of our Lord: comp. Mark xv. 44, 45. The article before the name of Joseph, the omission of which in some MSS. sprang from an inconsiderate comparison of the other Evangelists, points to the fact that Joseph was already known from the records of those predecessors of John, who introduce him formally, as one altogether unknown before: Matt. ver. 57; Mark, ver. 43; Luke, ver. 50. Matthew heads the list of his qualifications with his riches, ἄνθρωπος πλούσιος, with allusion to Isa. liii. 9, where the prophet represents the exaltation of Christ as beginning with His being buried with a *rich man*, instead of being entombed, according to His enemies' intention, with malefactors. Arimathea is now Ramlah, eight hours' journey from Jerusalem (v. Raumer, S. 217). That Joseph was a native of Arimathea, but a resident of Jerusalem, illustrates his position as a member of the council, Mark xv. 43, Luke xxiii. 51, and the fact of his having a sepulchre in the city, Matt. ver. 60. But the circumstance, that the sepulchre had never been used before, indicates that his removal to Jerusalem had taken place only a short time before. Matthew alone tells us expressly, that the sepulchre in which Jesus was placed belonged to Joseph. The correspondence between "of Arimathea" and the new grave, serves to anticipate and confirm that statement. Probably the consideration that he had a new grave in the neighbourhood of the place of crucifixion, and his reflection upon the hand of Providence in this, was the impulse to his coming out from his previous concealment. He had hitherto been only *in secret* a disciple of Jesus. It is true that, according to Luke, ver. 51, he had not consented to the deed of the Jews; but he had known how to clothe his protest in such a form as to avoid being known as a disciple of Christ. Lampe: Non directe, atque eapropter invalide: indirectly, and therefore ineffectually.

Ver. 39. " And there came also Nicodemus (which at the first came to Jesus by night), and brought a mixture of myrrh and aloes, about an hundred pound weight."—" Who came to Jesus by night" (comp. on ch. vii. 50) corresponds with what had been said about Joseph in ver. 38. Lampe: " They had been fellows in the imbecility and fear of faith; now they are fellows in the fortitude of love." The myrrh and aloes point to Ps. xlv. 9. There it is said of the apparel of the great King, in the day of the joy of His heart, in the day of His espousals to the Gentile world (comp. ch. xii. 32: " And I, if I am lifted up, will draw all men unto Me"), that all His garments " were of myrrh and aloes"—nothing but myrrh and aloes: they were so fragrant, that they might have been nothing else. The figure of the psalm becomes here incorporated in a symbol. In respect to the abundance of the material, comp. 2 Chron. xvi. 14. There it is said, that Asa was laid " in the bed, which was *filled* with sweet odours, and divers kinds of spices."

Ver. 40. " Then took they the body of Jesus, and wound it in linen clothes with the spices, as the manner of the Jews is to bury."—The ὀθόνια, linen clothes, with which the whole body was enveloped, are to be distinguished from the κειρίαις in ch. xi. 44, these having been mere bands, which pertained only to the hands and feet, and which were there connected with the winding-sheet. Only in the case of our Lord are ὀθόνια mentioned : comp. Luke xxiv. 12 ; John xx. 6, 7.

Ver. 41. " Now in the place where He was crucified there was a garden; and in the garden a new sepulchre, wherein was never man yet laid."—The place must naturally be taken with a wide meaning. The circumstance that the sepulchre had never been used before is made so emphatically prominent by the Evangelists (Matthew, " in his new sepulchre;" Luke xxiii. 53, " wherein yet never man lay :" John takes " new" from Matthew, and " never man yet" from Luke), that it must have been regarded as an important fact. They discerned in it a Divine hand, so ordering it that the Prince of life was never laid in a place of corruption. Something analogous we may note in the " new cart," with the " two milch kine on which there hath come no yoke," whereon the ark of the covenant was to be brought back from the Philistines, 1 Sam. vi. 7.

Ver. 42. " There laid they Jesus therefore, because of the Jews' preparation-day ; for the sepulchre was nigh at hand."—The meaning is not that they intended afterwards to remove Him again, but that, under these circumstances, the nearness of the sepulchre decided in its favour ; whereas otherwise there would have arisen a keen emulation among the disciples of Christ. The reason for choosing the nearest place, was simply the proximity of the Sabbath. How entirely different would it have been if the following day, beginning with the evening, is regarded as the first day of the Passover ! Thus the interment of Jesus would have been almost simultaneous with the slaying of the paschal lamb.—In the Divine care of the body of Jesus, there has always been observed a type and pledge of God's care of the Christian Church, when brought to the lowest point. The circumstances were all the more significant, as Isaiah in ch. liii. had made the honourable burial of the servant of God the beginning of His exaltation.

CHAPTER XX.

THE RESURRECTION.

THE SEVENTH GROUP OF THE WHOLE GOSPEL; THE THIRD OF ITS SECOND PART: THE RESURRECTION.

IN ch. xx. 1-18, John learns in the empty sepulchre to believe in the resurrrection, and the risen Lord appears to Mary Magdalene.

Ver. 1. "The first day of the week cometh Mary Magdalene early, when it was yet dark, unto the sepulchre, and seeth the stone taken away from the sepulchre."—The plural τὰ σάββατα, which often occurs in the Sept. and in Josephus as well as in the New Testament, was supposed to point to the high dignity of the day. It is the *pluralis excellentiæ*, of such wide use in Hebrew. The Sabbath is termed in Isa. lviii. 13 "the holy of the Lord." From a similar cause it sprang that all days of the week were distinguished by their relation to the Sabbath (the one day, or first day, μία, of the Sabbath, and so forth); and that the Sabbath, for instance in Luke xviii. 12, embodied in itself the whole week. It is incorrect to say that the Sabbath of itself signified the week. The first day of the week was peculiarly appropriate for the resurrection, inasmuch as on it the creation of the world had begun, and *light* had been brought into being. With the resurrection of Christ a new creation began, and a new light went forth into the darkness.

"Cometh Mary Magdalene:" Matt. xxviii. 1 mentions Mary Magdalene and the other Mary; Mark, besides these, Salome, xvi. 1. Luke is most copious; he mentions, xxiv. 10, with Mary Magdalene Joanna, now first appearing in his Gospel, and Mary mother of James, and "others with them:" comp. xxiii. 55, xxiv. 1, according to which those women went to the sepulchre who had remained together watching the interment (his predecessors had mentioned as such Mary Magdalene and the other Mary), and "certain others with them." The whole circle of Galilean women, as might have been expected, joined the pilgrimage. John, who everywhere, and especially in the narrative of the resurrection, is extremely sparing in the communication of what was already known through his predecessors, touching it only so far as was necessary for the introduction of his own peculiar contributions, goes no further than the mention of Mary Magdalene, who also with his predecessors is the central personage, and always is placed first. But we find in John a definite allusion to the fact that he passed over the others only for brevity. That lies in the οἴδαμεν, *we know*, in ver. 2, which cannot without the utmost violence be interpreted otherwise than "I and the women who went out with me." Ewald remarks, with strict propriety: "That Mary Magdalene went out alone to visit the sepulchre is in itself improbable, and at the same time opposed to the older narrative, besides being out of keeping with his own bent in ver. 2." The impossibility of sundering Mary Magdalene from the other women becomes very plain when we note Luke xxiv. 10. There, in conjunction with the others, she brings the Apostles the report; just as, according to Matthew and Mark, she came together with them to the sepulchre.

The fact that John does not mention the *intention* with which Mary and her companions went to the sepulchre, is as good as an express allusion to his predecessors, according to whom the women went out to *anoint* the body of Jesus: Mark xvi. 1; Luke xxiv. 1, xxiii. 55.—Mary came *early*, while it *was yet dark* at the sepulchre. This statement, and Luke's "very early in the morning, ὄρθρου βαθέος," are supposed to contradict Mark's "at the rising of the sun." Certainly his ἀνατείλαντος τοῦ ἡλίου can be interpreted only as *orto sole*. But this does not imply that the sun had fully risen. Many passages in the New Testament, and the frequently occurring ἀνατολαί in classical writers, show that the rising of the sun was an act not limited to one moment. The sun is really risen, though the disc of the sun may not be visible in the heaven; for the dawn is created by it before it rises. Mark precedes his sunrise by the remark "*very early*," and shows that he meant only the first glimmering of dawn. His ch. i. 35, καὶ πρωῒ ἔννυχον λίαν, furnishes a comment on this λίαν πρωΐ. Fritzsche: Mane, multa adhuc nocte = bene mane. In the ἔννυχον there, we have a parallel to the σκοτίας ἔτι οὔσης here. Mark speaks of the sunrise in the broader sense, as opposed to dark night; but John does not say "when it was yet night," but only that the light of day had not yet altogether dispelled the darkness. It was precisely the time which Homer describes by κροκόπεπλος ἠώς : comp. Eustatius ad Hom. xi. p. 181, "having something of the night's darkness remaining, although the sun's rays shed upon it a golden tinge." In the nature of the case we should expect neither perfect darkness nor perfect light. In the Old Testament, the dawn was consecrated as a symbol of transition from misery to happiness, from suffering to joy : Isa. lviii. 8, comp. ver. 10, xlvii. 11, viii. 20; Hos. vi. 3, x. 15; 2 Sam. xxiii. 4, and specifically Ps. xxii. 1 : there the hind of the morning is the suffering righteous, to whom salvation is come. There seems to be a special reference to this psalm, the same which throughout the crucifixion both our Lord and His apostles had continually in view.—" Unto the sepulchre" must, from what follows, be *to* the sepulchre, not *into* it : comp. ch. xviii. 28; Mark, ver. 2, ἐπὶ τὸ μνημεῖον ; Luke xxiv. 1, ἐπὶ τὸ μνῆμα. Yet the preposition εἰς was designedly chosen. If Mary had not actually visited the sepulchre itself, the Evangelist would have used ἐπί instead : comp. εἰσελθοῦσαι, Luke xxiv. 3 ; ἐξελθοῦσαι ἀπὸ τοῦ μνημείου, Matt. xxviii. 8.—John had mentioned the *stone* in connection with the resurrection of Lazarus, xi. 38, but not in connection with our Lord's sepulchre : Anton : "An instance to show that John refers back to the other Evangelists. For he had said nothing before of any stone. He knew that it was a matter well known to believers through the earlier accounts."

Ver. 2. "Then she runneth, and cometh to Simon Peter, and to the other disciple whom Jesus loved, and saith unto them, They have taken away the Lord out of the sepulchre, and we know not where they have laid Him."—The women had received a command to carry to the Apostles the angels' report concerning the resurrection, Matt. xxviii. 7, and especially, as Mark xvi. 7 adds, to Peter as their head. According to Luke xxiv. 9, they reported all that they had learnt at the sepulchre "to the eleven, and to all the rest." As it is improbable that all these,—not only the Apostles, but all other believers,—were assembled in one place, we have to assume that they divided the commission among them. It then was obvious that to Mary Magdalene, who everywhere takes the first place among the holy women, would be assigned the communication of the angels' message to Peter, especially named by the angel, as well as to his faithful companion, the disciple whom Jesus loved. According to Luke, the message embraced all that he records in vers. 3–8,—that they found not the body of Jesus in the sepulchre, that two angels appeared to them in their anxiety, and announced to them the resurrection. John, however, contents himself with communicating the *first* part of the message—the fact that the women found the sepulchre empty. This is in harmony with his pervading habit of touching lightly what his predecessors had narrated; and of introducing their details with the utmost brevity, and merely as a basis for incorporating and adjusting his own independent matter. If it were a matter of condensation, then the narrative of the appearance of the angels, and the transitory manifestation of our Lord Himself in the way (Matt. xxviii. 9), must have been postponed to that of the report of the sepulchre being found empty. This last reproduced what the women had seen with their bodily eyes, and stated on personal evidence a firm fact; those other reports moved in a sphere where excited imagination might play a considerable part. The question in them was one of an ὀπτασία, Luke, ver. 23, that certainly might have objective significance, but in regard to which it was needful to be very guarded. The really central matter in the message of the women seems to be that which John alone selects, that of Luke xxiv. 24, where the disciples of Emmaus say: "And certain of them which were with us went to the sepulchre, and found it even so as the women had said; but Him they saw not:" this latter word intimates, in harmony with Matt. xxviii. 9, that the women had asserted that they had seen Jesus. The Apostles gave full acceptance only to that part of the message, only to that which every one with a sound eye to the testimony must have believed. The remainder awakened only presentiments and indefinite hopes. Until further confirmation it was not spoken of, a mere rumour, λῆρος, Luke ver. 11. But we may prove from John himself that Mary Magdalene must have said more than what he so briefly communicates. The facts reported by him point us to the supplement which we find in Luke. It is striking at the outset that Mary *runs*. Accordingly she must have already experienced something which did not paralyse her feet, but gave them wings. Further, if Mary had nothing further to report, she would have come *weeping* to the Apostles. But she does not weep till ver. 12, when that seems to be vanishing from her which she had thought she held fast. If Mary, besides mentioning the fact which was evident to her sense, the emptiness of the grave, had not alluded to some *explanation* of that fact which she believed she had received, the conduct of the two disciples is hardly to be accounted for. The report of Mary must have deposited in them the germ of a faith in the Lord's resurrection; but that could not have been the case if she merely reported the emptiness of the sepulchre. For the fact that the sepulchre was empty furnished no evidence in favour of the resurrection; it was rather evidence to the contrary, since the resurrection of Jesus was inseparably connected with His making Himself known to His disciples. If the words of Mary had not given the two disciples some ground of hope, why did they run so fast to the sepulchre? How was it that John should record the circumstance, indifferent in itself, that he outran Peter and came first to the sepulchre, if their difference of speed did not reveal a difference of sentiment with regard to the report received by Mary,—a prelude to the subsequent difference in their faith and wonder? The running of the two men presupposes a germ of faith in the Lord's resurrection; a germ which was implanted solely by the report brought to them through Mary. Without some such faith they would have gone to the sepulchre, if they went at all, with faltering steps and downcast faces. In the disciple whom Jesus loved this germ was more energetically developed through the influence of that personal and individual love to Jesus which distinguished him beyond all the other disciples. So also the fact that John came to a mature faith in the resurrection while still in the sepulchre, ver. 8, assumes that the message of Mary had already given him ground for hoping it.—With "they have taken away," etc., we may compare Luke xxiv. 3, "And they entered in, and found not the body of the Lord Jesus," provided we include ver. 4, according to which they were in consequence filled with grief and anxiety: "And it came to pass, as they were much perplexed thereabout." What Mary here said was the result which observation with the natural eye would lead to. That she knew how to distinguish accurately between the sphere of lower sense and that of the higher, itself awakens in our minds a prejudice in favour of her trustworthiness.

Ver. 3. "Peter therefore went forth, and that other disciple, and came to the sepulchre."—Luke, after mentioning the cold reception which the women with their message met with at the hands of the Apostles, ver. 11, says in ver. 12, "Then arose Peter, and ran unto the sepulchre;" he singles out Peter from the rest. John completes his account by adding that he was with Peter. That Luke knew more than he recorded, is plain from ch. xxiv. 23, when the disciples of Emmaus say, "And *certain* of them that were with us went to the sepulchre." If Peter accordingly did not go alone, we might naturally enough suppose that John would go with him: for these two appear everywhere, and in Luke particularly, united in the most perfect manner (compare on ch. xiii. 24); and certainly there was not one in the whole company of the Apostles more disposed than John to faith in the resurrection. Luke limits himself to the mention of Peter, simply as being the *head* of the Apostles. John of course had a personal interest in recording his participation.

Ver. 4. "So they ran both together: and the other disciple did outrun Peter, and came first to the sepulchre."—Augustin: "After he had said that they came to the sepulchre, he returns back to say how they went." We have here John's supplement to Luke's word, "Peter ran." That it may be very plain where his more copious and exact narrative is to be inserted, John takes almost all the words of the summary account in Luke, and adapts his additions to them: Luke says, that Peter *ran* to the grave; John, that Peter *and John* ran, the latter faster than the former: Luke, that he stooped down and beheld the linen clothes laid by themselves; John uses the very same words, so that there can be no idea of mere accident in the matter: Luke speaks of the linen clothes *alone;* John says, that the napkin did not lie with the linen clothes: Luke, that he went home (ἀπῆλθε πρὸς ἑαυτόν); and John uses the very same words, "went away again unto their own home" (ἀπῆλθον πρὸς ἑαυτούς). If we attach their real value to these designed allusions, we shall not be misled by John's ver. 8, "And he saw and believed," in its plain reference to Luke's ver. 11, "And they believed them not." Now, says John, the earlier unbelief of the disciples gave way in the case of at least *one* of those disciples. It was not fortuitous that John in this way linked his narrative to Luke among the three Evangelists. Matthew breaks off his account of the holy women, after recording how the Lord appeared to them, and gave them a commission to the disciples; Mark still earlier, after his communications on the appearance and commission of the angel. Both fail to narrate the reception which they and their tidings concerning the resurrection and their message met with from the Apostles. Luke alone of the three Evangelists mentions this. Now, as it was John's design to furnish supplements to the first three accounts, it was natural that he should take up the thread where that Evangelist laid it down who had carried the common narrative furthest. There was all the more reason why John should refer to Luke, because Luke had not, like the other Evangelists, passed over in silence the event which John wished to record fully, the journey of the two to the sepulchre, but had related it imperfectly; so that it was of moment, in order to obviate the semblance of contradiction, to take up the earlier account again, and to indicate the places where the additions were to be inserted.

What made John run faster? We must reject all such external reasons as the more advanced age of Peter. If the difference had rested upon that ground, it would have been a trifling thing to mention. It is opposed also by the analogy of the following incident, where John yields in turn to Peter: John does not go into the sepulchre, Peter does. If in this the difference must be referred to the spiritual sphere, so also in the case of the running. The true interpretation will approve itself true, by referring both differences between the two Apostles to the same grounds. The reason why John ran faster was this, that he was the disciple whom Jesus loved. Personal love to Jesus, which kept pace with the love of Jesus to him, gave wings to his feet. (Quesnel: John must outrun Peter; we must be loved before we can love or run.) If the matter had been one of duty in his vocation, had there been anything to do or to suffer for Jesus and His Church, Peter would certainly not have been behindhand. Hence the reason was the same for which the Lord committed His mother, not to Peter, but to John. The Apostle had, in fact, in ver. 2, all but expressly assigned the reason, by there designating himself the disciple whom Jesus loved, ὃν ἐφίλει ὁ Ἰησοῦς:—φιλεῖν, stronger than the ἀγαπᾶν, used elsewhere.

Ver. 5. "And he stooping down, and looking in, saw the linen clothes lying; yet went he not in."—Luke had used the words, "And stooping down, he beheld," etc., of Peter. John, taking up the same narrative, does not purpose to correct Luke: that would have been contrary to all analogy. He simply intimates that this was what was common to him and Peter; and then, in ver. 6, introduces supplementarily the statement of that in which Peter anticipated him. Peter, too, had naturally first looked into the sepulchre, and had then entered into it, in order to investigate the matter more closely. The ὀθονία, linen clothes, with which the whole body was swathed: comp. on xix. 40.—Why did not John go at once into the sepulchre? His tender feeling, the gentle inwardness of his love to Christ, feared a shock. He left it to the stronger and bolder Peter to make the first essay. As soon as this gave a satisfactory result, he followed after. John here records his own weakness with the same openness as, in ver. 4, he records his strength.

Vers. 6, 7. "Then cometh Simon Peter following him, and went into the sepulchre, and seeth the linen clothes lie, and the napkin, that was about His head, not lying with the linen clothes, but wrapped together in a place by itself."—Luke says, "the linen clothes laid by themselves (*alone*)." This μόνα would have been very hard of explanation, if we had not John's commentary on it: it might seem, so to speak, as if he had expected a supplementary commentator. Θεωρεῖν, in contradistinction to the mere βλέπειν, signifies the more careful view which was secured by approaching nearer. The significance of this circumstance, so minutely recorded, out of which, according to ver. 8, John's faith derived its strength, has been well stated by Lampe: "It was because He who altered the condition of the grave did nothing in haste, but designedly, and for specific purpose, unwound the bandages from the body, and disposed them decently in their several places."

Ver. 8. "Then went in also that other disciple which came first to the sepulchre, and he saw and believed."—We must not interpret, "He believed what Mary had said about the emptiness of the grave," as, strangely enough, Augustin, Luther, and Bengel do. (Augustin: "What did he see, what did he believe? He saw the empty sepulchre, and believed what the woman had said, that He was taken away from the sepulchre.") For that would have required to be more specifically stated; it is opposed to the emphatic meaning of the term *believe*, especially in the writings of John (comp. on xix. 35); and it is not in keeping with the parallel words of Luke concerning Peter, "wondering in himself at that which was come to pass," θαυμάζων τὸ γεγονός,—wherein there was at least a dawn of faith, and which shows, as Calvin says, that something greater and higher came into his mind than mere wonder. But we must not at once explain, "He saw and believed that Jesus was risen." That also would have required to be more expressly declared. The faith here meant must needs be a faith in Christ absolutely, in the same general sense as the word πιστεύειν is used also in ver. 25. The faith developed here was faith that Jesus was the Christ the Son of God, ver. 31, and that which Thomas avowed, ver. 28, "My Lord and my God:" comp. the πεπίστευκας, in ver. 29, which is based upon this word of Thomas. Faith in the resurrection was involved in this broader faith; it was a part of the whole.—Faith in Christ is an empty delusion, if there is no faith in His resurrection, which is the immediate effect and evidence of His Messianic dignity and Divine Sonship.—That so slender a circumstance evoked faith in John, is explained by the fact, that this event had in a variety of ways been prepared for:—by the intelligence of Mary Magdalene; by all his experiences of the Divine dignity of Christ; by decisive foreannouncements of His own resurrection; by all that which in the Old Testament was predicted (as in Ps. cx.; Isa. liii.; Zech. ix. 9, 10) concerning Christ, as the Ruler over all His enemies, as entering through sufferings into His glory, as dividing the prey with the strong, as attaining a dominion over the earth, extending to its utmost bounds. Had not these solid grounds been existing, John might have been charged with the reproach of credulity. So also he would have been amenable to the charge of incredulity if he had not believed:

compare what Jesus says, Luke xxiv. 25, to the disciples of Emmaus, " O fools, and slow of heart to believe all that the prophets have spoken." In ver. 9, the Apostle himself points to these foundations of his faith. If we compare " He saw and believed" with the words to Thomas, " Blessed are they that have not seen, and yet have believed"—to which they have an undeniable allusion—we must perceive in them the Apostle's self-accusation, that he believed not altogether without seeing, that he still required some small hold on the visible, and that for a season he had still doubted whether the Divine nature of his Lord would declare itself in the resurrection. We might draw from this self-accusation of the Apostle the conclusion that, apart from the Apostle's hardness to believe, the manifestations of the risen Lord would have been altogether needless. But, even as it was becoming that the Apostles should believe in the resurrection without these appearances of the risen Redeemer, it seemed, on the other hand, good to Him to confirm this faith by actual evidence, and thus to give it such mighty power as to overcome the world, so that the Apostles, strong in its strength, might go forth and convince all men. So is it ever with faith generally. It must be present before experience; but if it were not surely and variously confirmed by experience, it would soon become feeble, and die by degrees. " The singular ἐπίστευσε," observes Meyer, " serves to satisfy *his own* personal experience, never to be forgotten, of that crisis; but it is not to be regarded as excluding Simon Peter's simultaneous faith." But this singular concurs with another singular, the θαυμάζων which Luke says of Peter: he attained to a developed faith, while Peter went no further than wonder. " He believed" gives probably a key to the fact, that the disciple whom Jesus loved had no specific manifestation vouchsafed to him, while one was vouchsafed to Peter. We may, however, seek it in the pre-eminence of Peter himself.

Ver. 9. " For as yet they knew not the scripture, that He must rise again from the dead."—The Apostle gives the reason why he *then* first believed in the resurrection, and that he required to *see* in order to believe, notwithstanding the existence of such abundant and express utterances of the Old Testament in relation to the resurrection, which, it might have been supposed, would have from the beginning rendered it a certainty to them all. It is true that the scripture loudly proclaims the resurrection, but that scripture was not *understood* or *known* by these disciples, entangled in subjectivity; just as even now the Scripture testifies and declares much that we do not know and understand until Divine dispensations to us, and manifold experiences, sometimes very bitter, or richer communications of the Holy Spirit, raise us to a higher spiritual intelligence.— John speaks here only of the foreannouncements of the resurrection as contained in the Scriptures of the Old Testament: comp. Luke xxiv. 25–27, 44–47, where Jesus similarly, speaking of His resurrection, points to the prophecies of the Old Testament. Our Lord's own declarations concerning His coming resurrection are not simply apart from and with "Scripture:" they are to be regarded only as interpretations and deductions drawn from it, and were declared to be such when uttered: comp. the δεῖ, Matt. xvi. 21, Luke ix. 22, with Luke xxiv. 26, 44. He had, before His resurrection, as after it, done no more than open their understanding to comprehend the Scripture, Luke xxiv. 45.

The "knew not" must not be too absolutely taken. It only says that the disciples' knowledge of the scripture had no such living power as of itself to lead them to faith. We must accept "they knew not" with the same slight modification as "they believed not," ch. vii. 5 (comp. on that passage). John is particularly partial to the expression of a relative contrast in an absolute form: comp. on i. 17, vii. 39. Compared with the knowledge which the Apostles afterwards attained, their present knowledge scarcely deserved the name. Seen from the point he then occupied, it seemed to have vanished. The Apostle makes with deep humiliation his confession here. The scripture was in itself so clear, and Jesus had, before His passion, so thoroughly and so impressively expounded it to His disciples, that it was incomprehensible how he had first to *see* in order to believe! But the seeing would never have led him to faith if this "not knowing the scripture" had been an absolute ignorance.

Ver. 10. "Then the disciples went away again unto their own home."—The disciples waited at their homes for further intelligence. However certainly John believed, he also waited for further intelligence of the Redeemer. For He had given His disciples certain assurance that, presently after His passion,

He would see them, and they should see Him again : ch. xvi. 16, 22. This promise, with all others like it, had now become matter of living expectation to John; in some sense also to Peter. Πρὸς ἑαυτόν in Luke, πρὸς ἑαυτούς here, the only instances in which this peculiar phraseology occurs in the New Testament :[1] explained by the fact that the dwelling is regarded as part of the dweller, so that he who comes home comes to himself. Because the expression was so entirely peculiar and strange, John adopted it into his language. It seems like an express reference to Luke, like a declaration that he was supplementing that Evangelist.

In the narrative of our Lord's appearance to Mary Magdalene, vers. 11–18, John dilates upon what Mark, in ch. xvi. 9, had already briefly hinted : " Now when Jesus was risen, early the first day of the week, He appeared first to Mary Magdalene, out of whom He had cast seven devils." That the appearance in Mark is not that of which Matt. xxviii. 9 speaks, but that in our text, is plain from a comparison of ver. 10 in Mark with ver. 18 here. Hastening to the end, he passes over the former in silence; because that manifestation had been less important, more transitory and superficial, and not adequate to produce in the minds of those who were favoured with it a perfectly undoubting faith. The "*first*" in Mark does not exclude that earlier manifestation: it notes this one only as the first among those mentioned by him. This is evident from the relation between the *first* and the *after that* in ver. 12, and the *afterward*, ver. 14.

Ver. 11. "But Mary stood without at the sepulchre weeping: and, as she wept, she stooped down, and looked into the sepulchre."—The disciples had run to the grave: Mary Magdalene came more slowly. She remains there, after the disciples had gone away: they went away so soon, doubtless because it was their task to carry intelligence to their fellow-Apostles, and with them to wait for that manifestation of the risen Lord which had been promised to the whole apostolical circle. Peter and John had both received a *joyful* influence from the sepulchre: Peter marvelled, John believed. Mary, on the contrary, *weeps*, notwithstanding that the Apostles had communicated their impressions to her. The result of the whole gave no

---

[1] Josephus has it in Antiq. viii. 5, 6 : πρὸς αὐτοὺς ἕκαστοι τοῦ βασιλέως ἀπολύσαντος ἀπῄεσαν.

satisfaction to her. The reason of this could be only that she had earlier been more favoured; and had expected, therefore, that the Apostles would have been more favoured also. She had seen, in company with the other women, a vision of angels who announced Christ's resurrection; on the way home she had seen the Lord Himself, although only in a transitory way. Now she has nothing but the empty grave, before which she indulges in sorrow, especially as the Apostles had seen nothing more. She is thrown into doubt as to her earlier experience, and this doubt breaks her heart. Her weeping for Jesus, however, is heard: first the angels become visible to her again, and then Jesus Himself appears to her.

Ver. 12. "And seeth two angels in white sitting, the one at the head, and the other at the feet, where the body of Jesus had lain."—The angels appear as the answer to Mary's weeping. This sets aside the question, How was it that Peter and John did not see the angels? The weeping was the condition not merely of their being seen, but also of their appearing. The angels had nothing more to do in the sepulchre. This is evident from their position, their *sitting*. Bengel: Sedentes quasi opera perfunctos,—sitting as having done their work. They appear there only because Mary seeks the living among the dead. That they sat on the place where the Lord had lain, one at the head, and the other at the feet (comp. Ps. xxxiv. 8, "The angel of the Lord encampeth about them that fear Him, and delivereth them"), intimated to her that no impiety had been permitted here: when God's angels kept their guard, no impious hands could enter.—It was appropriate that the angels in the New Testament should serve Him who, in the Old Testament, is exhibited as the Head of the angels, *the* Angel of the Lord, the Captain of the Lord's host, Josh. v. They appeared at His birth, after His temptation, in Gethsemane, at the resurrection, at the ascension.—Ἐν λευκοῖς, *in white*, is found elsewhere only in Rev. iii. 4, 5. In every other place of the New Testament, white *garments* are mentioned. White was the colour of glory, its symbolic shadow: comp. on Rev. iv. 4. The white garments of the angels correspond to the name of "holy ones," that is, glorious ones, which they bear in the Old Testament.

Vers. 13, 14. "And they say unto her, Woman, why weepest thou? She saith unto them, Because they have taken away my Lord, and I know not where they have laid Him. And when she had thus said, she turned herself back, and saw Jesus standing, and knew not that it was Jesus."—Mary, although invigorated by the aspect of the angels, could not at once be comforted. Her heart desires to see another, to see Jesus Himself. Had not that taken place which is recorded in Matt. xxviii. 9, the vision of angels alone would have been sufficient for her satisfaction. That her heart longed for more was made plain by her very action, as she turned away from the sepulchre and the angels towards the side whence, if He should appear at all, Jesus would come.—She sees Jesus standing, and knows not that it is Jesus. The reason of her not knowing must not be sought in Mary alone. What Mark says, ch. xvi. 12, with regard to the two disciples of Emmaus, holds good here: Christ appeared to them and to her in another form, ἐν ἑτέρᾳ μορφῇ. So also ch. xxi. 4, where Jesus appears to the disciples by the Galilean lake, and they knew not that it was Jesus; whereas, in His two manifestations to the apostolic circle in Jerusalem, Jesus at once made Himself known. Analogies are found in the angel-manifestations of the Old Testament, especially Judges xiii. 16, where we read, "For Manoah knew not that it was the angel of the Lord,"—a passage to which John, in ch. xxi. 4, literally alludes. The reason of their not knowing was not simply the weakness of spiritual vision in Manoah and his wife; but especially this, that the angel of the Lord would not, until afterwards, announce himself plainly as such: comp. ver. 17–21. In consequence of this, "Manoah knew not that it was an angel of the Lord," ver. 21. Glorified corporeity is distinguished from ordinary corporeity, in that it serves the spirit absolutely, and assumes at its desire various forms of manifestation. Jesus would not at once be known to Mary, otherwise than in Matt. xxviii. 9. This time, the *voice* was to be the token of recognition. It was in the name Mary, into which He condensed the whole relation in which He stood to her soul, that He would be made known. He would, at the same time, teach His Church of all ages, that in the guidance of His people He might be expected to assume many strange appearances, and that He would often be present among those who were still bemoaning His absence, and weeping for His presence.

Ver. 15. "Jesus saith unto her, Woman, why weepest thou? whom seekest thou? She, supposing Him to be the gardener, saith unto Him, Sir, if thou have borne Him hence, tell me where thou hast laid Him, and I will take Him away."—When Mary knew not Jesus, it was obvious that she should first think of the gardener: garden and gardener pertain to each other. What she says to the supposed gardener is not so much the real meaning of her heart, as the expression of her glowing desire to have her Lord again, were it only His dead form. The κύριε, Sir, which in its respectfulness goes beyond the position of the gardener, must be explained by the consideration that she thought herself dependent upon him for what was her dearest treasure.

Ver. 16. "Jesus saith unto her, Mary! She turned herself, and saith unto Him, Rabboni! which is to say, Master!"—The *Mary!* which Jesus here spoke went deeper into her heart, and was thus much more fitted to remove all doubt in the reality of the resurrection, than all that was said at the first manifestation. The superscription of this was the "Fear ye not," and its characteristics were strangeness and suddenness. The women ventured to touch His feet and worship Him. But here Mary, in the overmastering love of her heart, would actually embrace Him. The στραφεῖσα here, compared with the ἐστράφη εἰς τὰ ὀπίσω, ver. 14, shows that the former turning was only partial. Now, when she knows Jesus, she turns away entirely from the sepulchre and the angels towards Him. Rabboni, here only and Mark x. 51, is רבן, a dialectical variety of Rabban with the suffix. In process of time the suffix lost its meaning, like the pronoun in the Dutch *Mynheer*, and the Evangelist rightly omits it in the interpretation he gives. The address Rabboni is in harmony with the place at Jesus' feet which Mary loved; that was the place of a disciple in relation to her Master. It was natural that she who was formerly too masterless and free, should be especially thankful that she had found in Jesus the great Master.

Ver. 17. "Jesus saith unto her, Touch Me not; for I am not yet ascended to My Father: but go to My brethren, and say unto them, I ascend unto My Father, and your Father; and to My God, and your God."—The "Touch Me not" presupposes that Mary was in the act of touching the Lord, for

He would refuse only that which was proffered. "Ἅπτεσθαι is always used in the Old Testament of bodily touching; in Luke vii. 39 it is used specifically of Mary in relation to Jesus; and as there is nothing to limit the meaning here, we may regard the Lord as forbidding bodily touching as such. The women in Matt. xxviii. 9 embraced the feet of Jesus, and He forbade them not. The disciples are challenged by the Lord in Luke xxiv. 39 to handle Him, ψηλαφήσατέ με; and to Thomas He said, "Reach hither thy hand, and thrust it into My side." Therefore the reason of the prohibition must be sought in the personal character of Mary, and in the passionate nature of the touch which sprang from that character. Mary would embrace the Lord. She thought that the limits which had formerly existed between her Lord and herself (many very incorrectly make her suppose that she could continue to act towards her Lord "in the old style of confidence") were, now that the Saviour had passed into another form of existence, removed; and that she might now give free course to her feelings, without fearing the admixture of anything human in her sentiment towards her Lord. But the Lord repelled her. " Touch Me not, *for* I am not yet ascended to My Father:" My glorification is not yet perfect; the partition still remains in part which the infirmity of human nature erected between you and Me; but soon, when I have gone to the end of the way which I have now entered, this partition will be withdrawn. Every one will be able to express, without any reservation, love to Him who sitteth at the right hand of the Father.

The ascension appears here, as in Mark and Luke, to be a stage of the Redeemer's course quite distinct from the resurrection, while inseparably connected with it and its necessary complement. John mentions the ascension thrice, in ch. iii. 13, vi. 62, and this passage. His silence, therefore, as to the historical event must not be considered as implying unacquaintance with it,—an ignorance which his relation to Mark and Luke, apart from every other consideration, renders it impossible to maintain. Matthew does not record the ascension; and yet he mentions, ch. xxvi. 64, comp. xxviii. 8, Christ's sitting at the right hand of God, which presupposes the ascension. If, in opposition to all the Evangelists, we make the resurrection simply the restoration of Christ to life as before, then the ascension assumes the character of a new stage, and it is difficult to understand how any Evangelist could omit the record of it. But if, on the other hand, we admit that Christ rose in a glorified body, the resurrection and the ascension are, as it were, one, and bound up together. The latter event, in that case, must take place so soon as Christ had sufficiently attested His resurrection, and given the instructions and commissions which rested on the resurrection. Anton: " The resurrection placed the Redeemer in a new kind of life. Therefore He could not remain upon earth; but there was an ascension to come." It was all the less necessary for John to narrate the fact of the ascension, as his predecessors had given the narrative in a very complete manner.

The prohibition is followed by a commission. Mary must go to the Apostles, and give them information of the approaching ascension of the Redeemer. Why did the Lord send them intelligence of His approaching ascension, and not of His resurrection already accomplished? Why does He say nothing about His appearing in their midst, and His manifold intercourse with them afterwards? The answer is, that the essential consolation of the resurrection lay in the ascension which was connected with it, by which Christ would enter into the full possession of His Divine glory, and thus be able in the most effectual manner to care for His disciples and help His Church. Christ sitting at the right hand of the Father is the proper and all-sufficient consolation of the Church. Not until He should be with the Father, who was greater than He, ch. xiv. 28; not until the Father had glorified Him with the glory which He had before the foundation of the world, ch. xvii. 5, could He equip His disciples with irresistible might. The appearances of the risen Lord, far from being excluded by this message, which only gave prominence to the great central fact, were all the more to be expected after that message. If Christ was truly going to His Father, it was needful that He should give His disciples, before His departure, indubitable proofs that the bands of death could not hold Him. The entire position of the Apostles demanded that Christ should appear in their midst. Paul, in 1 Cor. xv., pretermits the appearances of Christ to the women, in token that the faith of the Church could not be based upon them; that they were only the prelude of the proper fundamental manifestations. But if our Lord had pre-announced His appearances in the apostolic circle, they would have lost that character of abruptness which it was manifestly appropriate that they should bear.—Jesus says, "I ascend," not "I will ascend," in order to intimate that His whole being already tended towards the ascension, which would have immediately taken place had it not been necessary to give the Apostles demonstration that He had risen, and to leave with them His last injunctions.

Our Lord here for the first time calls His disciples *brethren*. This He did primarily with allusion to Ps. xxii. 23, where the Righteous One delivered from the bands of death says, "I will declare Thy name unto my brethren." But this designation had a deeper reason. It pointed to that more profound fellowship between Jesus and His people,—a fellowship created by that redeeming death of which the resurrection was the seal. Christ having given His life for them, translated them from friends into brethren, ch. xv. 15. Anton : " Christ used this term first after His resurrection, because the resurrection was the seal of the atonement with its satisfaction, so that they might be assured now of their fellowship with Christ and in Christ. Although He has gone into glory, He makes His disciples already, as it were, sharers of it ; He clothes them with His dignity, and is not ashamed to call them brethren (Heb. ii. 12)." How full of consolation this new designation was to be, the sequel shows. As brethren they were the partakers of that glory which He had obtained by His death ; His God, who received Him into that glory, became their God.—He does not say " to our Father, to our God," because He was Christ's God and Father in a different sense from that in which He was their God and Father. He was their God only because He was Christ's God and they Christ's brethren. Augustin : Naturâ meum, gratiâ vestrum : Mine by nature, yours by grace.

Ver. 18. "Mary Magdalene came and told the disciples that she had seen the Lord, and that He had spoken these things unto her."—Compare Mark xvi. 10.

Chap. xx. 19-23.

Now follows, in vers. 19-22, the appearance of Christ in the midst of the disciples.

The appearances of the risen Lord had a twofold end: 1. To give assurance to His disciples of the reality of His resurrection; and 2. To communicate to them the new authority which He had obtained by His atoning death. Both ends are expressly noted by Luke, Acts i. 3 : 1. He was seen, during forty days, in many manifestations and acts which gave infallible proof of His resurrection. 2. He spoke to them of the things pertaining to the kingdom of God, this being a more comprehensive statement of the second design. This twofold design explains how all the four Evangelists, without being on that account in any respect imperfect, might restrict themselves to individual manifestations; indeed, it shows that they must have given prominence severally to individual manifestations, or otherwise they could not have avoided the accumulation of like narratives,—a repetition which they all show themselves careful to avoid. The two essential points noted above are found in them all; and as almost every individual appearance involved both, they might very well distribute them as they have done.

After the appearance of Christ to Mary Magdalene, followed His appearance to the two disciples who were journeying into the country. This Mark, ch. xvi. 12, 13, summarily narrates, and places it between the appearance to Mary in the morning and the appearance to the Apostles in the evening of the day of resurrection. Luke gives the narrative in all its fulness. According to him, the appearance was in the late afternoon of the day, ch. xxiv. 29.

About the same time occurred the manifestation to Peter which is passingly mentioned by Luke, ver. 34, and which Paul alludes to in his narrative of the appearances of our Lord, 1 Cor. xv. 5. He places it at the head, and before that to the Twelve, the appearances to the women being carefully excluded. That interview with Peter could not have taken place when the two went out of Jerusalem to go to Emmaus, for they knew of no other authority for the resurrection of Christ than the rumour of the women, Luke xxiv. 22 seq. And when they returned in the evening to Jerusalem, and entered the apostolic circle, it had occurred; for the Apostles met them with the intelligence that the Lord was risen indeed, and had appeared unto Simon.

We now come to the appearance of Christ on the evening of the day in the circle of the Apostles. This is recorded briefly by Mark, ver. 14, copiously by Luke, vers. 33–43, and by John in the present passage. In the statements as to time there is a perfect agreement. According to Mark, the Apostles were at the table when Jesus entered into their midst. Luke mentions no time; but Jesus, in his account, asks, " Have ye anything to eat?" and the Apostles have at once in readiness a little fish and honey. According to John, the occurrence fell in the evening. The suddenness, unexpectedness, and unearthliness of the appearance, all make prominent; the trait that it took place when the doors were shut is peculiar to John, but is required by the statement of Luke, that the Apostles thought they saw a spirit. The words of our Lord to the Apostles have two elements of importance. 1. He demonstrated to them the reality of His resurrection, and that gradually: first offering Himself to their sight, then challenging their touch, and finally asking them for meat. 2. He gave them the authority of their vocation, and at the same time the spiritual powers which that vocation presupposed. Luke's account is limited to the first of these points, because he reserves the authority committed to the Apostles for Christ's final interview with them before the ascension. John, on the other hand, refers to Luke for the former point,—what *is* there copiously stated, vers. 37–43, he touches briefly, ver. 20: after "He showed them His hands and His feet," inserted merely to adjust the position of what Luke recorded, we are to understand, as it were, " and so forth." He further supplements him, according to his characteristic thoroughness, by dwelling on the second point in vers. 21–23; while afterwards, for the same reason which made Luke abbreviate, he passes over in silence the final interview before the ascension.

Out of the several incomplete narratives a perfect one may easily be formed. The Lord enters with the customary greeting, " Peace be to you," which from His lips, and under these circumstances, had unusual significance. Then He convinces the astounded Apostles of the reality of His resurrection, which they must be assured of before the mission resting upon it could be committed to them. Thereupon He repeats the " Peace be unto you," assuredly with stronger emphasis, as introductory to His commission, which would bring upon them so much care and danger; and with the communication of this commission, and the gifts and prerogatives necessary to it, He concludes.

Ver. 19. "Then the same day at evening, being the first day of the week, when the doors were shut where the disciples were assembled for fear of the Jews, came Jesus, and stood in the midst, and saith unto them, Peace be unto you."—When our Lord entered into their midst, the Apostles had been in many ways prepared for His coming: by the first message of the women, by the experience of Peter and John at the sepulchre, by the report brought by Mary Magdalene of the appearance she had seen, by the appearance also to Peter, and by the tidings of the Emmaus disciples. We can hardly doubt that their whole soul was rapt in desire and in expectation of the coming of their Master. When we reflect upon the fundamental importance of that visitation of the Apostles, it will be clear that all these preceding preparations were no more than absolutely necessary.

According to strict Jewish computation, the *evening* was no part of this first day of the week. But in common life the Jews were in the habit of reckoning the evening with the day that it closed; and this we must do here, if we would preserve the integrity, as one whole, of the events which had their climax in the Lord's visitation of the Apostles. Matthew, in ch. xxviii. 1, reckons the day as continuing until the dawn of the following. It must have been already very late, for, according to Luke, the disciples of Emmaus were present at this appearance.—Luke says, ch. xxiv. 36, " And as they thus spake, Jesus Himself ἔστη ἐν μέσῳ αὐτῶν, and saith unto them, εἰρήνη ὑμῖν, Peace be unto you." There is here an intentional adherence to Luke's phraseology. What is peculiar to John, becomes all the more emphatic when what is common to both is expressed in the same words. Moses in ancient times pursued the same method, when returning to the same matter. He recapitulates earlier details as much as possible in the same words, and then inserts what was newly to be communicated.—The Greek plural θύραι was often used for a door, on account of the two leaves which frequently formed it, corresponding to the Hebrew דלתים. It was evidently the one door of the place in which the Apostles were assembled. If the Lord's entrance was not of a character transcending the ordinary limits of corporeity, if Jesus had knocked at the door, or if the door of itself had sprung open (comp. Acts xii. 10), John must have expressly stated it; since the person of our Lord, especially as delineated by John after the resurrection, would lead us to take a miracle for granted rather than otherwise. The circumstance that the doors were shut, was in itself not important enough to be mentioned; and it is very noteworthy that the mention of the closed doors occurs precisely in that part of the narrative where John simply recapitulates what Luke had already recorded. The more concise he is here, the less probable will it seem that he would have mentioned the fact of the door being shut if it had had to do with our Lord's entrance. And, in that case, the repeated mention in ver. 26 must be very strange. Further, why were the disciples so terrified? why did they believe they saw a spirit? This question, which Luke's narrative suggests, is answered only when we find in John that the doors remained shut after our Lord's entrance. We are led to regard this as the reason of its being mentioned, by comparing Matt. xiv. 26, "And when the disciples saw Him walking on the sea, they were troubled, saying, It is a spirit." They there regarded Him as a spirit, because He was above the law of a material body. So was it here. Finally, we are led to the conclusion that the doors remained shut, by a consideration of the manner in which the risen Lord is represented elsewhere as appearing and vanishing: compare ἐφανέρωσεν ἑαυτόν, ch. xxi. 1; ἐφανερώθη, Mark xvi. 12; ἔδωκεν αὐτὸν ἐμφανῆ γενέσθαι, Acts x. 40; ἄφαντος ἐγένετο ἀπ' αὐτῶν, Luke xxiv. 31. It is not said that Jesus came *through* the closed doors. That would have made John travel beyond the region of his own observation, and forsake the sphere of the historian. The apparent contradiction, that Jesus entered into their midst when the doors were shut, and yet presented Himself to His disciples' touch, and ate before them, is removed by the simple remark, that after His resurrection the glorified body of our Lord was absolutely under the dominion of the spirit. Augustin: "After His resurrection, He did with His body what He listed." Of this our Lord in the days of His flesh gave an earnest, when He walked upon the sea, ch. vi. 19. What was then an isolated act, became after the resurrection the rule. " Peace be unto you " (Bengel: " The same formula is thrice repeated," vers. 19, 21, 36) points back to ch. xiv. 27. The peace which Jesus there promised He *brings* them here, whilst He announces Himself as the risen

Lord. In His resurrection His disciples received the pledge of victory over all their enemies and His.

Ver. 20. " And when He had so said, He showed unto them His hands and His side. Then were the disciples glad when they saw the Lord."— Luke, in vers. 24, 40, mentions the hands and the feet; John, the hands and the side. Since the side is mentioned only on account of the wound (comp. ch. xix. 34), the hands and the feet must have been introduced for the same reason. The wounds received by our Lord on the cross were, to the Apostles, demonstration that they had not now to do with an unessential φάντασμα or " spirit," but with the selfsame Jesus who suffered for them on the cross. A comparison of John with Luke leads to the firm conclusion that our Lord's hands and feet as well as His side were pierced, which Bähr, Hug, and others, show to have been usual at crucifixions. As the εἰρήνη ὑμῖν points back to ch. xiv. 27, so does ἐχάρησαν to ch. xvi. 22, " I will see you again, and your heart shall rejoice, χαρήσεται."

Ver. 21. " Then said Jesus to them again, Peace be unto you: as My Father hath sent Me, even so send I you."—The first " peace" was directed to the *disciples;* the second to the *Apostles.* Before He gave them their commission, our Lord assured His servants of their protection against all their enemies. This peace, guaranteed to them in respect to their *office,* had its foundation in the fact of the resurrection; and, as connected with that, or immediately springing from it, the Lord's speedy assumption into the full participation of the glory of the Father. Instead of πέμπω, the other word, ἀποστέλλω, might, in itself considered, have been used: this is evident from the name of the Apostles, and ch. xvii. 18. But there is an intentional variation in the word, in order to avoid placing the mission of the Apostles on a level with that of their Master. That this *sending* was so directly connected with their assurance of the resurrection, reminded the Apostles that the significance of the resurrection extended far beyond the narrow circle of those to whom the Lord announced Himself as risen; that it was a resurrection œcumenical and for all the world; that the great concern would now be to enter upon the work of spreading the Gospel to the ends of the earth, according to the manifold predictions of the prophets; and that they must not think to enjoy in passive contemplation the blessedness obtained for them, but gird up their loins, and take up the sword, for contest with all the powers of the world. The mission of Jesus now had its end; and its end was the beginning of the mission of the Apostles. (Calvin: "His own course being fulfilled, He commits the same functions to them, who should govern the Church to the end of the world.") Jesus does not say, "I will send you," but "I send you." With their own conviction of the reality of the resurrection began in them a new life, which should urge them mightily forth into the world. The day of Pentecost only brought to consummation what was already begun here. It was not the Feast of Pentecost, but the resurrection announced to them, that Jesus had already referred to as the great crisis and turning-point in ch. xvi. 23, 26.

Ver. 22. "And when He had said this, He breathed on them, and saith unto them, Receive ye the Holy Ghost."—The breathing here stands in relation to Gen. ii. 7, where Jehovah breathes into the first man the breath of life, and thus man becomes a living soul: Sept. καὶ ἐνεφύσησεν. By this allusion our Lord places Himself on a level with Jehovah Elohim, with Jehovah who there possessed the fulness of divinity. The same πνεῦμα ζωοποιοῦν which there went forth from Jehovah Elohim, and produced in man the Divine image, proceeds here from Christ, in order to reinstate the Divine image, first in the Apostles, and then in those who should believe through their word, ch. xvii. 20. The relation to Gen. ii. 7, which speaks of an immediately effectual inbreathing, such as at once created a "living nature," shows that our Lord's act here was not of merely prophetic significance—that it did not simply pretypify what was to become a reality on the day of Pentecost. We are led to the same result by the present πέμπω in ver. 21, as well as by the nature of the case: it could not be otherwise than that their conviction of the truth of the Lord's resurrection should be a great turning-point in the life of the Apostles, and that with this crisis they would receive an advanced susceptibility, and a concurrent enlargement of the influence of the Spirit. What they now received was the preliminary and condition of what they were to receive at Pentecost; according to the Lord's word, "Unto him that hath it shall be given." The beginnings of the

Holy Spirit were imparted according to the universal law of our Lord's operation, viz. to perform in prelude and earnest, while still upon earth, all that He would afterwards in heaven perform universally, even down to the resurrection of the dead, "in order," says Quesnel, "that we may know that He is the real ground of all, in His true humanity."—If the breathing was an actual impartation, how was it with Thomas, not present on this occasion? The answer is, that those who were present received in and with the breathing the Holy Ghost; but that the influence was not necessarily bound to the symbol which was its medium. The great essential was living faith in the resurrection. When Thomas uttered the words, "My Lord and my God," he also was made partaker of the Holy Ghost, or rather he must already have been partaker of the Holy Ghost, to utter the words at all: comp. 1 Cor. xii. 3. Had it not been for its profound and important relation to Gen. ii. 7, Jesus would probably have altogether omitted the symbolical action. The essential factor was not the proper breathing, but the resurrection and faith in Him who rose.

We have here an interpenetration of personal grace and official grace; of such as was common to all believers and such as was peculiar to the Apostles, and, as represented by them, to all the bearers of ministerial office in the Church. That the former is not to be excluded, the relation of the act to Gen. ii. 7 plainly shows: as there, so here also, the act was one which pertained to the human race. That the second is not to be excluded, is plain from the connection in which "Receive the Holy Ghost" here stands, on the one hand, to "I send you," ver. 21, and, on the other hand, to the remitting and retaining of sins in ver. 23. Such a combination of personal and official grace often occurs in the Old Testament: for example, in the case of Saul, 1 Sam. x. 6, xvi. 14; and David, 1 Sam. xvi. 13. Quesnel: "The Christian receives the Holy Ghost only for himself; priests and bishops for others also. It is a frightful thing in the Church, to be in office a channel of the Holy Ghost, and an instrument of the wicked spirit through disorderly and carnal living."

Ver. 23. "Whose soever sins ye remit, they are remitted unto them; and whose soever sins ye retain, they are retained." —Jesus would fill His disciples with the consciousness of the dignity of their vocation, that they might make it the labour of body and soul worthily to discharge its functions. They should in Christ's place have the authority to remit and to forgive sins. The former is the main function, the proper end of the spiritual office. " But if," says Anton, " a minister of the Gospel is despised in the administration of this grace, it turns from the ἀφιέναι to the κρατεῖν. The remitting takes place primarily in the case of those who believe and are baptized; the retaining in the case of those who are unbelievers, and accordingly reject baptism." But then both functions are more generally exercised in the continuous history of the Christian Church. Examples of the remission are furnished by Cornelius and his house, Acts x. 47, 48, and the man of Lystra, Acts xiv. 8–10: examples of retaining, Acts viii. 20, where Peter says, "Thy money perish with thee;" Acts xiii. 10, 11, where Paul condemns Elymas, as in ch. xviii. 6 the Jews of Corinth. He who has to do with office held in the Holy Ghost, is cut off from all appeal. Strictly speaking, it is Christ who " hath the key of David; who openeth, and no man shutteth; who shutteth, and no man openeth," Rev. iii. 7. But Christ has given this key to the ministry in His Church, and placed in their hands the decision of salvation and perdition. But the foundation of this high authority is the Holy Ghost. The office in the Church holds it only so far as it possesses the Holy Ghost. When not led by the Holy Spirit, its remission and its retention are of no moment. Thus the high prerogative assigned to its representatives cannot lead to self-exaltation, but rather to fear and trembling.[1] That which is here conferred on the whole apostolical circle, and in it to the ministerial office of all times, had been already prospectively conferred on Peter, Matt. xvi. 19, as the centre of the apostolical circle. The remitting here explains the loosing in Matthew; the retaining here, the binding there. In Matthew, both had their comment in the preceding, " And I will give unto thee the keys of the kingdom of heaven." Accordingly, it is only admission into the kingdom of God, and exclusion from it, that is meant; and if this be so, the binding can only be the retaining

---

[1] Erasmus: They who lift their crests, and arrogate to themselves a kind of tyranny, should remember what went just before. Shall we swell with the spirit of the world, and complacently exult in our power to forgive and remit sins? Hold your authority, but take care that it has the Spirit through whom Christ gave the authority.

of sins that exclude from the kingdom of God; the loosing only the forgiveness of the same, and the consequent admission into the kingdom of God.

THE SECOND APPEARANCE TO THE APOSTLES.

Chap. xx. 24–29.

This appearance is to be regarded as the *complement* of the former, since it had special reference to that one among the Apostles who still doubted of the Lord's resurrection. Many have been disposed to transfer it to Galilee. But it is in itself improbable that the Apostles had set out for Galilee before the end of the seven days' feast; and then ver. 26 intimates that they were in the same place where they received the former manifestation, " when the doors were shut," showing, as in ver. 19, that their fear of the Jews continued,—a fear which would not have been felt in Galilee. Finally, the conviction of the Apostles as to the reality of the resurrection seems always to pertain to Jerusalem, the manifestations in Galilee having another end; and as Thomas' unbelief was the only reason for this new visitation, his conviction its only result, we should not, without urgent argument, leave Jerusalem and betake ourselves to Galilee. Thus this manifestation formed the conclusion of the Apostles' abode in Jerusalem, removing every further reason for that abode. On the Sabbath the Apostles were resting there, according to the law: the first day of the week was spent by them in calm celebration of the resurrection, and of the first visit of the risen Lord, by which this day was for ever sanctified. To *sanction* this celebration the Lord appeared again in their midst on that day, and on none of the intervening days, thus accomplishing the last work which remained to be done in Jerusalem. On the second day of the week they set out for Galilee, awaiting there the manifestation of their Lord.—It has been often assumed that the disciples reported to Jesus the unbelief of Thomas. But when could this have taken place? Was it in some visit not revealed? But such a visit could not have occurred in Jerusalem, since the object to be attained there, the full conviction of the Apostles, was perfectly gained by the two visits that are narrated; and that it did not take place there, is incontrovertibly plain from ch. xxi. 14, according to which only two appearances of our Lord to the Apostles belong to Jerusalem. Or was it on occasion of this second visit itself? But this second appearance had this unbelief of Thomas for its ground, and presupposed it. If we assume that the Lord previously knew nothing of his unbelief, we do away with the meaning of this manifestation, we abolish the distinction which existed between the appearances in Jerusalem and those in Galilee, and we cannot enter into the real design of our Lord's previous reference to the seeing Himself in Galilee.

Ver. 24. "But Thomas, one of the twelve, called Didymus, was not with them when Jesus came."—As to $\Delta i\delta \upsilon \mu o\varsigma$, see the remarks on ch. xi. 16. The surname stands here in direct connection with the event now related. "The Twelve" is the appellation of the Apostles in all the Evangelists. Account is not taken of the fact that one place was vacant. It is all the less regarded, because the Twelve was not a fortuitous number, but rested on theological grounds; in the Old Testament twelve having been the consecrated signature of the Church. Why Thomas was not with them,—whether it was for the reason indicated in Heb. x. 25, "Forsake not the assembling of yourselves together, as the manner of some is;" whether, with his doubts concerning Christ, the bond that united him to his brethren became relaxed,—we cannot with certainty determine. But Anton rightly observes: "They did not separate from Thomas, who was so unrestful; for he was not even then an enemy of Christ, but a dear friend, only that he gave too much place to his *postulatis*. This teaches us an important lesson—to distinguish whether those in error are friends or foes, and not to be too swift to separate. Let this be noted."

Ver. 25. "The other disciples therefore said unto him, We have seen the Lord. But he said unto them, Except I shall see in His hands the print of the nails, and put my finger into the print of the nails, and thrust my hand into His side, I will not believe."—"We have seen the Lord:" this is the summary only of their report. It is self-understood that they told him the whole occurrence. But he, in his hardness to believe, accused them of credulity. $T\acute{\upsilon}\pi o\varsigma$ is *impression, trace*. In the second clause, $\tau \acute{o}\pi o\varsigma$ is more suitable (Grotius: $\tau \acute{\upsilon}\pi o\varsigma$, *videtur*; $\tau \acute{o}\pi o\varsigma$, *impletur*), and the rather to be preferred, as it is so easy to account for the substitution of $\tau \acute{\upsilon}\pi o\varsigma$. Thomas' affirmation has three members: the number three is often in the Old Testament the mark of emphasis, *e.g.* Ezek. xxi. 32. Thomas had doubtless seen the crucifixion in common with the rest: this we may infer from the vivid impression made upon him by the image of the Crucified. According to Luke xxiii. 49, there stood beside the women πάντες οἱ γνωστοὶ αὐτοῦ, at a certain distance from the cross. That John alone is mentioned as being present, may be explained by the fact that to him a word was addressed. Thomas does not mention the *feet*, because the hands and the feet were one whole to him; and the experiment on the hands would suffice.

Vers. 26, 27. " And after eight days, again His disciples were within, and Thomas with them. Then came Jesus, the doors being shut, and stood in the midst, and said, Peace be unto you. Then saith He to Thomas, Reach hither thy finger, and behold My hands; and reach hither thy hand, and thrust it into My side: and be not faithless, but believing."—It must incline in favour of Thomas that he was found again in the midst of the disciples. The declarations of his fellow-disciples doubtless made a deeper impression upon him than he was willing to allow. " Eight days:" this is, in Luke ix. 28, the definition of a week, the time ἀπὸ σαββάτου ἐπὶ σάββατον. Thomas had demanded three things: the first and second are here inverted, because Thomas' emphasis lay upon his touching; he did not depend upon his eye alone, since that might be deceived by a φάντασμα: comp. Luke xxiv. 39. But the perception through the hands might not be omitted, because the whole declaration of Thomas was to be perfectly reproduced. That the Lord knew what he had said, was a more convincing demonstration of the reality of the resurrection than any seeing and feeling; hence all further thought of them vanishes from Thomas' mind, and he at once bursts into the cry, " My Lord and my God." With the "hither" the Lord offered him His hand. " Behold" is the antithesis to feeling, and must be thought of as emphasized. Although Thomas believed not, ver. 25, yet he was not on that account an " unbeliever." The term ἄπιστος denotes a settled state of unbelief. It is not altogether correct to speak so much of the *unbelieving* Thomas. He would have ceased to be Thomas if he had become an unbeliever. It was the vibrating between faith and unbelief which obtained him his name. The Lord does not say, "Be not unbelieving," so much as "*Become* not unbelieving." He must turn from the evil way which, continued in, would lead to unbelief as its goal.

Ver. 28. "And Thomas answered and said unto Him, My Lord and my God."—It runs εἶπεν αὐτῷ: therefore "My Lord and my God" is a concise expression of deep feeling, instead of "*Thou art* my Lord and my God." We have here the first passage in which Jesus is expressly by His disciples called God,— a confession which was soon to be the common one of the whole Christian Church; as Pliny, in the Epistle to Trajan, records that the Christians sang hymns to Christ as God. Thomas utters here, as his confession, only what Jesus had constantly set before His disciples as His doctrine. When, for example, He said to Philip, ch. xiv. 9, "He that seeth Me hath seen the Father," and ver. 10, "I am in the Father, and the Father in Me," He taught that the existences of the Father and the Son were perfectly co-extensive, and that in Himself dwelt all the fulness of the Godhead. Much vain industry has been spent in evading this confession of Thomas, by those who do not accept the doctrine of Christ's divinity. He addressed to Christ precisely the same words which are elsewhere addressed to the supreme God: *e.g.* Ps. xxxv. 23, "Stir up Thyself, and awake to my judgment, even unto my cause, my God and Lord," ὁ Θεός μου καὶ ὁ κύριός μου; Ecclus. i. 1, Ἐξομολογοῦμαι σοι κύριε βασιλεῦ καὶ αἰνέσω Θεόν. We are in a sphere in which the boundary between God and the creature is drawn with the most rigid precision: comp. Deut. vi. 4; Mark xii. 29, 30. The address of Thomas would have been blasphemy if there had been in the Father's essence anything that came not to manifestation in the Son. That Thomas, in the excitement of the moment, passed from one extreme to another, cannot be asserted by any one who observes that Christ accepted his invocation at once. (Calvin: Never would He have suffered that the honour of the Father should be wrested and transferred to Himself.) "Thou hast believed," referring to Himself, shows that to recognise in Christ the Lord and God, and specifically *his own* Lord and God, is the necessary condition of *faith*. (Calvin: He emphatically calls Him his own twice, to show that he spoke from a living and solemn sense of faith.) To talk of an "exaggerated cry," is altogether out of the question, in relation to a Gospel which everywhere discloses a tendency to place the divinity of Christ in the clearest light.

Ver. 29. "Jesus saith unto him, Thomas, because thou hast seen Me, thou hast believed: blessed are they that have not seen, and yet have believed."—Christ recognises therefore that faith also which has sight for its condition. That He will receive to Himself the well-disposed though weak in faith, that He will help their unbelief by actual demonstration, is a blessed truth, of which His treatment of Thomas is a most consolatory pledge. But the Lord places higher that faith which is present and energetic before sight comes. Thomas is here blamed for not exhibiting that faith. John had seen but little; and yet he reproves himself for not having believed without seeing: comp. ver. 8. The case was much worse with Thomas. He had, in the testimony of his brother Apostles, received such help for a faith grounded upon the word of God, that if the faith had been in any sense strong within him, he would not have required any further seeing. As then, so now, it becomes believers to believe without seeing: compare the saying of Peter, which alludes to this word of our Lord, 1 Pet. i. 8. But then, as now, it pleases Christ to crown and confirm that faith by making Himself known in many ways as its Lord and God. Faith would languish if its actual experience were in continual contradiction to it.—The Aorist participles are to be explained by this, that the process is represented as a closed one, and the μακάριοι is its result.

Chap. xx. 30, 31.

These two verses are not the conclusion of the whole book, but the conclusion of the main body of it, extending from ch. i. 19 downwards. The closing chapter xxi. corresponds to the prologue in ch. i. 1-18. So also the Apocalypse has introduction, body, and conclusion. If we forget that we have here only the conclusion of the body of the Gospel, ch. xxi. must become a mystery. These verses, 30, 31, as a conclusion of the whole Gospel, would in their brevity be out of harmony with the diffuseness of the prologue, as also with the conclusion of the Apocalypse, ch. xxii. 6-21. The body of the work needed a conclusion, such as we have it here, in order to mark it off from the epilogue, which must needs declare itself to be such by its position. We expect such a conclusion all the more, inasmuch as we find that in the body of the Gospel itself there is such a conclusion, ch. xii. 37–50, dividing between the first four groups and the last three.

Vers. 30, 31. "And many other signs truly did Jesus in the presence of His disciples, which are not written in this book: But these are written, that ye might believe that Jesus is the Christ, the Son of God; and that believing ye might have life through His name."—The words πολλὰ—μαθητῶν αὐτοῦ are in allusion, like ch. xii. 37, x. 32, to Ps. lxxviii. 11, 12. We must not limit the *signs* to demonstrations given by the risen Lord to His resurrection; for there is nothing to indicate such a restriction, and a comparison of ch. xii. 37 and xxi. 25 declares against it. But we must not, on the other hand, *exclude* those infallible proofs of the risen Lord: for they fall under the idea of the σημεῖα which Jesus did; they are testimonies in act that Jesus was Messiah: comp. Acts i. 3, where the appearances of the risen Lord are described as τεκμηρία. (Hesychius, τεκμηρίον σημεῖον ἀληθές; Suidas, ἀληθινὸν σημεῖον.) Moreover, these appearances have just before been recorded, and reference to them therefore seems obvious. The included reference to the resurrection alone makes "in the presence of His disciples" intelligible. Only the manifestations of the risen Lord were restricted to the Apostles: all the earlier σημεῖα belonged to a much wider circle, although the disciples were present at them, and indeed, as witnesses chosen of the Lord, ch. xv. 27, must have been present. We must seek this specific reason for the words "in the presence of His disciples;" otherwise "in the presence of all the people," Luke xxiv. 19, would have been the more obvious record. Ch. xxi. 1 also leads us to include the resurrection and its demonstrations. Τοῖς μαθηταῖς there obviously points back to ἐνώπιον τῶν μαθητῶν here.

The σημεῖα which this Gospel copiously records are *ten* in number, which was certainly not fortuitous: seven before the resurrection,—three in Galilee, and four in Judea; and three after the resurrection,—the appearance to Mary Magdalene, and the two appearances among the Apostles. That the "signs" are here made distinctively prominent without including the *words*, is in harmony with the strong emphasis laid upon the ἔργα, the works, throughout John's Gospel, ch. v. 36, x. 38, xv. 24. A reason may be found for it in the fact that the three earlier Evangelists had made these words prominent in their records. By this observation he intimates that he had written not *the* Gospel, but *a* Gospel; and suggests that the supplement of what he failed to record, because it was perfectly given by his predecessors, should be sought in their narratives. On the connection between the concluding words of the Evangelist and the preceding events, Bengel aptly remarks : " To the mention of the faith of Thomas, is very appropriately attached a commendation of faith to all, as the scope of his book." The connection is all the closer, as Thomas had believed on the evidence of a " sign."

THE CONCLUSION OF THE GOSPEL IN CHAPTER XXI.

The introduction of the Gospel, ch. i. 1-18, goes up to the eternal existence of Jesus. In the conclusion, now lying before us, John communicates what refers to the continuation of His Divine-human being in the *Church*, founded upon His death and His resurrection. So also Matthew and Mark closed their Gospels with an express reference to the missionary work of the Apostles. This closing chapter forms a transition from the Gospels to the Acts. First, in vers. 1-14, we have the missionary work of the Apostles, and their heavenly reward. Then, in vers. 15-17, the institution of Peter in his pastoral office; in 18-23, the prediction of their final departure made to the two most eminent Apostles, Peter and John; and finally, in vers. 24, 25, the proper epilogue, in which John announces himself as the author of the Gospel, affirms his own trustworthiness, and alludes to the reason why he had communicated only a *selection* of facts.

The notion that ch. xxi. is a postscript has sprung from a lack of insight into the construction of the Gospel. It leads to the assumption of a fortuitousness in the composition which is altogether unworthy of the apostolical character, and inconsistent with the tenor of this Gospel; and it altogether fails to give any reason why the Apostle did not strike out the conclusion in ch. xx. 30, 31, after the addition of the postscript had rendered it unsuitable.

Ver. 1. "After these things Jesus showed Himself again to the disciples at the sea of Tiberias; and on this wise showed He Himself."—"After these things;" μετὰ ταῦτα, the transition formula so common in John: comp. ch. ii. 12, v. 1, 14, vi. 1. The ἐφανέρωσεν ἑαυτόν (comp. φανέρωσον σεαυτόν, ch. vii. 4) intimates that the risen Lord was ordinarily inaccessible and invisible to His disciples; that He had entered into a manner of existence altogether different from His earlier life: compare the ἐφανερώθη in Mark xvi. 12, 14. Jesus had earlier manifested forth His hidden glory, ch. ii. 11; now His person has become hidden, and it never could be discovered or met unless it voluntarily came forth from its seclusion. To the manifestation here corresponds the appearance in the midst when the doors were shut, ch. xx. 19, 26. Both intimate plainly that the present corporeity of Jesus was altogether different from the former. He who could appear with closed doors was not confined to the region of sensible observation; He was then only manifest when it pleased Him to enter that domain, so that the dim eyes of flesh (Job x. 4) might be able to discern Him.—The *disciples* at the two former appearances were the Apostles, and so were they here.—The sea of Tiberias; a denomination peculiar to John among the Evangelists: comp. on ch. vi. 1. Ἐπί is literally as in ch. vi. 19, and means simply "*on* the sea." The bank is, in Biblical phrase, on or over the waters; hence על very frequently in Hebrew: e.g. Ps. i. 3. And as ἐπί is here Hebraistically used, so ἀπό in ver. 6, corresponding to the Heb. מן of the cause.—The second ἐφανέρωσεν is not to be supplemented by ἑαυτόν—He showed *Himself*—but, in allusion to the *first* Galilean sign, ch. ii. 11, by τὴν δόξαν αὐτοῦ. The mention of Nathanael in ver. 2, pointing to that same first sign, is in favour of this view. The word, needing its object and standing without it, represents as it were an express reference to that first sign. "He showed Himself *thus*, οὕτως," is not a needless diffuseness of narration, but intimates by its circumstantiality the importance of the facts and the attention they claim. It is the manner of Scripture, from Genesis downwards, to draw attention to the importance of events by this kind of repetition and circumstantiality. Thus "he lifted up his eyes and looked" is always, as in Gen. xviii. 2, said when the matter is of great moment, and attention was to be drawn to its importance. So in John we have, for example, "These things therefore the soldiers did," ch. xix. 24. Both seem to stand for a *Nota Bene*.

According to Matt. xxviii. 7, the angel gave the women a commission that they should go tell the disciples, "Behold, He goeth before you into Galilee." That the going before does not mean going *earlier* than they, but a going before them as Pastor and Guide, is plain from a comparison with the Lord's saying in Matt. xxvi. 32, the fulfilment of which the angel announces to be at hand. (Fritzsche: Ecce jam fit quod declaratum est, προάγει. This verb, in the sense of preceding any one, Matt. xxi. 9, Mark xi. 9, Luke xviii. 39, is used as here with the accusative of the person, Matt. ii. 9, Mark x. 32, καὶ ἦν προάγων αὐτοὺς ὁ Ἰησοῦς.) "I will go before you" forms in Matt. xxvi. 32 the antithesis to the *scattering* of the flock caused by the death of the Shepherd; but this meaning it could have only on the supposition that the going before was His leading the regathered flock to Galilee. If, therefore, we perceive that the gathering of the flock was, according to Matthew, to be the condition of Christ's going before them, and to precede the departure into Galilee,—if He was to lead His gathered flock to Galilee, after having gathered them simply and alone by revealing Himself to them, and convincing them of the reality of His resurrection,—then we must assume that the silence of Matthew as to the manifestation of Christ, recorded by the other Evangelists, in the midst of the Apostles on the evening of the day of resurrection in Jerusalem, was not due to his ignorance of the fact, but to his design to give prominence to those records by which Isaiah's prophecy, quoted in his ch. iv. 15, 16, concerning the glorification of the neighbourhood of the Galilean sea, might be shown to have been fulfilled. On the other hand, in perfect harmony with the commission quoted by Matt. xxviii. 10, "Go tell My brethren that they go before Me into Galilee," the manifestations of the Lord in Jerusalem, as recorded by John, were limited in their design to the full conviction of the Apostles that Christ was risen; with the single exception of ch. xx. 21–23, where something is said that *must* have been spoken emphatically at the first meeting with the Apostles. The proper *intercourse* with the Apostles, the "speaking of the things pertaining to the kingdom of God," Acts i. 3, was reserved, even according to John, for Galilee. We have here the *beginning* of that discourse concerning His kingdom. The contents of this chapter are well described by those words of Luke, in Acts i. 3.

Ver. 2. "There were together Simon Peter, and Thomas called Didymus, and Nathanael of Cana in Galilee, and the sons of Zebedee, and two other of His disciples."—All the names mentioned here are introduced with a definite reason. In the case of *Simon*, his surname Peter hinted that reason. The first of the Apostles could not be wanting; and it is in keeping with this, that in the entire narrative he has the first place. Hence he necessarily opens the list. Why *Thomas* was associated with him, is shown by the clause "called Didymus:" comp. on ch. xi. 16. The key to the mention of Nathanael is furnished by the clause "of Cana in Galilee." That could not have been intended to make Nathanael more known; for in ch. i. it was not said that Nathanael was born in Cana, although immediately after the narrative of the meeting between Christ and him we read of the marriage at Cana. Nathanael of Cana was important to the Evangelist, as a representative of the first miracle by which Jesus manifested forth His glory in Cana: comp. ch. ii. 11. Our present manifestation forms the counterpart of that first Galilean miracle. This end is kept in view by the additional clause, " of Galilee." If it had been intended only to note the origin of Nathanael, that would have been inadequate or needless. There was no Cana out of Galilee; and Cana had been three times mentioned as Cana of Galilee, ch. ii. 1, 11, iv. 46 Considering how economical of repetitions the Evangelist is, we cannot regard this as merely a repeated statement of Nathanael's country. The clause was almost equivalent to an express reference to the earlier passages. Why the presence of *John* and his *brother* is expressly mentioned, is explained by their designation as "sons of Zebedee." Zebedee is never elsewhere mentioned in the Gospel of John. With the same appellation of *sons* of Zebedee (the indefinite expression, οἱ τοῦ Ζεβεδαίου, is here designedly used in order to intimate that a more exact definition of their relation is found elsewhere), these two brothers appear in connection with the first fishing at the commencement of our Lord's ministry, the counterpart of which is the fishing in this chapter, deriving its interpretation from the earlier one, and having "I will make you fishers of men" in common with it: comp. Matt. iv. 21, 22; Mark i. 19, 20; Luke v. 10. The two *unnamed* brethren must at any rate have been Apostles; for μαθηταί stands before and after, ver. 14, of the disciples in a narrower sense, the Apostles; and Apostles were especially concerned in this fishing, which symbolized their future apostolical work. The reasons which are discernible for the mention of the five names lead us to suppose that the silence preserved as to the names of the other two was not a disparaging silence. They were not named, only because there was no particular reason for it; and to have named them would have been to obscure the design in the naming of the five. For the rest, they are as good as named; and the Evangelist might reckon upon their being detected. When Peter went a fishing, his brother Andrew would needs accompany him: comp. Matt. iv. 18; Mark i. 29; Luke vi. 14; John vi. 8. And where Andrew was, there we should expect Philip: comp. ch. i. 45, xii. 22; Mark iii. 18. The latter we might expect with all the more confidence, as he was connected also with Nathanael or Bartholomew by a very close bond: comp. i. 46; Matt. x. 3; Luke vi. 14.

The high importance of this event is indicated in the artistic grouping of those concerned in it. The number seven is divided, as commonly in the Apocalypse, into three and four. At the head of the three stands Peter; Thomas, *the divided*, in the middle; on one side of him the man of rock, on the other Nathanael, the true Israelite without guile, ch. i. 48. At the head of the four stand the sons of Zebedee, with Peter, the Apostles of the more intimate circle. The seven are moreover divided again: Peter at the head, then three pairs. The number seven is fixed; but that it was not a fortuitous number, is plain from the details of this grouping. Similarly exact is the grouping in Rev. vi. 15. Other examples of the significance of number in the Gospel of John have been collected in my Commentary on the Apocalypse (vol. ii. Clark's Trans.).

—The seven represented the collective apostolical circle (comp. ver. 14), with Paul included, so far as he was later received with full rights into this circle. They were a majority; only four of the Apostles were wanting; and the more intimate circle was complete. It is remarkable, that in the catalogue of the Apostles, Matt. x. 2–4, the seven here numbered as present take precedence of the absent ones.—" And two other of His disciples" may be compared with " and two of His disciples," ch. i. 35.

Ver. 3. " Simon Peter saith unto them, I go a fishing. They say unto him, We also go with thee. They went forth, and entered into a ship immediately; and that night they caught nothing."—It was shown, in ch. i. 43, that Matt. iv. 18–22 does not indicate the Apostles' having entirely abandoned their vocation. They still pursued it, so far as their new vocation left them time. Augustin refers to Paul, who, with all his superabundant apostolical labour, *victum manibus suis transigebat*. From the resurrection to Pentecost there was an interval to the Apostles wherein they might appropriately seek their maintenance with their own hands. Gregory the Great says justly, however: " Peter returned to his fishing, but Matthew did not return to his tax-gathering. There are things which cannot be applied to altogether without sin, to which after conversion we cannot return." " They went forth" from the town in which Peter resided: Capernaum, according to Matt. xvii. 24, 27; Bethsaida, the fishing town of Capernaum: comp. on ch. vi. 3, according to ch. i. 45. " Immediately:" εὐθύς (comp. ch. xiii. 32, xix. 34) appeared superfluous to many transcribers, and hence was omitted. But it intimates, in keeping with " all the night" in Luke v. 5, the long continuance of the fruitless labour. If the Apostles as soon as they met, thus before the coming of night proper, entered the ship, their unrewarded labour must have lasted through the night. Πιάζω occurs in John six times, besides this passage, and ver. 10; never in the first Gospels.

The detail with which the incident is recorded, has in it something " un-Johannean," if we fail to discern the symbolical character of the whole; but that symbolical design gives weight to things otherwise inconsiderable. The argument, that John must in that case have expressly declared this symbolical character, is ungrounded; for here, no less than in the record of the blighted fig-tree, of which no interpretation is given, the symbolical meaning is plain enough to all thoughtful and reflecting readers, and such only had John in view. The Old Testament gives us, with regard to this, a plain hint, in Ezek. xlvii. 9, 10: comp. on ch. i. 43. If the fishes there were men, to be brought to life by the Messianic salvation, then the fishers could only be the messengers of that salvation, who gather the living into the kingdom of God, and lead them into the fellowship of the Church. The word which our Lord spake at the first fishing, "I will make you fishers of men," applies to the present fishing; for John always presumes upon the records of the three Evangelists being known. We have a key also in the parable of the net in Matt. xiii. Accordingly the sea signifies the world, the net the kingdom of God, in its capacity to receive men into itself. But the demonstration that we have here before us an allegory in act, lies in this, that the narrative only in this point of view is clear, luminous, and significant in every particular; and that thus only it is suitable to the character of an epilogue, to which only that pertained which was transitional from the Gospel to the history of the Acts. If we reject the spiritual interpretation, the narrative of vers. 1–14 has certainly a strange aspect; and we must, if we would be sincere, confess that we would rather pass over it. The emphasis would then fall upon the fact that Jesus generally manifested Himself to His disciples, and not upon the communications which He made to them; nor can we then see precisely why the narrative stands in the *epilogue;* and moreover, the demarcation is disturbed which separates the appearances of Jesus in Galilee from those in Jerusalem. The doubts which have been entertained as to the genuineness of ch. xxi. have their root in the inability to discern this spiritual meaning,—an inability natural enough to those who are not trained by the exposition of the Old Testament to understand the New. Those who yield to such doubts, however, are obliged to confess, that the record is throughout and entirely Johannean in its cast.

That Simon Peter's energy took the initiative in regard to this ordinary fishing, was an intimation that he would take the lead of his brethren in the spiritual fishing also. But when he only intimates his own firm resolution, expecting the free determination of the rest, we are led to presume that his precedence would not be in the spiritual domain a primacy of tyranny; that it was not one established formally by rule, but that it was to result from that pre-eminence of energy which would attach the others to himself in free subordination and joyful recognition of the gift imparted to him by the Lord.—" And that night they caught nothing:" on the first fishing Simon said, " We have toiled all the night, and have taken nothing." As the fact was in both cases brought about by Divine disposal, we are led at once to assume that it was eminently significant. A passage in the Old Testament, which is here as it were dramatically expounded, gives us the solution. In Isa. xlix. the prophet depicts, vers. 1–3, the vocation and destiny which the Lord appointed to His servant, the Messiah. In ver. 4 he exhibits the contradiction between the mission and its result: the people of the covenant, to whom it was first addressed, requite that faithful labour with ingratitude! " Then I said, I have laboured in vain; I have spent my strength for nought and in vain:" Sept. Κενῶς ἐκοπίασα, εἰς μάταιον καὶ εἰς οὐδὲν ἔδωκα τὴν ἰσχύν μου. In compensation for refractory Israel, the Lord gives His Servant for an inheritance the *heathen*, who also in Ezekiel are the proper object of the fishing: the fishes there also are won from the dead sea of the heathen world. The historical commentary is found in the Acts (comp. especially ch. xiii. 46), and in Rom. xi. 9–11, according to which Israel as a people despised the Gospel salvation, and only a small proportion of individuals received it. *Night* signifies, in the symbolism of Scripture, an unsaved state—comp. on ch. xiii. 30, xi. 9, 10—and thus here the fruitlessness of work. Weitzel (in his valuable treatise On the Testimony borne by the fourth Evangelist to himself, S. and K. 49) gives us the right interpretation, when he sees in the fact a " type of the long fruitless labour of the original Apostles among the Jews, after the first sudden pentecostal successes." An objection has been raised against this view, that it represents the abundant success among the Gentiles as vouchsafed to the original Apostles, whereas it was vouchsafed to Paul; but Gal. ii. 9, which is appealed to, affords no support to that notion, inasmuch as that verse only treats of a temporary arrangement. Peter in Rome, John in Ephesus, proved that the contrary was the truth. The impossibility of the permanent limitation of the original Apostles to the Jews, is evident from the conclusion of Matthew's Gospel. Moreover, the entire contrast between the original Apostles and Paul is based on error. We have already shown that the disciples present at this fishing represented the collective apostolical circle, and that as including Paul with his abundant labour, which was vouchsafed to him only as a member of the body combined under Peter as its head.

Ver. 4. " But when the morning was now come, Jesus stood on the shore; but the disciples knew not that it was Jesus."—*Morning* is the type of dawning salvation : comp. on ch. xx. 1; Ps. xxx. 6, lix. 17, xc. 14, cxliii. 8. For πρωίας, comp. ch. xviii. 28, xx. 1, in both cases πρωί. We have in Matt. xxvii. 1 the full πρωίας δὲ γενομένης literally. That passage and Matt. xx. 1 are the only two besides this in the New Testament where πρωΐα occurs; and both times in a connection where the guilt and the rejection of the Jews are spoken of, when the new day of Christ's glorification breaks among the Gentiles : comp. ἡ ἀποβολὴ αὐτῶν, καταλλαγὴ κόσμου, Rom. xi. 15 ; and τῷ αὐτῶν παραπτώματι ἡ σωτηρία τοῖς ἔθνεσι, Rom. xi. 11.—" On the shore :" the combination of ἔστη and εἰς is as in ch. xx. 19, 26. Here Jesus stands on the margin. At the first fishing, Luke v. 4, He went up into the ship; in ch. vi. 19, He came to the disciples on the sea. That He here remained standing on the bank, points to the fact that now, withdrawn from the sea of the world, He belonged to another stage of being. To Him applied what will one day be true of all His people, " There was no more sea," Rev. xxi. 1 (compare my commentary on this passage). That He was on the bank, and His disciples on the sea, was an illustration of His word, ch. xvii. 11, " I am no longer in the world, but these are in the world." In the parable of the net, in Mark xiii., the margin signifies in ver. 48, according to ver. 49, the future state, the " end of the world."[1]

" The disciples knew not that it was Jesus :" so precisely of Mary Magdalene, ch. xx. 14, " And she knew not that it was Jesus." Here again our Lord appeared " in another form," because it was not His will to be recognised at once. In this

[1] The careful Grotius saw in this, as in many other points of our chapter, the true meaning: " Signifying that He through the resurrection had reached the shore ; they were still on the deep."

manner the impression upon the disciples would be deepened; at the same time they would be led into a perception of the truth, that Jesus was always with them, although their eyes might not always be able to discern Him.

Ver. 5. "Then Jesus saith unto them, Children, have ye any meat? They answered Him, No."—*Τέκνα* : thus does the Lord address the disciples in Mark x. 24. *Παιδία* is distinguished from this here. *Τέκνα* might be adults; *παιδία*, on the contrary, designates the age of childhood : comp. Luke i. 80, *τὸ δὲ παιδίον ηὔξανε*, xi. 40; 1 Cor. xiv. 20. *Παιδία* is the term by which age addresses youth, authority those subordinate, and wisdom the ignorant and inexperienced : comp. 1 John ii. 13, 18. Jesus here by the term *παιδία* assumes the position of *καθηγητής*, Matt. xxiii. 8, which was appropriate to Him, especially in relation to the *fishing* of His Apostles. The diminutive form gives the expression a certain tenderness.

Προσφάγιον, what was eaten with bread. Jesus condescends to the language of the *fishermen*, who ordinarily ate only fish with bread : compare what was said upon *ὀψάριον*, ch. vi. 9. This last word could not be used here; for that in John always signifies the individual article of food eaten with the bread, the single fish : comp. ch. vi. 9, *δύο ὀψάρια*, ver. 11, and vers. 9, 10, 13 of the present chapter. But here the general idea of food eaten with the bread was meant. "Have ye any meat?" *μὴ* stands where a negative answer is presupposed or expected (Winer, 453). Jesus shows by the style of the question that He knew how the matter was, and indeed wished it otherwise. The *οὐ* of the disciples, confirming His supposition, is followed by an intimation of the way in which they might alter the state of things. That Jesus put the question for His own sake, that He would have fish for Himself, is shown by a comparison with Luke xxiv. 41, and yet more definitely by ver. 10, where, after the state of things was *changed*, He caused the fish to be brought forward which the disciples had taken. As formerly He hungered for the fruit of the fig-tree, so now does He hunger for the fishes which the disciples might have taken, but had not; not for the natural fishes as such,—the risen Redeemer had no need of bodily food, and vers. 9, 12, 14 show that that would not have been wanting to Him,—but for the men whom the fishes signified : comp. ch. iv. 7, where our Lord says to the woman of Samaria, " Give Me to drink." Jesus would spiritually eat of the food which the disciples had provided, and they, on the other hand, should eat of His food.

Ver. 6. " And He said unto them, Cast the net on the right side of the ship, and ye shall find. They cast therefore; and now they were not able to draw it for the multitude of fishes."— The ship signifies the Church, the net her missions. The left side is, in the Divine fishery, the side of the Jews, the right side that of the Gentiles. The right is the better hand, and therefore the right side is the good side. The meaning of the name Benjamin, the son of the right hand, is, " His father loveth him," Gen. xliv. 22, and, " the beloved of Jehovah," Deut. xxxiii. 12: compare my commentary on Ps. lxxx. In Gen. xlviii. the youth on whom the right hand was laid is more blessed than he on whom the left. "The right hand," says Gesenius (Thes. ימן), "*boni ominis erat.*" Because the right hand is the better, Matt. v. 20, the Lord places His sheep on the right hand and the goats on the left. The multitude of the fishes here represents the " great multitude which no man could number, out of every nation, and tribe, and people, and tongue," Rev. vii. 9. That the disciples without hesitation acted on the suggestion of the Unknown, shows that His being had for them an imposing majesty.

Ver. 7. " Therefore that disciple whom Jesus loved saith unto Peter, It is the Lord. Now, when Simon Peter heard that it was the Lord, he girt his fisher's coat unto him (for he was naked), and did cast himself into the sea."—The thoughtful John first recognises the Lord; the energetic Peter, who on another occasion, Matt. xiv. 28, said, " Lord, if it be Thou, bid me come unto Thee on the water," casts himself into the sea to reach Him. We see here that the primacy of Peter had its limits, that it extended no further than the energy of action came into consideration. As here, so certainly in later times, he *heard* John, and in many things listened to him in his Christian vocation. Ὁ κύριος: John so designates Jesus before His resurrection only twice: comp. on ch. xiii. 23. Thus he names the risen Saviour also in ch. xx. 18, 20, 25, 28, and several times in the sequel of this chapter. Διαζώννυμι occurs in John only here and ch. xiii. 4, 5. The middle voice signifies " Gird oneself." Τὸν ἐπενδύτην is the accusative of closer definition, so frequent in Hebrew: comp. τὸν ἀριθμόν, ch. vi. 10 (Winer). It does not mean that he drew on the garment, but that he girded himself in it: therefore he was already clothed with it. "He was naked" explains this girding: the connection shows with what restriction we must take the "naked." It can refer only to the circumstance that Peter was not provided with the outside garment, the ὑποδύτης. The ἐπενδύτης (comp. ἐπενδύσασθαι, superinducere, 2 Cor. v. 4) intimates by its very name that it took a subordinate place in the clothing. That *naked* stands often for slight clothing, needs no further demonstration: Grotius has done all that is necessary to show that the idea of absolute nakedness is to be repelled, even if Gen. iii. 7, 21 were not sufficient. Peter had on him a mere wrapper. Theophylact says, "a linen shirt, such as the Phœnician and Syrian fishermen were wont to wear." This in his labour he had worn ungirt; but now he girded himself, the better to swim. Swimming is suggested by the "*throwing himself into the sea.*" As to any further preparation of his person in order to appear fitly before the Lord, the text says nothing, whatever the expositors may say.—The Apostle enters into this detail because this sudden decision of Peter symbolized the gift which was afterwards developed in the government of the Church. With the same impetuous promptitude with which he threw himself into the Galilean sea, he afterwards threw himself into the sea of the world. Always to be first, not to leave the initiative to others, and even to restrain those who take it, seems to be one of the first marks of a vocation to govern the Church. Our verse might be applied to the present spirit of church government in evangelical Germany. It cannot be in this respect according to the heart of Jesus; were it so, He could not have placed Peter at the head of His Apostles.

Ver. 8. "And the other disciples came in a little ship (for they were not far from land, but as it were two hundred cubits), dragging the net with fishes."—Γάρ explains and justifies the disciples' having come, without following Peter's example, to shore. So slight was the distance from the land, that the difference between them could not be great. Their justification is completed by the σύροντες, "dragging the net." Peter did right in leaving the ship, and the others did right in remaining. The exact statement of the distance on the lake corresponds to that in ch. vi. 19. John here, as in Rev. xxi. 17, measures by ells. The peculiar use of ἀπό with the meaning "distance *from*" is only found in John, in the Gospel and the Apocalypse: comp. on ch. xi. 18; with the "about fifteen furlongs off" corresponds very strictly the "as it were two hundred cubits" here. Πλοιάριον is here used; previously πλοῖον. We find the same interchange between the two words in ch. vi. 17 seq.

Ver. 9. "As soon then as they were come to land, they saw a fire of coals there, and fish laid thereon, and bread."—'Ανθρακία is only here and ch. xviii. 18. On κειμένην, comp. ch. ii. 6, 19, 29; on ἐπικείμενον, ch. xi. 38. 'Οψάριον is used by John only of single fishes; and the *one* fish is suggested by the single loaf. John describes simply in genuine historical manner what he with the rest *found*. As to whence the fire of coals, the fish and the bread, came, he keeps silence; just as in ch. xx. 19, 26 he limits himself to saying that Jesus came when the doors were shut, without travelling beyond the sphere of his observation to enter into the question as to *how* the Lord came. The supposition that Jesus provided these things as men do, rests upon a misconception of the new sphere in which the risen Lord moved. If Jesus was, in truth, "The Lord," there is no reason for bringing down the fact by such explanations into the region of ordinary life. Jesus, who, according to ch. vi., fed thousands in the days of His flesh with five loaves and two fishes; at whose command, according to Matt. xvii. 27, Peter caught the fish with the stater in its mouth; who, at the first Galilean miracle, turned water into wine,—retained here also the name of "Wonderful," which the ancient prophecy had given Him.

Ver. 10. "Jesus saith unto them, Bring of the fish which ye have now caught."—John speaks of the fishes, ἰχθύες, vers. 6, 8, 11. Jesus describes the same thing by another word, προσφάγιον, ver. 5, ὀψάρια here. The difference had some significance. The disciples spoke as in the style of fishermen; Jesus for him who was to eat. He regards the fish only in the light of food.—Why did the Lord cause His disciples to bring of their fish?—not that they might serve, together with the one fish which already lay on the fire of coals, for the disciples' repast. The symbolical character of the whole incident opposes this; as also does ver. 13, which shows that the disciples ate only of that one fish and one loaf which were provided already before the landing of the net. That important circumstance, further, would not have been omitted. Manifestly the end was answered, when the fish, or rather one representing the whole, was brought to Jesus; for nothing more was done with them. The fishes were regarded under the aspect of *food*, as the very term used has shown. But materially the Lord did not eat of them any more than the disciples. This shows that they bore a symbolical character. If they represented men or nations gathered into the kingdom of God, then our Lord's eating was simply spiritual: it signified the Lord's participation in the fruit of His servants' labours, the joy which their labour would provide for Him in the future: comp. Jer. xv. 16, "Thy words were found, and I did eat them; and Thy word was unto me the joy and rejoicing of mine heart," where eating is equivalent to the finding pleasure in it, as the succeeding words show. Ezekiel says, ch. iii. 3, concerning the Divine revelation, "Then did I eat it; and it was in my mouth as honey for sweetness." This spiritual eating which His disciples were to prepare for Jesus, was to be the condition on which their own eating should depend. So Isaac ate of his son's venison before he blessed him: that was the condition of the paternal blessing, that he should first show himself a son by providing the venison; and in the enjoyment of the venison the blessing was uttered.

Ver. 11. "Simon Peter went up, and drew the net to land full of great fishes, an hundred and fifty and three: and for all there were so many; yet was not the net broken."—The same word, ἀνέβη, is used, Mark vi. 51, for entering the ship. Peter must first go up into the ship, in order to release the net which adhered to it. He performed this task, doubtless, not alone: he, however, was the chief personage; and his act only is mentioned, because he was the centre of the spiritual fishery which was here symbolized. In this spiritual fishery the drawing of the net to land signified, according to Matt. xiii. 48, 49, the "end of the world," and what will take place then. Accordingly, Peter here represents not the mere individual apostolate, but at the same time the whole ministry of teaching and preaching, which has continued that apostolate from age to age. The net full of fishes represents not merely the "first-fruits of the Gentiles," as they were gathered in by the Apostles themselves, but the whole "fulness of the Gentiles," their πλήρωμα, Rom. xi. 25, as it is to be gathered down to the end of the world: comp. Matt. xxiv. 14. It follows from this as a direct consequence, that we must not limit our views here to the Apostles as individuals.

That the number one hundred and fifty and three must have a deep significance, is urgently felt by all who discern the symbolical meaning of the whole; otherwise the minuteness of specification would have a character of pettiness: comp. Bengel. It is bootless to object that the historical character of the chapter must suffer if we make the number here of any importance. For the distinction between the great fishes, which alone are reckoned, and the little ones, is a mere passing allusion; so that there is a certain latitude allowed here for theological speculation. The deep meaning of the number was acknowledged in ancient times. Jerome suggested that there were a hundred and fifty-three kinds of fishes, and that it was thereby signified that the Church was a net which received of every kind. But it cannot be established that any one in ancient times counted precisely that number of genera; not to say that such an enumeration was current at the time (Lampe), which however it must have been on that supposition. Then again there is absolutely no analogy for such a *natural-historical* allusion. All such secret hints in John's Gospel and in the Apocalypse remain within the domain of *Scripture.* Grotius perceived rightly that the number had some connection with 2 Chron. ii. 17 : " And Solomon numbered all the strangers that were in the land of Israel, after the number wherewith David his father had numbered them; and there were found an hundred and fifty thousand, and three thousand and six hundred :" comp. 1 Kings ix. 20. On the " strangers," Kimchi remarks: " The remnant of the Canaanites, who were no longer given over to the worship of false gods." It has been shown, in the commentary on Zech. ix. 7 (Christology, vol. iii. Clark's Trans.), that proselytes were here spoken of; and that the reception of strangers in Israel during David's life was a type of the future entrance of the fulness of the Gentiles among the people of God. As our present passage is related to 2 Chron. ii. 17, so is Rev. xiii. 18 related to Ezra ii. 13. Without the Old Testament key, both passages entirely baffle us. The objection, that John omits the six hundred of the calculation in Chronicles, has but little force. John counts one fish for every thousand; and therefore an incomplete thousand would go for nothing.

Τοσούτων, so great in *number*: comp. on ch. xii. 37. The "net broken" stands in no antithesis to Luke's "and their net brake," ch. v. 6. There it was only its being in *danger* of breaking,—a danger which, as we read, was at once obviated. But here also there is the urgent danger of breaking, as is evident from the τοσούτων ὄντων. Where all is significant, this trait also is of moment. Grotius discerned in it a "presage of the wonderful unity of those who should be gathered into the Church by the labour of the Apostles." Of this we can the less doubt, because already, in John's time, the word σχίσμα was also established to denote divisions in the Church (comp. 1 Cor. i. 10, xi. 18, xii. 25), and is used in John's Gospel itself for spiritual discord: ch. vii. 43, ix. 16, x. 19. The words are of very considerable importance, as we are all too much inclined to look at the divisions which seem to exist, and to forget the bond of unity that is there. We need not take refuge from the visible in the invisible Church, any more than we need fly from the past and the present into the "millennial reign." The net was *never* broken, οὐκ ἐσχίσθη; and it is better for us to purge our eyes, that we may see the unity which still obtains in the Christian world. One Lord, one Spirit, one baptism, one Holy Scripture, the common heritage of the three confessions of the ancient Church,—all these show that, despite all σχίσματα, springing from the τοσούτων ὄντων, the necessary concomitants of so many nations with all their peculiarities brought into one fellowship, there is yet an indissoluble bond of unity that encircles the whole Christian Church.

Ver. 12. "Jesus saith unto them, Come and dine. And none of the disciples durst ask Him, Who art Thou? knowing that it was the Lord."—Δεῦτε: comp. ch. iv. 29. 'Αριστάω signifies here, as in Luke xi. 37, and like ἄριστον, Matt. xxii. 4, Luke xi. 38, xiv. 12, the chief meal of the day, the midday repast. This was never in ordinary life bound strictly to the hour; and the symbolical character of all here makes the precise hour of the less importance. An "early morning meal," however, is unsuitable to the meaning of the event. The phrase and the symbol here go hand in hand, and both point to something later than the early repast. It was only to the mid-day meal and the supper that guests were wont to be invited.— Ἐξετάζειν is stronger than ἐρωτᾶν: although the disciples were sure that it was the Lord, yet they would gladly have heard from His own lips, for blessed confirmation and more full assurance, had not the Lord's majesty restrained them. In the presence of that majesty, the question seemed to them to have a derogatory character. The ἐτόλμα shows that the words εἰδότες, κ.τ.λ., were to represent the question, not as superfluous, but as unbecoming. They durst not demand satisfaction of the Lord, as of an indifferent person.

Ver. 13. "Jesus then cometh, and taketh bread, and giveth them, and fish likewise."—Jesus *came* at the head of the disciples, from the net brought to the shore to the fire of coals. After the disciples had received Him as their guest, He took the place of host. Grotius: "He showed Himself to be *Paterfamilias* to the Church, whose it was to give every man his portion." The feast which He gave them consisted only of one fish and one loaf; the loaves were in those days small, and the fish was not a large one. This was sparing hospitality (Bengel is wrong: "*satiavit* omnes"), if we forget the symbolical character of the whole; rather the scantiness of the fare was intended to intimate that its end was not in itself, but that it signified something different, something higher. It has been regarded as meaning, that Jesus provides for His disciples in the present life (compare "The labourer is worthy of his hire," Matt. x. 10); but such an interpretation is far from satisfactory, inasmuch as it makes Christ's hospitality but small towards His people; and moreover, it is altogether refuted by the fact that the meal did not take place until the net was drawn to the shore. We must therefore carry the interpretation into the next world. The meal signified the heavenly reward of faithful labour: compare "Great is your reward in heaven," Matt. v. 12, and "He that reapeth receiveth a reward, and gathereth fruit unto life everlasting," ch. iv. 36. This heavenly reward is often introduced under the figure of a feast, which Jesus provides for His people, Luke xii. 37; xxii. 30, "That ye may eat and drink at My table in My kingdom;" Matt. xxvi. 29, xxii. 1 seq., xxv. 10; Rev. vii. 17, xix. 9. The Apostles here received not merely a symbol, but also an earnest of that heavenly feast. Regarding this entirely symbolical meaning, we understand how it was that the breaking of bread was wanting, Luke xxiv. 30; and more than that, the benediction and thanksgiving: comp. ch. vi. 11. These took place only in feasts which were limited in their design to themselves. Here, where the meal represented benefits which were not to be imparted until a future state, they would have been out of keeping. The purport of the entertainment also explains the circumstance, that Jesus Himself did not eat: He did not say, "Let us dine;" but, "Come and dine." The Apostles all the while spake not a word. They knew that they had to do with the majesty that must be waited for to begin. Silence was appropriate to this meal; speech would have obscured its symbolical meaning. The feast interpreted itself.

Ver. 14. "This is now the third time that Jesus showed Himself to His disciples after that He was risen from the dead." —In this connection the disciples are the disciples in the stricter sense,—the majority of the apostolical circle, represented by their most eminent members. To them Christ had appeared only twice before—on the evening of the resurrection, and eight days afterward. The manifestation to Mary Magdalene, to Peter, to the Emmaus disciples, come not here into view. John enumerates only the manifestations which were granted to the apostolical college. He further indicates, that there were afterwards other appearances, which John, however, would not record. John *counts* elsewhere also, ch. ii. 11, iv. 54, which latter passage has close affinity with the present, so far as the expression goes. Even when he does not expressly enumerate, he evidently attaches much importance to number; as is plain from the fact, that he narrates three miraculous occurrences in Judea, four in Galilee,—seven in all. On ἐγερθεὶς ἐκ νεκρῶν, comp. ch. ii. 22, xii. 9, 17.

Vers. 15-23.

Jesus commits to Peter the care of His flock, and exhorts him to labour after that love which is the necessary condition of the worthy discharge of his duty. He foreannounces also by what death, in the discharge of that duty, he should glorify God, and answers his question as to the end which would befall his fellow-disciple John.

With this general glance at the future development of the Church, is fitly connected his institution in office whom Jesus, when He first met him, ch. i. 43, described as the rock on which He would build His Church.

Ver. 15. " So, when they had dined, Jesus saith to Simon Peter, Simon, son of Jonas, lovest thou Me more than these? He saith unto Him, Yea, Lord ; Thou knowest that I love Thee. He saith unto him, Feed My lambs."—John speaks of Simon Peter: Jesus addresses him as Simon, son of Jonas. The reason lay not in any allusion to Peter's denial, which might be supposed to have rendered him unworthy of his other name. During the whole of this colloquy there does not occur the faintest allusion to the denial of Peter. Such allusions have been introduced and forced upon the text by expositors. Peter's denial—of which too much every way is made— was long over. Even Stier, who holds fast the current notion, is obliged to confess, " There is no trace, in vers. 3, 7, of any timorousness in Peter's entrance into the apostolical circle." The true reason of the address is rather to be sought in a comparison with ch. i. 43: " Thou art Simon, the son of Jonas; thou shalt be called Peter." To the second clause there corresponds here, " Feed My sheep." The promotion would have been anticipated, the condition of that promotion would have been lowered in significance, if Simon had at the outset here received the appellation Peter. He is remanded back, as it were, into his natural position, in order that he may be exalted out of it into new dignity. Hitherto he had been only *Peter designate.* Now he was to be inducted into his office as Peter. The designation is, so to speak, pretermitted, in order to lay all the stress upon the *condition* of it. So also, in Matt. xvi. 17, the Lord first addressed Peter as Simon Barjona, and announced to him that He would make him Peter. Those who explain the omission of the name Peter by a reference to his denial, rend our passage violently from its connection with ch. i. 43 and Matt. xvi. 17.

Jesus asks Peter if he loved Him more than *these,* the other disciples. The question about the *more* takes it for granted that there was conceded to Peter a position excelling that of all the rest (comp. Matt. xvi. 18),—that he was to be truly Peter, the rock upon which the Church was to be built, the pastor of the flock of Christ.—The Lord might have said, "Thou lovest Me more than these, therefore feed My sheep." That this was the actual fact, is plain from his having the flock committed to him. From the presence of the result, we may argue the presence of the condition on which that result depended. But in naming the condition, the Lord puts it in the form of a question; and that because the loving more was not a fixed and unalterable experience, but something that might at any time be lost, something that must be preserved and increased by watching and praying, something that was always questionable, and therefore matter of earnest self-examination.—Asher, in Deut. xxxiii. 24, is spoken of as the most favoured among his brethren, and as blessed before the sons. The same might have been said of every other son of Jacob. Each was such in his own sphere. So also love to Jesus has its various spheres. Which of these spheres comes into notice here, must be estimated by the position which Peter was to assume. Peter had just shown that his love was more energetic in one particular direction than that of the others, inasmuch as he threw himself into the sea while the others followed after in the ship. This constant girding himself in the service of the Lord, comp. ver 18, was his loving more than the rest. The government of the Church demanded pre-eminently a practically energetic and effective love. In this Peter was superior to John, even as Martha was to Mary.

Peter assures the Lord that he loved Him; he says nothing about "more than others." He knew well that he might, in a certain sense, answer in the affirmative (comp. 1 Cor. xv. 10, where, instead of "I have laboured more than they all," it might have been "I have loved more than they all"); but the affirmation would not pass his lips, because he felt how much in other respects he fell behind his fellow-Apostles, and John especially. But while in one point his answer lagged behind the question, in compensation it went before it in another. Peter substituted for the ἀγαπᾶν the φιλεῖν, which rather denotes the tenderness of love: comp. on ch. xi. 5. Probably he used רחם, *diligere ex intimis visceribus*, with allusion to the beginning of Ps. xviii., "I will love Thee heartily, O Lord, my strength."—"Thou knowest" refers to Ps. xl. 10, where the singer, after the assurance of his thankful love, says, "O Lord, Thou knowest," precisely as here. That Peter really meant the Supreme Lord by his Κύριε,—to which in the original יהוה corresponds, rendered by the Septuagint here, as commonly, Κύριε,—is evident from what follows, "Thou knowest all things," ver. 17: to know all things is the prerogative of the Lord God alone. The design of the appeal to the omniscience of the Lord, was the same as in the psalm. In my commentary there I observed: "'O Lord, Thou knowest,' intimates how easily we may delude ourselves and others by the semblance of readiness for God's praise. Let us see to it always that we can appeal to the omniscience of God in this matter." "Lord, Thou knowest," occurs also in Ezek. xxxvii. 3; but this passage does not stand in such close relation to our present one. It is the original of the "Lord, Thou knowest," in Rev. vii. 14.

Jesus says first, "Feed My lambs:" ἀρνίον, the diminutive of ἀρήν. On occasion of the second and third questions, He substitutes the usual πρόβατα, sheep. The ἀρνίον, occurring elsewhere only in the Apocalypse, points back to Isa. xl. 11, where it is said of Jehovah the Good Shepherd, "He will gather the lambs in His arms." Christ, Jehovah manifest in the flesh, commits His tender lambs, when He leaves the earth, to Peter. The spiritual sheep are at the same time *lambs*, needing tender and vigilant care; "if overdriven, they may soon die."—"*My* lambs:" Christ is the "chief Shepherd," 1 Pet. v. 4, whose own the sheep are, John x. 12; He commits His sheep to Peter as His chief pastor; He again commits them, 1 Pet. v. 1-3, to the presbyters as the under-shepherds, for that is involved in his styling himself their fellow-elder (comp. my Comm. on the Revelation).[1]—Instead of βόσκω, Jesus the second time uses ποιμαίνω. Βόσκω, the Latin *pasco*, is properly to *pasture*: care for their own nourishment is one of the first obligations of the good shepherd: compare "shall find pasture," ch. x. 9. Ποιμαίνω is more general, and signifies the whole pastoral care. The third time our Lord recurs to βόσκω,

---

[1] Beza: *Meos:* Not therefore as their Lord, as Peter acknowledges; nor as ἀρχιποίμην (that was Christ alone, the Lord of the sheep, who gave His blood for their redemption), but as His faithful minister.

to impress it thoroughly upon Peter, that he must make this portion of his pastoral office his main and first concernment.

Ver. 16. "He saith to him again the second time, Simon, son of Jonas, lovest thou Me? He saith unto Him, Yea, Lord; Thou knowest that I love Thee. He saith unto him, Feed My sheep."—The second question differs from the first, in that Jesus omits the "more than these." Peter again substitutes for ἀγαπῶ his φιλῶ. Not until he had done this twice, does our Lord take up his φιλῶ into His question, as if in recognition of it. Πάλιν is connected with δεύτερον also in ch. iv. 54. "Again" indicates that Jesus went beyond the first question; "a second time" points forward to the third in ver. 17. The reading προβάτια, here and ver. 17 is merely an imitation of ἀρνία. Προβάτιον is not known in the Old Testament, or in the Septuagint, or in the Apocrypha. Everywhere we have only πρόβατα and ἀρνία: the latter in the Sept. of Jer. l. 45, and Ps. cxiii. 4, 6.

Ver. 17. "He saith unto him the third time, Simon, son of Jonas, lovest thou Me? Peter was grieved because He said unto him the third time, Lovest thou Me? And he said unto Him, Lord, Thou knowest all things; Thou knowest that I love Thee. Jesus saith unto him, Feed My sheep."—Jesus asks thrice, because three, the first number of completeness, is the signature of emphasis; therefore for the same reason that John in ch. xix. 35, gave a triple assurance of the fidelity of his narrative. As in the Old Testament the number three, in a number of cases, occurs with this meaning (comp. *e.g.* the priestly benediction, the triple Holy in Isa. vi.), and as the New Testament presents undeniable instances of the same (comp. 2 Cor. xii. 8), there is no reason to assume any special reference to the triple denial of Peter. There is but a connection of form between the two; and in the case of the denial, the number three was the number of completeness. Peter is *grieved*. The triple question of his Lord showed that there was a distrust of his love, and Peter felt how well grounded that distrust was: comp. "I am a sinful man, O Lord," Luke v. 8. But though with sorrow, he can also with confidence appeal to the Searcher of hearts for the sincerity of his love.

That Jesus, by a threefold repetition, and therefore with the strongest emphasis, represents love to Himself as the great requirement for feeding the flock of God; that He does not mention the love of God, which in the Old Testament law is the one thing supreme,—can be explained and justified only on the ground of Christ's perfect and absolute divinity: not acknowledging His divinity, we cannot but regard it as an invasion of the rights of Him who will not give His honour to another. Concurrently with "Lovest thou *Me*?" our Lord speaks only of *His* sheep, while in the Old Testament the flock of Jehovah is always spoken of.—" Lord, Thou knowest all things," absolutely transcends the creaturely sphere. To know all things is ever in the Old Testament the prerogative of God: comp. *e.g.* Ps. vii. 10, cxxxix. That Jesus shared this prerogative, Peter had variously experienced in fact. We have a parallel generally in ch. xvi. 39, where the Apostles say, "Now we know that Thou knowest all things:" comp. also ch. ii. 24.

Ver. 18. "Verily, verily, I say unto thee, When thou wast young, thou girdedst thyself, and walkedst whither thou wouldest: but when thou shalt be old, thou shalt stretch forth thy hands, and another shall gird thee, and carry thee whither thou wouldest not."—The delivery to Peter of his office is followed by a foreannouncement of the sufferings which he would have to endure in the discharge of it, and of the issue which was reserved for him: Luke ix. 31; 2 Pet. i. 15. The foreknowledge of this departure was part of Peter's preparation for his duty; it served also to still in him all lust of dominion, to extinguish in him all desire to "lord it over God's heritage," 1 Pet. v. 3: moreover, it drove him to seek from above all needful help for so perilous an office. (Grotius: "How difficult an office he received! The matter was one that involved the sacrifice of liberty and life.")—Νεώτερος, younger, is the comparative: the point of comparison must be sought only in the γηράσης that follows, "became old." Accordingly the whole period is included from the present until old age, and the death of crucifixion to ensue. "Thou wast," ἧς, is to be explained on the ground that Jesus looks back over Peter's life from its end. If we overlook this, and refer the ἧς, not to the ideal, but to the actual past, the whole long and important space between the youth of Peter and his death fails to come into view. The expression would also be somewhat harsh, since it was in this very interval that Peter's girding himself was so momentous for the Church, while the girding of the actual past was not brought into consideration. "Thou girdedst thyself" stands in undeniable relation to the girding of himself in ver. 7. In that act the Lord beheld a symbol of the unrestrained energy with which Peter would strongly and independently execute his vocation. Men gird themselves when they go to labour or travel (Buchner: "We gird ourselves when we prepare and raise ourselves to undertake something difficult"): comp. "Let him gird himself and serve me," Luke xvii. 8; Ex. xii. 11, 2 Kings iv. 29; Acts xii. 8, where the angel said to Peter, "Gird thyself, and put on thy sandals." In Prov. xxxi. 17, the girding the loins runs parallel with strengthening the hands.—The opposite of "Thou girdedst thyself, and wentest whither thou wouldest," is, "And another shall gird thee, and lead thee whither thou wouldest not." The contrast must be simply the general one between independence or unrestrained energy, and dependence or passiveness. To substitute *binding* for girding is in itself inadmissible, as girding is never used in that sense; and it is further opposed by the antithesis. We then read "shall bring," not "shall lead:" in order to make the passiveness more emphatic, comp. the $\phi\acute{\epsilon}\rho\epsilon\iota\nu$ in relation to Christ on His way of suffering, Mark xv. 22. The "*Other*" is not expressly defined. The only point was to express the contrast of autonomy, or self-rule, and heteronomy, or the rule of others. The "not willing" refers to the sensitive flesh, shrinking even in those most advanced in the spiritual life: comp. Matt. xvi. 22, 23.

We have not yet remarked on the $\grave{\epsilon}\kappa\tau\epsilon\nu\epsilon\hat{\iota}\varsigma\ \tau\grave{\alpha}\varsigma\ \chi\epsilon\hat{\iota}\rho\acute{\alpha}\varsigma\ \sigma o\nu$. Were this not there, we should have only the general antithesis of activity and passiveness, self-rule and the rule of others. But "Thou shalt stretch forth thine hands," standing first, points to the special fact in which the heteronomy and the passiveness would be shown. We cannot doubt that his *crucifixion* is meant; for the *Crucified* is speaking to Peter, whose feelings had been ineffaceably impressed by the outstretched hands which he had so lately seen. Any other interpretation must tend to embarrassment; no other outstretching of the hands can be safely thought of. The stretching out of the hands is elsewhere noticed as a characteristic of crucifixion: compare the classical passages in Wetstein. Artemidorus mentions, as belonging to crucifixion, $\tau\grave{\eta}\nu\ \tau\hat{\omega}\nu\ \chi\epsilon\iota\rho\hat{\omega}\nu\ \check{\epsilon}\kappa\tau\alpha\sigma\iota\nu$; and Plautus says, Dispessis manibus patibulum cum habebis. Finally, the "Follow Me" points to the cross, vers. 19, 22, compared with ch. xiii. 36, where Jesus had said to Peter, "Thou shalt follow Me afterwards:" thus we have here the unfolding of the hint already given there. The Lord makes prominent this particular point in the crucifixion, because in it *impotence* and *restriction* were most clearly exhibited. The hands are the instruments of action; they being bound, all action ceases. Passiveness being the state generally indicated, this must also, in the crucifixion, be made prominent.—If "thou shalt stretch forth thine hands" refers to the crucifixion, we have a clue to the meaning of "another." The punishment of the cross was specifically Roman, ch. xviii. 32. The Romans inflicted it on Christ; and His servants would have to endure it at their hands.—This utterance is referred to by Peter in his second Epistle, ch. i. 14. We must not interpret that of any new revelation. Peter combines the event we now dwell upon with the *circumstances of time*. But still plainer is 1 Pet. v. 1, where he, in prospect of martyrdom, terms himself the μάρτυς τῶν τοῦ Χριστοῦ παθημάτων. Then had the fulfilment of this present prophecy already begun. The Epistle was written from Babylon—that is, Rome in its capacity as an enemy of the people of God—at a time when Satan already went about as a roaring lion seeking whom he might devour, ch. v. 8. *Witness* of the sufferings of Christ was the Apostle, inasmuch as he would represent those sufferings in a living image.—The crucifixion of Peter is attested to us by the most trustworthy testimonies; among others by Tertullian, who says, *Petrus passioni Dominicæ æquatur*: compare also Eusebius, Hist. Ecc. ii. 25. Peter was, so far as we know, the only one among the Apostles who suffered the same death as our Lord.—The appearance to James, which Paul mentions in 1 Cor. xv., forms the complement to that which here concerns Peter, and presently afterwards John. (Compare, for the chronological position of this appearance, my treatise on the Supposed Contradictions in the Narration of the Resurrection of Jesus and the Appearances of the Risen Lord.) This manifestation to James probably referred to the departure which he also had to expect.

Ver. 19. "This spake He, signifying by what death he should glorify God. And when He had spoken this, He saith unto him, Follow Me."—We have the explanation of "glorify God" in Matt. v. 16, "that they may see your good works, and glorify your Father which is in heaven." God is glorified in the joyful death of martyrs, which can have its source only in Him, and apart from Him cannot be found. It appears that John had Peter's saying, 1 Pet. iv. 16, in his eyes: "But if any man suffer as a Christian, let him not be ashamed; let him glorify God on this behalf," δοξαζέτω δὲ τὸν Θεὸν ἐν τῷ μέρει τούτῳ. Martyrdom in which Christian virtue exhibits its highest bloom, appears there also to be a glorification of God. The ecclesiastical use of the phrase "glorify God" for the death of martyrs evidently sprang from this passage.—"By what death:" this cannot refer to violent death generally, but to the special kind of death; for only such a kind of death is referred to as would serve to glorify God. The genus was not death generally, but the death of martyrdom. The *species* of death was crucifixion only.—"Follow Me" must primarily refer to the external following, to the fact that Peter was then and there to follow Christ's steps: this is plain from the ἀκολουθοῦντα in ver. 20. According to that verse, the following was such as might be *seen*. But, on the other hand, it is obvious that "Follow Me" must also be understood of a following in the way of the cross. To this we are led by the connection, thus only established, with the words that preceded; to this we are led also by the obvious parallel of Matt. x. 38, "Whosoever taketh not up his cross, and followeth after Me, is not worthy of Me," a word which must involuntarily have occurred to Peter's mind when he heard the "Follow Me," the rather as the Lord had repeated it in prospect of His own passion, Matt. xvi. 24; by the fact that we cannot see any sufficient end in the mere external following, which would have been without meaning to the reader, and alone would not have been mentioned by John; and finally by ver. 22, where "Follow thou Me" forms the opposite of another destiny which awaited John. The seemingly discordant views are reconciled by the assumption that the Lord primarily meant an external following, but that this had a real symbolical significance, and was to foreshadow Peter's imitation of Christ in the death of crucifixion,—an assumption which is all the more obvious, as the whole chapter bears so pre-eminently a symbolical character. This view, represented by Grotius,[1] will satisfy the grounds of both interpretations. The typical following would mitigate the later actual fellowship of the cross to Peter, and quell in his work all emotion of pride. In it was given to him the most emphatic *memento mori.*—With regard to the two points in our Lord's words of prophecy to Peter, J. Gerhard remarks: " In the first Christ sets before him His own example in feeding the flock; in the second, His own example in the endurance of death."

Ver. 20. " Then Peter, turning about, seeth the disciple whom Jesus loved following; which also leaned on His breast at supper, and said, Lord, which is he that betrayeth Thee?" —As Peter followed Jesus, John also followed unbidden. He understood the words of Christ; and by his following also he expressed, without dictating to his Master, his own willingness to suffer martyrdom, with especial allusion to " whither thou wouldest not" spoken by the Lord to Peter. Peter turned when he heard some one following (on ἐπιστραφείς, comp. ch. xii. 40, Rev. i. 12: this last passage leads to the conclusion that he had special occasion to turn. Bengel says: " He had begun therefore to follow"); and when he saw John, he was seized with a desire to have him as his companion in martyrdom, according to the saying, *dulce est solamen miseris socios habere malorum.* And as, in his own case, the prediction of the cross had followed so soon upon the triple " Lovest thou Me?" he thought that the disciple who stood in a peculiarly affectionate relation to Christ might lay more special claims to martyrdom than himself; and therefore he made a faint endeavour to obtain from the Lord a decree to that purpose. This was his only fault. Peter did not desire to impose upon John a death of martyrdom against his will; but the fact was, as Anton says, " Peter perceived that John would go with him." In the words, "whom Jesus loved," " which also leaned on His breast at supper, and said, Lord, which is he that betrayeth Thee?" John points to the facts on which the question and the desire of Peter were based. The triple number gives perfectly the motive which

---

[1] " As before He had made the things done signs of things which He spoke, so now He expresses what He had said in a conspicuous sign. For ' Follow Me' had a common meaning first, which Peter obeyed, and then another and mystical meaning. He alluded to what He had said in Matt. x. 38."

impelled him. First, "whom Jesus loved:" we have already shown that this formula arose out of a signification of the name of John which Jesus Himself had uttered. John could not content himself with that, however; since, as he had often used the phrase as a mere personal designation, it would not have been sufficient of itself to explain Peter's motive. The second is, "which also leaned on Jesus' breast at supper:" ἀναπίπτειν is always used by John of placing oneself at table: comp. ch. vi. 10, xiii. 12; as also in the first three Evangelists. We must therefore adhere to the same meaning here: "which also placed himself near Jesus' breast at supper." In the passage alluded to, John xiii., the ἦν δὲ ἀνακείμενος εἷς ἐν τῷ κόλπῳ τοῦ Ἰησοῦ, in ver. 23, corresponds with the present; not the ἐπιπεσὼν ἐπὶ τὸ στῆθος of ver. 25. We have already remarked, that the place which John occupied at the table betokened the altogether peculiar internal relation of love subsisting between his Lord and him. But the Apostle now adds in the *third* clause a reference to an occurrence which had exhibited, and that with regard to *Peter* also, the greater intimacy between Christ and John,—to the incident of ch. xiii. 23–25, where Peter used the instrumentality of John in asking the Lord about the traitor. Anton's observation here is of profound practical application: "Because the kinds of suffering, especially of bodily suffering, vary, men fall into making comparisons about it. Why should I suffer this? Why not the other? One ought not thus to look at the other. For the tempter obtains great power when children of God make such comparisons. Here is something to be guarded against diligently!"

Ver. 21. "Peter, seeing him, saith to Jesus, Lord, and what shall this man do?"—What will this man receive or suffer? He who stands so near to Thee and me will not surely be separated in death from Thee, or from me: comp. 2 Sam. i. 23. The cautionary and repelling word of Christ throws light upon the question: the blame does not fall upon the curiosity, but upon unauthorized interference.

Ver. 22. "Jesus saith unto him, If I will that he tarry till I come, what is that to thee? Follow thou Me."—Jesus gives His express utterance concerning the end of John's life; and beneath "If I will," etc., lies concealed "I will." The conditional form was introduced simply because Peter, who had ventured to prescribe laws to Christ, was not worthy to receive His utterance in the direct form. The language is that of majesty, which suffers no invasion of prerogative, even from those standing nearest: comp. ch. ii. 4; Matt. xii. 48. But the repulse was only formal. Jesus, who always entered so kindly into the wishes of His disciples (Bengel: "The Lord never inflicted a pure repulse upon His friends, however unreasonably they might ask"), did in fact respond to Simon's request for a declaration as to the future of his fellow-disciple. His utterance was interpreted as such not only by the "brethren," ver. 23, but also by John himself. To the same conclusion we are led by its correspondence with the utterance concerning Peter. On $\theta\acute{\epsilon}\lambda\omega$, Bengel says: The power of Jesus over the life and death of His people. $M\acute{\epsilon}\nu\epsilon\iota\nu$, remain, could in this connection only have referred to abiding in this life: comp. 1 Cor. xv. 6; Phil. i. 24, 25. The *coming* of Jesus could not have had an individual meaning in relation to John; not the coming to take him in the hour of death, ch. xiv. 3, for in this sense the Lord came even to Peter. But we must find a sense in which John remained, and Peter did not, until Christ came. If the coming was one of universal import, we must needs think at once of the Lord's coming in judgment upon Jerusalem, concerning which He had said, Matt. xvi. 28, "Verily I say unto you, There be some standing here who shall not taste of death until they see the Son of man coming in His kingdom:" comp. Mark ix. 1; Matt. xxiv. 34, which teaches that that generation was not to pass before the sign of the Son of man would be seen in heaven. Peter fulfilled his course in martyrdom some few years before that catastrophe: John, on the other hand, survived that great and solemn coming of Jesus. Meanwhile, we must not limit ourselves to this first phase of the historical coming of Jesus. When the Lord spoke of John's remaining until He should come, He seems to have intimated that soon after His coming John should depart. But that will not suit the coming in judgment on Jerusalem; for John survived that event nearly thirty years. *Further*, it appears that the link between the abiding of John and the coming of Jesus was not a merely external one; but that before his departure John was to do his own part in connection with the coming of Christ. Now there was nothing of this sort in connection with the destruction of Jerusalem.

But it is altogether decisive, that John actually survived a second coming of the Lord, which could not therefore be excluded. In his lifetime fell the beginning of the great conflict between Christ and Rome. With the Roman persecution, as it, under Domitian, partook of an ecumenical character, followed simultaneously the coming of the Lord. This is one of the fundamental principles of the Apocalypse. That book is occupied, after its first verse, with that "which should shortly come to pass." According to ch. i. 3 and xxii. 10, the time was near. "I come quickly," the Lord declares, ch. xxii. 7, 12, 20, iii. 11, ii. 5, 16. On Rev. i. 1 it was observed: "'The keeper of Israel neither slumbers nor sleeps.' 'I am with you always unto the end of the world.' Of these truths, the 'shortly coming to pass' and the 'I come quickly' of this book are the necessary consequence. The boundless energy of the Divine nature admits here of no delay. There is nothing of quiescence or indolent repose in God. His appearing often to linger is merely on account of our shortsightedness. He is secretly working for salvation and destruction when He seems to us to be standing aloof" (Com. on Rev. vol. i. p. 47, Clark's Transl.). At the same crisis, when the world came with its prince, the Lord came. In this second historical coming of Christ, John was himself *pars aliqua*. He was the *herald* of His coming; and that he might be such, was the reason that the Lord willed that he should tarry. Yet not that alone: the Apocalypse is included in the coming of the Lord. In it He came with His consolation to His people, groaning under the oppression of the world's power. That was the specific purport of the Apocalypse. Hence Bengel says, with perfect propriety: "To Peter the cross, to John that great Apocalypse, were in mystery promised here."—Bengel also says on "Follow Me:" "The future is involved in the imperative. Do thy part: leave to the survivor his." It is only a following in the most pregnant sense that is here assigned to Peter: the following of Christ in the way of the cross, in the more general sense, pertains to all Christians; and that John's desire, as expressed in his following with Peter, was satisfied, and that he was also a partaker of the cross of his Lord, is evident from Rev. i. 9, 10. With "Follow thou Me" the colloquy ends. Here, as in Luke xxiv. 31, it might be said, "And He vanished out of their sight."

Ver. 23. "Then went this saying abroad among the brethren, that that disciple should not die: yet Jesus said not unto him, He shall not die; but, If I will that he tarry till I come, what is that to thee?"—The λόγος rested upon the assumption that the coming referred to was the last coming, that with which the παλιγγενεσία was connected, Matt. xix. 28: thus it was as to those then living the period of the great change, 1 Cor. xv. 51, 52, and of the rapture into the air, 1 Thess. iv. 17,—passages which probably had their influence upon the formation of this opinion. The Apostle opposes to this opinion that there was a difference between not dying and surviving till the coming of the Lord; he intimates that there was to be a coming of the Lord *before* the end of the present world, so that one might live till the coming of the Lord, and then afterwards die. Heumann touches the right point here: "John teaches his readers what return of the Lord was not to be understood here. Since, that is, some Christians supposed that the Lord was speaking of His coming to the general judgment, concerning which an angel said at the ascension, 'This Jesus will in like manner come again as ye have seen Him go into heaven,' Acts i. 11, and inferred therefore that John would not die, but remain in the world until the last day, and then be taken up with all other surviving believers into heaven,—John here testifies that Jesus had not said *that he would not die.* He gives it to be understood, that he, like his fellow-Apostles, would die, and consequently not survive to the last day, and the coming of the Lord in judgment; and that they therefore erred who understood the Lord's words of that His final coming."—John describes Christians as "brethren." The bond of brotherhood girded the disciples of Christ from the time that the Lord had termed them His brethren, ch. xx. 17. Αὐτῷ: What is said in relation to any one is in a certain sense said to him, although the words were primarily addressed to another. It is after the manner of the Old Testament: comp. *e.g.* Gen. xx. 2, "And Abraham said of Sarah his wife, She is my sister."

CONCLUDING FORMULA OF THE GOSPEL.

VERS. 24, 25.

Ver. 24. "This is the disciple which testifieth of these things, and wrote these things; and we know that his testimony is true."—Lampe: "He names himself simply disciple, as his constant custom is." Τούτων, ταῦτα, can refer only to all *that* from the beginning of the Gospels down to ver. 23. What Lampe further says must remain true: "Then he adds, 'This is the disciple which testifieth of these things, and wrote these things;' which cannot be defended from the imputation of falsehood, if any other than the Apostle affixed this chapter." In the οἴδαμεν the spirit of John is one with the spirit of his readers: compare "When ye are gathered together, and my spirit," 1 Cor. v. 4, and 3 John 12, "Yea, and we also bear record; and ye know that our record is true." The profound conviction of the truth of his testimony, of which the Holy Spirit was the source, ch. xiv. 26, filled him with the assurance that it would be acknowledged as true by all who were of the truth. Not only he knew it, but the Church, all Christendom upon earth, knew it. That John's confidence did not delude him, has been proved by the experience of all ages. All brethren, ver. 23, all sincere Christians (compare ἡμεῖς πάντες, ch. i. 16), have ever set to it their seal. This enlargement of personal conviction into that of the Church is extraordinarily frequent in the Old Testament. Habakkuk, for example, speaks throughout his third chapter as the *microcosmos* of the whole community. In the New Testament all those passages are analogous where the Apostles speak of themselves in the plural, as Rom. i. 5; 2 Cor. i. 8 seq.; 1 John i. 1 (Winer). For the reason of this so-called *pluralis majestaticus* is the central position of the Apostles—the fact that they were not so much individual persons, as the epitome of the Church: compare the τὸ ἐν ὑμῖν ποίμνιον τοῦ Θεοῦ, 1 Pet. v. 2, which makes the shepherds include as it were the flock. According to 1 John i. 3, the object of the Apostle's declaration and teaching was, that his readers should walk in fellowship with him, and through him with the Father and His Son Jesus Christ. There also we are met by him as a central figure. The theory of another author adding his postscript, which has no ground whatever to rest upon, is refuted by the impossibility that this Gospel could have been issued without some such conclusion as we have in vers. 24, 25; by the unmeaningness of οἴδαμεν in the mouth of one unknown; by the present participle ὁ μαρτυρῶν, and the singular οἶμαι, ver. 25; by the close affinity between this assurance of the truth of a testimony and ch. xix. 35; by its relation with 3 John 12; finally, by the correspondence of this concluding formula for the whole Gospel with the concluding formula of the main body in ch. xx. 30, 31, and the circumstance that in both formulæ there is contained the hint that the Gospel was only a selection from a much more abundant mass.

Ver. 25. "And there are also many other things which Jesus did, the which, if they should be written every one, I suppose that even the world itself could not contain the books that should be written. Amen."—Instead of ὅσα, quæcunque, which points to the great mass of things omitted, many MSS. have the simple ἅ. On "which Jesus did," comp. ch. ii. 23. John in all his books makes frequent mention of *writing*. For καθ' ἕν, comp. Acts xxi. 19; and for οἶμαι, Gen. xli. 1, Sept. Objection has been needlessly taken to the singular "I suppose," because John never speaks in the singular. For there is really here no speaking in the first person, no actual obtrusion of his own personality: οἶμαι means no more than "so to speak." Κόσμος is the whole world as such, and not in a moral sense. On χωρεῖν, *hold*, comp. ch. ii. 6. Heumann is right in interjecting, "which we four Evangelists have not written;" for John everywhere takes his three predecessors into account. Here he is speaking generally of what had not been written. Much has been idly said about "hyperbole quite foreign to John's simplicity and thoughtfulness." But there is no hyperbole here. Internal, transcendent greatness, simply takes the array of the external—takes dimensions of space; after the precedent of Amos vii. 10, where Amaziah, the priest of Bethel, says to Jeroboam, "Amos hath conspired against thee in the midst of the house of Israel: the land is not able to bear all his words:" it is not large enough; they find no place therein. That the external here only represents the internal—that we must distinguish between the thought and its clothing, is plain from the οἶμαι, *opinor*, "I suppose." Bengel: "οἶμαι, *opinor*; the amplification is softened by this word." The idea is that of the absolute unfitness of the world for the spiritual acceptance and use of a perfect history of Christ. Hyperbole could be alleged only if this unfitness were other than absolute. We may find many analogies in the Apocalypse (compare my Commentary). There is no more exaggeration here than in the verse of Luther's well-known hymn, " And were the world," etc. There also spiritual greatness is made to assume the dimensions of space. Wetstein rightly observes: "Coronis evangelio imposita respondet τῷ προσώπῳ τηλαυγεῖ in principio, i. 1, 2, 3." The world which was made by Christ is even for that reason too small to hold the perfect knowledge of Him,—all that might be said of Him. How weighty is the practical conclusion which may be drawn from the fact, that precisely these words form the conclusion of this Gospel and of the Four, of all that is delivered in the Gospel verbally written! How anxious should we be to receive this fourfold Gospel into our hearts!

CONCLUDING OBSERVATIONS.

After our investigations in detail, there still remain several questions to be discussed which refer to the Gospel as a whole. Of these the most important is its *design*. John himself tells us clearly and decisively what that was, at the close of the main body of it. He says, ch. xx. 31, " These are written, that ye might believe that Jesus is the Christ, the Son of God; and that believing ye might have life through His name." In harmony with this is the prologue, which sets forth as the great theme, " The Word was made flesh." The Evangelist gives in the prologue the sum of what he would unfold throughout the work.

So also in the first three Evangelists we have the full confession that Jesus was the Messiah; and the Messiah not in the ordinary Jewish sense, but in a sense that makes Messiah and Son of God equivalent and synonymous terms. Testimonies to the Divine nature of Christ we find throughout Matthew: for instance, in all those countless passages where Jesus is spoken of as the *Son of man* (comp. on ch. i. 52); in the record, occurring

CONCLUDING OBSERVATIONS. 499

at the very outset, of the incarnation through the Holy Ghost; then in ch. iii. 11, 12, 14, x. 37, where Christ arrogates for Himself that supreme love which throughout the Old Testament is spoken of as the prerogative of God alone, ch. xi. 27, xvi. 16, 27, xvii. 5, xxii. 41-46, xxv. 31, xxvi. 63-65, xxviii. 18-20. In Luke we refer simply to ἑνὸς δὲ ἐστι χρεία, " one thing is needful," ch. x. 42. If devotion to Jesus was the one thing needful, He must be God over all; and that must apply to Him which is written in Deut. vi. 4, 5, a passage which the Lord evidently had in view. It would have been pure blasphemy for another than the Son of God in the fullest and most essential sense to have described devotion to himself as the one thing needful. The first three Evangelists make it generally their aim also to show that Jesus the Christ was the Son of God: in Matthew this constantly appears in the comparison of prophecy with fulfilment. But he does not expressly lay this down as his design; and we may say that it does not rule in his narrative to anything like the same degree as it does in the narrative of John. All that Jesus said and did had profound interest for the Evangelists; and they do not ask at every step how far every detail serves to demonstrate the proposition that Jesus was the Christ. They have their joy in the history as such. John is the only one who, as a rule, retains that design unchangeably in view. His Gospel was, so to speak, the first *apology*. He exhibits the proposition that Jesus is the Christ, the Son of God, in a certain systematic completeness, and by a series of arguments he demonstrates it. These arguments we shall now glance at, in order that we may have a clear view of the character of the entire Gospel.

That Jesus is the Christ, and as such the Son of God, is first the Lord's own testimony to Himself. When the woman of Samaria says, " I know that the Messias cometh," Jesus answers with decisive clearness, " I am He," ch. iv. 26. He evermore assumes that central place which in the Old Testament was the prerogative of Jehovah. He describes Himself as the way, the truth, and the life; as the light of the world, as the true bread from heaven, as He who could give water to drink that would quench all thirst for ever, as the good Shepherd, as the door of the sheep. At the very outset, in His conversation with Nicodemus, He declares Himself to be the only-begotten

Son of God, who came down from heaven, and would go back to heaven, and who, during His sojourn upon earth, was at the same time in heaven. He utters the lofty word, "I and the Father are one," ch. x. 30. Jesus Himself testifies that His own utterance concerning His own person furnished a sure ground for faith in Him, and that it was only a concession to infirmity when He appeals to other grounds, ch. x. 38, xiv. 11. He defends, in ch. viii. 14, the validity of this testimony against the Pharisees, intimating to them that He might not be measured by a human standard, that He moved in a sphere in which the mists of vanity and self-complacency exist not, and in which the saying, "Let another praise thee, and not thyself," had no force. Accordingly Jesus could bear testimony to Himself; and the truth of His testimony is confirmed by the whole impression of His personality. Men had only to regard Him in His majestic dignity, in His glory as the only-begotten of the Father, and the thought must instantly vanish, that He had in proud self-delusion arrogated to Himself a dignity that did not belong to Him, or that He had in intentional deception given Himself out to be the Son of God. Men who make themselves God are always either madmen or knaves. Who but a blasphemer would dare to place Jesus in the one or the other of these classes?

Those who were not satisfied with His testimony to Himself Jesus refers to His *works*, especially to His miracles, as being a testimony borne to Him by the Father. "The works," He says, in ch. v. 36, "which the Father hath given Me to finish, the same works that I do bear witness of Me, that the Father hath sent Me." So also He appeals to the works in ch. x. 25, 37, 38: "The works that I do in My Father's name, they bear witness of Me.—If I do not the works of My Father, believe Me not. But if I do, though ye believe not Me, believe the works: that ye may know and believe that the Father is in Me, and I in Him." Similar references to the works are found in ch. viii. 18, xiv. 11. According to ch. xv. 24, it was the works that made the Jews inexcusable, and proved that in hating Jesus they hated the Father. In ch. xi. 15, He rejoices that Lazarus had died before His arrival, because He thus had opportunity, by the performance of a glorious *work*—the raising one a considerable time dead—to strengthen the faith of His

CONCLUDING OBSERVATIONS. 501

disciples. According to ver. 42, He formally utters the petition for the raising of Lazarus, that the connection of the work with His own person might be set in full light, and that thus faith in His Divine mission might be wrought in the hearts of those who were present.—The Apostle often points to the deep impression which the works of Jesus produced upon the men of his day and all eye-witnesses. Nicodemus says to Jesus, ch. iii. 2, "We know that Thou art a teacher come from God; for no man can do the miracles that Thou doest, except God be with him." According to ch. ii. 23, many in Jerusalem believed in His name when they saw the miracles that He did. According to ch. iv. 45, when Jesus came to Galilee the Galileans received Him, because they had seen all that He had done in Jerusalem at the feast. In ch. vii. 31 we read: "And many of the people believed on Him, and said, When Christ cometh, will He do more miracles than those which this man hath done?" What significance the Apostle attached to the works of Christ, is shown by the narrative of the man born blind. Everything is ordered in true apologetic style, with the design to obviate all hostile attack. The same holds good of the narrative of Lazarus' resurrection.

The fact that the Evangelist attached such high importance to the Lord's miracles, would lead us to expect in his Gospel a series of detailed miraculous events. Nor are we deceived in our expectation. It is true that, so far as their number goes, the miracles are not so prominent in his Gospel as in those of his predecessors; it is true, as Ewald says, that "his entire work contains, if we look at the matter as a quantity, for the most part Christ's words and discourses;" but, as it is John who gives most prominence to the miraculous element, this must be explained by the fact that he assumes the existence of his predecessors' narratives. The miracles which he describes in detail are representatives of classes; and with regard to each the design of the Evangelist was, that those analogous facts should be inserted which his predecessors had already recorded. Baur observes (die Evangelien, S. 2557): "Only one kind of miracles is here altogether wanting, the casting out of demons; which is all the more strange, as precisely this class of miracles is most amply and frequently detailed in the Synoptists." But the explanation of the matter is simply this, that the material had been already exhausted by them. Mere repetition is carefully avoided by the Evangelist.—To the works belong also those facts by which Christ declares Himself to be the risen and glorified Lord. Their apologetic significance is referred to in ch. vi. 62, ii. 18, 19, viii. 28, xx. 31. The assurance of the resurrection commended itself not only to faith, but also, in the person of Thomas, to doubt itself.

The witness borne to Jesus by the Father is connected with a series of other Divine hints and confirmations: for example, that Caiaphas must utter the word, "It is expedient that one man should die for the people," ch. xi. 50, the deep significance of which the Apostle, in ver. 51, expressly comments on; that Pilate, despite the opposition of the Jews, described Jesus as the King of the Jews in the superscription of the cross; that blood and water from the side of Jesus followed the piercing of the spear, as a symbol of redemption and justification obtained by His passion,—a circumstance so marvellous, that the Apostle expressly and emphatically declares himself to have seen what he records, ch. xix. 35. The apologetic import of this occurrence he alludes to when he makes the design of his testimony to be, "that ye might believe."

Concurrent with the works of Jesus are the *words*. Jesus Himself makes the argument from them valid in ch. vi. 63. There He tells those who were in danger of mistaking Him, "The words which I have spoken to you, are spirit and are life." According to ch. xv. 22, the words of Christ constitute so decisive a demonstration of His Divine mission that they are sufficient of themselves to render those inexcusable, and to involve them in condemnation, who had heard without attaining to faith. In ch. xvii. 8, our Lord says, "For I have given unto them the words which Thou hast given Me; and they have received them, and have known surely that I came out from Thee, and they have believed that Thou didst send Me." All this they learnt from the words of Christ, which so manifestly had their source in another world, and could never have sprung from this poor earth. According to the Baptist's word, in ch. iii. 31, he that is of the earth speaketh of the earth; and the only-begotten Son of God testifies in His sayings what He had heard and seen in the supermundane sphere. By the side of the self-testimony of Jesus, the works and the words are made prominent in ch. xiv. 10, "Believest thou not that I am in the Father, and the Father in Me? The *words* that I speak unto you, I speak not of Myself; but the Father that dwelleth in Me, He doeth the *works.*" And if in ver. 11, in connection with His self-testimony, the works only are emphasized, "Believe Me that I am in the Father, and the Father in Me; or else believe Me for the very works' sake," that was not because the works were better demonstration than the words; but the Lord appeals to them simply as being the more obvious and palpable demonstration.

The Apostle frequently points to the deep impression which the words of Christ produced; he makes it very prominent that this testimony approved itself in its effect. When Jesus, at a season when many misconceived and deserted Him, said to the Apostles, "Will ye also go away?" Peter, as the mouthpiece of all, ch. vi. 68, answered, "Lord, to whom shall we go? Thou hast the words of eternal life." This is the response of the confessing Church to that which Jesus had Himself said concerning the high significance of His words. Even the servants of the high priest are constrained to avow, ch. vii. 46, "Never man spake like this man."—The direct consequence of the high position conceded to the words of Christ is this, that in the Gospel a series of His Divine discourses is communicated. Especially the discourses delivered before His departure are to be looked upon in this light. They enforce from every heart not hardened, from every soul not under the ban of its own perverted inclinations and lusts (comp. ch. v. 44), the avowal that Jesus is the Christ, the Son of God. They are, not less than the miracles, signs, $\sigma\eta\mu\epsilon\hat{\iota}\alpha$, although John, following the current phraseology, has used that word only with regard to the *works* of Christ.—The effect of this testimony is, indeed, dependent on a subjective condition; but wherever this condition is not wanting, where the heart is found right with God, it cannot but prove its might.—" My *doctrine*," says Christ, in ch. vii. 16, 17, "is not Mine, but His that sent Me. If any man will do His will, he shall know of the doctrine, whether it be of God, or whether I speak of Myself." The doctrine of Christ approves itself to the conscience of him who has a sincere will to do the will of God. He shall find in it the solution of the mystery of his inner being, the satisfaction of the desires of his longing heart, and all help for his struggling and wrestling spirit. The place of doubt is only departure from God, the perverted heart that will do the will of the flesh, and will not be disturbed in the gratification of its lusts and passions.

By the side of these three great arguments the Gospel presents a series of others.

The *Baptist's testimony to Christ* could not be omitted, especially as it was that testimony which led John himself to the Lord. It was his personal experience of the force of that witness that made John attach to it such importance, and assign it such prominence. So early as the prologue, ch. i. 7, he alludes to it: "The same came for a witness, to bear witness of the light, that all men through Him might believe." In ch. i. 19–36, the Evangelist, at the outset of the body of the Gospel, communicates the threefold testimony which the Baptist bore to Jesus at the period of His first appearing. In ch. iii. 22–36, John abases himself profoundly under Christ at the end of his own course, and utters a glorious testimony concerning Him: "He must increase, but I must decrease.—He that believeth on the Son hath everlasting life: and he that believeth not the Son shall not see life; but the wrath of God abideth on him." It has been shown (in vol. i.), that in these communications touching the Baptist, the Evangelist had no polemical reference to imaginary disciples of John. He had rather the followers of Thomas in view, the δίψυχοι of his time, who vibrated uneasily between faith and unbelief. The testimony of John is only one link of a chain of demonstrations to the proposition that Jesus is the Christ, the Son of God. This is not only suggested in ch. xx. 31; we learn it definitely from ch. v. 33–35, where Jesus appeals to John's witness in opposition to the Jews. There this testimony opens the series of those which the Father bore to the Son. There it is a power against unbelief generally, not a weapon to resist the pretensions of an obscure sect. And the importance of this testimony (with regard to which compare vol. i.) was approved by its effects. According to ch. i., it led to Jesus His first disciples; according to ch. x. 41, 42, the people were induced to believe, by comparing what John had said concerning Christ with the works which they beheld in Him.

How Jesus was accredited by the *predictions* of the Old Testament, Matthew had shown in a very complete series of instances. But John also, although taking for granted what his predecessor had written, does not omit all reference to them. Jesus, in ch. v. 39, appeals, in opposition to the hostile Jews, to the "scriptures" that testified of Him, to the whole body of Messianic prophecies in the Old Testament, which were fulfilled in Him; and then, in vers. 45-47, He specifically challenges the testimony of Moses. At the entrance of our Lord into Jerusalem on an ass, the Evangelist expressly points out that the event was a fulfilment of Zechariah's prophecy, ch. xii. 16. At the distribution of the garments, and the casting lots for the vesture, he points to the coincidence of prophecy and fulfilment, ch. xix. 23, 24. So also with regard to the vinegar given Him to drink, ver. 28. And in the circumstance that the legs of Jesus were not broken, and that one of the soldiers pierced Him with a lance, John sees the hand of God, which brought about this harmony between prediction and accomplishment.

Hand in hand with the prophecies of the Old Testament, we have the testimony of *Christ's own predictions.* By the clearness with which the future lay open before Him, He was proved to be the Sent of God, who partook of the omniscient prerogative of the Divine nature. For God alone can reveal secret things, Dan. ii. 28; and He to whom He reveals hidden things is thereby authenticated and declared to be trustworthy, so that all must believe the testimony that He bears to Himself. Jesus ever has His own destiny open before Him. He foreannounces, as early as ch. iii. 14, His *death on the cross.* After the words in ch. xii. 32, "And I, if I be lifted up, will draw all men unto Me," John adds, "This He said, signifying what death He should die:" comp. further ch. viii. 28, xviii. 32. He utters, in ch. ii. 19 (comp. ver. 22), a prophecy of His resurrection. In ch. xvi. 16, He foreannounces to the Apostles His impending departure, and that speedy reappearance which the resurrection fulfilled. The same clear view of the future our Lord displays with regard to His *disciples.* This is seen in the promises of protection to be afforded them, ch. xvii. 12 (comp. ch. xviii. 9), and of the Holy Spirit whom they should receive, ch. vii. 38, 39, xiv. 16, 17, 25, 26, xv. 26, xvi. 7, 13, as connected with the glorious and public accomplishment at Pentecost. Our Lord says to Peter, ch. i. 42, at the first meeting, "Thou art Simon, the son of Jonas: thou shalt be called Cephas, which is, by interpretation, A stone," or Peter. The man of rock had justified his name, at the time when John wrote, by the whole course of his life, and by his death. Jesus predicts to Peter his denial, ch. xiii. 38, comp. ch. xviii. 25–27; so also his mode of departure, in which he should follow his Master by a death on the cross, ch. xiii. 36, xxi. 18. And the life of John, different from that of Peter, lies clearly before His vision, ch. xxi. 22. Through all the discourses of our Lord there runs a prophecy of the doom to befall the *Jewish people* (comp. *e.g.* ch. viii. 21, 24, 28, xv. 2, 6), the fearful fulfilment of which had already taken place, threatening those with similar judgment who should walk in the footsteps of the Jews' unbelief in Christ. How plainly the Lord saw the course of the Church down to the end, is shown especially in ch. xxi. He proclaimed from the beginning that His Church would be entirely severed from the temple at Jerusalem, ch. iv. 21, 23; saw that the consequence of His death on the cross would be an extension of His kingdom over the heathen world, ch. xii. 32 (comp. ch. iv. 35, 38); that the seedcorn falling into the earth would bring forth much fruit, ch. xii. 24; that the converted Jews and Gentiles would be formed into one fold, ch. x. 16. He gives, after the resurrection, a figure of the prosperous labour of His servants among the Gentiles. He predicts that His Church would withstand all the assaults of the world, and conquer the whole earth, ch. xvi. 33.—In harmony with the Lord's own predictions, there are other evidences that His knowledge penetrated all things, into depths inaccessible to the human mind. He assumes the prerogative of the Searcher of hearts: He knows what is in man, ch. ii. 25. He looks through Judas the traitor from the beginning, ch. vi. 64. When Nathanael comes to Him, He says of him, "Behold an Israelite indeed, in whom there is no guile," ch. i. 48; and as He looks into his inner being, so also He knows his external relations, ver. 49. He says to the Samaritan woman, "Thou hast had five husbands; and he whom thou now hast is not thy husband;" and the woman herself, with many of the town, are led to faith in Jesus by the fact that He told her all things that ever she did. When the Apostles had fished all night, and taken nothing, He says to them, "Cast the net on the right side of the ship, and ye shall find," ch. xxi. 6. On the ground of the accordance between the word and the result, John says, "It is the Lord." There was uttered the design for which John recorded all the facts which proclaimed that the knowledge of Jesus transcended all human limits. They were to bring his readers to the conviction that Jesus is the Lord.

In 1 John v. 6, great stress is laid upon the *effects of Christianity*. These are asserted to be the testimony which God gives to His Son. The Apostle there gives prominence to a triad of those testimonies: the *water*, or the forgiving of sins imparted by Christ; the *blood*, or the atonement accomplished by Him; and the *spirit*, who bears witness that the Spirit—that is, the Divine nature in Christ—is truth. That there is upon earth a fellowship of those who are partakers of these great gifts,—who have received reconciliation with God, the forgiveness of sins, and the Holy Ghost,—is the best demonstration that He from whom these gifts come is the Son of God in truth. To this argument from effects which apart from Christ are never found, the Gospel also frequently points. In the prologue we read, "As many as received Him, to them gave He power to become the sons of God," ch. i. 12; and, "Out of His fulness have all we received, and grace for grace," ch. i. 16. Jesus Himself, in ch. iii. 5, represents regeneration of water and the Spirit as the privilege of His people. He describes Himself, ch. iv. 10, as One who can give the living water and allay the thirst of the human spirit; in ch. vi. as giving *life* to His people, when He gives them His flesh and blood to eat. They have in Him blood and water, ch. xix. 34; through Him they obtain the gift of the Holy Ghost, ch. vii. 38, xv. 26, xvi. 7, xx. 22; knowledge of the truth, and, as the result of it, freedom from the slavery of sin, ch. viii. 32, as well as purification from its pollution, ch. xv. 3; the power of acceptable prayer, ch. xv. 7; peace, ch. xiv. 27; deliverance from the terror of death, ch. viii. 51, xi. 26. Who would not believe on the name of Him who can impart to His people gifts so transcendent, and in no other way to be obtained!

John delights to communicate the *confessions* which Jesus evoked by the influence of His personal manifestation. In them also he discerns testimonies to His Divine dignity, evidences in favour of the proposition that Jesus is the Christ, the Son of God. Nathanael cries, "Thou art the Son of God," ch. i. 50; Peter, in the name of the Apostles, "Thou art the Christ, the Son of God," ch. vi. 69; Martha utters the same avowal, ch. xi. 29; Thomas, overpowered by facts, must cry, "My Lord and my God;" the Samaritans testify, "We have heard Him ourselves, and know that this is indeed the Christ, the Saviour of the world:" comp. further ch. vii. 31. When Jesus enters Jerusalem, the people meet Him, and cry, "Hosanna, blessed is the King of Israel, that cometh in the name of the Lord," ch. xii. 13. Many also of the rulers of the people believe on Him, and keep back their confession only through fear of the Pharisees, ch. xii. 42. The reason why men refuse their confession to Christ is perfectly plain: they come not to the light, because their deeds are evil. Their hatred is not less a testimony in favour of Christ than the love of the men whose hearts are right.

The Evangelist not only adduces positive arguments for his proposition that Jesus is Christ, the Son of God: he also refutes all *objections* to that doctrine. It might be a disparagement to the divinity of Christ, that so large a proportion of the Jews disbelieved: he enters into this frequently, in the Lord's discourses which he communicates, *e.g.* in ch. v. 8, and in his own observations, ch. xii. 37 seq. So also he meets the objection that might be derived from the treachery of Judas, one of the Twelve, ch. vi. 64, 70, 71, according to which Jesus was not surprised by the traitor, but knew him as such from the beginning, ch. xiii. 18, 19, 21–30, xvii. 12. The stumblingblock which might be found in our Lord's capture he removes also, by showing in fact that Jesus freely delivered Himself up. Moreover, He cast His captors to the ground by a word.

We have shown that the aim to demonstrate that Jesus is the Christ, the Son of God, rules the whole Gospel. But the question now arises, Does the Apostle design in this merely to raise those who stood in a lower stage of faith to a higher one, or has he in view the *doubts* which were already stirring in his own time?

Of itself, the simple proposition would not lead us to the assumption of any polemical or apologetical design. That Jesus is the Christ, the Son of God, is in fact the centre of

Christianity; and it may be thought that the Apostle who himself, before all others, rested on that centre, would make it his great task to give the utmost prominence to this one thing needful, merely for the furtherance of the faith of those who were not yet firmly established on this foundation. Meanwhile there is much in the Gospel itself which forbids us to adhere absolutely and alone to this positive design.

If the Apostle wrote merely for the advantage of a faith not yet perfect, his treatment would have been less systematic. The aim would not, to such an extent, have pervaded the whole book down to its minutest detail; the Evangelist would have involuntarily, oftener than he does, abandoned the centre and wandered to the circumference. The matter would not have been such as to allow the section of the adulteress to be, as it were, a foreign element in a Gospel directed to one great end. The Evangelist would have been less disposed to array, as he does, a whole battalion of orderly reasons. In the record of miracles, he would not have been so careful at once to deduce from them a dogmatic result. On occasion of the very first miracle, he remarks, ch. ii. 11, that Jesus in that miracle manifested forth His glory. It is *he* pre-eminently who exhibits the miracles as signs, σημεῖα, means of placing the person of Jesus in the true light, ch. ii. 11, 23, iv. 54, xii. 37. The style in which the miracles on the man born blind and Lazarus are narrated, the manifest intention to fortify these facts against all objections, can hardly be accounted for on the supposition that John wrote only to simple faith.

It must be regarded as noteworthy, that the last figure who appears before the words in which John lays down the scope of his Gospel, "These are written, that ye might believe that Jesus is the Christ, the Son of God; and that believing ye might have life through His name," is that of *Thomas*, and that the words of Christ addressed to him, "Be not faithless, but believing," and, "Because thou hast seen Me, thou hast believed: blessed are they that have not seen, and yet have believed," undeniably connect themselves with that conclusion. We are led by this to the inference that the Apostle aimed not merely to further an imperfect faith, but to furnish antidotes to doubt.

That the Apostle had to do with doubt and doubters, seems

plain from his assuring us of the truth of his record in ch. xxi. 24: comp. ch. xix. 37. There is nothing of the same kind in the earlier Evangelists.

The seasonable and opportune character of Holy Scripture generally affords a presumption in favour of a polemic and apologetic design in this Gospel. Those scriptures especially, which furnish predominantly doctrinal elements, display, as a rule, a relation to the special needs and errors of the time. It is because scripture commonly presents truth in its reference to concrete relations and living errors, that it has had such a living power, penetration, and effect. What in any one age is mighty in its operation, may be presumed to be mighty in its influence upon all times.

It is true that the arguments for a polemical design in this Gospel are not perfectly obvious; and he who rejects them cannot have them enforced upon him. But it was in the nature of the case that the design should not be palpable. The Apostle would have taken the edge from his weapon, if he had made his aim more expressly and evidently prominent. To the reasonings and devices of heretics, he would not oppose the like; not fictions to fictions, but what he had heard and seen, beheld and handled with his hands (1 John i. 1): to the Christological image of mist, he would oppose the historical Christ in His full historical truth. That was the weapon with which he warred. To this was necessary the strictest historical fidelity. This the Apostle has so carefully maintained, that, in spite of his aim for the times, not one word occurs which leaves the region and sphere of our Lord Himself. There can be no doubt, if we compare the Epistles of John and the Apocalypse, that in the section ch. xv. 18-xvi. 11, the theme of which is the position of the disciples in the world, the Apostle had the relations of his own time in view, the hatred with which the heathen part of the world persecuted the Christians; and that it was his purpose to meet the temptations to offence which this persecution supplied. But, this notwithstanding, everything refers directly to the hatred of the Jewish part of the world which Jesus had before Him: ch. xv. 15, 22, 24, suit only the Jews: so also "they shall cast you out of the synagogues," ch. xvi. 2; "of sin, because they believe not on Me," ch. xvi. 9, refer only to that phase of the world which by unbelief had already sinned against Christ. Generally, all is concretely Jewish, and never is there one word of generalization. The emphasis which in the high-priestly prayer is laid upon the disciples being one, the urgent exhortations to brotherly love in ch. xv. 12–17, receive in the Epistles of John and the Apocalypse a striking historical illustration. But here also every word refers primarily to the relations which existed in the time of the Son of man. His one aim rules in the Gospel, but yet it bears everywhere a rigidly historical character. Hence the exactitude in the notes of time and place; the precise specification of historical relations and persons which produces in every unbiassed mind the impression of perfect historical truth. He who would, in support of a theory, doubt this, will find his conviction in Josephus, as our commentary has abundantly shown.

Owing to the rigidly historical strain of the Gospel, we cannot arrive at perfect assurance with regard to the question whether John had a polemical design, unless we compare with it his other writings. The first of his Epistles is of special moment in this relation. It presents such abundant and manifestly intentional points of contact with the Gospel, that we may regard it as a kind of historical commentary on it, as its key or introduction, opening up the way for its application to the relations of the time when it was written.

The situation presented to us in the first Epistle is as follows. The time stood in danger of the "sin unto death," of that sin which had ruined the Jews (comp. the Gospel, ch. xv. 22, xvi. 9). Many false prophets had gone out into the world, ch. iv. 1, through whom the world, or heathenism, sought to penetrate the Church, ch. ii. 19, v. 21; and the Apostle at the end of his Epistle cries to his readers, "Little children, keep yourselves from idols." The fundamental error of these false prophets was the denial of Christ, ch. ii. 18. "Little children, it is the last time; and as ye have heard that antichrist shall come, even now are there many *antichrists*, whereby we know that it is the last time." John regards this error, so perilously spreading in the Church of the Gentiles, as the beginning of the end. As it was the last hour of Judaism when it gave itself up to this hour, so would the Church of the Gentiles make shipwreck on the same rock if the germ of this error were allowed to develop, and it obtained the mastery.[1] With the denial of the saving truth that Jesus is the Christ, there was connected another double error: first, the violation of brotherly love; and secondly, the neglect of God's commandments, the abolition of those distinguishing marks which He had set between the world and His people. The three points are blended in ch. iii. 23, 24: "And this is His commandment, That we should believe on the name of His Son Jesus Christ, and love one another, as He gave us commandment. And he that keepeth His commandments dwelleth in Him." The same three points encounter us in the *second* Epistle of John. He describes it there as the great business required by the times, that "we love one another," ver. 5; then, "that we walk after His commandments," ver. 6; and finally, he comes to the cardinal point, ver. 7, "Many deceivers are entered into the world, who confess not that Jesus Christ is come in the flesh. This is a deceiver and an antichrist." In harmony with the first Epistle, vers. 8–11 of the second show how much in danger the Church then was of losing Christ, and God with Christ; and that only the most severe and unshrinking opposition could secure the Church from this greatest of all dangers.

The genesis of that error, and the cause of its wide extension, we may gather with some probability from Matt. xiii. 20, 21. There oppression and *persecution* on account of the world appears as the chief reason of the fall of unsettled minds. To the same points our Lord's word in Matt. xxiv. 9–13. There He represents it as a consequence of the hatred of the *people*, that many would be offended, that many false prophets would arise and find entrance into the Church, and that the love of many would wax cold. Historical observation tends to the confirmation of this. The theology of compromise is ordinarily a product of the infusion of the world in the Church. Its leading principle is the endeavour to relax the Church's severity, and to relieve it from all pressure as it regards the ruling power, and to reconcile itself with that power by all means. That this principle was

---

[1] Lampe: He set all the legions of the spirit of antichrist before their eyes, fashioned in various ways, fighting against the Divine glory of our Saviour, without whom there was no salvation to be expected, some by snares, and some by open warfare, and continuing that warfare through a long course of ages.

CONCLUDING OBSERVATIONS. 513

then at work, we may gather from many definite hints in the first Epistle. In ch. iii. 13 we read, "Marvel not, my brethren, if the world hate you." Before this, and after it, the Apostle zealously condemns their lack of brotherly love. It is obvious that this lack was the result of the world's hatred: men denied their brethren because they were afraid of suffering persecutions with them, and would avoid encountering with them all the evils which the minority, the "little flock," would have to endure at the hands of the world. According to ch. iii. 16, it was a time when it was needful to lay down life for the brethren; according to ch. iii. 12, a time when the remembrance of Cain was suggested, who slew his brother. The endeavour to propitiate a persecuting world might well lead them to deliver up their brethren to the world's hatred: compare the ἀλλήλους παραδώσουσι of Matt. xxiv. 10.

The Epistles of John form a counterpart to the Epistle to the Hebrews. As the latter came to the succour of the churches exposed to internal danger from the Jewish persecution, so the Epistles of John encounter the internal dangers which the influence of the preponderance of *Gentile* authority introduced. These dangers were the same which the present day presents to view. He who would be at peace with the great world around him, must before all things give up the true and perfect divinity of Christ; for that is the fundamental ground of the enmity which exists between the Church and the world. He must renounce all rigour in his zeal for the commandments of Christ, especially those which are most contrary to the world, those which enforce the crucifixion of the flesh, with its affections and lusts, which demand absolute self-denial, and which maintain the ordinances of God inviolate against the caprice of subjective inclination. Finally, he must erect a wall of partition between himself and the true confessors.

The scope of the first Epistle is, in ch. v. 13, described, like that of the Gospel, in ch. xx. 31: "These things have I written unto you that believe on the name of the Son of God; that ye may know that ye have eternal life, and that ye may believe on the name of the Son of God:" comp. ch. v. 5, "Who is he that overcometh the world, but he that believeth that Jesus is the Son of God?" The accordance between the Epistle and the Gospel is too plain, the designed relation of the former to the latter is too manifest, to allow of their being sundered from each other. Then, if the Epistle was written with reference to certain particular relations in the age, the same must hold good of the Gospel. When could a Gospel, the design of which was to maintain the proposition that Jesus is the Christ, the Son of God, have more fitly issued, than at a time when "many antichrists" were abroad, who, according to ch. ii. 22, 23, denied that Jesus was the Christ?

In opposition to all novelties, the Apostle, in 1 John iii. 11, refers Christian people to the message which they had heard from the beginning. So also in the second Epistle, vers. 5, 6, John opposes to the deceivers the Gospel as originally received by word of mouth. From these passages—with which may be connected the injunction in Rev. ii. 25, iii. 11, "That which ye have already, hold fast;" the praise of the Philadelphian Church, Rev. iii. 8, "Thou hast kept My word;" and Rev. ii. 26, "And he that overcometh, and keepeth My works unto the end," My works, which I have performed, and I have commanded—there is only a step to the written Gospel, which repeated and fixed the oral Gospel as a firm bulwark against all the attacks of the deceivers.

The third Epistle of John, no less than the first and second, bears a polemical character. The joy of the Apostle over Gaius, who walked in the truth, was based upon the fact that the truth was then greatly endangered by false teachers. And Diotrephes is mentioned as one of the most prominent of these seducers.

But the *Apocalypse* carries us further than the Epistles into the issues and objects of John's writings. In the epistle to the Church of Ephesus, ch. ii. 2, we read: "I know thy works, and thy labour, and thy patience, and how thou canst not bear them that are evil: and thou hast tried them which say they are apostles, and are not, and hast found them liars." We see here that the false prophets were desirous to introduce an entirely new Christianity. This is evident from their having given themselves out to be *apostles*, and therefore displacing the old Apostles, the bearers and representatives of original Christianity. It is quite in harmony with this, that John, in the third Epistle, says of Diotrephes, "He receiveth us not, prating against us with malicious words." This was one of the new apostles, who went so far, according to ver. 10, as to cast out of the Church those who remained faithful to the old apostolate. We are provided with a still more express description of the character of their false doctrine in Rev. ii. 6, 13, 20, where the deceivers of that time are exhibited as Nicolaitanes or Balaamites, and as dependants of Jezebel. We learn from this that the matter was one of "mediation theology," or a compromise with the world, and the absorption of heathenism into the Church of God; as it is hinted in the close of the first Epistle, "Little children, keep yourselves from idols," where the power that endangered Christianity was heathenism clothed in Christian disguise. Balaam, in Greek Nicolaus, who, according to Num. xxv., compared with ch. xxxi. 16, seduced the Israelites, by means of the Moabitish and Midianite women, to lust and participation in idol worship; and Jezebel, the daughter of Ethbaal, king of Sidon, consort of Ahab, king of Israel, who, as a murderer of the prophets, introduced the worship of idols into Israel,—are the two Old Testament representatives of heathen perversion penetrating the Church of Christ, who live again in the false doctrines of the present time.

But the Apocalypse not merely presents the error to us in sharp outlines; it gives us also information as to its origin, and the reason of the great influence which it exerted over men's minds, so as to bring the very existence of God's Church into danger. Concurrently with warnings against heretical teachers, there are in the apocalyptic Epistles exhortations to stedfastness in face of this world's persecutions. It is obvious that these two—persecution and false doctrine—stood in internal connection; that persecution paved the way for error, as being the means of escaping danger; that this error was in fact a concession to the persecuting power on the part of those who were internally vanquished,—an attempt to remove the enmity which existed between the Church and the world.

In the epistle to the Church of Pergamos, the connection between persecution and false doctrine comes out very plainly. There the angel of the Church is first *praised*, because he had held fast the name of Jesus, and had not denied His faith, even in the days when Antipas the faithful witness was martyred. Then he is *blamed*, because he tolerated those who retained the doctrine of Balaam. These were evidently the men who, in the place where "Satan's throne" was,—that is, the capital seat of the persecutions of Christians in Asia,—fell internally before the Gentile persecutions, sought some method of compromise with the enemy, some scheme of mediation by which they might propitiate the throne of Satan.

We are led to the same result by the passage, ch. ii. 14: "But I have a few things against thee, because thou hast there them that hold the doctrine of Balaam, who taught Balak (*for* Balak) to cast a stumblingblock before the children of Israel, to eat things sacrificed unto idols, and to commit fornication." It is here made emphatic that Balaam, in his seducing arts, had Balak, king of Moab, always in view. From him he expected his reward, if his schemes succeeded. Doubtless "in behalf of Balak" had reference to the relations of the time present. "The Balaamites in Pergamos," says Bengel, "also sought the favour of eminent heathen powers." The Balak of the present was the Roman dominion, with which the false teachers sought to make common cause; that which was called just before "the seat of Satan," or his throne.

"To him that overcometh," we read in ch. ii. 17, "will I give to eat of the hidden manna." Those who overcome are the opposite of the Balaamites, who *yielded* to the pressure of heathenism, and, in fear of the persecuting power, committed themselves to concessions.

In ch. ii. 26 we read: "And he that overcometh, and keepeth My works unto the end, to him will I give power over the nations." He who does not, like the Balaamites of the day, yield himself up to the spiritual bondage of the Gentiles, shall obtain as his reward dominion over the Gentiles.

In Rev. xi. 1, 2, also, we have evidence that false doctrine was a product of heathen persecution: "And there was given me a reed like unto a rod: and the angel stood, saying, Rise, and measure the temple of God, and the altar, and them that worship therein. But the court which is without the temple leave out, and measure it not; for it is given unto the Gentiles: and the holy city shall they tread under foot forty and two months." Here we have in apocalyptic form a parallel to Matt. xxiv. 9-13. The temple is the Church. The proper temple consists of those who are thoroughly penetrated and filled with the spirit of the Church; the external forecourt consists of those who are only superficially touched. The measuring is the extent of the preservation. Where the measuring ceases, there begins the region of abandonment. That the forecourt was given up to the Gentiles, was related to their treading the holy city, as effect is related to cause. The world overflowing the Church caused that from many who had not was taken that which they had. Nothing but a perfect faith could be a sure breakwater against the violent waves of the world. All who are without it must, at such conjunctures. like Issachar, Gen. xlix. 15, bow their shoulders to serve.

After these investigations, we may then determine the question of the genesis of John's authorship. All the Johannean writings have for their starting-point the overflowing of the Church by the persecuting Gentile world. The Apostle had been told by the risen Lord, ch. xxi. 22, that he should tarry till He came. This coming of the Lord implied a previous coming of the prince of this world. John was not to be an idle spectator of this coming, or of the Lord's coming to encounter him; he was rather to serve as an instrument in the coming of Christ. That was the reason why he must remain so long. This mission he fulfilled in three ways. In his Gospel he gave an historical foundation to the faith of Jesus as the Christ, the Son of God, which was shaken by Gentile persecution, and showed that the deceivers who attacked this faith are, in the true history of Christ, brought to shame. In the first Epistle he gave a contemporary commentary to the rigidly historical Gospel, and showed how that Gospel was to be applied to the errors of the present time. The second and third Epistles are a kind of appendage to the first; they are concerned with a particular manifestation of the compromising theology which had been evoked by heathen persecution. Finally, in the Apocalypse John overturns the dread felt for the persecuting heathen world; shows that it was doomed to the destructive judgments of God, while the Church was to remain victorious: so that it was simple folly to condescend through fear to concessions, and true wisdom to hold faithful to Christ and His Church. The Apocalypse shows how God avenges His people on the persecuting world; how He secures for His Church the victory over the Gentile state, and for her sake binds Satan a thousand years, so that he could no longer mislead the heathen into great assaults; how, finally, He creates a new heaven and a new earth, and brings down the new Jerusalem from heaven to earth.

The Gospel and the Apocalypse concur in this, that they only take their point of departure from the relations of the present: they do not regard those relations in their accidental individual characteristics, but view the general in the particular, and thus maintain their full significance for all ages of the Church. The Apocalypse does not confine itself to the then present phase of the power of this world. Of Domitian, the author of the heathen persecution of the day, it furnishes no trace. It embraces in its view the whole conflict which the Church has to wage with heathenism and its invisible head down to the end of time. Its theme is, according to ch. i. 7, the whole coming of Christ in the clouds, His judicial power as displayed from generation to generation. Domitian is merged in the whole to which he belonged, in the heathen state hostile to God. The glance of the seer embraces all the vast spaces of the history of the world. So also in the Gospel, as in the first Epistle, the Apostle does not confine himself to the fortuitous form which an evil theology of compromise had assumed in his own time; he has not to do with the changing vesture of error, but with its essential substance, permanent in all times, ever recurring under fleeting forms, as oft as the Church is overflowed anew by the world. Had the Apostle conferred upon the heresiarchs of his time the undeserved honour of entering into the details of all their inventions, then his Gospel would have become obsolete with the errors which it overthrew. The Apostle beheld in these only the *beginning* of the end, and that of itself would preserve him from entering into them too minutely. "The dogmatic proportions and allusions of the prologue," says Lücke, "are stated very generally, and the opposites are only indirectly reflected in them." Olshausen perceived the fact, but he deduced from it an erroneous inference: "The love and the gentleness of the Apostle of love not only permitted no trace of severity and bitterness to escape, but declined all specific and direct attack." That such soft-hearted love and gentleness were not characteristic of this Apostle, may be abundantly seen in the Epistles, as confirmed by the narrative of his encounter with Cerinthus. Ewald's unsupported

CONCLUDING OBSERVATIONS. 519

opinion, that the Apostle "determined that his Gospel, as a legacy of love, should not be made public until his death," is upset at once by the consideration of the polemical undertone of those general propositions, as it is established by a comparison between the Epistles and the Gospel. The Gospel itself was thrown into the midst of the strife of parties.

Baur (über der Evang. S. 380) remarks in reference to the Gospel and the Apocalypse: "Here as there we find the development of a great conflict, in which the idea of Christianity is realized. There the conflict is with antichristian heathenism, in which the idea of Christianity is realized; here the conflict is with unbelieving Judaism, which Jesus Himself had to maintain." This antithesis establishes a close relation between the two writings. But that relation is made closer when we discern that even in the Gospel there is a background. The victory of our Lord over the Jews is the pledge of His future victory over the heathen. The Apostle, by his exhaustive delineation of the warfare of Christ against the Jews, which, in the eyes of all the world, was ended by their utter downfall, cries out to heathenism, *Mutato nomine de te fabula narratur*, and fills with courage the hearts of all those who had to continue the war with heathenism.

The result at which we have arrived by an examination of the Johannean writings themselves,—that the Gospel of John bears a polemical, or, if it be preferred, aims at an apologetic design,—is confirmed by the testimony of antiquity. Of special importance in relation to this is the declaration of Irenæus, a man in whose character truth in opposition to tradition is a fundamental trait, whose home was in the scene of St John's labours, who stood in intimate connection with many eminent men who had known the Apostle himself, and who in all his assertions concerning the Johannean writings shows himself to be always trustworthy (compare, for the confirmation of his remarks upon the date of the Apocalypse, the introduction of my commentary on that book).

He says, iii. 11, that John wrote his Gospel to root out the error which had been propagated by Cerinthus, and before him by the Nicolaitanes: "Announcing this faith, John, the disciple of our Lord, desired by the publication of his Gospel to abolish that error which Cerinthus had sown among men, and long previously those who are called Nicolaitanes, a fragment of falsely called science," or Gnosticism.

Coincident with this statement is the well-known narrative of Irenæus, iii. 3 (comp. Eusebius, iii. 28, iv. 21), touching the encounter of John and Cerinthus in the bath, and John's precipitate departure with the words, " Let us flee, lest the bath fall in, Cerinthus, the enemy of truth, being in it." Irenæus refers this story back to those who heard it from Polycarp, who had known John himself. If we doubt the literal truth of the account, we cannot deny that it so far historically holds, that John stood in decided opposition to Cerinthus, as the great enemy of the truth in his time.

Irenæus thus describes the error of Cerinthus, i. 26 : " A certain Cerinthus, in Asia, taught that the world was not made by the Supreme God, but by some power very distinct from that which is over all things, and ignorant of the God who is above all. He said that Jesus was not born of the Virgin (that seemed to him impossible), but that He was the son of Joseph and Mary after the manner of other men, and was pre-eminent among men for justice and prudence and wisdom; that after His baptism Christ descended upon Him, from that sphere which is over all things, in the figure of a dove; that He then announced His unknown Father, and wrought miracles; but that Christ departed again from Jesus in the end, and Jesus died and rose again, Christ remaining impassible as a spiritual existence." The lost Greek text of this passage in Irenæus may mainly be recovered from Theodoret (Hæret. Fab. ii. 3), who drew from his sources. Cerinthus, according to this account, denied the proposition which John in his Gospel and Epistles laid down with such decision, " that Jesus is the Christ, the Son of God." He denied the perfect incarnation of God in Christ, which is the essential pillar of Christianity, and thus gave occasion to the theme, " The Word was made flesh." He placed Christ and Jesus in a very loose connection, which was only the prelude to the entire dissolution of the relation between the two, and from which there was only one step to the assertion that Jesus was a mere man. Before the baptism, and from the beginning of the passion onwards, Jesus was without Christ; even from the baptism to the passion there was no real union between them, only a loose connection, merely a stronger form

CONCLUDING OBSERVATIONS. 521

of that which is the privilege of other pious men. Thus was the stone of stumbling set aside; the offence was removed which the wisdom of this world found in the perfect incarnation of God, and the bridge was formed between the Church and the world. The difference between Jesus and Socrates was no longer essential, but only one of degree. The miraculous birth of Jesus, this offence to the natural reason, was done away with. Men might now say many beautiful things about Jesus, without wounding the Gentile consciousness, whose motto was, " Live and let live," and was hard only upon exclusiveness. He still remained in reality on the same level with those great ones whom the heathen marvelled at and reverenced; on the same level with those also who could not tolerate that a son of man should be placed absolutely above them, and arrogate to himself Divine honour and unconditional obedience, with the denial and suppression of all the dearest passions of their soul.

As it respects the doctrine of Cerinthus, we must confine ourselves to Irenæus. Later authorities, especially the untrustworthy Epiphanius, have made him into a thorough scarecrow. According to Epiphanius, he declared the Jewish law to be good, and the observance of it necessary. Then there was attributed to him a coarse millenarianism, which certainly must have sprung from Jewish sources. These representations are not consistent with the doctrine of Cerinthus as exhibited by Irenæus. According to the latter, he taught that the world was not made by the Supreme God, but by a power subordinate to Him, who knew Him not. (Theodoret: " He taught that there was one God of all things, but that He was not the framer of the world, which was made by certain powers widely sundered from Him, and knowing Him not.") All Jewish-Christian tendencies are shut out by this. The judgments of the Gnostics upon the Demiurge were, according to Baur (Gnosis, S. 28), so many judgments upon the internal worth of Judaism, and its religious laws and institutions. " The Christian religion," he says elsewhere, " was represented by Christ; the Jewish by the Demiurge." " The Demiurge was declared by the Gnostics generally to be the God of the Jews." Assuredly there are men of confusion, who unite things the most irreconcilable; but they are not dangerous, and not worthy of study or refutation. The earnest consideration which John vouchsafed to

Cerinthus presupposes that he was a thoroughly dangerous enemy of the truth,—a man who might be regarded as the actual representative of heathenism pressing into the Christian Church. Theodoret also exhibits Cerinthus as a pure philosopher. He says: "This man having lived a long time in Egypt, and having studied the philosophers, afterwards came into Asia." The later disfiguration of the historical character of Cerinthus may be traced to two reasons: first to the fact, that Irenæus, in the passage, i. 36, which lies at the foundation of all the later accounts of Cerinthus, immediately after mentioning him, speaks of the Ebionites. The reason he does so is, that both taught falsely concerning the Lord's person: consimiliter[1] ut Cerinthus et Carpocrates opinantur. But the connection was pushed further, and it was thought that the other Jewish-Christian errors were also common to Cerinthus with the Ebionites, that what was said of the Ebionites held good of Cerinthus also: "They persevere in those customs which are according to the law, and in the Jewish mode of life." A second occasion of the mistake was furnished by a passage of Caius, communicated in Eusebius, iii. 29. Caius justified his deep disinclination to the Apocalypse, which he did not understand, by denying the authorship of John, and attributing it to Cerinthus; and this latter for no other reason, than because Cerinthus bore a particularly hateful name as a heretic, and was specifically opposed to the Apostle. He says of Cerinthus, that he sought to make his name imposing by supposititious revelations, written by him as by a great Apostle, and which angels had been sent to teach him. This passage was rightly understood by Dionysius of Alexandria (Eusebius, iii. 28, vii. 25). He said that Caius pointed to the Apocalypse of John. Others, however, referred it, in its designedly ambiguous wording, to a writing of Cerinthus distinct from the Apocalypse; and thus arose the notion about Cerinthus' millenarianism,—a notion altogether untenable, from the very fact that the doctrine of a thousand years' reign never occurs apart from the Apocalypse, from which Cerinthus could not yet have drawn it. Massuet

---

[1] So must we read, instead of *non* similiter. This is evident from the connection, and from the passage referred to in Theodoret. There we read of Cerinthus: "Τὸν Ἰησοῦν δὲ τοῖς Ἑβραίοις παραπλησίως ἔφησε κατὰ φύσιν ἐξ ἀνδρὸς γεγεννῆσθαι καὶ γυναικός."

(in his Dissertationes præviæ in Irenæum, pp. 64, 65) was in the right track with regard to the later misrepresentations of the historical character of Cerinthus. But he did not pursue the track to the end : even he held that Cerinthus was, " if not by nation, at least by religion, a Jew." Baur (Gnosis, S. 404) has altogether lost the clue. He follows Epiphanius, but without applying criticism where it is wanted.

The doctrine of Cerinthus concerning the Demiurge, and his doctrine concerning Christ, stand in strict internal connection. By the former, the Old Testament, with its hateful Jews presenting so many stumblingblocks to the cultivated heathen, was set aside; by the latter, the God-man was abolished, who so deeply abased heathenism, and laid claim to such absolute subjection and devotion at their hands.

The later authorities, however, agree with Irenæus in exhibiting it as a settled fact, that the Gospel of John had a polemic aim. Jerome, for example, says in the Proœm. in Matt.: " John, when he was in Asia, and already the seed of the heretics began to germinate, was constrained by almost all the bishops of Asia, and deputations of many churches, to write profoundly concerning the divinity of the Saviour."

From the investigation of the design of the Gospel, we now turn to the *relation it bears to the first Gospels*, as their complement.

It has been shown in the Commentary, that John everywhere assumes the existence of the first Gospels, and especially connects his Gospel with that of Luke; that his relation to his predecessor, however, is not that of a corrector, but of a corroborating witness and supplementer; that his design is always and most manifestly to make his Gospel with the former one whole. He who will ponder the multiplied evidences which we have adduced in support of this point during the course of the Commentary, will hardly fail to yield assent.

The result arrived at by an investigation of details is confirmed by a view of the Gospel as a whole. His entire character shows that it was designed to serve only as a topstone; and that it was constructed on the assumption that the others were already in being. Weizsäcker (in his work on the Characteristics of John's Gospel) makes here some pertinent remarks: "We must put the question to ourselves, what we should have if the Gospel of John were our only source of the life of Christ. We should possess in it a sublime sketch; but it would be without a clear and definite view. We should have information as to the great deeds of Jesus, but no notion of His usual and common course of life and action. We should have the most profound declarations of His nature and mission; but, strictly speaking, no examples how He approved that mission in the teaching. The many individual statements could not hinder our having only a very dim apprehension of the whole.— As John passes over the whole Galilean life of Jesus with few exceptions, he gives us no luminous picture of our Lord's ordinary commerce with men; we do not see how He, in particular matters, influenced their moral life, how He led His disciples into the way of faith, and the discipline of religion, and the exercises of prayer. We lack here, so to speak, the wealth of the common real life in the Gospel.—Thus the Johannean picture is of itself almost ideal and cloudy; it is like a centre without a plainly defined circumference; a manifestation of great sublimity, but without clear concomitants; the exhibition of an internal nature, but without those confirmatory traits that should proceed from it. Hence Jesus ever speaks with the deepest pathos, and His manifestation lacks that character of naturalness which that of the Synoptists displays. On this account the Johannean picture demands such a complement as those other Evangelists supply."

In this Gospel we find Jesus, as we find Him in the first three, surrounded by multitudes: ch. vi. 2, 22, xii. 12. How did He attract these crowds? What did He say to attract them into the way of salvation? In the Gospel of John we find no traces of a popular style of speaking. This fact of itself throws us back upon the first three records.

But as John refers back to his predecessors, so also they seem to have written in the expectation of a future supplement. Why do they confine themselves so almost entirely to Galilee? Why do they abstain, until the Lord's last journey, from touching upon events of great importance in the metropolis, which, according to their own statements, He must have often visited? comp. *e.g.* Luke xiii. 34. Why do they omit those momentous discourses which were connected with the feeding of the five thousand? Why do they say nothing of the resurrection of Lazarus?

The following observations will serve to place in its true light the relation of John's Gospel to those of his predecessors.

Our Lord expressly assigned it to His Apostles as their vocation to bear witness of what they had heard and seen in their intercourse with Himself: ch. xv. 27, "And ye also shall bear witness, because ye have been with Me from the beginning:" comp. Luke xxiv. 48; Acts v. 32. And He had declared this testimony to be a power for the conversion of the unbelieving world. The functions of this vocation they discharged at first by oral announcement. And this was in the case of John all the more important, as the sphere of his labour was first Jerusalem and afterwards Ephesus, each a centre of the Christian Church. Pliny (Hist. Nat. v. 29) terms Ephesus *lumen Asiæ*; Strabo, ἐμπόριον μέγιστον τῶν κατὰ τὴν Ἀσίαν τὴν ἐντὸς τοῦ ταύρου; Seneca, Ep. 102, compares Ephesus, for extent of space and multitude of inhabitants, with Alexandria; and a coin of the time of Vespasian bears the inscription, Εφεσιων πρωτων Ασιας.[1]

In the nature of the case, John's Gospel was published from the time of the resurrection and ascension, and known as far as the Christian Church extended.[2]

Doubtless the Apostle had from the beginning, and apart from any polemical or contemporaneous requirements, purposed to commit his Gospel to writing; and the whole Christian world must have looked for it. The importance of writing was firmly established by the Old Testament; and the Apostle had grown up in the experience of its salutary influence. What gave its stability to the Old Testament, could not be wanting to the New. It was obvious that oral proclamation would be valid only so long as the "witnesses of the word" were alive; and that

[1] Lampe, p. 50·: Ephesus, as the metropolis of Asia Minor, was a noble emporium, well adapted by situation for commerce, being on the coast of Asia, and in the heart of the Mediterranean Sea, central to the three regions of the habitable globe, Asia, Africa, and Europe; whence passage was easy into Syria and Egypt, and so into Greece and Latium.

[2] Eusebius, Hist. Eccl. iii. 25, appealing to tradition, mentions the oral Gospel of John: "It is said that John the whole time made use of an unwritten Gospel in his preaching; but that at the last he committed it to writing."

the Christian Church would be in the greatest danger if these "eye-witnesses" did not, before their departure, take care to secure their testimony in writing. John had been called at the very outset of the Lord's ministry; he had been His inseparable attendant; he had been one of three elect Apostles; he was the only witness for many isolated occurrences, such as the examinations before Annas, Caiaphas, Pilate; and he could with special truth and meaning say what we find him saying in 1 John i. 2. But what is more than this, the Apostle knew well that he, with his profound knowledge of the heart of Jesus, had received a special commission for some portions of the evangelical history, especially for a certain class of the longer discourses of our Lord. This specific vocation was so fully acknowledged in the Church, that neither of his predecessors ventured to occupy this region, all expecting his future supplement. This held good especially of the discourses delivered in Jerusalem. In the centre of Jewish culture, at the same time the chief seat of Pharisaic opposition, Jesus had taken occasion to enter into the profoundest discussions, to reproduce which in their connection John alone, in the apostolic centre, was adapted. Even Peter, the first of the Apostles, must recede in this province. That his gift extended not to this, is evident from the fact of a Gospel having been written by Mark under his influence. But the discourses delivered at Capernaum after the feeding of the multitude, and preserved by John, show that, in the Galilean work of Jesus, there were departments which none of the first Gospels ventured to occupy, but which were regarded as the reserved province of John. That the unfitness of the others referred not merely to the discourses, but that there were also *works* of our Lord which they abstained from recording in deference to John's claims, we see in the narrative of the resurrection of Lazarus, which is peculiar to John, and would wear a strange aspect in any of the others. John would have been unfaithful to his vocation if he had not always contemplated the final committal of his Gospel to writing. But as to the accomplishment of this design he was not in haste. The oral communication which filled up a large sphere was, to his nature, altogether given up to the person of Jesus, the most engaging part of his duty; and this oral communication would have been much interfered with, or disparaged, if the Gospel had first been written and circulated. He had not to fear being surprised by death. The Lord had assured him of continuance until a certain definite term. He awaited a Divine call, which would appear in the shaping of circumstances. This call came in the time of the first great heathen persecution, in which the words of our Lord, in ch. xxi. 22, had assigned him an important work to do. The preparation of the Gospel was one of the means by which he executed that mission. To delay longer after that would have been impossible, inasmuch as the same word of Christ had intimated to him that not long after this catastrophe the Apostle's own departure would take place.

The written Gospel coincided in substance with the unwritten, since in both the Apostle declared what he had heard and seen with his eyes, 1 John i. 1. In his Epistles, John makes it very prominent, that in his contest with the deceivers of the time he brought nothing forward that they had not heard "from the beginning," 1 John ii. 7; 2 John 5, 6. Yet there would be found differences not unimportant between the written and the oral Gospel. These were occasioned first by the presence of the first three Gospels, which John did not desire to render superfluous, but only to supplement; the first of them having been written by a fellow-Apostle, and the two others with the co-operation of two fellow-Apostles, Peter and Paul. Probably these Gospels themselves had already exerted considerable influence before his own oral communications. Then a regard to the perils of the Church led to a certain difference between the written and the oral. John would complement the first Gospels; but with this predominant object, and under this particular aspect, that he must communicate all that which would serve, besides their contribution to the same object, to demonstrate that Jesus was the Christ, the Son of God. Undoubtedly John's eye had been fixed upon this even in his oral communications. But, in view of the troubled circumstances of the time, he would strike a bolder chord; the rather as he discerned the end in this beginning, and foresaw that the stone of stumbling on which Judaism was ruined would one day prove ruinous to the Gentile Church also. In order to this, the discourses delivered by Christ in Jerusalem, which the other Evangelists passed over, offered abundant material. It was natural that in the metropolis, the seat of antichristian Pharisaism, opposition to Jesus and His claims was systematized; that this opposition would concern itself mainly with the claims of Jesus to be the Christ, the Son of God, making this its cardinal point; and that Jesus, in His defence against this attack, would thoroughly and clearly lay down the evidences of His Divine mission. But we should exaggerate if we were to refer all that the Gospel contains to one design, the demonstration that Jesus was the Christ, the Son of God. This must be regarded only as the main scope. It would have been unnatural if John, the eye-witness, had not communicated, out of mere joy in the history, and pleasure in the remembrances which made up the fibre of his life, much that stood in no direct relation to that leading scope. The very exactitude with which he treats the chronology of Christ's life, shows that, by the side of his polemical or apologetical aim, he pursued one generally historical. To the same result we are led by a number of other individual historical traits. The passion-history, in particular, cannot be understood if we fix our attention too rigidly upon the Apostle's design to demonstrate that Jesus was Christ, the Son of God.

John could not appropriately write until other exhibitions of the evangelical history had given him a foundation on which to rest his own. The first Gospels are the necessary preliminary to his; as the Apostle himself acknowledges, in that he always adjoins his narrative to theirs, and passes over all that they had exhaustively recorded. The vocation and gift of the Apostle were directed only to one aspect of the manifestation and work of Christ. The popular aspect, so important and indispensable to the Church, had been represented by others, who had the gift for it in a larger measure than he.

The results thus obtained are supported by the testimonies of antiquity.

Eusebius (Hist. Ecc. iii. 24), expressly appealing to tradition, records that John acknowledged the writings of the first three Evangelists which he had received, and bore witness to their truth (ἀλήθειαν αὐτοῖς ἐπιμαρτυρήσαντα); but that he completed the first three Gospels, having described the first beginnings of Christ's preaching omitted by them; that he passed by the human genealogy of Christ, as having been already recorded by Matthew and Luke, but made his own commencement with the Divine nature of Christ, to present which clearly had been reserved by the Holy Spirit as his prerogative (τῆς δὲ θεολογίας ἀπάρξασθαι, ὡς ἂν αὐτῷ πρὸς τοῦ θείου πνεύματος οἷα κρείττονι παραπεφυλαγμένης). John's aim to supplement is too much circumscribed here, when it is referred only to the beginnings of Christ's teaching. But Eusebius may have intended this only as a specimen; just as, when he refers to John's design to set Christ's divinity in a steady light, he adduces only the prologue, to which, however, he certainly would not limit the Apostle's design.

Clemens Alexandrinus has this second point exclusively in view, when he says (Eusebius, vi. 14) that "John, seeing that things earthly had been fully set forth in the Gospels, passed by what was already known, and, inspired by the Spirit, composed a spiritual Gospel." A spiritual Gospel, that is, in which the attention is mainly directed to the Spirit indwelling in Christ, His Divine nature: compare on ch. vi. 63.

These witnesses are followed by later ones, whom we may now pass over.

"These four Gospels," says Credner (Gesch. der neutest. Kanon, S. 87), "came at length to be regarded as together the perfect and sealed witness and voucher of the Gospel, as τὸ εὐαγγέλιον itself; so that each one of them contained an individual view, not exhaustive, but apostolically accredited, of the Gospel (τὸ εὐαγγέλιον κατά): the Gospel, which in itself was one, is presented in a fourfold form, according to the presentation of Matthew, etc.—It was from the beginning firmly held that the four Gospels were to be regarded as one whole. Irenæus says, iii. 11, 8: τετράμορφον τὸ εὐαγγέλιον ἑνί τε πνεύματι συνεχόμενον.—Eusebius (vi. 25) declares the acceptance of only four Gospels to be a fundamental law of the Catholic Church; recording of Origen, that he, 'guarding the ecclesiastical canon, knew only the four Gospels.' Accordingly he terms our four canonical Gospels τὴν ἁγίαν τῶν εὐαγγελίων τετρακτύν.— Clemens Alexandrinus rejects a saying of Christ, which Julius Africanus had adduced from the Gospel of the Egyptians, with the remark, 'In the four Gospels handed down to us there is no such word.'" The unanimity of the early Church in its view of the four Gospels, which Credner establishes by a series of other testimonies, must have had its ground in this, that John closed the canon of the Gospels. In the time of Luke it was otherwise. According to his ch. i. 2, there were many Gospels in the Church. All doubt, all uncertainty, all capricious choice, was utterly shut out by the authority of the last of the Apostles, the disciple whom Jesus loved.

But we must not limit ourselves to this conclusion. John is, by the old ecclesiastical writers, described as the Apostle "from whom the *collection* of our four canonical Gospels proceeded, in such manner that his own Gospel, the last, and therefore placed at the end, should serve as the complement and seal of the rest. This view soon rose into ecclesiastical supremacy; as Eusebius (Hist. Ecc. iii. 21), Jerome (Catalog. ix.), Theodore of Mopsuestia, and many others prove" (Credner).

For what readers did John design his Gospel? That he wrote for *Christians*, is plain from the general analogy of the books of the New Testament, which have collectively an inward reference to the Church. It was the province of the oral preaching to secure its first entrance to those who were not Christians. Luke, in his dedication to Theophilus, ch. i. 4, defines the scope of his Gospel, "that thou mayest know the certainty of the things wherein thou hast been instructed." In John's prologue, the ἐθεασάμεθα, "we beheld," ch. i. 14, combining the writer and readers in one, intimates that the book was written for the Christian world, which had either directly or indirectly (comp. 1 John i. 3) beheld the glory of the Lord. So also " of His fulness have all we received," ch. i. 16. If we discern the internal connection between the narrative of Thomas and ch. xx. 30, 31, we shall come to the conclusion that those there addressed are such as, like Thomas, stood in a lower degree of faith. To them the Apostle furnishes in his Gospel weapons against doubt, for their furtherance in the faith. "We know," also, in ch. xxi. 20, embracing in one the Apostle and his readers, suggests that the latter belonged to the Christian fellowship, and that the Apostle writes for the "brethren," ver. 23. This term the Apostle could apply to Christians, only if he were writing to Christians. It is an appellation that belongs to the inner circle. That the whole Gospel bears an esoteric character, that those without could not understand it, that to them it was a sealed book, needs no proof. Many have thought that the Gospel was intended specifically for the "Johannean Church in Asia." That there was a circle of Johannean churches, and that the personal labour of the Apostle was not limited to Ephesus, is evident from the seven epistles in the Apocalypse, the second and third Epistles of John, and the current of ecclesiastical tradition. Clemens Alexandrinus (Euseb. iii. 24) testifies to John's official activity in all the district round Ephesus, and says that he travelled round it, instituted bishops, raised churches, and introduced into the ministry men marked out to him by the Holy Ghost. It is obvious, in the nature of things, that John, in the preparation of his Gospel, had this circle *primarily* in view; the rather as the epistles in the Apocalypse, and his own second and third Epistles, show that this district was especially beset by the false teachers and false doctrine that he stedfastly opposed. But it would be altogether wrong to limit the design of the Gospel to this region. In strict truth, the personal work of John was itself not restricted to this circle. He was not a bishop, he was an Apostle. Had his physical strength permitted, he would have occupied the same position throughout the world which he assumed in the churches round Ephesus. No such limitations were thrown round the written Gospel. It bears in itself no trace of restriction to any one region in particular. The "we all," ch. i. 16, decidedly opposes such an idea. The book was meant for the whole Christian world. This is plain from its being an adjunct of the first three Gospels, and from its aim to be their complement, forming with them one whole. The universal design of the Gospel concurs with the universal character of the Church: comp. "I will draw all men unto Me," ch. xii. 32, x. 16. The Apostle, whose mission was to the whole world, Matt. xxviii. 19, John xvii. 18, would have denied his own characteristic if he had not from the first intended a document of such importance for the universal Church.

At what time did John compose his Gospel?

Doubtless it was written after the destruction of Jerusalem. It is true that the reasons adduced by Ewald and others— "When the Gospel was written, Jerusalem was destroyed, as we may see in the description of localities, ch. xi. 18, xviii. 1,

xix. 41"—are not of any weight. These passages do not establish the affirmative, any more than ch. v. 2 the negative. The use of $\mathring{\eta}\nu$, "was," may be explained in all those places by the fact that the Evangelist and his readers were interested only in what existed at that earlier time, whether still continuing or not being in itself matter of indifference. But in all three cases local relations are pointed to, which could have been little if at all affected by the destruction of the city. Bethany exists to the present day, so also the garden of Gethsemane.—But there are other adequate reasons for our conclusion that the Gospel was written after the fall of Jerusalem.

According to the testimonies of history, the Apostle as such had his proper abode only in two places: first in Jerusalem, and then in Ephesus. There can be no doubt that his Gospel was written, not in Jerusalem, but in Ephesus: for the Apostle beholds everything Jewish as from a distance; and we everywhere see that he lived amidst a predominantly Gentile population, for whom he explains that which was Jewish: ch. ii. 6, iv. 9, vii. 2, xi. 18, 55. But if it was composed in Ephesus, it must have been after the destruction of Jerusalem; for the Apostle, of whom a pious feeling towards all existing relations was characteristic, would not certainly have left the sphere of his first work until facts themselves had so interpreted to him the Divine will. According to Gal. ii. 9, John held himself bound primarily to the circumcision. The limit of that obligation the Lord Himself had prescribed to him, in Luke xxi. 20, 21. When Jerusalem was surrounded by armies, flight was not only permitted, but enjoined; for then its condition was hopeless. During the whole period of Paul's labours in Asia, we find no trace there of John. Acts xxi. 18, "And the day following Paul went in with us unto James; and all the elders were present," cannot prove that John was then no longer in Jerusalem; for the Apostles themselves were included among the elders. John so terms himself, 2 John 1; 3 John 1. James soon afterwards died by martyrdom. Of the three pillars, in Gal. ii. 9, John alone remained. It is not probable that he would have abandoned the important post assigned him by God, before the last hour of Jerusalem was come. The character of John's phraseology and composition points also to a long abode in Palestine. It is entirely Hebraistic in its colouring. Ewald rightly remarks: "In its true spirit and tone, no language can be more thoroughly Hebraistic than that of our author." This goes so far as the frequent use of Hebrew words; but it shows itself especially in the great simplicity of the construction of his propositions.

Its composition after the fall of Jerusalem is attested also by the care with which many sayings of our Lord referring to that catastrophe are introduced. Remembering the apologetic scope of the work, this is to be explained on the ground that these utterances had been confirmed by their accomplishment, and thus helped to establish the great conclusion, that Jesus was the Christ, the Son of God.

There are, however, many other facts which lead to the inference that the Gospel was composed in the extreme age of the Apostle.

It must have been written after the first Epistle of Peter; for ch. xxi. 9 refers back to 1 Pet. iv. 16. The same passage establishes, that when it was written, Peter had already suffered death on the cross. What death Peter should die, was certainly involved in the words of Christ; but without the commentary afforded by the event, it would have been hard to detect it with certainty. The prophecy was to have light shed upon it by the fulfilment. A similar remark is made by the Apostle in ch. xii. 33, xviii. 32, with reference to the sayings of Christ pointing to His own death. There also history has already come to his aid.

The Gospel was constructed at a time when the division between Christianity and Judaism was already perfectly accomplished, comp. on ch. i. 19; at the same period in which the Apocalypse moves, which, in ch. ii. 9 and iii. 9, describes Judaism as the "synagogue of Satan."

The relation to the first three Gospels shows that these, at the time of its composition, were extant, and in common use among Christians.

That the Gospel cannot be sundered from the Apocalypse by a long interval, is shown by references to the latter in ch. xvi. 13 and xxi. 22, this last all the more noteworthy as standing at the close of the Gospel, and, as it were, forming a kind of transition from this to the Apocalypse.

The appearance of Cerinthus, whose errors the Gospel

opposes, Theodoret (Hæret. Fab. ii. 3) places in the time of Domitian.

The entire works of John bear a unique character, and have one end. They were designed to withstand the ruinous effects of the Gentile world's incursions on the Church. The Apocalypse treats, in reference to the heathen, and specially the Roman dominion, the theme, "Be of good courage, I have overcome the world." It describes, for the inspiriting of dejected souls, Christ's victory over heathenism. The Epistles and the Gospel confront the relaxing influences which the heathen admixture had exerted upon the doctrine and life of Christians,—upon the former directly and the latter indirectly,—by bringing forward the historical demonstration of the faith, which these heretics gainsaid, that Jesus was the Christ, the Son of God. But the heathen oppression, which the Gospel, and also John's writings, assume as present, did not come upon the Church until the time of Domitian. How wide-spread and how severe was his persecution, we have established at length in the Introduction to the Commentary on the Apocalypse. The only earlier persecution, based upon public authority, that of Nero, bore only a local character, and did not extend over Asia; it had, moreover, only a brief duration.

The Gospel of John is distinguished from those of the former Evangelists by its pre-eminently systematic character; as also by its more artificial arrangement. It consists of prologue and epilogue, and the main body divided into seven groups. These groups, again, are divided into four and three: at the end of the four there is the boundary of a final word; as also at the end of the three, ch. xx. 30, 31, a conclusion which separates the main body from the epilogue. At the close of the epilogue there is an identification of the author, with the intimation that the book lays no claim to perfect completeness. Concurrent with this systematic character and artificial arrangement, there are the precision and exactitude in historical statements which betray an author who is everywhere set on preparing his work for critical eyes. So also the accurate chronology carried throughout the whole, by means of which we are able to regulate the chronological relations of the historical matter contained in the first three Gospels. These peculiarities of the Gospel refer its composition to a late period, in which Christian doctrine had to encounter the doubts of those who had been cultivated in the school of Greek science. The rich genius of the Apostle had, in its intercourse and conflict with these, had opportunity to develop itself. The contest with the Gnostics, who ever had deep things on their lips, promising to lead all into the depths (comp. Rev. ii. 24), had, as it were, armed his spirit, and prepared him, in contrast with their false depth, to disclose the true deep things of the Church, now more susceptible to those revelations than at an earlier period. His glowing love to Christ filled him, the only Apostle left alive, the only bulwark against the great temptation and peril of the time, with an urgent impulse to meet to the utmost all its exigencies. The Gospel and the Apocalypse show that the Apostle, at the time of their composition, was no longer, as formerly, in the sphere of the "unlearned and ignorant men," Acts iv. 13. They are, even in their human aspect, perfect works of art. Every word in them is in its place.

With the results which we have independently gained, tradition here also entirely accords. According to Irenæus, ch. iii. 1, the Gospel of John was issued during his residence in Ephesus ("John, the Lord's disciple, who lay in His bosom, sent forth himself a Gospel, living at the time at Ephesus, in Asia"), which extended, according to xi. 22, down to the time of Trajan. Jerome and others repeat this statement. Later writers, who represent the Gospel as written in Patmos, nevertheless agree with Irenæus that it was the production of the Apostle's late age. According to the Chronicon Alexandrinum (p. 246), John came to Ephesus at the commencement of the reign of Vespasian, and composed there his Gospel, during the closing years of his life. Epiphanius states that he wrote it when he was more than ninety years old, and therefore in the reign of Domitian, Hær. li. 12: ἐπὶ τῇ γηραλέᾳ αὐτοῦ ἡλικίᾳ, μετὰ ἔτη ἐνενήκοντα τῆς ἑαυτοῦ ζωῆς.

We are led to the assumption of a comparatively late period for the authorship of the Gospel by the order of the Gospels, and the fact that John takes the last place among them. Credner says: "Simultaneously with the reception of the four Gospels, as containing together the entire Gospel, the order of these Gospels also has been very firmly established from the beginning; and that order is the one we now have." "In the oldest list we have (Muratori), and in the Epistle to Diognetus (ch. xi. 12), the last place is assigned to John's Gospel."

We shall not enter into any discussion of the *genuineness* of the Gospel. Multiplied evidences of an external character, however strong and sufficient, have but little attraction, as the matter is at once decided by the testimony of Eusebius, who, in Hist. Ecc. iii. 25, terms the Gospel one of the "writings not controverted" of the Apostle, and describes it as accepted by all the churches under heaven.[1] But internal reasons have been exhibited during the progress of the commentary, which, for all who can and will see, are abundantly convincing. May all others cease their laborious frivolity! Rev. xxii. 11. We shall, however, enter at some length into the question, whether John has communicated the discourses of Christ in the form in which they were delivered, or whether he has dealt with them after a freer fashion. We maintain the former; yet with the unessential and self-evident limitation, that the verbal coincidence extended only so far as that the word is faithful to the thought. That we cannot go further, is shown by all scriptural analogies, and by the citations of God's word which John himself gives. Absolute literalness is excluded at once by the fact that our Lord spoke in Aramæan.

The arguments alleged against John's fidelity in the reproduction of Christ's discourses have no force.

It has been urged that His discourses bear a quite different character in the first three Evangelists. But the difference is really not so absolute. It has been shown in the commentary, that there are everywhere the finest points of union between John's record and theirs. But, so far as the difference is real, and may be established, its reason is plain, viz. that our Lord had two manners of teaching: that the second or more profound was adopted specially in Jerusalem, the capital of Jewish culture and science; and that John from the beginning had this vocation, to provide for the conservation of this kind of our Lord's discourses. It was essential to the Redeemer's character that He should be able to pay its tribute to every kind of culture, and to change His voice according to the dispositions and tendencies of His hearers. This was known to His "brethren,"

---

[1] Those who desire to enter more fully into this question would do well to consult the little work of Schneider, *Die Æchtheit der Joh. Evang.*

who, in ch. vii. 4, address to Him the challenge, "If Thou doest these things, show Thyself to the world." He was to come out of the Galilean corner, and approve His mission in the presence of intellect and science. Moreover, there are not wanting traces, even in the first three Evangelists, of a profounder style of teaching, such as was needful for the disciples in order to exercise their spiritual senses: comp. for example, Matt. xi. 27–30, xxi. 21; Luke x. 41, 42; even as in John's Gospel we meet with the popular style of teaching occasionally, when circumstances rendered it desirable: comp. for example, ch. iv. 48–50, xviii. 23.

An argument has also been based upon the similarity between our Lord's discourses in John and John's own Epistles. But the disciple whom Jesus loved had, in a sense in which no other had, eaten the flesh of Jesus, and drunk His blood. He had become entirely fashioned and moulded into Christ, and how could he have done otherwise than employ the Lord's style of speaking? Of the two kinds of discourse adopted by Christ, John's appropriation would be limited to that one which was most in unison with his own nature, and which found most response in his own spirit, with its affinities for deep things; so that the assumption of such an assimilation cannot tend to the disparagement of the former Evangelists' fidelity in their reproduction of our Lord's discourses.—But there is another reason for the harmony between the Gospel discourses and the Epistles. Those Epistles, especially the first, stand in close connection with the Gospel. They run parallel with it as a kind of commentary. They place the Gospel in the light of the contemporary age. And if they were to fulfil this function, they must needs as closely as possible adapt themselves in their expression to the discourses recorded in the Gospel. Literal contact with the phraseology of those discourses of Christ served the purpose of direct reference. Especially in regard to the three main points, around which the warfare of the time revolved—faith in Christ, the keeping of His commandments, and brotherly love—we clearly perceive an endeavour as closely as possible to adhere to Christ's words in the Gospel, in order to facilitate their application to the evils of the present time. But we also find certain peculiarities in the phraseology of the Epistles, of which the Gospels furnish no parallel. We long ago pointed out that the Logos, which we meet in the first Epistle, as also in the prologue of the Gospel and the Apocalypse, never occurs in the Lord's discourses, although they contain the express doctrine which found its expression in this word. But it is not less remarkable that there is such a difference in the use of the words light and darkness. In the Gospel discourses of our Lord, the word light, after the precedent of the Old Testament, means salvation (comp. on ch. i. 4), while darkness describes an unsaved state. But in the first Epistle light designates that which is morally good; darkness that which is morally evil, ch. i. 5, 6, ii. 9, 11. This phraseology was first fashioned in opposition to the Gnostics, who had the word light for ever in their mouths; who fancied that in the "light" of their intellectual contemplation they possessed access to God, whom they loved to designate as Light, in the sense of the supreme Intellect. John sets against their light of error the true light. The word light is everywhere in the first Epistle to be understood, so to speak, within quotation marks. This is specially evident in ch. ii. 9: "He that saith he is in the light," ἐν τῷ φωτὶ εἶναι. Similarly as the light in these passages, the ambitious *gnosis* of the Gnostics is parodied by John in 1 John ii. 3: καὶ ἐν τούτῳ γινώσκομεν ὅτι ἐγνώκαμεν. This polemical use of light and darkness is unknown to the Gospel; and its exposition has been much damaged by a neglect of this distinction.

Stress has been laid on the impossibility that such long discourses could have been reproduced. But length has nothing to do with the matter. Between the discourses of Jesus, and the Gospel as compiled and written, there lies the oral Gospel. The question, therefore, can only be, whether John was capable of making the discourses of Jesus his own. In favour of his ability, and his actual retention of the entire discourses, we need only appeal to the high degree of John's receptivity, the aid of other Apostles, to whom he might have recourse at need, the assistance of the Holy Spirit, promised by the Lord's words, ch. xiv. 26,—with which we may find some slight analogy in the fact, that believers often find, and especially in times of sorrow, long forgotten utterances of holy writ recurring with marvellous clearness to the soul. But that John was in a position faithfully to reproduce the Lord's discourses, follows simply from the circumstance of his having *undertaken* to communicate them. The Apostle who, beyond all others, lays stress upon *truth*, whose whole nature breathed truth, who held all lies in such abomination, and excluded whosoever loveth and maketh a lie from the new Jerusalem, 1 John ii. 21, 27, Rev. xxi. 27, xxii. 15, could not possibly have put into our Lord's lips imaginary and invented words. Let it not be urged that such freely reported discourses would belong to Christ, inasmuch as the Apostle had the Spirit of Christ. For the Apostle does not give us discourses which might in some certain sense be attributed to Christ: he gives us discourses which the Son of man, in the days of His flesh, delivered; and with these to introduce any admixture of his own would have been deception, even though his own had sprung from the suggestion of the Spirit of Christ. It could not, however, in that case have proceeded from the Spirit of Christ, for that Spirit could never minister to deception. Nor should reference be made to the speeches of antiquity interwoven with the narratives of classical historians; for here we have to do with the "words of eternal life," not with such as were designed for the entertainment of the reader, or were, in a lower domain, for his instruction. The Apostle, whose reverence towards Christ was supreme, who so constantly presents the discourses of Christ as His own sole prerogative and as evidences of His eternal divinity, would surely have counted it blasphemy to have put these or any discourses into His mouth. Throughout the entire Scriptures generally there is no room for the analogy of classical authors. There is something in them too solemn and too true.

Finally, it has been already shown in the Commentary, that the arguments which have been adduced in favour of John's freer treatment, from ch. iii. 16 seq. and ch. xii. 44, have absolutely no force.

For his entire fidelity in the communication of our Lord's discourses, we may bring forward, among others, the following reasons.

The Evangelist represents himself to be conscious of his own truthfulness in this matter. According to ch. xxi. 24, his Gospel, as a whole, was a *testimony*; he records only that which he had heard and seen, for that is the simple province of a witness. He gives there the express assurance that his witness was *true*; and therefore that he recorded nothing which he had *not* seen and heard. He communicates, in ch. xv. 27, a saying of Christ that assigns to His Apostles the task of testifying concerning Him, "because ye have been with Me from the beginning,"—a reason which would have force only on the supposition that the Lord meant historical fidelity to be observed in the communication of what they had seen and heard. He opposes himself, in the first Epistle, to the phantasts of his time, as one who declared only what he had heard and seen with his eyes. How could he have said this, if, in the record of our Lord's discourses, he had himself strayed into the region of imagination?

In ch. xiv. 26 the work of the Holy Spirit is said to be the bringing to their remembrance all that Christ had said. This shows what importance the Lord attached to the true and unadulterated delivery of His own words.

In ch. xv. 3 our Lord says, "Now ye are clean through the word which I have spoken unto you." The word of Jesus, to which John owed his sanctification, he certainly would not have dishonoured by any additions of his own.

In ch. xv. 7 Jesus declares, "If ye abide in Me, and My words abide in you, ye shall ask what ye will." There the faithful maintenance of the words of Jesus is represented as the condition of a state of grace. Those words were a power ruling the Apostles, to which they must entirely and unconditionally be in subjection.

The most rigid criticism has failed to detect a single word which Jesus might not have spoken, and in which the later relations of John are reflected. That would have been inevitable, if the discourses of Christ had not been faithfully reproduced.

Evidence may further be found in the multitude of points of contact between the discourses in John and the discourses in the three Evangelists, as these have been indicated in the Commentary.

John's exactitude in the specification of time, place, and occasion of the individual discourses, is a guarantee of a similar exactitude in the communication of the discourses themselves. Compare, for example, ch. viii. 20: "These things He spake in the treasury;" vii. 37, "in the last and great day of the feast;" vi. 1 seq., where the historical basis of the discourse on the

CONCLUDING OBSERVATIONS. 541

eating of His flesh and blood is given with great care; ch. x. 22-24. To the same result we are led by the rigidly historical bearing of the whole Gospel, as it is exemplified, for instance, in the description of characters. The woman of Samaria, the man born blind, Mary, Martha, Pilate,—what life-like forms are these!

John is so exact in the record of the discourses of others, that he often even retains the Hebrew word, and adds, for the benefit of his readers, the Greek translation, ch. i. 39, 42, iv. 25, xx. 16,—evidence that to his historical fidelity the translation into Greek was itself a matter of solicitude.

The historical truth of our Lord's discourses appears in the effects which were connected with them: *e.g.* in ch. x. 19-21, 31-33, where the Jews would stone Christ because He arrogated to Himself divinity, ch. viii. 59.

John's faithfulness in the reproduction is attested also by ch. xxi. 23, where, over against a misinterpretation of one of our Lord's words, he simply sets the word itself, without addition and without explanation; by the illustrations which he adjoins to hard and mysterious words, ch. xii. 33, vii. 39, xxi. 19; by the intimations he gives when certain words were unintelligible to the disciples, ch. ii. 21, 22, xvi. 17, 18, comp. ver. 29, which show that these words had for the Apostles an objective character (in ch. xi. 11-13, we first have a word of Jesus; then it is recorded that the disciples misunderstood it; then the Apostle corrects the misapprehension); by the expressions of the hearers, evoked by Christ's words, *e.g.* in ch. iii. 8, vi. 28, 34, 60, viii. 13, 33, xiv. 5, 22, xvi. 29, 30, which John must also have invented, if the sayings of our Lord were not reproduced as He uttered them; finally, by the references to the word of Christ ch. ii. 19, which is found in Matt. xxvi. 61, Mark xiv. 58, and to the word of ch. xxi. 18 in 2 Pet. i. 14, 1 Pet. v. 1. The charge brought against Christ before the Council, that He had arrogated to Himself a divine Sonship, points back pre-eminently to the discourses of our Lord in John's Gospel.

The author closes this work with devout thankfulness to Almighty God, whose strength has been made perfect in his weakness, and who has enabled him to finish his task under the pressure of a heavy cross. To His name be the glory!

www.ingramcontent.com/pod-product-compliance
Lightning Source LLC
Chambersburg PA
CBHW071219290426
44108CB00013B/1222